9781337620284

*To Rosie, Clare, Camila, Sofia, Eliana, Julian, Carson, and Owen*

# BRIEF

## CONTENTS

Ninth Edition

# Leadership

## Research Findings, Practice, and Skills

**ANDREW J. DuBRIN**

*Rochester Institute of Technology*

CENGAGE

Australia • Brazil • Mexico • Singapore • United Kingdom • United States

**Leadership: Research Findings,**
**Practice and Skills, Ninth Edition**
**Andrew J. DuBrin**

Senior Vice President: Erin Joyner

Product Director: Bryan Gambrel

Project Manager: Julie Dierig

Content Developer: Stacey Lutkoski, MPS

Product Assistant: Rhett Ransom

Marketing Manager: Emily McLellan

Manufacturing Planner: Ron Montgomery

Intellectual Property Analyst: Diane Garrity

Intellectual Property Project Manager: Sarah
Shainwald

Art Director: Bethany Bourgeois

Text Designer: Cindy and Lou Beckmeyer/
Beckmeyer Design

Cover Image Credit: robertharding/Alamy Stock
Photo

Production Management and Composition:
Lumina Datamatics Inc.

For product information and technology assistance, contact us at
**Cengage Customer & Sales Support, 1-800-354-9706**

For permission to use material from this text or product,
submit all requests online at **www.cengage.com/permissions**
Further permissions questions can be emailed to
**permissionrequest@cengage.com**

Library of Congress Control Number: 2017954048

ISBN-13: 978-1-337-62028-4

**Cengage**
20 Channel Center Street
Boston, MA 02210
USA

Cengage is a leading provider of customized learning solutions with
employees residing in nearly 40 different countries and sales in more than
125 countries around the world. Find your local representative at
**www.cengage.com.**

Cengage products are represented in Canada by
Nelson Education, Ltd.

To learn more about Cengage Solutions, visit
**www.cengage.com**

Purchase any of our products at your local college store or at our
preferred online store **www.cengagebrain.com**

Printed in the United States of America
Print Number: 03    Print Year: 2021

# CONTENTS

**CHAPTER 3**      Charismatic and Transformational Leadership    57

## CHAPTER 4

# Leadership Behaviors, Attitudes, and Styles   86

## CHAPTER 5

# Contingency and Situational Leadership   117

**CHAPTER 7**

## Power, Politics, and Leadership   169

**CHAPTER 8**

## Influence Tactics of Leaders   201

## CHAPTER 12

## Communication and Conflict Resolution Skills   310

# PREFACE

Welcome to the ninth edition of *Leadership: Research Findings, Practice, and Skills*. The new edition of this text is a thorough update of the eighth edition, which has been used widely in both graduate and undergraduate courses in leadership.

Many scholars and managers alike are convinced that effective leadership is required to meet most organizational challenges. Today, organizations recognize that leadership transcends senior executives. As a result, organizations require people with appropriate leadership skills to inspire and influence others in small teams, task forces, and units at all organizational levels.

Without effective leadership at all levels in organizations, it is difficult to sustain profitability, productivity, and good customer service. In dozens of different ways, researchers and teachers have demonstrated that leadership does make a difference. Many curricula in business schools and other fields, therefore, now emphasize the development of leadership skills. With the continuing exposures of the dark side of business leadership, such as CEOs finding ways to create fortunes for themselves at the expense of employees and stockholders, more attention than ever is being paid to the values and personal characteristics of leaders. Toward that end, this text continues to emphasize the qualities of effective leaders, including an entire chapter on leadership ethics and social responsibilities.

## Purpose of the Text

The purpose of this text is implied by its title—*Leadership: Research Findings, Practice, and Skills*, ninth edition. It is designed for undergraduate and graduate courses in leadership that give attention to research findings about leadership, leadership practice, and skill development. The text best fits courses in leadership that emphasize application and skill building. *Leadership* is also designed to fit courses in management development that emphasize the leadership aspect of management.

The student who masters this text will acquire an overview of the voluminous leadership literature that is based both on research and experience. Information in this text is not restricted to research studies and syntheses of research and theories; it also includes the opinions of practitioners, consultants, and authors who base their conclusions on observations rather than empirical research.

What the text is *not* also helps define its nature and scope. This book does not attempt to duplicate the scope and purpose of a leadership handbook by integrating theory and research from several thousand studies. At the other extreme, it is not an evangelical approach to leadership espousing one leadership technique. I have attempted to find a midpoint between a massive synthesis of the literature and a trade book promoting a current leadership fad. *Leadership: Research Findings, Practice, and Skills*, ninth edition, is designed to be a mixture of scholarly integrity, examples of effective leadership in action, and skill development.

*Leadership* is not intended to duplicate or substitute for an organizational behavior text. Because almost all organizational behavior texts are survey texts, they will mention many of the topics covered here. My approach, however, is to emphasize skill development and prescription rather than to duplicate basic descriptions of concepts and theories. I have tried to minimize overlap by emphasizing the leadership aspects of any concept presented here that might also be found in an organizational behavior or management text. Often when overlap of a topic exists, the presentation here focuses more on skill development than on a review of theory and research. For example, the section on motivation emphasizes how to apply basic explanations of motivation such as expectancy theory and worker engagement, but I do not present an overview of motivation theories as is found in an organizational behavior text.

One area of intentional overlap with organizational behavior and management texts does exist: a review of most basic leadership theories. In such instances, however, I emphasize skill development and ideas for leadership practice stemming from these older theories. This edition, however, recognizes that it is time to omit several basic leadership theories that have not been researched for decades, such as the Leadership Grid and Situational Leadership II.

## Features of the Book

To accomplish its purpose, this textbook incorporates many features into each chapter in addition to summarizing and synthesizing relevant information about leadership:

- **Chapter Outlines** giving the reader a quick overview of the topics covered
- **Learning Objectives** to help focus the reader's attention on major outcomes
- Boldfaced key **terms** listed at the end of the chapter and defined in a **Glossary** at the back of the textbook
- Real-life and hypothetical **examples** throughout the textbook
- **Leader in Action** inserts describing the leadership practices, behaviors, and personal attributes of real-life leaders
- **Leadership Self-Assessment Quizzes** relating to both skills and personal characteristics
- **Leadership Skill-Building Exercises**, including role plays, to emphasize the activities and skills of effective leaders
- End-of-chapter **Summaries** that integrate all key topics and concepts
- End-of-chapter **Guidelines for Action and Skill Development**, giving additional suggestions for improving leadership skill and practice
- **Discussion Questions and Activities** suited for individual or group analysis
- Two **Leadership Case Problems** per chapter, which illustrate the major theme of the chapter and contain questions for individual or group analysis
- **Role plays** accompanying all the case problems to help reinforce the opportunity for learning interpersonal skills within the case problems
- A **Leadership Portfolio** skill-building exercise in each chapter that instructs the student to record progress in developing leadership skills and behaviors

### Framework of the Text

The text is a blend of description, skill development, insight development, and prescription. Chapter 1 describes the meaning, importance, and nature of leadership, including leadership roles and the importance of followership. Chapter 2 identifies personal attributes associated with effective leaders, a subject that has experienced renewed importance in recent years. Charismatic and transformational leadership, an extension of understanding the personal attributes of leadership, is the subject of Chapter 3.

Chapter 4 surveys behaviors and practices associated with effective leadership in a variety of situations, and describes leadership styles. Chapter 5 extends the study of styles by describing the contingency and situational aspects of leadership. Chapter 6 focuses on leadership ethics and social responsibility. Chapter 7 describes how leaders use power and politics. Chapter 8 extends this topic by analyzing the tactics leaders use to influence people. Chapter 9 describes how leaders foster teamwork and empower team members.

The next five chapters deal with specific leadership skills: motivating and coaching skills (Chapter 10), which constitute the basis of many leadership positions; creativity and innovation (Chapter 11); communication (including nonverbal, social media, and cross-cultural communication) and conflict resolution skills (Chapter 12); vision and strategy creation and knowledge management (Chapter 13); and effective leadership in international and culturally diverse settings (Chapter 14).

Chapter 15 concludes the book with an overview of approaches to leadership development and learning. In addition, there is a discussion of leadership succession and the challenges facing a new leader.

## Changes in the Ninth Edition

The ninth edition of *Leadership: Research Findings, Practice, and Skills* is an update but not an overhaul of the eighth edition. The structure and key subject areas of the previous edition are retained. Some of the changes in this edition reflect the recent leadership information I felt should be included in the new edition. To make way for the new material, I have selectively pruned older examples and research findings, and deleted some concepts that seem to be only slight variations of another concept in the text. I have also deleted some of the research findings that basically duplicate other findings on the same topic. As a result of selective pruning, the textbook is now about 90 pages shorter. The following list highlights the changes in the ninth edition, in addition to updating research and opinion.

### Changes Throughout the Text

- Fifteen new chapter introductions plus updating of introductions in Chapters 1 and 15
- Fifteen Leader in Action boxes are new
- Fifteen new cases are new plus an update of one case
- New research findings presented in each chapter
- New examples throughout
- Four Guidelines for Action and Skill Development are supplemented with additional information
- Fifteen new Skill-Building Exercises, plus three of them with new components
- Seven new or modified figures (Chapters 1, 5, 7, 9, 12, 13, and 14)
- Seven new Leadership Self-Assessment Quizzes

### Content Changes Within Chapters

Chapter 1 summarizes research about how leadership has an impact on sales performance in organizations. A slightly revised framework for leadership is presented in Figure 1-2. Chapter 2 describes mindfulness as a task-related personality trait. A self-assessment quiz about thinking big is included to reinforce the discussion of conceptual thinking. Chapter 3 adds new company vision statements. A separate section describes the narcissism component of charisma. A checklist of narcissism attitudes and behaviors is provided to reinforce the discussion of narcissism.

Chapter 4 adds a section on the relationship-oriented leadership behavior of reducing task ambiguity, therefore lowering stress for workers. Servant leadership is now included as a separate leadership style. Chapter 5 presents several new findings about the leader–member exchange (LMX) model as they relate to contingency leadership. Dividing major problems into smaller chunks is added as a component of crisis leadership.

Chapter 6 now includes a section on minimizing abusive supervision throughout the organization. Information is presented about unethical behavior at Wells Fargo that involved assigning unwanted accounts and services to customers. Chapter 7 adds the empowerment practice of practicing an optimal amount of empowerment. A new political tactic is offered: reach out to your boss's boss. A brief section is added about overcoming political blunders.

Chapter 8 expands the discussion of leadership influence for organizational change, including holding people accountable for the changes in behavior that support the cultural shift. A new self-assessment quiz supports the discussion about leader ingratiating behavior.

Chapter 9 includes collective leadership as part of serving as a model of teamwork, and the use of positive feedback for fostering teamwork. Information is presented about how the gig economy fits into virtual teams. Mention is made of how good relationships with the supervisor lead to better satisfaction with teamwork, and better role clarity in dealing with patients. Chapter 10 includes a new section on how a positive relationship with the leader can enhance employee engagement. A self-assessment quiz about work engagement tendencies helps personalize the discussion of engagement. Mention is made of defining the issues as a stat to coaching a subordinate.

Chapter 11 provides information about soliciting feedback on your performance as a self-help technique for creativity improvement. Two self-assessment quizzes are provided to personalize the discussion about creativity traits: one about the intuitive problem-solving style, and another about attitudes and behaviors reflecting good concentration and focus. A revamped section provides information about leadership practices geared specifically toward enhancing innovation.

Chapter 12 presents a section on using group chat as a leadership communication network. A seventh principle of persuasion is added about putting people in a receptive mood before asking them for something. A negotiation tactic is added about how to minimize looking or feeling anxious during the negotiation. Chapter 13 replaces the section about the nature of business strategy with a section about the development of business strategy. Several elements of the previous section are retained, and a discussion of the importance of strategic thinking is added, reinforced by a new self-assessment quiz on the topic. The section about knowledge management and the learning organization now includes a separate section about knowledge sharing.

Chapter 14 presents new data about the work orientation of American workers versus those in other countries. Mention is made of how eliciting ideas and giving feedback can be influenced by cultural values. A section is added about understanding which leadership and management practices function well in a specific culture. Another new section deals with the conduct of anti-bias training.

Chapter 15 now includes a self-assessment quiz about self-discipline to personalize the discussion of self-discipline for leadership development. Information is now included about how formal education contributes to learning agility because of its importance for leadership success. A new section is added about the characteristics of an effective leadership development program.

## Acknowledgments

Any project as complex as this one requires a team of dedicated and talented people to see that it achieves its goals. First, I thank the many effective leaders whom I have observed in action or read about for improving my understanding of leadership. Second, I thank the following professors who offered suggestions for improving this and previous editions:

Steve Barnett, *Unitec New Zealand*

Steven Barry, *University of Colorado-Boulder*

John Bigelow, *Boise State University*

Meika Bowden McFarland, *Albany Technical College*

Bruce T. Caine, *Vanderbilt University*

Felipe Chia, *Harrisburg Area Community College*

Jeewon Cho, *Montclair State University*

Conna Condon, *Upper Iowa University*

Emily J. Creighton, *University of New Hampshire*

Michael de Percy, *University of Canberra*

Rawlin Fairbough, *Sacred Heart University*

Michael Fekula, *The Citadel*

Janice Feldbauer, *Austin Community College*

Justin Frimmer, *Jacksonville University*

Barry Gold, *Pace University*

George B. Graen, *University of Cincinnati*

Stephen G. Green, *Purdue University*

Nathan Hanson, *Palm Beach Atlantic University*

James R. Harris, *North Carolina Agricultural and Technical State University*

Paul Harris, *Lee College*

Nell Hartley, *Robert Morris College*

Linda Hefferin, *Elgin Community College*

Winston Hill, *California State University, Chico*

Katherine Hyatt, *Reinhardt University*

Avis L. Johnson, *University of Akron*

Marvin Karlins, *University of South Florida*

Nelly Kazman, *University of La Verne*

David Lee, *University of Dayton*

Alan Lockyer, *Unitec New Zealand*

Brian McNatt, *University of Georgia*

Ralph Mullin, *Central Missouri State University*

Linda L. Neider, *University of Miami*

Andreas Nilsson, *Umeå School of Business, Sweden*

Rhonda S. Palladi, *Georgia State University*

Jeff Perlot, *Green River Community College*

Joseph Petrick, *Wright State University*

Mark Phillips, *University of Texas at San Antonio*

Judy Quinn, *Kutztown University*

Diana Rajendran, *Swinburne University of Technology at Lily dale*

Clint Relyea, *Arkansas State University*

Gary Renz, *Webster University*

Howard F. Rudd, *College of Charleston*

Silvia Sala, *University of Massachusetts at Lowell*

Tom J. Sanders, *University of Montevallo*

Robert Scherer, *Wright State University*

Marianne Sebok, *Community College of Southern Nevada*

Charles Seifert, *Siena College*

Kimberley L. Simons, *Madisonville Community College*

Randall G. Sleeth, *Virginia Commonwealth University*

Steven Tello, *University of Massachusetts at Lowell*

Ahmad Tootoonchi, *Frostburg State University*

David Van Fleet, *Arizona State University West*

John Warner, *University of New Mexico*

Velvet Weems-Landingham, *Kent State University—Geauga*

The editorial and production team at Cengage Learning also receives my gratitude. By name, they are Erin Joyner, Mike Schenk, Bryan Gambrel, Stacey Lutkoski, and Carol Moore. Jenny Ziegler and the staff of Lumina Datamatics Ltd also receive my gratitude for their contributions to this book. Writing without loved ones would be a lonely task. My thanks, therefore, also go to my family members—Drew and Heidi, Douglas and Gizella, Melanie and Will, Rosie, Clare, Camila, Sofia, Eliana, Carson, Julian, Owen, and Drake. Thank you also to Stefanie and her daughter Sofia for their contribution to my well-being.

A.J.D.

## About the Author

Andrew J. DuBrin is a professor of management emeritus in the Saunders College of Business at the Rochester Institute of Technology, where he teaches courses and conducts research in leadership, organizational behavior, and career management. He also served as department chairman and team leader in previous years. He received his PhD in industrial psychology from Michigan State University.

DuBrin has business experience in human resource management and in consulting with organizations and individuals. His specialties include leadership, influence tactics, and career development. DuBrin is an established author of both textbooks and trade books, and he has contributed to professional journals. He has written textbooks on organizational behavior, management, human relations, organizational politics, and edited a handbook of crisis leadership. His trade books cover many topics, including charisma, the proactive personality, coaching and mentoring, office politics, and self-discipline.

# The Nature and Importance of Leadership

ilikiss Adebiyi, a former corporate software engineer at IBM, was taking a development ventures class as part of her MBA program at the MIT Sloan School of Management. She was assigned a project aimed at finding ways to help people at the bottom socioeconomic level in her native Lagos, Nigeria. (Lagos is the capital of the state of Lagos.) In Nigeria, about 70 percent of the natives are very poor. Basic sanitation and healthcare are lacking. Adebiyi wanted to make a difference by helping poor Nigerians.

She was also very interested in the application of waste management and noted how managing waste through recycling had gained a hold in the U.S. environment but not in her native land. Thinking about how recycling might help poor people and the environment in Lagos, Adebiyi founded Wecyclers in 2012 and holds the position of CEO. The company is a waste collection social enterprise. Waste collection is carried out through delivery tricycles (or "cargo bikes") that ride around poor neighborhoods and collect waste, such as empty soda bottles, from inhabitants. Participants receive rewards for every kilogram of recycled material, via points sent by SMS. The points are redeemable for goods the participants value such as cellphone minutes or household supplies.

Wecyclers sorts the trash picked up by the delivery tricycles and sells it to local recyclers. The business is possible because Logos generates about 735,000 tons of plastic annually, worth about $300 million to waste brokers. According to Adebiyi, "That's money lying on the street."

Adebiyi has been labeled a "Lioness of Africa" based on her leadership accomplishments. Her most obvious accomplishment is rebuilding Nigeria's recycling center. Partner families receive an average of $10 per month from Wecyclers, which often amounts to 20 percent of family income. About 3,400 families from poor neighborhoods are active partners. So far the company has created more than 50 jobs, including 37 full-time managers and collectors. The average income is $125 per month, which is $8 above the Lagos minimum wage. Wecyclers also has an impact on the local economy because the tricycles are purchased in Lagos, and the software used to handle the text message stream is purchased from a Nigerian company. Wecyclers pays about $1,600 in annual taxes to the Nigerian government. Furthermore, most company employees are from poor neighborhoods, and working for Wecyclers is their first official job.

In commenting on her work, Adebiyi says, "Wecyclers gives low-income communities a chance to develop waste and clean up their neighborhoods through an incentive-based recycling program." In addition to her MBA from MIT, Adebiyi holds a master's degree from Vanderbilt University.[1]

The description of Bilikiss Adebiyi touches on many leadership topics to be covered in this book, including the following ideas: that providing direction is part of a leader's job, that technical expertise is an important leadership role, and that a strong leader can create meaningful work for people and enrich their lives.

Our introductory chapter begins with an explanation of what leadership is and is not. We then examine how leaders make a difference, the various roles they play, and the major satisfactions and frustrations they experience. This chapter also includes an explanation of how reading this book and doing the various quizzes and exercises will enhance your own leadership skills. It concludes with a discussion of followership—giving leaders good material to work with.

## The Meaning of Leadership

You will read about many effective organizational leaders throughout this text. The common characteristic of these leaders is their ability to inspire and stimulate others to achieve worthwhile goals. Therefore, we can define **leadership** as the ability to inspire confidence and support among the people who are needed to achieve organizational goals.[2]

A Google search of articles and books about leadership in organizations indicates 69 million entries. In all those entries, leadership has probably been defined in many ways. Here are several other representative definitions of leadership:

- A process in which an individual influences a group of individuals to achieve a common goal.
- The influential increment over and above mechanical compliance with directions and orders.
- An act that causes others to act or respond in a shared direction.
- The art of influencing people by persuasion or example to follow a line of action.
- An effort to maintain control and power over others.

- The principal dynamic force that motivates and coordinates the organization in the accomplishment of its objectives.[3]
- The exercise of social influence between and among many sources of leadership (including the leader, follower, and setting), working toward a common goal by using various mechanisms including the leader's traits, behavior, and emotion.[4]

Importantly, leadership is not only found among people in high-level positions. Quite the contrary: Leadership is needed at all levels in an organization and can be practiced to some extent even by a person not assigned to a formal leadership position. For example, working as a junior accountant, a person might take the initiative to suggest to management that they need to be more careful about what they classify as a true sale. It has been suggested that for improved business results to come about, it will be because managers below the C-suite (such as CEO, COO, and CFO) take the initiative and risks to drive the company in a different direction. Change needs to come about from leaders at lower levels, rather than relying exclusively on leadership from the top.[5]

Another way of understanding that leadership can be exercised by many people in the organization is the presence of people who provide leadership to others yet do not have a job title suggesting that they are managers or leaders. You can also rise to leadership when people come to respect your opinion and personal characteristics and are thus influenced by you. **Emergent leaders** are group members who significantly influence other group members even though they have not been assigned formal authority.[6] You, therefore, can exert some leadership by being an influential coworker. A team member who is influential based on personal attributes and behaviors will often be regarded as a leader by peers.

The ability to lead others effectively is a rare quality. It becomes even rarer at the highest levels in an organization because the complexity of such positions requires a vast range of leadership skills. This is one reason that firms in search of new leadership seek out a select group of brand-name executives with proven track records. It is also why companies now emphasize leadership training and development to create a new supply of leaders throughout the firm.

## Leadership as Shared Responsibility and Collaboration

Many leadership theorists and managers agree that the leadership role within a team is seldom the responsibility of one person. Rather, several individuals within the team may serve as leaders, both by formal assignment and informally. Leadership may shift, depending on whose expertise is the most relevant at the moment,[7] such as one member of a marketing team having advanced expertise in using social media for product promotion.

The essence of shared and collaborative leadership is reflected in the comments of Nick Petrie who conducted a study on leadership development. He said, *"There is a transition occurring from the old paradigm in which leadership resided in a person or role, to a new one in which leadership is a collective process that is spread throughout networks of people."*[8] A recent experiment conducted with both college students and working adults supported the usefulness of shared leadership. Participants in the study who experienced shared leadership showed good performance on the simulated decision-making tasks, and also high job satisfaction.[9]

A key force driving collaborative leadership is the hyperconnected organizational world fostered by e-mail and social media, along with globalization. The collaborative leadership style is well suited to harness the power of this multitude of connections.[10] For example, a head of marketing can readily gather and welcome the input of thousands of people on broadening the market for a product. In this way, the head of marketing collaborates with people from afar instead of developing the strategy alone.

More will be presented and shared about collaborative leadership throughout the book, especially in the discussion in Chapter 4 about leadership styles, and Chapter 9 about developing teamwork.

## Leadership as a Relationship

Leadership is usually a relationship between the leader and the people being led. A theoretical analysis by Gail T. Fairhurst and Mary Uhl-Bien explains that leadership is not a trait or behavior of an individual but rather a phenomenon generated in the interactions among people acting in a given setting. The social actions between and among people enable them to work together in meaningful ways to produce leadership outcomes. For example, a leader at a vehicle dealership might be pursuing the outcome of generating more revenue per vehicle purchase. By building good relationships with dealer associates, he or she gains their cooperation in generating useful ideas for generating more revenue, such as pushing harder to get customers to purchase a navigation and security system that generates monthly revenue.

The *given setting* mentioned previously refers to the context of the relationship. In a high-power and authority context, such as an entry-level employee working with the CEO, the communication is likely to be both task based and relationship oriented. The entry-level worker, having much less power and authority, is likely to emphasize politeness, speak formally, and be complimentary.[11]

How leaders build relationships has changed somewhat in the modern era and its emphasis on interacting with people electronically. It is common practice for leaders to give recognition and praise via e-mail or a posting on the company social media site, or a public social media site such as Facebook or Twitter. The late Steve Jobs, the Apple Company cofounder, however, emphasized that leaders should not let communication technology block them from interacting face-to-face with work associates. *"There's a temptation in our networked age to think that ideas can be developed by e-mail and iChat. That's crazy. Creativity comes from spontaneous meetings, from random discussions."*[12] In addition to sparking innovation, the face-to-face encounters help develop relationships.

## Leadership Versus Management

To understand leadership, it is important to grasp the difference between leadership and management. We get a clue from the standard conceptualization of the functions of management: planning, organizing, directing (or leading), and controlling. Leading is a major part of a manager's job; yet a manager must also plan, organize, and control.

Broadly speaking, leadership deals with the interpersonal aspects of a manager's job, whereas planning, organizing, and controlling deal with the administrative aspects. Leadership deals with change, inspiration, motivation, and influence.

If these views are taken to their extreme, the leader is an inspirational figure, and the manager is a stodgy bureaucrat mired in the status quo. But we must be careful not to downplay the importance of management. Effective leaders have to be good managers themselves or be supported by effective managers. A germane example is the inspirational entrepreneur who is so preoccupied with motivating employees and captivating customers that he or she neglects internal administration. As a result, costs skyrocket beyond income, and such matters as funding the employee pension plan and paying bills and taxes on time are overlooked. In short, the difference between leadership and management is one of emphasis. Effective leaders also manage, and effective managers also lead.

John O'Leary, a leadership development specialist, investigated whether leaders and managers really carry out different activities. His method was to conduct interviews of eight experienced leaders in business, government, and upper-level college sports. O'Leary's general finding was that leaders and managers tend to have a different focus on the same set of activities. One finding was that managers delegate largely as a method of increasing efficiency. In contrast, leaders delegate as an approach to empowerment. Another key finding was that leaders focus more on people, and mangers focus more on results.[13]

Management guru Henry Mintzberg, a professor at McGill University, based on first-hand information, strongly supports the position that the difference between leadership and management should not be overdrawn. Mintzberg writes:

> How would you like to be managed by someone who doesn't lead? That can be awfully dispiriting. Well, then, why would you want to be led by someone who doesn't manage? That can be terribly disengaging; how are such "leaders" to know what is going on?[14]

An example of how a company might recognize the difference between leadership and management took place at the Boston investment firm, GMO LLC. The company brought on the first chief executive in its thirty-two-year history, Marc Mayer. His role was to take care of running the company (management) so that senior officials could focus more on navigating the treacherous market (strategic leadership).[15]

# The Impact of Leadership on Organizational Performance

An assumption underlying the study of leadership is that leaders affect organizational performance. Boards of directors—the highest-level executives of an organization—make the same assumption. A frequent antidote to major organizational problems is to replace the leader in the hope that the newly appointed leader will reverse performance problems. Here, we will review some of the evidence and opinions, pro and con, about the ability of leaders to affect organizational performance.

## Research and Opinion: Leadership Does Make a Difference

The idea that leaders actually influence organizational performance and morale is widely believed, and there has been a moderate amount of research and opinion that deals with this issue.

A case history example of how the right approach to leadership can make a positive impact on organizational performance is the situation of chairman and CEO Mark Leslie at Veritas Software. When he joined the company in 1990, he knew the type of culture he wanted to create. The culture included making decision making more transparent, which included a monthly staff meeting with managers worldwide being invited to listen in. Leslie emphasized sharing information, including earning projections. During the eleven years Leslie spent at Veritas, the number of employees increased from 12 to 6,000, and annual revenues increased from $95,000 to $1.5 billion. As Leslie looks back on his time at Veritas, he is convinced that the culture of openness was a driver of success.[16]

The Center on Leadership & Ethics at Duke University conducted a survey about executive leadership based on 205 executives from public and private companies. One of the issues explored was whether leadership actions can affect performance. It was concluded that they can indeed, but only if the leader is perceived to be responsible and inspirational. Such behaviors included engaging employees in the company's vision and inspiring employees to elevate their goals. Another contributor to organizational performance was promoting an environment in which employees have a sense of responsibility for the entire organization.[17]

In another study, a group of researchers analyzed 200 management techniques as employed by 150 companies over ten years. The aspect of the study evaluating the effects of leadership found that CEOs influence 15 percent of the total variance (influencing factors) in a company's profitability or total return to shareholders. The same study also found that the industry in which a company operates also accounts for 15 percent of the variance in profitability. So, the choice of a CEO leader is as important as the choice of whether to remain in the same industry or enter a different one.[18]

An overview of research on managerial succession over a recent twenty-year period provides more support for the idea that leadership has an impact on organizational performance. A consistent relationship was found between who is in charge and how well an organization performed as measured by a variety of indicators. Using different methodologies, these studies arrived at the same conclusion that changes in leadership are followed by changes in company performance. Statistical analyses suggest that the leader might be responsible for somewhere between 15 percent and 45 percent of a firm's performance.[19]

Leadership researcher Bruce J. Avolio from the University of Washington, along with four colleagues, conducted a comprehensive synthesis of 200 studies about the impact of leadership. The studies analyzed included those conducted in laboratories and in work settings. The many outcomes of leadership studied included the satisfactions of subordinates and organizational performance. One of the many study findings was that the leader's activities had a 66 percent probability of achieving a positive outcome.[20]

A specific outcome of how leadership has an impact on organizational performance is sales performance. Julian Barling synthesized the results of many studies exploring how leadership influences sales results—a key metric of organizational success. Although leadership can influence sales performance, the link between the two is complicated.[21] An example of this complicated relationship stems from a series of studies conducted by Adam Grant. In a company involved in the sales of educational and marketing software, new hires were divided into four different groups for their first training.

In addition to their regular training, the eighteen employees in one group also met with a senior company director for fifteen minutes. The executive explained the company's vision and was optimistic and enthusiastic that employees could achieve this vision. Members of this group also met with someone from a different department who was a beneficiary of their work. (An example of a beneficiary of the work of a sales representative might be a software engineer whose software the sales representative was successful in selling.) A key finding was that the combined influence of interacting with a company leader *and* meeting with an internal beneficiary led to the group attaining more sales and higher revenue than the other three groups.[22]

How leaders impact organizational (or unit) performance is the essential subject of this book. For example, good results are attained by developing teamwork and formulating the right strategy.

## Research and Opinion: Formal Leadership Does Not Make a Difference

In contrast to the previous argument, the anti-leadership argument holds that the impact of the leader on organizational outcomes is smaller than the impact of forces within the situation. To personalize this perspective, imagine yourself appointed as the manager of a group of highly skilled investment bankers. How well your group performs could be attributed as much to their talent and to economic conditions as to your leadership. Several of the arguments that leadership can be overrated are presented next.

At times, competent leadership is not necessary, and incompetent leadership can be counterbalanced by certain factors in the work situation. Under these circumstances, leadership itself is of little consequence to the performance and satisfaction of team members. According to this viewpoint, many organizations have **substitutes for leadership**. Such substitutes are factors in the work environment that provide guidance and incentives to perform, making the leader's role almost superfluous,[23] as shown in Figure 1-1.

1. ***Closely knit teams of highly trained individuals.*** When members of a cohesive, highly trained group are focused on a goal, they may require almost no leadership to accomplish their task.

2. ***Intrinsic satisfaction.*** Employees who are engaged in work they find strongly self-motivating, or intrinsically satisfying, require a minimum of leadership. Part of the reason is that the task itself grabs the worker's attention and energy. The worker may require little leadership as long as the task is proceeding smoothly.

3. ***Professional norms.*** Workers who incorporate strong professional norms often require a minimum of supervision and leadership. A group of certified professional accountants may not need visionary leadership to inspire them to do an honest job of auditing the books of a client or advising against tax fraud.

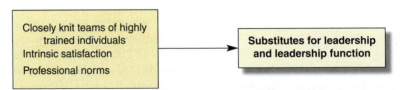

**FIGURE 1-1**   Substitutes for Leadership.

Another argument for leadership being overrated is that in the modern organization, effective leadership means widespread collaboration in obtaining ideas, rather than the heroic leader doing all the innovating. According to this point of view, instead of centralizing leadership in the hands of a few, authority and power are shared, and people lead themselves.[24] (The concept of shared leadership was mentioned above in relation to the meaning of leadership and will surface at several places in the text.)

The argument that leadership is not very important would have greater practical value if it were recast as a leader constraint theory, which would hold that leaders are constrained in what they can do but still have plenty of room to influence others.

A useful perspective on whether leadership makes a difference is to ask the right question as framed by J. Richard Hackman and Ruth Wageman. Instead of asking if leaders make a difference, we should be asking under what conditions leaders make a difference.[25] A crisis mode is an example of a situation in which a strong leader usually makes a difference, such as getting field units back on track after a hurricane or product recall.

## Leadership Roles

Another way to gain an understanding of leadership is to examine the various roles carried out by leaders. A role in this context is an expected set of activities or behaviors stemming from one's job. Leadership roles are a subset of the managerial roles studied by Henry Mintzberg and others.[26] Before reading ahead to the summary of leadership roles, you are invited to complete Leadership Self-Assessment Quiz 1-1.

Leading is a complex activity, so it is not surprising that Mintzberg and other researchers identified ten roles that can be classified as part of the leadership function of management.

1. **Figurehead.** Leaders, particularly high-ranking managers, spend some part of their time engaging in ceremonial activities, or acting as a figurehead. Four specific behaviors fit the figurehead role of a leader:
   a. entertaining clients or customers as an official representative of the organization
   b. making oneself available to outsiders as a representative of the organization
   c. serving as an official representative of the organization at gatherings outside the organization
   d. escorting official visitors

2. **Spokesperson.** When a manager acts as a spokesperson, the emphasis is on answering letters or inquiries and formally reporting to individuals and groups outside the manager's direct organizational unit. As a spokesperson, the managerial leader keeps five groups of people informed about the unit's activities, plans, capabilities, and possibilities (vision):
   a. upper-level management
   b. clients or customers
   c. other important outsiders such as labor union
   d. professional colleagues

   Dealing with outside groups and the general public is usually the responsibility of top-level managers.

3. **Negotiator.** Part of almost any manager's job description is trying to make deals with others for needed resources. Four illustrative negotiating activities are as follows:
   a. bargaining with superiors for funds, facilities, equipment, or other forms of support
   b. bargaining with other units in the organization for the use of staff, facilities, equipment, or other forms of support
   c. bargaining with suppliers and vendors for services, schedules, and delivery times
   d. bargaining with job candidates about starting compensation and benefits

4. **Coach and motivator.** An effective leader takes the time to coach and motivate team members, and sometimes to inspire large groups of people inside the organization. This role includes five specific behaviors:
   a. informally recognizing team members' achievements

# LEADERSHIP SELF-ASSESSMENT QUIZ 1-1

### Readiness for the Leadership Role

**Instructions:** Indicate the extent to which you agree with each of the following statements, using the following scale: 1, disagree strongly; 2, disagree; 3, neutral; 4, agree; 5, agree strongly.

|  |  | DS | D | N | A | AS |
|---|---|---|---|---|---|---|
| 1. | I like having people count on me for ideas and suggestions. | 1 | 2 | 3 | 4 | 5 |
| 2. | I have definitely inspired other people. | 1 | 2 | 3 | 4 | 5 |
| 3. | It is a good practice to ask people provocative questions about their work. | 1 | 2 | 3 | 4 | 5 |
| 4. | It is easy for me to compliment others. | 1 | 2 | 3 | 4 | 5 |
| 5. | I have many more friends and followers on social working websites than do most people. | 1 | 2 | 3 | 4 | 5 |
| 6. | I like to cheer people up even when my own spirits are down. | 1 | 2 | 3 | 4 | 5 |
| 7. | What my team accomplishes is more important than my personal glory. | 1 | 2 | 3 | 4 | 5 |
| 8. | Many people imitate my ideas. | 1 | 2 | 3 | 4 | 5 |
| 9. | Building team spirit is important to me. | 1 | 2 | 3 | 4 | 5 |
| 10. | I would enjoy coaching other members of the team. | 1 | 2 | 3 | 4 | 5 |
| 11. | It is important to me to recognize others for their accomplishments. | 1 | 2 | 3 | 4 | 5 |
| 12. | I would enjoy entertaining visitors to my firm even if it interfered with my completing a report. | 1 | 2 | 3 | 4 | 5 |
| 13. | It would be fun for me to represent my team at gatherings outside our unit. | 1 | 2 | 3 | 4 | 5 |
| 14. | The problems of my teammates are my problems too. | 1 | 2 | 3 | 4 | 5 |
| 15. | Resolving conflict is an activity I enjoy. | 1 | 2 | 3 | 4 | 5 |
| 16. | I would cooperate with another unit in the organization even if I disagreed with the position taken by its members. | 1 | 2 | 3 | 4 | 5 |
| 17. | I am an idea generator on the job. | 1 | 2 | 3 | 4 | 5 |
| 18. | It is fun for me to bargain whenever I have the opportunity. | 1 | 2 | 3 | 4 | 5 |
| 19. | Team members listen to me when I speak. | 1 | 2 | 3 | 4 | 5 |
| 20. | People have asked me to assume the leadership of an activity several times in my life. | 1 | 2 | 3 | 4 | 5 |
| 21. | I have always been a convincing person. | 1 | 2 | 3 | 4 | 5 |
| 22. | I enjoy imagining a bright future for a group to which I belong. | 1 | 2 | 3 | 4 | 5 |
| 23. | Several people have told me that I have good ability to see the big picture. | 1 | 2 | 3 | 4 | 5 |
| 24. | I am willing to listen to people gripe and complain about their job. | 1 | 2 | 3 | 4 | 5 |
| 25. | I enjoy the opportunity to work with people from cultures different than my own. | 1 | 2 | 3 | 4 | 5 |

**Scoring and Interpretation:** Calculate your total score by adding the numbers circled. A tentative interpretation of the scoring is as follows:

- **90–100:** High readiness for the leadership role
- **60–89:** Moderate readiness for the leadership role
- **40–59:** Some uneasiness with the leadership role
- **39 or less:** Low readiness for the leadership role

If you are already a successful leader and you scored low on this questionnaire, ignore your score. If you scored surprisingly low and you are not yet a leader, or are currently performing poorly as a leader, study the statements carefully. Consider changing your attitude or your behavior so that you can legitimately answer more of the statements with a 4 or a 5. Studying the rest of this text will give you additional insights that may be helpful in your development as a leader.

   **b.** providing team members with feedback concerning ineffective performance

   **c.** ensuring that team members are informed of steps that can improve their performance

   **d.** implementing rewards and punishments to encourage and sustain good performance

   **e.** inspiring people through such means as being charismatic, creating visions, telling interesting stories, and being highly ethical

5. ***Team builder.*** A key aspect of a leader's role is to build an effective team. Activities contributing to this role include:

   **a.** ensuring that team members are recognized for their accomplishments, such as through letters of appreciation

   **b.** initiating activities that contribute to group morale, such as giving parties and sponsoring sports teams

   **c.** holding periodic staff meetings to encourage team members to talk about their accomplishments, problems, and concerns

6. ***Team player.*** Related to the team-builder role is that of the team player. Three behaviors of team players are:

   **a.** displaying appropriate personal conduct

   **b.** cooperating with other units in the organization

   **c.** displaying loyalty to superiors by fully supporting their plans and decisions

7. ***Technical problem solver.*** It is particularly important for supervisors and middle managers to help team members solve technical problems. Two activities contributing to this role are:

   **a.** serving as a technical expert or adviser, such as helping the group make optimum of social marketing to promote the company

   **b.** performing individual contributor tasks on a regular basis, such as making sale calls or repairing machinery

8. ***Entrepreneur.*** Although not self-employed, managers who work in large organizations have some responsibility for suggesting innovative ideas or furthering the business aspects of the firm. Three entrepreneurial leadership role activities are:

   **a.** reading trade publications and professional journals to keep up with what is happening in the industry and profession

   **b.** talking with customers or others in the organization to keep aware of changing needs and requirements

   **c.** getting involved in situations outside the unit that could suggest ways of improving the unit's performance, such as visiting other firms, attending professional meetings or trade shows, and participating in educational programs

9. ***Strategy developer.*** Top-level managers develop strategy, usually assisted by input from others throughout the organization. Carrying out the strategy developer role enables the manager to practice strategic leadership. The strategist role is concerned with shaping the future of the organization, or a unit within the larger organization. Specific activities involved in this role include:

   **a.** setting a vision and direction for the organization and providing innovative ideas to pursue

   **b.** helping the firm deal with the external environment

   **c.** helping develop organizational policies

   **d.** being a thought leader in the sense of the organization being widely respected for advancing a field or producing a superior product

10. ***Executor.*** In carrying out the executor role, the leader makes things happen, often helping translate plans into action. Parts of this role include:

   **a.** translating strategy into action, such as helping develop action plans

   **b.** making change happen

   **c.** holding people accountable to ensure that productive work is accomplished

A common thread in the leadership roles of a manager is that the managerial leader in some way inspires or influences others. An analysis in the *Harvard Business Review* concluded that the most basic role for corporate leaders is to release the human spirit that makes initiative, creativity, and entrepreneurship possible.[27] An important practical implication is that managers at every level can exercise leadership. For example, a team leader can make an important contribution to the firm's thrust for efficiency by explaining to team members how to minimize duplications in a mailing list. Leadership Skill-Building Exercise 1-1 provides an opportunity to apply role analysis to yourself.

# LEADERSHIP SKILL-BUILDING EXERCISE 1-1

## My Leadership Role Analysis

Here is an opportunity for you to think through your current level of skill or potential ability to carry out successfully the ten leadership roles already described. Each role will be listed along with a reminder of one of its key aspects. Check next to each role whether it is an activity you could carry out now, or something for which you will need more experience and preparation. For those activities you check as "capable of doing it now," jot down an example of your success in this area. For example, a person who checked "capable of doing it now" for Role 7, technical problem solver, might have written: "I helped the restaurant where I was an assistant manager bring in more revenue during off-peak hours. I promoted an early-bird supper for senior citizens."

Few readers of this book will have had experience in carrying out most of these roles. So relate the specific roles to any leadership experience you may have had, including full-time work, part-time work, volunteer work, clubs, committees, and sports.

| LEADERSHIP ROLE | CAPABLE OF DOING IT NOW | NEED PREPARATION AND EXPERIENCE |
|---|---|---|
| 1. Figurehead (Engage in ceremonial activities; represent the group to outsiders.) | ☐ | ☐ |
| 2. Spokesperson (Answer inquiries; report information about the group to outsiders.) | ☐ | ☐ |
| 3. Negotiator (Make deals with others for needed resources.) | ☐ | ☐ |
| 4. Coach and motivator (Recognize achievements; encourage; give feedback and advice; inspire people.) | ☐ | ☐ |
| 5. Team builder (Contribute to group morale; hold meetings to encourage members to talk about accomplishments and concerns.) | ☐ | ☐ |
| 6. Team player (Correct conduct; cooperate with others; be loyal.) | ☐ | ☐ |
| 7. Technical problem solver (Help group members solve technical problems; perform individual contributor tasks.) | ☐ | ☐ |
| 8. Entrepreneur (Suggest innovative ideas and further business activity of the group; search for new undertakings for the group.) | ☐ | ☐ |
| 9. Strategy developer (Set direction for others based on external environment.) | ☐ | ☐ |
| 10. Executor (Makes things happen, often helping translate plans into action.) | ☐ | ☐ |

**Interpretation:** The more of the ten roles you are ready to perform, the more ready you are to function as a leader or carry out leadership roles. Your study of leadership will facilitate carrying out more of these roles effectively. For purposes of skill development, choose one of the roles in which you need preparation and experience. Read some information in this text or elsewhere about the role, and then practice that role when the opportunity arises. Or create an opportunity to practice that role. For example, assume you have a valuable skill such as gathering followers on a social media website. During the next couple of weeks, coach a beginner in creating effective social media posts.

The accompanying Leader in Action helps illustrate both leadership roles and the fact that a leader can make a difference.

## LEADER IN ACTION

### Apple Car Chief Bob Mansfield Has Provided Direction to Many Key Product Groups

Over the years when Apple Inc. needed a leader to direct the hardware engineering for a key project, top management frequently turned to veteran Bob Mansfield. So it was logical when CEO Tim Cook wanted a strong leader to take over the reins of the autonomous driving system that he chose Mansfield.

Previous to the car project, Mansfield was the senior vice president of Technologies at Apple, a group that combined all of Apple's wireless teams into one unit, fostering innovation at an even higher level. He was also previously the leader in charge of some of the company's biggest hits, such as the original iPad, the iMac, and the MacBook Air. Although not an automobile specialist, he is skilled at converting Apple's hardware division into reality. Mansfield, along with design chief Jony Ive, was one of the few executives to appear in Apple's carefully designed product announcement videos.

Under Mansfield's leadership, the company has not abandoned its effort to build an Apple Car, but it has begun to focus more heavily on developing an autonomous driving system. Such a system could make it more feasible to partner with a traditional automobile manufacturer in the future. Mansfield has three teams in his division: one for software, one for sensors, and one for hardware engineering.

One of the implied purposes of appointing Mansfield to the car project was to get it back on track because the project had been mired in problems. One of the challenges, for example, was for Apple to find a way to differentiate its proposed vehicle for automotive companies entering the self-driving field.

### QUESTIONS

1. Identify at least two roles that Mansfield occupies, and explain your reasoning.
2. What do you see as Mansfield's most important qualification for heading up the Apple Car project?
3. Even if Apple is a great company and Mansfield is a strong leader, would you ever purchase a self-driving car produced by a maker of electronic gadgets and small computers?

*Sources:* Original story created from facts and observations in the following sources: Daisuke Wakabayashi, "Apple Taps New Leader for Car," *The Wall Street Journal*, July 26, 2016, p. B1; Matt Burns, "Apple's Car Project to Be Led by Bob Mansfield," *TC* (https://techcrunch.com), July 25, 2016, pp. 1–7; Jon Fingas, "Apple Picks a Well-Known Executive to Lead Its Electric Car Team," *www.engadget.com*, July 25, 2016, pp. 1–2; Juli Clover, "Apple's Car Project Shifts Toward Autonomous Driving System Under Mansfield's Direction," July 28, 2016, pp. 1–3; Steven Max Patterson, "Opinion: Why Bob Mansfield Was Cut from Apple's Executive Team," *Network Word* (www.ndetworkworld.com), July 29, 2013, pp. 1–5.

## The Satisfactions and Frustrations of Being a Leader

The term *leader* has a positive connotation for most people. To be called a leader is generally better than to be called a follower or a subordinate. (The preferred term for a person who reports to a leader or manager is *team member, group member,* or *associate.* Researchers, however, continue to use the terms *subordinate* and *follower* for technical purposes.) Yet being a leader, such as a team leader, vice president, or COO (chief operating officer), does not always bring personal satisfaction. Some leadership jobs are more fun than others, such as being the leader of a successful group with cheerful team members.

Because most of you are contemplating becoming a leader or moving further into a leadership role, it is worthwhile to examine some of the potential satisfactions and frustrations that many people find in being an organizational leader.

### Satisfactions of Leaders

The types of satisfactions that you might obtain from being a formal leader depend on your particular leadership position. Factors such as the amount of money you are paid and the type of people in your group influence your satisfaction. Leaders often experience seven sources of satisfaction.

1. *A feeling of power and prestige.* Being a leader automatically grants you some power. Prestige is forthcoming because many people think highly of people who are leaders. In some organizations, top-level leaders are addressed as Mr., Mrs., or Ms., whereas lower-ranking people are referred to by their surnames. Yet most leaders encourage others to address them by their first names.

2. *A chance to help others grow and develop.* A leader works directly with people, often teaching them job skills, serving as a mentor, and listening to personal problems. Part of a leader's job is to help other people become managers and leaders. A leader often feels as much of a people helper as does a human resource manager or a counselor. Kip Tindell, founder of the Container Store, served as CEO for thirty-eight years before leaving that role to become chairman in 2016. He says that one of the most rewarding aspects of his job is enriching people's lives.[28]

3. *High income.* Leaders, in general, receive higher pay than team members, and executive leaders in major business corporations typically earn several million dollars per year. A handful of business executives receive compensation of over $100 million per year, and several have received over $150 million as compensation for being fired. If money is an important motivator or satisfier, being a leader has a built-in satisfaction. In some situations, a team leader earns virtually the same amount of money as other team members. Occupying a team leadership position, however, is a starting point on the path to high-paying leadership positions.

4. *Respect and status.* A leader frequently receives respect from group members. He or she also enjoys a higher status than people who are not occupying a leadership role. Status accompanies being appointed to a leadership position on or off the job. When an individual's personal qualifications match the position, his or her status is even higher.

5. *Good opportunities for advancement.* Once you become a leader, your advancement opportunities increase. Obtaining a leadership position is a vital first step for career advancement in many organizations. Staff or individual contributor positions help broaden a person's professional experience, but most executives rise through a managerial path.

6. *A feeling of being in on things.* A side benefit of being a leader is that you receive more inside information. For instance, as a manager you are invited to attend management meetings. In those meetings, you are given information not passed along to individual contributors. One such tidbit might be plans for expansion or downsizing.

7. *An opportunity to control money and other resources.* A leader is often in the position of helping to prepare a department budget and authorize expenses. Even though you cannot spend this money personally, knowing that your judgment on financial matters is trusted does provide some satisfaction. Many leaders in both private and public organizations control annual budgets of several million dollars.

Leadership Skill-Building Exercise 1-2 provides you an opportunity to think about the satisfactions of being a leader.

## Dissatisfactions and Frustrations of Leaders

About one out of ten people in the workforce is classified as a supervisor, administrator, or manager. Not every one of these people is a true leader. Yet the problems these people experience often stem from the leadership portions of their job. Many individual contributors refuse to accept a leadership role because of the frustrations they have seen leaders endure. These frustrations include the following:

# LEADERSHIP SKILL-BUILDING EXERCISE 1-2

### Appreciating the Satisfactions of Being a Leader

An indirect way of building leadership skills is to identify which aspects of leadership appear to be particularly satisfying and then plan to emphasize those aspects in your current or future leadership activities. Toward this end, interview two people in leadership positions in any field whom you consider to be successful. The interview can be conducted in-person, over the phone, by e-mail, or through texting. Ask your subject one or two basic questions such as "What's really fun about your job?" or "What is the most satisfying aspect of your leadership position?"

Observe whether the key satisfactions you uncover match those in the text. If the satisfactions you uncover resonate with you, think about how you could emphasize that aspect of leadership. For example, one of the people you interview might say, "It's great fun celebrating victories with the group." The skill you would then aim for be to make a point of celebrating any victories the group you lead might have.

1. ***Too much uncompensated overtime.*** People in leadership jobs are usually expected to work longer hours than other employees. Such unpaid hours are called casual overtime. People in organizational leadership positions typically spend about fifty-five hours per week working. During peak periods of peak demands, this figure can surge to eighty hours per week.

2. ***Too many headaches***. It would take several pages to list all the potential problems leaders face. Being a leader is a good way to discover the validity of Murphy's law: "If anything can go wrong, it will." A leader is subject to a batch of problems involving people and things. Many people find that a leadership position is a source of stress, and many managers experience burnout.

3. ***Facing a perform-or-perish mentality.*** Many leaders face an enormous amount of pressure to either perform or be fired. These pressures often can be found in companies owned by private equity (or buyout) firms. The head of each company owned by an equity firm is expected to make the company profitable through such means as slashing costs, boosting sales in international markets, and paying down debt. There is also considerable pressure on the CEO to improve operations by making them more efficient.[29]

4. ***Not enough authority to carry out responsibility.*** People in managerial positions complain repeatedly that they are held responsible for things over which they have little control. As a leader, you might be expected to work with an ill-performing team member, yet you lack the power to fire him or her. Or you might be expected to produce high-quality service with too small a staff and no authority to become fully staffed.

5. ***Loneliness.*** The higher you rise as a leader, the lonelier you will be in a certain sense. Leadership limits the number of people in whom you can confide. It is awkward to confide negative feelings about your employer to a team member. It is equally awkward to complain about one group member to another. Some people in leadership positions feel lonely because they miss being one of the gang.

6. ***Too many problems involving people.*** A major frustration facing a leader is the number of human resource problems requiring action. The lower your leadership position, the more such problems you face. For example, the office supervisor spends more time dealing with problem employees than does the chief information officer. If you do not like dealing with people problems, you are not suited for a leadership or management position.

7. ***Too much organizational politics.*** People at all levels of an organization, from the office assistant to the chairperson of the board, must be aware of political factors. Yet you can avoid politics more easily as an individual contributor than you can as a leader. As a leader you have to engage in political byplay from three directions: below, sideways, and upward. Political tactics such as forming alliances and coalitions are a necessary part of a leader's role. Another troublesome aspect of organizational politics is that there are people who seek to discredit you, perhaps even by fabricating mistakes you have made.

8. ***The pursuit of conflicting goals.*** A major challenge facing leaders is to navigate among conflicting goals. The central theme of these dilemmas is attempting to grant others the authority to act independently, yet still getting them aligned or pulling together for a common purpose.[30] Many of the topics relating to these conflicting goals are discussed at later points in the text.

9. ***Being perceived as unethical, especially if you are a corporate executive.*** The many corporate financial scandals made public in recent years have led to extreme perceptions that CEOs, in particular, are dishonest, unethical, and almost criminal in their behavior. Even if 95 percent of corporate leaders are honest and devoted to their constituents, the leader still has to deal with the possibility of being perceived as dishonest.

10. ***Job fatigue and burnout as a result of the preceding nine problems.*** Leaders occupying high-level positions face so many pressures that many of them experience fatigue and even burnout—intense fatigue and resentment caused by dealing with heavy stress over a prolonged period of time. According to a study conducted by Harvard Medical School faculty, 96 percent of senior leaders reported at least some burnout, with one-third describing their burnout as extreme. The round-the-clock attention to responsibilities contributes to the excessive fatigue. Another major contributor to leader burnout is being responsible for an action that hurts so many people, such as laying off workers.[31]

## A Framework for Understanding Leadership

Many different theories and explanations of leadership have been developed because of the interest in leadership as a practice and as a research topic. Several attempts have been made to integrate the large number of leadership theories into one comprehensive framework.[32] The framework presented in Figure 1-2 and described here focuses on the major sets of variables that influence leadership effectiveness. The framework suggests that the leadership process is a function of the leader, group members (or followers), and other situational variables.

The basic framework presented in Figure 1-2 emphasizes this situational perspective (referring to the situational variable just mentioned). According to this model, leadership can best be understood by examining its key variables: leader characteristics and traits, behavior and style, group member characteristics, and the internal and external environment. At the left side of the framework, **leadership effectiveness** refers to attaining desirable outcomes such as productivity, quality, and satisfaction in a given situation. Whether or not the leader is effective depends on the three sets of variables in the box.

The left box, *leader characteristics* refers to the inner qualities, such as self-confidence and problem-solving ability that help a leader function effectively in many situations. *Leader behavior and style* refers to the activities engaged in by the leader, including characteristic approach, that relate to his or her effectiveness. A leader who frequently coaches group members and practices participative leadership, for example, might be effective in many circumstances.

*Group member characteristics* refers to attributes of the group members that could have a bearing on how effective the leadership attempt will be. Intelligent and well-motivated group members, for example, help the leader do an outstanding job. The *internal and external environment* also influences leadership effectiveness. A leader in a culturally diverse environment,

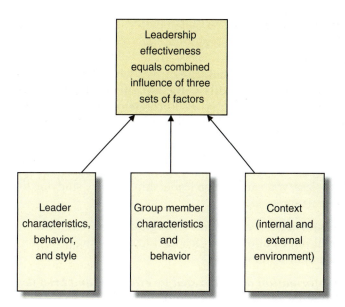

**FIGURE 1-2**    A Basic Framework for Understanding Leadership.

Leader Characteristics And Behavior Are Described In Chapters 2, 3, 4, 8, 11, And 12. Group Member Characteristics And Behavior Are Described In Chapters 5, 9, And 12. The Context Of Leadership Is Described In Chapters 13, 14, And 15.

for example, will need to have multicultural skills to be effective. All of the topics in this text fit somewhere into this model, and the fit will be more obvious at some places than at others.

The information at the bottom of Figure 1-2 outlines how the elements of leadership line up with chapters in the text. A key point of this model is that leadership is a multilevel phenomenon. The leader interacts with group members one at a time, and also with the group. At the same time, leadership takes place in the context of the organization and the external environment. As noted by leadership scholars Francis J. Yammarino and Fred Danjsereau, leadership involves a movement from one level (person level) to a higher level (leader–follower group level).[33] After that come the organizational and societal levels. A brief example of leadership as a multilevel phenomenon follows:

> Team leader Ashley decides to coach team member Li on how to express her ideas more forcibly when making a PowerPoint presentation. Ashley recognizes that Li is shy, so she moves slowly with her coaching. Ashley also recognizes that she is working with a supportive team, so she thinks that the team will be encouraging toward Li in whatever progress she makes. In addition, Ashley recognizes that the organization as a whole encourages assertiveness, so she feels justified in coaching Li toward being more assertive in her presentations. Yet at the same time Ashley understands that Li was raised in a culture (society level) that values humility and timidity so she does not push Li too fast to make improvements.

A recently developed integrative process model of leadership provides two implications[34] of the framework presented in Figure 1-2. The first implication is that *context influences leadership at any given moment.* Context in this sense refers to any external stimuli that may impact the nature of leadership. For example, if the organization is facing a crisis, the leader might have to emphasize compassion for people and provide clear guidance about a plan to deal with the crisis.

The second implication is that leadership is a process with intrapersonal and interpersonal mechanisms (or modes of transmission). The intrapersonal mechanisms include the leader's traits and emotions. Among the traits are cognitive skills and personality factors that influence leadership effectiveness. For example, an intelligent person would be effective at developing strategy. The interpersonal mechanisms refer to the impact of the leader on the behavior of others. For example, a leader who is perceived to be charismatic might influence others to make personal sacrifices for the good of the organization.

## Skill Development in Leadership

Leadership skills are in high demand. Executives who recruit candidates for high-level management jobs list leadership skills as the top attributes they want. Leadership skills are also sought in candidates for entry-level professional positions. Two reasons are that a job candidate with leadership skills is more likely to be self-reliant and also he or she can be placed in charge of a part of a project.[35] Although students of leadership will find this information encouraging, developing leadership skills is more complex and ambiguous than developing a structured skill such as inserting an additional memory card into a computer. Nevertheless, you can develop leadership skills by studying this textbook, which follows a general learning model:

1. *Conceptual information and behavioral guidelines.* Each chapter in this textbook presents useful information about leadership, including a section titled "Guidelines for Action and Skill Development."

2. *Conceptual information demonstrated by examples and brief descriptions of leaders in action.* Students can learn much from reading about how effective (or ineffective) leaders operate.

3. *Experiential exercises.* The textbook provides an opportunity for practice and personalization through cases, role plays, and self-assessment quizzes. Self-quizzes are emphasized here because they are an effective method of helping you personalize the information, thereby linking conceptual information to yourself. For example, you will read about the importance of assertiveness in leadership and also complete an assertiveness quiz.

4. *Feedback on skill utilization, or performance, from others.* Feedback exercises appear at several places in the text. Implementing some of the skills outside of the classroom will provide additional opportunities for feedback.

5. *Practice in natural settings.* Skill development requires active practice. A given skill has to be practiced many times in natural settings before it becomes integrated comfortably into a leader's mode of operation. A basic principle of learning is that practice is necessary to develop and improve skills. Suppose, for example, that you read about giving advice in the form of questions, as described in Chapter 10. If you practice this skill at least six times in live settings, you will probably have acquired an important new skill for coaching others.

Leadership Skill-Building Exercise 1-3 gives you the opportunity to begin developing your leadership skills systematically.

## LEADERSHIP SKILL-BUILDING EXERCISE 1-3

### My Leadership Portfolio

Here, we ask you to begin developing a leadership portfolio that will be a personal document of your leadership capabilities and experiences. In each chapter, we will recommend new entries for your portfolio. At the same time, we encourage you to use your imagination in determining what constitutes a suitable addition to your leadership portfolio.

We suggest you begin your portfolio with a personal mission statement that explains the type of leadership you plan to practice. An example might be, "*I intend to become a well-respected corporate professional, a key member of a happy and healthy family, and a contributor to my community. I aspire to lead many people toward constructive activities.*" Include your job résumé in your portfolio, and devote a special section to leadership experiences. These experiences can be from the job, community and religious activities, and sports. (See Leadership Self-Assessment Quiz 1-2.)

# LEADERSHIP SELF-ASSESSMENT QUIZ 1-2

**The Leadership Experience Audit**

*Instructions:* Readers of this book vary considerably in their leadership, managerial, and supervisory experience. Yet even readers who have not yet occupied a formal leadership position may have had at least a taste of being a leader. Use the following checklist to record any possible leadership experiences you might have had in the past or have now.

1. Held a formal leadership position, such as vice president, department head, manager, assistant manager, team leader, group leader, or project manager ☐

2. Seized the opportunity on the job to take care of a problem, although not assigned such responsibility ☐

3. Headed a committee or task force ☐

4. Was captain or cocaptain of an athletic team ☐

5. Held office in a club at high school, career school, or college ☐

6. Was editor of a campus newspaper or section of the newspaper such as sports ☐

7. Organized a study group for a course ☐

8. Organized an ongoing activity to sell merchandise at people's homes, such as for Avon, Mary Kay, or Tupperware ☐

9. Worked in multilevel sales and recruited and guided new members ☐

10. Organized a charity drive for a school or religious organization ☐

11. Organized a vacation trip for friends or family ☐

12. Took charge during a crisis, such as by helping people out of a burning building or a flooded house ☐

13. Was head of a choir or a band ☐

14. Headed a citizens' group making demands on a company or the government ☐

15. Organized a group of friends to help out people in need, such as physically disabled senior citizens ☐

16. Other ☐

*Interpretation:* The more experiences you checked, the more leadership experience you already have under your belt. Leadership experience of any type can be valuable in learning to work well with people and coordinate their efforts. Many CEOs in a variety of fields got their start as assistant fast-food restaurant managers.

# Followership: Being an Effective Group Member

To be an effective leader, one needs good followers. According to followership expert Robert Kelley, about 70–90 percent of all work in organizations is performed by people in follower roles.[36] As we mentioned at the outset of this book, the word *followers* suffers from political incorrectness; yet it is a neutral term as used by leadership researchers. A point of view that represents a modern view of leadership, as explained by J. Richard Hackman and Ruth Wageman, is that leaders are also followers, and followers also exhibit leadership. Each boss is also a subordinate, such as a team leader reporting to a middle manager.[37] Moreover, each subordinate will often carry out a leadership role, such as heading up a short-term project—or even organizing this year's holiday party. Another perspective on followers is that they are the people who get things done and that the bright ideas of leaders would go nowhere without the doers.[38]

Followership has become so important that some organizations offer training in the subject. Training in followership often focuses on how to take responsibility for shared goals, being a self-starter, and providing constructive feedback to leaders when they make mistakes. In some high-risk occupations, such as an airplane crew member, followership skills are so important that formal training in this behavior is a formal requirement.[39]

Most of the topics in our study of leadership are aimed at inspiring, motivating, and influencing group members to achieve organizational goals. It is also valuable, however, to focus on three key aspects of being an effective group member: types of followers, the personal characteristics of productive followers, and the importance of collaboration between leaders and followers.

## Types of Followers

A major challenge in being a leader is to recognize that followers differ substantially in talent and motivation. Similarly, a challenge in becoming an effective follower is to understand your basic approach to being a group member. Barbara Kellerman offers a typology that helps explain how followers differ from one another. She focuses on the defining factor of the level of engagement with the leader or group to arrive at five types of followers, as illustrated in Figure 1-3. At one end of the continuum is "feeling and doing nothing." At the other end is "being passionately committed and deeply involved."[40]

1. *Isolates* are completely detached and passively support the status quo by not taking action to bring about changes. They do not care much about their leaders and just do their job without taking an interest in the overall organization. Isolates need coaching, yet sometimes firing them is the only solution.

2. *Bystanders* are free riders who are typically detached when it fits their self-interests. At a meeting, a bystander is more likely to focus on the refreshments and taking peeks at his or her personal text messages. Bystanders have low internal motivation, so the leader has to work hard to find the right motivators to spark the bystander into action.

3. *Participants* show enough engagement to invest some of their own time and money to make a difference, such as taking the initiative to learn new technology that would help the group. Participants are sometimes for, and sometimes against, the leader and the company. The leader has to review their work and attitudes carefully to determine whether or not the participant is being constructive.

   Participants have also been regarded as *active followers*, or those who make a major contribution to the mission of the group. The term derives from experiences at the space shuttle activities at NASA, and the National Outdoor Leadership School that includes mountain climbing, expeditions, and adventure paths. Leaders at both activities said that success in their ventures requires a single-minded focus on the goal and a team of active followers.[41] Such individuals will inform the leader and the group

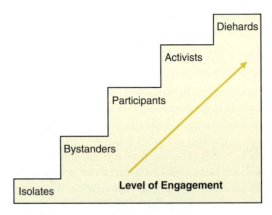

**FIGURE 1-3**   Followers Classified by Level of Engagement.

about what they think is necessary for success, or survival, such as alerting the leader to a potential avalanche.

4. **Activists** are considerably engaged, heavily invested in people and processes, and eager to demonstrate their support or opposition. They feel strongly, either positively or negatively, about their leader and the organization and act accordingly. An activist might be enthusiastic about reaching company goals, or so convinced that the company is doing the wrong thing that he or she blows the whistle (reports the company to an outside agency). The leader has to stay aware of whether the activist is for or against the company.

5. **Diehards** are super-engaged to the point that they are willing to go down for their own cause, or willing to oust the leader if they feel he or she is headed in the wrong direction. Diehards can be an asset or a liability to the leader. Diehards have an even stronger tendency to be whistleblowers than do activists. A diehard, for example, might take it on her own to test the lead quantity of paint in children's furniture sold by the company. Leaders have to stay in touch with diehards to see if their energy is being pointed in the service of the organization.

The categorization of followers just presented adds a touch of realism to understanding the challenging role of a leader. Not everybody in the group is supercharged and eager to collaborate toward attaining organizational goals.

## Essential Qualities of Effective Followers

As observed by Robert E. Kelley, effective followers share four essential qualities:[42]

1. **Self-management.** The key to being a good follower is to think for oneself and to work well without close supervision. Effective group members see themselves as being as capable as their leaders.

2. **Commitment.** Effective followers are committed to something beyond themselves, be it a cause, product, department, organization, idea, or value. To a committed group member, the leader facilitates progress toward achieving a goal.

3. **Competence and focus.** Effective followers build their competence and focus their efforts for maximum impact. Competence centers on mastering skills that will be useful to the organization. Less-effective group members rarely take the initiative to engage in training and development.

4. **Courage.** Effective followers establish themselves as independent, critical thinkers, and fight for what they believe is right. A good follower, for example, might challenge the company's policy of taking ninety days to make good on accounts payable, or of recruiting key people almost exclusively from people with demographic characteristics similar to those of top management.

This list is illustrative, since almost any positive human quality would contribute directly or indirectly to being an effective group member or follower. Another way of framing the qualities of effective followers is to say that such followers display the personal characteristics and qualities of leaders. Although leaders cannot be expected to change the personalities of group members, they can take steps to encourage these qualities. Interventions such as coaching, empowerment, supportive communication, and frequent feedback would support effective followership.

## Collaboration Between Leaders and Followers

A key role for followers is to collaborate with leaders in achieving organizational goals, as reflected in the emphasis on collaborative leadership. As described by leadership guru Warren Bennis, the post-bureaucratic organization (a type of organization that came after the bureaucratic era, such as team-based organizations) requires a new kind of alliance between leaders and the led. When high-level leaders do not make all of the decisions but solicit input from knowledgeable group members, leaders and followers work together more closely.[43]

A related point here is that the new leader and the led are close allies. Great leaders are made by great groups; every organizational member needs to contribute energy and talent to help leaders carry out their roles successfully. We emphasize again that in the modern organization, leaders and followers often switch roles, such as a group member being assigned leadership responsibility for a group task. In the words of Petros G. Malakyan, "In reality, one cannot claim that he or she is a leader or a follower at all times and in all circumstances."[44]

## SUMMARY

Leadership is the ability to inspire confidence in and support among the people who are needed to achieve organizational goals. Leading is a major part of a manager's job, but a manager also plans, organizes, and controls. Leadership is said to deal with change, inspiration, motivation, and influence. In contrast, management deals more with maintaining equilibrium and the status quo. Leadership is often regarded as a partnership or collaboration between leaders and group members.

Many people attribute organizational performance to leadership actions. Some research evidence supports this widely accepted view. For example, one study showed that leadership actions can affect performance, but only if the leader is perceived to be responsible and inspirational. Others argue that certain factors in the work environment, called substitutes for leadership, make the leader's role almost superfluous. Among these factors are close-knit teams of highly trained workers, intrinsic satisfaction with work, and professional norms. Another anti-leadership argument is that the leader is irrelevant in most organizational outcomes because the situation is more important, and the leader has unilateral control over only a few resources. Moreover, since new leaders are chosen whose values are compatible with those of the firm, those values actually are more important.

Examining the roles carried out by leaders contributes to an understanding of the leadership function. Ten such leadership roles are the figurehead, spokesperson, negotiator, coach and motivator, team builder, team player, technical problem solver, entrepreneur, strategy developer, and executor. An important implication of these roles is that managers at every level can exert leadership.

Leadership positions often are satisfying because they offer such things as power, prestige, the opportunity to help others, high income, and the opportunity to control resources. At other times, being a leader carries with it a number of frustrations, such as facing a perform-or-perish mentality, insufficient authority, having to deal with human problems, and too much organizational politics. The leader also has the difficult task of balancing workers' need to be independent with their need to commit to a common purpose.

The framework for understanding leadership presented here is based on the idea that the leadership process is a function of the leader, group members, and other situational variables. According to the model, leadership can best be understood by examining its key variables: leader characteristics and traits, leader behavior and style, group member characteristics, and the internal and external environment. Leadership effectiveness is dependent on all three sets of variables. Another point of the model is that leadership is multilevel, involving the individual, the small group, and the organization. The society and culture might also need to be taken into account. Two implications of the model are that context influences leadership at any given moment and that leadership is a process with intrapersonal and interpersonal mechanisms.

Leadership skills can be developed by following a general learning model that involves acquiring conceptual knowledge, reading examples, doing experiential exercises, obtaining feedback, and practicing in natural settings.

A major challenge facing leaders is that followers differ substantially in characteristics, including level of engagement from feeling and doing nothing to total passion, commitment, and involvement. To be an effective leader, one needs good followers with characteristics such as self-management, commitment, competence and focus, and courage. A key role for followers is to collaborate with leaders in achieving organizational goals. The post-bureaucratic organization requires a new kind of alliance between leaders and the led.

## KEY TERMS

**leadership** 02
**emergent leaders** 03

**substitutes for leadership** 06

**leadership effectiveness** 14

## GUIDELINES FOR ACTION AND SKILL DEVELOPMENT

Vast amounts of information have been gathered about leaders and leadership, and many different leadership theories have been developed. Many leadership research findings and theories are confusing and contradictory. Nevertheless, from this thicket of information emerge many useful leadership concepts and techniques to guide you toward becoming a more effective leader.

As you work toward leadership effectiveness, first be familiar with the approaches to leadership described in this text. Then choose the formulation that seems best to fit the leadership situation you face. For example, if you are leading a team, review the information about team leadership. Typically, an effective leader needs to combine several leadership approaches to meet the demands of a given situation. For instance, a leader might need to combine creative problem solving and emotional support to members to help the team rebound from a crisis.

The eclectic (choosing from among many) approach we recommend is likely to be more effective than accepting an idea such as "there are six secrets to leadership success."

### Discussion Questions and Activities

1. Why bother studying leadership when fields such as petroleum engineering and physician assistant pay high starting salaries?
2. Give an example of how you have exerted leadership on or off the job in a situation in which you did not have a formal leadership position. Explain why you describe your activity as leadership.
3. What would a boss of yours have to do to demonstrate that he or she is an effective leader and an effective manager?
4. Identify a business or sports leader whom you think is highly effective and explain why you think he or she is highly effective.
5. Many people who were voted "the most likely to succeed" in their high school yearbooks become leaders later on in their career. How can you explain this finding?
6. Why might experience in managing entry-level workers, such as in a fast-food restaurant, be valuable leadership experience?
7. If so much useful information is available about leadership, why do we still find so many managers who cannot gain the respect of their subordinates?
8. Considering that so many people of all ages do much of their communication with text messages, what would be wrong with leaders communicating with group members mostly through texting?
9. Which one or two of the ten leadership roles described in this chapter do you think require the highest level of skill? Why?
10. In what way might being an effective follower help prepare a person for becoming an effective leader?

## LEADERSHIP CASE PROBLEM A

### Hailey Wants to Make a Difference

Hailey was recently promoted to the position of production manager in the manufacturing plant of a company that makes desktop printers for commercial and home use. Her department is responsible for producing the printer drums that house the cartridges. Hailey has an undergraduate degree in industrial engineering and an MBA. She aspires toward eventually holding a high-level leadership position in manufacturing or operations. Hailey therefore considers her promotion to production manager to be a building block in her career. She says: "Our country became great by building things. That's why I love manufacturing. Here's my chance at age 26 to make a difference as a manufacturing leader."

Having worked as an industrial engineer for two years at the plant, Hailey understands the technology behind printer drums, as well as the manufacturing process. During her first week in her new assignment, Hailey spent a lot of time talking with her two supervisors and many production technicians. She was particularly looking for ways in which she could provide leadership to the group.

Hailey asked Jud, an experienced supervisor, what changes needed to be made in the functioning of the department. Jud replied: "Right now things are going well. Despite the worldwide decline in the number of desktop computers purchased, we have a nice steady demand for new drums. The office-supply stores still sell a lot of replacement drums for existing printers. I notice too that morale is okay in my department. Just keep the year-end raises and bonuses flowing (said with a laugh)."

Hailey asked Jenna, a supervisor with five years of experience, the same question. Jenna said: "I think the biggest problem we face is not having enough new, qualified production technicians. Maybe making drums is hum-drum, but you need skill to do the job right. These days, most young people don't want to make things. They just want to stay glued to their mobile devices. Also, a lot of the people we recruit for entry-level jobs can't do much math, and they don't want to talk. We need to find a pipeline of new blood for our basic production jobs."

Hailey spoke with Barney, a production technician with twenty-five years of experience, about what changes he thought a department leader should bring about. Barney replied: "Not much, Hailey. I know that you are well educated and very smart, but don't worry much about changes right now. The other guys and gals in the department and I are all happy that our jobs have not been shipped to another country. We also like the idea that we have not been replaced by robots so far."

Hailey was particularly interested in the comments of Gloria, another production technician, who said: "I am a little worried about the future of our department. We are making printer drums, but how long can this last? Maybe you as the leader can find another product for us to make that will keep us going at least until I retire."

Hailey reflected: "I have been collecting a lot of information. But what do I do with the information. As the department leader, how can I make a difference now and in the near future?"

#### QUESTIONS

1. Advise Hailey on where she should get started in making a difference as a leader in the drum-manufacturing department.
2. To what extent do you think it is advisable for Hailey to interview workers in the department to get some input as to what she should do as their leader?

## ASSOCIATED ROLE PLAY

One student plays the role of Hailey who decides to meet with Jud and Jenna to discuss a few exciting leadership initiatives she has planned. Two other students play the role of Jud and Jenna. Jud is a little skeptical of changes being made, and Jenna seems focused on the issue of recruiting the right type of workers. Hailey may have to be persuasive today to sell her initiatives. Feedback from other class members about Hailey's success today is welcomed.

## LEADERSHIP CASE PROBLEM B

### Elon Musk, Business Leader and Serial Entrepreneur

While still in his early forties, Elon Musk had established himself as one of the world's best known entrepreneurs and corporate leaders. He has been considered in the same category as Steve Jobs, Henry Ford, and Thomas Edison. Musk's extraordinary intellect, vision, and the breadth of his ambition make him symbolic of the future. His rise to fame began in 1999 when he founded X.com, an online payment company that eventually became PayPal, and was later sold to eBay for $1.5 billion in stock. In a few years, Musk invested this large amount of money into three start-up companies.

Musk wanted to start a low-cost Mars mission that would capture the imagination of thousands of people about space travel. To make life interplanetary, Musk reasoned that a transport system was needed that would be completely and rapidly reusable. To meet this need, in 2002, he founded Space Exploration Technologies (or SpaceX). The company has promised NASA and several satellite makers that the reusable rockets he is developing can deliver their payloads at substantially lower costs than competitors. SpaceX has contracts worth $4.2 billion for transporting U.S. astronauts and supplies to the International Space Station.

In 2012, the Dragon spacecraft of SpaceX delivered 500 pounds of provisions and equipment to the International Space Station. Dragon returned nine days later, landed in the Pacific Ocean precisely on target two minutes ahead of schedule and in excellent condition. Yet not all of SpaceX's launches have proceeded smoothly. In September 2016, a massive fireball and explosion took place at SpaceX's main launching pad in Cape Canaveral, Florida. The explosion destroyed a rocket as well as a satellite that Facebook planned to use to widen Internet service to Africa. SpaceX was still scrambling to get back on track with satellite deliveries following a launch accident in 2015.

In his quest to help Earth become less dependent on carbon-generating fuels, Musk cofounded Tesla, the electric car company, and SolarCity, which manufactures and markets solar-energy systems. Musk believes that Tesla is heading the world into a future without gasoline. In 2015, he predicted that in ten years Tesla would equal the market capitalization of Apple, which at the time was the world's most valuable company. Robots are used extensively in building Tesla cars, often eight at a time. Tesla automobiles are sold directly to consumers, often through two dozen stores or galleries in the United States. Traditional dealers dislike this direct approach to sales because they say it violates state franchise laws.

Musk has also built a battery factory that will supply batteries for both Tesla vehicles and the solar systems built by SolarCity. The batteries will store energy in homes, with larger batteries that store energy for utility and business firms. Musk describes his large batteries as "a fundamental transformation of how the world works." Musk believes that Powerpacks paired with solar panels could eliminate conventional power plants in some cities.

Musk is a strong believer in simplicity in technical design, in manufacturing, and in running an organization. Tim Mueller, the director of propulsion systems at SpaceX, says that the bureaucracy is much simpler in his company than in an organization such as NASA, which has to satisfy so many constituents. He says: "If you want to change something of fix something, just talk to Elon. It keeps the signal-to-noise ratio high."

Musk displays a strong belief in his own capabilities and creativity, seen as a sign of hubris by some observers. He believes that he has a design that will allow for the colonization of Mars. Musk has filed for almost no patents because he believes that he is so strongly ahead of the field that nobody else could copy his technology. Musk's reasoning is that if you move fast enough, nobody can catch you.

Several people who worked for Musk in the past describe him as autocratic and blunt, often to the point of being offensive. Steve Jurveson, a SpaceX board member, said about Musk: "Like Steve Jobs, Elton does not tolerate C or D players. But I'd say he's nicer than Jobs and a bit more refined than Bill Gates." In 2013, when three battery-related fires erupted in Tesla cars, Musk responded combatively to critics via his blog. He pointed out that gasoline fires were a greater potential danger than battery fires in an electric vehicle.

Musk is strongly interested in human resource management and selects key employees primarily on their ability to solve complex problems, rather than industry-relevant experience. Musk asks candidates what types of complex problems they have solved before, and presses for details.

Musk is such a fanatic about design that he devotes hours to personally inspecting every Tesla car. He will notice a headlamp misaligned by a few millimeters. He once said that the wrong type of screw in a sun visor, "feels like daggers in my eyes."

Musk was raised in South Africa and Canada before coming to the United States to complete his college education  He holds undergraduate degrees in physics and business from the University of Pennsylvania. Musk acquired his expertise in aerospace engineering on his own, including being guided by textbooks on subjects such as fundamentals of liquid propellants as well as propulsion elements. Musk has also carefully studied a biography of Albert Einstein.

### Questions

1. Which roles does Musk appear to occupy as a leader of his companies?

2.  What would you perceive to be a key advantage, and a key disadvantage of reporting directly to Musk?

3.  What is your overall evaluation of Elon Musk as both a business leader and a leader in society?

4.  What factors might have Musk, similar to the late Steve Jobs, going for him as a leader that people will put up with his blunt approach to people?

5.  Incidentally, do you think that Musk's reliance on problem-solving ability as a criterion for hiring would be helpful, or harmful, to new graduates? Explain your reasoning.

*Sources*: Original case based on facts and observations in the following sources: Max Chafkin, "Tunnel Vision: There's a Huge Hole in Musk's Trump-Era Business Plan," *Bloomberg Businessweek*, February 20–March 5, 2017, pp. 52–55; Rolfe Winkler, "Tesla's Musk Dream Big About Traffic," *The Wall Street Journal*, May 1, 2017, p. B4; Winkler, "Brain Is Musk's New Frontier," *The Wall Street Journal*, March 28, 2017, p. B4; John Lippert, "Will Tesla Make Money?" *Bloomberg Markets*, April 2015, pp. 34–42; Max Chaflin, "Elon Musk Thinks Bigger," *Fast Company*, December 2015–January 2016, pp. 118–116, 139–140; Jeff Dyer, Hal Gregersen, and Nathan Furr, " Tesla's Secret Formula," *Forbes*, September 7, 2014, pp. 90–118; Chris Woodyard, "Tesla's CEO Standing Firm," *USA Today Money*, November 20, 2013, p. 5B; Anne Vandermey, "The Shared  Genius of Elon Musk and Steve Jobs," *Fortune*, December 9, 2013, p. 105; "Explosion at Space X Launch Pad Destroys Rocket, Satellite," www.yahoo.com, September 2, 2016, p. 1.

## ASSOCIATED ROLE PLAY

### Expressing Disagreement with Your Boss, Elon Musk

One student plays the role of a direct report to Musk who believes that he should stop trying to sell Tesla automobiles directly to the public. You think, for example, that Tesla Motors Inc. might be better off distributing his vehicles through Toyota or Ford dealers, or perhaps establishing a network of Tesla dealers.

Another person plays the role of Elon Musk who may not take kindly to a direct report who disagrees with his marketing strategy. Run the role play for about six minutes and observe how effectively the direct report is in gaining acceptance of his or her opinion. Observe also the leadership skills of Musk in dealing with dissent.

## NOTES

1.  Original story created from facts and observations in the following sources: "Small Is Powerful," *Wecyclers* (www.smallispowerful.fr). Retrieved July 23, 2016, pp. 1–5; Jaclyn Trop, "Bilikiss Adebiyi-Abiolaq: Turning Trash into Treasure," *Fast Company*, February 2015, pp. 42–43; "Lionesses of Africa: Bilikiss Adebiyi" (www.lionessesof Africa.com), pp. 1–10. Retrieved July 23, 2016; "Welcome to Wecyclers," http://wecyclers.com, pp. 1–3. Retrieved July 23, 2016.

2.  W. Kan Kim and Rene A. Maubourgne, "Parables of Leadership," *Harvard Business Review*, July–August 1992, p. 123.

3.  Derived from a literature review in Bernard M. Bass (with Ruth Bass), *The Bass Handbook of Leadership: Theory, Research, and Managerial Applications*, Fourth Edition (New York: The Free Press, 2008), pp. 15–23.

4.  Marion B. Eberly, Michael D. Johnson, Morela Hernandez, and Bruce J. Avolio, "An Integrative Process Model of Leadership: Examining Loci, Mechanisms, and Event Cycles," *American Psychologist*, September 2013, p. 439.

5.  James Kelly and Scott Nadler, "Leading from Below," *The Wall Street Journal*, March 3–4, 2007, p. R4.

6.  Sankalp Chaturvedi, Michael J. Zyphur, Richard D. Arvey, Bruce J. Avolio, and Gerry Larsson, "The Heritability of Emergent Leadership: Age and Gender as Moderating Factors," *Leadership Quarterly*, April 2012, p. 219.

7.  Tamara L. Friedrich, et al., "A Framework for Understanding Collective Leadership: The Selective Utilization of Leader and Team Expertise Within Networks," *The Leadership Quarterly*, December 2009, pp. 933–958.

8.  Christopher Hann, "We're All in This Together," *Entrepreneur*, March 2013, pp. 157–158.

9.  Gesche Drescher and Yvonne Garbers, "Shared Leadership: A Policy-Capturing Study," *The Leadership Quarterly*, April 2016, pp. 200–217.

10. Herminia Ibarra and Morten T. Hansen, "Are You a Collaborative Leader?" *Harvard Business Review*, July–August 2011, p. 71.

11. Gail T. Fairhurst and Mary Uhl-Bien, "Organizational Discourse Analysis (ODA): Examining Leadership as a Relational Process," *The Leadership Quarterly*, December 2012, pp. 1043–1062.

12. Quoted in Walter Isaacson, "The Real Leadership Lessons of Steve Jobs," *Harvard Business Review*, April 2012, p. 100.

13. John O'Leary, "Do Managers and Leaders Really Do Different Things?" *Harvard Business Review* (https://hbr.org), June 26, 2016, pp. 1–5.

14. Henry Mintzberg, *Managing* (San Francisco: Berrett-Koehler Publishers, 2009), p. 8.

15. Diya Gullapalli, "GMO Taps 1st CEO in 32-Year History," *The Wall Street Journal*, February 13, 2009, p. C9.

16. Christopher Hann, "The Masters," *Entrepreneur*, March 2012, pp. 54–63.

17. *Duke University Executive Leadership Survey*, Center on Leadership & Ethics, March 2009, pp. 1–17.

18. Nitin Nohria, William Joyce, and Bruce Roberson, "What Really Works," *Harvard Business Review*, July 2003, p. 51.

19. Robert B. Kaiser, Robert Hogan, and S. Bartholomew Craig, "Leadership and the Fate of Organizations," *American Psychologist*, February–March 2008, p. 103.

20. Bruce J. Avolio, Rebecca J. Reichard, Sean T. Hannah, Fred O. Walumbwa, and Adrian Chan, "A Meta-Analytic Review of Leadership Impact Research: Experimental and Quasi-Experimental Studies," *The Leadership Quarterly*, October 2009, pp. 764–784.

21. Julian Barling, *The Science of Leadership: Lessons from Research for Organizational Leaders* (New York: Oxford University Press, 2014), pp. 37–41.

22. Adam M. Grant, "Leading with Meaning: Beneficiary Contact, Prosocial Impact, and the Performance Effects of Transformational Leadership," *Academy of Management Journal*, April 2012, pp. 458–476.

23. Jon P. Howell, David E. Bowen, Peter W. Dorfman, Steven Kerr, and Philip Podaskoff, "Substitutes for Leadership: Effective Alternatives to Ineffective Leadership," *Organizational Dynamics*, Summer 1990, p. 23.

24. Thomas H. Hout, "Are Managers Obsolete?" *Harvard Business Review*, March–April 1999, pp. 161–162. (Books in Review); John E. Masthieu, Michael Kukenberger, Lauren D'Innocenzo, and Greg Reilly, "Modeling Reciprocal Team Cohesion-Performance Relationships, as Impacted by Shared Leadership and Members' Competence," *Journal of Applied Psychology*, May 2015, pp. 713–734.

25. J. Richard Hackman and Ruth Wageman, "Asking the Right Questions About Leadership," *American Psychologist*, January 2007, p. 43.

26. Updated and expanded from Henry Mintzberg, *The Nature of Managerial Work* (New York: Harper & Row, 1973); Kenneth Graham Jr. and William M. Mihal, *The CMD Managerial Job Analysis Inventory* (Rochester, NY: Rochester Institute of Technology, Center for Management Development, 1987), pp. 132–133; Mary Jo Hatch, Monika Kostera, and Andrzej K. Koz'min'ski, "The Three Faces of Leadership: Manager, Artist, Priest," *Organizational Dynamics*, vol. 35, no. 1, 2006, pp. 49–68; Dave Ulrich, Norm Smallwood, and Kate Sweetman, *The Leadership Code: Five Rules to Lead By* (Boston: Harvard Business Press, 2008).

27. Christopher A. Bartlett and Sumantra Ghosal, "Changing the Role of Top Management Beyond Systems to People," *Harvard Business Review*, June 2002, pp. 132–133.

28. Cited in Justin Fox, "Employees First!" *Time*, July 7, 2008, p. 45; Phil Wahba, "Why Container Store's Found Is Quitting CEO Job," *Fortune.com*, May 9, 2016, pp. 1–3.

29. Emily Thornton, "Perform or Perish," *BusinessWeek*, November 5, 2007, p. 40.

30. Thomas A. Stewart, "The Nine Dilemmas Leaders Face," *Fortune*, March 18, 1996, pp. 112–113.

31. Leslie Kwoh, "When the CEO Burns Out: Job Fatigue Catches Up to Some Executive Amid Mounting Expectations; No More Forced Smiles," *The Wall Street Journal*, May 8, 2013. The study mentioned is cited in this source.

32. Two examples are Marion B. Eberly, Michael D. Johnson, Morela Hernandez, and Bruce J. Avolio, "An Integrative Process Model of Leadership: Examining Loci, Mechanisms, and Event Cycles," *American Psychologist*, September 2013, pp. 427–443; Francis Yammarino, Fred Dansereau, and Christina J. Kennedy, "A Multiple-Level Multidimensional Approach to Leadership: Viewing Leadership Through an Elephant's Eye," *Organizational Dynamics*, Winter 2001, pp. 149–162.

33. Francis J. Yammarino and Fred Dansereau, "Multi-Level Nature of and Multi-Level Approaches to Leadership," *The Leadership Quarterly*, April 2008, p. 136.

34. Eberly, Johnson, Hernandez, and Avolio, "An Integrative Process Model of Leadership," pp. 436–438.

35. Ronnie Ann, "Why Do Entry-Level Jobs Require Leadership Skills?" *CAREER NOOK*, May 2016, pp. 1–12; Reem Boudraa, "Are Your Skill Sets in Demand and What You Can Do About It," http://blog.bayt.com, August 22, 2013. pp. 1–4.

36. Sue Shellenbarger, "Leader? No, Be a Follower," *The Wall Street Journal*, September 30, 2015, p. D1.

37. Hackman and Wageman, "Asking the Right Questions," p. 45.

38. Nancy Lublin, "Let's Hear It for the Little Guys," *Fast Company*, April 2010, p. 33.

39. Shellenbarger, "Leader? No, Be a Follower," p. D1.

40. Barbara Kellerman, "What Every Leader Needs to Know About Followers," *Harvard Business Review*, December 2007, pp. 84–91.

41. "The Power of 'Active Followers,' from Mission Control to Mountain Climbing," *Knowledge@Wharton*, http://knowledge. wharton.upenn.edu, July 03, 2012, pp. 1–3.

42. Robert E. Kelley, "In Praise of Followers," *Harvard Business Review*, November–December 1988, pp. 142–148.

43. Warren Bennis, "The End of Leadership: Exemplary Leadership Is Impossible Without Full Inclusion, Initiatives, and Cooperation of Followers," *Organizational Dynamics*, Summer 1999, pp. 76–78. (This statement has become increasingly true over the years.)

44. Petros G. Malakyan, "Followership in Leadership Studies: A Case of Leader-Follower Trade Approach," *Journal of Leadership Studies*, no. 4, 2014, p. 17.

## CHAPTER 2

# Traits, Motives, and Characteristics of Leaders

## LEARNING OBJECTIVES

After studying this chapter and *doing* the exercises, you should be able to

- Identify general and task-related traits that contribute to leadership effectiveness.
- Describe how emotional intelligence contributes to leadership effectiveness.
- Identify key motives that contribute to leadership effectiveness.
- Describe cognitive factors associated with leadership effectiveness.
- Discuss the heredity versus environment issue in relation to leadership effectiveness.
- Summarize the strengths and weaknesses of the trait approach to leadership.

## CHAPTER OUTLINE

After working at Macy's for thirty-three years, Jeff Gennette was appointed as the new chief executive officer (CEO), succeeding another company long-timer, Terry Lundgren, in early 2017. Gennette began his career with Macy's as an executive trainee in 1983. The CEO appointment was expected since Gennette's promotion to president of Macy's in 2014. He served as the chief merchandising officer of the company for five years before becoming president. Macy's operates about 870 stores in 45 states, including the stores labeled Macy's, Bloomingdale's, Blue Mercury, and the off-price stores, Macy's Backstage.

Gennette had developed as a skilled retail operator thoroughly familiar with the operations of the famous department store chain.

Gennette became CEO at a very difficult time for Macy's as well as other department store chains. Shoppers were making more purchases online, searching for bargains, and shopping more at off-price stores. (The Backstage stores were opened to help Macy's compete with discount chains.) Craig Johnson, the president of a retail consulting and research firm, said that Gennette was facing a very daunting task as he began his role as CEO. Johnson said, "Macy's is facing some very difficult challenges. I think it's the right move at the right time."

During his over three-decade tenure with Macy's, Gennette has steadily climbed the ranks. The company board looked to him to find a lasting solution to the shifting shopping habits of consumers, as he builds on what his predecessor already accomplished. In addition to his deep knowledge of merchandising, the board decided that Gennette has the courage to make the shifts Macy's need to survive and prosper in the new retail environment. One of Gennette's first initiatives was to simplify pricing to more effectively communicate the value offered to customers. He also planned to make it easier for customers to find their color or size or get the help they need in-store or online. "We are used to winning and we will win again," said Gennette.

Gennette regularly studies information about the retail industry, and is a business administration graduate of Stanford University.[1]

The vignette just presented describes a highly placed manager who has several of the leadership traits discussed in this chapter, particularly the ability to think conceptually (see the big picture), knowledge of the business, as well as showing courage. Gennette's career path also suggests a person with high emotional stability.

When people evaluate managers in terms of their leadership effectiveness, they often scrutinize the managers' traits and personal characteristics. Instead of focusing only on the results the managers achieve, those making the evaluation assign considerable weight to the manager's attributes, such as adherence to high standards. Many people believe intuitively that personal characteristics strongly determine leadership effectiveness.

The trait-based perspective on leadership has reemerged in recent years after having fallen out of favor for decades. A group of researchers analyzed the results of many syntheses of studies about leadership effectiveness. The traits groupings covered were personality and intelligence, and the leadership effectiveness criteria included group performance and satisfaction with the leaders. The behaviors studied included factors such as providing structure to subordinate and being considerate. A major conclusion for this study of many studies is that traits and behaviors combined explain a minimum of 31 percent of leadership effectiveness, with behaviors accounting for even more of the differences.[2]

The trait-based perspective also acknowledges that the situation often influences which trait to emphasize, such as a supervisor of highly technical workers needing to emphasize problem-solving ability. In contrast, a supervisor of workers performing nontechnical, repetitive work might need to emphasize enthusiasm as a motivator.

This chapter and the following chapter concentrate on personal characteristics. Chapter 4 describes the behaviors and skills that contribute to leadership effectiveness. Recognize, however, the close association between personal characteristics and leadership skills and behaviors. For example, creative thinking ability (a characteristic) helps a leader formulate an exciting vision (leadership behavior). The combination of traits and behaviors helps to explain why leaders show individual differences in effectiveness.[3] For example, a leader who is highly intelligent, trustworthy, and passionate about the mission of the group is likely to achieve more success than his or her counterpart who has average intelligence, is untrustworthy, and is indifferent about what work the group is performing.

## Personality Traits of Effective Leaders

Characteristics associated with leadership can be classified into three broad categories: personality traits, motives, and cognitive factors. These categories of behavior serve as helpful guides, but they are not definitive categories. Nevertheless, no matter how personal characteristics are classified, they point toward the conclusion that effective leaders are made of the *right stuff*. Published research about the trait perspective first appeared in the mid-nineteenth century, and it continues today. Since a full listing of every personal characteristic ever found to be associated with leadership would take several hundred pages, this chapter discusses only the major and most consistently found characteristics related to leadership effectiveness. In this section of the chapter, we focus on personality traits.

Personality traits contribute to leadership effectiveness in many situations, as long as the leader's style fits the situation reasonably well. For example, an executive might perform admirably as a leader in several different high-technology companies with different organizational cultures. However, his or her intellectual style might make him or her a poor fit with production workers. Leaders' personality traits can be divided into two groups: general personality traits such as self-confidence and trustworthiness, and task-related traits, such as proactivity.

### General Personality Traits

We define a general personality trait as a trait that is observable both within and outside the context of work. That is, the same general traits are related to success and satisfaction in both work and personal life. Figure 2-1 lists the general personality traits that contribute to successful leadership.

*Self-Confidence*   Self-confidence improves one's performance in a variety of tasks including leadership.[4] A leader who is self-assured without being bombastic or overbearing

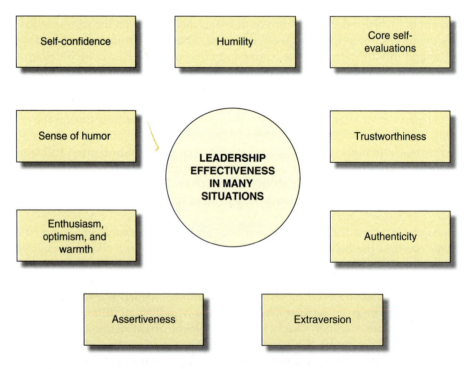

**FIGURE 2-1**   General Personality Traits of Effective Leaders.

instills self-confidence in team members. A self-confident team leader of a group facing a seemingly impossible deadline might tell the group, "We are understaffed and overworked, but I know we can get this project done on time. I've been through tough demands like this before. If we work like a true team, we can pull it off."

Self-confidence was among the first leadership traits researchers identified, and it still receives considerable attention as a major contributor to leadership effectiveness. As explained by executive coach Sally Ward, "Want to be seen as a leader? Confidence is the underpinning. Those who have it are more sought after, more trusted, more promoted, more influential."[5] In addition to being self-confident, the leader must project that self-confidence to the group. He or she may do so by using unequivocal wording, maintaining good posture, and making appropriate gestures such as pointing an index finger outward. Taking long strides, and walking with the chest held high, also projects self-confidence.

Self-confidence is not only a personality trait. It also refers to a behavior and an interpersonal skill that a person exhibits in a number of situations. It is akin to being cool under pressure. We can conclude that a person is a self-confident leader when he or she maintains composure when dealing with a crisis, such as while managing a large product recall. The interpersonal skill comes into play in being able to keep others calm during turmoil. In speaking about the suitability of job candidates who were recently military officers, Noel Tichy, director of the Global Business Partnership at the University of Michigan said, "There's a big pool of these officers who had had the kind of under-fire judgment experience that makes them really valuable."[6]

Leadership Self-Assessment Quiz 2-1 gives you an opportunity to think about your level of self-confidence.

*Humility*    Although self-confidence is a key leadership trait, so is humility, or being humble at the right times. Part of humility is admitting that you do not know everything and cannot do everything, as well as admitting your mistakes to team members and outsiders. A leader, upon receiving a compliment for an accomplishment, may explain that the group deserves the credit (a standard practice). The case for humility as a leadership trait is made strongly by Stephen G. Harrison, the president of a consulting firm, in his comment about how the definition of great leadership has changed: "Great leadership is manifested or articulated by people who know how to understate it. There is leadership value in humility, the leadership that comes from putting people in the limelight, not yourself. Great leadership comes from entirely unexpected places. It's understatement, it's dignity, it's service, it's selflessness."[7]

*Core Self-Evaluations*    Self-confidence is one way of looking at the self that contributes to leadership effectiveness. Extensive research suggests that a set of four other related self-perceptions also contributes to leadership effectiveness. **Core self-evaluations** is a broad personality trait that captures bottom-line self-assessment that is composed of self-esteem, locus of control, generalized self-efficacy, and emotional stability. All four traits are positively related to each other. Self-esteem deals with feeling positive toward the self, and generalized self-efficacy means roughly the same thing as being self-confident in many situations. Locus of control refers to whether a person feels personally responsible for events happening to him or her, helping the leader deliver a take-charge attitude. Emotional stability refers to having emotional control, not being neurotic, and having good mental health.

A leader with positive core evaluations is more likely to make decisions more rapidly and pursue initiatives to implement the decisions. Such a leader will feel confident, be steady under pressure, and believe that he or she can control the external environment to some extent.[8] Jeff Gennette, the CEO described in the chapter opener section, is admired for his stability during these difficult times for most department store chains.

*Trustworthiness*    Evidence and opinion continue to mount that being trustworthy and/or honest contributes to leadership effectiveness. An effective leader or manager is

# LEADERSHIP SELF-ASSESSMENT QUIZ 2-1

### How Self-Confident Are You?

Indicate the extent to which you agree with each of the following statements. Use a 1 to 5 scale: (1) disagree strongly; (2) disagree; (3) neutral; (4) agree; (5) agree strongly.

| | | DS | D | N | A | AS |
|---|---|---|---|---|---|---|
| **1.** | I frequently say to people, "I'm not sure." | 5 | 4 | 3 | 2 | 1 |
| **2.** | I have been hesitant to take on any leadership assignments. | 5 | 4 | 3 | 2 | 1 |
| **3.** | Several times, people have asked me to be the leader of the group to which I belonged. | 1 | 2 | 3 | 4 | 5 |
| **4.** | I perform well in most situations in life. | 1 | 2 | 3 | 4 | 5 |
| **5.** | At least several people have told me that I have a nice, firm handshake. | 1 | 2 | 3 | 4 | 5 |
| **6.** | I am much more of a loser than a winner. | 5 | 4 | 3 | 2 | 1 |
| **7.** | I am much more of a winner than a loser. | 1 | 2 | 3 | 4 | 5 |
| **8.** | I am cautious about making any substantial change in my life. | 5 | 4 | 3 | 2 | 1 |
| **9.** | I dread it when I have to learn a new skill, such as reading a foreign language. | 5 | 4 | 3 | 2 | 1 |
| **10.** | I freely criticize other people, even over minor matters such as their hair style or word choice. | 5 | 4 | 3 | 2 | 1 |
| **11.** | I become extremely tense when I know it will soon be my turn to present in front of the group or class. | 5 | 4 | 3 | 2 | 1 |
| **12.** | Speaking in front of the class or other group is a frightening experience for me. | 5 | 4 | 3 | 2 | 1 |
| **13.** | When asked for my advice, I willingly offer it. | 1 | 2 | 3 | 4 | 5 |
| **14.** | I feel comfortable attending a social event by myself. | 1 | 2 | 3 | 4 | 5 |
| **15.** | It is rare that I change my opinion just because somebody challenges me. | 1 | 2 | 3 | 4 | 5 |

***Scoring and Interpretation:*** Calculate your total score by adding the numbers circled. A tentative interpretation of the scoring is as follows:

- **65–75:** Very high self-confidence, with perhaps a tendency toward arrogance
- **55–64:** A high, desirable level of self-confidence
- **35–54:** Moderate, or average, self-confidence
- **15–34:** Self-confidence needs strengthening

supposed to *walk the talk,* thereby showing a consistency between deeds (walking) and words (talk). In this context, **trust** is defined as a person's confidence in another individual's intentions and motives and in the sincerity of that individual's word.[9] Leaders must be trustworthy, and they must also trust group members. Trust is closely related to *transparency,* in which organizational leadership is open rather than secretive about activities that affect the welfare of stakeholders. Given that so many people distrust top-level business leaders, as well as political leaders, gaining and maintaining trust is a substantial challenge. The following trust builders are worthy of a prospective leader's attention and implementation:[10]

- Make your behavior consistent with your intentions. Practice what you preach, and set the example. Let others know of your intentions and invite feedback on how well you are achieving them.
- When your organization or organizational unit encounters a problem, move into a problem-solving mode instead of looking to blame others for what went wrong.
- Honor confidences. One incident of passing along confidential information results in a permanent loss of trust by the person whose confidence was violated.
- Maintain a high level of integrity. Build a reputation for doing what you think is morally right in spite of the political consequences.
- Listen with compassion and attentiveness when interacting with others. Appear attentive by your body language such as maintaining eye contact, moving toward the person, and put away electronic interrupters such as a smartphone.
- Tell the truth in ways people can verify. It is much easier to be consistent when you do not have to keep patching up your story to conform to an earlier lie. An example of verification would be for a group member to see if the manager really did attempt to buy new conference room furniture as promised.
- Admit mistakes. Covering up a mistake, particularly when everybody knows that you did it, destroys trust quickly.
- Make trust pay in terms of receiving rewards. Trust needs to be seen as a way of gaining advantage.
- Making eye contact is a basic gesture that most people associate with trust.

It takes a leader a long time to build trust, yet one brief incident of untrustworthy behavior can permanently destroy it. Leaders are usually allowed a fair share of honest mistakes. In contrast, dishonest mistakes quickly erode leadership effectiveness.

When a leader is perceived as trustworthy, the organization benefits. Kurt T. Dirks and Donald L. Ferrin examined the findings and implications of research during the last four decades about trust in leadership. The review involved 106 studies and 27,103 individuals. The meta-analysis (quantitative synthesis of studies) emphasized supervisory leadership based on the importance of trust in day-to-day interactions with group members. Trusting a leader was more highly associated with a variety of work attitudes of group members. The highest specific relationships with trust were as follows: more job satisfaction, more commitment to the organization, less intention to leave the company, and more satisfaction with the leader. The relationship of trust to job performance was statistically significant but quite low.[11] One reason may be that many people perform well for a leader they distrust out of fear of being fired or bad listed.

Michael E. Palanski and Francis J. Yammarino conducted an online experiment, a study in a healthcare organization, and a lab study to investigate how integrity relates to job performance. (*Integrity* was defined as the consistency between words and actions.) No direct relationship between integrity and job performance was found, yet integrity facilitated the leader being trusted, which, in turn, was associated with higher performance. Leader integrity also enhanced job satisfaction to some extent, which, in turn, can sometimes enhance job performance.[12]

Leadership Self-Assessment Quiz 2-2 gives you the opportunity to examine your own tendencies toward trustworthiness.

*Authenticity*    Embedded in the trait of being trustworthy is **authenticity**—being genuine and honest about your personality, values, and beliefs as well as having integrity. Bill George, a Harvard Business School professor and former chairman and CEO of Medtronic, developed the concept of authentic leadership. In his words, "Authentic leaders demonstrate a passion for their purpose, practice their values consistently, and lead with their hearts as well as their heads. They establish long-term meaningful relationships and have the self-discipline to get results. They know who they are."[13] George has explained more

# LEADERSHIP SELF-ASSESSMENT QUIZ 2-2

## Behaviors and Attitudes of a Trustworthy Leader

**Instructions:** Listed here are behaviors and attitudes of leaders who are generally trusted by their group members and other constituents. After you read each characteristic, check to the right whether this is a behavior or attitude that you appear to have developed already, or whether it does not fit you at present.

| | FITS ME | DOES NOT FIT |
|---|---|---|
| 1. Tells people he or she is going to do something, and then always follows through and gets it done. | ☐ | ☐ |
| 2. Is described by others as being reliable. | ☐ | ☐ |
| 3. Is good at keeping secrets and confidences. | ☐ | ☐ |
| 4. Tells the truth consistently. | ☐ | ☐ |
| 5. Minimizes telling people what they want to hear. | ☐ | ☐ |
| 6. Is described by others as "walking the talk." | ☐ | ☐ |
| 7. Delivers consistent messages to others in terms of matching words and deeds. | ☐ | ☐ |
| 8. Does what he or she expects others to do. | ☐ | ☐ |
| 9. Minimizes hypocrisy by not engaging in activities he or she tells others are wrong. | ☐ | ☐ |
| 10. Readily accepts feedback on behavior from others. | ☐ | ☐ |
| 11. Maintains eye contact with people when talking to them. | ☐ | ☐ |
| 12. Appears relaxed and confident when explaining his or her side of a story. | ☐ | ☐ |
| 13. Individualizes compliments to others rather than saying something like "You look great" to many people. | ☐ | ☐ |
| 14. Does not expect lavish perks for himself or herself while expecting others to go on an austerity diet. | ☐ | ☐ |
| 15. Does not tell others a crisis is pending (when it is not) just to gain their cooperation. | ☐ | ☐ |
| 16. Collaborates with others to make creative decisions. | ☐ | ☐ |
| 17. Communicates information to people at all organizational levels digitally and in person. | ☐ | ☐ |
| 18. Readily shares financial information with others. | ☐ | ☐ |
| 19. Listens to people and then acts on many of their suggestions. | ☐ | ☐ |
| 20. Generally engages in predictable behavior. | ☐ | ☐ |

**Scoring and Interpretation:** The more of these statements that fit you, the more trustworthy you are—assuming you are answering truthfully. The usefulness of this self-quiz increases if somebody who knows you well also answers it about you. Your ability and willingness to carry out some of the behaviors specified in this quiz could have an enormous impact on your career because so many business leaders in recent years have not been perceived as trustworthy. Being trustworthy is therefore a career asset.

recently that people who follow their leadership compass toward *true north* can achieve authentic leadership. True north refers to a person's most deeply held beliefs, his or her values, and the principles that lead the person.[14]

To become an authentic leader and demonstrate authenticity, be yourself rather than attempting to be a replica of someone else. Others respond to your leadership, partly because you are genuine rather than phony. The authentic leader can emphasize different values and characteristics to different people without being phony. For example, a corporate-level manager at Goodyear service centers might engage in more banter when he or she visits a service center than when meeting with financial analysts.

George and several colleagues conducted an intensive leadership development study of 125 diverse business leaders to understand how they became and remain authentic. The authentic leaders typically learned from their experiences by reflecting on them. They also took a hard look at themselves to understand what they really believe, such as whether they really care if their workers are satisfied. The authors of the study concluded that the leader being authentic is the only way to create long-term, positive business results.[15]

A team of researchers conducted two studies to better understand the relationship between authentic leadership and job performance. The settings chosen were a police organization and a training camp at a U.S. Army base. These difficult, or extreme, settings were chosen because such contexts provide greater opportunity for leaders to encourage positive attitudes and reduce negativity among subordinates. The results of both studies showed that leaders rated as being more authentic had subordinates rated as more effective performers. The underlying mechanism appeared to be that group members who reported to an authentic leader reported experiencing more positive emotions and fewer negative emotions than those individuals reporting to a less authentic leader.[16] In short, having an authentic leader puts you in a better mood and can elevate your job performance.

*Extraversion*    Extraversion (the scientific spelling for *extroversion)* has been recognized for its contribution to leadership effectiveness because it is helpful for leaders to be gregarious, outgoing, and upbeat in most situations. Also, extraverts are more likely to want to assume a leadership role and participate in group activities. A meta-analysis of 73 studies involving 11,705 subjects found that extraversion was the most consistent personality factor related to leadership effectiveness and leadership emergence.[17] (*Emergence* refers to someone being perceived as having leadership qualities.) Extraversion is also the personality trait most consistently and strongly related to the type of leadership that brings about major changes (the transformational type).[18]

Extraversion may be an almost innate personality characteristic, yet most people can move toward becoming more extraverted by consciously attempting to be friendlier toward people including smiling and asking questions. An example is, "How are things going for you today?"

Research evidence suggests that an extraverted leader may be more effective in stimulating good job performance among laid back than proactive workers. (The proactive worker takes the initiative to solve problems and seize opportunities.) Adam M. Grant, Francesca Gino, and David A. Hofmann sent questionnaires to managers and their employees at 130 franchises of a U.S. pizza delivery company. Managers were asked to rate their own extent of extraversion. Employees were asked to estimate how often they and their coworkers "try to bring about improved procedures," among other proactive behaviors. Data were also collected on store profitability, yet controlling for location such as being close to a college campus. Among the study that provide clues to the best leadership approach to proactive employees were the following:

- In stores where employees were below average in proactive personality, extraverted leadership was associated with 16 percent higher profits than average.
- In stores where employees offered ideas, extroverted leadership was associated with 14 percent lower profits.

A key conclusion drawn from the study is that when employees are proactive, extraverted leadership is associated with lower performance. The problem is that extraverted leaders may attempt to come up with most of the ideas for improvement themselves, rather than listening carefully to employee suggestions. Furthermore, with proactive employees leaders need to be receptive to suggestions from the group. When employees are not proactive, extraverted leadership was associated with higher group performance.[19] The implication is that with less proactive group members, the leader needs to act more demonstratively and set a clear direction.

The fact that extraversion contributes to effective leadership does not mean introverts cannot be effective in leadership roles. Susan Cain who has studied introverted CEOs. She observes that they are more likely to have qualities such as restraint, humility, and composure when interacting with stakeholders. They tend to be more careful and deliberate, and less likely to dominate discussion which facilitates collaborative leadership.[20]

*Assertiveness*   Letting others know where you stand contributes to leadership effectiveness, and also contributes to being or appearing extraverted. **Assertiveness** refers to being forthright in expressing demands, opinions, feelings, and attitudes. Being assertive helps leaders perform many tasks and achieve goals. Among them are confronting group members about their mistakes, demanding higher performance, setting high expectations, and making legitimate demands on higher management. A director of her company's mobile phone service unit was assertive when she said to her staff, "Our mobile service is the worst in the industry. We have to improve." An assertive person is reasonably tactful rather than being aggressive and obnoxious. A leader with good sensitivity knows when assertiveness crosses the line into aggressiveness, such as insulting subordinates or making unreasonable demands.

*Enthusiasm, Optimism, and Warmth*   In almost all leadership situations, it is desirable for the leader to be enthusiastic. Group members tend to respond positively to enthusiasm, partly because enthusiasm may be perceived as a reward for constructive behavior. Enthusiasm is also a desirable leadership trait because it helps build good relationships with team members. A leader can express enthusiasm both verbally ("Great job"; "I love it") and nonverbally (making a fist-bump or high-five gesture). Kevin A. Plank, the founder and CEO of Under Armour, is known for his hand-clapping style of enthusiasm, described later in this chapter.

Enthusiasm often takes the form of optimism, which helps keep the group in an upbeat mood and hopeful about attaining difficult goals. The optimistic leader is therefore likely to help bring about exceptional levels of achievement. Yet, there is a potential downside to an optimistic leader. He or she might not develop contingency plans to deal with projects that do not go as well as expected.[21] An overly optimistic marketing manager at a solar energy, for example, might not take into account that most homeowners are skeptical that an investment in solar panels will be cost effective.

Being a warm person and projecting that warmth is part of enthusiasm and contributes to leadership effectiveness in several ways. First, warmth helps establish rapport with group members. Second, the projection of warmth is a key component of charisma. Third, warmth is a trait that helps provide emotional support to group members. Giving such support is an important leadership behavior. Fourth, being warm is engaging, whereas being cold tends to create distance from others.

Experimental evidence has been collected suggesting that a leader with a positive emotional state can have a positive impact on job performance. As framed by James B. Avey, Bruce J. Avolio, and Fred Luthans, being positive is part of having positive psychological capital that includes self-efficacy, optimism, hope, and resilience. As part of a broader experiment, engineers in an aerospace company were assigned to leaders with a high or low positive psychological capital. (Low positive psychological capital means that the leader has a negative emotional state.) Leaders in the experiment were given either positive or negative scripts to reflect the two differences in positive psychological states. The experimental task for the engineers was to solve a complex aerospace engineering task. A positive relationship was found between the leader's positive state and the follower's

## LEADERSHIP SKILL-BUILDING EXERCISE 2-1

### Enthusiasm, Optimism, and Warmth on the Job

One person plays the role of the CEO of an American company that makes medical devices, including a computerized leg prosthesis that enables the wearer to engage in everyday activities comfortably, as well as play demanding physical sports such as tennis, soccer, and half-court basketball (within limits). The CEO and the top-management team have just learned that a medical device manufacturer located in Malaysia has produced an equally good prosthetic leg that will be sold in the United States for one-half the price of their device. The CEO has scheduled an 8:30 a.m. Monday meeting to discuss the problem. The CEO believes that enthusiasm, optimism, warmth, as well as the display of positive psychological capital will be necessary to help the team deal with this peril. About five other students will play the role of the top-management team members who attend the meeting.

positive state and performance. The study therefore supports the conventional wisdom that leaders with a positive attitude can facilitate group members developing a positive attitude and performing well.[22]

Leadership Skill-Building Exercise 2-1 provides an opportunity to use display positive psychological capital to group members.

*Sense of Humor*    Whether humor is a trait or a behavior, the effective use of humor is an important part of the leader's role. Humor adds to the approachability and people orientation of a leader. Laughter and humor serve such functions in the workplace as relieving tension and boredom and defusing hostility. Because humor helps the leader dissolve tension and defuse conflict, it helps him or her exert power over the group. Self-effacing humor is the choice of comedians and organizational leaders alike. By being self-effacing, the leader makes a point without insulting or slighting anybody. Instead of criticizing a staff member for being too technical, the leader might say, "Wait, I need your help. Please explain how this new product works in terms that even I can understand."

Humor as used by leaders has been the subject of considerable serious inquiry, and here are a few recommendations based on this research:[23]

- People who occupy high-status roles joke at a higher rate than those of lesser status and tend to be more successful at eliciting laughter from others. (A possible reason that high-status people elicit more laughter is that lower-status people want to please them.)
- Executives and other managers who use self-deprecating humor appear more approachable and likeable to subordinates.
- Aggressive humor can be used to victimize, belittle, and cause others some type of disparagement—and will lead to negative outcomes such as stress and counter-hostility among group members. (No surprise to readers here.)

## Task-Related Personality Traits

Certain personality traits of effective leaders are closely associated with task accomplishment. The task-related traits described here are outlined in Figure 2-2.

*Proactive Personality*    Leadership is often perceived to mean about the same thing as taking the initiative. Initiative, in turn, is closely related to being proactive, or creating or controlling a situation by causing something to happen, rather than reacting after the event happens. According to its original research-based definition, a person with a **proactive personality** has a relatively stable tendency to effect environmental change.[24] Proactive behavior usually stems from a proactive personality and refers to self-initiated anticipatory action with the intent of either changing the situation or one's own behavior

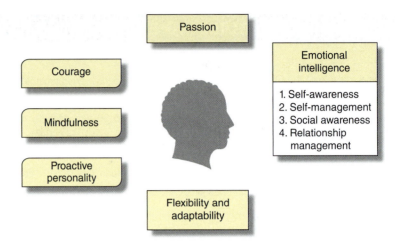

**FIGURE 2-2**    Task-Related Personality Traits of Leaders.

and attitudes.[25] An effective leader therefore often has a proactive personality, and therefore exhibits proactive behavior.

Most of the leaders, you will read about in this book, show high proactivity including also those who initiate change. An example of evidence for the importance of leader proactivity is found in a study of district managers and their business units from a large U.S.-based consumer packaged goods company. The managers were rated on their proactivity by their immediate managers, using statements such as "Takes charge in situations where a leader is needed." Part of the study found that proactive high-level managers establish more challenging goals for their business units, which, in turn, are associated with higher sales performance.[26]

Leadership Self-Assessment Quiz 2-3 gives you an opportunity to think through your own tendencies toward having a proactivity personality and therefore being proactive.

*Mindfulness*    *Mindfulness* has become a buzz word during the past thirty-five years, referring to concentrating on the present moment without making judgments about what is happening. For example, you are being mindful when you listen to a subordinate's creative suggestion, concentrate intensely on the idea. Furthermore, you make no immediate judgments about the value of the idea, and do not think about the past or future. A technical definition of **mindfulness** is "a state of nonjudgmental attentiveness to and awareness of moment-to-moment experiences."[27]

The mindful leader has traits and engages in behaviors that have long been associated with successful leadership, such as being observant, perceptive, and attentive to details that could affect important outcomes. An effective leader is supposed to look at the big picture, yet key details contribute to the big picture. Visualize Angela, the vice president of human resources at a large bank. Part of the big picture for here is for the bank to have a committed, engaged workforce. On a recent tour of the bank, Angela is mindful enough to recognize that very few workers are smiling. To Angela, this limited amount of smiling could indicate that employee morale is too low to contribute to an engaged workforce. Angela now swings into action by conferring with bank supervisors about potential morale problems, and what can be done to elevate morale.

Several behaviors of a mindful leader are presented next:[28]

- The mindful leader is usually calm, and has clarity and focus. He or she can help the group see the way out of a crisis, such as criticism of the company having gone viral, by providing a clear path to recovery.
- Being aware of his or her feelings, as well as the feelings of group members, the mindful leader displays compassion.
- As part of being observant, the mindful leader listens carefully and attempts to extract meaning from what people are saying. As the leader interacts with subordinates both

# LEADERSHIP SELF-ASSESSMENT QUIZ 2-3

## My Tendencies Toward Being a Proactive Personality

Indicate on a 1 to 5 scale the extent of your agreement with the following statements: (1) agree strongly (AS); (2) agree (A); (3) neutral (N); (4) disagree (D); and (5) disagree strongly (DS).

| | | AS | A | N | D | DS |
|---|---|---|---|---|---|---|
| 1. | I plan carefully for things that might go wrong. | 5 | 4 | 3 | 2 | 1 |
| 2. | I don't worry about problems until after they have taken place. | 1 | 2 | 3 | 4 | 5 |
| 3. | If I see something that is broken, I fix it. | 5 | 4 | 3 | 2 | 1 |
| 4. | I have been told several times that I am good at taking the initiative. | 5 | 4 | 3 | 2 | 1 |
| 5. | I often let things like a computer password expire without making the necessary changes. | 1 | 2 | 3 | 4 | 5 |
| 6. | When something important needs doing, I wait for somebody else to take the initiative. | 1 | 2 | 3 | 4 | 5 |
| 7. | I think that having a home security system is a good investment in money. | 5 | 4 | 3 | 2 | 1 |
| 8. | I look around for good opportunities that would help me in my career or personal life. | 5 | 4 | 3 | 2 | 1 |
| 9. | I don't give much thought to the future because there is not much I can do about it. | 1 | 2 | 3 | 4 | 5 |
| 10. | It is a good idea to start saving or investing for retirement at the beginning of your career. | 5 | 4 | 3 | 2 | 1 |
| 11. | I begin projects and tasks by myself, without requiring prompting from somebody else. | 5 | 4 | 3 | 2 | 1 |
| 12. | The old saying, "The early bird gets the worm," doesn't make much sense in real life. | 1 | 2 | 3 | 4 | 5 |
| 13. | I let the future take care of itself without giving it much thought. | 1 | 2 | 3 | 4 | 5 |
| 14. | I set my own goals rather than have others set them for me. | 5 | 4 | 3 | 2 | 1 |
| 15. | I create a lot of change both in work and personal life. | 5 | 4 | 3 | 2 | 1 |
| 16. | I have often asked for feedback on my job performance. | 5 | 4 | 3 | 2 | 1 |
| 17. | If your job is going well, it is a bad idea to explore new job possibilities from time to time. | 1 | 2 | 3 | 4 | 5 |
| 18. | Once you have chosen a satisfactory career, it is a bad idea to explore the possibilities of another career from time to time. | 1 | 2 | 3 | 4 | 5 |
| 19. | I readily express my opinion about the effectiveness of a work process. | 5 | 4 | 3 | 2 | 1 |
| 20. | It is best to stick carefully to your job description rather than create responsibilities for yourself. | 1 | 2 | 3 | 4 | 5 |
| 21. | I regularly take positive steps to increase the chances that I will stay healthy and physically fit. | 5 | 4 | 3 | 2 | 1 |
| 22. | I am quite innovative both in work and personal life. | 5 | 4 | 3 | 2 | 1 |

**Scoring and Interpretation:** Total the numbers corresponding to your answers.

- **100–125:** Scores in this range suggest that you have strong tendencies toward being a proactive personality. Such proactivity should be (or already is) an asset to you in your career and personal life. Yet scoring 115 points or more could suggest that you sometimes annoy people with your constant need for taking on new responsibility and creating change.
- **70–99:** Scores in this range suggest that you have about average tendencies toward being proactive. To enhance your success and have more fun in life, you might attempt to become more proactive.
- **25–69:** Scores in this range suggest that you have a problem with proactivity. Both your work and personal life would probably be enhanced if you became more proactive.

*Source:* The idea for this scale and several of its statements stem from Thomas S. Bateman and J. Michael Grant , "The Proactive Component of Organizational Behavior: A Measure and Correlates," *Journal of Organizational Behavior*, March 1993 , p. 112.

in formal meetings and in casual interactions, he or she looks for directly expressed and implied meanings. A retail chain executive might be on a tour of stores, and asks a store manager how things are going at the store. The manager replies, "Could be a lot worse." The mindful leader recognizes that "could be a lot worse," is hardly a glorious condition, so he asks, "What is preventing things from being outstanding?" The store manager feeling understood, replies, "Our inventory shrinkage from customers and employees is far too high." Now the executive and the store manager have an important problem to work on jointly.

- The mindful leader is open to new ideas and multiple perspectives. Although an effective leader is likely to have an agenda he or she believes is worth pursuing, the mindful leader stays alert to what could be new and significant. The mindful leader is nonjudgmental within limits. Being nonjudgmental is part of mindfulness, and this characteristic will often help the leader. The limits are that being judgmental is important when the behavior of group members is illegal, unsavory, or nonproductive such as workers using company credit cards to pay for casino betting.

**Passion for the Work and the People**    A dominant characteristic of effective leaders is their passion for their work and to some extent for the people who help them accomplish the work. The passion goes beyond enthusiasm and often expresses itself as an obsession for achieving company goals. Many leaders begin their workday at 6:00 A.M. and return to their homes at 7:00 P.M. After dinner, they retreat to their home offices to conduct business for about two more hours. Communication technology devices feed the passion for work, making it possible to be in touch with the office even during golf or a family picnic. The downside to extreme passion for work is that it can lead to work addiction, thereby interfering with other joys in life.

Passion for their work is especially evident in entrepreneurial leaders, no matter what size and type of business. A given business, such as refurbishing engines, might appear mundane to outsiders. The leader of such a business, however, is willing to talk for hours about tearing down old engines and about the wonderful people who help do the job.

One of the ways for an entrepreneur to inject passion into a business is to tell a *creation-of-the-enterprise story*. The story should inspire people to understand how your product or cause will make the world a better place. Howard Schultz, the founder and chairman of Starbucks, provides an example.[29]

Schultz's story begins in 1961, when his father broke his ankle at work and was left without income, insurance or any way to support his family. The family's fear inspired change. Schultz grew up driven to create a company in which employees have a safety net woven of respect and dignity.

**Emotional Intelligence**    Many different aspects of emotions, motives, and personality that help determine interpersonal effectiveness and leadership skill have been placed under the comprehensive label of *emotional intelligence*. **Emotional intelligence** refers to the ability to do such things as understanding one's feelings, have empathy for others, and regulate one's emotions to enhance one's quality of life. This type of intelligence generally has to do with the ability to connect with people and understand their emotions. Many of the topics in this chapter (such as warmth) and throughout the text (such as political skill) can be considered related to emotional intelligence. In addition to being an ability, emotional intelligence is also a trait, or part of the leader's personality.[30]

Based on research in dozens of companies, Daniel Goleman discovered that the most effective leaders are alike in one essential way: They all have a high degree of emotional intelligence. Without a high degree of emotional intelligence, a person can have excellent training, superior analytical skills, and loads of innovative suggestions, but he or she still will not make a great leader. His analysis also revealed that emotional intelligence played an increasingly important role in high-level management positions. (Keep in mind, however, that most high-level managers would not have advanced to their position if they lacked good technical skills or business knowledge.) Furthermore, when star performers were compared with average ones in senior leadership positions, differences in emotional intelligence were more pronounced than differences in cognitive abilities.[31] Recent research conducted by Travis Bradberry also indicates that emotional intelligence is a powerful measure of leadership performance because emotions play a key role in driving behavior.[32]

Four key domains in emotional intelligence are described next, along with a brief explanation of how each factor links to leadership effectiveness. The domains (components) of emotional intelligence have gone through several versions, and the version presented here is tied closely to leadership and interpersonal skills. The leader who scores high in emotional intelligence is described as *resonant*.[33]

1. **Self-awareness.** Having high self-awareness allows people to know their strengths and limitations and have high self-esteem. Self-awareness helps accurately measure their own moods, and they intuitively understand how their moods affect others. (Effective leaders seek feedback to see how well their actions are received by others. A leader with good self-awareness would recognize such factors as whether he or she was liked or was exerting the right amount of pressure on people.) The associated competency is emotional self-awareness.

2. **Self-management.** This is the ability to control one's emotions and act with honesty and integrity in a consistent and adaptable manner. The right degree of self-management helps prevent a person from throwing temper tantrums when activities do not go as planned. Resonant leaders do not let their occasional bad moods ruin their day. (A leader with high self-management would not suddenly decide to fire a group member because of one difference of opinion.) The four specific competencies are emotional self-control, adaptability, achievement orientation, and positive outlook.

3. **Social awareness.** This includes having empathy for others and intuition about organizational problems. Empathy has surged in importance as a key leadership quality.[34] Socially aware leaders go beyond sensing the emotions of others by showing they care. In addition, they accurately size up political forces in the office. (A team leader with social awareness, or empathy, would be able to assess whether a team member had enough enthusiasm for a project to assign it to him.) The two specific competencies are empathy and organizational awareness.

4. **Relationship management.** This includes the interpersonal skills of being able to communicate clearly and convincingly, disarm conflicts, and build strong personal bonds. Resonant leaders use relationship management skills to spread their enthusiasm and solve disagreements, often with kindness and humor. (A leader with good relationship management skills would not burn bridges and would continue to enlarge his or her network of people to win support when support is needed.) The four specific competencies are influence, coach and mentor, teamwork, and inspirational leadership.

It is also helpful to recognize that emotional intelligence has relevance for people who are beginning their leadership careers. Two studies with students taking a course in organizational behavior, and assigned small-group projects, examined how emotional intelligence was related to emergent leadership. Among the dimensions of emotional intelligence measured, it was found that the ability to understand emotions was the most consistently related to leadership emergence.[35] The study participants with the best skill in understanding emotions in others were more therefore likely to be perceived as having leadership qualities.

If leaders do not have emotional intelligence, they may not achieve their full potential despite their high cognitive intelligence. Almost daily, a scanning of newspapers will reveal an organizational leader who was disgraced or dismissed because of displaying poor emotional intelligence. Sometimes the business leader is a person of outstanding reputation and accomplishment. Among the frequent errors in emotional intelligence are lying about credentials, repeated sexual harassment of subordinates and customers, and insider trading.

A broad application of emotional intelligence is for leaders to understand the emotional culture of the organization. The *emotional culture* refers to which feelings people have at work, feelings they should have, and feeling they keep to themselves. A company in which most employees were enthusiastic and had high job satisfaction would have a positive emotional culture. Understanding these emotions is important because employee emotions have an impact on creativity, decision making, quality of work, and involuntary turnover. Two basic examples are that a positive mood enhances creativity, and being angry with an employee may prompt an employee to quit. Managing the emotional culture is a complex topic involving many leadership actions. A specific example, however, would be for to encourage employees to post positive feelings and compliments about each other, which could result in the spread of positive emotion in the company (emotional contagion).[36]

A study of emotional intelligence and leadership also recognizes the importance of the leader's mood in influencing performance. Daniel Goleman, Richard Boyatzis, and Annie McKee believe that the leader's mood and his or her associated behaviors greatly influence bottom-line performance. One reason is that moods are contagious. A cranky and ruthless leader creates a toxic organization of underachievers (who perform at less than their potential). In contrast, an upbeat and inspirational leader breeds followers who can surmount most challenges. Thus, mood finally affects profit and loss. The implication for leaders is that they have to develop emotional intelligence regarding their moods. It is also helpful to develop a sense of humor, because lightheartedness is the most contagious of moods.[37]

Emotional intelligence highlights the importance of leaders making effective use of emotions. Information about emotional intelligence also leads to a better understanding of how leadership emerges, leadership behaviors, and leadership effectiveness. Nevertheless, some proponents of emotional intelligence go too far in their claims about its importance in relation to leadership effectiveness. Specifically, we cannot overlook the contribution of general mental ability (cognitive intelligence) to being an effective leader. Several syntheses of research studies suggest that emotional intelligence is only one of various factors (including other personality traits, cognitive ability, and functional skills) that influences what leaders accomplish.[38]

*Flexibility and Adaptability*    A leader is someone who facilitates change. It therefore follows that a leader must be flexible enough to cope with such changes as technological advances, downsizings, global outsourcing, a shifting customer base, and a changing work force. **Flexibility**, or the ability to adjust to different situations, has long been recognized as an important leadership characteristic. Leaders who are flexible are able to adjust to the demands of changing conditions, much as antilock brakes enable an automobile to adjust to changes in road conditions. Without the underlying trait of flexibility, a person might be an effective leader in only one or two situations. The manufacturing industry exemplifies a field in which situation adaptability is particularly important. This is true because executives are required to provide leadership on the production floor and in the executive suite where the norms of behavior might be quite different.

*Courage*    Leaders need courage to face the challenges of taking prudent risks and taking initiative in general. Courage comes from the heart, as suggested by the French word for heart, *coeur*. Leaders must face up to responsibility and be willing to put their reputations on the line. It takes courage for a leader to suggest a new undertaking, because if the undertaking fails, the leader is often seen as having failed. Courageous leadership has also been described as *gutsy*. Many people criticized the late Steve Jobs (the former Apple Inc. CEO and then chairman) and his management team when they initiated Apple stores because they saw no useful niche served by these retail outlets. Apple stores were an immediate and long-lasting success, vindicating the judgment of Jobs and his team. The more faith people place in the power of leaders to cause events, the more strongly they blame leaders when outcomes are unfavorable.

## Leadership Motives

Effective leaders have frequently been distinguished by their motives and needs. In general, leaders have an intense desire to occupy a position of responsibility for others and to control them. Figure 2-3 outlines four specific leadership motives or needs. All four motives can be considered task related.

### The Power Motive

Effective leaders have a strong need to control resources. Leaders with high power motives have three dominant characteristics: (1) they act with vigor and determination to exert their power, (2) they invest much time in thinking about ways to alter the behavior and thinking of others, and (3) they care about their personal standing with those around them.[39] The power motive is important because it means that the leader is interested in influencing others. Without power, it is much more difficult to influence others. Power is not necessarily good or evil; it can be used for the sake of the power holder (personalized power motive) or for helping others (socialized power motive).[40]

*Personalized Power Motive*    Leaders with a personalized power motive seek power mostly to further their own interests. They crave the trappings of power, such as status symbols, luxury, and money. The wealthiest of CEOs purchase luxury condominium apartments in major cities, even when they have another home. Some leaders with strong personalized power motives typically enjoy dominating others. Their need for dominance can lead to submissive subordinates who are frequently sycophants and yes-persons. Another characteristic of leaders with a personalized power motive is that they do not worry about everybody liking them. They recognize that as you acquire power, you also acquire enemies.

*Socialized Power Motive*    Leaders with a socialized power motive use power primarily to achieve organizational goals or a vision. In this context, the term *socialized* means that the leader uses power primarily to help others. As a result, he or she is likely to provide more effective leadership. Leaders with socialized power motives tend to be more emotionally mature than leaders with personalized power motives. They exercise power more for the benefit of the entire organization and are less likely to manipulate others through the use of power. Leaders with socialized power motives are also less defensive and more willing to accept expert advice. Finally, they have longer-range perspectives.[41]

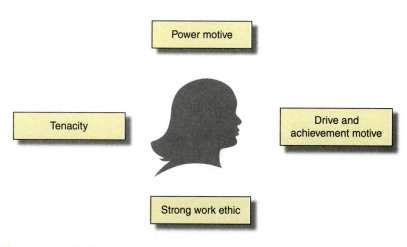

**FIGURE 2-3**    Leadership Motives.

It is important not to draw a rigid line between leaders with personalized power motives and those with socialized power motives. The distinction between doing good for others and doing good for oneself is often made on the basis of very subjective criteria. A case in point is Denise Morrison, the president and CEO of Campbell Soup. The many nutritious, relatively low-priced foods her company manufactures facilitate the well-being of millions of people throughout the world. At the same time, Morrison is growing in power and stature because the company she leads is so successful.

## The Drive and Achievement Motive

Leaders are known for working hard to achieve their goals. **Drive** refers to a propensity to put forth high energy into achieving objectives and to persistence in applying that energy. Drive also includes **achievement motivation**—finding joy in accomplishment for its own sake. Entrepreneurs and high-level corporate managers usually have strong achievement motivation. Such people have a consistent desire to:

1. achieve through their efforts and take responsibility for success or failure;
2. take moderate risks that can be handled through their own efforts;
3. receive feedback on their level of performance;
4. introduce novel, innovative, or creative solutions; and
5. plan and set goals.[42]

Drive usually requires a high level of physical energy, especially because many leadership positions require long hours and heavy travel. In recognition of the energy requirements of their position, many business executives emphasize physical fitness.

Whether at home or in a hotel, many of these executives exercise on a treadmill or stationary bicycle, often watching news on television at the same time.

## Tenacity and Resilience

A final observation about the motivational characteristics of organizational leaders is that they are *tenacious*. Tenacity multiplies in importance for organizational leaders because it takes a long time to implement a new program or to consummate a business deal, such as acquiring another company. *Grit* has become synonymous with tenacity because grit refers to an unswerving focus on long-term goals, and is considered to be a success factor in most fields.[43] The gritty person has the stamina to keep pushing forward even when setbacks surface.

Resilience is part of tenacity because the tenacious person will bounce back from a setback through continuous effort. An extraordinary example of a resilient leader is Oscar Munoz, the chief executive of United Continental Holdings Inc. Five months after having a heart transplant operation, he was back on the job leading the airline that was struggling at the time. Although his right hand was not fully functional, he was jogging and biking again. Munoz had a heart attack just two weeks after being appointed CEO.[44]

# Cognitive Factors and Leadership

Mental ability as well as personality is important for leadership success. To inspire people, bring about constructive change, and solve problems creatively, leaders need to be mentally sharp. Another mental requirement is the ability to sort out essential information from less essential information and then store the most important information in memory. Problem-solving and intellectual skills are referred to collectively as **cognitive factors**. We discuss five cognitive factors that are closely related to cognitive intelligence, as shown in Figure 2-4. The descriptor *cognitive* is helpful to differentiate traditional mental ability from emotional intelligence.

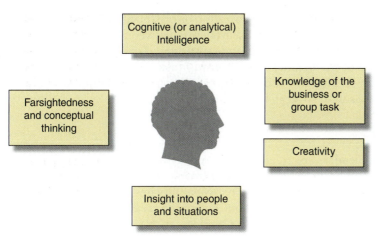

**FIGURE 2-4**   Cognitive Factors and Leadership.

## Cognitive (or Analytical) Intelligence

Being very good at solving problems is a fundamental characteristic of effective leaders in all fields. Business leaders, for example, need to understand how to analyze company finances, use advanced software, manage inventory, and deal with international trade regulations. Research spanning over 100 years has demonstrated that leaders receive higher scores than most people on mental ability tests, including IQ (a term for a test score that for many people is synonymous with intelligence). A meta-analysis of 151 studies found a positive relationship between intelligence and job performance of leaders in many different settings. The relationship is likely to be higher when the leader plays an active role in decision making and is not overly stressed. The researchers also found support for the old idea that intelligence contributes the most to leadership effectiveness when the leader is not vastly smarter than most group members.[45] Again, group members prefer that their leaders be smarter than the average group member even if the difference is not huge.

The top 1 percent in combined mental ability (as measured by intelligence tests) and income includes large numbers of successful professionals such as doctors, lawyers, and business executives.[46]

Cognitive intelligence is all the more useful for leadership when it is supplemented by **practical intelligence**, the ability to solve everyday problems by using experience-based knowledge to adapt to and shape the environment. Practical intelligence is sometimes referred to as street smarts, and also includes wisdom.[47] Recent evidence suggests that specific problem-solving skills, such as wisdom, are more closely related to leader performance than general intelligence.[48]

A leader with good practical intelligence would know, for example, not to deliver a vision statement on a day most of the company employees were worried about a power outage in their homes created by a massive lightning storm. Another example of displaying practical intelligence and wisdom is the leader mentioned in Chapter 1 who had the wisdom to figure out how poor people in Nigeria could make money from collecting garbage.

## Knowledge of the Business or Group Task

Intellectual ability is closely related to having knowledge of the business or the key task the group is performing. An effective leader has to be technically competent in some discipline, particularly when leading a group of specialists. It is difficult for the leader to establish rapport with group members when he or she does not know what the group members are doing and when the group does not respect the leader's technical skills.

The importance of knowledge of the business is strongly recognized as an attribute of executive leadership. Leaders at every level are expected to bring forth useful ideas for carrying out the mission of the organization or organizational unit. A representative example is that according to a team of researchers, a key requirement for the chief supply chain management officer is "end-to-end understanding of the supply chain."[49]

Knowledge of the business or the group task is particularly important when developing strategy, formulating mission statements, and sizing up the external environment. Chapter 13 deals with strategy formulation at length.

## Creativity

Many effective leaders are creative in the sense that they arrive at imaginative and original solutions to complex problems, such as thinking of an idea for a new product or service, or how to recruit talented employees. Creative ability lies on a continuum, with some leaders being more creative than others. At one end of the creative continuum are business leaders who think of innovative products and services, such as Elon Musk of Tesla (described in a case in Chapter 1).

At the middle of the creativity continuum are leaders who explore imaginative—but not breakthrough—solutions to business problems. At the low end of the creativity continuum are leaders who inspire group members to push forward with standard solutions to organizational problems. Creativity is such an important aspect of the leader's role in the modern organization that the development of creative problem-solving skills receives separate attention in Chapter 11.

## Insight into People and Situations

Another important cognitive trait of leaders is **insight**, a depth of understanding that requires considerable intuition and common sense. Intuition is often the mental process used to provide the understanding of a problem. Insight helps speed decision making. Jeff Bezos, the founder of **Amazon.com,** and Tim Cook, the CEO of Apple Inc., believe that the bigger the decision, such as whether or not to enter a particular business, the greater the role of insight and intuition.

Insight into people and situations involving people is an essential characteristic of organizational leaders because it helps them make the best use of both their own and others' talents. For example, it helps them make wise choices in selecting people for key assignments. Insight also enables managers to do a better job of training and developing team members because they can wisely assess the members' strengths and weaknesses. Another major advantage of being insightful is that the leader can size up a situation and adapt his or her leadership approach accordingly. For instance, in a crisis situation, group members welcome directive and decisive leadership. Being able to read people helps the manager provide this leadership.

You can gauge your insight by charting the accuracy of your hunches and predictions about people and business situations. For example, size up a new coworker or manager as best you can. Record your observations and test them against how that person performs or behaves many months later. The feedback from this type of exercise will help sharpen your insights.

## Farsightedness and Conceptual Thinking

To develop visions and corporate strategy, a leader needs **farsightedness**, the ability to understand the long-range implications of actions and policies. A farsighted leader recognizes that hiring talented workers today will give the firm a long-range competitive advantage. A more shortsighted view would be to hire less-talented workers to satisfy immediate employment needs. The farsighted leader/manager is not oblivious to short-range needs but will devise an intermediate solution, such as hiring temporary workers until people with the right talents are found.

Conceptual thinking refers to the ability to see the overall perspective, and it makes farsightedness possible. A conceptual thinker is also a *systems thinker*, because he or she understands how the external environment influences the organization and how different parts of the organization influence each other. A good conceptual thinker recognizes how his or her organizational unit contributes to the firm or how the firm meshes with the outside world.

The CEO of PepsiCo, Indra Nooyi, believes that the single most important skill needed for any CEO today is strategic acuity (meaning conceptual thinking and farsightedness). She notes that over twenty-five years ago, when she was chosen to run the European business for PepsiCo, Roger Enrico, the company CEO at the time, said, "I'm pulling you back." When Nooyi asked why, Enrico replied, "I can get operating executives to run a profit-and-loss-center. But I cannot find people to help me re-conceptualize PepsiCo. That's the skill in shortest supply."[50]

Leadership Self-Assessment Quiz 2-4 provides you an opportunity to think through your tendencies toward conceptual (or big) thinking.

## LEADERSHIP SELF-ASSESSMENT QUIZ 2-4

### How Big Is My Thinking?

Indicate your strength of agreement with each of the following statements: (1) strongly disagree (SD); (2) disagree (D); (3) neutral (N); (4) agree (A); (5) strongly agree (SA).

| | | SD | D | N | A | SA |
|---|---|---|---|---|---|---|
| 1. | I get upset if my checkbook does not balance even to the dollar. | 5 | 4 | 3 | 2 | 1 |
| 2. | I often think about the meaning and implication of news stories. | 1 | 2 | 3 | 4 | 5 |
| 3. | A top-level manager is usually better off finding ways to cut costs than thinking about the future of the business. | 5 | 4 | 3 | 2 | 1 |
| 4. | I like to argue (or used to) with an instructor about what should be the correct answer to a multiple-choice question. | 5 | 4 | 3 | 2 | 1 |
| 5. | So long as a company provides good customer service with its present product line, its future is very secure. | 5 | 4 | 3 | 2 | 1 |
| 6. | I prefer acquiring knowledge and skills that can help me with my job during the next month rather than those that might help me in the future. | 5 | 4 | 3 | 2 | 1 |
| 7. | It makes me laugh when a CEO says a big part of his or her job is creating visions. | 5 | 4 | 3 | 2 | 1 |
| 8. | I have already created a vision for my life. | 1 | 2 | 3 | 4 | 5 |
| 9. | I am a "big picture" thinker. | 1 | 2 | 3 | 4 | 5 |
| 10. | If people take care of today's problems, they do not have to worry about the future. | 5 | 4 | 3 | 2 | 1 |
| 11. | World events have very little impact on my life. | 5 | 4 | 3 | 2 | 1 |
| 12. | An organization cannot become great without an exciting vision. | 1 | 2 | 3 | 4 | 5 |

*Scoring and Interpretation:* Find your total score by summing the point values for each question.

- **52–60:** You probably already a big-picture thinker which should help you in our career.
- **30–51:** You probably have a neutral, detached attitude toward thinking big.
- **12–29:** Your thinking probably emphasizes the here and now and the short term. People in this category usually do not focus on the implications of their work.

The accompanying Leader in Action insert gives you a CEO in the sports apparel field to study in terms of his personal attributes including cognitive skills.

## LEADER IN ACTION

### Kevin A. Plank, Founder of Under Armour Inc.

Kevin A. Plank is the entrepreneurial leader who founded Under Armour Inc., the popular line of sports apparel. In 2014, Under Armour overtook Adidas to become the second largest sportswear brand in the United States, trailing only Nike. Plank launched a basic idea, tight, breathable, sports clothes, and built into a company of $5 billion in annual sales.

While a student at the University of Maryland, Plank started several businesses, including Cupid's Valentine, a small firm that delivered roses on Valentine's Day. Savings from the rose-delivery business became the startup money for Under Armour, As Plank became frustrated with the inability of his tee shirts to absorb perspiration and keep him dry, he searched for material that would wick the sweat from his body, making him lighter and faster. Plank did find the right type of synthetic fabric, used in women's lingerie. He had a tailor create a handful of prototypes, and asked his teammates to give the T-shirts a try, suggesting that the sweat-absorbing shirts would enhance their performance. Plank later sent sample T-shirts to professional football players, asking them to pass them out to other players in the locker room.

To market his new business, Plank traveled extensively, visiting locker rooms across the country to introduce athletes and equipment managers to a novel item—a tight-fitting, moisture-wicking T-shirt that provides muscle support and regulates the body temperature. Over the years, the product line has expanded including professional and amateur team uniforms, footwear, and even loose fitting garments such as tennis shirts.

A major part of the company image Plank has created is that of a youthful, athletic lifestyle. The average employee age is in the low thirties, and most are physically fit, and were athletic team members in high school and, or college. Employees work out physically on company premises, and food in the company cafeteria is coded according to its level of healthiness.

Plank has made Under Armour a place where anyone with a creative idea will be listened to carefully, and encouraged. Many suggestions for improvement come from employees in their early twenties. Plank will sometimes clap his hands in enthusiasm when he and an employee agree on a course of action, such as a product improvement. Plank stays actively involved in the details of the business such new product development and seeking the most appropriate professional athletes for product endorsements.

A key part of Plank's management style is to incorporate athletic values into the office environment. Instead of meetings, the company holds "huddles." Employees are encouraged to "manage the clock," "executive the play," and "respect your teammates." The company culture is team focused, and often breaks into huddles for a meeting instead of sitting around a table.

Plank believes that motivation should start from the top of the organization, and that a positive attitude is contagious. He communicates regularly with his team, and solicits their opinions on company objectives. A few years ago when Under Armour began acquiring manufacturers of activity- and diet-tracking apps, some of the company's most experienced employees were skeptical. In response, Plan spent hours holding one-on-one conversations with these veteran workers trying to persuade them that the acquisitions were a good business idea. Plan said, "It was important that this was not just my decision."

Plank also holds MVP lunches where he meets with a small group of employees who are regarded as potential stars, and listens to them about they think is working or not working at Under Armour.

As company CEO, Plank devotes considerable time to drawing elaborate plans for the future of Under Armour, and contributing to the economic development of Baltimore. At one point, Plank owned a five-acre parcel in an industrial section of Baltimore, Port Covington, where he planned to build a whisky distillery. Over the next few years, he invested more than $100 million of his own money buying up nearby real estate. He eventually acquired 266 acres through his real estate investment arm, Sagamore Development.

In 2016, Sagamore revealed its plans for the future of Port Covington, which include a 4 million-square-foot headquarters for Under Armour. Over a twenty-year span, Sagamore intends to build a new neighborhood from virtually abandoned land that will be one of the largest urban renewal projects in the United States. The hope is to find part of the project with over $1 billion in support from local, state, and federal governments.

Plank graduated from the University of Maryland with a bachelor's degree in business administration, and has been a long-time believer in the promise of Baltimore as a city.

## LEADER IN ACTION (continued)

### QUESTIONS

1. What evidence is presented in this story that Kevin Plank has good cognitive skills?

2. Which personality traits does Plank appear to possess?

3. Assuming that he had a job available in your field, how would you enjoy reporting directly to Plank?

*Source:* Original story created from facts and observations in the following sources: Shana Lebowitz, "Under Armour CEO Kevin Plank Reveals His Smart Strategy for Making Big Decisions," *Business Insider* (www.businessinsider.com), January 11, 2016, pp. 1–2; Kurt Blazek, "Inspirational Leadership Style: Under Armour CEO Kevin Plank," *Revolve* (www.boothcom.com), September 15, 2015, pp. 1–2; Rachel Monroe, "Stomping Grounds," *Bloomberg Businessweek*, July 4–July 10, 2016, pp. 42–47; Jean Marbella, "Under Armour Founder Kevin Plank Sees Himself as the Underdog: CEO Grounds Myriad Ambitions in His Maryland Roots," *Baltimore Sun* (http://articles.baltimoresun.com), May 09, 2013, pp. 1–2; Jason Fagone, "Kevin Plank, the Man Under the Armour," *Men's Journal* (www.mensjournal.com), September 2013, pp. 1–8.

## The Influence of Heredity and Environment on Leadership

Which contributes more to leadership effectiveness, heredity or environment? Are leaders born or made? Do you have to have the right stuff to be a leader? The most sensible answer is that the traits, motives, and characteristics required for leadership effectiveness are caused by a combination of heredity and environment. Leaders are both born and made. Personality traits and mental ability traits are based on certain inherited predispositions and aptitudes that require the right opportunity to develop. Cognitive intelligence is a good example. We inherit a basic capacity that sets an outer limit to how much mental horsepower we will have. Yet people need the right opportunity to develop their cognitive intelligence so that they can behave brightly enough to be chosen for a leadership position.

Evelyn Williams, who directs the leadership development program at Stanford University, makes the following metaphor: "I think leadership is a combination of nature and nurture. Just as some musicians have a special talent for playing instruments, some people seem to be born with leadership abilities. But whatever their natural talent, people can certainly learn to be better musicians—and better leaders."[51] The conclusion Williams reaches is supported by the extensive review of the evidence conducted by Julian Barling. He concludes that both environmental and genetic factors contribute to leadership emergence and leadership behavior.[52]

The physical factor of energy also sheds light on the nature-versus-nurture issue. Some people are born with a biological propensity for being more energetic than others. Yet unless that energy is properly channeled, it will not help a person to become an effective leader.

Advances in neuroscience provide additional evidence that there is most likely a genetic and biological component to leadership. David Rock, founder of the NeuroLeadership Institute in Australia, points out that an effective leader is adaptive, such as knowing when to be dogmatic versus collaborative, or when to focus on details versus the big picture. To be adaptive, a person needs an integrated brain. Such integration requires strong connections across all regions of the brain. These connections are mostly genetic although they can be enhanced though mental activities such as creativity training. When the brain is well integrated, the leader can switch between different approaches with ease, such as being tough and unforgiving in one situation and displaying empathy in another.[53]

A convincing example of how brain structure can influence leadership behavior comes from a study about the use of neurological imaging to classify transformational versus nontransformational leaders. As will be explained in the next chapter, transformational leaders bring about major positive changes. In the brain imaging study referenced here,

## LEADERSHIP SKILL-BUILDING EXERCISE 2-2

### My Best Leadership Attribute

Each class member takes a few moments to think about what appears to be his or her best leadership trait, motive, or characteristic as a leader or future leader from among those mentioned in this chapter. Next, about ten volunteers, or the entire class, makes about a two-minute presentation identifying the attribute, and explains the basis for his or her conclusion. For example, a student might say, "Creativity is my best leadership attribute. People have been telling me for many years that I am imaginative, and some of my best ideas have worked well." If the course is being taken online, students can post their responses. Other class members are free to provide any observations that what the person is saying make sense from their perspective.

leaders were classified as transformational versus nontransformational based on psychological test results. The 200 leaders studied came from a variety of industries as well as the military. A complex analysis of electroencephalogram (EEG) recordings was able to classify leaders as transformational versus nontransformational with an astonishing 92.5 percent accuracy.

A key finding was that transformational leadership is linked to dominance of the frontal part of the brain—precisely the part of the brain associated with executive functions such as planning and foresight.[54] Keep in mind that the frontal part of the brain can be developed through concentrated intellectual activity over time, suggesting that becoming a transformational leader requires more than having inherited a brain with a dominant frontal lobe.

To help personalize the information about key leadership traits presented in this chapter, do Leadership Skill-Building Exercise 2-2.

## The Strengths and Limitations of the Trait Approach

A compelling argument for the trait approach is that there is convincing evidence that leaders possess personal characteristics that differ from those of non-leaders. Based on their review of the type of research reported in this chapter, Kirkpatrick and Locke concluded: "Leaders do not have to be great men or women by being intellectual geniuses or omniscient prophets to succeed. But they do need to have the 'right stuff' and this stuff is not equally present in all people."[55] The current emphasis on emotional intelligence, charisma, innovative thinking, and ethical conduct, which are really traits, attitudes, and behaviors, reinforces the importance of the trait approach.

Understanding the traits of effective leaders serves as an important guide to leadership selection. If we are confident that honesty and integrity, as well as creativity and imagination, are essential leadership traits, then we can concentrate on selecting leaders with those characteristics. Another important strength of the trait approach is that it can help people prepare for leadership responsibility and all of the issues that accompany it. A person might seek experiences that enable him or her to develop vital characteristics such as self-confidence, good problem-solving ability, and assertiveness.

A limitation to the trait approach is that it does not tell us which traits are absolutely needed in which leadership situations. We also do not know how much of a trait, characteristic, or motive is the right amount. For example, some leaders get into ethical and legal trouble because they allow their ambition to cross the borderline into greed and gluttony. In addition, too much focus on the trait approach can breed an elitist conception of leadership. People who are not outstanding on key leadership traits and characteristics might be discouraged from seeking leadership positions.

A subtle limitation to the trait approach is that it prompts some people to believe that to be effective, you have to have a high standing on almost every leadership characteristic. In reality, the majority of effective leaders are outstanding in many characteristics but are low on others. Another possible limitation to the trait approach is that some leaders might be convinced that they must be strong on one trait at the exclusion of its polar opposite, such as always being extraverted and avoiding introversion. Peter Grauer, the CEO of Bloomberg Ltd., believes that a combination of opposite traits is often required for leadership effectiveness. For example, a leader who is a big-picture thinker might also need to be strong at details. He says that such a leader can give direction on little things and also encourage big ideas.[56]

A balanced perspective on the trait approach is that certain traits, motives, and characteristics increase the probability that a leader will be effective, but they do not guarantee effectiveness. The leadership situation often influences which traits will be the most important. At the same time, different situations call for different combinations of traits. Visualize yourself as managing a restaurant staffed by teenagers who had never worked previously. You would need to emphasize warmth, enthusiasm, flexibility, and adaptability. Less emphasis would be required on cognitive skills and the power motive.

## READER'S ROADMAP

In this chapter, we focused on the traits, motives, and characteristics of the leader—his or her inner qualities. In the next chapter, we dig further into leadership qualities by studying charismatic and transformational leadership.

## SUMMARY

The trait-based perspective of leadership contends that certain personal characteristics and skills contribute to leadership effectiveness in many situations. General personality traits associated with effective leadership include (1) self-confidence; (2) humility; (3) core self-evaluations; (4) trustworthiness; (5) authenticity; (6) extraversion; (7) assertiveness; (8) enthusiasm, optimism, and warmth; and (9) sense of humor.

Some personality traits of effective leaders are closely associated with task accomplishment. Among them are (1) proactive personality, (2) mindfulness, (3) passion for the work and the people, (4) emotional intelligence, (5) flexibility and adaptability, and (6) courage. Emotional intelligence is composed of four key domains : self-awareness, self-management, social awareness, and relationship management. Each domain has one or more associated competencies.

Certain motives and needs associated with leadership effectiveness are closely related to task accomplishment. Among them are (1) the power motive, (2) the drive and achievement motive, (3) strong work ethic, and (4) tenacity and resilience.

Cognitive factors are also important for leadership success. They include cognitive (or analytical) intelligence and knowledge of the business or group task (or technical competence.). Practical intelligence contributes to cognitive intelligence. Creativity is another important cognitive skill for leaders, but effective leaders vary widely in their creative contributions. Insight into people and situations, including the ability to make effective judgments about business opportunities, also contributes to leadership effectiveness. Farsightedness and conceptual thinking help leaders to understand the long-range implications of actions and policies and to take an overall perspective.

The issue of whether leaders are born or bred frequently surfaces. A sensible answer is that the traits, motives, and characteristics required for leadership effectiveness are a combination of heredity and environment.

The trait approach to leadership is supported by many studies showing that leaders are different from nonleaders, and that effective leaders are different from less-effective leaders. Nevertheless, the trait approach does not tell us which traits are most important in which situations or how much of a trait is required. Also, different situations call for different combinations of traits.

## KEY TERMS

| | | |
|---|---|---|
| core self-evaluations 29 | mindfulness 36 | cognitive factors 42 |
| trust 30 | emotional intelligence 38 | practical intelligence 43 |
| authenticity 31 | flexibility 40 | insight 44 |
| assertiveness 34 | drive 42 | farsightedness 44 |
| proactive personality 35 | achievement motivation 42 | |

## GUIDELINES FOR ACTIONS AND SKILL DEVELOPMENT

Because emotional intelligence is so important for leadership success, many organizations sponsor emotional intelligence training for managers. Even if emotional intelligence is really a group of traits, those component traits are important for leadership success. One way to get started on improving emotional intelligence would be to attend such a training program. However, like all forms of training, emotional intelligence training must be followed up with consistent and determined practice. A realistic starting point in improving your emotional intelligence is to work with one of its four components at a time, such as the empathy aspect of social awareness.

Begin by obtaining as much feedback as you can from people who know you. Ask them if they think you understand their emotional reactions, and how well they think you understand them. It is also helpful to ask someone from another culture or someone who has a severe disability how well you communicate with him or her. (A higher level of empathy is required to communicate well with somebody much different from you.) If you have external or internal customers, ask them how well you appear to understand their position. Another way of gaining insight into one's level of emotional intelligence would be a complete professional assessment of EQ (emotional intelligence quotient), combined with an interview by a skilled professional to supplement the assessment.

If you find any area of deficiency, work on that deficiency steadily. For example, perhaps you are not perceived as taking the time to understand a point of view quite different from your own. Attempt to understand other points of view. Suppose you believe strongly that money is the most important motivator for practically everybody. Speak to a person with a different opinion, and listen carefully until you understand that person's perspective.

A few months later, obtain more feedback about your ability to empathize. If you are making progress, continue to practice. Then, repeat these steps for another facet of emotional intelligence. As a result of this practice, you will have developed another valuable interpersonal skill.

Another way of developing emotional intelligence is through mindfulness. Reflect carefully on how you react to people and what you are thinking. As with meditation, pay careful attention to the moment. For example, you might be a participant in an intense meeting, and you think of a witty comment that at first you feel cannot wait. Through mindfulness, you might decide to postpone the comment until a less intense moment.

A constructive approach to applying trait theory to attain your goals in a given situation is to think through which combination of traits is the most likely to lead to positive outcomes in the situation at hand. Finding the right cluster of traits to emphasize is usually much more useful than emphasizing one trait. You might be leading a group, for example, that is worried because it needs a creative idea to become more productive. Here you might emphasize your cognitive skills, be assertive about expressing your ideas, and also express enthusiasm about the group's chances for success.

Although personality traits are a stable part of an individual's makeup, they usually lie on continuum from low to high. For example, people range in proactivity from very low proactivity to very high proactivity. Select a leadership trait that you would like to strengthen, such as proactivity. You can gain in proactivity by being aware of the importance to take the initiative in a wide range of situations. For instance, you might volunteer to create a schedule for a series of online meetings for your team.

### Discussion Questions and Activities

1. Identify two strong traits, motives, and characteristics of the current president of the United States. Also identify two attributes that appear to be weak. Explain your reasoning for both answers.
2. Suppose a college student graduates with a major for which he or she lacks enthusiasm. What might this person do about becoming a passionate leader?

3. What have you observed personally to be helpful about a leader displaying a sense of humor?

4. What would lead you to conclude that a leader was nonauthentic (phony)?

5. Under what circumstances do you think it is acceptable for a leader to lose emotional control, such as ranting, swearing, or crying?

6. If cognitive ability is so important for high-level leadership, why not have a fifteen-year-old genius be the CEO of a large organization?

7. Provide an example of a leader you have observed who appears to have good cognitive intelligence, yet lacks practical intelligence.

8. Which do you think is the most outstanding leadership trait, motive, or characteristic of the person teaching this class? Explain your answer.

9. If leadership ability is partially inherited, to what extent is it still worthwhile for a person without any family members who have held leadership positions to pursue a career as a high-level business leaders?

10. Many people who disagree with the trait approach to leadership nevertheless still conduct interviews when hiring a person for a leadership position. Why is conducting such interviews inconsistent with their attitude toward the trait approach?

# LEADERSHIP CASE PROBLEM A

### A True Warrior Jumps into the Electric Car Race

Padmasree Warrior, one of Silicon Valley's best-known technology executives, shifted industries in 2016 to be part of the global competition to develop electric automobiles. Several months after leaving her position as chief technology officer at Cisco Systems Inc. she joined the Chinese electric auto startup, NextEv Inc. Warrior was appointed as the company's U.S. chief executive officer and head of software development.

The Indian-born Warrior said that she was looking to enter a new field after her days at Cisco where her thirty years of technology experience would be relevant. "I wanted to be part of creating something that is bigger and different," she said. When Warrior joined NextEv, the company had not yet produced electric cars for the consumer market. NextEv, however, had developed a single-passenger race car that had competed in major racing events for electric vehicles. The company plans to sell its electric cars first in China, and then branch into other markets. NextEv is intent on competing directly with Tesla.

Warrior's experience and values fit well into the NextEv mission that reads in part: "Our aspiration is to shape an exciting lifestyle for our users by delivering next-generation connected vehicles. We are a company dedicated to becoming a user enterprise that transforms vehicle ownership to a pure delight. We are passionate about user experience." Warrior envisions developing a new mode of transportation that leverages all of the technology advances that have been incorporated into the Internet and mobile devices. Although NextEv USA is not yet selling any vehicles, the company is able to operate and hire people with approximately $1 billion in startup funding.

Warrior advises young people to take risks in their career. She says, "A lot of people stay in the same industry sometimes for their entire lives." From her viewpoint, it is better to go after new opportunities and take new challenges, and see what else you can do with your career.

As a NextEv leader, Warrior is committed to creating a culture that outlasts changes in technology. The culture should be passionate about starting a movement in an industry with a hundred-year legacy. She envisions the new culture to be international in scope, sparked by smart people who work collaboratively to combine their experiences from different specialties. She believes that hiring great talent is the leader's job. Warrior handpicked the first hundred hires to NextEv USA. A key selection criterion was whether the candidate was passionate about developing a car that will be the smartest device people will own. She contends that passion is more important than years in a job when selecting among job candidates. "In my book, tech chops + drive + hunger to learn scores over experience any day."

Warrior says that as a leader, she is passionate about technology, entrepreneurship, and global business. She says that she is a tireless advocate on behalf of women in technology.

### Questions

1. To what extent to do think that Warrior is taking on too big a risk by trying to be competitive in the electric car business?

2. Which personality-related leadership traits does Warrior appear to demonstrate?

## LEADERSHIP CASE PROBLEM A *(Continued)*

3. Which cognitive skills does Warrior possess that are particular relevant in her role as CEO of NextEv?
4. What is your evaluation of Warrior's belief that passion about electric cars and technology skills are more important than experience in hiring people to work at the company?

*Source:* Original story created from facts and observations in the following sources: Sarah Buhar, "Padmasree Warrior on Why She Chose to Take on Her New Role as NextEv CEO," *TC* (https://techcrunch.com), December 16, 2015. pp. 1–5; Claire Dodson, "The Road Warrior: Padmasree Warrior," *Fast Company*, May 2016, p. 20; Don Clark, "Warrior Joins Electric-Car Startup," *The Wall Street Journal*, December 16, 2015, p. B5; "Padmasree Warrior: CEO at NextEV USA," *www.linkedin.com*, July 27, 2016, pp. 1–7; Padmasree Warrior, "Why Building a Great Team Is the Key to an Ideal Workplace," *www.linkedin.com*, July 26, 2013, pp. 1–3.

## ASSOCIATED ROLE PLAY

One student plays the role of Padmasree Warrior who is interviewing a candidate for a marketing position at NextEv USA. She believes strongly that "technology chops" and passion are more important than experience in filling this marketing position. Another student plays the role of the candidate who is excited about being interviewed by such a well-known technology leader. The candidate wants to stand out by demonstrating his or her passion for electric cars, technology, and marketing a consumer product. Run the role play for about ten minutes with observers providing some feedback after the role players have completed their task.

## LEADERSHIP CASE PROBLEM B

### Blunt Brittany

Brittany is the director of merchandising for Auto Pal, a large chain of automotive supply stores in the United States and Canada. The company has continued to grow in terms of stores and income, as so many more people keep their vehicles longer, and also perform more maintenance, such as oil changes, by themselves. Merchandising is a core function of Auto Pal because the chain distributes thousands of products in its stores, from floor mats to transmissions.

With profit margins thin, and heavy competition, the pace of conducting business at Auto Pal is hectic. Brittany moves quickly when dealing with her direct reports, sometimes to their surprise.

Sid, a merchandise specialist for vehicle cleaning and polishing supplies, recently requested a two-week paternity leave because he and his wife were expecting a baby any moment now. Brittany replied that such a request was kind of wimpy, and a little bit out of the ordinary. *"Don't you have a mother-in-law who can help with the new baby? Or, are you so poor that you can't hire a nanny for two weeks?"*

Katie, a merchandising specialist for batteries, regulators, and radiators, sent Brittany a detailed report about new procurement software that might save thousands of dollars for Auto Pal in the long run. Brittany sent back an e-mail stating in part, *"Does this great new software come from a company that employs a relative of yours? We are already using state-of-the art software."*

Jeff, the office manager, and one of Auto Pal's most senior employees, sent Brittany an e-mail asking if he could take his ten days of vacation in five two-day pieces next year instead of ten consecutive working days. The next day, Brittany wrote back, *"I like your idea Jeff. In this way your work flow would be less disrupted. And besides, an old-timer like you needs a few more long weekends than the rest of us do."*

One day, Auto Pal CEO Derek asked Brittany how well she was proceeding with her strategic plan for next year. Brittany replied, *"Not much progress yet. I'm running around putting out fires and dealing with the realities of making sure my team gets the right merchandise into the stores. Maybe you could have one of those overpaid marketing specialists dream up a strategic plan that I could sign off on."*

### Questions

1. In which leadership trait or characteristic does Brittany seem to need the most development?
2. How would you rate Brittany's warmth and enthusiasm as a leader?
3. What action would you recommend that Derek take to improve Brittany's leadership effectiveness?

## ASSOCIATED ROLE PLAY

CEO Derek has heard some rumors that Brittany is insensitive in dealing with her direct reports, and he has also observed some of this insensitivity in his interactions with Brittany. At the same time, Derek recognizes that her leadership in merchandising has helped Auto Pal grow and prosper. Derek decides to schedule a one-on-one meeting with Brittany. She thinks that perhaps the meeting will be a good opportunity for her to complain about how thin-skinned some of her direct reports appear to be. Run the role play for about eight minutes with observers, providing some feedback after the role players have completed their task.

## LEADERSHIP SKILL-BUILDING EXERCISE 2-3

### My Leadership Portfolio

For this addition to your leadership portfolio, first select five of the traits, motives, and characteristics described in this chapter that you think you have already exhibited. For each of these attributes, explain why you think you have it. An example would be as follows:

> Insight into people and situations: As a restaurant manager, my job was to help hire an assistant manager who would share some of the responsibilities of running the restaurant. I invited a friend of mine, Laura, to apply for the position, even though she had never worked in a restaurant. I noticed that she was businesslike and also had a good touch with people. Laura was hired, and she proved to be a fantastic assistant manager. I obviously sized her up correctly.

Second, select several leadership traits, motives, or characteristics that you think you need to develop to enhance your leadership skills. Explain why you think you need this development, and how you think you might obtain it. An example would be as follows:

> Passion for the work and people: So far I am not particularly passionate about any aspect of work or any cause, so it is hard for me to get very excited about being a leader. I plan to read more about my field and then interview a couple of successful people in this field to find some aspect of it that would be a joy for me to get involved in.

## LEADERSHIP SKILL-BUILDING EXERCISE 2-4

### Analyzing the Traits, Motives, and Characteristics of a Well-Known Leader

Choose one or two well-known leaders as a topic for discussion. *Well-known* in this context refers to somebody whom the majority of the class has observed, either in person or through the media, including the Internet, newspapers, and on YouTube. Take a few class moments to agree on which leader or leaders will be analyzed. Possibilities include (1) your college president, (2) your country president or prime minister, or (3) a well-known NFL or professional soccer coach.

The next step is for the class to discuss this leader's traits, motives, and characteristics, using ideas from this chapter of the text. Look to see if you can find consensus about the leader's strongest and weakest personal attributes.

## NOTES

1. Original story based on facts and observations in the following sources: Suzanne Kapner and Joann Lublin, "Macy's Chief to Exit Amid Store Struggles," *The Wall Street Journal*, June 24, 2016, pp. B1, B2; Hadley Malcolm, "Shake Up at Macy's: Jeff Gennette to Become CEO, Terry Lundgren to Step Down," *USA Today* (www.usatoday.com), August 10, 2016, pp. 1–3; Annalyn Kurtz and Rachel Abrams, "Jeff Gennette to Succeed Terry Lundgren as Macy's Chief," *The New York Times* (www.nytimes.com), June 23, 2016, pp. 1–2; Karl Utermohlen, "Jeff Gennette: 5 Things to Know About Macy's (M) New CEO," *http://investorplace.com*, June 23, 2016, pp. 1–2; Walter Loeb, "Expect Evolutionary Changes From Macy's Next CEO, Jeff Gennette," *www.forbes.com*, June 23, 2016, pp. 1–6.

2. D. Scott DeRue, Jennifer D. Nahrgang, Ned Wellman, and Stephen E. Humphrey, "Trait and Behavioral Theories of Leadership: An Integration and Meta-Analytic Test of Their Relative Validity," *Personnel Psychology*, no. 1, 2011, pp. 7–52D; Scott DeRue, Jennifer D. Nahrgang, Ned Wellman, and Stephen E. Humphrey, "Trait and Behavioral Theories of Leadership: An Integration and Meta-Analytic Test of Their Relative Validity," *Personnel Psychology*, no. 1, 2011, pp. 7–52.

3. Stephen J. Zaccaro, "Individual Differences and Leadership: Contributions to a Third Tipping Point," *The Leadership Quarterly*, August 2012, pp. 718–728.

4. George P. Hollenbeck and Douglas T. Hall, "Self-Confidence and Leader Performance," *Organizational Dynamics*, no. 3, 2004, p. 254.

5. Sally Ward, "Invaluable: Appropriate Self-assurance," *Democrat and Chronicle*, December 15, 2015, p. 6A.

6. Quoted in Brian O'Keefe, "Battle-Tested: How a Decade of War Has Created a New Generation of Elite Business Leaders," *Fortune*, March 22, 2010, p. 112.

7. Stephen G. Harrison, "Leadership and Hope Go Hand in Hand," *Executive Leadership*, June 2002, p. 8.

8. Timothy A. Judge, Ronald F. Picccolo, and Tomek Kosalka, "The Bright and Dark Sides of Leader Traits: A Review and Theoretical Extension of the Leader Trait Paradigm," *The Leadership Quarterly*, December 2009, p. 866.

9. Roy J. Lewicki, Daniel McAllister, and Robert J. Bies, "Trust and Distrust: New Relationships and Realities," *Academy of Management Review*, July 1998, p. 439.

10. "4 Keys to Building Trust Quickly," *Manager's Edge*, March 2005, p. 4; David Horsager, *The Trust Edge: How Top Leaders Gain Faster Results, Deeper Relationships, and a Stronger Bottom Line* (Minneapolis, MN: Summerside Press, 2011); "A Conversation with Rick Miller: Build Trust Over Time," *Executive Leadership*, April 2015, p. 3.

11. Kurt T. Kirks and Donald L Ferrin, "Trust in Leadership: Meta-Analytic Findings and Implications for Research and Practice," *Journal of Applied Psychology*, August 2002, pp. 611–628.

12. Michael E Palansaki and Francis J. Yammarino, "Impact of Behavioral Integrity on Follower Job Performance: A Three-Study Examination," *The Leadership Quarterly*, August 2011, pp. 765–786.

13. Bill George, Peter Sims, Andrew N. McClean, and Diana Mayer, "Discovering Your Authentic Leadership," *Harvard Business Review*, February 2007, p. 130.

14. Interview of George by James Tehrani, "'Northern Exposure' to Leadership," *Workforce*, September 2015, p. 12.

15. George, Sims, McClean, and Mayer, "Discovering Your Authentic Leadership," pp. 129–138.

16. Suzanne J. Peterson, Fred O. Walumba, Bruce J. Avolio, and Sean T. Hannah, "The Relationship Between Authentic Leadership and Follower Job Performance: The Mediating Role of Follower Positivity in Extreme Contexts," *The Leadership Quarterly*, June 2012, pp. 502–516.

17. Timothy A. Judge, Joyce E. Bono, Remus Ilies, and Megan W. Gerhardt, "Personality and Leadership: A Qualitative and Quantitative Review," *Journal of Applied Psychology*, August 2002, pp. 765–780.

18. Research reported in Judge, Piccolo, and Kosalka, "The Bright and Dark Sides of Leader Traits," p. 865.

19. Adam M. Grant, Francesca Gino, and David A. Hofmann, "Reversing the Extraverted Leadership Advantage: The Role of Employee Proactivity," *Academy of Management Journal*, June 2011, pp. 528–550; Adam M. Grant, Francesca Gino, and David A. Hofmann, "The Hidden Advantages of Quiet Bosses," *Harvard Business Review*, December 2010, p. 28.

20. Meghan McGrath, "Introverts Can Make Great Leaders," *Chief Learning Officer* (www.clomedia.com), November 10, 2015, pp. 1–3.

21. Jared Sandberg, "The Office Pessimists May Not Be Lovable, but Are Often Right," *The Wall Street Journal*, November 27, 2007, p. B1.

22. James B. Avey, Bruce J. Avolio, and Fred Luthans, "Experimentally Analyzing the Impact of Leader Positivity on Follower Positivity and Performance," *The Leadership Quarterly*, April 2011, pp. 282–294.

23. Eric J. Romeo and Kevin W. Cruthirds, "The Use of Humor in the Workplace," *Academy of Management Perspectives*, May 2006, pp. 60, 63–64; Additional research reported in Sue Shellenbarger, "Comedic Gold or Clunker? Secrets of Effective Office Humor," *The Wall Street Journal*, August 14, 2013, pp. D1–D2.

24. Thomas S. Bateman and J. Michael Crant, "The Proactive Component of Organizational Behavior: A Measure and Correlates," *Journal of Organizational Behavior*, March 1993, p. 103.

25. Uta K. Bindle and Sharon Parker, "Proactive Work Behavior: Forward Thinking and Change-Oriented Action in Organizations," in Sheldon Zedeck (ed.), *APA Handbook of Industrial and Organizational Psychology* (Washington, DC: American Psychological Association, 2010).

26. Craig D. Crossley, Cecily D. Cooper, and Tara S. Wernsing, "Making Things Happen Through Challenging Goals: Leader Proactivity, Trust, and Business-Unit Performance," *Journal of Applied Psychology*, May 2013, pp. 540–549.

27. Ute R. Hülsheger, "Benefits of Mindfulness at Work: The Role of Mindfulness in Emotion Regulation, Emotional Exhaustion, and Job Satisfaction," *Journal of Applied Psychology*, March 2013, p. 310.

28. Manish Chopra, "Want to Be a Better Leader? Observe More and React Less," *McKinsey Quarterly* (www.mckinsey.com), February 2016, pp. 1–6; Christy Cassia, "The Truly Mindful Workplace: A Reality Whose Moment is Arriving," *UCSD Center for Mindfulness* (http://ucsdefm), December 11, 2012, pp. 1–4; Leigh Buchanan, "13 Ways of *Looking at a Leader*," www.inc.com/magazine, May 29, 2012, pp. 1–5; Erika Garms, "Practicing Mindful Leadership," *www.td.org*, March 08, 2013, pp. 1–5.

29. "Starbucks: More Than a Caffeine High," *Executive Leadership*, August 2006, p. 4.

30. Rashimah Rajah, Zhaloi Song, and Richard D. Arvey, "Emotionality and Leadership: Taking Stock of the Past Decade of Research," *The Leadership Quarterly*, December 2011, p. 1110.

31. Daniel Goleman, "What Makes a Leader?" *Harvard Business Review*, November–December 1998, p. 94; Goleman and Richard E. Boyatis, "Emotional Intelligence Has 12 Elements. Which One Do You Need to Work On?" *Harvard Business Review* (https://hrb.org), February 6, 2017, pp. 1–6; Annie McKee, "How the Most Emotionally Intelligent CEOs Handle Their Power," *Harvard Business Review* (https:hbr.org) December 8, 2016, p. 4.

32. Travis Bradberry, "Is Emotional Intelligence a Good Measure of Leadership Ability? Yes," *HR Magazine*, November 2015, p. 22.

33. Daniel Goleman, Richard Boyatzis, and Annie McKee, "Primal Leadership: The Hidden Driver of Great Performance," *Harvard Business Review*, December 2001, pp. 42–51.

34. Adam Waytz, "The Limits of Empathy," *Harvard Business Review*, January–February 2016, pp. 68–73.

35. Stéphane Côté, Paulo N. Lopes, Peter Salovey, and Christopher T. H. Miners, "Emotional Intelligence and Leadership Emergence in Small Groups," *The Leadership Quarterly*, June 2010, pp. 496–508.

36. Sigal Barsade and Olivia A. O'Neil, "Manage Your Emotional Culture," *Harvard Business Review*, January–February 2016, pp. 58–66.

37. Goleman, Boyatzis, and McKee, "Primal Leadership," pp. 42–51.

38. John Antonakis, "Is Emotional Intelligence a Good Measure of Leadership Ability? No, the Scientific Evidence Isn't There," *HR magazine*, November 2015, p. 23; Antonakis, Neal M. Ashkanasy, and Marie T. Dasborough, "Does Leadership Need Emotional Intelligence?" *The Leadership Quarterly*, April 2009, pp. 247–26.

39. David C. McClelland and Richard Boyatzis, "Leadership Motive Pattern and Long-Term Success in Management," *Journal of Applied Psychology*, December 1982, p. 727

40. Locke and Associates, *The Essence of Leadership: The Four Keys to Leading Successfully* (New York: Lexington/Macmillan, 1992), p. 22.

41. Locke and Associates, *The Essence of Leadership*, p. 22.

42. John B. Miner, Normal R. Smith, and Jeffrey S. Bracker, "Role of Entrepreneurial Task Motivation in the Growth of Technologically Innovative Firms," *Journal of Applied Psychology*, August 1989, p. 554.

43. Angela Duckworth and Lauren Eskreis-Winkler, "True Grit," *Observer* (www.psychologicalscience.org), vol. 26, no. 4, April 2013, pp. 1–3.

44. Susan Carey, "CEO Says United Now Ready for Lift-off," *The Wall Street Journal*, September 1, 2016, p. B3.

45. Timothy A. Judge, Amy E. Colbert, and Remus Ilies, "Intelligence and Leadership: A Quantitative Review and Test of Theoretical Propositions," *Journal of Applied Psychology*, June 2004, pp. 542–552.

46. Jonathan Wai, "The Braniac-Billionaire Connection," *Psychology Today*, July/August 2012, p. 80.

47. Robert J. Sternberg, "The WICS Approach to Leadership: Stories of Leadership and the Structures and Processes That Support Them," *The Leadership Quarterly*, June 2008, pp. 360–371.

48. Michael D. Mumford, Logan L. Watts, and Paul J. Partlow, "Leader Cognition: Approaches and Findings," *The Leadership Quarterly*, June 2015, p. 303.

49. Boris Groysberg, L. Kevin Kelly, and Bryan McDonald, "The New Path to the C-Suite," *Harvard Business Review*, March 2011, p. 66.

50. Jessica Shambora and Beth Kowitt, "The Queen of Pop," *Fortune*, September 28, 2009, p. 108.

51. "How Stanford Is Grooming Next Business Leaders," *The Wall Street Journal*, May 29, 2007, p. B6.

52. Julian Barling, *The Science of leadership: Lessons from Research for Organizational Leaders* (New York: Oxford University Press, 2014), p. 143.

53. Adrienne Fox, "Leading with the Brain: David Rock Explains How Scientists' Growing Understanding of the Brain Illuminates Techniques for Leadership and Decision Making," *HR Magazine*, June 2011, pp. 52–53.

54. Pierre A. Balthazard, David A. Waldman, Robert W. Thatcher, and Sean T. Hannah, "Differentiating Transformational and Non-transformational Leaders on the Basis of Neurological Imaging," *The Leadership Quarterly*, April 2012, pp. 244–258.

55. Shelly Kirkpatrick and Edwin A. Locke, "Leadership: Do Traits Matter?" *Academy of Management Executive*, no. 2, 1991, p. 59.

56. "Bloomberg's Peter Grauer: How the 'And Factor' Defines Leadership," *Knowledge@Wharton* (http://knowledge.wharton.upenn.edu/), July 31, 2013, p. 1.

# Charismatic and Transformational Leadership

After twenty-two years of holding a variety of leadership positions at Microsoft Corp., Satya Nadella was appointed chief executive officer (CEO). He began his new position by establishing a new mission and vision for Microsoft. Nadella's primary focus was to make the company more innovative as the company was losing some of its dominance in software for business and personal use. He said that information technology only respects innovation, not tradition. A new mission and vision for the company was needed also because throughout the industry, software as a product was gradually being replaced by software as a service. Many companies now run their IT infrastructure off cloud-based servers.

As articulated by Nadella, the mission of Microsoft is "to empower every person and every organization on the planet to achieve more." Nadella admits that the mission is ambitious, but that the company has the unique capability to harmonize the needs of both individuals and organizations because this capability is in Microsoft's DNA.

Nadella also explains that the mission must be grounded in the present world and the future the company is trying to create. He believes that we live in a mobile-first, cloud-first world, and that Microsoft products and services enable customers to thrive in this world. Nadella explains that his vision of technology is transformational, and that he wants leaders to use technology to make a difference in the world. Microsoft envisions a new platform that is going to be as powerful, if not more powerful, than the Web or mobile apps. The platform centers on making more use of human language in computing. Nadella contends that the world is facing

a "fourth Industrial Revolution" that follows the mechanical, electrical, and digital.

Nadella says, "As a leader, I'm interested in fighting the new battles. You need new concepts with new innovation, and you have to have new capability and culture to go after those new concepts." Nadella also strongly believes that leaders should help create a culture that enables people to attain high performance. He says, "If you don't focus on creating a culture that allows people to do their best work, then you've created nothing."

To help him sharpen his insights into how Microsoft products are used, Nadella reserves time for children in his tours of the United States and other countries. Nadella notes that children are the next generation of customers, and they also help keep him grounded in reality.

Nadella holds a bachelor's degree in electrical engineering from the Manipal Institute of Technology (India), an MS degree in computer science from the University of Wisconsin-Milwaukee, and an MBA from the University of Chicago, Booth School of Business. Nadella enjoys watching and playing cricket.[1]

---

The words and actions of Satya Nadella illustrate a couple of key points about charismatic and transformational leaders. They think big, are committed to their strong beliefs, and are willing to pursue a bold new path. The study of charismatic and transformational leadership, an extension of the trait theory, has become an important way of understanding leadership. One of the many reasons that charisma is important is that it facilitates leaders in carrying out their roles. Charisma makes the leader's job much easier. In today's fiercely competitive global economy, leaders need to energize their constituents more than ever. Helping people attain stretch goals and understand why change is necessary is done more quickly with charisma than relying solely on reasoning and logic.[2] (A stretch goal tests most of your capabilities but is not so difficult to attain that you are likely to fail.)

In this chapter, we examine the meaning and effects of charismatic leadership, the characteristics of charismatic leaders including narcissism, how such leaders form visions, and how one develops charisma. We also describe the closely related and overlapping subject of transformational leadership. Finally, we look at the dark side of charismatic leadership.

## The Meanings of Charisma

Charisma, like leadership itself, has been defined in various ways. Nevertheless, there is enough consistency among these definitions to make charisma a useful concept in understanding and practicing leadership. *Charisma* is a Greek word meaning "divinely inspired gift." In the study of leadership, **charisma** is a special quality of leaders whose purposes, powers, and extraordinary determination differentiate them from others.[3] In general use, the term *charismatic* means to have a charming and colorful personality, such as that shown by many talk-show hosts.

The various definitions of charisma have a unifying theme. Charisma is a positive and compelling quality that makes many others want to be led by the person that has it. The phrase *many others* is chosen carefully. Few leaders are perceived as charismatic by *all* of their constituents. A case in point is the late Steve Jobs of Apple Inc., whose name surfaces frequently in discussions of charisma. *Fortune* magazine once declared Jobs to be the CEO of the Decade in part because he had cheated death (overcome pancreatic cancer for a while) and changed our world.[4] In contrast, a news reporter and novelist described Jobs as *"a brilliant but short-tempered figure known for his outsized ego and penchant for control."* He was also known to be stubborn and arrogant.[5] Furthermore, Jobs was cruelly insulting toward people who challenged him. Such behavior is hardly a characteristic of an inspiring leader.

Given that charisma is based on perceptions, an important element of charismatic leadership involves the *attributions* made by group members about the characteristics of leaders and the results they achieve. According to attribution theory, if people perceive a leader to have a certain characteristic, such as being visionary, the leader will more likely be perceived as charismatic. Attributions of charisma are important because they lead to other behavioral outcomes, such as commitment to leaders, self-sacrifice, and high performance.

A study of attributions and charisma found that the network a person belongs to influences the attributions he or she makes. The subjects in the study were police workers who rated the director of a police organization and students in an introductory business course who rated the charisma of their professors. The study found that network members influenced to some extent whether the study participants perceived their leader or professor to be charismatic and that perceptions of charisma were the closest among friends within networks.[6] What about you? Are your perceptions of the charisma of your professors influenced by the opinions of your network members?

A study of both U.S. presidential elections and business organizations conducted by Philippe Jacquart and John Antonakis points to the relevance of charisma as a leadership attribute. It was shown that a charismatic leader was more likely to be reelected as president or reappointed as a CEO. Past performance was also a key factor for a U.S. president or CEO to be reelected or reappointed.[7]

## Charisma: A Relationship Between the Leader, Group Members, and Other Stakeholders

A key dimension of charismatic leadership is that, like all leadership, it involves a relationship or interaction between the leader and the people being led. Charismatic leaders use impression management to deliberately cultivate a certain relationship with group members. In other words, they take steps to create a favorable, successful impression, recognizing that the perceptions of constituents determine whether they function as charismatic leaders.[8] Impression management seems to imply that these leaders are skillful actors in presenting a charismatic face to the world. But the behaviors and attitudes of truly charismatic leaders go well beyond superficial aspects of impression management, such as wearing fashionable clothing or speaking well. For example, a truly charismatic leader will work hard to create positive visions for group members.

A notable aspect of charismatic and transformational leaders is that their influence extends beyond the immediate work group and beyond reporting relationships. An example is that some consumers are influenced to purchase products from a company, and some suppliers want to do business with it, based partly on the charisma of a company leader.[9] An example is Kevin A. Plank, the CEO of Under Armour, described in Chapter 2, who inspires many people in the community to wear Under Armour products.

Another way in which the highly charismatic leader influences external stakeholders is that he or she becomes the symbol of the organization. If the leader meets the stakeholders' (or followers') needs, such as wanting to identify with a powerful figure, the stakeholders will have favorable interactions with the organization. Plank fits this role in part because he is athletic and was a college football player.

## The Effects of Charisma

The study of charisma grows in importance when its effects are recognized, such as whether by being charismatic a leader can enhance productivity, lower accidents, and enhance job satisfaction. Much of the impact of charisma is based on the positive affect (emotion) the charismatic leader triggers among the group members. A group of researchers conducted a study of firefighters and their leaders to explore how the emotional component of charisma affects the mood and happiness of subordinates.

The firefighter study followed a preliminary laboratory study with college students designed to explore how the leader's emotion might affect subordinate behavior. The field study involved 216 firefighters and 48 officers. Happiness, including positive affect and negative affect (unhappiness), was measured through a questionnaire. Leader charisma was measured by a questionnaire quite similar to one presented later in this chapter. The results suggested that firefighters under the command of a charismatic officer were happier than those under the command of a noncharismatic officer. Charismatic leaders who expressed positive emotion and thoughts tended to have an even stronger impact on the positive emotional state of firefighters. The positive affect of the officers also tended to reduce negative affect among the firefighters.

A conclusion of the study going beyond firefighters is that one of the ways by which charismatic leaders emotionally touch subordinates is through enhancing their positive affect. Furthermore, happier leaders spread their positive mood to group members.[10]

Another major impact of a charismatic leader in a senior-level position is that he or she leaves a personal stamp on the organization. For example, Mark Zuckerberg, the CEO of Facebook, has become one of the world's best-known business leaders. At the same time, he is "the face of Facebook."

## Three Types of Charismatic Leaders

The everyday use of the term *charisma* suggests that it is a straightforward and readily understood trait. As already explained, however, charisma has different meanings and dimensions. As a result, charismatic leaders can be categorized into various types, with the three most relevant for today described here: socialized charismatics, personalized charismatics, and celebrities.[11]

Following the distinction made for the power motive, some charismatic leaders use their power for the good of others. A **socialized charismatic** is a leader who restrains the use of power in order to benefit others. This type of leader also attempts to bring group members' values in line with his or her values. The socialized charismatic formulates and pursues goals that fulfill the needs of group members and provide intellectual stimulation to them. Followers of socialized charismatics are autonomous, empowered, and responsible. A study conducted in a healthcare organization indicated that direct reports of leaders perceived to be socialized charismatics are less likely to engage in workplace deviance (e.g., lying, stealing, and cheating). Part of the reason is that the socialized charismatic imparts positive values to group members.[12]

The effect of the socialized charismatic on followers provides more insight into this type of charismatic. In the socialized relationship, the followers have a clear sense of who they are and a clear set of values. The charismatic relationship gives them an opportunity to express their important values within the framework of being a group member, such as wanting to work together to preserve the planet. In a socialized relationship, the followers derive a sense of direction and self-expression not from identifying with the leader but from the leader's message.[13] The message of the socialized charismatic in this situation might be, "We want to make money but we want to contribute to a sustainable environment at the same time."

A second type of charismatic leader is the **personalized charismatic**. Such individuals serve primarily their own interests and so exercise few restraints on their use of power.

Personalized charismatics impose self-serving goals on constituents, and they offer consideration and support to group members only when it facilitates their own goals. Followers of personalized charismatics are typically obedient, submissive, and dependent. They also identify more with the leader than the leader's message and therefore might follow the leader down an unethical path, such as granting homeowner loans that will most likely result in a high foreclosure rate.

The *celebrity charismatic* can be found in organizational life as well as in the political and entertainment realms. Charismatic people of this type may overlap with the other types such as being socialized and personalized. Howard Schultz, the founder and CEO of Starbucks, has emerged into a celebrity CEO. He often takes a stand on national and political issues, such as urging people to get the federal debt under control, or calling for improved race relations in the United States.

## Characteristics of Charismatic Leaders

The outstanding characteristic of charismatic leaders is that they can attract, motivate, or lead others. They also have other distinguishing characteristics. Because charisma is a key component of transformational leadership, many of these characteristics also apply to transformational leaders. A **transformational leader** is one who brings about positive, major changes in an organization. Many charismatic leaders, however, are not transformational. Although they inspire people, they may not bring about major organizational changes. As we look at the characteristics of charismatic leaders,[14] you will note that many of these characteristics apply to leaders in general.

First, charismatic leaders are *visionary* because they offer an exciting image of where the organization is headed and how to get there. Charismatic leaders also possess *masterful communication skills.* To inspire people, the charismatic leader uses colorful language and exciting metaphors and analogies. (More about the communication skills of charismatic leaders is presented later in this chapter.) Another key characteristic is the *ability to inspire trust.* Constituents believe so strongly in the integrity of charismatic leaders that they will risk their careers to pursue the chief's vision. Charismatic leaders are also *able to make group members feel capable.* Sometimes they do this by enabling group members to achieve success on relatively easy projects. They then praise the group members and give them more demanding assignments.

Charismatic people are typically tactful in social situations based partly on their ability to read other people's emotions (part of emotional intelligence). Related to reading emotions is the ability to connect with people, as in the now overdone phrase, *"I feel your pain."* For example, during a severe business downturn, a company leader might say, *"I know a lot of you are worried about losing your jobs. Working with you as a team, we are fighting to avoid layoffs."*

In addition, charismatic leaders demonstrate an *energy and action orientation.* Like entrepreneurs, most charismatic leaders are energetic and serve as role models for getting things done on time. *Emotional expressiveness and warmth* are also notable. A key characteristic of charismatic leaders is the ability to express feelings openly. A bank vice president claims that much of the charisma people attribute to her can be explained very simply: *"I'm up front about expressing positive feelings. I praise people, I hug them, and I cheer if necessary. I also express my negative feelings, but to a lesser extent."* Nonverbal emotional expressiveness, such as warm gestures and frequent (nonsexual) touching of group members, is also characteristic of charismatic leaders.

Another trait of charismatic leaders is that they *romanticize risk.* They enjoy risk so much that they feel empty in its absence. Jim Barksdale, now a venture capitalist for online startup companies and former CEO of Netscape, says that the fear of failure is what increases your heart rate. As great opportunists, charismatic people yearn to accomplish activities others have never done before. Risk taking adds to a person's charisma because others admire such courage. In addition to treasuring risk, charismatic leaders use *unconventional strategies* to achieve success.

Another characteristic observed in many charismatic leaders is that they *challenge, prod, and poke*. They test your courage and your self-confidence by asking questions like "Do your employees really need you?" Larry Elison, the celebrity charismatic who is founder and CEO of Oracle Corporation, often asks workers to explain how their job contributes to the organization.

Recent research conducted by William von Hippel of the University of Queensland suggests that people who think fast tend to be perceived as charismatic. Participants in the study were given intelligence and personality tests, and then asked thirty common-knowledge questions, such as "How many continents are there?" Participants also rated their friends' charisma and social skills. Individuals who answered the questions more rapidly were perceived to be more charismatic regardless of their cognitive ability, personality, or knowledge.[15]

Another major characteristic of charismatic leaders is amalgam of the ideas already introduced: Being *dramatic and unique* in significant, positive ways is a major contributor to charisma. This quality stems from a combination of factors, such as being energetic, self-promotion, romanticizing risk, and being emotionally expressive. The late leadership scholar Warren G. Bennis contends that great leaders, particularly those in public life, are great actors. The effective leader sells people on a vision to elevate their spirits.[16]

To personalize charisma characteristics, go through the charisma checklist presented in box Leadership Self-Assessment Quiz 3-1. If you can respond to checklist with a reasonable degree of objectivity, the quiz should enhance your understanding of how you might or might not be perceived as charismatic by many people at this stage of your career.

## The Narcissism Component of Charismatic Leadership

Narcissism is a characteristic of charismatic leadership that warrants separate mention because of its major link with charisma. **Narcissism** is a relatively stable personality trait characterized by a sense of personal superiority, a desire for power, and a sense of self-importance. Narcissists have little empathy for others because they are so focused on themselves.[17] Many charismatic leaders are narcissistic, or self-adoring in excess. The narcissistic leader is likely to be charming except when engaging in excessive self-puffery and blaming others for mistakes.

Part of being charismatic is having a *self-promoting personality*. They frequently toot their own horn and allow others to know how important they are. Richard Branson, the colorful chairman of the Virgin Group, has relied on self-promotion to build his empire, a collection of about 400 companies with the Virgin trademark. Among his antics have been flying around the world in a balloon, and sliding down the side of a silver ball attached to a New York City building. He also conducts much of his business electronically from his private island in the Virgin Islands.

Narcissistic CEOs tend to make riskier decisions, often to attain dramatic results which enhance their image. A study of CEOs of thirty-two prominent high-technology firms investigated whether narcissism was related to compensation, consisting of salary, bonus, and stock options. Degree of narcissism was measured by an online checklist sent to people who worked for the CEOs studied. The study found that among the CEOs have longer tenures, tended to receive the highest compensation.[18]

At their best charismatic leaders who are narcissistic are effective in their roles. On the positive side, the air of confidence and dominance so characteristic of narcissism often inspires followers. During a crisis, for example, followers might want a narcissistic leader who believes he or she is talented enough to get through a crisis. Leaders who combine narcissism with a touch of humility tend to have positive effects on their subordinates. A study in a large health insurance company found that leaders who tempered

## LEADERSHIP SELF-ASSESSMENT QUIZ 3-1

**A Checklist of Behaviors and Attitudes Reflecting Charisma**

***Instructions:*** Indicate whether each of the following statements applies to you now, or whether it does not apply now or probably never will.

| | APPLIES NOW | DOES NOT APPLY OR PROBABLY NEVER WILL |
|---|---|---|
| 1. Many people have said that I am likeable and charming. | ☐ | ☐ |
| 2. In groups, I have been part of or led, I have offered a vision that others accepted. | ☐ | ☐ |
| 3. I have more physical energy than most people, and the energy is apparent to other people. | ☐ | ☐ |
| 4. I do a good job of telling true stories and anecdotes to others on the job. | ☐ | ☐ |
| 5. My appearance in terms of dress and personal grooming is well above average. | ☐ | ☐ |
| 6. I communicate a lot of passion about my own work, or about the task of the group. | ☐ | ☐ |
| 7. I am successful at making other people feel important. | ☐ | ☐ |
| 8. I am candid without being offensive. | ☐ | ☐ |
| 9. I make frequent use of a firm handshake or fist-bumps when greeting people I know or first-time introductions. | ☐ | ☐ |
| 10. My posture is good and I look people in the eye without being accused of staring at them. | ☐ | ☐ |
| 11. I have taken sensible risks at least several times in my life. | ☐ | ☐ |
| 12. I am comfortable in letting other people know of my accomplishments. | ☐ | ☐ |
| 13. I have been told that I have a warm smile. | ☐ | ☐ |
| 14. People listen to me when I talk at a meeting. | ☐ | ☐ |
| 15. I have an exceptional number of social media friends and followers. | ☐ | ☐ |

***Scoring and Interpretation:*** The more of these fifteen statements that apply to you now, the greater the probability that you are perceived to be charismatic by many people. If twelve or more of the statements in the checklist apply to you now, you have above average charismatic tendencies. Answering these statements is so subjective that it would be helpful for one or two people who know you well to also respond to the checklist in relation to you. You might then compare your responses to the responses of the other person or persons.

narcissism with humility tended to be perceived as effective. Furthermore follower job engagement and job performance as rated by supervisors and production data tended to be higher.[19]

Leadership Self-Assessment Quiz 3-2 provides you an opportunity to look closely at symptoms, or attitudes and behaviors, of narcissism.

# LEADERSHIP SELF-ASSESSMENT QUIZ 3-2

### The Narcissism Attitudes and Behavior Checklist

Listed here are fifteen attitudes or behaviors experienced by people who have varying degrees of narcissism. Check "Yes" or "No" whether each attitude or behavior is something that applies to you. People who are highly narcissistic, however, often do not perceive their negative attitudes or behaviors. To verify the accuracy of your responses to the checklist, have a person who knows you well verify the accuracy of your responses.

| NARCISSISTIC ATTITUDE OR BEHAVIOR | YES | NO |
|---|---|---|
| 1. Patronizes and criticizes others. | ☐ | ☐ |
| 2. Strongly dislikes other people disagreeing with him or her. | ☐ | ☐ |
| 3. Becomes quite upset when cannot control a situation. | ☐ | ☐ |
| 4. Very little empathy for others. | ☐ | ☐ |
| 5. Very little concern for others. | ☐ | ☐ |
| 6. Thinks more about extraordinary achievements than carrying out daily responsibilities. | ☐ | ☐ |
| 7. Convinced of own superiority. | ☐ | ☐ |
| 8. Dependent on others for frequent does of admiration and affection. | ☐ | ☐ |
| 9. Abuses and insults others without feeling the least bit guilty. | ☐ | ☐ |
| 10. Has an unusually high level of self-confidence. | ☐ | ☐ |
| 11. Believes that he or she can accomplish anything with proper effort. | ☐ | ☐ |
| 12. Poor team player because of need to be the center of attention. | ☐ | ☐ |
| 13. Often bullies others. | ☐ | ☐ |
| 14. Quick to blame somebody else for own mistakes. | ☐ | ☐ |
| 15. Abuses and insults others without feeling the least bit guilty. | ☐ | ☐ |

*Scoring and Interpretation:* The more of these attitudes and behaviors you have felt or demonstrated, the more problems your level of narcissism is creating, or will create, problems for you in the workplace. If you checked twelve or more of these attitudes or behaviors, you might be annoying too many work associates. Attaining work goals often requires collaboration, so if you decrease your narcissistic attitudes and behaviors, you will most likely be more productive.

# The Vision Component of Charismatic Leadership

A major buzzword in leadership and management is **vision**, the ability to imagine different and better future conditions and ways to achieve them. A vision is a lofty, long-term goal. An effective leader is supposed to have a vision, whereas an ineffective leader either lacks a vision or has an unclear one. Being a visionary is far from an ordinary task, and recent research in neuroscience suggests that visionary leaders use their brain differently than others. (See the discussion in Chapter 2 about heredity versus environment in relation to being visionary.)

Many people use the terms *vision* and *mission* interchangeably, yet management theorists see them differently. A mission is a purpose, and reason for being, whereas a vision is a picture or image of the future we seek to create. A mission of a company that rents private warehouse space to consumers and small business might be, "To extend the living and working space of responsible people." The same company's vision might be, "To create a more comfortable, less cramped world for the decades ahead."

Creating a vision is one of the major tasks of top management, yet quite often vision statements fail to inspire constituents. According to Jim Collins, a vision statement is likely to be more inspirational when it combines three elements:

1. A reason for being beyond making money
2. Timeless, unchanging core values
3. Ambitious but achievable goals

Mechanisms should then be established that set the values into action.[20] At Google, for example, engineers have "20 percent time," in which they are free to pursue projects about which they are passionate. (In recent years, many fewer engineers have been allocated 20 percent of their time to dream up new ideas.) This policy supports the company vision of being a world-class innovator. A vision is also considered an important part of strategy implementation. Implementing the vision (or ensuring that the vision is executed) is part of the leader's role. This is true despite the opinion that the leader creates the vision and the manager implements it.

Vision statements typically relate to the entire organization, yet a leader or manager responsible for an organizational unit can have a vision about what he or she is attempting to accomplish. For example, the over-the-counter medicine unit of a larger pharmaceutical company might have the vision of "Creating a world in which people can work and play without arthritis pain."

Visions have become so popular that some companies have them reproduced on wallet-size plastic cards, key rings, and coffee mugs. It has been said that an effective vision fits on a T-shirt. Here are seven sample vision statements:

*Google:* To make nearly all information accessible to everyone all the time.
*AT&T:* Our vision is to design and create in this decade the new global network, processes, and service platforms that maximize automation, allowing for a reallocation of human resources to more complex and productive work.
*Kellogg Company:* To enrich and delight the world through foods and brands that matter.
*Caterpillar:* Our vision is a world in which all people's basic needs—such as shelter, clean water, sanitation, food and reliable power–are fulfilled in an environmentally sustainable way and be a company that improves the quality of the environment and the communities where we live and work.
*Marriott:* To be the #1 hospitality company in the world
*Microsoft Corporation:* To enable people throughout the word to realize their potential.
*GM:* GM's vision is to be the world leader in transportation products and related services. We will earn our customers' enthusiasm through continuous improvement driven by the integrity, teamwork, and innovation of GM people.

Although many vision statements appear as if they could be formulated in fifteen minutes, managers invest considerable time in their preparation and often use many sources of data. To create a vision, obtain as much information from as many of the following sources as necessary:[21]

- Your own intuition about developments in your field, the market you serve, demographic trends in your region, and the preferences of your constituents. Think through what are the top industry standards.
- The work of futurists (specialists in making predictions about the future) as it relates to your type of work.
- A group discussion of what it takes to delight the people your group serves. Analyze carefully what your customers and organization need the most.
- Annual reports, management books, business magazines, and Internet search engine results to uncover the type of vision statements formulated by others.
- Group members and friends; speak to them individually and collectively to learn of their hopes and dreams for the future.
- For a vision of the organizational unit, support the organization's vision. You might get some ideas for matching your unit's vision with that of the organization.

## LEADERSHIP SKILL-BUILDING EXERCISE 3-1

### Formulating a Vision

Along with your teammates, assume the role of the top-management group of an organization or organizational unit that is in need of revitalization. Your revitalization task is to create a vision for the organization. Express the vision in not more than twenty-five words, using the guidelines for developing a vision described in the text. Come to an agreement quickly on the organization or large organizational unit that needs a vision. Or choose one of the following:

- The manufacturer of turbines for wind power
- An online store that sells used designer clothes for women and men
- A waste disposal company
- A chain of home-improvement and hardware stores
- A manufacturer of watches retailing for a minimum of $25,000

After vision statements have been formulated, a wide range of employees must be involved in implementing the vision. Research conducted with 340 employees from a health maintenance organization (HMO) found that two-way communication between leaders and group members had an impact on employees actually integrating the vision into their work.

An example of a vision integration statement was, "The vision serves as a 'mental guideline' on how to do my job."[22] A vision for an HMO to be integrated into work behavior would include an idea such as, "Become a regional standout in helping out patients prevent becoming ill in the future."

Leadership Skill-Building Exercise 3-1 gives you an opportunity to practice vision formulation. Keep in mind that a critic of vision statements once said that it is often difficult to tell the difference between a vision and a hallucination. Google's vision statement about making nearly all the information in the world accessible to everyone appears to be close to a hallucination.[23] Also a vision that is extremely grandiose might invite cynicism from employees. For example, the amount of information available is nearly infinite, and not everybody on the planet has access to Google.

## The Communication Style of Charismatic Leaders

Charismatic and transformational leaders typically communicate their visions, goals, and directives in a colorful, imaginative, and expressive manner. In addition, they communicate openly with group members and create a comfortable communication climate. To set agendas that represent the interests of their constituents, charismatic leaders regularly solicit constituents' viewpoints on critical issues. They encourage two-way communication with team members while still promoting a sense of confidence.[24] Here we describe three related aspects of the communication style of charismatic leaders: leadership by inspiration, leadership by storytelling, and communication via social networking.

### Leadership by Inspiration

According to Jay A. Conger, the era of managing by dictate is being replaced by an era of leadership by inspiration. An important way to inspire others is to articulate a highly emotional message. An example would be the CEO explaining to her top-management team, "If we continue to provide such outstanding customer service we will double our market share within one year." Conger has observed two major rhetorical techniques of inspirational leaders: the use of metaphors and analogies, and the ability to gear language to different audiences.[25]

*Using Metaphors and Analogies*    A well-chosen analogy or metaphor appeals to the intellect, to the imagination, and to values. The charismatic Mary Kay Ash (now deceased), founder of the cosmetics company Mary Kay, Inc., made frequent use of metaphors during her career. To inspire her associates to higher performance, she often said: *"You see, a bee shouldn't be able to fly; its body is too heavy for its wings. But the bumblebee doesn't know that and it flies very well."* Mary Kay explained the message of the bumblebee metaphor in these terms: "Women come to us not knowing they can fly. Finally, with help and encouragement, they find their wings—and then they fly very well indeed."[26]

*Gearing Language to Different Audiences*    Metaphors and analogies are inspiring, but effective leaders must also choose the level of language that will suit their audience. This is important because constituents vary widely in verbal sophistication. One day, for example, a CEO might be attempting to inspire a group of Wall Street financial analysts, and the next day he or she might be attempting to inspire first-level employees to keep working hard despite limited salary increases.

An executive's ability to speak on a colloquial level helps create appeal. A person with the high status of an executive is expected to use an elevated language style. When the person unexpectedly uses the everyday language of an operative employee, it may create a special positive response. One of the reasons Mary Barra, the Chairman and CEO of GM is so popular is that her family background and work experience in production facilitate her being able to establish rapport with manufacturing workers. (See the Leader in Action section in the chapter.)

## Leadership by Storytelling

Another significant aspect of the communication style of charismatic and transformational leaders is that they make extensive use of memorable stories to get messages across. **Leadership by storytelling** is the technique of inspiring and instructing team members by telling fascinating stories. The technique is a major contributor to building a strong company culture. Storytelling also helps bring out the need for organizational change. A Coca-Cola company executive might tell a story about how the company's clean-water efforts prevented deaths of thousands of children in an African village. At the same time, the executive might emphasize that Coca-Cola must move more quickly to help thousands of other people throughout the world who lack safe drinking water.

Storytelling as a leadership tool has been elevated to such a level that some companies hire corporate storytelling consultants to help their executives develop the art. Storytelling is regarded as a useful tool for getting people to embrace change, because a well-crafted story captures people's attention.

A team of researchers in Germany conducted an experiment to investigate whether story telling by a leader had an impact on subordinates. The leaders in the experiment were actors whose stories were videotaped, and the stories told were related to life experiences of the leader. A modest amount of evidence indicated that leaders are perceived to be more authentic when they tell life stories that include negative turning point.[27] An example of a negative turning point for an entrepreneurial leader would be, "My savings were down to zero, I was unemployed, and my family and I faced eviction when I thought of the idea for founding this company. The first day we opened for business I had no customers and no employees. Today we have hundreds of customers across the country, and 75 employees."

To get started developing the skill of leadership by storytelling, do Leadership Skill-Building Exercise 3-2.

# LEADERSHIP SKILL-BUILDING EXERCISE 3-2

## Charismatic Leadership by Storytelling

**Instructions:** Gather in a small problem-solving group to develop an inspiring anecdote about something that actually happened, or might have happened, at a current or former employer. Search for a scenario that illustrates an important value of the firm. For example, the CEO of a large international bank while on vacation discovered a company ATM that was not working properly. He immediately went inside the bank branch to investigate the problem and what could be done about it.

Share your stories with other members of the class, and discuss whether this exercise could make a contribution to leadership development.

## Extensive Use of Social Networking

To help facilitate their interpersonal communication, charismatic leaders make extensive use of social networks—both in face-to-face interactions and through social media websites. The members of the network are basically contacts with whom the leader has some kind of relationship. The vast majority of managers and professionals also rely on social networking, yet charismatic leaders are particularly aware of its relevance for accomplishing their purposes.

*Face-to-Face Networks*    Charismatic leaders are aware of the importance of face-to-face interactions for establishing effective relationships with constituents. A charismatic leader is therefore likely to invest time in such activities as the following: having lunch with group members, visiting group members at their offices or cubicles, chatting with subordinates in the parking lot or cafeteria, dropping by break rooms to chat for a few moments, and attending as many company social functions as feasible.

In recognition of the importance of internal networks for building relationships and accomplishing goals, some large firms establish formal networking groups. An example is the GE Women's Network, which has 100,000 active members worldwide. The Women's Network was created in 1997 to help women working at GE advance their careers and contribute to company success. A key focus of the initiative includes sharing the experience, best practices, and knowledge of successful women role models. Members of the network cultivate their leadership skills, business practices, and career opportunities.

The focus on the network on leadership, advancement, and career-broadening opportunities has helped the company get to the point where women run businesses generating 20 percent of total company revenues. For example, one of the networks' top priorities is "Enhance women's professional growth by providing information on coaching career paths, flexibility, and role models." Women outside GE are invited to some of the key networking events, which help the GE women strengthen their external as well as internal networks. Also, the company outsiders are key customers who might develop ties with the GE women that lead to a better working relationship and more sales.[28]

*Social Networking Sites*    The charismatic leader goes beyond the ordinary use of public social networking sites (e.g., Facebook, Twitter, G+, and LinkedIn), and company-special social media sites. The ordinary use of these websites would be to post status reports, present due dates, ask questions, and perhaps post trivial personal information. A more charismatic use of social networking sites would be to post messages designed to inspire, motivate, and make group members feel good about themselves and the organization. A few examples of messages that might project charisma are as follows:

- I liked the cost-saving suggestion you made in this morning's meeting. I think it will result in cost-effective savings.
- Congratulations on having attained your certification as a professional office administrator. Our company can use more professionalism like that.

- I am so sorry that Taboo, your fifteen-year-old cat, passed away. Yet it's wonderful to know that you had all the love and friendship for so long. (A charismatic leader will often show empathy.)

## LEADERSHIP SKILL-BUILDING EXERCISE 3-3

### Identifying the Characteristics of a Charismatic Leader on YouTube

Now that you have studied many of the characteristics of a charismatic leader go to YouTube, or similar source, to observe a leader who is probably charismatic. Perhaps your target person is making a presentation, such as a CEO talking about the success of his or her organization. As you watch the video, perhaps two or three times, identify three characteristics that you think make the person charismatic. Would any of these characteristics be helpful for you to develop?

Despite the positive use of social networking sites to project charisma, the leader has to guard against posting sensitive information, such as an idea for a new product or service, or legal problems the company might be facing.

Leadership Skill-Building Exercise 3-3 is designed to give you additional insights into the characteristics of charismatic leaders.

## The Development of Charisma

A person can increase charisma by developing some of the traits, characteristics, and behaviors of charismatic people. Several of the charismatic characteristics described earlier in the chapter are capable of development. For example, most people can enhance their communication skills, become more emotionally expressive, take more risks, and become more self-promoting. In this section, we examine several behaviors of charismatic people that can be developed through practice and self-discipline.

### Techniques for Developing Charisma

*Create Visions for Others*    Being able to create visions for others will be a major factor in your being perceived as charismatic. A vision uplifts and attracts others. To form a vision, use the guidelines presented previously in the chapter. The visionary person looks beyond the immediate future to create an image of what the organization, or unit within, is capable of becoming. A vision is designed to close the discrepancy between current and ideal conditions. The vision thus sees beyond current realities.

Another characteristic of an effective vision formulated by the leader is that it connects with the goals and dreams of constituents.[29] For example, the leader of a group that is manufacturing fuel cells for electric cars might listen to team members talk about their desires to help reduce pollution in the atmosphere and then base the vision statement on a "desire to save the planet" or "reduce global warming."

*Be Enthusiastic, Optimistic, and Energetic*    A major behavior pattern of charismatic people is their combination of enthusiasm, optimism, and high energy. Without a great amount of all three characteristics, a person is unlikely to be perceived as charismatic by many people. A remarkable quality of charismatic people is that they maintain high enthusiasm, optimism, and energy throughout their entire workday and beyond. Elevating your energy level takes considerable work, but here are a few feasible suggestions:

1. Get ample rest at night, and sneak in a fifteen-minute nap during the day when possible. If you have a dinner meeting where you want to be impressive, take a shower and nap before the meeting.

2. Exercise every day for at least ten minutes, including walking. No excuses are allowed, such as being too busy or too tired or the weather being a handicap.
3. Switch to a healthy, energy-enhancing diet.
4. Keep chopping away at your To Do list, so you do not have unfinished tasks on your mind—they will drain your energy.

An action orientation helps you be enthusiastic, optimistic, and energetic. "Let's do it" is the battle cry of the charismatic person. An action orientation also means that the charismatic person prefers not to agonize over dozens of facts and nuances before making a decision.

*Be Sensibly Persistent*   Closely related to the high energy level of charismatics is their almost-never-accept-no attitude. I emphasize the word almost because outstanding leaders and individual contributors also know when to cut their losses. If an idea or a product will not work, the sensible charismatic absorbs the loss and moves in another, more profitable direction.

*Remember People's Names*   Charismatic leaders, as well as other successful people, can usually remember the names of people they have seen only a few times. (Sorry, no charisma credits for remembering the names of everyday work associates.) This ability is partly due to the strong personal interest charismatic leaders take in other people.

The surest way to remember names, therefore, is to really care about people. Failing that, the best way to remember a name is to listen carefully to the name, repeat it immediately, and study the person's face. You can also use the many systems and gimmicks available for remembering names, such as associating a person's name with a visual image. For example, if you meet a woman named Betsy Applewhite, you can visualize her with a white apple (or a white tablet computer) on her head. The best system of name retention remains to listen carefully to the name, repeat it immediately, and study the person's face.

*Develop Synchrony with Others*   A subtle, yet defining, aspect of a truly charismatic person is one who connects well with others. Psychology professor Frank Bernieri studies physical signals that people send to each other, and concludes that being in synch physically with other people is part of charisma. If someone is in synchrony with you, you tend to think he or she is charismatic. A practical method of being in synch with another person is to adjust your posture to conform to his or her posture. The other person stands up straight, and so do you; when he or she slouches, you do also. Charismatic people make these postural adjustments almost subconsciously, or at least without giving the process much thought. Highly skilled charismatic people through the timing of their breaths, gestures, and cadence can entrap listeners into synchrony to the point that they "breathe and sway in tune with the speaker."[30] (Developing synchrony is almost the same idea as the nonverbal communication technique of mirroring.)

*Develop a Personal Brand, Including Making an Impressive Appearance*   A popular career advancement technique is to build a personal brand. Understanding your basket of strengths forms the basis for developing your **personal brand**. Your identity as shown on the Internet, including social networking sites such as Facebook, is also part of your personal brand. Your personal brand makes you unique, thereby distinguishing you from the competition.[31] Perhaps your brand will not reach the recognition of Nike or Rolex, but it will help develop your reputation. Your personal brand also helps you attract people to accept your leadership.

Another component of your personal brand is your appearance. By creating a polished appearance, a person can make slight gains in projecting a charismatic image. In most cases, the effect of appearance depends on the context. If exquisite clothing and good looks alone made a person a charismatic leader, those impressive-looking store associates in upscale department stores and boutiques would all be charismatic leaders. Therefore, in attempting to enhance your charisma through appearance, it is necessary to analyze your work environment to assess what type of appearance is impressive. A highly polished appearance would create a negative image at most high technology firms.

**Be Candid**    Charismatic people, especially effective leaders, are remarkably candid with people. Although not insensitive, the charismatic person is typically explicit in giving his or her assessment of a situation, whether the assessment is positive or negative. Charismatic people speak directly rather than indirectly, so that people know where they stand. Instead of asking a worker, "Are you terribly busy this afternoon?" the charismatic leader will ask, "I need your help this afternoon. Are you available?"

**Display an In-Your-Face Attitude**    The preferred route to being perceived as charismatic is to be a positive, warm, and humanistic person. Yet some people, including business and sports figures, earn their reputation for charisma by being tough and nasty. An in-your-face attitude may bring you some devoted supporters, although it will also bring you many detractors. The tough attitude is attractive to people who themselves would like to be mean and aggressive.

Experimental evidence exists that charismatic leadership can be taught. John Antonakis, Marika Fenley, and Sui Liechti of the University of Lausanne tested whether individuals could be taught to behave more charismatically, and whether changes in charisma affected the impact of leaders. One study involved middle managers, and a second study involved videotapes of MBA students giving a speech. Participants in both studies were trained in charismatic techniques quite similar to those previously mentioned here. Charisma was measured by ratings of coworkers or other students on behaviors and attitudes similar to the checklist presented earlier in the chapter. Training had a significant impact on charisma ratings given by coworkers and other students. In addition, the charisma of individuals had a significant impact on ratings of being a prototypical (conforming to a stereotype) leader, and the probability of the personal emerging as a leader.[32]

## Transformational Leadership

Transformational leadership focuses on what the leader accomplishes, yet it still pays attention to the leader's personal characteristics and his or her relationship with group members. As mentioned previously, the transformational leader helps bring about major, positive changes by moving group members beyond their self-interests and toward the good of the group, organization, or society. Because of its importance, transformational leadership has become the most widely researched leadership theory. The essence of transformational leadership is developing and transforming people.[33] As a result, the organization is transformed. In contrast, the *transactional* leader focuses on more routine transactions, rewarding group members for meeting standards (contingent reinforcement). Extensive research by the late Bernard M. Bass indicates that the transformational-versus-transactional distinction has been observed in a wide variety of organizations and cultures.[34]

So, who is a transformational leader? One example from the retail business is Hubert Joly, a turnaround specialist, who came in from outside the company to be appointed as CEO of Best Buy. Over a period of fifteen years, Joly had developed a track record of successfully turning around companies in the media technology and service sectors.

Best Buy had been losing market share to competitors, the stock price was falling rapidly, and the former CEO was dismissed because he was having an affair with an employee. Joly helped limit Best Buy from functioning as a showroom in which many consumers would visit the stores mostly to try out merchandise, and then purchase the product online. Under Joly, Best Buy soon matched online prices but also offered the experience of touching merchandise and asking questions. Joly cut costs and reduced the workforce, particularly at company headquarters. He also emphasized selling large appliances and promoting the Geek Squad.

Joly earned a reputation as a respected turnaround artist, yet investors say he does not fit the negative stereotype of many other such executives. "He's more of a leader than just one of those guys that comes in and cuts everything and leaves," said one analyst. In Joly's approach to a turnaround, there are four "levers" to improve profits. First, leaders must do all they possibly can do to increase revenue. Second, to trim costs, begin by cutting nonsalary expenses, such as travel. Third, eliminate luxury perks and purchase an efficient health insurance plan for the company. Fourth, only reduce headcount if the first three steps do not generate enough savings. Joly also closed stores and sold off foreign divisions to help Best Buy survive.

Under the transformational leadership of Joly, both profits and employee morale showed some improvement, but enhancing sales and profits consistently proved to be a problem. Several years after the transformation began, Joly and his executive team were still looking for path to sustainable growth.[35]

## How Transformations Take Place

Leaders often encounter the need to transform organizations from low performance to acceptable performance or from acceptable performance to high performance. At other times, a leader is expected to move a firm from a crisis mode to high ground. To accomplish these lofty purposes, the transformational leader attempts to overhaul the organizational culture or subculture. His or her task can be as immense as the process of organizational change. To focus our discussion specifically on the leader's role, we look at ten ways in which transformations take place.[36] (See also Figure 3-1.)

1. **Raising people's awareness.** The transformational leader makes group members aware of the importance and values of certain rewards and how to achieve them. He or she might point to the pride workers would experience should the firm become number one in its field. At the same time, the leader should point to the financial rewards accompanying such success.

2. **Helping people look beyond self-interest.** The transformational leader helps group members look to the big picture for the sake of the team and the organization. The executive vice president of a bank told her staff members, "I know most of you dislike doing your own support work. Yet if we hire enough staff to make life more convenient for you, we'll be losing money. Then the government might force us to be taken over by a larger bank. Who knows how many management jobs would then have to be cut."

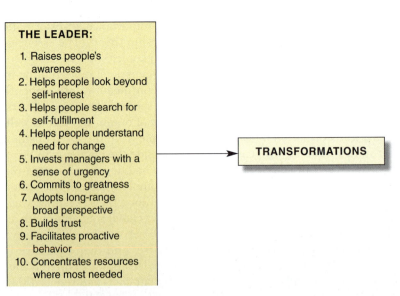

**THE LEADER:**

1. Raises people's awareness
2. Helps people look beyond self-interest
3. Helps people search for self-fulfillment
4. Helps people understand need for change
5. Invests managers with a sense of urgency
6. Commits to greatness
7. Adopts long-range broad perspective
8. Builds trust
9. Facilitates proactive behavior
10. Concentrates resources where most needed

**TRANSFORMATIONS**

**FIGURE 3-1** How Transformations Take Place.

3. *Helping people search for self-fulfillment.* The transformational leader helps people go beyond a focus on minor satisfactions to a quest for self-fulfillment. The leader might explain, "I know that making sure you take every vacation day owed you is important. Yet if we get this proposal out on time, we might land a contract that will make us the envy of the industry." (Being the envy of the industry satisfies the need for self-fulfillment.)

   Related to helping people search for self-fulfillment is for transformational leaders to help workers understand how their values fit the values of the organization (person–organization value congruence). A study conducted with 140 managers enrolled in an MBA program suggested that transformational leadership influenced work group effectiveness. The impact on effectiveness tended to be positive because of the leader's ability to help workers understand that there was a good fit between their values and those of the organization. Visualize a leader of a group of workers engaged in the fabrication of cement pipes, and that many of the group members value helping people.[37] The transformational leader would be able to enhance group effectiveness by explaining how the pipes are instrumental in delivering potable water to a wide variety of people.

4. *Helping people understand the need for change.* The transformational leader must help group members understand the need for change both emotionally and intellectually. The problem is that change involves dislocation and discomfort. An effective transformational leader recognizes this emotional component to resisting change and deals with it openly. Dealing with the emotional conflicts of large numbers of staffers is obviously an immense task. One approach taken by successful leaders is to conduct discussion groups in which managers and workers are free to discuss their feelings about the changes.

5. *Investing managers with a sense of urgency.* To create the transformation, the leader assembles a critical mass of managers and imbues in them the urgency of change. The managers must also share the top leader's vision of what is both necessary and achievable. To sell this vision of an improved organization, the transformational leader must capitalize on available opportunities.

6. *Committing to greatness.* Peter Koestenbaum argues that business can be an opportunity for individual and organizational greatness. By adopting this greatness attitude, leaders can ennoble human nature and strengthen societies. Greatness encompasses striving for business effectiveness such as profits and high stock value, as well as impeccable ethics. An emphasis on ethical leadership instills a desire for customer service and quality and fosters feelings of proprietorship and involvement.[38] (A commitment to greatness is, of course, important for all leaders, not just those who are transformational.)

7. *Adopting a long-range perspective and at the same time observing organizational issues from a broad rather than a narrow perspective.* Such thinking on the part of the transformational leader encourages many group members to do likewise. Unless many people think with a future orientation, and broadly, an organization cannot be transformed.

8. *Building trust.* Another useful process for transforming a firm is to build trust between leaders and group members, particularly because distrust and suspicion are rampant during a company revival. Dave Cote, CEO of one of the world's largest conglomerates, Honeywell International, led one of the best corporate comebacks in recent history. His greatest accomplishment in the turnaround was unifying Honeywell's formerly fractured, disenchanted culture. At the same time, he developed a successful business strategy, including a cooperative approach in dealing with asbestos lawsuits. Cote also shifted the company to a less aggressive type of accounting, and a shift to manufacturing efficiencies.[39] Such moves in a highly ethical direction helped Cote gain the trust of the workforce including managers.

9. *Facilitating proactive behavior.* Another way in which transformational leaders bring about transformations is to facilitate proactive behavior on the part

of subordinates. By being proactive, subordinates take the initiative to bring about positive change. Imagine a Best Buy store manager who responds positively to the change efforts of the CEO Hubert Joly. The store manager is likely to encourage store associates to listen more attentively to customer inquiries and provide useful suggestions. Proactive behavior is facilitated by giving group members more autonomy, or the opportunity to make decisions independently, as revealed in a study of sixty-nine companies in the Netherlands.[40]

10. *Concentrating resources on areas that need the most change.* The turnaround artist or transformational leader cannot take care of all problems at once in a troubled organization. A practical strategy is to get around limitations on funds, staff, or equipment by concentrating resources on problem areas that are most in need of change and have the biggest potential payoff. Assume that the tax bureau of a state government is not performing well because tax collections are too low. The agency might invest money in hiring specialists who would search for tax evaders, including those who under-report income.

## Attributes of Transformational Leaders

Transformational leaders possess the personal characteristics of other effective leaders, especially charismatic leaders. In addition, a compilation of studies suggests that eight qualities are particularly helpful in enabling leaders to bring about transformations.[41] Our discussion of those qualities follows.

Above all, transformational leaders are *charismatic*. Two key personality factors enhancing their charisma are agreeableness and extraversion, which combine to enhance their interpersonal relationships. Of these, extraversion had the biggest impact.[42] Included in the charisma of transformation leaders are their optimism and their openness to the viewpoints of others. An example of a charismatic, transformational leader is Akio Toyoda, the president of Toyota Motor Corporation. Among his charismatic behaviors are race car driving, being a TV pitchman for his company, and having a rock star persona. Among the transformations he is credited with are helping Toyota overcome the effects of an embarrassing 2009 recall, and the effects of the 2011 earthquakes that severely damaged the company's production facilities. A few years later, Toyoda was planning to make the Mirai a mass-market hydrogen (using hydrogen fuel cells) car. He said, "The automobile industry can contribute to the sustainable growth of earth itself."[43]

Unless they are the brutal slash-and-burn type of turnaround manager, transformational leaders have the respect, confidence, and loyalty of group members. One reason is that managers who use the transformational leadership style tend to score higher on *emotional intelligence*. A specific attribute here is that transformational leaders read emotions well.[44]

Similar to effective leaders in general, transformational leaders often have positive core self-evaluations. (As described in Chapter 2, this composite personality factor is composed of self-esteem, locus of control, generalized self-efficacy, and emotional stability.) A study conducted with three high-tech companies in China found that leaders with positive core evaluations were more likely to be perceived as transformational by subordinates.[45]

Charismatic, transformational leaders create a *vision*. By communicating a vision, they convey a set of values that guide and motivate employees. The vision describes an optimistic picture of what the organization will become after the transformation is complete, such as a division being threatened with being shut down becoming the leading division in a conglomerate.

Although transformational leaders are often greatly concerned with organizational survival, they also take the time to *encourage the personal development of their staff*. As group members develop, their performance is likely to increase. Transformational leaders also give *supportive leadership*, such as by giving positive feedback to group members and recognizing individual achievements. Supportive leadership also contributes to the development of group members. Transformational leaders frequently use *empowerment* to help develop group members.

*Innovative thinking*, another important characteristic, helps transformational leaders achieve their goals; for example, they might develop innovative ways to raise cash and cut costs quickly. Transformational leaders encourage their staff to think innovatively as well and give them challenging assignments.

Not every leader classified as transformational will have the eight characteristics just described. For example, some transformational leaders are brusque with people rather than agreeable. Furthermore, it is not always easy to determine whether a given leader can be accurately described as transformational. Sometimes situational forces contribute more heavily to the turnaround than do the leader's personal qualities. The director of an indoor tennis club was complimented about how he transformed the club from one that was close to bankruptcy and short on membership. He replied, "It wasn't me. Two of our competitors closed down and we picked up a lot of their membership."

Leadership theorist Julian Barling notes that it is not possible or necessary for leaders to engage in all of the characteristics and behaviors mentioned earlier to be classified as transformational. Leaders and subordinates do not even see each other every day, and may be geographically dispersed.[46] Yet an effective transformational leader will choose the right time to engage in the right behavior, such as thinking innovatively when the group needs a new direction.

## The Impact of Transformational and Charismatic Leadership on Performance and Behavior

Although the present discussion deals primarily with transformational leadership, we also include the impact of charismatic leadership because the two overlap. The general picture of the impact of transformational leadership is that, at its best, it can arouse followers to a higher level of thinking. Transformational leaders appeal to the ideals and values of their constituents, thereby enhancing commitment to a carefully crafted vision. Followers are inspired to develop new ways of thinking about problems. Group members become more responsible because they are inspired, and they engage in more constructive behavior such as organizational citizenship behavior—or helping out even without the promise of a reward.[47] Workers who report to transformational leaders are even more likely to have a positive mood throughout the workday.[48]

Here we look at two empirical studies about the effects of charismatic and transformational leadership in work settings. The studies summarized here are also useful in understanding how transformational leadership affects behavior.

*Overall Validity of Transformational Leadership*    Timothy A. Judge and Ronald F. Piccolo reviewed eighty-seven studies to examine the impact of transformational leadership on various measures of performance. The researchers also evaluated the impact of transactional leadership and laissez-faire leadership on performance. Laissez-faire leadership is a style that gives group members the freedom to do basically what they want with almost no direction. The three approaches to leadership were measured by questionnaires based on subordinates' perceptions.

Transformational leadership showed the highest overall relationships on six criteria: (a) follower job satisfaction, (b) follower leader satisfaction, (c) follower motivation, (d) leader job performance, (e) group or organization performance, and (f) rated leader effectiveness. Interestingly, transactional leadership was also shown to produce good results, and laissez-faire leadership was associated with negative results. Unlike previous studies, transactional leadership showed a strong positive relationship to transformational leadership. (Ordinarily, transformational leadership and transactional leadership are negatively related because transformational leaders are said not to engage in routine transactions with group members.) Transformational leadership was negatively related to laissez-faire leadership.[49] The explanation is most likely that transformational leaders are actively involved with group members.

*Organizational Level Performance*    A group of researchers studied the impact of leadership effectiveness on organizational performance that reinforces several of the ideas already presented in this book. Data were collected from 134 mid-level managers from a large Brazilian energy company. The personality traits of the participants and transformational leadership were measured by questionnaires completed by subordinates, and performance was measured by both ratings from superiors and company records. The findings indicated that leadership effectiveness as measured by organizational outcomes (or business results) was a direct function of the leader's transformational behavior. Furthermore, intelligence and conscientiousness are the individual differences that contribute the most to being a transformational leader. A study of this nature emphasizes how transformational leadership can benefit organizations.[50]

The accompanying Leader in Action box illustrates a leader who helps bringing about major changes in one of the world's best known business corporations.

 **LEADER IN ACTION**

### Mary Barra, CEO of GM

Mary Barra is Chairman and chief executive officer of General Motors Company, the dual title she has held since January 2016. In early 2014, when she was the product global chief of General Motors Co., Barra, was named the new company CEO. When Barra, age fifty-one at the time, was appointed to this position, she was the first woman to become CEO of a major vehicle manufacturer. Departing CEO Dan Akerson stated that he picked Barra to be his successor based on her ability to "make order out of chaos."

In March 2014, Barra faced the chaos of the recall of 2.53 million cars for faulty switches, and 1.3 million vehicles for power steering problems. In 2014, the company spent $2.9 billion on recalls related to the switches. GM was held legally responsible for 124 deaths due to faulty ignition switches. The company has already paid $1.5 billion in penalties and settlements. After an internal probe conducted by a former U.S. attorney, Barra fired fifteen employees, and instituted a policy of "If you see something, say something." She also restructured engineering operations to facilitate quicker responses to potential safety violations.

Under Barra's leadership, the company has focused on strengthening its core business of manufacturing cars, trucks, and crossover. At the same time, GM has strived to lead the transformation of personality mobility through advanced technologies such as connectivity, autonomous driving, and vehicle sharing. A specific example is that GM is close to releasing self-driving cars for the Lyft ride-hailing service, and Barra intends for the company to be the first in introducing fully autonomous technology. Also of note, GM introduced the 2017 Chevy Bolt EV, winning over rival Tesla in the race to engineer the first affordable electric car with a range of 200 miles. In referring to changes in the automobile industry, Barra said, "In this era of rapid transformation, you have to have a culture that's agile. We still have a lot of work to do."

As the head of product development as well as global purchasing and supply chain, Mary Barra was already the highest-ranking woman in the global automobile and truck industry. She was promoted to head of product development in 2011. Previous to her appointment as head of product development, Barra spent four years as vice president, global human resources. Joining GM after graduation as an electrical engineer, she was soon identified as a person with executive potential. She moved up the corporate ladder steadily in jobs in manufacturing, administration, and internal communications before the HR position. As the CEO, Barra was expected to change the culture of a company for which she had worked her entire career.

The GM board regards Barra as one of his key change agents in his efforts to remake the often slow-moving company culture. The CEO before Barra identified her as "a strong leader and change agent who knows the business inside and out."

In 2017, Barra spearheaded a major initiative to improve GM profits. Her plan was to withdraw from markets where GM was not highly profitable, including Russia, India, and Europe, in favor of more profitable locales, particularly the United States. Another approach to boosting profits is to cut back on the low-margin business of selling cars to rental fleets.

In one of her initiatives to change the culture, Barra has helped GM loosen the controls over engineers, allowing them more creative freedom with vehicles. She said her approach is "empowering them to make the decisions, and I think you see it with some of the vehicles we just put out, whether it's the Chevrolet Impala or the Cadillac CTS or the Corvette." One of the organizational complexities Barra wants to change is that there a twelve executive chief engineers responsible for every

*(Continued)*

## LEADER IN ACTION *(Continued)*

automobile, truck, or crossover that the company makes around the world. Another culture-changing initiative is for senior executives to participate in a year-long course in transformational leadership.

Barra believes that her thrust for creative freedom and simplicity will strengthen GM in the long term. She is adamant about leading by persuasion rather than direct commands. Barra said that when employees say "I'm doing it because Mary told me to do it" is the day she loses. Barra recognizes that culture change only takes place when people change their behavior, such as taking more responsibility for problems.

During her first month as CEO Barra revealed her goals to expand GM's profit margins in North America, while increasing its global market share. Part of her plan for attaining these goals was to strive for innovation on both business processes and product development. Several years later, she emphasized that the ultimate proof point of whether the changes she has introduced are working "will be when we deliver exceptional financial results."

Barra received a bachelor of science in electrical engineering (BSEE) from the General Motors Institute (now the Kettering University). Later she graduated with an MBA from Stanford University. She was raised in a GM family, with her father having been a die-maker in a Pontiac plant for thirty-nine years.

### QUESTIONS

1. Why might Barra be classified as a transformational leader?

2. What relevance might Barra's experience in HR have for the product development of vehicles?

3. Based on whatever information you might have available, how well is Mary Barra doing as GM's top executive?

*Source:* Original story created from facts and observations in the following sources: Christopher Ross, "A Day in the Life of GM CEO Mary Barra," *The Wall Street Journal* (www.wsj.com), April 25, 2016, pp. 1–4; David Kiley, "Has GM Doomed CEO Mary Barra By Making Her Chairman?" *Forbes* (www.forbes.com), January 7, 2016, pp. 1–6; Jeff Bennett, "Forget the Concept Cars, Here Comes Mary Barra," *The Wall Street Journal*, January 14, 2014, p. B1; TTAC Staff, "GM Puts Mary Barra In Charge of Purchasing Too, Says 'No Excuses…No More Crappy Cars,'" *The Truth About Cars* (www.thetruthaboutcars.com), October 24, 2013, pp. 1–28; Geoff Colvin, "GM's Mary Barra Continues to Surprise, and Impress," *Fortune* (www.fortune.com), March 17, 2016, pp. 1–6; "Mary T. Barra," *General Motors* (https://www.gm.com/company/leadership/corporate-officers/mary-barra.html), 2016; "Fortune's Most Powerful Women List: No. 1, Mary Barra," *Fortune*, September 15, 2015, p. 90; David Welch, "All about the Benjamins," *Bloomberg Businessweek*, May 2–May 28, 2017, p. 22.

## Concerns About Charismatic and Transformational Leadership

Up to this point, an optimistic picture has been painted of both the concept of charisma and charismatic leaders, as well as transformational leaders. For the sake of fairness and scientific integrity, contrary points of view must also be presented. The topic of charismatic leadership has been challenged from two major standpoints: the validity of the concept and the misdeeds of charismatic leaders.

### Challenges to the Validity of Charismatic Leadership

Some leadership researchers doubt that charisma can be accurately defined or measured. Conducting research about charisma is akin to conducting research about high quality: You know it when you see it, but it is difficult to define in operational terms. Furthermore, even when one leader is deemed to be charismatic, that leader has many detractors. According to the concept of **leadership polarity**, leaders are often either revered or vastly unpopular. Many leaders in public office experience the same problem. Charisma needs to be mixed with humility for full effectiveness.

Another problem with the concept of charisma is that it may not be necessary for leadership effectiveness. Warren Bennis and Burt Nanus hypothesized that instead of charisma resulting in effective leadership, the reverse may be true: People who are outstanding leaders are granted charisma (perceived as charismatic) by their constituents as a result of their success.[51] A representative example is that when retailing executive Ron Johnson had major successes at Target and Apple, he was regarded as highly charismatic. Yet, when his business strategy failed as CEO of J.C. Penney, he was ridiculed being insensitive to his customer base—a perception of weak charisma. The take-away lesson here is that if you are successful in attaining goals, it will enhance your charisma.

## The Dark Side of Charismatic Leadership

Some people believe that charismatic leadership can be exercised for evil purposes. This argument was introduced previously in relation to personalized charismatic leaders. Many years ago, Robert Tucker warned about the dark side of charisma, particularly with respect to political leaders:

> The magical message which mesmerizes the unthinking (and which can often be supplied by skilled phrase makers) promises that things will become not just better but perfect. Charismatic leaders are experts at promising Utopia. Since perfection is the end, often the most heinous actions can be tolerated as seemingly necessary means to that end.[52]

When charismatic leaders are highly narcissistic, organizational performance may suffer. One reason is that the highly narcissistic leader will be disliked and resented. A meta-analysis of many studies revealed that a moderate amount of narcissism is associated with leadership effectiveness, but both low and high levels of the trait lowered leadership effectiveness.[53] (Leaders with too little narcissism may be perceived as bland and lacking much self-confidence.)

A recent analysis by Dan Ciampa points to other negative consequences of a highly charismatic organizational leader. Two of these concerns follow. One is that because the charismatic leader's views and actions are the only ones that matter, followers become less proactive. A group member might thing, "Why should I suggest a new course of action when only his (or her) ideas count?" Another concern is that people still comply with what the charismatic leader wants, but the passion vanishes because the people do not feel they are contributing. Eventually, the subordinates stop listening and become cynical.[54]

Some charismatic leaders are unethical and lead their organizations and outsiders toward illegal and immoral ends. People are willing to follow the charismatic leader down a quasi-legal path because of his or her personal magnetism. Perhaps the most widely publicized financial fraud in history was carried out by Bernard M. Madoff. Investors lost about $50 billion before approximately 10 percent of their money was recovered a few years later. Madoff, whose career included a term as the president of NASDAQ, a popular stock exchange, was well liked and considered by many to be warm and charismatic. His ability to defraud people depended somewhat on his ability to be well liked and entrusted.

A broad perspective on the downside of both charismatic and transformational leadership is that emphasizing these behaviors directs attention away from other important aspects of leader-follower relationships. David Collinson and Dennis Tourish note, for example, that the idea of transformational leadership suggests that power should be vested in the hands of a few heroic leaders, and neglects the potential contribution of follower dissent.[55]

Boards of directors currently seek CEOs who do not overemphasize charisma and celebrity status at the expense of concentrating on running the business. In this way, the dark side of charisma can be minimized. Recognize that a true charismatic and transformational leader is highly concerned about human welfare and attaining outstanding organizational performance.

## READER'S ROADMAP

In Chapter 2, we focused on the traits, motives, and characteristics of the leader—the inner qualities. Here we dug further into leadership qualities by studying charismatic and transformational leadership. In the next chapter, we focus more sharply on the actions of leaders in terms of their behaviors, attitudes, and styles.

# SUMMARY

Charisma is a special quality of leaders whose purposes, powers, and extraordinary determination differentiate them from others. It is also a positive and compelling quality of a person that makes many others want to be led by that person. An important element of charismatic leadership involves the attributions made by group members about the characteristics of leaders and the results they achieve. Social network members often influence a person's attributions of charisma. The relationship between group members and the leader is important because of these attributions. Charismatic leaders frequently manage their impressions to cultivate relationships with group members.

Much of the impact of charisma is based on the positive effect the charismatic leader triggers among group members. A study with firefighters showed that having a charismatic leader contributed to their happiness. In a top-level executive position, being perceived as not having enough charisma can lead to your downfall.

Three major charismatic leader subtypes are socialized (helping others), personalized (self-interested), and celebrity. Charismatic leaders have characteristics that set them apart from noncharismatic leaders: They have a vision, masterful communication skills, the ability to inspire trust, and the ability to make group members feel capable. They are tactful; they have energy and an action orientation; they are emotionally expressive and warm; they romanticize risk; they use unconventional strategies; they have self-promoting personalities; and they challenge, prod, and poke. Also, they tend to think fast; and they emphasize being dramatic and unique.

Many charismatic leaders are narcissistic, or self-adoring in excess, and are self-promoting. At their best, narcissistic leaders are effective in their roles, particularly when narcissism is combined with humility.

The idea of vision is closely linked to charisma because charismatic leaders inspire others with an uplifting and attractive vision. Visionaries may have different levels of brain activities than nonvisionaries in certain areas of the brain. A vision is more future oriented than a mission. In formulating a vision, it is helpful to gather information from a variety of sources, including one's own intuition, futurists, and group members.

Charismatic and transformational leaders communicate their visions, goals, and directives in a colorful, imaginative, and expressive manner. Communication effectiveness allows for management by inspiration. One technique for inspiring others is to use metaphors, analogies, and organizational stories. Another is gearing language to different audiences. Charismatic and transformational leaders also extensively use memorable stories or anecdotes to get messages across. Social networking sites can be used to communicate the leader's charisma.

A person can increase his or her charisma by developing some of the traits, characteristics, and behaviors of charismatic people. The suggestions presented here include creating visions for others; being enthusiastic, optimistic, and energetic; being sensibly persistent; remembering people's names; developing a personal brand and making an impressive appearance; being candid; and displaying an in-your-face attitude.

To bring about change, the transformational leader attempts to overhaul the organizational culture or subculture. Specific change techniques include raising people's awareness of the importance of certain rewards and getting people to look beyond their self-interests for the sake of the team and the organization. Transformational leaders help people search for self-fulfillment and understand the need for change, and they invest managers with a sense of urgency. The transformational leader also commits to greatness, adopts a long-range perspective, builds trust, facilitates proactive behavior by subordinates, and concentrates resources where change is needed the most.

Transformational leaders have characteristics similar to those of other effective leaders. In addition, they are charismatic, extraverted, create a vision, encourage personal development of the staff, and give supportive leadership. Emphasis is also placed on empowerment, innovative thinking, and leading by example.

Transformational leadership can arouse followers to a higher level of thinking and to engage in more constructive behavior. Transformational leadership is positively related to the criteria of follower job satisfaction, leader satisfaction, follower motivation, leader job performance, group or organization performance, and rated leader effectiveness. Transactional leadership attains the same results to a lesser degree, whereas laissez-faire leadership is negatively related to such criteria. A study showed that leadership effectiveness as measured by business results was a direct function of the leader's transformational behavior.

One concern about charismatic and transformational leadership is that the concept is murky. Many noncharismatic leaders are effective. Another concern is that some charismatic leaders are unethical and devious, suggesting that being charismatic does not necessarily help the organization. When charismatic leaders are highly narcissistic, organizational performance may suffer. A true charismatic and transformational leader is highly concerned about human welfare and attaining organizational goals. Too much attention paid to charismatic and transformational leadership can divert attention away for other important aspects of the leader–follower relationship.

## KEY TERMS

charisma  58
socialized charismatic  60
personalized charismatic  60

transformational leader  61
narcissism  62
vision  64

leadership by storytelling  67
personal brand  70
leadership polarity  77

## GUIDELINES FOR ACTIONS AND SKILL DEVELOPMENT

Following are suggestions to help a person act in a charismatic manner. All of them relate to well-accepted interpersonal skill techniques.

1. **Be sure to treat everyone you meet as the most important person you will meet that day.** For example, when at a company meeting, shake the hand of every person you meet.

2. **Multiply the effectiveness of your handshake or fist bump.** Shake firmly without creating pain or use a fist bump of moderate impact and make enough eye contact to notice the color of the other person's eyes. When you take that much trouble, you project care and concern. Think a positive thought about the person whose hand you shake or whose fist you bump.

3. **Stand up straight, and use other nonverbal signals of self-confidence.** Practice good posture. Minimize fidgeting, scratching, floor tapping, and speaking in a monotone. Walk at a rapid pace without appearing to be anxious. Dress fashionably without going to the extreme that people notice your clothes than they notice you. A fist can project confidence, power, and certainty. Waving a hand, pointing, or rapping a table can help get attention focused on you.

4. **Give sincere compliments.** Most people thrive on flattery, particularly when it is plausible. Attempt to compliment only those behaviors, thoughts, and attitudes you genuinely believe merit praise. At times you may have to dig to find something praiseworthy, but it will be a good investment of your time.

5. **Thank people frequently, especially your own group members.** Thanking others is still so infrequently practiced that it gives you a charismatic edge.

6. **Smile frequently, even if you are not in a happy mood.** A warm smile seems to indicate a confident, caring person, which contributes to a perception of charisma. A smile generally says, "I like you. I trust you. I'm glad we're together."

7. **Maintain a fascination for your world.** Express enthusiasm for and interest in the thoughts, actions, plans, dreams, and material objects of other people. Your enthusiasm directed toward others will engender enthusiasm in you.

8. **Be more animated than others.** People who are perceived to be more charismatic are simply more animated than others. They smile more frequently, speak faster, articulate better, and move their heads and bodies more often.[56]

9. **Think big.** If you want to become a charismatic and transformational leader, you must develop the capacity to spin beautiful, sweeping visions, and, in general, think big. It is so easy to become preoccupied with small problems that we face daily, such as high prices at the gas pump or a smartphone battery running low on power. Such problems require attention but can block visionary and charismatic thinking if they become preoccupying.

10. **Inspire trust and confidence.** Make your deeds consistent with your promises. Get people to believe in your competence by making your accomplishments known in a polite, tactful way.

The information just presented is useful for the aspiring charismatic leader. Using charisma and a positive mood to help workers become happy is valuable. Productivity might increase as stress might be reduced, resulting in less time lost to illness. Also, not being charismatic enough can sometimes make it difficult to hold on to a high-level leadership position.

### Discussion Questions and Activities

1. Identify a business, government, education, or sports leader whom you perceive to be charismatic. Explain the basis for your judgment.

2. Identify a business, government, education, or sports leader whom you perceive to have very little charisma. What other factors appear to compensate for his or her limited charisma?

3. How might being charismatic contribute to the effectiveness of the manager of entry-level workers, such as those employed as cashiers or fast-food preparers?

4. Describe how a person might write e-mail messages of social media posts to give an impression of being charismatic.

5. Explain why the presence of a charismatic leader tends to enhance the job satisfaction of group members.

6. To what extent do you think dressing expensively and fashionably really contributes to the charisma of a leader within an organization?

7. If a transformational leader is supposed to be so smart and visionary, why would he or she emphasize empowerment in his or her leadership approach?

8. How might a major retailer such as Sears or J.C. Penney benefit from having a transformational leader as CEO?

9. Do you think a true transformational leader should ever lay off thousands of workers to help make a company profitable?

10. What opportunities might a first-level supervisor or team leader have to be a transformational leader?

## LEADERSHIP CASE PROBLEM A

### Baxter, the Self-Adoring Charismatic

Baxter is the marketing and sales director of Train and Subway Interiors, a niche company that makes interiors for railroad and subway cars. The interior components include ceilings, overhead storage compartments, holding bars, and kitchenettes. As the demand for public transportation has increased, so has the business of Train and Subway Interiors.

Baxter attributes much of the sales growth of Train and Subway Interiors to his magnetic personality, and the way in which he has inspired the four sales representatives on his team. Baxter says, "I'm a positive thinker. I know that we can win together. I smile at everybody, and my customers love me. I'm good, my sales staff is good, and we all know it. The competition is jealous."

Baxter decorates his office to project his personal pride. An 8x10 photo shows him front and center on his college football team. Another photo shows him shaking hands with the U.S. Transportation secretary. A large cabinet is filled with sales trophies and employee-of-the-month plaques Baxter has won at various employers. Another photo shows Baxter smiling in front of an Amtrak high-speed train. The landscape on Baxter's laptop consists of a photo of Baxter seated between two Labrador retrievers.

Phil, the head if engineering at Train and Subway, made this comment about Baxter as the head of marketing and sales:

A lot of people go for Baxter's hype and bravado. He shakes a lot of hands, gives lots of pep talks, and smiles most of the time. But what Baxter doesn't realize is that without our design and engineering, he and his team would have nothing to sell. He tells me, of course, that without his great marketing and sales skills, the company would have nothing but scrap.

Francesca, the head of HR and administration, had collected some feedback about Baxter's approach to leadership from his subordinates, colleagues, and customers. She commented, Baxter is well liked and charming. He is great at entertaining railway train and subway manufacturing executives, both from the United States and other companies. Yet a lot of people are tired of his bragging and self-congratulations. He talks about being the driving force behind this business, even though Train and Subway Interiors has existed for over fifty years. A clerk said that "Baxter makes more use of mirrors that anybody she knows."

Megan, a sales representative who left the company to take a sales position with a steel company, made this comment about Baxter: "I liked most of the marketing strategy Baxter developed for the company. He also has a warm personality. Yet, I couldn't take the way he never really listened to me. When I began talking about a tough sales problem I was facing, Baxter would start talking about his self and the sales challenges he had conquered. If Baxter dropped by my work area in the office, he would begin by describing in great detail what his beloved Labradors did recently."

### Questions

1. What hints do you get from this case that Baxter is charismatic?

2. What hints do you get from this case that Baxter is narcissistic?

3. What suggestions can you offer Baxter so he can make more effective use of his charisma?

## ASSOCIATED ROLE PLAY

One person plays the role of Baxter who is feeling great about himself today, and is looking for an opportunity to talk about his leadership effectiveness. Another person plays the role of a sales representative who wants to talk about the possibility of a major sale, but the customer is looking for a suspiciously high gift for approving the sale. Baxter is dropping by her cubicle. Observers might make note of the effectiveness of the communication between Baxter and the sales representative.

## LEADERSHIP CASE PROBLEM B

### Turnaround Ashley

At age thirty-two, Ashley believed that she had landed an opportunity to accelerate her career as a leader and manager. Ashley had worked four years as a manufacturing manager in the industrial pump division of a conglomerate. Based on her outstanding performance, she was offered the opportunity to be the division head of a small and troubled unit of the company, Ultra Covers. The division in question manufactures after-market stylish covers for smartphones, laptops, and tablet computers. Although the products are of high quality, Ultra Covers has been losing money for several years. Competition in the field of stylish covers for electronic devices is intense, and profit margins are thin. Despite these challenges, Ashley took just one hour to accept the offer. She told the top-management committee, "I know I can convert Ultra Covers into a proud and profitable business unit."

Thirty days later, Ashley began her new position as division president. The former president was reassigned to a plant manager position in another unit of the conglomerate. Ashley's first move was to conduct a listening tour of the company, interacting with workers and managers at all levels of the division. She also spoke with the major customers and several kiosk operators who sold Ultra Covers at shopping malls.

After listening to so many people, making observations of her own, and analyzing financial and production data from the Ultra Cover division, Ashley swung into action. Her first step was to inform the manufacturing group that if they could not reduce manufacturing costs by 10 percent within six months, she might shut down domestic manufacturing and outsource all manufacturing to China. Ultra Covers would then become a sales and distribution unit, with almost no manufacturing.

Ashley's next major initiative came in a meeting with the sales manager, Ken. She told him that his goal for the upcoming fiscal year is to increase sales by 15 percent, and that no excuses would be acceptable. Ken explained that his sales force is highly motivated, and that they are doing everything they can to boost sales, including intense Internet marketing. He said, "The channels are already saturated with decorative covers for portable electronic devices. A 15 percent jump in sales is unrealistic." Ashley told Ken it was his job to find a way to increase sales—particularly if he wanted to keep his job.

Another initiative Ashley took was to order managers and supervisors to find ways to reduce division costs by 10 percent in the upcoming fiscal year. "Do whatever it takes," said Ashley. "Our costs are too high for our sales volume. Adjust the thermostats, do not replace some of the workers who quit or retire, cut back on scrap. And when you make photocopies, remember to print on both sides of the sheet of paper."

Ashley began to sense from comments she heard from her staff that perhaps her turnaround efforts appeared to be a little harsh. Based on this feedback, she decided to prepare a video that would be distributed on the Ultra Cover intranet. A central part of her message was that about four billion people in the world use some type of mobile device or computer, and that only 3 percent of them are purchasing a cover for these devices. She concluded, "We have a potential market of about 3.9 billion people throughout the world who could use at least one Ultra Cover. We have just begun our journey to greatness."

### Questions

1. How successful do you think Ashley will be as a transformational leader at Ultra Cover?

2. What might Ashley be doing right as a transformational leader?

3. What suggestions might you offer Ashley to be more successful as a transformational leader?

## ASSOCIATED ROLE PLAY

One student plays the role of turnaround leader Ashley who is driven to transform Ultra Covers into a high-performing unit within the conglomerate. Today she has a face-to-face meeting with Ken to hammer home the point that sales must increase by 15 percent. Another student plays the role of Ken who wants to cooperate but thinks that Ashley is being unrealistic considering the business climate. Ken also wants to preserve his job. One focal point for observers will be the extent to which Ashley is being inspirational and transformational.

## LEADERSHIP SKILL-BUILDING EXERCISE 3-3

### My Leadership Portfolio

How much charisma, or how many charismatic behaviors, have you exhibited this week? Think back to all your interactions with people in this last week or two. What have you done that might have been interpreted as charismatic? Review the characteristics of a charismatic leader described in the text and in the Guidelines for Action and Skill Development. For example, did you smile warmly at someone, did you wave to a person you see infrequently and address him or her by name? Did you help your team, club, or group think seriously about its future? As part of this same exercise, record your charismatic behaviors for the upcoming week. Be alert to opportunities for displaying charisma.

## LEADERSHIP SKILL-BUILDING EXERCISE 3-4

### Finding Inspirational Messages on a Social Networking Site

The purpose of this exercise is to find a few inspiring messages on social media websites. For example, track down your followers on Twitter to see if you can find at least two inspirational messages such as those posted by Tim in the above case. Reflect on the effect these messages have on you. What impact do these messages have on your perception of the charisma of the sender? Compare your results to those of one or two other classmates.

## NOTES

1. Original story created from facts and observations in the following sources: Marco della Cava, "Nadella Counts on Culture Shock to Drive Microsoft Growth," *USA Today*, February 20, 2017, p. 4B; Anita Campbell, "Microsoft CEO Challenges Business Leaders: 'Make a Difference in the World,'" *Small Business Trends* (http://smallbiztrends.com), April 5, 2016, pp. 1–5; Andrew Nusca, "Satya Nadella's Traveling Road Show," *Fortune*, December 1, 2016, pp. 76–83; Marco della Carva, "Karma and the Cloud," *USA Today*, October 20, 2014, pp. 1B–2B; Shira Ovide, "The Quiet Evolution at Microsoft's Office," *The Wall Street Journal*, September 30, 2015, p. B6; Dina Bass, "Beyond Windows," *Bloomberg Businessweek*, February 23–March 1, 2015, pp. 30–31; Richard Hay, "Satya Nadella Lays Out New Mission and Vision for Microsoft," *SuperSite Windows* (http://winsupersite.com), June 25, 2014, pp. 1–4.
2. Jack and Suzy Welch, "It's Not About Empty Suits," *BusinessWeek*, October 16, 2006, p. 32.
3. Jay A. Conger and Rabindra N. Kanungo, *Charismatic Leadership in Organizations* (Thousand Oaks, CA: Sage Publications, 1998).
4. Stephanie N. Mehta, "Why Him?" *Fortune*, November 23, 2009, pp. 89–90.
5. Daniel Lyons, "Digital Tools: Big Brother," *Forbes*, October 1, 2007, p. 51.

6. Juan-Carlos Pastor, James R. Meindl, and Margarit C. Mayo, "A Network Effects Model of Charisma Attributions," *Academy of Management Journal*, April 2002, pp. 410–420.

7. Philippe Jacquart and John Antonakis, "When Does Charisma Matter for Top-Level Leaders? Effects of Attributional Ambiguity," *Academy of Management Journal*, August 2015, pp. 1051–1074.

8. William L. Gardner and Bruce J. Avolio, "The Charismatic Relationship: A Dramaturgical Perspective," *Academy of Management Review*, January 1998, pp. 32–58.

9. Angelo Fanelli and Vilmos F. Misangyi, "Bringing Out Charisma: CEO Charisma and External Stakeholders," *Academy of Management Review*, October 2006, p. 1053.

10. Amir Erez, Vilmost Misangyi, Diane E. Johnson, Marcie A. LePine, and Kent C. Halverson, "Stirring the Hearts of Followers: Charismatic Leadership as the Transferal of Affect," *Journal of Applied Psychology*, May 2008, pp. 602–613.

11. Bernard M. Bass with Ruth Bass, *The Bass Handbook of Leadership: Theory, Research, & Managerial Applications*, Fourth Edition (New York: The Free Press, 2008), pp. 578–580.

12. Michael E. Brown and Linda K. Treviño, "Socialized Charismatic Leadership, Values Congruence, and Deviance in Work Groups," *Journal of Applied Psychology*, July 2006, pp. 954–962; Michael E. Brown and Linda K. Treviño, "Leader-Follower Values Congruence: Are Socialized Charismatics Leaders Better Able to Achieve It?" *Journal of Applied Psychology*, March 2009, pp. 478–490.

13. Jane M. Howell and Boas Shamir, "The Role of Followers in the Charismatic Leadership Process: Relationships and Their Consequences," *Academy of Management Review*, January 2005, p. 100.

14. Mark Greer, "The Science of Savoir Faire," *Monitor on Psychology*, January 2005, pp. 28–39; Jane M. Howell and Bruce Avolio, "The Ethics of Charismatic Leadership: Submission or Liberation?" *The Academy of Management Executive*, May 1992, pp. 43–52; Andrew J. DuBrin, *Narcissism in the Workplace* (Cheltenham, UK: Edward Elgar, 2012), pp. 108–119.

15. Research cited in Nicole Torres, "Defend Your Research: Fast Thinkers are More Charismatic," *Harvard Business Review*, March 2016, pp. 28–29.

16. Warren Bennis, "Acting the Part of a Leader," *BusinessWeek*, September 19, 2009, p. 80.

17. Charles A. O'Reilly III et al., "Narcissistic CEOs and Executive Compensation," *The Leadership Quarterly*, April 2014, p. 219.

18. O'Reilly et al., "Narcissistic CEOs and Executive Compensation," pp. 218–231.

19. Bradley P. Owens, Angela S. Wallace, and David A. Waldman, "Leader Narcissism and Follower Outcomes: The Counterbalancing Effect of Leader Humility," *Journal of Applied Psychology*, July 2015, pp. 1203–1213.

20. Jim Collins, "Aligning Action and Values," *Leader to Leader Institute*, http://leadertoleader.org, as reported in "Actions: Louder than Vision Statements," *Executive Leadership*, May 2004, p. 8.

21. A couple of the ideas in the list are from "Nailing Down Your Vision: 8 Steps," *Executive Leadership*, September 2007, p. 2.

22. Jeffrey C. Kohles, Michelle C. Bligh, and Melissa K. Carsten, "A Follower-Centric Approach to the Vision Integration Process," *The Leadership Quarterly*, June 2012, pp. 476–487.

23. Ellen Florian, "Dr. Mehmet Oz: The Crown Prince of Medical Media on Leadership," *Fortune*, February 27, 2012, p. 20.

24. Howell and Avolio, "The Ethics of Charismatic Leadership," p. 46.

25. Jay A. Conger, "Inspiring Others: The Language of Leadership," *The Academy of Management Executive*, February 1991, p. 39.

26. Ibid.

27. Anna Elisabeth Weischer, Jürgen Weibler, and Malte Petersen, "'To Thine Own Self Be True': The Effects of Enactment and Life Storytelling on Perceived Leader Authenticity," *The Leadership Quarterly*, August 2013, pp. 477–495.

28. "2015 Women's Network Conference and Leadership Summit," *www.gewomensnetwork*.com, ©copyright 2011–2015 event Power; Diane Brady and Jena McGregor, "What Works in Women's Networks," *Business Week*, June 18, 2007, pp. 58–60.

29. Dennis A. Romig, *Side by Side Leadership: Achieving Outstanding Results Together* (Marietta, GA.: Bard Press, 2001), p. 157.

30. Research cited in Greer, "The Science of Savoir Faire," p. 30.

31. Thomas Smale, "5 Steps to Build Your Personal Brand," *Entrepreneur* (www.entrepreneur.com), September 25, 2015, p. 1.

32. John Antonakis, Marika Fenley, and Suie Liechti, "Can Charisma Be Taught? Test of Two Interventions," *Academy of Management Learning & Education*, September 2011, pp. 374–396.

33. Marshall Sashkin and Molly G. Sashkin, *Leadership That Matters: The Critical Factors for Making a Difference in People's Lives and Organizations' Success* (San Francisco: Berrett-Koehler, 2003).

34. Bernard M. Bass, "Does the Transactional–Transformational Leadership Paradigm Transcend National Boundaries?" *American Psychologist*, February 1997, p. 130.

35. Frank Vasceilaro, "New CEO Single-Handedly Turing Best Buy Around," *CBS Minnesota* (http://minnesota.cbslocal.com), November 6, 2013, pp. 1–4; Jen Wieczner, "Best Buy CEO On How to Lead a Corporate Turnaround (without Making Employees Hate You)," *Fortune* (www.fortune.com), October 29, 2015, pp. 1–6; Shelly Banjo, "Best Buy's Turnaround May Already Be Over," *Bloomberg Gadfly* (www.bloomberg.com), June 7, 2016, pp. 1–4.

36. Many of the items in the list are derived from John J. Hater and Bernard M. Bass, "Superiors' Evaluations and Subordinates' Perceptions of Transformational and Transactional Leadership," *Journal of Applied Psychology*, November 1988, p. 65; Noel M. Tichy and Mary Anne Devanna, *The Transformational Leader* (New York: Wiley, 1990); Shaul Oreg and Yair Berson, "Leadership and Employees' Reactions to Change: The Role of Leaders' Personal Attributes and Transformational Leadership Style," *Personnel Psychology*, no. 3, 2011, pp. 627–659.

37. Brian J. Hoffman, Bethany H. Bynum, Ronald F. Piccolo, and Ashley W. Sutton, "Person–Organization Value Congruence: How Transformational Leaders Influence Work Group Effectiveness," *Academy of Management Journal*, August 2011, pp. 779–790.

38. Peter Koestenbaum, *Leadership: The Inner Side of Greatness* (San Francisco: Jossey-Bass, 1991).

39. Shawn Tully, "The Man Who Got Honeywell's Groove Back," *Fortune*, May 21, 2012, pp. 176–184.

40. Deanne N. Den Hartog and Frank D. Belschak, "When Does Transformational Leadership Enhance Employee Proactive Behavior? The Role of Autonomy and Roles Breadth Self-Efficacy," *Journal of Applied Psychology*, January 2012, pp. 194–202.

41. Literature reviewed in Sally A. Carless, Alexander J. Wearing, and Leon Mann, "A Short Measure of Transformational Leadership," *Journal of Business and Psychology*, Spring 2000, pp. 389–405; Joyce E. Bono and Timothy A. Judge, "Personality and Transformational and Transactional Leadership: A Meta-Analysis," *Journal of Applied Psychology*, October 2004, pp. 901–910; Taly Dvir, Dov Eden, Burce J. Avolio, and Boas Shamir, "Impact of Transformational Leadership on Follower Development and Performance: A Field Experiment," *Academy of Management Journal*, August 2002, pp. 735–744; Bass, *The Bass Handbook of Leadership*, pp. 633–636.

42. Timothy A. Judge and Joyce E. Bono, "Five-Factor Model of Personality and Transformational Leadership," *Journal of Applied Psychology*, October 2000, pp. 751–765; Bono and Judge, "Personality and Transformational and Transactional Leadership," pp. 901–910.

43. Chester Dawson, "Toyota Chief Grabs the Wheel to Turn Around Humbled Auto Giant," *The Wall Street Journal*, July 13, 2012, pp. A1, A8; Bryan Bremner, Craig Trudell, and Yuki Hagiwara, "Remaking Toyota," *Bloomberg Businessweek*, December 28, 2014, pp. 44–49.

44. Robert S. Rubin, David C. Munz, and William H. Bommer, "Leading from Within: The Effects of Emotional Recognition and Personality on Transformational Leadership Behavior," *Academy of Management*, October 2005, pp. 845–856.

45. Jia Hu, Zhen Wang, Robert C. Liden, and Jianmin Sun, "The Influence of Leader Core Self-Evaluation on Follower Reports of Transformational Leadership," *The Leadership Quarterly*, October 2012, pp. 860–868.

46. Julian Brkling, *The Science of Leadership* (New York: Oxford University Press, 2014), p. 20.

47. Ronald F. Piccolo and Jason A. Colquitt, "Transformational Leadership and Job Behaviors: The Mediating Role of Core Job Characteristics," *Academy of Management Journal*, April 2006, p. 327.

48. Joyce E. Bono, Hannah Jackson Foldes, Gregory Vinson, and John P. Muros, "Workplace Emotions: The Role of Supervision and Leadership," *Journal of Applied Psychology*, September 2007, pp. 1357–1367.

49. Timothy A. Judge and Ronald F. Piccolo, "Transformational and Transactional Leadership: A Meta-Analytic Test of Their Relative Validity," *Journal of Applied Psychology*, October 2004, pp. 755–768.

50. Flavia Cavazotte, Valter Moreno, and Mateus Hickmann, "Effects of Leader Intelligence, Personality, and Emotional Intelligence on Transformational Leadership and Managerial Performance," *The Leadership Quarterly*, June 2012, pp. 443–455.

51. Warren G. Bennis and Burt Nanus, *Leaders: Strategies for Taking Charge* (New York: Harper & Row, 1985), p. 223.

52. Robert C. Tucker, "The Theory of Charismatic Leadership," *Daedalus*, Summer 1968, pp. 731–756.

53. Emily Grijalva et al., "Narcissism and Leadership: A Meta-Analytic Review of Linear and Nonlinear Relationships," *Personnel Psychology*, no. 1, 2015, pp. 1–47.

54. Dan Ciampa, "When Charismatic Leadership Goes Too Far," *Harvard Business Review* (https://hbr.org), November 21, 2016, p. 4.

55. David Collinson and Dennis Tourish, "Teaching Leadership Critically: New Directions for Leadership Pedagogy," *Academy of Management Learning & Education*, December 2015, pp. 576–594.

56. Items 1, 2, 4, 5, and 6 on the list are from Roger Dawson, *Secrets of Power Persuasion: Everything You'll Need to Get Anything You'll Ever Want* (Upper Saddle River, NJ: Prentice Hall, 1992), pp. 179–194; the eighth item is from James M. Kouzes and Barry Z. Posner, *The Leadership Challenge*, Third Edition (San Francisco: Jossey-Bass, 2002), p. 158.

# Leadership Behaviors, Attitudes, and Styles

Chris Cox is the chief product officer at Facebook in charge of such major projects as developing Reactions, a possible approach to offering uses more options that simply "liking" a post, including being sad. His major responsibility is to run the Facebook social network itself. Cox is known for his ability to carefully guide the introduction of new products as well as for his superior ability to engage in warm interpersonal relationships with his team as well as other Facebook employees. He is also well liked by financial analysts who meet periodically with the Facebook executive team. Cox has become a pitchman in company videos about Facebook presented to analysts. "Team Cox" consists of Julie Zhou, Adam Mosseri, Fidji Simo, Will Cathart, and Cox himself.

Facebook founder and chief executive officer (CEO), Mark Zuckerberg, says Cox is one of his closest friends, and also an individual who has made the company a really special place. Zuckerberg makes note of Cox's cognitive skills and emotional intelligence. He said, "It's really rare to find people who are very good at both." Facebook director of engineering Mark Slee, once said, "One of Chris' biggest skills is emotional intelligence. He's just one of those rare people from an engineering background who excels at that."

At one point, Cox served as Facebook's first human resources chief. In this role, he helped establish the Facebook culture, as well as defining the company's mission: "To make the world more open and connected." As a Facebook leader, Cox strives to make the company more social by encouraging positive interactions among employees. He also stays on top of product details such as trying to perfect the "Like" function.

Cox holds a bachelor's degree in symbolic systems with a concentration in artificial intelligence from Stanford University.[1]

The story about a world-leading technology executive illustrates how leaders' behaviors can influence their effectiveness. Among these behaviors are providing direction and establishing positive interpersonal relationships. This chapter describes a number of key behaviors and attitudes that help a manager function as a leader. We also describe the closely related topic of leadership styles.

Frequent reference is made in this chapter, and at other places in the text, to leadership effectiveness. A working definition of an **effective leader** is one who helps group members attain productivity, including high quality and customer satisfaction, as well as job satisfaction. Leadership effectiveness is typically measured by two key criteria.

The first criterion relates to objective data, such as those dealing with sales, production, safety, number of patents produced by the group, cost cutting, or staying within budget. Measures of job satisfaction and turnover are also used to measure leadership effectiveness. The second criterion focuses on judgments by others about the leader's effectiveness, such as a plant manager rating a supervisor or the board rating a CEO. Most of the research reported throughout this text includes measures of leadership effectiveness in the study design.

## The Classic Dimensions of Consideration and Initiating Structure

Studies conducted at Ohio State University in the 1950s identified 1,800 specific examples of leadership behavior that were reduced to 150 questionnaire items on leadership functions.[2] The functions are also referred to as *dimensions of leadership behavior*. This research became the foundation for most future research about leadership behavior, attitudes, and styles. The researchers asked team members to describe their supervisors by responding to the questionnaires. Leaders were also asked to rate themselves on leadership dimensions. Two leadership dimensions accounted for 85 percent of the descriptions of leadership behavior: *consideration* and *initiating structure*.

**Consideration** is the degree to which the leader creates an environment of emotional support, warmth, friendliness, and trust. The leader creates this environment by being friendly and approachable, looking out for the personal welfare of the group, keeping the group abreast of new developments, and doing small favors for the group.

Leaders who score high on the consideration factor typically are friendly and trustful, earn respect, and have a warm relationship with team members. Leaders with low scores on the consideration factor typically are authoritarian and impersonal in their relationships with group members. Three questionnaire items measuring the consideration factor are as follows:

1. Do personal favors for people in the work group.
2. Treat all people in the work group as your equal.
3. Do little things to make it pleasant to be a member of the staff.

The relationship-oriented behaviors described later in this chapter are specific aspects of consideration. Another key example of consideration is *making connections* with people. For example, much of the time Sheryl Sandberg, the chief operating officer (COO) of Facebook, spends outside the office on business is devoted to making connections with key people who could advance the cause of the company, as well as help women succeed in their careers.

Being soft-spoken is a leadership style element that contributes to consideration because workers feel respected when the leader does not attempt to dominate the discussion. Adam Silver, the National Basketball Association (NBA) commissioner, is regarded as dispassionate, congenial, and practical—and rarely argumentative.[3]

**Initiating structure** means organizing and defining relationships in the group by engaging in such activities as assigning specific tasks, specifying procedures to be followed, scheduling work, and clarifying expectations for team members. A team leader who helped group members establish realistic goals would be engaged in initiating structure. The task-related leadership behaviors and attitudes described later in this chapter are specific aspects of initiating structure.

Leaders who score high on this dimension define the relationship between themselves and their staff members, as well as the role that they expect each staff member to assume. Such leaders also endeavor to establish well-defined channels of communication and ways of getting the job done. Three self-assessment items measuring initiating structure are as follows:

1. Try out your own new ideas in the work group
2. Emphasize meeting deadlines.
3. See to it that people in the work group are working up to capacity.

An example of an emphasis on initiating structure is the way Joe Kasser, the CEO of the industrial conglomerate Siemens provides leadership to the organization. During his first three years as CEO, Kasser simplified the organization structure, sold off business units, and trimmed the workforce by 12,000 people.[4] Workers throughout the organization were given many specific directives in order to achieve such large objectives.

Leaders have been categorized with respect to how much emphasis they place on consideration and initiating structure. As implied by Figure 4-1, the two dimensions are not mutually exclusive. A leader can achieve high or low status on both. For example, an

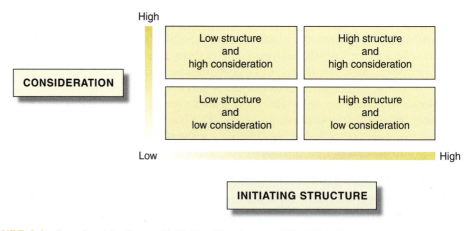

**FIGURE 4-1**  Four Combinations of Initiating Structure and Consideration.

effective leader might contribute to high productivity and still place considerable emphasis on warm human relationships. The four-cell grid of Figure 4-1 is a key component of several approaches to describing leadership style. For many years, the Leadership Grid™ was a standard method of understanding leadership styles. The Grid is a framework for specifying the extent of a leader's concern for production (initiating structure) and people (consideration), and stemmed from the four-cell grid.[5] We return to leadership styles later in this chapter and in Chapter 5.

A study of the validity of consideration and initiating structure indicates that these classic dimensions do indeed contribute to an understanding of leadership because they are related to leadership outcomes. A meta-analysis showed that consideration is strongly related to the job satisfaction of group members, satisfaction with the leader, worker motivation, and leader effectiveness. Initiating structure was slightly more strongly related to job performance, group performance, and organization performance. However, initiating structure was also associated with satisfaction and performance.[6] These results are encouraging because they reinforce the importance of this pioneering research.

More recent research conducted with an online research group and U.S. Air Force officers provides additional insight into the effects of initiating structure and consideration on employee work-related attitudes. The focus of the research was the fit between consideration and initiating structure needed and received. One key result of the study was that when employees did not receive the amount of consideration and initiating structure they thought they needed, unfavorable attitudes were forthcoming. Among these attitudes were less trust in the supervisor, lower job satisfaction, and less commitment to the organization. The study also found that excess levels of consideration were associated with favorable attitudes, and excess levels of initiating structure were associated with unfavorable attitudes. (Apparently, employees don't mind being treated with excess kindness, but they do object to being over controlled.)[7]

## Task-Related Attitudes and Behaviors

The task-related versus relationship-related classification remains a useful framework for understanding leadership attitudes, behaviors, and practices. This section identifies and describes task-related attitudes and behaviors that are characteristic of effective leaders, as outlined in Table 4-1. *Task-related* in this context means that the behavior, attitude, or skill focuses more on the task to be performed than on the interpersonal aspect of leadership.

A synthesis of many studies indicates that the combination of leadership traits and behaviors (both task and relationship) accounts for a minimum of 31 percent of the differences in leadership effectiveness. Yet, according to the research in question, leader behaviors have a bigger impact on effectiveness than do traits. Although certain traits may predispose individuals to certain behaviors, behaviors are the more important predictor of leadership effectiveness. For example, a leader who is assertive may take naturally to providing clear guidelines and providing feedback to subordinates. It is also noteworthy to recognize that it is easy to develop behaviors than to develop or modify traits.[8]

**TABLE 4-1** Task-Related Leadership Attitudes and Behaviors

1. Adaptability to the situation
2. Direction setting
3. High performance standards
4. Concentrating on strengths of group members
5. Risk taking and execution of plans
6. Hands-on guidance and feedback
7. Ability to ask tough questions
8. Organizing for collaboration

1. ***Adaptability to the situation.*** Effective leaders adapt to the situation. Adaptability reflects the contingency viewpoint: A tactic is chosen based on the unique circumstances at hand. A leader who is responsible for psychologically immature group members will find it necessary to supervise them closely. If the group members are mature and self-reliant, the leader will use less supervision. The adaptive leader also selects an organization structure that is best suited to the demands of the situation, such as choosing between a brainstorming group and a committee.

2. ***Direction setting.*** Given that a major responsibility of leadership is to produce change, the leader must set the direction of that change. Direction setting is part of creating a vision and a component of strategy. The strategy describes a feasible way of achieving the vision. Assume that the vision of a website company were to get millions of people in emerging countries connected to the Internet. A supporting strategy would have to include producing low-cost devices for accessing the Internet, and finding a way to distribute the devices.

3. ***High performance standards.*** Effective leaders consistently hold group members to high standards of performance. High performance standards can also take the form of challenging the thinking of others. In the given example, a member of the top management team might say, "There is no way we find a manufacturer to produce tablet computers for less than $50." The CEO might respond, "Why not? Has anybody tried it?"

   When performance is measured against high standards, productivity is likely to increase, since people tend to live up to the expectations of their superiors. This is called the **Pygmalion effect**, and it works in a subtle, almost unconscious way. When a managerial leader believes that a group member will succeed, the manager communicates this belief without realizing it. Conversely, when a leader expects a group member to fail, that person will not disappoint the manager. The manager's expectation of success or failure becomes a self-fulfilling prophecy because the perceptions contribute to success or failure.

4. ***Concentrating on the strengths of group members.*** An axiom of effective leadership and management is to make good use of the strengths of group members rather than concentrating effort on patching up areas for improvement. The effective leader helps people improve, yet still capitalizes on strengths. A team member might have excellent interpersonal skills, yet poor technical skills. It would be best to assign that person a role that emphasizes interpersonal skills, while at the same time helping him or her improve technical skills. Marcus Buckingham emphasizes that capitalizing on each person's unique pattern of skills saves time because group members are not laboring at tasks outside their capability and interest. The manager might even develop a job description that best fits each employee's uniqueness.[9] Suppose you are the leader of a call center, and one staffer is great at calming down angry customers. Other call center members are then asked to refer customers who have gone ballistic to your team member who can handle customer rage well.

5. ***Risk taking and execution of plans.*** To bring about constructive change, the leader must take risks and be willing to implement those risky decisions. The relevance of risk taking to leadership effectiveness is emphasized by Sarah Mensah, the General Manager (GM) vice president (VP) of Jordan Brand North America. She believes that the ability to welcome and seek out risks is a valuable skill: "I've learned that if there is no risk, there will be no reward."[10] Former major business executive turned consultant, Larry Bossidy says about the importance of execution: "I'm an impatient person, and I get more satisfaction from seeing things get done than I do about philosophizing or building sand castles. Many people regard execution as detail work that's beneath the dignity of a business leader. That's wrong. It's a leader's most important job."[11]

6. ***Hands-on guidance and feedback.*** You will recall that technical competence and knowledge of the business are important leadership characteristics. They enable the leader to provide group members with hands-on guidance about how to accomplish important work. The leader who provides such guidance helps the group accomplish

important tasks; at the same time, group members learn important skills. Too much guidance of this nature, however, can be a symptom of poor delegation and micro-management (managing too closely). Too little guidance, and macromanagement is the result, in which the manager gives too little or no direction to group members. Henry Mintzberg observes that the leader's strategy might suffer because he or she does not understand the operations of the business.[12]

Closely related to guidance is giving frequent feedback on performance. The leader can rarely influence the actions of group members without appropriate performance feedback. This feedback tells group members how well they are doing so that they can take corrective action if needed. It also serves as reinforcement that prompts group members to continue favorable activities. Leadership Skill-Building Exercise 4-1 provides practice in developing feedback skills.

7. ***Ability to ask tough questions.*** Often, leaders can be effective by asking tough questions rather than providing answers. A **tough question** is one that makes a person or group stop and think about why they are doing or not doing something. (A tough question might also be considered the *right* question.) In this way, group members are forced to think about the effectiveness of their activities. They might ask themselves, "*Why didn't I think of that? It seems so obvious.*" Asking questions is important because quite often group members may have the solutions to difficult problems facing the organization.

8. ***Organizing for collaboration.*** A leadership behavior on the borderline between a task orientation and a relationship orientation is to demand that workers collaborate with each other. The task focus is that the information sharing takes place, whereas the relationship focus is that group members must work collaboratively with each other. The Corporate Executive Board, a research and advisory service company, recommends three steps for the leader who wants to use information technology to increase collaboration:

- First, identify the high-value business outcomes desired, such as accelerating new-product development, before selecting collaboration technologies.

## LEADERSHIP SKILL–BUILDING EXERCISE 4-1

### Feedback Skills

After small groups have completed an assignment such as answering the case questions or discussion questions, hold a performance feedback session. Also use observations you have made in previous problem-solving activities as the basis for your feedback. Each group member provides some feedback to each other member about how well he or she thinks the other person performed. Use only volunteers, because this type of feedback may be uncomfortable and disturbing to some individuals. Students not receiving feedback can serve as observers and later present their views on what took place during the exercise. To increase the probability of benefiting from this experience, feedback recipients must listen actively. Refer to the section in Chapter 10 on coaching skills and techniques for more information on feedback and active listening.

A convenient way to do this exercise is for everyone to sit in a circle. Choose one feedback recipient to begin. Going clockwise around the circle, each group member gives that person feedback. After all people have spoken, the feedback recipient gives his or her reactions. The person to the left of the first recipient is the next one to get feedback.

After everyone has had a turn receiving performance feedback, hold a general discussion. Be sure to discuss three key issues:

1. How helpful was the feedback?
2. What was the relative effectiveness of positive versus negative feedback?
3. Were some group members better than others in giving feedback?

    • Second, identify collaboration hot spots. Speak with employees to understand their communication patterns and workflows. (A specialist might be required here to help map workflows, such as who is interacting with whom. More will be said about this topic in Chapter 12.)

    • Select technologies that will improve or speed up existing workflows. For example, a search engine dedicated to in-company practices might be effective.[13] A wide variety of collaboration software is available today.

    Now that you have studied various components of task-oriented attitudes and behaviors, do Leadership Self-Assessment Quiz 4-1. It will further sensitize you to the task activities of leaders and managers.

## LEADERSHIP SELF-ASSESSMENT QUIZ 4-1

### Task-Oriented Attitudes and Behaviors

**Instructions:** Indicate whether you mostly agree or mostly disagree with the following statements. Relate the statements to any work situation—including sports, community activities, and school activities—in which you have been responsible for others' work. If a work situation does not come to mind, imagine how you would act or think.

|  | MOSTLY AGREE | MOSTLY DISAGREE |
|---|---|---|
| **1.** I keep close tabs on productivity figures and interpret them to the group. | ☐ | ☐ |
| **2.** I send frequent e-mail and text messages to group members, giving them information about work procedures. | ☐ | ☐ |
| **3.** I clearly specify the quality goals our group needs to achieve. | ☐ | ☐ |
| **4.** I maintain clear-cut standards of performance. | ☐ | ☐ |
| **5.** When I conduct a meeting, the participants can count on a clear-cut agenda. | ☐ | ☐ |
| **6.** I feel good about my workweek only if our team has met or exceeded its productivity goals. | ☐ | ☐ |
| **7.** Workers should not access e-mail, text messages, or the Internet during working hours unless the activity is actually increasing productivity. | ☐ | ☐ |
| **8.** I freely criticize work that does not meet standards. | ☐ | ☐ |
| **9.** I spend at least 5 percent of my workweek either planning myself or helping team members with their planning. | ☐ | ☐ |
| **10.** I spend a good deal of time solving technical or business problems myself, or helping group members do the same. | ☐ | ☐ |

**Interpretation:** If you responded "mostly agree" to eight, nine, or ten of these statements, you have a strong task orientation. If you responded "mostly disagree" to four or more of the statements, you have below-average task-oriented behaviors and attitudes.

**Skill Development:** A task orientation is important because it can lead directly to goal attainment and productivity. Nevertheless, a task orientation must be balanced with a strong people orientation and interpersonal skills for maximum effectiveness.

    The accompanying Leader-in-Action insert illustrates how task-related attitudes and behavior can contribute to organizational effectiveness, and how these behaviors might include a human touch.

# LEADER IN ACTION

### Ford Executive Joe Hinrichs Is a Troubleshooter with a Human Touch

When he was thirty years old, Joe Hinrichs was regarded as a boy wonder in automobile manufacturing. Less than twenty years later, he became the executive VP and president, The Americas, Ford Motor Company, placing him in charge of a business that generates 70 percent of the company's business. Much of his career has involved taking the leadership of difficult manufacturing problems. This includes getting the vehicles critical to Ford's future out the door without any glitches.

Hinrichs joined Ford in 2000 as a plant manager at a transmission plant, after holding positions at GM and the investment firm, Ryan Enterprises Group. He has had a variety of roles at Ford including president and CEO of Ford Motor Company of Canada, group VP, Global Manufacturing and labor Affairs, and group VP and president of Asia Pacific and Africa.

In 2007, Hinrichs was placed in charge of global manufacturing, with the key assignment of integrating Ford's 104 factories across the world. At the same time, he was expected to accelerate the pace of Ford's globalization efforts. As GM youngest plant manager at age twenty-nine Hinrichs facilitated a turnaround of an inefficient GM Powertrain manufacturing facility in Fredericksburg, VA. His approach was so innovative that it became the subject of a Harvard Business School case study.

In December 2012, Hinrichs returned to Dearborn, Michigan, to become president of Ford America's most profitable business unit. During his tenure in that assignment, Ford America attained record profits. Hinrich has also been placed in charge of the manufacture of vehicles that were experiencing glitches during their product launches—the Lincoln MKZ, and Ford Escape, and the Ford Fusion. Hinrich was given responsibility also for leading an effort to fix the MyFord Touch infotainment system.

Hinrichs was once visiting a Ford assembly plant in Louisville, Kentucky where he pored over an early production version of the Lincoln MKC sports utility vehicle with a team responsible for its release. He carefully examined the hatchback on the SUV. The complex shape of the opening presented a challenge in aligning the door. Hinrichs suggested, "We knew this would was going to be hard to do going in. But we have to get it right." The same day he told the chief engineer that he would like to

see a small light in the cubby that enabled phone chargers to be plugged in.

Hinrichs was once assigned to a major company trouble spot—Ford, China where the company trailed GM and Volkswagen in sales. He worked hard to learn Mandarin, often practicing with a company chauffeur. Hinrichs pushed for the boosting sales by offering its SUV, which were gaining acceptance with Chinese consumers. The strategy worked, and Ford soon gained over 4 percent of the Chinese auto market.

In terms of his approach to people, Hinrichs is perceived to have a small-town, Midwestern style. A Ford dealer said that Hinrichs "has a common touch and a lot of the qualities Alan [Alan Mulally, the legendary former CEO of Ford] possesses. He seems very dedicated to Ford."

In 2016, Hinrichs accepted the position of Chairman of National Minority Supplier Development Council (NMSCD). The organization advances business opportunities for certified minority business enterprises and connects them to corporate members. NMSCD is committed to advancing Asian, Black, Hispanic, and Native American suppliers in an international supply chain.

Hinrichs earned a bachelor's degree in electrical engineering from the University of Dayton, and MBA from Harvard Business School as a GM Fellow.

### QUESTIONS

1. In what way does it appear that Hinrichs highly emphasizes a task orientation and initiating structure in his approach to leadership?

2. What evidence do you see that Hinrichs emphasizes consideration (or humanistic) in his approach to leadership?

*Source:* Original story created from facts and observations in the following sources: Mike Ramsey, "Ford Boss Tees Up for Key Releases," *The Wall Street Journal*, February 15–16, 2014, pp. B1, B4; "Joseph R. Hinrichs Named Chairman of NMSDC," *NMSDC*, June 9, 2016, pp. 1–4; Adrienne Selco, "Joe Hinrichs Named Ford's Manufacturing Chief," *IndustryWeek* (www.industryweek.com), December 14, 2017, pp. 1–4; Bradford Wernle, "After High-Profile Successes, Ford's Hinrichs Tackles Launch Problems," *Automotive News* (www.autonews.com), July 29, 2013, pp. 1–13; "Joseph R. Hinrichs," *The Ford Motor Company Media Center* (https://media.ford.com), June 14, 2016, pp. 1–2.

# Relationship-Oriented Attitudes and Behaviors

Leadership involves influencing people, so it follows that many effective leadership attitudes, behaviors, and practices deal with interpersonal relationships. Table 4-2 lists the seven relationship-oriented attitudes and behaviors that we will discuss next. (Most other parts of this book describe the interpersonal skill aspects of leadership.)

1. *Aligning people.* Getting people pulling in the same direction and collaborating smoothly is a major interpersonal challenge. To get people pulling together, it is necessary to speak to many people. The target population can involve many different stakeholders. Among them are managers and team leaders, higher-ups, peers, and workers in other parts of the organization, as well as suppliers, government officials, and customers. Anyone who can implement the vision and strategies or who can block implementation must be aligned.[14] After being aligned, organizational members can pull together toward a higher purpose. Alignment also incorporates getting the group working together smoothly.

2. *Openness to worker opinions.* A major part of relationship-oriented leadership is to engage in **management openness**, or a set of leader behaviors particularly relevant to subordinates' motivation to voice their opinion.[15] When the leader is open in this way, subordinates perceive that their boss listens to them, is interested in their ideas, and gives fair consideration to suggestions. Being open to worker opinions is part of the consideration dimension, and it is also central to participative leadership. A representative example being open to worker opinions is Frank Blake, the chairman of Home Depot. During his time as CEO, he incorporated face-to-face meetings with almost all new store managers or assistant managers at the home-improvement chain, as well as occasional meetings with other store managers.[16] During these meetings, Blake listened attentively to suggestions for improving store operations and customer experience.

3. *Creating inspiration and visibility.* As described in the discussion of charismatic and transformational leadership, inspiring others is an essential leadership practice. Inspiring people usually involves appealing to their emotions and values, such as when the head of a snowmobile business unit encourages workers to believe that they are making winters more enjoyable for people who live in regions that accumulate snow as well as facilitating rescue missions.

   Because human contact and connections reinforce inspiration, another part of being inspirational is being visible and available. One factor contributing to the popularity of Apple Inc. CEO Tim Cook is that he communicates freely with his executive team and many other workers. A market researcher said "Tim is down to Earth and approachable."[17]

4. *Satisfying higher-level needs.* To inspire people, effective leaders motivate them by satisfying higher-level needs, such as needs for achievement, personal growth, a sense of belonging, recognition, self-esteem, and a feeling of control over one's life. Many

TABLE 4-2 Relationship-Oriented Attitudes and Behaviors

| | |
|---|---|
| 1. | Aligning people |
| 2. | Openness to worker opinions |
| 3. | Creating inspiration and visibility |
| 4. | Satisfying higher-level needs |
| 5. | Giving emotional support and encouragement |
| 6. | Promoting principles and values |
| 7. | Reducing task ambiguity |

leaders in organizations express an awareness of the importance of need satisfaction for building good relationships with workers. A robust method of satisfying workers' higher-level needs is to help them grow professionally. W. James McNerney, the former long-time executive at Boeing Company, says that he has been a successful executive at three major companies primarily through helping people perform better. McNerney contends that people who grow are open to change, have the courage to do so, work hard, and are good team players. In his words, "What I do is figure out how to unlock that in people, because most people have that inside of them. But they often get trapped in a bureaucratic environment where they've been beaten about the head and shoulders."[18]

5. *Giving emotional support and encouragement.* Supportive behavior toward team members usually increases leadership effectiveness. A supportive leader gives frequent encouragement and praise and also displays caring and kindness even about non-work-related matters such as the health of a worker's ill family member. Keep in mind that encouragement means to fill with courage. One of the many work-related ways of encouraging people is to ask for their input about important decisions. Emotional support generally improves morale and sometimes improves productivity. In the long term, emotional support and encouragement may bolster a person's self-esteem. Being emotionally supportive comes naturally to the leader who is empathetic and warm.

Giving encouragement was also the eighth leadership principle of Dale Carnegie, the famous early proponent of human relations principles, in work and personal life. Recently, Tessa E. Basford and Andrea Molberg searched for empirical evidence for the validity of Carnegie's leadership principles, including encouragement. Overall, they found support for Carnegie's recommendations to use encouragement. Encouragement is linked to improvement of job performance and attitudes, probably because encouragement boosts feelings of self-worth.[19]

An indirect, but effective, way of giving emotional support to group members is to make them happy by creating conditions that foster happiness. Psychology professor Sonja Lyubomirsky has found that employees are happier when they are helping others. Based on a study at Coca-Cola in Madrid, she found that acts of kindness make employees feel more connected to each other and their jobs. Furthermore, coworkers observed what was happening and were inspired to replicate kindness in such ways as complimenting each other and bringing coffee.[20] The leader's role here would be to encourage employees to be kind to each other. Many of the techniques of employee engagement to be described in Chapter 10 would foster employee happiness.

6. *Promoting principles and values.* A major part of a top leader's role is to help promote values and principles that contribute to the welfare of individuals and organizations. This promotion can be classified as relationship oriented because it deals directly with the emotions and attitudes of people, and indirectly with the task. The late Stephen Covey, who is widely quoted for his uplifting messages, advises that an organization's mission statement must be for all good causes.[21] Leaders who believe in these good causes will then espouse principles and values that lead people toward good deeds in the work place. To encourage managers and all other employees to conduct their work affairs at a high moral level, many companies put their values in written form. The values might be placed in employee handbooks, on company intranets, or on company websites.

Another value that often helps an enterprise is a strong focus on the welfare of employees. A notable example is the leadership of Rich Snyder, CEO of the successful fast-food chain, In-N-Out Burger. Wages and benefits are relatively high, and managers who meet their goals are eligible for company-paid luxury vacations. The Snyder family was committed to viewing employees as if they were family members. As a result, In-N-Out Burger boasts one of the lowest turnover rates in the industry. Snyder met an early death at age forty-nine, but the family kept the business operating based on the same values.[22]

Providing moral leadership begins with understanding one's own values. Leadership Skill-Building Exercise 4-2 gives you an opportunity to think through your work-related values so that you can better provide moral leadership to others. Also, more will be said about values and ethics in Chapter 6.

7. ***Reducing task ambiguity.*** A useful by-product of relationship-oriented leadership behaviors is that they reduce ambiguity in the minds of subordinates. Ambiguity leads to stress for many workers, so stress is reduced when more structure is provided. A study with 129 people in a variety of occupations measured approaches to leadership through questionnaires. Stress level was measured objectively by measuring the amount of the stress hormone, cortisol found in hair samples provided voluntarily by the participants. Two hypotheses were supported: (1) Ambiguity-increasing leadership behaviors of providing very little direction and identifying a vision tended to increase follower's general stress levels. (2) Clarifying leadership behaviors such as producing an appropriate model, fostering the acceptance of group goals, and intellectual stimulation tended to reduce follower's stress levels.[23]

Based on this study, leaders probably should not abandon establishing high-performance standards and establishing visions in order to reduce stress. Yet, they might simultaneously look for ways to reduce ambiguity.

Leadership Skill-Building Exercise 4-3 provides an opportunity for you to practice relationship-oriented and task-oriented behaviors. Combined, these are sometimes referred to as the nuts and bolts of leadership.

## LEADERSHIP SKILL-BUILDING EXERCISE 4-2

### Clarifying Your Interpersonal Work Values

***Instructions:*** To provide effective value leadership, it is essential that you first understand your own values with respect to dealing with others. Rank from 1 to 15 the importance of the following values to you as a person. The most important value on the list receives a rank of 1; the least important, a rank of 15. Use the space next to "Other" if we have left out an important value related to interpersonal relations on the job.

—— Having respect for the dignity of others

—— Ensuring that others have interesting work to perform

—— Earning the trust of others

—— Earning the respect of others

—— Impressing others with how well my group performs

—— Giving others proper credit for their work

—— Inspiring continuous learning on the part of each member in our group, myself included

—— Holding myself and others accountable for delivering on commitments

—— Helping others grow and develop

—— Inspiring others to achieve high productivity and quality

—— Developing the reputation of being a trustworthy person

—— Being in contact regularly with work associates using social networking sites

—— Contributing to the job satisfaction of work associates

—— Avoiding creating intense job dissatisfaction for any work associate

—— Other

1. Compare your ranking of these values with that of the person next to you, and discuss your observations.

2. Perhaps your class, assisted by your instructor, might arrive at a class average on each of these values. How does your ranking compare to the class ranking?

3. Look back at your own ranking. Does your ranking surprise you?

4. Are there any surprises in the class ranking? Which values did you think would be highest and lowest?

Clarifying your values for leadership is far more than a pleasant exercise. Many business leaders have fallen into disgrace and brought their companies into bankruptcy because of values that are unacceptable to employees, stockholders, outside investigators, and the legal system. For example, a CEO who valued "developing the reputation of being a trustworthy person" would not borrow $400 million from the company while paying thousands of employees close to the minimum wage.

# LEADERSHIP SKILL-BUILDING EXERCISE 4-3

### Applying Relationship-Oriented and Task-Oriented Attitudes and Behaviors

About six role players who can tolerate brutal outdoor conditions are needed for this exercise. The setting is an oil drilling rig in the Arctic Circle, where deep underground oil reserves have been discovered, and energy companies are now digging. Today, the wind chill factor is −40 degrees Fahrenheit. The crew of five is uncomfortable and a little confused about how to get the drilling started this morning. The leadership task of the supervisor is to help the crew get the digging accomplished.

Supervisor A attempts to engage in relationship-oriented attitudes and behavior with the group. He or she will use several of the behaviors mentioned in the text. The other five or so role players will react to his or her leadership. Work the role play for about ten minutes.

After the first scenario is complete, Supervisor B will engage in task-oriented attitudes and behaviors, using several of the behaviors mentioned in the text. The other five or so role players will react to this leadership. Continue the role play for about ten minutes.

Class members not thrown into the frozen tundra will observe the interactions of the supervisor with the workers. Provide feedback as to (1) how well the leadership attitudes and behaviors were carried out, and (2) how likely these attitudes and behaviors were helpful in accomplishing the task of getting the drilling started.

# Leadership Styles

A leader's combination of attitudes and behaviors leads to a certain regularity and predictability in dealing with group members. **Leadership style** is the relatively consistent pattern of behavior that characterizes a leader. Studying leadership style is an extension of understanding leadership behaviors and attitudes. Most classifications of leadership style are based on the dimensions of consideration and initiating structure. Comments such as "He's a real command-and-control-type" and "She's a consensus leader" have become commonplace.

An important insight into leadership style is that personality traits influence which style will be natural for a given individual. The same association exists between the leadership behaviors already described in this chapter. Imagine a person who is authoritarian and controlling; this person would gravitate toward being an authoritarian leader. And a person who scores high on the traits of agreeableness and extraversion might take naturally to a shared type of leadership.

Reinout E. de Vries conducted a study with 113 leaders and 201 subordinates at several companies to explore the relationship between personality traits and leadership style. His key findings support information presented at several places in this book in addition to being directly related to the styles to be described in this section. The study concluded that (1) honesty–humility was positively related to ethical leadership, (2) extraversion is positively related to charismatic leadership, (3) agreeableness is positively related to supportive leadership, and (4) conscientiousness is positively related to task-oriented leadership.[24]

Here, we describe the participative leadership style, the autocratic leadership style, servant leadership, the entrepreneurial leadership style, gender differences in leadership style, and choosing the best style. Chapter 5 continues the exploration of leadership styles by presenting several contingency leadership theories.

## Participative Leadership

Sharing decision making with group members and working with them side by side has become the generally accepted leadership approach in the modern organization. Consultant Maria Collar observes that in today's volatile markets where abilities to explore and innovate are highly valued, collective approaches to leadership can help foster creative problem solving.[25] A useful perspective for understanding collective and participative leadership is that they are based on networks of people working together and sharing information. A social network consists of a set of individuals and the relationships that bind them, such as people within a work group who trust each other enough to accept their advice on a problem.[26] (*Social network* in this context refers more to physical than virtual groups).

**Participative leaders** share decision making with group members. The terms *shared leadership, collaborative leadership,* and *team leadership* all refer to the same idea as participative leadership. Participative leadership encompasses so many behaviors that it can be divided into three subtypes: consultative, consensus, and democratic.

**Consultative leaders** confer with group members before making a decision. However, they retain the final authority to make decisions. **Consensus leaders** strive for consensus. They encourage group discussion about an issue and then make a decision that reflects general agreement and that group members will support. All workers who will be involved in the consequences of a decision have an opportunity to provide input. A decision is not considered final until it appears that all parties involved will at least support the decision. **Democratic leaders** confer final authority on the group. They function as collectors of group opinion and take a vote before making a decision.

The participative style is based on management openness because the leader accepts suggestions for managing the operation from group members. Welcoming ideas from below is considered crucial because as technology evolves and organizations decentralize, frontline workers have more independence and responsibility. These workers are closer to the market, closer to seeing how the product is used, and closer to many human resource problems. Frontline knowledge can provide useful input to leaders for such purposes as developing marketing strategy and retaining employees.

The participative style encompasses the teamwork approach. Predominant behaviors of participative leaders include coaching team members, negotiating their demands, and collaborating with others. Often, the team member who has the most relevant knowledge for the task at hand slips into a leadership role. Research indicates that poor-performing teams are often dominated by the team leader, whereas high-performing teams are characterized by shared leadership.[27]

The participative style is well suited to managing competent people who are eager to assume responsibility. Such people want to get involved in making decisions and giving feedback to management. Because most graduates from business and professional programs expect to be involved in decision making, participative leadership works well with the new breed of managers and professionals.

Participative leadership does have some problems. It often results in extensive and time-consuming team meetings and committee work. Also, consensus and democratic leaders are sometimes accused of providing too little direction, or being *macromanagers*. Sometimes, participative leadership is carried to extremes. Team members are consulted about trivial things that management could easily handle independently. Another problem is that many managers still believe that sharing decision making with members reduces their power.

If democratic leadership goes one step further, the result is extreme macromanagement, which is referred to as the laissez-faire leadership style. A study conducted with 4,500 Norwegian employees found that employees managed by a laissez-faire (the French term for "let do") leader experienced role ambiguity. The ambiguity led them to anxiously guess what criteria their supervisor would follow when evaluating their performance, and also guess about which tasks should receive the highest priority.[28] You will recall that such a lax approach to leadership also creates ambiguity for workers.

## Autocratic Leadership

In contrast to participative leaders are **autocratic leaders**, who retain most of the authority. They make decisions confidently, assume that group members will comply, and are not overly concerned with group members' attitudes toward a decision. Autocratic leaders are considered task oriented because they place heavy emphasis on getting tasks accomplished. Typical autocratic behaviors include telling people what to do, asserting authority, and serving as a model for team members.

In some situations, and in some organizational cultures, autocratic leadership is called for. Jeff Bezos, the founder and CEO of Amazon, makes many product and technology decisions by himself. Bezos is also the owner of the *Washington Post* and Blue Ocean, a rocket-ship company. His extraordinary cognitive intelligence and business acumen are so well recognized that his decisions are accepted without resistance. As with other effective autocratic leaders, Bezos moves quickly in making many decisions but does seek some input from trusted advisors. In recent years, he has become more empowering to supplement his autocratic style. An Amazon board member said, "He was at the center of everything at the beginning. The leadership *was* Jeff and Bezos. Today, it's not a hub-and-spoke connecting to him. He has become a great leader of leaders."[29] To be described as *autocratic* does not necessarily mean the leader is impulsive or stubborn.

Employee attitudes toward acceptance of power and authority can also influence how well employees adapt to authoritarian leadership. A study of employees in a Chinese technology company suggested such an influence. It was found that in units where workers strongly accepted leaders having power, authoritarian leadership did not have negative effects such as lowered performance, commitment to the organization, and intention to leave. Acceptance of authority (or power distance) was measured by questionnaire items, such as "Managers should be able to make the right decision without consulting others."[30]

Part of your skill development as a leader involves gaining insight into your own leadership style or potential style. To this end, do Leadership Self-Assessment Quiz 4-2.

## LEADERSHIP SELF-ASSESSMENT QUIZ 4-2

**What Style of Leader Are You or Would You Be?**

*Instructions:* Answer the following statement, keeping in mind what you have done, or think you would do, in the scenarios and attitudes described.

|  |  | MOSTLY TRUE | MOSTLY FALSE |
|---|---|:---:|:---:|
| 1. | I am more likely to take care of a high-impact assignment myself than turn it over to a group member. | ☐ | ☐ |
| 2. | I would prefer the analytical aspects of a manager's job to working directly with group members. | ☐ | ☐ |
| 3. | An important part of my approach to managing a group is to keep the members informed almost daily of any information that could affect their work. | ☐ | ☐ |
| 4. | It is a good idea to give two people in the group the same problem and then choose what appears to be the best solution. | ☐ | ☐ |
| 5. | I like to have updates a few times a day on the work progress of subordinates, even if the update is simply a text message or instant message. | ☐ | ☐ |
| 6. | I look for opportunities to obtain group input before making a decision, even on straightforward issues. | ☐ | ☐ |

*(Continued)*

| | MOSTLY TRUE | MOSTLY FALSE |
|---|---|---|
| **7.** I would reverse a decision if several of the group members presented evidence that I was wrong. | ☐ | ☐ |
| **8.** Differences of opinion in the work group are healthy. | ☐ | ☐ |
| **9.** I think that activities to build team spirit, like fixing up a poor family's house on a Saturday, are an excellent investment of time. | ☐ | ☐ |
| **10.** If my group were hiring a new member, I would like the person to be interviewed by the entire group. | ☐ | ☐ |
| **11.** An effective team leader today uses e-mail or other digital media for about 98 percent of communication with team members. | ☐ | ☐ |
| **12.** Some of the best ideas are likely to come from the group members rather than from the manager. | ☐ | ☐ |
| **13.** If our group were going to have a banquet, I would get input from each member on what type of food should be served. | ☐ | ☐ |
| **14.** I have never seen a statue of a committee in a museum or park, so why bother making decisions by committee if you want to be recognized? | ☐ | ☐ |
| **15.** I dislike it intensely when a group member challenges my position on an issue. | ☐ | ☐ |
| **16.** I typically explain to group members how (what method) they should use to accomplish an assigned task. | ☐ | ☐ |
| **17.** If I were out of the office for a week, most of the important work in the department would get accomplished anyway. | ☐ | ☐ |
| **18.** Delegation of important tasks is something that would be (or is) very difficult for me. | ☐ | ☐ |
| **19.** When a group member comes to me with a problem, I tend to jump right in with a proposed solution. | ☐ | ☐ |
| **20.** When a group member comes to me with a problem, I typically ask that person something like, "What alternative solutions have you thought of so far?" | ☐ | ☐ |

**Scoring and Interpretation:** The answers for a participative leader are as follows:

| | | |
|---|---|---|
| 1. Mostly false | 8. Mostly true | 15. Mostly false |
| 2. Mostly false | 9. Mostly true | 16. Mostly false |
| 3. Mostly true | 10. Mostly true | 17. Mostly true |
| 4. Mostly false | 11. Mostly false | 18. Mostly false |
| 5. Mostly false | 12. Mostly true | 19. Mostly false |
| 6. Mostly true | 13. Mostly true | 20. Mostly true |
| 7. Mostly true | 14. Mostly false | |

Give yourself a score of 1 for each answer that matches the answer key.

If your score is 15 or higher, you are most likely (or would be) a participative leader. If your score is 5 or lower, you are most likely (or would be) an authoritarian leader.

**Skill Development:** The quiz you just completed is also an opportunity for skill development. Review the twenty statements and look for implied suggestions for engaging in participative leadership. For example, statement 20 suggests that you encourage group members to work through their own solutions to problems. If your goal is to become an authoritarian leader, the statements can also serve as useful guidelines. For example, statement 19 suggests that an authoritarian leader first looks to solve problems for group members.

# The Servant Leadership Style

A style of leadership anchored in the desire to help others has surged in popularity in recent years. A **servant leader** serves constituents by working on their behalf to help them achieve their goals, not the leader's own goals. The idea behind servant leadership, as formulated by Robert K. Greenleaf, is that leadership derives naturally from a commitment to service.[31] Serving others, including employees, customers, and community, is the primary motivation for the servant leader. Servant leadership focuses on ethical behavior and constructive relationships between leader and follower.

A study with CEOs found, not surprisingly, that narcissism as measured by a personality test is negatively related to servant leadership.[32] True leadership emerges from a deep desire to help others. A servant leader is therefore a moral leader. Servant leadership has been accomplished when group members become wiser, healthier, and more autonomous. The following are key aspects of servant leadership.[33]

1. *Place service before self-interest.* A servant leader is more concerned with helping others than with acquiring power, prestige, financial reward, and status. The servant leader seeks to do what is morally right, even if it is not financially rewarding. He or she is conscious of the needs of others and is driven by a desire to satisfy them. An example of a questionnaire item measuring this behavior is "My leader puts my best interests ahead of his or her own."[34] (You will recall that wanting to satisfy the needs of others is a relationship behavior.)

2. *Listen first to express confidence in others.* The servant leader makes a deep commitment to listening in order to get to know the concerns, requirements, and problems of group members. Instead of attempting to impose his or her will on others, the servant leader listens carefully to understand what course of action will help others accomplish their goals. After understanding others, the best course of action can be chosen. Through listening, for example, a servant leader might learn that the group is more concerned about team spirit and harmony than striving for companywide recognition. The leader would then concentrate more on building teamwork than searching for ways to increase the visibility of the team.

3. *Inspire trust by being trustworthy.* Being trustworthy is a foundation behavior of the servant leader. He or she is scrupulously honest with others, gives up control, and focuses on the well-being of others. Usually, such leaders do not have to work hard at being trustworthy because they are already moral.

4. *Focus on what is feasible to accomplish.* Even though the servant leader is idealistic, he or she recognizes that one individual cannot accomplish everything. Therefore, the leader listens carefully to the array of problems facing group members and then concentrates on a few. The servant leader thus systematically neglects certain problems. A labor union official might carefully listen to all the concerns and complaints of the constituents and then proceed to work on the most pressing issue.

5. *Lend a hand.* A servant leader looks for opportunities to play the role of the Good Samaritan. As a supermarket manager, he or she might help out by bagging groceries during a busy period. Or a servant leader might help clean out mud in the company lobby after a hurricane.

6. *Provide emotional healing.* A servant leader shows sensitivity to the personal concerns of group members, such as a worker being worried about taking care of a disabled parent. A recurring example of the need for emotional healing is when a natural disaster such as a tornado or sinkhole strikes an employee's home. The servant leader would likely grant the employee time off with pay to manage the problem, and also direct the employee toward any company resources available for emergency help.

7. ***Act as a role model for other organizational members to emphasize service.*** As a result of the behaviors just described, servant leaders often ignite a cycle of service by acting as a role model servant behavior. A study conducted in a large retail chain found that the leader's servant behavior is mirrored through modeling the helping behavior of coworkers and high-quality customer service.[35]

A later study conducted in seventy-one restaurants of a restaurant chain found similar results. It was found that leaders created a serving culture in which the restaurant workers placed the needs of others before their own. The serving culture was positively related to the performance of the restaurants, as well as to individual job performance. Restaurant performance was measured by a composite of factors including carryout accuracy and customer satisfaction. Employee job performance was rated by managers, and included creativity and customer service behaviors.[36]

8. ***Focus on employee growth that leads to need satisfaction.*** A study in a Quebec, Canada, company that makes high-technology products helps explain why servant leadership might lead to improved job performance and being a good organizational citizen. (A good organizational citizen goes beyond the job description to help others without the promise of a reward.) It was found that the servant leader's focus on employee's development help them satisfy the psychological needs for autonomy (working independently), competence, and relatedness (relating to other people). The satisfaction of these three needs fuels employees to perform better and be good organizational citizens.[37]

Research evidence suggests that servant leadership at the top of the organization has a positive impact on the performance of a firm. The study involved 126 CEOs in the United States from the software and hardware technology industries. Servant leadership was measured by a self-report questionnaire, and firm performance was measured by return on assets (annual income divided by net assets). Analysis of data revealed that CEO servant leadership tendencies were significantly related to firm performance. Another part of the study suggested that CEOs who were company founders were more likely to be servant leaders,[38] reinforcing the idea that founders are often passionate about their company and its employees.

Leadership Skill-Building Exercise 4-4 gives you an opportunity to try your hand at servant leadership.

## Entrepreneurial Leadership

Many entrepreneurs use a similar leadership style that stems from their personality characteristics and circumstances. Although there are different types and definitions of entrepreneurs; in general, an entrepreneur is a person who founds and operates an innovative business. Not all business owners, including franchise operators, are therefore entrepreneurial leaders. The general picture that emerges of an entrepreneur is a task-oriented and charismatic person. Entrepreneurs drive themselves and others relentlessly, yet their personalities also inspire others.

# LEADERSHIP SKILL-BUILDING EXERCISE 4-3

### The servant leader

Several students play the role of a group of financial analysts working at a large investment bank. Among the group's responsibilities are to seek new real estate investments for the bank, with an emphasis on large office buildings and apartment buildings. The group is aware that top management is looking for superior returns to make up for big losses from investments in the energy sector. The members of the group are excited about their professional challenge, yet they are apprehensive about attaining the returns top-level management expects. Another student plays the role of their supervisor who wants to function as a servant leader to get the group started on its mission and to provide guidance as the work continues. The group members will be quite candid in expressing their concerns, and the servant leader will be quite explicit about his or her role.

The entrepreneurial leadership style often incorporates the behaviors described in the following paragraphs. Although some authorities disagree about whether an entrepreneurial personality exists, evidence is accumulating that many entrepreneurs share a recognizable personality pattern.[39] Leadership Self-Assessment Quiz 4-3 gives you the opportunity to think about the type of entrepreneurial thinking and behavior typical of the entrepreneurial personality.

## LEADERSHIP SELF-ASSESSMENT QUIZ 4-3

### Entrepreneurial Thinking and Behavior

**Instructions:** Indicate how well each of the following statements reflects your attitudes or behavior, using this scale: very inaccurately (VI), inaccurately (I), moderately well (MW), accurately (A), very accurately (VA).

| | | VI | I | MW | A | VA |
|---|---|---|---|---|---|---|
| 1. | I have actually started a business of my own. | 1 | 2 | 3 | 4 | 5 |
| 2. | The thought of starting my own business appeals to me. | 1 | 2 | 3 | 4 | 5 |
| 3. | So many new products are being introduced practically every week that it seems senseless to bother dreaming up an idea for another new product. | 5 | 4 | 3 | 2 | 1 |
| 4. | In enjoy the challenge of meeting new people and explaining what I do. | 1 | 2 | 3 | 4 | 5 |
| 5. | I get excited about thinking of a new idea for a product or service. | 1 | 2 | 3 | 4 | 5 |
| 6. | My career advice to young people is to pursue a well-established occupation with a high demand for newcomers to the field. | 5 | 4 | 3 | 2 | 1 |
| 7. | Betting money on sports is exciting and fun. | 1 | 2 | 3 | 4 | 5 |
| 8. | Taking care of administrative details is boring for me. | 1 | 2 | 3 | 4 | 5 |
| 9. | I am (or would be) comfortable working outside of regular working hours. | 1 | 2 | 3 | 4 | 5 |
| 10. | The best job for me would be one that offers a stable salary, regular working hours and vacations, and a guaranteed pension. | 5 | 4 | 3 | 2 | 1 |
| 11. | Self-employment fits (or would fit) my personality. | 1 | 2 | 3 | 4 | 5 |
| 12. | What a horrible life it would be for me to get paid strictly on commission. | 5 | 4 | 3 | 2 | 1 |
| 13. | I enjoy the challenge of selling my ideas and myself to people I have not met before. | 1 | 2 | 3 | 4 | 5 |
| 14. | I need at least eight hours of sleep and regular rest breaks during the day to perform well. | 5 | 4 | 3 | 2 | 1 |
| 15. | If I personally knew a family that had been a disaster victim, I would be willing to attempt to raise money for that family. | 1 | 2 | 3 | 4 | 5 |
| 16. | I enjoy purchasing lunch from a street vendor when the opportunity arises. | 1 | 2 | 3 | 4 | 5 |
| 17. | If you are not a scientist or an engineer, it is useless to try to invent something that is intended for the marketplace. | 5 | 4 | 3 | 2 | 1 |
| 18. | Most people who become rich and famous got there by luck. | 5 | 4 | 3 | 2 | 1 |
| 19. | I would enjoy the experience of working on developing new products in a company department located away from where most employees worked. | 1 | 2 | 3 | 4 | 5 |
| 20. | If I were self-employed or worked from home for an employer, I would probably start my workday at about 10 A.M. | 5 | 4 | 3 | 2 | 1 |
| | **Total Score:** _____ | | | | | |

*(Continued)*

## LEADERSHIP SELF-ASSESSMENT QUIZ 4-3 *(Continued)*

**Scoring and Interpretation:** Add the numbers that you have circled.

- **85–100:** The results suggest that you have many of the tendencies of an entrepreneurial personality. You probably enjoy risk taking and change, and would be willing to take the risk of earning your income through self-employment.

- **50–84:** You most likely have average tendencies toward being an entrepreneurial personality. You probably would not enjoy a career filled with risk and uncertainty.

- **20–49:** Your personality makeup most likely does not resemble that of an entrepreneurial personality. You might place a high value on stability and security. A regular paycheck is probably quite important to you.

1. ***Strong achievement drive and sensible risk taking.*** Entrepreneurs have stronger achievement motives than most leaders. Building a business is an excellent vehicle for accomplishment and risk taking. To accomplish what they think needs to be accomplished, entrepreneurs are willing to work extraordinary hours, with twelve-hour days, seven days a week not being unusual. Because entrepreneurs take sensible risks, many do not perceive themselves as being risk takers—just as many tightrope walkers believe they are not taking risks because they perceive themselves to be in control.

2. ***High degree of enthusiasm and passion.*** Entrepreneurs are highly enthusiastic, partially because they are so excited about their achievements. As *Entrepreneur* magazine puts it, "Something about being an entrepreneur is, for them, a five-star, butt-kicking, rocket-boosting blast." Entrepreneurs' enthusiasm, in turn, makes them persuasive. As a result, they are often perceived as charismatic. Some entrepreneurs are so emotional that they are regarded as eccentric. Jack Ma, the founder of the enormous e-commerce website, Alibaba, displayed enthusiasm for his enterprise in its early days that reflected enormous self-confidence. When he attempted to sell the vision of his Internet marketplace in China, he took to quoting Bill Gates: "The Internet will change every aspect of human beings' lives." He also said he wanted his venture to become number one in the world.[40]

   The enthusiasm of entrepreneurs often develops into passion. A theoretical analysis of entrepreneurial passion suggests that it is invested in three roles. First is the inventor role of recognizing an opportunity such as seeing the need for a product or service. Second is the founder role of creating the venture, with all its associated managerial and leadership responsibilities. Third is the developer role of growing the venture, such as expanding into the global market.[41]

   A potential downside to entrepreneurial passion is that it can prompt an entrepreneur to pursue an idea for a business or product that was never, or is no longer, worth pursuing. Harvard Business School professor Noam Wasserman has studied 10,000 business founders, and has noted a consistent theme of passion. Yet some of these founders believe in their ideas so strongly that they quit comfortable jobs and risk their life savings to pursue their dreams. One problem is that being too passionate about an idea can lead to overlooking that fact that the market for the idea is very limited or does not exist. The passionate entrepreneur might fail to run careful tests to accurately assess consumer demand.[42]

3. ***Typical pattern of being proactive.*** Leon C. Prieto argues that the proactive personality has potential for providing additional insight into how personality traits are related to entrepreneurship. The natural link is that entrepreneurship is inherently proactive—to be an entrepreneur one has to scan the environment to find an opportunity, and then capitalize on the opportunity. Individuals with a proactive personality may be more inclined to mobilize resources and gain the commitment required for value creation that the entrepreneur requires.[43]

Proactive personality types may have a strong desire to become entrepreneurial leaders to create value for the firm. An assistant manager at a large restaurant, for example, might explore the possibilities of establishing a team-building component based on the preparation of gourmet meals. The program would be sold to organizations, as has been done successfully by a handful of elite restaurants.

4. ***Tendency to act quickly when opportunity arises.*** Entrepreneurs are noted for seizing upon opportunity, as part of their proactivity. When a deal is on the horizon, they push themselves and those around them extra hard. Entrepreneurs are always in a hurry. While engaged in one meeting, their minds typically begin to focus on the next meeting. Their flurry of activity rubs off on group members and those around them. Entrepreneurs often adopt a simple dress style in order to save time, and they typically allow little slack time between appointments

5. ***Visionary perspective combined with tenacity.*** Entrepreneurs, at their best, are visionaries. As with other types of effective leaders, they see opportunities others fail to observe. Specifically, they have the ability to identify a problem and arrive at a solution. Ted Turner of CNN is a legendary example of an entrepreneurial visionary. Turner picked up on a trend that people wanted—an all-news cable channel that they could access anytime. Not only is CNN a commercial success, but it also revolutionized the way people get their news all over the globe. After the vision is established, the entrepreneur tenaciously implements the vision, working an eighty-hour week if need be.

    For many entrepreneurs, just growing their businesses requires tenacity. A relevant example is none other than Mark Zuckerberg, the founder of Facebook, who in his early twenties became one of the best-known entrepreneurs of all time. During the Great Recession, he sank money and time into developing Facebook and grew its engineering ranks by 50 percent.[44]

6. ***Dislike of hierarchy and bureaucracy.*** Entrepreneurs are not ideally suited by temperament to working within the mainstream of a bureaucracy. Many successful entrepreneurs are people who were frustrated by the constraints of a bureaucratic system. The implication for leadership style is that entrepreneurs deemphasize rules and regulations when managing people.

7. ***Preference for dealing with external customers.*** One reason that entrepreneurs have difficulty with bureaucracy is that they focus their energies on products, services, and customers, rather than on employees. Some entrepreneurs are gracious to customers and moneylenders but brusque with company insiders. A blind spot many entrepreneurs have is that they cannot understand why their employees do not share their passion for work and customer focus. As a result, they may be curt with employees who do not share their dedication to the firm.

8. ***Eye on the future.*** Entrepreneurs have the pronounced characteristic of thinking about future deals and business opportunities even before a current business is running smoothly. "Where is my next deal coming from?" is the mantra of the true entrepreneur. Even after accumulating great wealth from a current business activity, the entrepreneurial leader looks toward future opportunities. A good example is Richard Branson, whose empire contains about 400 companies with the Virgin label, yet he continues to look for the next company to start or acquire.

One reason many entrepreneurs focus on the future is that their enthusiasm and passion for their present product or service may fade over time. A recommended way to avoid the fading enthusiasm is to change and refine ideas rather than sticking to the same plan. As the entrepreneur learns more about his or her product, customers, and the market, the original idea might evolve.[45] Imagine an entrepreneur who establishes a company that provides IT services to small- and medium-size companies, a service that includes technicians making repairs at customer sites. For the entrepreneur to remain passionate, he or she might have to shift to offering cloud services.

A caution, however, is that the entrepreneurial personality carried to an extreme can lead to addictive behavior, including substance abuse.[46] A representative example of this problem would be the entrepreneur who stays at work regularly up until midnight searching the Internet for new customers and product ideas. Such behavior can lead to a dependence on caffeine and nonprescription drugs to sustain energy.

To practice one aspect of entrepreneurial leadership, do Leadership Skill-Building Exercise 4-5.

## Gender Differences in Leadership Style

Several researchers and observers argue that women have certain acquired traits and behaviors that suit them for relations-oriented leadership. Consequently, women leaders frequently exhibit a cooperative, empowering style that includes nurturing team members. According to this same perspective, men are inclined toward a command-and-control, task-oriented leadership style. Women find participative management more natural than do men because they appear to feel more comfortable interacting with people. Furthermore, it is argued that women's natural sensitivity to people gives them an edge over men in encouraging group members to participate in decision making. Here, we look briefly at some of the evidence and reasoning whether gender differences exist in leadership style.

*The Argument for Male–Female Differences in Leadership Style*  The pioneering work of Judy Rosener concluded that men and women do tend toward opposite styles. Based on self-reports, she found that men tended toward a command-and-control style. In contrast, women tended toward a transformational style, relying heavily on interpersonal skills.[47] Recent research suggests that hormonal differences may account for many of these gender differences in leadership style.

Based on years of laboratory and field research, Paul J. Zak of the Claremont Graduate University has explored the role of oxytocin in interpersonal relationships. His findings suggest that women tend to release more oxytocin than men. As a result, women are more likely to display empathy, cooperation, and trust when working with subordinates and other work associates. Women would therefore gravitate more naturally to participative leadership than do men. Another important finding is that positive social interactions stimulate the release of more oxytocin, thereby making trusting relationships more likely. Given participative leadership often results in positive relationships, this style of leadership leads to more hormonally induced trust.[48]

As corporate leaders, women tend to place greater emphasis on forming caring, nurturing relationships with employees. Women are also more likely than men to praise group members. And when an employee falls short of expectations, women are more likely to buffer criticism by finding something praiseworthy.

# LEADERSHIP SKILL-BUILDING EXERCISE 4-5

## Entrepreneurial Leadership

An important part of the entrepreneurial role is convincing others of the merit of your idea so that they will invest in your company or lend you money. Two students play the role of a team of entrepreneurs who have a new product or service and want to launch a business. (The two entrepreneurs choose the product or service.) About five other students play the role of a group of venture capitalists or bankers listening to the presentation to decide whether to invest or lend money. The entrepreneurs will communicate excitement and commitment about their product, along with a good business plan. (You might want to quickly review the material about persuasive communication in Chapter 12.) The students who are not participating will evaluate how well the two entrepreneurs displayed aspects of the entrepreneurial leadership style.

Gender differences in communication also are reflected in leadership style. Above all, women are more likely than men to use spoken communication for building relationships and giving emotional support.[49] Men focus more on disseminating information and demonstrating competence. Women are therefore more likely to choose a relationship-oriented leadership style.

An experiment was conducted with working adults by administering questionnaires about how men and women exhibit certain aspects of transformational leadership, and which aspects they should emphasize to get promoted. Conforming to stereotypes about gender differences, it was found that women display more transformational behavior and give rewards more based on merit. It was also believed that women engage in fewer management-by-exception (only intervening when a problem exists) and laissez-faire behaviors than do men. In terms of getting promoted, inspirational motivation was perceived as of higher importance for men than women, especially to be promoted to CEO. In contrast, individualized consideration (responding to the needs of individuals) was perceived as more important for women than men, and especially important for promotion to CEO.[50]

*Placing Gender Differences in Leadership Style in Perspective*    To what extent the stereotypes of men and women leaders are true is difficult to judge. Even if male and female differences in leadership style do exist, they must be placed in proper perspective. Both men and women leaders differ among themselves in leadership style. Plenty of male leaders are relationship oriented, and plenty of women are highly task oriented. Many women believe that women managers can be more hostile and vindictive than men managers.

Perhaps the best approach to leadership takes advantage of the positive traits of both men and women. To compete in the global marketplace, companies need a diverse leadership team including men and women. Not recognizing that both male and female styles are needed can lead to confusion for women managers.

Even if gender differences in leadership style do exist, a review of the scientific evidence indicates that they do not have a meaningful impact on leadership effectiveness. A group of researchers attempted to shed light on the debate about when men or women are perceived to be more effective in leadership positions. The research combined the results of ninety-nine independent samples from ninety-three studies, in a wide variety of situations. The results showed that when all leadership contexts are considered, men and women do not differ in perceived leadership effectiveness. Yet when rated by others, women tended to be perceived as more effective than men in leadership roles. In contrast, according to self-ratings, men rate themselves significantly more effective than women rate themselves.[51]

## 360-Degree Feedback for Fine-Tuning a Leadership Approach

In most large organizations, leaders not only provide feedback to group members but also receive feedback that gives them insight into the effects of their attitudes and behaviors. This feedback is systematically derived from a full sampling of parties who interact with the leader. In particular, **360-degree feedback** is a formal evaluation of superiors based on input from people who work for and with them, sometimes including customers and suppliers. It is also referred to as multirater feedback. The multiple inputs become another way of measuring leadership effectiveness. The specific 360-degree form is often customized to a particular firm's needs, but standardized forms are widely used.

Specialists in the field, view 360-degree feedback as more suited for its original purpose of development for a manager or leader than for administrative purposes, such as performance evaluation and salary administration. When used for development, 360-degree feedback should emphasize qualitative comments rather than strictly quantitative ratings.[52]

For example, being told, "You do not maintain eye contact with me during meetings," is more helpful than simply receiving a low rating on "Makes others feel comfortable." The feedback is communicated to the leader and interpreted with assistance from a HR professional or an external consultant.

The data from the survey can be used to help leaders fine-tune their attitudes and behavior. For example, if all the interested parties gave the leader low ratings on "empathy toward others," the leader might be prompted to improve his or her ability to empathize, such as by reading about empathy, attending a seminar, or simply making a conscious attempt to empathize when involved in a conflict of opinion with another person. Recent research with pairs of leaders and their subordinates (dyads) indicates that leaders are more likely to trust and respect those feedback reports that were given by raters who know well the person they are rating.[53]

An example of a 360-degree feedback form is shown in Figure 4-2. When used for purposes of development, the leader will often provide a self-rating on each dimension and then compare self-ratings with those of subordinates as well as other work associates. Statement 10, "Has constructive interpersonal relationships" is particularly significant because it reflects a *derailment factor*. A leader who does not have constructive interpersonal relationships is likely to derail his or her career.[54]

When there is a large gap between self-ratings and ratings by others, professionally trained counselors or business coaches should be involved in 360-degree feedback. Some people feel emotionally crushed when they find a wide discrepancy between their self-perception on an interpersonal skill dimension and the perception of others. A middle manager involved in a 360-degree evaluation prided herself on how well she was liked by others. The feedback that emerged, however, depicted her as intimidating, hostile, and manipulative. Upon receiving the feedback, the woman went into a rage (proving the feedback true!) and then into despondency. Professional counseling can sometimes help a person benefit from critical feedback and place it in perspective.

For best results, it is extremely important that 360-degree surveys reflect those behaviors and attitudes that the organization values most highly. Care should also be taken that

| Leadership Behavior or Attitude | Ratings (1 to 10) |
|---|---|
| 1. Provides guidance and direction to the group related to the work we are performing. | |
| 2. Creates an exciting vision. | |
| 3. Gives useful feedback to group members. | |
| 4. Sets high performance standards. | |
| 5. Motivates the group to perform well, including getting us engaged in the work | |
| 6. Coaches team members as needed. | |
| 7. Provides emotional support and encouragement to group members. | |
| 8. Gets people working together as a team. | |
| 9. Thinks strategically in terms of the future of our group. | |
| 10. Has constructive interpersonal relationships. | |

**FIGURE 4-2** A 360-Degree Feedback Chart.

the dimensions measured reflect important aspects of leadership functioning. Following are some suggestions for making better use of 360-degree surveys.[55]

- The person receiving the multiple feedback should have some say about who the raters will be. The supervisor of the person receiving the survey is also invited to suggest who should provide the feedback.
- Customize the assessment dimensions based on the leadership competencies that are associated with success in your organization.
- Train workers in giving and receiving feedback. Giving constructive feedback takes coaching, training, and practice. It is helpful to inform the workers who provide the feedback that feedback should be constructive, not punitive.
- Create an action plan for improvement for each leader based on the feedback. For example, a leader rated low on interpersonal skills might benefit from training in emotional intelligence. When a serious leadership problem exists, the regular sessions might be scheduled with an industrial psychologist or executive coach.
- Ensure that the managers rated have full ownership of the feedback information so that they will perceive the feedback as being geared toward personal development rather than administrative control.

A potential problem with 360-degree feedback is its anonymity. Much like people who post nasty comments about people on social media websites, an angry subordinate can write an insulting and crushing comment about a manager on the 360-degree feedback form. The criticism might be without merit.

## Selecting the Best Leadership Style

An underlying theme of our discussion of leadership styles in this and the next chapter is that there is no one best or most effective leadership style. A study of 3,000 executives revealed that leaders who get the best results do not rely on one style. Instead, they use several different styles in one week, such as being autocratic in some situations and democratic in others.[56] Another consideration is the national culture in which the leadership takes place. An effective leadership style for most German workers would be a high performance (task) orientation and a modest amount of compassion (consideration).[57] Scandinavian workers, however, respond best to a democratic leadership style.

The organizational culture also influences which leadership style will be tolerated and effective. A friendly, collaborative culture calls for more of a consensus style of leadership. In contrast, in a perform-or-perish culture, a more directive or autocratic leadership style will be effective.

At several places in this book, we mention the leader–member exchange (LMX) theory. A key point of the theory is that the leader establishes different quality relationships with each group member.[58] Part of establishing a high-quality relationship would be for the leader to vary his or her style to meet the needs of each subordinate. For example, Randy might need more guidance, and Suzanne might want to work more independently.

Close to forty-five years ago, pioneering researcher Ralph Stogdill made a statement about selecting a leadership style that still holds today: "The most effective leaders appear to exhibit a degree of versatility and flexibility that enables them to adapt their behavior to the changing and contradictory demands made on them."[59] A more recent suggestion urges leaders to follow a similar path of changing with the times, and customize a culture that is specific to each company, and the personality of its work force.[60]

Before moving on to the end-of-chapter activities, do Leadership Skill-Building Exercise 4-5 that deals with flexibility and adaptability.

## LEADERSHIP SKILL-BUILDING EXERCISE 4-6

### Contrasting Leadership Styles

One student plays the role of a new associate working for a financial services firm that sells life insurance and other investments. The associate has completed a six-week training program and is now working full time. Four weeks have passed, and the associate still has not made a sale. The associate's boss is going to meet this associate today to discuss progress. Another student plays the role of a task-oriented leader. The two people participate in the review session.

Before playing (or assuming) the role of the associate or the boss, think for a few minutes how you would behave if you were placed in that role in real life. Empathize with the frustrated associate or the task-oriented leader. A good role player is both a scriptwriter and an actor.

Another two students repeat the same scenario, except that this time the manager is a strong relationship-oriented leader. Two more pairs of students then have their turn at acting out the task-oriented and relationship-oriented performance reviews. Another variation of this role play is for one person to play the roles of both the task-oriented and the relationship-oriented boss. Other class members observe and provide feedback on the effectiveness of the two styles of leadership.

## READER'S ROADMAP

So far in this book, we have examined the nature of leadership and the inner qualities of leaders, along with their behaviors, attitudes, and styles. In the next chapter, we describe some of the specific approaches to adapting one's leadership approach to the situation.

## SUMMARY

Effective leadership requires the right behaviors, skills, and attitudes, as emphasized in the classic Ohio State University studies. Two major dimensions of leadership behavior were identified: consideration and initiating structure. Consideration is the degree to which the leader creates an environment of emotional support, warmth, friendliness, and trust. Making connections with people is a current aspect of consideration. Initiating structure is the degree to which the leader organizes and defines relationships in the group by such activities as assigning tasks and specifying procedures. Both consideration and initiating structure are related to important leadership outcomes such as job satisfaction and performance.

Many task-related attitudes and behaviors of effective leaders have been identified. Among them are (1) adaptability to the situation, (2) direction setting, (3) high performance standards, (4) concentrating on strengths of group members, (5) risk taking and execution of plans, (6) hands-on guidance and feedback, (7) ability to ask tough questions, and (8) organizing for collaboration. Many relationship-oriented attitudes and behaviors of leaders have also been identified.

Among them are (1) aligning people, (2) openness to workers' opinions, (3) creating inspiration and visibility, (4) satisfying higher-level needs, (5) giving emotional support and encouragement, (6) promoting principles and values, and (7) reducing task ambiguity.

Understanding leadership style is an extension of understanding leadership attitudes and behavior. Participative leaders share decision making with group members. The participative style can be subdivided into consultative, consensus, and democratic leadership. The participative style is well suited to managing competent people who are eager to assume responsibility. Yet the process can be time consuming, and some managers perceive it to be a threat to their power. Autocratic leaders retain most of the authority for themselves.

Servant leaders are committed to serving others rather than achieving their own goals. Aspects of servant leadership include placing service before self-interest, listening to others, inspiring trust by being trustworthy, focusing on what is feasible to accomplish, lending a hand, emotional healing, and acting as a role model to emphasize service.

Another important style of leader is the entrepreneur. The entrepreneurial style stems from the leader's personal characteristics and the circumstances of self-employment. It includes a strong achievement drive and sensible risk taking; a high degree of enthusiasm (including passion) and creativity; a typical pattern of being proactive; the tendency to act quickly on opportunities; hurriedness and impatience; a visionary perspective; a dislike of hierarchy and bureaucracy; a preference for dealing with external customers; and an eye on the future.

Male–female differences in leadership style have been observed. Women have a tendency toward relationship-oriented leadership, whereas men tend toward command and control. Perhaps the best approach to leadership takes advantage of the positive traits of both men and women. Even if gender differences in leadership style do exist, a review of the scientific evidence indicates that they do not have a meaningful impact on leadership effectiveness.

Many leaders receive extensive feedback on their behaviors and attitudes in the form of 360-degree feedback, whereby people who work for or with the leader provide feedback on the leader's performance. Such feedback is likely to be useful when the feedback relates to business goals and strategy and to important aspects of leadership, when training is provided in giving and receiving feedback, when action plans are developed, and when managers own the feedback evaluation. The anonymous comments in 360-degree feedback can be a problem.

Rather than searching for the one best style of leadership, managers are advised to diagnose the situation and then choose an appropriate leadership style to match. To be effective, a leader must be able to adapt style to circumstance.

## KEY TERMS

effective leader  87
consideration  87
initiating structure  88
Pygmalion effect  90
tough question  91

management openness  94
leadership style  97
participative leaders  98
consultative leaders  98
consensus leaders  98

democratic leaders  98
autocratic leaders  99
servant leader  101
360-degree feedback  107

## GUIDELINES FOR ACTIONS AND SKILL DEVELOPMENT

A major consideration about choosing a leadership style is that you may have to modify your style to fit the occasion. For example, your group members may need close direction at one point, and at other times, they may require less direction (as explained in several of the leadership theories presented in this chapter).

Most leadership-style classifications are based on the directive (task-oriented) dimension versus the nondirective (relationship-oriented) dimension. In deciding which of these two styles is best, consider the following questions:

1. **What is the structure of your organization and the nature of your work?** You might decide, for example, that stricter control is necessary for some types of work, such as dealing with proprietary information.
2. **Which style suits you best?** Your personality, values, and beliefs influence how readily you can turn over responsibility to others.
3. **Which style suits your boss and the organization culture?** For example, a boss who is highly directive may perceive you as weak if you are too nondirective. In a tough-minded, perform-or-perish culture, you might want to use a highly directive leadership style.

It is probably better for you to lead in the style you consider to be the most effective rather than be concerned with a gender stereotype dictating the style you should be using. For example, many male leaders are the most effective when being conciliatory and supportive. And many female leaders prefer to be more task-oriented in their leadership and are less concerned with building cordial relationships and being supportive.

### Discussion Questions and Activities

1. Give an example of a high-consideration behavior that a supervisor of yours showed on your behalf. What was your reaction to his or her behavior?
2. Why is direction setting still an important leadership behavior in an era of empowerment and shared leadership?

3. How might both task-oriented and relationship-oriented leadership styles contribute to the bottom line (a company being profitable)?
4. Why do so many CEOs say they want entrepreneurial style leaders in their company even though the company is essentially a large bureaucracy?
5. Why would being a highly narcissistic person interfere with being an effective servant leader?
6. Why might it be helpful to have a mentor or coach who is a hands-on leader?
7. How would you characterize the leadership style of your favorite executive, athletic coach, or television character who plays a boss?
8. Why is shared or participative leadership likely to be effective with well-educated and intelligent team members?
9. Which, if any, style differences have you noticed between men and women leaders?
10. Several people have commented that this chapter deals with the "nuts and bolts of leadership." What makes them say that?

## LEADERSHIP CASE PROBLEM A

### Lola Asks Tough Questions

Lola majored in business administration with a concentration in marketing, and she is delighted with her career progress. She joined the frozen-food division of a large company ten years ago as a product specialist for frozen Indian food. Lola says with a smile, "I was torn between Asian studies and marketing. My first job was therefore a perfect fit for my interests."

Lola now holds the position of general manager of frozen foods, with a team of 6 people directly reporting to her, and 350 total employees. Lola has learned that a leader does not have all the answers, so he or she should ask lots of questions. She also believes that the right questions will get people thinking.

During a recent meeting with her sales manager, Marvin, Lola asked her, "What's to prevent consumers from serving mostly inexpensive fresh food instead of purchasing our expensive products?" Marvin responded, "Let me think about that one. It never occurred to me that our industry was in jeopardy."

The next day Lola sent a text message to Quinn, a new product development specialist, that asked, "How have you justified your pay this month?" Quinn sent a message back, "I've been working forty-five hours a week. Isn't that enough?"

The following day, Lola dropped by the cubicle of Brooklyn, the department administrative assistant,

and asked her, "How can I improve my communication with you?" Brooklyn responded, "I thought that our communication was pretty good."

While having lunch with Geoff, the director of human resources, Lola asked, "Can you please explain to me how your group is increasing our revenue, improving our products or saving us money?" Geoff replied, "With all due respect Lola, you need more information about what HR does for an organization."

The following week during a staff meeting, Lola asked her team, "What should I be doing to help make our group the best frozen-food division in the industry?" Margot, the director of supply chain management, responded: "I'm going to need time to think about this one."

### Questions

1. How effective does Lola appear to be in her approach of asking tough questions as a leadership technique?
2. What suggestion can you offer Lola to make her questioning technique more effective?
3. Which style of leadership does Lola appear to be demonstrating when she asks her team, "What should I be doing to help make our division the best pet-food division in the industry?"

## ASSOCIATED ROLE PLAY

In this group role play, one student plays the role of Lola who wants to ask tough questions of her team. Four other students play the roles of Marvin, Brooklyn, Quinn, and Geoff, each of whom receives the "tough question" asked by Lola in the case just presented. The team members who receive the questions will answer

in the manner that seems best without entering into strong conflict with Lola. Other class members will provide feedback on both the effectiveness of Lola's questioning, and the effectiveness of the response of the team members.

## LEADERSHIP CASE PROBLEM B

### Tricia and Her Facebook Friends and Twitter Followers

Tricia is the human resources team leader in the regional headquarters of an international bank. She has five direct reports plus considerable individual responsibility for carrying out various human resource initiatives. About six months ago, Tricia started thinking about how she could improve her leadership effectiveness with her team of human resource professionals, plus one support person. As she reflected on feedback she had received from their boss, the VP of administration, Tricia thought that perhaps she was a little too business-like and task oriented. The insight came to her that perhaps she should become Facebook friends, and have Twitter exchanges with her staff of five.

Tricia's first step was to invite each staff member to become a Facebook friend and also follow each group member on Twitter. Tricia began her social media initiative by writing about strictly work-related topics, with posts such as the following:

"I feel good about the response we are getting to our proposed wellness program."

"Did you catch how the regional VP of administration said in her monthly intranet post that our team was doing a great job?"

"Our new group interview program seems to be working. Most of our new hires are turning in above-average performance, and turnover among them is below average."

After a couple of months of these business-like posts on Facebook and Twitter, Tricia did not observe that she and the group were developing a better personal relationship. Consequently, she decided to send posts that were more personal, including the following:

- "How about you and I spending a little quality time at the shopping mall this weekend?"
- "My two-year-old nephew is having a birthday party October 10 at noon. You are warmly invited. Let me know ASAP."
- "I thought that taupe and beige combination you wore to the office today was stunning. The way you dress picks up morale."
- "My boyfriend was angry with me last night because he said I don't like his parents."
- "Don't let the fact that I'm the team leader interfere with us being friends."

Tricia did receive a few positive responses from her posts, but a few responses to her posts suggested the team members were not comfortable receiving the personal messages. One tweet response was simply "????."

### Questions

1. What would you advise Tricia to do about future posts of a personal nature to the team?
2. Which one or two relationship-oriented behaviors does Tricia appear to be exaggerating?
3. If your team leader sent you a post about his or her team leadership role and your potential friendship, how would you respond?

## ASSOCIATED ROLE PLAY

One student plays the role of Tricia who happens to meet Ken, the benefits specialist, in the company cafeteria. Another student plays the role of Ken who wants to preserve a good working relationship with Tricia, but he thinks her social media posts to him have become unprofessional. Class members who provide feedback will be particularly observant of (1) how receptive Tricia is to the feedback from Ken, and (2) how diplomatic Ken is in expressing his concerns

## LEADERSHIP SKILL-BUILDING EXERCISE 4-7

**My Leadership Portfolio**

For this addition to your leadership portfolio, identify four leadership task-oriented behaviors or relationship-oriented behaviors that you have demonstrated this week. Your list can comprise any combination of the two sets of behaviors. Also jot down the result you achieved by exercising these behaviors. Here is an example:

"Thursday night, I applied direction setting and it really worked. We have a group assignment in our marketing class with each group consisting of about five people. Our assignment is to analyze how well employee self-service is

working in supermarkets and home-improvement stores. The group was hitting a wall because in their Internet searches, they were finding mostly advertisements for Home Depot and the like. I suggested that we each visit a supermarket or home-improvement store and make firsthand observations of the customers who were using the automated checkout system. I also suggested we ask a couple of questions of the store associate supervising the activity. The group loved my idea, and the project was a big success. We supplemented written articles with a firsthand field study. I set the group in the right direction."

## NOTES

1. Original story created from facts and observations in the following sources: Sarah Frier, "Facebook's Chris Cox is Messing with One of the Most Valuable Features on the Internet," *Bloombergbusinessweek*, February 1–February 7, 2016, pp. 44–49; Jessica Guynn, "Facebook's Chris Cox: A Very Likeable Pitchman," *Los Angeles Times* (http://articles.latimes.com), May 12, 2012, pp. 1–3; Josh Constine, "Facebook Promotes VP Of Product Chris Cox to Chief Product Officer, But No Organizational Change," *TC* (https://techcrunch.com), May 2, 2014, pp. 1–7.

2. Ralph M. Stogdill and Alvin E. Coons, eds., *Leader Behavior: Its Description and Measurement* (Columbus, Ohio: The Ohio State University Bureau of Business Research, 1957); Carroll L. Shartle, *Executive Performance and Leadership* (Upper Saddle River, N.J.: Prentice Hall, 1956).

3. Scott Cacciola, Matthew Futterman, and Ashley Jones, "The NBA's Calmer, Cooler New Boss," *The Wall Street Journal*, October 26, 2012, p. D10.

4. Christopher Alessi, "Pressure Is Mounting on Siemen's Chief," *The World Street Journal*, January 25, 2016, p. B3.

5. Robert R. Blake and Anne Adams McCanse, *Leadership Dilemmas—Grid Solutions* (Houston, Tex: Gulf Publishing, 1991), http://www.gridinternational.com/gridtheory.html, 2007.

6. Timothy A. Judge, Ronald F. Piccolo, and Remus Ilies, "The Forgotten Ones? The Validity of Consideration and Initiating Structure in Leadership Research," *Journal of Applied Psychology*, February 2004, pp. 36–51.

7. Lisa Schurer Lambert, Bennett J. Tepper, Jon C. Carr, Daniel T. Holt, and Alex J. Barelka, "Forgotten but Not Gone: An Examination of Fit Between

Leader Consideration and Initiating Structure Needed and Received," *Journal of Applied Psychology*, September 2012, pp. 913–930.

8. D. Scott Derue, Jennifer D. Nahrgang, Ned Welman, and Stephen E. Humphrey, "Trait and Behavior Theories of Leadership: An Integration and Meta-Analytic Test of Their Relative Validity," *Personnel Psychology*, no. 1, 2011, pp. 7–52.

9. Marcus Buckingham, "What Great Managers Do," *Harvard Business Review*, March 2005, pp. 70–79.

10. Quoted in Sonja D. Mack, "Sarah Mensah: Chief Operating Officer & Chief Marketing Officer, Portland Trail Blazers," *Black Enterprise*, February 2011, p. 106.

11. Desa Philadelphia, "Q&A: Larry Bossidy on Execution," *Time Global Business*, July 2002, p. B5.

12. Henry Mintzberg, *Managing* (San Francisco: Berrett-Koehler, 2009), p. 88.

13. Mitch Betts, "How Job: Corporate Anthropologist to Boost Collaboration," *Computerworld* (www.computerworld.com), October 25, 2010.

14. John P. Kotter, "What Leaders Really Do," *Harvard Business Review*, May–June 1990, pp. 105–106.

15. James R. Detert and Ethan R. Burris, "Leadership Behavior and Employee Voice: Is the Door Really Open?" *Academy of Management Journal*, August 2007, p. 871.

16. Arielle Kass, "Going to School with Home Depot's CEO," *The Atlanta Journal Constitution* (www.ajc.com), July 29, 2012, p. 1.

17. Quoted in Jefferson Graham and Jon Swartz, "After 5 Years of Cook, More Cash, Less Splash," *USA Today*, August 24, 2015, p. 4B.

18. Geoffrey Colvin, "How One CEO Learned to Fly," *Fortune*, October 30, 2006, p. 98.

19. Tessa E. Basford and Andrea Molberg, "Dale Carnegie's Leadership Principles: Examining the Theoretical and Empirical Support," *Journal of Leadership Studies*, no. 4, 2013, pp. 37–38.

20. Cited in interview by Arianne Cohen, "What I Wear to Work: Sonja Lyubomirsky," *Bloomberg Businessweek*, January 12–January 18, 2015, p. 71.

21. "Covey Proposes Principle-Based Leadership," *Management Review*, September 1995, p. 21.

22. Stacy Perlman, "The Secret Sauce at In-N-Out Burger," (Book Excerpt), *Business Week*, April 20, 2009, pp. 68–69; "In-N-Out Burgers Inc.," *Encyclopedia of Business*, Second Edition. *https://en.wikipedia.org*. Accessed November 23, 2013.

23. Mathias Diebig, Kai C. Bormann, and Jens Rowold, "A Double-Edged Sword: Relationship between Full-Range Leadership Behaviors and Followers' Hair Cortisol Level," *The Leadership Quarterly*, August 2016, pp. 684–696.

24. Reinout E. de Vries, "Personality Predictors of Leadership Styles and the Self-Other Agreement Problem," *The Leadership Quarterly*, October 12, 2012, pp. 800–821.

25. Maria Collar, "Try Leading Collectively: Command-and-Control Leadership Gives Way to a More Democratic Style," *HR Magazine*, January 2013, p. 63.

26. Noshir S. Contractor, Leslie A. DeChurch, Jay Carson, Dorothy R. Carter, and Brian Keegan, "The Topology of Collective Leadership," *The Leadership Quarterly*, December 2012, pp. 994–1011.

27. Craig L. Pearse, "The Future of Leadership: Combining Vertical and Shared Leadership to Transform Knowledge Work," *Academy of Management Executive*, February 2004, pp. 47–57.

28. Anders Skogstad et al., "The Destructiveness of Laissez-Faire Leadership Behavior," *Journal of Occupational Health Psychology*, no. 1, 2007, pp. 80–92.

29. Adam Lashinsky, "The World's 50 Greatest Leaders: 1, Bezos Prime," *Fortune*, April 1, 2016, pp. 72–73.

30. John M. Schaubroeck, Yimo Shen, and Sinhui Chong, "A Dual Stage Moderated Mediation Model Linking Authoritarian Leadership to Follower Outcomes," *Journal of Applied Psychology*, February 2017, pp. 203–214; Robert K. Greenleaf, *The Power of Servant Leadership* (San Francisco: Berrett-Koehler Publishers, 1998).

31. Robert K. Greenleaf, *The Power of Servant Leadership* (San Francisco: Berrett-Koehler Publishers, 1998).

32. Suzanne J. Peterson, Benjamin M. Galvin, and Donald Lange, "CEO Servant Leadership: Exploring Executive Characteristics and Firm Performance," *Personnel Psychology*, no. 3, 2012, pp. 565–596.

33. Based on Robert K. Greenleaf, *Servant Leadership: A Journey into the Nature of Legitimate Power and Greatness* (Mahwah, NJ: Paulist Press, 1997); Robert C. Liden, Sandy J. Wayne, Hao Zhao, and David Henderson, "Servant Leadership: Development of a Multidimensional Measure and Multi-Level Assessment," *The Leadership Quarterly*, April 2008, pp. 161–177.

34. Robert C. Liden et al., "Servant Leadership: Validation of a Short Form of the SL-28," *The Leadership Quarterly*, April 2015, p. 256.

35. Emily M. Hunter et al., "Servant Leaders Inspire Servant Followers: Antecedents and Outcomes for Employees and the Organization," *The Leadership Quarterly*, April 2013, pp. 316–331.

36. Robert C. Liden, Sandy J. Wayne, Chenwei Liao, and Jeremy Meuser, "Servant Leadership and Serving Culture: Influence on Individual and Unit Performance," *Academy of Management Journal*, October 2014, pp. 1434–1452.

37. Myriam Chiniara and Kaathleen Bentein, "Linking Servant Leadership to Individual Performance: Differentiating the Mediating Role of Autonomy, Competence and Relatedness Need Satisfaction," *The Leadership Quarterly*, February 2016, pp. 124–141.

38. Suzanne J. Peterson, Benjamin M. Galvin, and Donald Lange, "CEO Servant Leadership: Exploring Executive Characteristics and Firm Performance," *Personnel Psychology*, no. 3, 2012, p. 585.

39. Andrew J. DuBrin, *Proactive Personality and Behavior for Individual and Organizational Productivity* (Cheltenham, UK; Northampton, MA: Edward Elgar, 2014), pp. 118–122; J. Robert Baum and Edwin A. Locke, "The Relationship of Entrepreneurial Traits, Skill, and Motivation to Subsequent Venture Growth," *Journal of Applied Psychology*, August 2004, pp. 587–598.

40. Duncan Clark, *Alibaba: The House That Jack Ma Built* (New York: Ecco, 2016).

41. Melissa S. Cardon, Joakim Wincent, Jagdip Singh, and Mateja Dronovsek, "The Nature and Experience of Entrepreneurial Passion," *Academy of Management Review*, July 2009, pp. 511–532.

42. Noam Wasserman, "How an Entrepreneur's Passion Can Destroy a Startup," *The Wall Street Journal*, August 25, 2014, p. R1.

43. Leon C. Prieto, "Proactive Personality and Entrepreneurial Leadership: Exploring the Moderating Role of Organizational Identification and Political Skill," *Academy of Entrepreneurship Journal*, July 1, 2010, pp. 1–16.

44. "The World's 50 Most Innovative Companies," *Fast Company*, March 2010, p. 67.

45. Veroniek Collewaert and Frederick Anseel, "Maintain Your Entrepreneurial Passion by Being Flexible,"

*The Management Tip of the Day from Harvard Business Review*, August 25, 2016, p. 1.

46. "Can Entrepreneurship Be Taught?" *The Wall Street Journal*, March 19, 2012, p. R4.

47. Judy Rosener, "Ways Women Lead," *Harvard Business Review*, November–December 1990, pp. 119–125.

48. Kenneth Nowack, "Are Women More Effective Leaders than Men?" *Pulse* (www.linkedin.com), June 9, 2015, pp. 1–4; Paul J. Zak and Lacek Kugler, "Neuroeconomics and International Studies: A New Understanding of Trust," *International Studies Perspectives,* no. 2, May 2011, pp. 136–152.

49. Much of the research on this topic is summarized in Mary Crawford, *Talking Difference: On Gender and Language* (London: Sage Publications, 1995).

50. Claartje J. Vinkenburg, Marloes L. van Engen, Alice H. Eagly, and Mary C. Johannesen-Schmidt, "An Exploration of Stereotypical Beliefs About Leadership Styles: Is Transformational Leadership a Route to Women's Promotion?" *The Leadership Quarterly*, February 2011, pp. 10–21.

51. Samantha C. Paustian-Underdahl, Lisa Slattery Walker, and David J. Woehr, "Gender and Perceptions of Leadership Effectiveness: A Meta-Analysis of Contextual Moderators," *Journal of Applied Psychology*, November 2014, pp. 1129–1145.

52. Ginka Toegel and Jay A. Conger, "360-Degree Assessment: Time for Reinvention," *Academy of Management Learning and Education*, September 2003, pp. 297–311.

53. Steven F. Markham, Ina S. Markham, and Janice Witt Smith, "At the Crux of Dyadic Leadership: Self-other Agreement of Leaders and Direct Reports—Analyzing the 360-Degree Feedback," *The Leadership Quarterly*, December 2015, p. 975.

54. Steven E, Markham, Janice Witt Smith, Ina S. Markham, and Kristian F. Braekkan, "A New Approach to Analyzing the Achilles' Heel of Multisource Feedback Program: Can We Really Trust Ratings of Leaders at the Group Level of Analysis?" *The Leadership Quarterly*, December 2014, p. 1120.

55. Harriet Edleson, "Do 360 Evaluations Work?" *Monitor on Psychology*, November 2012, pp. 58–60; Bruce Pfau and Ira Kay, "Does 360-Degree Feedback Negatively Affect Company Performance?" *HR Magazine*, June 2002, pp. 58–59; Tina Smagala, "Assessment Tool Can Be Used to Collect Anonymous Feedback," *Democrat and Chronicle*, October 8, 2013, p. 5B.

56. Daniel Goleman, "Leadership That Gets Results," *Harvard Business Review*, March–April 2000, pp. 78–90.

57. Felix Brodbeck, Michael Frese, and Mansour Havidan, "Leadership Made in Germany: Low on Compassion, High on Performance," *Academy of Management Executive*, February 2002, pp. 16–30.

58. David J. Henderson, Robert C. Liden, Brian C. Glibkowski, and Anjali Chaudhry, "LMX Differentiation: A Multilevel Review and Examination of Its Antecedents and Outcomes," *The Leadership Quarterly*, August 2009, pp. 517–534.

59. Ralph M. Stogdill, "Historical Trends in Leadership Theory and Research," *Journal of Contemporary Business*, Autumn 1974, p. 7.

60. Christopher Hann, "We're All in This Together," *Entrepreneur*, March 2013, p. 56.

# Contingency and Situational Leadership

A t age fifty, seasoned retail executive Marvin Ellison was appointed as CEO of J.C. Penney (JCP). He had spent the previous year as president, under the tutelage of chief executive officer (CEO) Mike Ullman. JCP was a hundred-year-old institution with a glorious past. Yet the present was less than glorious.

"JCP" as well as other department-store chains were struggling for survival. Hundreds of stores had been closed, a few big retailers had declared bankruptcy, and shopping malls were shrinking in size. Among the problems these stores faced were a sharp growth in online shopping, consumer preferences for specialty stores, people spending more money on services than physical goods, and young consumers who questioned the relevance of department stores.

JCP was also suffering with declining sales, a shrinking and aging customer base, shrinking sales per selling square foot, and excessive debt. When Ellison became CEO, company sales were down 37 percent from their 2006 high point. Another crisis point was the damage created by past CEO Ron Johnson whose strategy of going hipper almost destroyed the company, including the elimination of 43,000 jobs. (Johnson, the former retailing guru at Apple Inc., was replaced by Ullman as interim measure.)

The board at JCP believed that Ellison could step in and revitalize sales at the company's one hundred plus locations. He had spent twelve years at Home Depot, including three years as the executive vice president of U.S. stores. Ellison helped move the company back toward its former success, thereby developing the reputation of a successful crisis manager.

When Ellison joined JCP in 2014, he stated publicly, "As president, and ultimately CEO, I will be focused on positioning the Company to compete in a rapidly changing retail environment for the benefit of our customers, shareholders, suppliers, and associates. I am confident that we have the customer proposition, the brand, and the talent to make JC Penney successful over the long term."

Ellison combines his retailing intuition with data when making decisions. He says, "Pure intuition without any data gets you into trouble." As he spent more time analyzing the problems of the giant retailer, Ellison focused on three key initiatives to turnaround the company. First, he wanted JCP's eighty-seven million active customers to spend as much money at the stores as they did in the past. Inventory would be managed better so in-demand products would always be in stock. Second, because in-house brands, such as Liz Claiborne, account for more that 50 percent of sales, JCP would build on the clothing line by adding big and tall, and plus sizes, and also bring popular styles to the store more rapidly.

Third, enhance the technology experience for customers through such means as same-day in-store pickup of online orders, and overhauling the shopping app to facilitate shoppers finding discount items. The hope was that small but meaningful improvements will add up to a full recovery. For example, men's shoes had been placed next to the women's department, and Ellison boosted sales by moving men's shoes back to the men's department.

To sustain profitability, an analysis reported in *Forbes* suggested that Ellison must provide strong leadership that inspires every member of the management team and employees throughout the company to collaborate in generating sales, cut costs, and work more efficiently to succeed in a difficult, competitive marketplace. To help cut costs, in 2015, the company reduced its pension obligations by bout about $1.25 billion by paying a lump sum to approximately 13,900 retirees and former employees.

Retail experts admire Ellison's progress in getting JCP out of the crisis mode. As one retailing consultant observes, however, if JCP cannot become relevant to younger customers, it will reach a ceiling with respect to a comeback.

Ellison is one of a handful of African-American CEOs of a Fortune 500 company. He began his career as a part-time security guard at Target while a college student. Ellison is a graduate of the University of Memphis, and holds an MBA from Emory University.[1]

The story about retail executive illustrates an increasingly important leadership task: leading people and an organization through a crisis. Leadership of this type is a special case of the general subject of this chapter—adjusting one's approach to the situation. Contingency and situational leadership further expand the study of leadership styles by adding more specific guidelines about which style to use under which circumstance.

In this chapter, we present an overview of the situational perspective on leadership. We then summarize three classic contingency theories of leadership: Fiedler's contingency theory, path-goal theory, and the normative decision model. We also explain how a more contemporary theory, the leader–member exchange (LMX), contributes to understanding the contingency perspective. In addition, we describe crisis leadership because leading others through a crisis has become a frequent challenge in recent years. Finally, we describe how evidence-based leadership and management contribute to the contingency approach.

## Situational Influences on Effective Leadership Behavior

The situation can influence the leadership behavior or style a leader emphasizes. The essence of a **contingency approach to leadership** is that leaders are most effective when they make their behavior contingent on situational forces, including group member characteristics. Both the internal and the external environment have a significant impact on leader effectiveness. For example, the quality of the workforce and the competitiveness of the environment can influence which behaviors the leader emphasizes. A manager who supervises competent employees might be able to practice consensus leadership readily. And a manager who faces a competitive environment might find it easier to align people to pursue a new vision.

A useful perspective on implementing contingency leadership is that the manager must be flexible enough to avoid clinging to old ideas that no longer fit the current circumstances.[2] Being stubborn about what will work in a given situation and clinging to old ideas can result in ineffective leadership. The effective leader adapts to changing circumstances. For example, at one point, offering employees generous benefits might not have been motivational. In reality, with many employers having cut back on benefits such as health insurance, these benefits can actually be helpful in attracting and retaining workers.

The leader needs to take into account the major situational variable of organizational culture when choosing which approach to leadership will lead to favorable outcomes. A command-and-control leadership style may not be effective in a company with a collaborative, friendly organizational culture. If the culture seems at odds with what a highly placed leader wants to accomplish, the leader may attempt to change the culture.

Victor H. Vroom and Arthur G. Jago have identified three conclusions about the role of situations in leadership, and these findings support the model of leadership presented in Figure 1-2, Chapter 1. The conclusions are geared to support the idea that leadership involves motivating others to work collaboratively in the pursuit of a common goal.[3] We add a fourth conclusion, focused on the organization structure.

1. *Organizational effectiveness is affected by situational factors not under leader control.* The leader might be able to influence the situation, yet some situational factors are beyond the leader's complete control. The manager of a prosperous, independent coffee shop might be running her business and leading her employees successfully for ten years. Suddenly, a Starbucks opens across the street, thereby seriously affecting her ability to lead a successful enterprise. She might be smart enough to have a contingency plan of offering services Starbucks cannot equal, yet staying in business will be a struggle.

2. *Situations shape how leaders behave.* Contingency theorists believe that forces in the situation are three times as strong as the leader's personal characteristics in shaping his or her behavior. How the leader behaves is therefore substantially influenced by environmental forces. In the face of competition from Starbucks, our coffee shop proprietor might now act with a greater sense of urgency, be much more directive in telling her workers what to do, and become much less warm and friendly. Her normal level of enthusiasm might also diminish.

3. *Situations influence the consequences of leader behavior.* Popular books about management and leadership assume that certain types of leader behavior work in every situation. Situational theorists disagree strongly with this position. Instead, a specific type of leadership behavior might have different outcomes in different situations. The leader behavior of empowerment illustrates this idea. Perhaps empowerment will work for our coffee shop owner because she has a group of dedicated workers who want their jobs and her enterprise to endure. However, empowering incompetent workers with a weak work ethic is likely to backfire because the workers will most likely resist additional responsibility.

4. *The type of organization influences which leadership approach is best.* Henry Mintzberg has identified the form of organization as a key situational variable influencing which approach to leadership is likely to be most effective. Two examples will suffice here. In an *entrepreneurial organization*, the key leader will engage in considerable doing and dealing as well as creating visions. In a classic bureaucracy, the leader will engage in a considerable amount of controlling.[4]

In this chapter, as well as throughout the book, possible situational factors are mentioned that should be taken into consideration in leading others. A general approach to being aware of all these factors is for the leader to be *mindful* of events in the environment. If you are mindful, you are sensitive to what is happening around you. According to mindfulness researcher Jon Kabat-Zinn, you learn to pay attention on purpose to the present moment, in a nonjudgmental way, to whatever arises in your leadership situation.[5]

Leadership Self-Assessment Quiz 5-1 provides you an opportunity to think about your tendencies toward taking a situational perspective as a leader.

# LEADERSHIP SELF-ASSESSMENT QUIZ 5-1

## Measuring Your Situational Perspective

*Instructions:* Indicate how well you agree with the following statements, using the following scale: DS = disagree strongly; D = disagree; N = neutral; A = agree; AS = agree strongly. Circle the most accurate answer.

|  |  | DS | D | N | A | AS |
|---|---|---|---|---|---|---|
| 1. | Workers need to be carefully trained before you can place high expectations on them. | 1 | 2 | 3 | 4 | 5 |
| 2. | Workers who are more knowledgeable have less need of small, day-by-day goals. | 1 | 2 | 3 | 4 | 5 |
| 3. | Workers who are self-confident and intelligent require less supervision and guidance than do other workers. | 1 | 2 | 3 | 4 | 5 |
| 4. | Workers who are anxious usually need a lot of reassurance. | 1 | 2 | 3 | 4 | 5 |
| 5. | Most workers learn at about the same pace, so the manager can give about the same amount of instruction to each worker. | 5 | 4 | 3 | 2 | 1 |
| 6. | The same well-delivered pep talk will usually appeal to workers at all levels. | 5 | 4 | 3 | 2 | 1 |
| 7. | A manager will usually need to provide clear directions during a crisis. | 1 | 2 | 3 | 4 | 5 |
| 8. | As a manager, I would invest the least amount of time supervising the most competent workers. | 1 | 2 | 3 | 4 | 5 |
| 9. | An effective approach to supervising emotionally immature workers is to grant them a lot of freedom. | 5 | 4 | 3 | 2 | 1 |
| 10. | It is best not to put much effort into supervising unenthusiastic staff members. | 5 | 4 | 3 | 2 | 1 |
| 11. | An effective leader delegates equal types and amounts of work to group members. | 5 | 4 | 3 | 2 | 1 |
| 12. | If I noticed that a team member appeared to be insecure and anxious, I would give him or her especially clear instructions and guidance. | 1 | 2 | 3 | 4 | 5 |
| 13. | Many competent workers get to the point where they require relatively little leadership and supervision. | 1 | 2 | 3 | 4 | 5 |

| | | DS | D | N | A | AS |
|---|---|---|---|---|---|---|
| 14. | Whether a person is a young adult or old adult often influences the best approach to leading him or her. | 1 | 2 | 3 | 4 | 5 |
| 15. | A person's cultural background usually has no significance in providing him or her appropriate leadership. | 5 | 4 | 3 | 2 | 1 |

**Scoring and Interpretation**

- **46–75 points:** You have (or would have) a strong situational perspective as a leader and manager.
- **31–45 points:** You have (or would have) an average situational perspective as a leader and manager.
- **15–30 points:** You rarely take (or would take) a situational perspective as a leader and manager.

**Skill Development:** For the vast majority of leadership and management assignments, it pays to sharpen your situational perspective. If you scored lower than you want, sharpen your insights into situations by asking yourself, "What are the key factors in this situation that will influence my effectiveness as a leader–manager?" Study both the people and the task in the situation.

# Fiedler's Contingency Theory of Leadership Effectiveness

Fred E. Fiedler developed a widely researched and quoted contingency model many years ago that holds that the best style of leadership is determined by the situation in which the leader is working.[6] Here we examine how the style and situation are evaluated, the overall findings of the theory, and how leaders can modify situations to their advantage. Although this theory is no longer the subject of new research, it still provides a few useful suggestions for today's leader.

## Measuring Leadership Style: The Least Preferred Coworker (LPC) Scale

Fiedler's theory classifies a manager's leadership style as relationship motivated or task motivated. Style is therefore based on the extent to which the leader is relationship motivated or task motivated. According to Fiedler, leadership style is a relatively permanent aspect of behavior and thus difficult to modify. Leaders are regarded as having a consistent style of task or relations orientation. Fiedler reasons that once leaders understand their particular leadership style, they should work in situations that match that style. Similarly, the organization should help managers match leadership styles and situations.

The LPC scale measures the degree to which a leader describes favorably or unfavorably his or her LPC—that is, an employee with whom he or she could work the *least well*. The coworker is described by rating him or her on a series of eighteen polar-opposite adjectives, such as the following:

| Pleasant | 8 | 7 | 6 | 5 | 4 | 3 | 2 | 1 | Unpleasant |
|---|---|---|---|---|---|---|---|---|---|
| Tense | 1 | 2 | 3 | 4 | 5 | 6 | 7 | 8 | Relaxed |

The general idea of the LPC approach is that if you have a positive, charitable attitude toward people you had a difficult time working with, you are probably relationship oriented. In contrast, if you take a dim view of people who gave you a hard time, you are probably task oriented. The message here is that a relationship-oriented leader should be able to work well with a variety of personalities. The leadership style measure presented in Leadership Self-Assessment Quiz 4-1 is a more direct and less abstract way of measuring your style.

## Measuring the Leadership Situation

Fiedler's contingency theory classifies situations as high, moderate, and low control. The more control that the leader exercises, the more favorable the situation is for the leader. The control classifications are determined by rating the situation on its three dimensions: (1) *leader–member relations* measure how well the group and the leader get along; (2) *task structure* measures how clearly the procedures, goals, and evaluation of the job are defined; and (3) *position power* measures the leader's authority to hire, fire, discipline, and grant salary increases to group members.

Leader–member relations contribute as much to situation favorability as do task structure and position power combined. The leader therefore has the most control in a situation in which relationships with members are the best.

## Overall Findings

The key points of Fiedler's contingency theory are summarized and simplified in Figure 5-1. The original theory is much more complex. Leadership effectiveness depends on matching leaders to situations in which they can exercise more control. A leader should therefore be placed in a situation that is favorable to, or matches, his or her style. If this cannot be accomplished, the situation might be modified to match the leader's style by manipulating one or more of the three following situational variables.

The theory states that task-motivated leaders perform the best in situations of both high control and low control. Relationship-motivated leaders perform the best in situations of moderate control. The results of many studies indicated that the relationship-motivated leader outperformed the task-motivated leader in three of the eight situations but that the reverse was true in the other five situations. The eight situations result from each of the three situational variables being classified in one of two ways (good or poor, high or low, or strong or weak), as shown in Figure 5-2.

FIGURE 5-1   Summary of Findings from Fiedler's Contingency Theory.

**Situational Characteristics**

| Situation (Octant)<br>Number → | 1 | 2 | 3 | 4 | 5 | 6 | 7 | 8 |
|---|---|---|---|---|---|---|---|---|
| Leader–Member Relations | Good | Good | Good | Good | Poor | Poor | Poor | Poor |
| Task Structure | High | High | Low | Low | High | High | Low | Low |
| Position Power | Strong | Weak | Strong | Weak | Strong | Weak | Strong | Weak |

**FIGURE 5-2**    The Eight Different Situations in Fiedler's Contingency Theory.

Task-motivated leaders perform better in situations that are highly favorable for exercising control because they do not have to be concerned with the task. Instead, they can work on relationships. In moderately favorable situations, the relationship-motivated leader achieves higher group productivity because he or she can work on relationships and not get involved in micromanaging. In very-low-control situations, the task-motivated leader is able to structure and make sense out of confusion, whereas the relationship-motivated leader wants to give emotional support to group members or call a meeting.

## Making the Situation More Favorable for the Leader

A practical implication of contingency theory is that leaders should modify situations to match their leadership style, thereby enhancing their chances of being effective. Consider a group of leaders who are task motivated and decide that they need to exercise more control over the situation to achieve higher work unit productivity. To increase control over the situation, they can do one or more of the following:

- Improve leader–member relations through displaying an interest in the personal welfare of group members, having meals with them, actively listening to their concerns, telling anecdotes, and in general being a nice person.
- Increase task structure by engaging in behaviors related to initiating structure, such as being more specific about expectations, providing deadlines, showing samples of acceptable work, and providing written instructions.
- Exercise more position power by requesting more formal authority from higher management. For example, the leader might let it be known that he or she has the authority to grant bonuses and make strong recommendations for promotion.

Now imagine a relationship-motivated leader who wants to create a situation of moderate favorability so that his or her interests in being needed by the group could be satisfied. The leader might give the group tasks of low structure and deemphasize his or her position power.

## Evaluation of Fiedler's Contingency Theory

A major contribution of Fiedler's work is that it has prompted others to conduct studies about the contingency nature of leadership. At one time, it was used extensively as the basis for leadership training programs. The model has also alerted leaders to the importance of sizing up the situation to gain control. At the same time, Fielder pioneered in taking into account both traits and the situation to better understand leadership.[7] Despite its potential advantages, however, the contingency theory is too complicated to have much of an impact on most leaders.

# The Path-Goal Theory of Leadership Effectiveness

The **path-goal theory** of leadership effectiveness, as developed by Robert House, specifies what a leader must do to achieve high productivity and morale in a given situation. In general, a leader attempts to clarify the path to a goal for a group member so that the group member receives personal payoffs. At the same time, this group member's job satisfaction and performance increase.[8] Similar to the expectancy theory of motivation on which it is based, path-goal theory is multifaceted and has several versions. Its key features are summarized in Figure 5-3.

The theory is so complex that it is helpful to consider an overview before studying more of the details. The major proposition of path-goal theory is that the manager should choose a leadership style that takes into account the characteristics of the group members and the demands of the task. Furthermore, initiating structure will be effective in situations with a low degree of subordinate task structure but ineffective in highly structured task situations. The rationale is that in the first situation, subordinates welcome initiating structure because it helps to provide structure to their somewhat ambiguous tasks. Instead of just flailing around, the leader provides guidance. In the situation of highly structured tasks, more structure is seen as unnecessary and associated with overly close supervision.[9]

In his reformulated version of path-goal theory, House offered a meta-proposition, which provides a capsule summary of a dizzying amount of studies and theorizing in relation to the theory. Understanding this meta-proposition would be a good take-away from the theory: For leaders to be effective, they should engage in behaviors that complement subordinates' environments and abilities. They should engage in these behaviors in a manner that compensates for deficiencies and that enhances subordinate satisfactions as well as individual and work unit performance.[10] For example, if our coffee shop owner found that one of her workers was fearful of losing his or her job because of Starbucks competition, she would give him or her lots of encouragement and explain the survival plan of the coffee shop in detail.

Two key aspects of this theory will be discussed: matching the leadership style to the situation and steps the leader can take to influence performance and satisfaction.

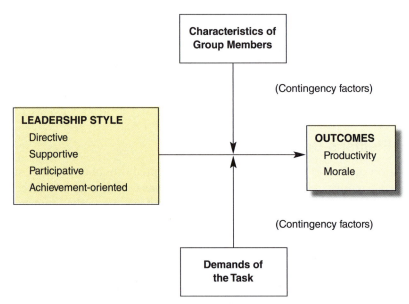

**FIGURE 5-3** The Path-Goal Theory of Leadership.

## Matching the Leadership Style to the Situation

Path-goal theory emphasizes that the leader should choose among four leadership styles to achieve optimum results in a given situation. Two important sets of contingency factors are the type of subordinates and the tasks they perform (a key environmental factor). The type of subordinates is determined by how much control they think they have over the environment (locus of control) and by how well they think they can do the assigned task.

Environmental contingency factors are those that are not within the control of group members but influence satisfaction and task accomplishment. Three broad classifications of contingency factors in the environment are (1) the group members' tasks, (2) the authority system within the organization, and (3) the work group.

To use path-goal theory, the leader must first assess the relevant variables in the environment. Then he or she selects one of the four styles listed next that fits those contingency factors best:

1. **Directive style.** The leader who is directive (similar to task motivated) emphasizes formal activities such as planning, organizing, and controlling. When the task is unclear, the directive style improves morale.

2. **Supportive style.** The leader who is supportive (similar to relationship motivated) displays concern for group members' well-being and creates an emotionally supportive climate. The supportive leader enhances morale when group members work on dissatisfying, stressful, or frustrating tasks. Group members who are unsure of themselves prefer the supportive leadership style.

3. **Participative style.** The leader who is participative consults with group members to gather their suggestions, and then considers these suggestions seriously when making a decision. The participative leader is best suited for improving the morale of well-motivated employees who perform nonrepetitive tasks.

4. **Achievement-oriented style.** The leader who is achievement oriented sets challenging goals, pushes for work improvement, and sets high expectations for team members, who are also expected to assume responsibility. This leadership style works well with achievement-oriented team members and with those working on ambiguous and nonrepetitive tasks.

A leader can sometimes successfully combine more than one of the four styles, although this possibility is not specified in path-goal theory. For example, during a crisis, such as a major product recall, the marketing manager might need to be directive to help the group take fast action. After the initial emergency actions have been taken, the leader, recognizing how stressed the workers must be, might shift to a supportive mode.

Few practicing leaders and managers attempt to systematically apply the path-goal theory, yet many effective leaders apply some aspects of the theory intuitively. An example is Mark Murphy, the president and CEO of the Green Bay Packers, a National Football League (NFL) team. Part of the reason Murphy is so well liked by team members and fans is that he uses a supportive style. At the same time, he emphasizes an achievement-oriented style to get the most from his staff and the players. After his playing days were over, Murphy earned a law degree and an MBA.

Joe Gibbs, a Hall of Fame coach, noticed Murphy's knack for leadership early on. "He was somebody I could go and talk to if I were having problems," he says. "Mark was so smart. He made the absolute most of his abilities."[11] Murphy, in turn, explains that his leadership style was influenced by Gibbs: "He had many leadership traits that I admired and incorporated into my own leadership style. He had a very natural way about him with the way he related to people, and he tried to be accessible. And when he worked with you, he was very fair and sincere. All those skills and traits fueled his awesome ability to motivate his teams."[12]

Murphy also practices participative leadership, as evidenced by his frequent use of *management by wandering around* (MBWA) with his senior management.[13] (MBWA refers to casually dropping by the work sites of subordinates and chatting with them about work and listening to their input.)

### Steps Leaders Can Take to Influence Performance and Satisfaction

In addition to recommending the leadership style to fit the situation, the path-goal theory offers other suggestions to leaders. Most of them relate to motivation and satisfaction, including the following:

1. Recognize or activate group members' needs over which the leader has control.
2. Increase the personal payoffs to team members for attaining work goals. The leader might give high-performing employees special recognition.
3. Make the paths to payoffs (rewards) easier by coaching and providing direction. For instance, a manager might help a team member be selected for a high-level project.
4. Help group members clarify their expectations of how effort will lead to good performance and how performance will lead to a reward. The leader might say, "Anyone who has gone through this training in the past came away knowing how to implement a 3D printing program. And most people who learn how to use this system wind up getting a good raise."
5. Reduce frustrating barriers to reaching goals. For example, the leader might hire a temporary worker to help with a seasonal work overload.
6. Increase opportunities for personal satisfaction if the group member performs effectively. The *if* is important because it reflects contingent behavior on the leader's part.
7. Be careful not to irritate people by giving them instructions on things they already can do well.
8. To obtain high performance and satisfaction, the leader must provide structure if it is missing and supply rewards contingent on adequate performance. To accomplish this, leaders must clarify the desirability of goals for the group members.[14]

As a leader, you can derive specific benefit from path-goal theory by applying these eight methods of influencing performance. Although research interest in path-goal theory has almost disappeared in recent years, the basic tenets of the theory are on target. Any comprehensive theory of leadership must include the idea that the leader's actions have a major impact on the motivation and satisfaction of group members.[15]

Despite the potential contributions of path-goal theory, it contains so many nuances and complexities that it has attracted little interest from managers. Implementing any of the eight points just mentioned would represent a potential contribution of the path-goal theory.

## The Normative Decision Model

Another contingency viewpoint is that leaders must choose a style that elicits the correct degree of group participation when making decisions. Since many of a leader's interactions with group members involve decision making, this perspective is sensible. The **normative decision model** views leadership as a decision-making process in which the leader examines certain factors within the situation to determine which decision-making style will be the most effective. Here we present the latest version of the model that has evolved from the work of Victor Vroom and his associates over thirty years, based on research with more than 100,000 managers.[16] The models have changed but they all include the basic idea of matching decision-making style to situational factors.

### Decision-Making Styles

The normative model (formerly known as the leader-participation model) identifies five decision-making styles, each reflecting a different degree of participation by group members:

1. *Decide.* The leader makes the decision alone and either announces or sells it to the group. The leader might use expertise in collecting information from the group or others who appear to have information relevant to the problem.
2. *Consult (Individually).* The leader presents the problem to the group members individually, gathers their suggestions, and then makes the decision.

3. **Consult (Group).** The leader presents the problem to group members in a meeting, gathers their suggestions, and then makes the decision.

4. **Facilitate.** The leader presents the problem and then acts as a facilitator, defining the problem to be solved and the boundaries in which the decision must be made. The leader wants concurrence and avoids having his or her ideas receive more weight based on position power.

5. **Delegate.** The leader permits the group to make the decision within prescribed limits. Although the leader does not directly intervene in the group's deliberations unless explicitly asked, he or she works behind the scenes, providing resources and encouragement.

## Contingency Factors and Application of the Model

The leader diagnoses the situation in terms of seven variables, or contingency factors, that contribute to selecting the most appropriate decision-making style. Based on answers to those variables, the leader or manager follows the path through decision matrices to choose one of five decision-making styles. The model has two versions: one when time is critical, and one when a more important consideration is developing group members' decision-making capabilities. When development of group members receives higher priority, the leader or manager relies more on the group to make a decision even if the process is time consuming.

The situational factors, or problem variables, make the model a contingency approach. The decision-making style chosen depends on following factors:

**Decision Significance:** The significance of the decision to the success of the project or organization (significance deals with decision quality).

**Importance of Commitment:** The importance of team members' commitment to the decision (commitment deals with decision acceptance).

**Leader Expertise:** Your knowledge or expertise in relation to the problem.

**Likelihood of Commitment:** The likelihood that the team will commit itself to a decision you might make on your own.

**Group Support:** The degree to which the team supports the organization's objectives at stake in the problem.

**Group Expertise:** Team members' knowledge or expertise in relation to the problem.

**Team Competence:** The ability of the team members to work together in solving problems.

Accurate answers to these seven situational factors can be challenging to obtain. The leader may have to rely heavily on intuition and also minimize distorted thinking, such as believing he or she has some expertise but in fact does not.

Although applying the model in its true form is complicated and subject to misinterpretation, the take-away from the model provides useful clues about making group versus individual decisions, as follows:[17]

1. A *consultative* or *collaborative* decision-making style is likely to bring about the best results when (a) you need information from others to solve the problem in question, (b) the problem is not clearly defined, (c) team member acceptance of the decision is important, and (d) you have sufficient time to deal with a group decision.

2. A *decide* decision-making style (making the decision by yourself) is recommended when (a) you have more expertise than the individual group members, (b) you are confident about your ability to make the decision in question, (c) the team will most likely accept your decision, and (d) the time available for decision making is limited.

The normative model provides a valuable service to practicing managers and leaders. It prompts them to ask questions about contingency variables in decision-making situations. At a minimum, the model prompts the leader to reflect on whether to make a group or unilateral decision in relation to an issue of consequence.

## Leader–Member Exchange and Contingency Theory

Another perspective on the contingency approach is suggested by the LMX theory. Leaders who adapt their style to different individuals within the group, or have different quality relationships with individual group members, are essentially practicing contingency leadership. Hundreds of studies have been conducted about LMX theory. One of the many questionnaires used to measure the quality of the relationship between the leader and the group member is presented in Leadership Self-Assessment Quiz 5-2. Here we present several conclusions from LMX research that indicate a contingency approach to leadership. LMX theory has been extensively researched, and only parts of the theory are about contingency leadership.

## LEADERSHIP SELF-ASSESSMENT QUIZ 5-2

### Quality of Leader–Member Relations

**Instructions:** Indicate whether you agree or disagree with each of the following statements in reference to a specific present or former supervisor.

| | STATEMENT ABOUT RELATIONSHIP | AGREE | DISAGREE |
|---|---|---|---|
| 1. | My manager likes me a lot. | ☐ | ☐ |
| 2. | When my boss does criticize me, it is almost always in a helpful, constructive way. | ☐ | ☐ |
| 3. | I welcome the opportunity to spend time with my boss in social settings. | ☐ | ☐ |
| 4. | My manager inspires me to perform at my best. | ☐ | ☐ |
| 5. | I think that my manager really cares about my career. | ☐ | ☐ |
| 6. | My boss asks me questions about my personal life without being nosy. | ☐ | ☐ |
| 7. | My manager and I easily laugh at each other's jokes. | ☐ | ☐ |
| 8. | I regard my manager as a true mentor for me. | ☐ | ☐ |
| 9. | My manager has exceptional technical and professional skills. | ☐ | ☐ |
| 10. | My manager listens to me carefully when I explain a work problem that I might be experiencing. | ☐ | ☐ |
| 11. | My manager has more than once complimented in a group setting or e-mail sent also to others. | ☐ | ☐ |
| 12. | My boss has commented more than once that I have good potential for advancement. | ☐ | ☐ |
| 13. | It is an enjoyable experience to work for and with my boss. | ☐ | ☐ |
| 14. | My manager and I trust each other a lot. | ☐ | ☐ |
| 15. | I think that my boss is a person of very fine character. | ☐ | ☐ |

**Scoring and Interpretation:** The more of the above statements you agree with, the higher the quality of your leader–member exchange. Agreeing with ten or more statements suggests a high-quality leader–member exchange. Agreeing with between five and ten statements suggests an average quality leader–member exchange. Agreeing with four or fewer suggests a poor-quality LMX.

1. Leaders tend to give members of their in-group more favorable performance ratings than they give to out-group members, even when their objective performance is the same. This finding reflects the idea that the leader might be kinder toward group members he or she likes.

2. Leaders do not always develop entirely different relationships with each group member, but may respond the same way to a few members of the group. For example, the leader might show equal care and trust for three members of an eight-person team.[18]

3. In larger groups, there tends to be more differences with respect to LMXs. As a result, the leader of a large group is more likely to use a slightly different style with various group members, such as being more authoritarian with several of the group members.

4. A manager is more likely to act as a servant leader toward subordinates with whom he or she has high-quality exchanges.[19] As a consequence, in-group members are likely to perceive that they have a leader who is working on their behalf.

5. Leaders are more likely to empower group members with whom they have a high-quality exchange (or good relationship) because they are more likely to trust those members. Research suggests, however, that better results for the organization will be attained if leaders attempt to have high-quality relationships with more group members and empower them at the same time.[20]

6. Larger differences in LMXs tend to lead to higher team performance when the LMX-quality median is low (meaning that group members tend to have poor exchanges with the leader). In contrast, when the LMX-quality median is high, differences in LMXs are not related to team performance. (If most group members feel that they have good exchanges with the leader, being treated a little differently by the leader does not affect their performance.) Similarly, when the LMX-quality median is low, more differentiation in exchanges leads to higher commitment to the group by its members. In contrast, when the LMX-quality median is high, differentiation has no effect on commitment.[21] (If you like your exchanges with the leader, your commitment is not affected by his or her different relationships with team mates.)

7. A study of 143 teams in three organizations suggested that moderate degrees of LMX differentiation yield the highest level of team performance. Moderate differentiation improves coordination within in the team which enhances performance.[22]

8. The quality of one's own LMX influences how leaders treating subordinates differently affects organizational commitment and organizational citizenship behavior. Surprisingly, LMX differentiation leads to more positive commitment and citizenship behavior when the LMX quality is lower rather than higher.[23] Apparently, when a worker does not have a good relationship with the boss, he or she will have better work attitudes when the leader treats most people differently.

Leadership Skill-Building Exercise 5-1 provides an opportunity for you to practice the contingency aspect of the LMX model.

## LEADERSHIP SKILL-BUILDING EXERCISE 5-1

### Leader–Member Exchange with In-Group Member and Out-Group Member

One student plays the role of the leader of a group of website developers. A second student plays the role of a member of the in-group, and a third student plays the role of a member of the out-group. The leader will have a brief interaction with the in-group member, exaggerating how he or she relates to this person. The leader will then have a brief interaction with the out-group member, and again exaggerating how he or she relates to this person. Observers might provide feedback as to the most likely impact of the two sets of behaviors on their targets.

The accompanying box Leader in Action illustrates how a manager uses the contingency approach to leadership.

**LEADER IN ACTION**

### Automotive Parts Company CEO Sarah Varies her Leadership Approach

Sarah, an automotive industry veteran, was appointed as CEO of Westwood Automotive, three years ago. Westwood supplies automobile and truck manufacturers with hundreds of parts and assemblies to use in vehicle production. Part of the reason Sarah was selected as the new CEO is that the company board of directors believed that the company needed revitalization. Sales had declined for nine consecutive quarters even though automobile sales in the United States were moving along at a healthy clip.

Part of Westwood's declining sales could be attributed to increased foreign competition. Another factor contributing to the decrease in sales at Westwood was that the many of the parts they supply to automotive manufacturers had decreased in demand, as vehicles became increasingly electronic. An extreme example is that the market for hand-operated window openers and closers, and carburetors, had virtually evaporated. Three years into her position, Sarah recognized that Westwood had some success in terms of stabilizing sales, market share, and profits, but much room for improvement remained.

As she analyzed the situation, the biggest change Westwood still needs is for employees, managers, and workers to understand the urgency of change. In the past, orders were almost automatic. For example, Westwood could manufacture thousands of brakes, place them in inventory, and know that orders from automobile and truck manufacturers would be forthcoming. In the present, orders for brakes must be carefully calculated because demand is so uncertain.

According to Sarah, "We have about one-half of our employees who understand the new automotive supplies environment. They can quickly shift their tactics, and respond well to changing customer needs. Yet about one half of our employees represent the 'frozen bottom.' They are stuck in the past, and resist change."

Sarah uses a different approach in dealing with the two groups. When she interacts with a department head, or the entire department of workers who respond well to the dynamic market conditions, she projects optimism and encouragement. She says, "I applaud what they are accomplishing, and I ask what I can do as CEO to overcome any hurdles they are facing. I laugh, I joke, and I allude to a better future for Westwood."

When Sarah interacts with the "frozen bottom," she has a different leadership approach. She says, "I emphasize the need for speed and more awareness of the need for change. I encourage the department heads to establish many short-term, specific goals. I also establish tight improvement goals for the department managers. With a couple of departments, I have even hinted that more layoffs could be possible if we do not attain our sales and profit goals."

#### QUESTIONS

1. In what way is Sarah practicing contingency leadership?
2. What risk do you see of Sarah being perceived as a two-faced (or dishonest) leader?

## Leadership During a Crisis

Among the potential crises facing organizations are a drastic revenue decline; pending bankruptcy; homicide in the workplace; scandalous or criminal behavior by executives; natural disasters, such as hurricanes, floods, or earthquakes; nuclear radiation spills; suicide bombings and other terrorist attacks; and a cruise ship being shipwrecked. Leading during a crisis can be regarded as contingency leadership because the situation demands that the leader emphasize certain behaviors, attitudes, and traits.

**Crisis leadership** is the process of leading group members through a sudden and largely unanticipated, intensely negative, and emotionally draining circumstance. Leadership is the key ingredient in successful crisis management. Effective crisis leadership ensures that a business is prepared before a crisis emerges, and that successfully navigates response and recovery.[24]

# LEADERSHIP SELF-ASSESSMENT QUIZ 5-3

**Checklist for Crisis Leadership**

***Instructions:*** Indicate whether you agree or disagree with each of the following statements in reference to dealing with a work-related crisis.

| | | AGREE | DISAGREE |
|---|---|:---:|:---:|
| 1. | I can make decisions and recommendations although under extreme time pressures. | ☐ | ☐ |
| 2. | I stay composed when I have to deal with an urgent problem that is suddenly facing me. | ☐ | ☐ |
| 3. | I almost never choke under pressure. | ☐ | ☐ |
| 4. | When the pressure is heavy, I can give clear direction to other people. | ☐ | ☐ |
| 5. | When someone else is facing a very difficult situation, I am reassuring and helpful. | ☐ | ☐ |
| 6. | When faced with an emergency, I can make a good decision even without all the facts I need. | ☐ | ☐ |
| 7. | When facing a major problem, I quickly get the input from people who might have useful suggestions for dealing with the problem. | ☐ | ☐ |
| 8. | If I am faced with a real mess that is mostly or partly my responsibility, I tell the truth about what happened. | ☐ | ☐ |
| 9. | When faced with an overwhelming problem, I can usually imagine what can be done to find a solution. | ☐ | ☐ |
| 10. | I can change my usual work activities immediately to take care of an urgent need. | ☐ | ☐ |

**Scoring and Interpretation:** The more of the given statements you agree with, the stronger your tendencies for being an effective crisis leader. Agreeing with eight or more statements suggests (and your perception is accurate) high ability to deal with and lead others through a crisis. Agreeing with between three and seven statements suggests an average degree of crisis leadership ability. Agreeing with two or fewer statements suggests a limited ability right now to lead others through a crisis.

*Source:* Statements 1 and 10 are adapted from Constance Noonan Hadley, Todd L. Pittinsky, S. Amy Sommer, and Weichun Zhu, "Measuring the Efficacy of Leaders to Assess Information and Make Decision in a Crisis: The C-LEAD Scale," *The Leadership Quarterly*, August 2011, p. 638.

Here we describe nine leadership attributes and behaviors associated with successfully leading an organization or organizational unit through a crisis. Leadership Self-Assessment Quiz 5-3 gives you an opportunity to think through your own tendencies toward being able to lead through a crisis.

***Be Decisive***    The best-accepted principle of crisis leadership is that the leader should take decisive action to remedy the situation. The greater the crisis, the less time the leader has to consult a wide array of people. After the plan is formulated, it should be widely communicated to help reassure group members that something concrete is being done about the predicament. After their physical facilities were destroyed in the terrorist attacks on the World Trade Center on September 11, 2001, several leaders announced the next day that their firms would move to nearby backup locations. Communicating plans helps reduce uncertainty about what is happening to the firm and the people in it. A leader who takes highly visible action to deal with a crisis is likely to be viewed as competent.

A corollary of being decisive during a crisis is not to be indecisive or to hide from the crisis in its midst. The first phase of crisis leadership is to stabilize the emergency situation and buy time.[25] Suppose that five key managers leave the company at the same time to join a competitor, and only one in-house replacement is available. To deal with the emergency, the CEO might hire four managers from an employment agency that specializes in providing temporary managers and professionals. The next step would be to prepare other company personnel to replace managers who quit in the near future.

Being decisive in response to a crisis also includes communicating widely the plans for resolving the problems that created the crisis, assuming that the organization had some responsibility for the crisis. Announcing these plans appeared to give many employees hope for better times ahead.

Another component of decisiveness is to avoid the fear of failure that can prevent taking the necessary action to exit the crisis. Chris Warner and Don Schmincke, authors of *High Altitude Leadership*, advise leaders that fear is the ultimate strategy killer. "It stops staff from making great decisions, stops change agents from disrupting the status quo, and stops leaders from leading."[26] The decision of Alan Mullaly when he was CEO of Ford Motor Company to bring back the defunct Taurus model is a good example of avoiding the fear of failure. Ford officials had discontinued the Taurus because of declining sales, but Mullaly thought the former popularity of the model warranted bringing it back to the public.

**Lead with Compassion**    Displaying compassion with the concerns, anxieties, and frustrations of group members is a key interpersonal skill for crisis leadership. The type of compassionate leadership that brings about organizational healing involves taking some form of public action that eases pain and inspires others to act as well. Compassionate leadership encompasses two related sets of actions. The first is to create an environment in which affected workers can freely discuss how they feel, such as a group meeting to talk about the crisis or disaster. The second is to create an environment in which the workers who experience or witness pain can find a method to alleviate their own suffering and that of others. The leader might establish a special fund to help the families of workers who were victims of the disaster or give workers the opportunity to receive grief counseling.[27]

A noteworthy example of a leader being compassionate and decisive at the same time took place after a massive flooding in Louisiana in 2016. Paul Kuserow, the chief executive of Amedisys Inc., based in Baton Rouge, showed active concern for the company employees and clients. (Amedisys provides home health and hospice care.) Among the thirteen people who died in the flooding was company founder Bill Borne.

The disaster left about 100 of the company's 400 employees with flooded homes, and the firm's local hospice patients were at risk. Limited supplies of gasoline were available in the community. Kuscrow arranged for fuel trucks to be brought in, and dispensed fuel to caregivers so they could visit their patients. Employees with substantial property damage were wired $2,500 into their bank accounts. Kuscrow went to a Lowe's in the middle of the night with the company general counsel. He said, "We bought mops, buckets, fans, bleach and anti-mold spray, anything that was on the shelf." Kuscrow's decisive and compassionate actions help the company, its employees, and patients get through the disaster.[28]

**Think Strategically (See the Big Picture)**    A success factor for the leader of an organization or a key organizational unit is to think strategically, including seeing the big picture. During an organizational crisis, this cognitive skill increases in importance because subordinates may become so mired in the crisis that they see no way out. The effective crisis leader helps the group understand that conditions will soon change for the better. A group of researchers headed by Leslie A. DeChurch used measures of historical events to elucidate the aspects of leadership essential in extreme contexts. Critical incidents, or key activities, taking place during the crisis situation were also studied. Published reports of events, including newspapers and books, constituted the qualitative data in this type of analysis. These extreme situations included responding to the aftermaths of natural disasters and orchestrating postwar stability, support, transition, and reconstruction efforts.

A major finding of the historical analysis of leadership events was that the leadership function of strategy was important in dealing with the crisis event. An aspect of strategy uncovered that is relevant here was *understanding the big picture*.[29] An example of seeing the big picture would be for a leader to recognize that a couple of months after a manufacturing plant was destroyed due to an explosion, another company plant could absorb its workload. Or the destroyed plant might be restored.

***Communicate Widely About the Problem***  When tough times hit, it pays to increase communication about the problems facing the company or unit, and what might be done to improve the situation. By communicating with workers throughout the organization, they will have an opportunity to provide leadership. In one company, a technician suggested the company focus more on servicing existing equipment than attempting to sell new equipment during the recession. Communicating with customers as well as their customers can bring forth useful information about how long the tough times will remain. The business can be reconfigured to meet the new reality, such as finding the least painful ways to cut costs.

Roger Ferguson had become CEO of the financial services giant TIAA-CREF (now TIAA) a few months before the financial crisis of 2008. He said that he and his team had a sense that thing were unraveling even more quick that others had observed. In addition to looking into the future (seeing the big picture), he said that it is essential to communicate. Employees must understand how you are seeing the world, and why you are making the decision you are making. In this way, they can align the decision making to your decision making.[30]

*Sensemaking* by the leader can be a helpful form of communication during a crisis. A crisis leader engages in sensemaking when he or she explains the nature of what is happening, or literally makes sense of the events.[31] Sensemaking also refers to helping stakeholders understand the implications of what has happened. Assume that a company is going through the crisis of bankruptcy. The CEO could help make sense of the situation by explaining that the company will continue to operate, employees will be paid, and there will only be a 5 percent reduction in force.

***Reestablish the Usual Work Routine***  A temporary drop in performance and productivity is almost inevitable for most workers after disaster strikes, such as an earthquake or terrorist attack—even if the organization was not directly affected. Although it may appear callous and counterintuitive, the leader should emphasize the temporary nature of the performance decline. An effective way of helping people deal with a workplace crisis is to encourage them to return to their regular work. It is important for workers to express their feelings about the crisis before refocusing on work, but once they have, returning to work helps ground them in reality and restores purpose to their lives. Randall Marshall, director of trauma studies for the New York State Office of Mental Health, said after 9/11, "A healthy response to this type of situation is to get back into a routine."[32]

***Stick with Constructive Core Values***  Leaders who keep their company or division focused on core values are likely to endure difficult times. Lowering core values to help overcome adversity can create permanent damage. Take this humble example: A well-known underwear company decided to cope with lower sales volume by cutting costs on the manufacture of men's briefs. The lower-cost briefs looked fine but they tore apart at the waistband after several washings. Word spread quickly about the defective briefs, and the company lost accounts with several major retail chains. The core value compromised here was offering only high-quality goods to the public.

***Divide Major Problems into Smaller Chunks***  Give workers bits of the major problem to work on so they feel less overwhelmed by the adversity facing them and the company. For example, if the company is hurting for cash, one group of employees might search for items in the office or factory that could be sold on an auction website. Another group of workers might search for ways to reduce shipping costs by 10 percent. Other groups would be assigned different adversity-fighting tasks. When an obstacle is framed as too large, too complex, or too challenging, workers might feel overwhelmed and therefore freeze in their tracks.

*Avoid a Circle-the-Wagons Mentality*   One of the worst ways to lead a group through a crisis is to strongly defend yourself against your critics or deny wrongdoing. The same denial approach is referred to as maintaining a bunker mentality or stonewalling the problem. Instead of cooperating with other stakeholders in the crisis, the leader takes a defensive posture. A case in point is how U.S. interior secretary Ken Salazar dealt with one aspect of the disastrous BP oil spill in the Gulf of Mexico in 2009. Part of the problem had been attributed to a too-friendly relationship between the Minerals Management Service and oil companies, which might have resulted in nonrigorous inspections of oil drilling. Instead of denying that problems existed at the Minerals Management Service, Salazar quickly reorganized the government unit with a new name: Bureau of Ocean Energy Management, Regulation, and Enforcement. Stricter ethical standards were also imposed to show that the new agency would act more independently in inspecting oil-drilling equipment and processes.[33]

*Display Optimism*   Pessimists abound in every crisis, so an optimistic leader can help energize group members to overcome the bad times. The effective crisis leader draws action plans that give people hope for a better future (as in strategic thinking). Barbara Baker Clark contends that the role of a leader during a crisis is to encourage hopefulness. She states:

> I'm not saying that you have to plaster a stupid grin on your face even
> if the bottom line is tanking or people are dying in battle. I am saying
> don't wallow in pessimism. Believe it or not, it matters to your employees
> that you remain reasonably optimistic. It will reduce anxiety and keep
> everyone motivated. That's the power of leadership.[34]

*Prevent the Crisis Through Disaster Planning: The Ideal Form of Crisis Leadership*   A key part of planning for a physical disaster, for example, is to anticipate where you would go, how you would get in touch with employees, and where you might set up a temporary workplace. Having a list of backup vendors in case they are hit by a physical disaster is also important. Small business owners should be networking with other business owners and agree to assist each other if a crisis strikes. Arranging in advance for support groups, such as grief counselors, is another key element of disaster planning. Even the fact of letting employees know that a disaster plan is in place can be an effective leadership act because it may lower worker anxiety. Also, the leader might communicate that the company has purchased disaster insurance.

The Deepwater Horizon oil-spill disaster was attributed, in part, to inadequate disaster plans. Former BP executive Tony Hayward said it was probably true that the company didn't do enough planning in advance of the disaster. He said that "there are some capabilities that we could have available to deploy instantly rather than creating as we go." Apparently, BP was not prepared for the long-term, round-the-clock process of coping with a deep-sea spill.[35]

*Stay Calm and Provide Stable Performance*   Effective leaders stay calm and are steady performers, even under heavy workloads and uncertain conditions. Remaining steady under crisis conditions contributes to effectiveness because it helps team members cope with the situation. When the leader remains calm, group members are reassured that things will work out. Stability also helps the managerial leader appear professional and cool under pressure. A representative example is Fréderic Oudén, the chairman and CEO of Société Générale. One of the major crises faced by this French banking giant were the stock market plunge in 2008, followed by a stock market scandal that cost the bank $7 billion (U.S.). Another crisis took place in 2011 when rumors arose that the bank had lost its liquidity as the Greek debt crisis swept Europe. Oudén says that the key to dealing with crisis of this magnitude is to remain calm, and manage your stress. Furthermore, to avoid creating useless turbulence, you must create a process to help the teams organize themselves to make the right decisions at the right time.[36]

***Be a Transformational Leader***    During times of large and enduring crisis, transformational leadership may be the intervention of choice. The transformational leader can often lead the organization out of its misery. Transformational leadership is likely to benefit the troubled organization both in dealing with the immediate crisis and in performing better in the long run. David Novak, the CEO of Yum! Brands (which includes KFC, Taco Bell, Pizza Hut, and Long John Silver's), has seen his share of crises, including vermin infestation in a restaurant that was broadcast on television and YouTube. He says that honesty, consistency, and continuity of communication is the key to managing through these issues and that the transformation may take six to nine months.[37]

Another way a transformational leader helps a company or work unit cope with crisis is to establish a climate of trust long before a crisis strikes.[38] If workers and other shareholders trust the leader, they will take more seriously his or her directives during the crisis. Leaders at both Walmart and McDonald's did a notable job of holding their workforce together after hurricane Katrina. Executives and store managers alike scrambled to get in touch with employees to assure them that they would all have their jobs back as soon as operations were up and running. In general, workers in the Gulf Coast area had trusted leadership at the two companies.

Leadership Skill-Building Exercise 5-2 provides you an opportunity to take a look at how crisis leadership is practiced.

## LEADERSHIP SKILL-BUILDING EXERCISE 5-2

### Crisis Leadership

Working in a small group, find a crisis that a business or not-for-profit organization is facing these days. Examples would include a pharmaceutical firm needing to recall an over-the-counter medicine that has triggered illnesses in hundreds of consumers, or an investment banking firm in which several key executives have been accused of insider trading. After agreeing on which crisis to tackle, develop a list of suggestions on how the CEO should deal with the situation. Use several ideas from the section about crisis leadership presented in this chapter to help you develop an action plan.

## Evidence-Based Leadership for the Contingency and Situational Approach

A leading-edge way for a person to practice contingency leadership would be to look for research-based evidence about the best way to deal with a given situation. Before taking action, the leader would ask, "What does the research literature tell me is most likely to work in this situation?" **Evidence-based leadership or management** is an approach whereby managers translate principles based on best evidence into organizational practices.[39] The systematic use of scientific evidence, along with evidence from other sources such as experience, had its origins in medicine about twenty-five years ago.[40]

Quite often the best evidence is empirical (based on experience) and recent. Yet, at times, old principles can still be useful. For example, it has been known for at least a century that when a manager has too many subordinates, coordinating the work of subordinates is difficult. The alternative to evidence-based leadership is to rely heavily on common sense and adopting practices used by other companies, whether or not they fit a particular situation. Many of the principles and suggestions presented throughout this text would help a manager practice evidence-based leadership.

An example of using evidence-based leadership follows: Research indicates that empowerment is more likely to succeed with group members whose cultural values favor a manager or leader sharing power. In contrast, empowerment is less likely to succeed when the group members expect the leader to retain most of the power. (See Chapter 14 for the evidence.) In this example, a *principle* (empowerment works best when cultural values are compatible) is translated into *practice* (using empowerment to motivate and satisfy workers when the cultural values of the workers are compatible with empowerment).

An example of using evidence-based leadership stemming from the experience of managers is to regularly express thanks for a job well done.[41] The thank you can be expressed orally or in writing and should focus on something specific the person has accomplished such as, "Your tracking down of potential candidates for our opening by using the social media produced four good prospects. Thanks so much for lending your expertise."

Evidence-based leadership and management is not yet widely practiced, but taking the study of leadership and management seriously will move managers and organizations toward basing their practices and decisions on valid evidence. The result is likely to be more precise contingency leadership.

## READER'S ROADMAP

So far in this book, we have examined the nature of leadership, the inner qualities of leaders, and leadership styles, including contingency leadership. In the next chapter, we focus on a topic that incorporates many of these ideas: leadership ethics and social responsibility.

## SUMMARY

Theories of contingency and situational leadership build on the study of leadership style by adding more specific guidelines about which style to use under which circumstances. Leaders are most effective when they make their behavior contingent on situational forces, including group member characteristics. Organizational effectiveness is affected by situational factors not under the leader's control. Situations shape how leaders behave, and they also influence the consequences of leader behavior.

Fiedler's contingency theory states that the best style of leadership is determined by the leader's work situation. Style, in Fiedler's theory, is measured by the LPC scale. If you have a reasonably positive attitude toward your LPC, you are relationship motivated. You are task motivated if your attitude is negative. Situational control, or favorability, is measured by a combination of the quality of leader–member relations, the degree of task structure, and the leader's position power.

The key proposition of Fiedler's theory is that in situations of high control or low control, leaders with a task-motivated style are more effective. In a situation of moderate control, a relationship-motivated style works better. Leaders can improve situational control by modifying leader–member relations, task structure, and position power.

The path-goal theory of leadership effectiveness specifies what the leader must do to achieve high productivity and morale in a given situation. The major proposition of the theory is that the manager should choose a leadership style that takes into account the characteristics of the group members and the demands of the task. Initiating structure by the leader works best when the group faces an ambiguous task. Effective leaders clarify the paths to attaining goals, help group members progress along these paths, and remove barriers to goal attainment. Leaders must choose a style that best fits the two sets of contingency factors—the characteristics of the subordinates and the tasks. The four styles in path-goal theory are directive, supportive, participative, and achievement oriented.

The normative decision model explains that leadership is a decision-making process. A leader examines certain contingency factors in the situation to determine which decision-making style will be the most effective in either a time-driven or developmental situation. The model defines five decision-making styles: two individual styles and three group styles.

By answering a series of seven diagnostic questions in a matrix, the manager follows the path to a recommended decision style. The most important take-away from the model is to know when to consult with the group versus making an independent decision.

LMX theory provides some insights into contingency leadership. Leaders who have different quality relationships with individual group members are essentially practicing contingency leadership. LMX influences such factors as the favorability of performance ratings, which group member receives servant leadership and are empowered, extent of empowerment, and team performance.

Leading others through a crisis can be considered a form of contingency leadership because the leader adapts his or her style to the situation. In a crisis, leaders should (a) be decisive, (b) lead with compassion, (c) think strategically, (d) communicate widely about the problem, (e) reestablish the usual work routine, (f) stick with constructive core values, (g) divide major problems into smaller chunks, (h) avoid a circle-the-wagons mentality, (i) display optimism, (j) prevent the crisis through disaster planning, (k) provide stable performance, and (l) be a transformational leader.

A leading-edge way for a person to practice contingency leadership would be to look for research-based evidence about the best way to deal with a given situation. This approach means using evidence-based leadership or management.

## KEY TERMS

**contingency approach to leadership** 119
**path-goal theory** 124

**normative decision model** 126
**crisis leadership** 130

**evidence-based leadership or management** 135

## GUIDELINES FOR ACTION AND SKILL DEVELOPMENT

1. A major contingency factor for a team or group leader is the talent and motivation of the individual being led. Although talented and well-motivated workers may not require close monitoring of their efforts, they still require encouragement and recognition to sustain high performance. Otherwise, the leader has very little impact on their performance or their intention to stay a member of the team or group.

2. When practicing the LMX theory of leadership by forming unique relationships with members of the group, it is important to minimize the potential unintended negative consequences of this type of leadership. For morale purposes, it is important to avoid establishing favorites or pets in the group, and having only superficial, mechanical relationships with other group members.

3. A subtle way of practicing contingency leadership is to adapt to times that may have changed in terms of the demands of your leadership position. You have to fine-tune your leadership approach to meet the new circumstances. Assume that hospital administrator Maggie has held her position for ten years. According to her perception of her role, the focus of her leadership would be to inspire her staff toward doing what is best for patient care. Yet her role has now changed. Focusing on what is good for patients still receives high priority, yet Maggie has to emotionally accept the reality that finding ways to inspire her group to reduce the cost of operating the hospital has become a key part of her leadership and management role.

### Discussion Questions and Activities

1. What relevance might contingency leadership have for dealing with generational differences in the workplace?
2. What are the potential risks of relying too heavily on stereotypes when practicing contingency leadership?
3. Identify a personality trait you think would help a manager function as a contingency leader. Also identify a trait you think might detract from a manager's ability to function as a contingency leader.

4. How might a leader modify the clothing he or she wore to different work situations to help practice contingency leadership?

5. How would a manager know which variables in a given situation should influence which approach to leadership he or she should take?

6. Which of the four path-goal styles do you think would be the best for managing a group of software engineers? Justify your answer.

7. To what extent do you think that battle-field experience would help a person become an effective crisis leader in a business situation?

8. Why are both a task emphasis and a relationship emphasis often necessary to get a group through a crisis, such as a hurricane having destroyed a company facility?

9. Ask two experienced managers you know whether they have ever heard of or practiced contingency leadership. What conclusion about contingency leadership do you draw from your answers?

10. In what way do effective teachers practice contingency leadership?

## LEADERSHIP CASE PROBLEM A

### Supervisory Styles at the Red Rascal

Jessica Perez is the manager of a thriving Red Rascal Restaurant, a chain of several hundred moderately priced restaurants throughout the country. Jessica recently returned from a regional conference in which she was informed about a new program of recruiting several developmentally disabled workers to work at each restaurant. The restaurants would work closely with local institutions that provided vocational training for individuals who are intellectually challenged. In many of the communities, these institutions coordinate their effort with both psychology and special education departments at local colleges.

The developmentally disabled workers would be hired into basic positions that fit their capabilities, such as salad chefs, bakers, dishwashing machine attendants, and custodial workers. Restaurant (store) managers would receive training into how to optimize the capabilities of developmentally disabled workers, as well as how to motivate or discipline the workers as needed.

Three months after the program was launched, Jessica's branch had hired three developmentally disabled young adults, all assigned jobs within the kitchen. Jessica spent a little time coaching her kitchen supervisors about supervising developmentally disabled workers. She emphasized the importance of providing clear, uncomplicated directions, and not overwhelming these workers by changing their assignments frequently. As instructed at regional headquarters, Jessica also explained the need to provide positive feedback and encouragement to the intellectually challenged recruits.

The program of hiring a few developmentally disabled kitchen workers appeared to be going generally well at the Red Rascal. No particular problems with the food prepared by the new workers were found, food preparation was not delayed, and their attendance was satisfactory. Yet as Jessica listened to several of the restaurant associates, the wait staff and kitchen staff included, she heard some grumbling. Head chef Tammy expressed her concerns in these terms: "I'm not exactly sure why this is happening, but these days my supervisor is treating me like I'm ten years old. She's so condescending, and she tells me what she wants done in tiny details. I asked Mindy (the supervisor) to taste a new salad dressing I prepared. She told me, 'Tammy, I'm so proud of you. You did a great job.' I mean, she's acting like I'm stupid or something."

Kurt, the host, made a similar comment about Jessica. He said, "All of a sudden you're treating me as if I'm a little slow. You made such a fuss just because my shoes were shined and my shirt was wrinkle free. Are you forgetting that I'm not developmentally challenged?"

Mindy began to think that maybe there were some supervisory style problems at the Red Rascal.

### Questions

1. What does the restaurant scenario presented have to do with contingency leadership?

2. In what ways might Jessica and the supervisors modify their leadership styles to adapt to the differences in intellectual levels of the Red Rascal staff?

3. What is the problem with the kitchen staff and wait staff at the Red Rascal? Should not all workers receive careful instructions, feedback, and encouragement?

## ASSOCIATED ROLE PLAY

One student plays the role of a supervisor whose responsibility is to show a developmentally challenged recruit how to prepare a salad in a giant bowl, that will then be divided into single-portion salads as needed.

Another student plays the role of the twenty-year-old recruit who has never previously prepared food. Observers should be particularly cognizant if the supervisor is using an effective leadership style.

## LEADERSHIP CASE PROBLEM B

### Emma Varies the Quality of Her Relationships

Emma is the president of the braces and support division of a pharmaceutical company. Her division develops, manufactures, and sells such devices as wrist, ankle, elbow, and back supports, plus knee and back supports that sold through prescription only. The various support devices are found in pharmacies, supermarkets, and department stores as well as directly to consumers online.

One day Emma was discussing how well she was performing as a leader with Jerald, the director of human resources. Jerald said, "We will review some of the multirater feedback with you. It appears to be consistent with some of the informal buzz I have heard about your leadership. Your direct reports like the strong leadership you bring to the division, but they think you play favorites."

"How so," said Emma?

Jerald replied, "Let's look at some of the written comments on the anonymous forms done online. I think you will find it helps explain the comments about having favorites:

Direct Report A says that you are a kind and caring manager who always takes into account her needs. When she needed time off to take care of a parent who moving to assisted living, you gave her three days off of paid leave. When she wanted some experience with analytics, you found the right project for her.

Direct Report B says that you can be a little callous and indifferent. He once told you that if you could hire one more online sales support representative, he

could boost sales by 20 percent. He said that you flatly rejected his demand, saying there was no money in the budget for an additional hire.

Direct Report C says that you never shut up in meetings, both face-to-face and virtual, about our director of product development and design. You talk as if that person were single-handedly responsible for the success of our division.

Direct Report D says that you practically ignore her. If she tries to tell you something funny, you don't even crack a smile. She thinks you are a good strategic leader, but that you act like a zombie toward her."

Emma said to Jerald, "It is good to know that I am perceived to be an effective leader. Yet I find some of this feedback troubling. I thought that an effective leader was supposed to have different relationships with different people. How else can you deal with the reality that people are unique?"

### Questions

1. In what way does this case illustrate the LMX model of leadership?
2. To what extent do you thinking the feedback presented by the direct reports could help Emma hone her leadership style?
3. If Emma does not want to be perceived as playing favorites, what should she do differently in her leadership approach?

## ASSOCIATED ROLE PLAY

One student plays the role of Emma, who will be meeting with two group members today. One student plays the role of Direct Report A. Run a six-minute role play interaction in which Emma reacts in a kind and caring way toward Direct Report A. Another student plays the role of Direct Report B who thinks

that Emma is cool and indifferent toward him. Run a six-minute role play interaction in which Emma reacts in a cold and indifferent way toward Direct Report B. Observers will provide feedback as to whether Emma really has different quality relationships with the two direct reports.

## LEADERSHIP SKILL-BUILDING EXERCISE 5-3

### My Leadership Portfolio

For this chapter entry in your leadership portfolio, visualize two different leadership scenarios that you witnessed directly, read about, or saw on television or in a movie. Think through how you would have used a different leadership approach for each one if you had been the leader. To illustrate, suppose you had passed a construction site for a skyscraper and noticed that the crane operator seemed confident and competent. You might conclude, "In this situation, I would have used a *delegating* style of leadership with the crane operator because she was so self-sufficient. Yet I would still have given her some recognition for a job well done at the end of her shift."

Another scenario might be that you witnessed a bloody fight at a professional hockey match. You might conclude, "In this situation, I would be as directive as possible. I would suspend and fine the players, with no room for negotiation. Decisive action must be taken to quell violence in professional sports."

## LEADERSHIP SKILL-BUILDING EXERCISE 5-4

### Crisis Leadership

Working in a small group, find a crisis that a business or not-for-profit organization is facing these days. Examples would include a pharmaceutical firm needing to recall an over-the-counter medicine that has triggered illnesses in hundreds of consumers, or an investment banking firm in which several key executives have been accused of insider trading. After agreeing on which crisis to tackle, develop a list of suggestions on how the CEO should deal with the situation. Use several ideas from the section about crisis leadership presented in this chapter to help you develop an action plan.

## NOTES

1. Original story is based on facts and observations in the following sources: Phil Wahba, "The Man Who's Re- [Re- Re-] Inventing J. C. Penney," *Fortune*, March 1, 2016, pp. 76–86; Walter Loeb, "Opportunities and Woes Faced By J. C. Penney's New CEO Marvin Ellison," *Forbes* (www.forbes.com), October 8, 2015, pp. 1–4; Rachel Graf, "J.C. Penney (JCP) Stock Slumps, Jim Cramer: Problems Don't Involve Appliances," *The Street* (www.thestreet.com), January 20, 2016, pp. 1–4; "Why Marvin Ellison Is an Ideal CEO for J. C. Penney (JCP, GE), *Investopedia* (www.investopedia.com), July 1, 2015, pp. 1–3; "J.C. Penney Names Marvin Ellison President and CEO Designee," *JC Penney Company News* (http://ir.jcpernney.com), October 13, 2014, pp. 1–3; Dana Blankenhorn, "Marvin Ellison Will Get His Chance at J. C. Penney," *Seeking Alpha* (http://seekingalpha.com), June 12, 2015, p. 1.

2. "Surprising and Effective Cure for Today's Biggest Workplace Crisis," *Executive Focus*, September 2004, p. 21.

3. Victor H. Vroom and Arthur G. Jago, "The Role of the Situation in Leadership," *American Psychologist*, January 2007, pp. 6–16.

4. Henry Mintzberg, *Managing* (San Francisco: Berrett-Koehler Publishers, 2009), pp. 106–107.

5. Cited in Karen Barrow, "Mindfulness Lets Leaders See More Possibilities," *Democrat and Chronicle* (New York: Rochester, January 18, 2009), p. 2E; Erika Garms, "Practicing Mindful Leadership," *Association for Talent Development* (www.td.org), March 8, 2013, pp. 1–5.

6. For a synthesis of contingency theory by one of its key researchers, see Martin M. Chemers, *An Integrative Theory of Leadership* (Mahwah, N.J.: Erlbaum, 1997), pp. 2838; Bernard M. Bass (with Ruth Bass), *The Bass Handbook of Leadership: Theory, Research, and Managerial Applications*, Fourth Edition (New York: The Free Press, 2008), pp. 522–527.

7. Vroom and Jago, "The Role of the Situation," p. 20.

8. Robert J. House, "A Path-Goal Theory of Leader Effectiveness," *Administrative Science Quarterly*,

September 1971, pp. 321–328; Robert T. Keller, "A Test of the Path-Goal Theory with Need for Clarity as a Moderator in Research and Development Organizations," *Journal of Applied Psychology*, April 1989, pp. 208–212; Robert J. House and Terence R. Mitchell, "Path-Goal Theory of Leadership," *Journal of Contemporary Business*, Autumn 1974, pp. 81–97.

9. Vroom and Jago, "The Role of the Situation," p. 20.

10. Robert House, "Path-Goal Theory of Leadership: Lessons, Legacy, and a Reformulated Theory," *The Leadership Quarterly*, Vol. 7, no. 3, 1996, p. 348.

11. Quoted in Jeff Bercovici, "The Power of the Packers: How Tiny Green Bay Became the NFL's Most Improbable Financial Juggernaut," *Forbes*, September 20, 2011, p. 90.

12. "Green Bay Packers: Mark Murphy," *www.packers.com*, p. 2. Retrieved October 7, 2016.

13. "Packers' CEO Conveys Keys to Leadership Success," *University of Wisconsin-Parkside* (http://www.uwp.edu/explore/media/), April 5, 2013, p. 1.

14. House and Mitchell, "Path-Goal Theory," p. 84; Bass, *The Bass Handbook of Leadership*, pp. 804–811.

15. Chemers, *An Integrative Theory of Leadership*, p. 48.

16. Victor H. Vroom, "Leadership and the Decision-Making Process," *Organizational Dynamics*, Vol. 28, Spring 2000, pp. 82–93; Victor H. Vroom, "Educating Managers in Decision Making and Leadership," *Management Decision*, Vol. 10, 2003, pp. 968–978.

17. "The Vroom-Yetton-Jago Decision Model: Deciding How to Decide," *Mind Tools* (www.mindtools.com), 1996–2013.

18. The first two statements are based on Li Ma and Qing Qu, "Differentiation in Leader–Member Exchange: A Hierarchical Linear Modeling Approach," *The Leadership Quarterly*, October 2010, pp. 733–744.

19. The second two statements are based on David J. Henderson, Robert C. Liden, Brian C. Glibkowski, and Anjali Chaudhry, "LMX Differentiation: A Multilevel Review and Examination of Its Antecedents," *The Leadership Quarterly*, August 2009, pp. 517–534.

20. Kenneth J. Harris, Anthony R. Wheeler, and K. Michele Kacmar, "Leader–Member Exchange and Empowerment: Direct and Interactive Effects on Job Satisfaction, Turnover Intentions, and Performance," *The Leadership Quarterly*, June 2009, p. 399.

21. Pascale M. Le Blanc and Vicente Gonzalez-Roma, "A Team Level Investigation of the Relationship Between Leader–Member Exchange (LMX), and Commitment and Performance," *The Leadership Quarterly*, June 2012, pp. 534–554.

22. Yang Sui, Hui Wang, Bradley L. Kirman, and Sing Li, "Understanding the Curvilinear Relationship between LMX Differentiation and Team Coordination and Performance," *Personnel Psychology*, Number 3, 2016, pp. 555–597.

23. Olli-Pekka Kauppila, "When and How Does LMX Differentiation Influence Followers' Work Outcomes? The Interactive Roles of One's Own LMX Status and Organizational Context," *Personnel Psychology*, no. 2, 2016, pp. 357–393.

24. Robin Kielkowski, "Leadership During a Crisis," *Journal of Leadership Studies*, no. 3, 2013, p. 65.

25. Ronald Heifetz, Alexander Grashow, and Marty Linsky, "Leadership in a (Permanent) Crisis," *Harvard Business Review*, July–August 2009, p. 64.

26. Chris Warner and Don Schmincke, *High Altitude Leadership: What the World's Forbidding Techniques Teach Us About Success* (San Francisco: Jossey-Bass, 2009), p. 6.

27. Andrew J. DuBrin, "Personal Attributes and Behaviors of Effective Crisis Leaders," in DuBrin (ed.), *Handbook of Research on Crisis Leadership in Organizations* (Cheltenham, UK: Edward Elgar, 2013), pp. 12–13.

28. Lauren Weber, "One CEO's Hands-On Crisis Management," *The Wall Street Journal*, September 21, 2016, p. B8.

29. Leslie A. DeChurch, C. Shawn Burke, Marissa. L Shuffler, Rebecca Lyons, Daniel Doty, and Eduardo Salas, "A Historiometric Analysis of Leadership in Mission Critical Multiteam Environments," *The Leadership Quarterly*, February 2011, pp. 152–169.

30. Geoff Colvin, "Running Retirement U." *Fortune*, March 1, 2015, p. 24.

31. Ian A. Combe and David J. Carrington, "Leaders' Sensemaking Under Crises: Emerging Cognitive Consensus Over Time Within Management Teams," *The Leadership Quarterly*, June 2015, pp. 308–309.

32. Suzanne Koudsi, "How to Cope with Tragedy," *Fortune*, October 1, 2001, p. 34.

33. Neil Simon, "Crisis Management: Department of Interior, Department of Labor," *Hispanic Business*, October 2010, p. 43.

34. Barbara Baker Clark, "Leadership During a Crisis," *Executive Leadership*, December 2001, p. 8.

35. Quoted in Ben Casselman and Guy Chazan, "Disaster Plans Lacking at Deep Rigs," *The Wall Street Journal*, May 18, 2010, p. 1A.

36. "Lead in the 21st Century: An Interview with Société Générale's Frédéric Oudéa," www.mckinsey.com, November 2013, p. 1.

**37.** Jia Lynn Yang, "A Recipe for Consistency," *Fortune*, October 29, 2007, p. 58.

**38.** Erika Hayes James and Lynn Perry Wooten, "How to Display Competence in Times of Crisis," *Organizational Dynamics*, Vol. 34, no. 2, 2005, p. 146.

**39.** Denise M. Rousseau, "Presidential Address: Is There Such a Thing as 'Evidence-Based Management'?" *The Academy of Management Review*, April 2006, pp. 256–269; Wayne F. Cascio, "Evidence-Based Management and the Marketplace for Ideas," *Academy of Management Journal*, October 2007, pp. 1009–1012.

**40.** Sara L. Rynes, Denise M. Rousseau, and Eric Barends, "From the Guest Editors: Change the World: Teach Evidence-Based Practice!" *Academy of Management Learning & Education*, September 2014, p. 305.

**41.** Quint Studer, "Evidence-Based Leadership," *Studer Group* (www.studergroup.com), January 14, 2008.

# Leadership Ethics and Social Responsibility

A s the founder and chief executive officer (CEO) of the Sama Group, and the cofounder and CEO of Laxmi, Leila Janah has become a well-publicized social entrepreneur. (The other companies in the Sama Group are essentially divisions or departments that conduct various phases of the work.) The mission of both companies is to decrease global poverty by obtaining work for very poor people, particularly women and children, and also to build better communities. Janah believes that creating work opportunities is the most effective approach to combatting poverty.

The idea for the social entrepreneurship traces back to an assignment Janah had while working as a management consultant and assigned to a major Indian outsourcing company. She encountered a man who was commuting in from the slums. An idea clicked: "If this guy can do this work and he's from a place with open sewers and cholera outbreaks, what if we can use this outsourcing and training model to grant more people access to work and get them out of poverty?" Funding Sama proved to be almost impossible. However, the persistent Janah won $30,000 from two business plan competitions in the Bay Area, to launch the firm.

The core of the business is the model, Impact Sourcing. This approach uses technology-based jobs to people in poor locations in Africa, India, parts of Haiti, and rural Arkansas in the United States. The Sama Group uses private sector methods in innovative ways to substantially improve poor people's access to meaningful work, essential medical care, and education.

Instead of relying on grants to fund the work of her companies, Janah outsources work for a few major technology companies and also sells luxury skin-care products through Laxmi. The Sama Group is self-funding based on contracts with business firms. Clients of the Sama Group include Getty Images, Microsoft, Google, eBay, LinkedIn, and Wal-Mart. Janah says, "They are shocked by the high quality of work that comes out of some of the most unlikely places." The Sama Group has over 80 employees, but the work has been outsourced to approximately 35,000 people.

Most of the work is Internet based including image tagging and content generation for websites. An educational program in the United States taught Americans how to find virtual work. The students faced stiff international competition from low-wage workers. To improve job placement, Sama changed the focus to skill such as social media marketing.

A core belief of Jana and her employees is that talent is equally distributed around the world, but opportunity is not, and that by capitalizing on technology and private sector methods the Sama Group can have a social impact. LXMI is a luxury skin-care brand whose natural ingredients are harvested from the earth by poor women in poor countries, enabling them to earn above-average wages. The foundation idea behind Laxmi is that impact sourcing can also applied to the luxury sector, and that if people spend a lot of money for a product, that product should do some social good. Laxmi grows, harvests, and processes the ingredients of its skincare products on exchange for a fair wage by local standards.

The Sama Group was cited by the magazine *Fast Company* as being among the most innovative companies in 2016. Janah graduated from Harvard University with a major in international economic development with a focus on development in Africa.[1]

The story just presented represents an unusual example of ethical and socially responsible leadership. In this chapter, we examine leadership ethics and social responsibility from several major perspectives: principles of ethical and moral leadership, an ethical decision-making guide, examples of ethical violations, examples of how leaders develop an ethical and socially responsible culture, and the link between business ethics and organizational performance.

## Principles and Practices of Ethical and Moral Leadership

Enough attention has been paid to what leaders at all levels *should* do that several principles of ethical and moral leadership have emerged. Because terms dealing with the ideal behavior of leaders are used so loosely, it is helpful to define what these terms have generally come to mean in the business community. **Ethics** is the study of moral obligations, or of separating right from wrong. *Ethics* can also be a plural noun meaning the accepted guidelines of behavior for groups or institutions.[2] In this sense, it means much the same as **morals**, which are an individual's determination of what is right or wrong; morals are influenced by a person's values. Values are tied closely to ethics because ethics become the vehicle for converting values into action. A leader who values fairness will evaluate group members on the basis of their performance, not personal friendships. And a moral leader will practice good ethics.

Edwin H. Locke, the goal theorist, argues that ethics is at the center of leadership because the goal of a rational leader is to merge the interests of all parties so that everyone benefits and the organization prospers.[3] The ethics link is that if everyone benefits, all people are being treated ethically.

In this section, we present a sampling of ethical and moral behaviors, all centering on the idea that a leader should do the *right* thing, as perceived by a consensus of reasonable people. None of these terms can be pinned down with great precision. We also present a brief explanation of why the ethical and moral behavior of leaders differs so widely and pay separate attention to the importance of an ethical mind. Before studying these principles, do Leadership Self-Assessment Quiz 6-1 to think through your work-related ethics and morality.

## LEADERSHIP SELF-ASSESSMENT QUIZ 6-1

### The Leadership Ethics Quiz

*Directions:* Circle the numbers to indicate how well each statement describes your current attitudes and behavior, or how you would behave if placed in the situation suggested by the statement. Response choices: 1 = disagree strongly; 2 = disagree; 3 = agree; 4 = agree strongly.

| | | DS | D | A | AS |
|---|---|---|---|---|---|
| 1. | A small bribe to make a sale is entirely reasonable. | 1 | 2 | 3 | 4 |
| 2. | As the manager, I would have no problem in taking credit for an innovative idea of a subordinate. | 1 | 2 | 3 | 4 |
| 3. | Supplying a customer with a prostitute to help win a big contract is justified. | 1 | 2 | 3 | 4 |
| 4. | I would be willing to use a video surveillance camera to see what my subordinates are doing when I am out of the office. | 1 | 2 | 3 | 4 |
| 5. | Cheating on your expense account up to about 10 percent of the total expenses is usually justifiable. | 1 | 2 | 3 | 4 |
| 6. | Honest guys and gals tend to finish last. | 1 | 2 | 3 | 4 |
| 7. | If I were fired, I would be willing to get revenge on my employer by taking away trade secrets. | 1 | 2 | 3 | 4 |
| 8. | I would avoid hiring someone into the work group who might become a competitor for my position. | 1 | 2 | 3 | 4 |
| 9. | Overcharging a government customer for goods or services is justified because most companies already pay too much in taxes. | 1 | 2 | 3 | 4 |
| 10. | All things being equal, I would give higher performance evaluations to people of my own ethnic group or race. | 1 | 2 | 3 | 4 |
| 11. | I deliberately give lower performance evaluations to subordinates who I dislike personally. | 1 | 2 | 3 | 4 |
| 12. | I typically play favorites within the group or team. | 1 | 2 | 3 | 4 |
| 13. | I am willing to fake productivity figures just to look good to upper management. | 1 | 2 | 3 | 4 |
| 14. | I would not take time from writing an important report to coach a group member who needed help at the moment. | 1 | 2 | 3 | 4 |
| 15. | I exaggerate the mistakes a subordinate might make just so he or she does not become too self-confident. | 1 | 2 | 3 | 4 |
| 16. | I look for ways to get revenge on any group member who makes me look bad. | 1 | 2 | 3 | 4 |
| 17. | I rarely praise an employee without also finding a way to criticize something he or she has done. | 1 | 2 | 3 | 4 |
| 18. | If a subordinate wants me to do something I do not want to do, I blame upper management for not letting me do it. | 1 | 2 | 3 | 4 |
| 19. | I think it is justified to ask group members to run errands for me, such as getting my car repaired or shopping. | 1 | 2 | 3 | 4 |
| 20. | I will ignore an employee's request to help him or her with a problem just so I can spend some personal time on the Internet. | 1 | 2 | 3 | 4 |

## QUIZ 6-1 (continued)

**Scoring and interpretation:** Add up your responses to the twenty statements. Recognize that people tend to perceive themselves as more ethical and honest than they really are, so your score could be positively biased.

- **20–25:** If you scored in this range, your self-image is that of a highly ethical and trustworthy leader or potential leader. Assuming that your answers are accurate, your ethics could be an asset to you as a leader.

- **26–45:** Scores in this range suggest the self-image of a leader or potential leader with an average level of ethics. There are probably times when you could behave more ethically.

- **46–80:** Scores in this range suggest the self-image of a highly unethical leader or potential leader. If your score is an accurate reflection of your behavior, you are (or would be) perceived as highly unethical and devious to the point that it could damage your career. You should study ethics seriously.

## Four Ethical Leadership Behaviors

*Be Honest and Trustworthy and Have Integrity in Dealing with Others*   Continuing reports of frauds and scandals in the media have placed ethical behavior high on the priority list of many organizations. The problem is that ethical problems erode the trust of both leaders and organizations. Despite the importance of leaders who are trustworthy, evidence suggests that business firms have many ethical problems. As part of an ongoing study of employee attitudes and opinions, the Ethics Resource Center surveyed 2,100 employees among Fortune 500 companies. Twenty-six of the respondents observed misconduct, and 41 percent said the unethical behavior had been repeated at least a second time. The employees surveyed indicated that members of management are responsible for six out of every ten instances of misconduct. Senior managers were cited in 24 percent of the rule-breaking incidents. More than one in five workers who reported misconduct said they experienced retaliation as a result.[4] Retaliation would include a low performance evaluation or the denial of a salary increase.

An ethical leader is honest and trustworthy and therefore has integrity. According to ethics researcher Thomas E. Becker, this quality goes beyond honesty and conscientiousness. **Integrity** refers to loyalty to rational principles; it means practicing what one preaches regardless of emotional or social pressure.[5] For example, a leader with integrity would believe that employees should be treated fairly, and the pressure to cut costs would not prompt him or her to renege on a commitment to reimburse an employee for relocation expenses. As another example, a leader who preaches cultural diversity would assemble a diverse team.

Ron Wallace began his 38-year-long-career at UPS International as a delivery driver, and eventually became CEO. He said that survey after survey indicates that the No. 1 thing people want in a leader is integrity. "It's doing the right thing when no one else is looking."[6]

*Pay Attention to All Stakeholders*   Ethical and moral leaders strive to treat fairly all interested parties affected by their decisions. To do otherwise creates winners and losers after many decisions are made. The traditional belief that a CEO's primary responsibility is to maximize shareholder wealth conflicts with the principle of paying attention to all stakeholders. A leader interested in maximizing shareholder wealth might attempt to cut costs and increase profits in such ways as (1) laying off valuable employees to reduce payroll costs, (2) overstating profits to impress investors, (3) overcharging customers, and (4) reducing health benefits for retirees. Although these practices may be standard, they all violate the rights of stakeholders.

Jim Goodnight, the CEO of software company SAS, is among the business leaders who contend that there is a strong link between employee satisfaction and increased productivity and profits. His commitment to work-life balance has led to SAS being consistently ranked as one of the best workplaces worldwide. Goodnight explains, "Because we put employee-oriented measures in place long ago, we have the benefit of years of experience to show that the long-term benefits far outweigh the short-term costs. Most companies don't know how to represent that kind of return in their annual reports."[7]

Another behavior of *authentic leaders* (see Chapter 2) is to perceive their role to include having an ethical responsibility to all of their shareholders. The welfare of others takes precedence over their own personal welfare (as in servant leadership). Authentic leaders have a deep commitment to their personal growth as well as to the growth of other stakeholders.[8]

**Build Community**   A corollary of taking into account the needs of all stakeholders is that the leader helps people achieve a common goal. Leadership researcher Peter G. Northouse explains that leaders need to take into account their own and their followers' purposes and search for goals that are compatible to all.[9] When many people work toward the same constructive goal, they build a community. A business leader who works with many people to help poor schoolchildren is an ideal example of someone who builds a community.

**Respect the Individual**   Respecting individuals is a principle of ethical and moral leadership that incorporates other aspects of morality. If you tell the truth, you respect others well enough to be honest. If you keep promises, you also show respect. And if you treat others fairly, you show respect.[10] Showing respect for the individual also means that you recognize that everybody has some inner worth and should be treated with courtesy and kindness. An office supervisor demonstrated respect in front of his department when he asked a custodian who entered the office, "What can we do in this department to make your job easier?"

## Factors Contributing to Ethical Differences

There are many reasons for differences in ethics and morality among leaders. Here we look at a variety of these factors.

1. *Leader moral identity.* A set of studies confirmed the idea that a leader's moral identity has a major influence on his or her level of ethical behavior. A moral identity involves a self-perception organized around a set of moral traits such as honesty, caring, and compassion. The moral identity acts as a self-regulatory mechanism rooted in a person's sense of what is right and wrong. The studies in question concluded that leaders set the ethical tone of an organization and are instrumental in encouraging ethical behavior among subordinates, as well as reducing interpersonal conflict. Leaders with a strong moral identity are more likely to achieve such good results.[11]

2. *Greed, gluttony, and avarice.* Many people seek to maximize personal returns, even at the expense of others. Exceptionally high executive compensation could be interpreted as signs of greed and avarice. Two examples are the recent total one-year compensation paid to Dara Khosrowshahi of Expedia ($94.6 million) and Safra A. Catz, of Oracle ($53.2 million).[12] Instead of taking so much money for themselves, how about sharing more of the money with employees and stockholders, and offering lower prices for customers? The counterargument is that supply and demand rules, with a limited supply of capable CEOs. So you have to pay talented executives loads of money to stay competitive, even if the compensation exceeds $100 million per year. Also, an effective CEO can point the firm in the right direction to enhance its prosperity and survival. Recognize also that many celebrities receive exceptional pay, such as the young singer Lady Gaga earning $59 million in a recent year.

3. *Rationalization and implied permission.* Timothy P. Flynn, chairman of the global accounting firm KPMG, has identified reasons why good people choose the wrong path. One reason is rationalization, which leads people to focus on the intent of the action rather than on the action itself. For example, people might say that they are doing something wrong (such as exaggerating profits) in order to help a client or that they are boosting the stock price to help investors. Another reason is implied permission—"Nobody is telling me to stop, so it must be OK."[13] For example, managers might continue to place only personal friends and relatives in key jobs because they were not told to stop.

4. ***Moral development level.*** A notable contributor to a leader's ethics and morality is his or her level of moral development. Some leaders are morally advanced, whereas others are morally challenged—a mental condition that often develops early in life. People progress through three developmental levels in their moral reasoning. At the preconventional level, a person is concerned primarily with receiving external rewards and avoiding punishment. A leader at this level of development might falsify earnings statements for the primary purpose of gaining a large bonus. At the conventional level, people learn to conform to the expectations of good behavior as defined by key people in their environment and societal norms. A leader at this level might be moral enough just to look good, such as being fair with salary increases and encouraging contributions to the United Way campaign. At the postconventional level, people are guided by an internalized set of universal principles that may even transcend the laws of a particular society. A leader at the postconventional level of moral behavior would be concerned with doing the most good for the most people, without regard for whether such behavior brought him or her recognition and fortune.[14] The servant leader described in Chapter 4 would be at this advanced level of moral development.

5. ***Sense of entitlement.*** The moral excesses of business leaders can occur because many of them have developed a sense of **entitlement**. In the opinion of several psychiatrists and corporate governance experts, some CEOs lose their sense of reality and feel entitled to whatever they can get away with or steal. Many executives feel entitled to extraordinary compensation, as implied from the mention of greed, gluttony, and avarice.

6. ***Situational influences.*** Unethical and immoral leadership behavior can also be influenced by the *situation,* particularly the organizational culture. If leaders at the top of the organization take imprudent, quasi-legal risks, other leaders throughout the firm might be prompted to behave similarly. The imprudent risks in subprime mortgages taken with investor money by investment banks in recent history might also reflect an aggressive culture. Financial executives were pushed to maximize profits, sometimes not taking into account investor welfare.[15] Many financial specialists believe that the federal government push for availability of mortgages to applicants with low credit ratings encouraged the availability of subprime mortgages to be invested.

Another potential situational influence on ethical behavior is that national culture in which the leader operates. In some national cultures, bribes are expected to carry out business transactions such as selling to companies or the government. As one participant told Mary Gentile, who was directing an ethics seminar in an Asian country, "Madam we are happy to have you here and we listen to what you have to say about ethics and values in the workplace. But this is _____, and we are entrepreneurs—we can't even get a driver's license without paying a bribe."[16]

7. ***Character of the person.*** A person's character contributes heavily to ethical differences. The higher the quality of a person's character, the more likely he or she will behave ethically and morally. For example, a leader who is honest and cooperative will tend to behave more ethically than a leader who is dishonest and uncooperative. A person's character is quite close in meaning to moral identity, discussed first in this list. Leadership Self-Assessment Quiz 6-2 digs into the behavioral specifics of good character as perceived by the U.S. Air Force.

8. ***Motivated blindness.*** A final factor to be considered here that contributes to unethical leadership behavior is motivated blindness, or seeing what we want to see and missing contradictory information. The result can be a conflict of interest, such as a compensation consultant being paid by the CEO to make recommendations about her financial compensation. Although the consultant is attempting to be honest, the desire to please the CEO leads him to recommend a pay package so generous that the CEO becomes overpaid. Another example of motivated blindness is that a manager who hires an individual may not notice the new hire's unethical behavior because the behavior would reflect an error in selecting the new hire.[17]

# LEADERSHIP SELF-ASSESSMENT QUIZ 6-2

## The Air Force Character Attributes Checklist

**Instructions:** Listed and defined next are character attributes the U.S. Air Force wants to see among the ranks of its leaders. For each attribute, note your standing as being high (H), average (A), or low (L). A checklist of this nature lends itself to self-serving bias, so work extra hard to be objective. When applicable, visualize an example of how you have exhibited, or have not exhibited, a particular character attribute.

| | | MY STANDING | | |
| --- | --- | --- | --- | --- |
| FACTOR | DESCRIPTION | H | A | L |
| Integrity | Consistently adhering to a moral or ethical code or standard. A person who consistently chooses to do the right thing when faced with alternative choices. | ☐ | ☐ | ☐ |
| Honesty | Consistently being truthful with others. | ☐ | ☐ | ☐ |
| Loyalty | Being devoted and committed to one's organization, supervisors, coworkers, and subordinates. | ☐ | ☐ | ☐ |
| Selflessness | Genuine concern about the welfare of others and a willingness to sacrifice one's personal interests for others and the organization. | ☐ | ☐ | ☐ |
| Compassion | Concern for the suffering or welfare of others and providing aid or showing mercy for others. | ☐ | ☐ | ☐ |
| Competency | Capable of excelling at all tasks assigned. Is effective and efficient. | ☐ | ☐ | ☐ |
| Respectfulness | Shows esteem for and consideration and appreciation of other people. | ☐ | ☐ | ☐ |
| Fairness | Treats everyone in an equitable, impartial, and just manner. | ☐ | ☐ | ☐ |
| Responsibility and self-discipline | Can be depended on to make rational and logical decisions and to do tasks assigned. Can perform tasks assigned without supervision. | ☐ | ☐ | ☐ |
| Decisiveness | Capable of making logical and effective decisions in a timely manner. Makes good decisions promptly after considering data appropriate to the decision. | ☐ | ☐ | ☐ |
| Spiritual appreciation | Values the spiritual diversity among individuals with different backgrounds and cultures and respects all individuals' rights to differ from others in their beliefs. | ☐ | ☐ | ☐ |
| Cooperativeness | Willing to work or act together with others in accomplishing a task toward a common end or purpose. | ☐ | ☐ | ☐ |

**Interpretation:** The more of the attributes you rated as *high*, the more likely it is that others perceive you as having a good character. The list may provide some clues to leadership development. For example, if you are perceived to be low on integrity and cooperativeness, you are less likely to be able to influence others.

*Note:* Although competency and decisiveness are not ordinarily considered character traits, being competent and decisive contributes to having good character.

*Source:* U.S. Air Force, as reprinted in Cassie B. Barlow, Mark Jordan, and William H. Hendrix, "Character Assessment: An Examination of Leadership Levels," *Journal of Business and Psychology,* Summer 2003, p. 568.

## The Ethical Mind for Leaders

Cognitive and educational psychologist Howard Gardner believes that for a leader to stay ethical, he or she must develop an **ethical mind** or a point of view that helps the individual aspire to good work that matters to their colleagues, companies, and society in general.[18] Developing an ethical mind begins with the belief that retaining an ethical compass is essential to the health of the organization. Early life influences, such as encouragement not to cheat on exams or plagiarize when writing papers, are a good start. Next, the leader must state his or her ethical beliefs and stick to them. (The ethical beliefs already mentioned in this chapter are relevant, such as being convinced that attention must be paid to all stakeholders.) The leader must also make a rigorous self-test to make sure values are being adhered to, such as checking to see if merit instead of favoritism is a key criterion for promotion. Taking the time to reflect on beliefs can help the leader stay focused on ethical behavior. Asking mentors to comment on the ethics of your behavior can be a useful reality check. Finally, to stay ethical, the leader should act quickly on strongly unethical behavior of others, such as confronting a colleague who is using the corporate jet for a family vacation.

So which leader has an ethical mind? You will probably find many of them as hardworking middle managers. A famous business leader with an ethical mind might be Sheryl Sandberg, the COO of Google, based on her high reputation to date. We never know, however, when a business leader with an outstanding reputation for ethical behavior will have a moral lapse at some point.

## Guidelines for Evaluating the Ethics of a Decision

Several guidelines, or ethical screens, have been developed to help leaders or other influence agents decide whether a given act is ethical or unethical. The Center for Business Ethics at Bentley College has developed six questions to evaluate the ethics of a specific decision:[19]

- *Is it right?* This question is based on the deontological theory of ethics that states there are certainly universally accepted guiding principles of rightness and wrongness, such as "thou shalt not steal."
- *Is it fair?* This question is based on the deontological theory of justice that certain actions are inherently just or unjust. For example, it is unjust to fire a high-performing employee to make room for a less competent person who is a relative by marriage.
- *Who gets hurt?* This question is based on the utilitarian notion of attempting to do the greatest good for the greatest number of people.
- *Would you be comfortable if the details of your decision or actions were made public in the media or through e-mail?* This question is based on the universalist principle of disclosure.
- *What would you tell your child, sibling, or young relative to do?* This question is based on the deontological principle of reversibility, which evaluates the ethics of a decision by reversing the decision maker.
- *How does it smell?* This question is based on a person's intuition and common sense. For example, counting a product inquiry over the Internet as a sale would smell bad to a sensible person.

Ethical issues that require a run through the guide are usually subtle rather than blatant, or a decision that falls into the gray zone. An example took place several years ago when General Motors (GM) and Ford offered to buy out the pensions of 140,000 employees, meaning that workers were offered a lump-sum payout instead of monthly payments for the rest of their lives. For example, an employee with 40 years of service might be

## LEADERSHIP SKILL-BUILDING EXERCISE 6-1

### Should "Dinosaur Power" Be Placed on the Market?

A manufacturer of niche beverages, such as vitamin water, canned tea drinks, and multivegetable bottled drinks, is looking to expand its product line in order to raise revenue. The product development team has been working for several months on an energy-boosting drink, called Dinosaur Power. Product development head Cliff explained to company leadership that energy drinks are among the fastest-growing products in the beverage sector. He pointed out that Dinosaur Power will differentiate itself from the many other products on the market because it will contain an extra-heavy dose of caffeine, will resemble the taste of an alcoholic beverage, and will have a thick cherry taste known to be habit forming, particularly with young adults. Cliff said, "Our test results show that the energy surge provided by this drink will keep people coming back for more. Consumers will be using it on and off the job to feel energized."

With company revenues showing signs of declines, sales could use a quick boost, yet there is some concern about releasing what would be the highest-power, and most habit-forming energy drink on the market. Work in a small group to take the contemplated decision about releasing Dinosaur Power into the market through the guidelines for evaluating the ethics of a decision.

offered $500,000, and then receive no more pension money from the company. Employees who refused the buyout would find their plan shifted to a private financial services firm. The ethics of this pension buyout plan might fall into the gray zone because the workers who accept the offer are receiving a large sum of money.[20] If these same workers die early, their beneficiaries will have profited handsomely. Also, the financial services firm would still provide them with at least a limited pension. Yet, most workers who accept the buyout will receive much less money than if they received monthly payments for the rest of their life.

Leaders regularly face the necessity of running a contemplated decision through an ethics test. Leadership Skill-Building Exercise 6-1 provides an opportunity to think through the ethics of a decision facing a beverage manufacturer.

## Sampling of Unethical Leadership Behaviors

We have been alluding to unethical behavior in this and previous chapters. Here, we present a sampling of unethical behaviors from the past and present. A statement often made is that about 95 percent of business leaders are ethical and that the 5 percent of bad apples (mostly senior executives) get all the publicity. However, the impact of unethical leadership has been enormous. Unethical behavior has thrown companies into bankruptcy, led to the layoffs of thousands of workers, diminished trust in stock investments, and discouraged many talented young people from embarking on a business career. Table 6-1 presents some unethical, immoral, and often illegal behaviors engaged in by business leaders whose acts have been publicly reported. All of these unethical acts resulted in convictions or indictments rather than simply accusations or allegations. Thousands of other unethical acts go unreported, such as a business owner who places a family member, friend, or lover on the payroll at an inflated salary for work of limited value to the firm.

**TABLE 6-1** Examples of Unethical Behavior by Business Leaders

The sampling of behaviors presented here includes behaviors that resulted in criminal prosecutions, and those that result in only embarrassment and negative press.

| LEADER AND COMPANY | OFFENSE AND OUTCOME |
|---|---|
| Bernard L. Madoff, former CEO of Bernard L. Madoff Investment Securities and also former chairman of Nasdaq (the stock exchange) | Convicted of defrauding investors out of about $17 billion over a period of years. Basically sold investors phantom investments, pocketed most of the money, and made some payments to new investors from money paid by earlier investors. Had worldwide network of brokers and other contacts sending him referrals. Sent to prison for 150 years for crimes including securities fraud, international money laundering, mail fraud, and wire fraud. At the time of conviction, said he was sorry. |
| | The Madoff finance chief, Frank DiPascali, pleaded guilty to ten counts of conspiracy, fraud, and other charges and faced a 125-year prison sentence. In hopes of gaining leniency, he testified against five former coworkers accused of participating in the fraud. |
| Prem Reddy, CEO, Prime Health-care Service Inc. | A lawsuit originally filed by a Prime employee in 2011 was joined by the Justice Department in 2016 under the False Claims Act. The claim is that Dr. Reddy pressured emergency room physicians in fourteen prime hospitals in California to admit patients instead of holding them for observation because Medicare payments are usually higher for admissions. Another charge was that Reddy pressured managers and physicians to meet admission quotas and to "embellish" medical records to legitimatize longer hospital stays. Reddy's attorney denies the charges and said that is client did not have the interest or ability to micromanage patient admissions by doctors. |
| Deon Anderson, former Boeing procurement officer | Anderson and three other executives were indicted by a federal grand jury and accused of engaging in a bribery and kickback scheme. He was accused of leaking nonpublic information to bidders for contracts on military aircraft parts in exchange for cash. Faced a wire fraud count that carries a maximum prison sentence of 20 years, and a $250,000 fine. |
| John Stumpf, Chairman and CEO of Wells Fargo & Co. | In 2016, federal investigators revealed that Wells Fargo had opened more than two million bank and credit card accounts for customers without obtaining their consent from 2011 to 2015. As a result of these bogus accounts, customers paid $2.6 million in unwarranted fees (such as draft overcharges) for tens of thousands of unaware customers. Stumpf and the executive team agreed to pay $185 million in penalties. The bank fired 5,300 employees for creating the unauthorized ban and credit-card accounts. Stumpf gave back $41 million of his compensation and said, "We never directed nor wanted our team members to provide products and services to customers that they did not want." Stumpf resigned in 2016, receiving a $134 million retirement package. |

*Source:* The facts in the table have been widely circulated in the media. Representative sources for the facts include the following: Kevin McCoy, "Madoff's Top Aide to Testify Today," USA Today Money, December 2, 2013, p. 5B; Roger Parloff, "As If a Credit Tsunami Weren't Enough: The Case of Accused Ponzi Schemer Bernard L Madoff," Fortune, January 19, 2009, p. 61; Melanie Evans, "Hospital Chain's CEO Faces Suit," *The Wall Street Journal*, August 1, 2016, p. B7; Evan Sweeney, "DOJ Complaint Levels New Allegations Against Prime Healthcare," Fierce Healthcare (www.fiercehealthcare.com), June 28, 2016, pp. 1–3; Massimo Calabresi, "Wells Fargo Customer Fraud Deals Political Setback to Banks," *Time*, October 3, 2016, p. 14; Stacy Cowley, "At Wells Fargo, Complains About Fraudulent Accounts Since 2005," *The New York Times* (www.nytime.com), October 11, 20016, pp. 1–6; Matt Krantz, "Under Cloud of Scandal, Wells Fargo CEO Retires, Gets $134M," *USA Today*, October 13, 2016, p. 1B.

# Leadership, Social Responsibility, and Creating an Ethical Organizational Culture

**Corporate social responsibility** is the idea that firms have obligations to society beyond their financial obligations to owners or stockholder, and also beyond those prescribed by law or contract. Such responsibility is part of external engagement, or the efforts a company makes to manage its relationship with the external world. The external engagement should be integrated into decision making at every organizational level. The external engagement should include a wide variety of activities including philanthropy, community

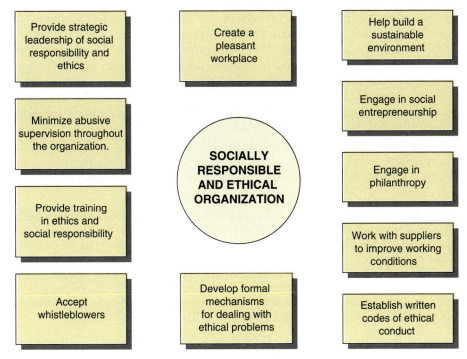

**FIGURE 6-1**   Initiatives for Achieving a Socially Responsible and Ethical Organization.

programs, aspects of product design, and recruiting policy.[21] The initiatives to be described in the following pages are examples of both corporate social responsibility and external engagement.

Being socially responsible fits into the Thou Shalt approach, or finding out better ways for leaders to make a positive contribution to society. In contrast, the Thou Shalt Not approach focuses on avoiding the kind of wrongdoing depicted in Table 6-1.[22] When corporate social responsibility generates value for shareholders and stakeholders, it is regarded as good business strategy.[23]

Our focus here is illustrative actions that leaders can take to enhance social responsibility, as well as create an organizational culture that encourages ethical behavior, as outlined in Figure 6-1.

## Providing Strategic Leadership of Ethics and Social Responsibility

The most effective route to an ethical and socially responsible organization is for senior management to provide strategic leadership in that direction. In this way, senior managers become ethics leaders: Their policies and actions set the ethical and social responsibility tone for the organization. If high ethics receive top priority, workers at all levels are more likely to behave ethically.

Strategic leadership of ethics and social responsibility includes leading by example. If workers throughout the firm believe that behaving ethically is in and behaving unethically is out, ethical behavior will prevail. Ethical behavior that is rewarded is likely to endure. In addition, workers who perform unethically should not be rewarded, and perhaps disciplined. A sales manager who uses a thirty-five-day month might not be rewarded for sales booked during those five days borrowed from the next month just to look good in the previous months.

## Creating a Pleasant Workplace

Creating a comfortable, pleasant, and intellectually stimulating work environment is a social responsibility initiative that directly affects employees' well-being. Because many people invest about one-third of their time at work, a pleasant work environment increases the chances that their lives will be enriched. Robert Levering and Milton Moskowitz of the Great Place to Work® Institute, in cooperation with *Fortune*, have institutionalized the idea of being a "best company to work for." Employers nominate themselves, and two-thirds of the score is based on how randomly selected employees respond to the Great Place to Work Trust Index,® a survey measuring organizational culture. An evaluation of the Culture Audit by staff members at the Great Place to Work Institute determines the rest of the score. The focus is on employee satisfaction, yet the firms that fall into "the 100 best companies to work for" are also typically profitable. Among the benefits these companies offer are flexible working hours; on-site day care; concierge services, such as dry-cleaning pickup; domestic-partner benefits to same-sex couples; and fully paid sabbaticals. Following are the three of the most highly rated companies:[24]

> *Google, Mountain View, California:* The business firm whose name has become a verb sets the standard for Silicon Valley. Google has placed first six times so far as a *Fortune* best company to work for. The company has a workforce of 45.000. Among its perks are free gourmet meals, free massages, a seven-acre sports complex, and free medical services on-site. Engineers are empowered to spend 20 percent of their time on independent projects. Google employees are empowered to award one another $175 on-the-spot peer spot bonuses, and more than two-thirds of "Googlers" made the awards. Hiring standards are tough, emphasizing brilliance, good team player skills, and diverse interests.

> New parents, both men and women of biological or adoptive children, are eligible for up to twelve weeks of fully-paid baby-bonding time. Google also allocated $500 in "bonding bucks" for all new parents to use during the first three months of their infant's life.

> *Devon Energy, Oklahoma City, OK:* This oil and gas driller employs 3,800 people and places 38 on the list. The company has a partnership with an inner-city school to provide one-on-one tutoring of students. In a recent year, Devon employees invested 3,000 hours at the school.

> *Navy Federal Credit Union, Vienna, VA:* Ranked number 72 on the list, Navy Federal is the world's largest credit union, with over 11,000 employees. The company has a generous award recognition programs. A recent career award winner received $10,000, and 73 employees were awarded $3.000 for providing excellent customer service.

The employee programs that qualify a company as a best place to work focus on employee benefits. However, the leaders of these companies also emphasize stimulating work.

## Helping Build a Sustainable Environment

Socially responsible leaders influence others to sustain and preserve the external environment through a variety of actions that go beyond mandatory environmental controls such as managing toxic waste. Helping build a sustainable environment can involve hundreds of different actions such as making packaging smaller; making more extensive use of fluorescent lighting; and, when feasible, using energy from solar panels and wind turbines to replace burning of fossil fuels. Furthermore, many companies sponsor team-building events, in which participants build a playground or refurbish an old house in a declining neighborhood. Preserving an old building uses less energy than constructing a new one, and it enhances the aesthetics of the environment, as well.

A leadership position has been created in several firms, bearing a title such as chief sustainability officer. At Nike Corporation, Hannah Jones is chief sustainability officer and also vice president of the Innovation Accelerator. She is responsible for stewarding Nike's global sustainability and labor rights strategies.[25]

A representative leadership initiative for helping create a sustainable environment is the logistical work of UPS. The company has improved the fuel efficiency of its domestic delivery fleet by 10 percent in recent years. To improve another 10 percent, the company has added more alternative fuel vehicles. A key gas save is to minimize left turns. Avoiding left runs conserves fuel and reduces emissions because less time is spent idling. UPS now has all-electric vehicles, hybrid-electric vehicles, vehicles that run on compressed natural gas, and those that run on liquid natural gas. A newer development is the use of trucks with plastic rather than aluminum panelling, creating a lighter, more fuel-efficient vehicle.[26]

Another way for a leader to help the environment is to be in the recycling business. Electronic recycling is particularly important because electronics are the fastest-growing solid waste stream in the world and contain toxins such as mercury and chromium. The largest company in the field is Electronic Recyclers International in Fresno, California. The company is licensed to de-manufacture and recycle everything from computers to drones. ERI chief executive John S. Shegerian takes performing a good deed for society one step further: One-third of the 200 full- and part-time employees are part of its second chance program, which includes primarily ex-cons and former addicts.[27] The social-good aspect is that being employed facilitates a person's not lapsing back into criminal behavior and drug addiction.

For company leadership to better evaluate their sustainability initiatives, it is important to rigorously evaluate the steps, the processes they are using, and the true impact on the environment. According to the research of Magali A. Delmas, Dror Etzion, and Nicholas Nairn-Birch, 80 percent of corporate environmental performance is accounted for by two factors. One is the environmental processes and practices implemented by the firm; and the other is the environmental outcomes they generate.[28]

A case in point is the Waste<Less denim collection of Levi-Strauss. In one year, 3.5 million recycled plastic bottles are used in the spring collection—an admirable process. Yet, the true impact on the environment would be how many plastic bottles are really removed from the environment. If landfills and waters became less clogged, the environmental impact would be substantial. However, if these same plastic bottles would have been converted to other uses anyway, such as plastic benches, driveways, and ball-point pens, the environmental impact would be zero.

As with any corporate social responsibility initiative, critical thinking is required to determine if a given sustainability initiative is doing any good. In some regions of the United States, recycling companies have closed because of an extremely limited market for the recycled material. In a recent year, more than 300 of the 2,100 recycling plants in California shut down because prices for scrap material have plummeted. A contributing factor was the plummet in the price of oil making it less expensive to produce, making new plastic cheaper than recycled.[29] Another problem is the decreased demand in China for such plastic.

# LEADERSHIP SKILL-BUILDING EXERCISE 6-2

### Conducting an Environmental Audit

To create an environmentally friendly workplace, somebody has to take the initiative to spot opportunities for change, thereby exercising leadership. Organize the class into groups of about five, with one person being appointed the team leader. You might have to do the work outside of class because your assignment is to do an environmental audit of a workplace that might include nonprofit setting such as a place of worship, a school, or an athletic facility. If the audit is done during class time, evaluate a portion of the school, such as a classroom, an athletic facility, or the cafeteria. Your task is to conduct an environmental audit with respect to the energy efficiency and healthfulness of the workplace. Make judgments, perhaps on a 1-to-10 scale, plus comments about the following factors:

### QUESTIONS

1. How energy efficient is the workplace in terms of such factors as building insulation, use of fluorescent lighting, heating and cooling, and use of solar panels?

2. How safe is the environment in terms of pollutants and steps to prevent physical accidents?

3. How esthetic is the environment in terms of protecting against sight and sound pollution?

Summarize your findings and suggestions in a bulleted list of less than one page. Present your findings to classmates and perhaps to a manager of the workplace. Classmates might comment on whether your findings will really improve the planet from an ecological standpoint.

Given the decreased demand for recycled plastic, a more constructive approach for a large company might be to encourage less use of plastic than using plastic generously, and then recycle what was used.

Leadership Skill-Building Exercise 6-2 provides an opportunity for you to practice conducting an environmental audit.

The accompanying text of box Leader in Action described how a leader of a major segment of one of the world's best-known companies cares about sustainability.

# LEADER IN ACTION

## David Cheesewright, President and CEO, Walmart International Focuses on Sustainability

David Cheesewright is president and CEO of Walmart International, a major and fast-growing segment of Walmart. The division has more than 6,300 stores, and more than 777,000 associates serving customers in 27 countries outside the United States. One factor contributing to Cheesewright's appointment to his position in 2013 is his passion for Walmart to contribute to a sustainable physical environment. At the time Cheesewright was appointed to lead the international division, Wal-Mart Stores Inc., president and CEO Doug McMillon said, "He is the ideal person to steer our next chapter of continued, long-term growth. David's passion for sustainability will drive change that will help improve the world."

During a company leadership conference, Cheesewright and Kathleen McLaughlin, the Walmart international chief sustainability officer, discussed how the company uses sustainability to make an impact. "Sustainability is really about where your food, clothes and other products come from—how they're made, shipped and sold," explained McLaughlin.

"Sustainability means doing these things in a way that's good for people and the planet."

Cheesewright notes that the company sets long-term goals to operate with 100 percent renewable energy. Creating a zero-waste future is another goal. Sustainability progress for Walmart includes having doubled the efficiency of U.S. trucks and recycling more than 75 percent of global waste.

Cheesewright and his team have found that going green has various meaning in different parts of the world, with the distinction between developed versus developing countries being noteworthy. A surprising finding for the company is that in developing markets, consumers are more passionate about green products. These consumers are much more pragmatic, related to the realities of life. If a consumer has to carry water from a pump a mile away from his or her home, that person will favor products like shampoo that don't require water or detergents that are very efficient.

Cheesewright and his team also search for sustainability throughout the supply chain to find creative ways of reducing waste. A basic example that if you have bought children's toys, you may have noticed the little wire ties that are difficult to undo, and bother a lot of people. You will no longer find these wires in any product sold at Walmart. Enough wire ties were saved to go around the world eight times. Cheesewright and his colleagues continue to search for creative ways to enhance sustainability.

Cheesewright has an unusual formal education for a business executive leader. He holds a first-class honors degree in sports science and mathematics from Loughborough University, U.K.

### QUESTIONS

1. How legitimate do you think it is for Cheesewright to concentrate so much of executive time and energy into green causes?

2. You might applaud Walmart for saving on the small wires used in wrapping toys, but how socially responsible is it to cut off the wire makers as suppliers?

3. If leadership at Wal-Mart is so concerned about sustainability, why not encourage its customers to purchase fewer products so there would be less physical goods, including wrappings, to throw away?

*Source:* Original story based on facts and observations in the following sources: Leslie Eaton, "Wal-Mart and the Green Consumer," *The Wall Street Journal*, March 31, 2015, p. R6; "Leadership Highlights from Shareholders 2016," *Walmart* (http://corporate.walmart.com), June 3, 2016, pp. 1–6; "David Cheesewright: President and CEO, Walmart International," *Walmart* (http://corporate.walmart.com), © 2016 Wal-Mart Stores, Ind., pp. 1–3; "David Cheesewright Named President and CEO of Walmart International," *Walmart* (http://corporate.walmart.com), December 10, 2013, pp. 1–5.

## Engaging in Social Entrepreneurship

A social responsibility initiative gaining momentum is **social entrepreneurship**, the use of market-based methods to solve social problems.[30] Social entrepreneurship is therefore an entrepreneurial approach to social problems such as homelessness, contaminated drinking water, damaged physical environments, and extreme poverty. (Recall the introductory case to this chapter.) Leaders at a business firm might also form a foundation to help a cause, or be a socially focused, for-profit company such as Better World Books. Through the sale of used and new books, one of the company's social initiatives is to fund literacy programs around the world. Partners of Better World build schools, launch libraries, and provide scholarships. Similar to other social entrepreneurships, Better World pursues a triple bottom line of profits, taking care of people, and protecting the planet.[31]

A research-based model of social entrepreneurship emphasizes that compassion encourages social entrepreneurship. Compassion in the model is viewed as a prosocial (helping others) motivation that connects the individual with a suffering community and triggers sensitivity to the pain and needs of others.[32] An exceptional example of a business leader with compassion is Father Gregory Boyle, the CEO of Homeboy Industries. The beginning mission of the company was to create jobs for former Los Angeles gang members, many of whom had prison records. The company takes former men and women gang members and trains them in job-related skills, starting with custodial work, followed by baking skills.

To create work for the former gang members, Boyle started a bakery. Homeboy has expanded into five other social enterprises besides the bakery, including Homegirl Café, and Homeboy Apparel & Merchandise. Despite all the social good Homeboy Industries continues to do, it does not mean that the enterprise is problem free. In 2015, federal U.S. officials said that the Mexican mafia had united three Northeast Lost Angeles gang. Several of the twenty-two gang members were using Homeboy Industries to hide their criminal activities. For example, one man convicted said he one time used Homeboy Industries as a place to meet a drug dealer who owed the gang "taxes" on drug sales.

Following the arrests, Homeboy Industries issued a statement that stated in part, "As a gang rehabilitation center, we exist to support all those who want to turn away from criminal pasts and transform their lives. We understand that while we successfully help; a majority of our clients, a small percentage attempt, but fail, to make that transformation."[33]

## Engaging in Philanthropy

A standard organizational leadership approach to social responsibility is to donate money to charity and various other causes. Most charities are heavily dependent on corporate support. Colleges, universities, and career schools also benefit from corporate donations. Many of the leading philanthropists donate money during their lifetime rather than giving through their estates. A striking example is Bill and Melinda Gates of Microsoft, who formed their own foundation with the primary global aims of reducing extreme poverty, combating AIDS, and vaccinating children against illnesses. Financier Warren Buffet is also a director of the foundation. In the United States, the focus is more on educational opportunities and access to information technology. In 2016, the foundation had an endowment of over $42 billion, with Buffet having doubled the endowment in 2006. Furthermore, Bill Gates has called for a revision of capitalism in which poor people receive more benefits. Gates said he is troubled because advances in technology, healthcare, and education tend to help the rich and neglect the poor.[34]

Many corporate donors want their charitable investments to benefit the end consumer, not get lost in red tape and overhead, and show measurable results. The new breed of philanthropist studies each charitable cause as he or she would a potential business investment, seeking maximum return in terms of social impact. This philanthropist might also seek follow-up data, for example, on how many children were taught to read or by what percentage new cases of AIDS declined.

## Working with Suppliers to Improve Working Conditions

An opportunity for practicing social responsibility is for company leaders to work with suppliers to improve physical and mental working conditions. Instead of refusing to deal with a supplier who operates a sweatshop, management might work with the supplier to improve plant working conditions. The justification for helping the supplier improve conditions is that the supplier's employees are often in dire need of a paying job. Almost any job is better than no job to a person facing extreme poverty or who is dependent on modest wages for food and shelter. Helping suppliers improve working conditions has been conceptualized as corporations being vehicles for positive social change—yet another way of demonstrating corporate social responsibility.[35] Another form of helping to improve working conditions is to assist factory management to repair potential hazards such as inadequate escape routes in case of fire.

Apple Inc. is one example whereby company leadership took action to work with suppliers to improve substandard working conditions. Worker advocates and Apple representatives found that workers assembling iPhones, iPads, and other Apple devices often work in harsh and dangerous conditions. It was found that many employees worked excessive overtime, lived in crowded dorms, and often stood at the assembly tables for such a long time that their legs swelled until they could barely walk. Underage workers were often included in the workforce of subcontractors.

In recent years, Apple made significant progress in improving the factories. The company now has a supplier code of conduct that provides specific guidelines on labor standards and safety protection. Apple conducts thorough audits, and when abuses are discovered, corrections are required for the subcontractor to continue to be an Apple supplier. [36]A specific example of an Apple initiative with overseas suppliers was to end bonded servitude across its chain. Furthermore, $3.96 million was refunded to workers who had paid exorbitant fees to secure a job in an iPhone factory.[37] Apple leadership has to stay vigilant to labor abuses, because labor abuses have a tendency to resurface, as reported by China Labor Watch, a nonprofit group.

## Establishing Written Codes of Ethical Conduct

Many organizations use written codes of conduct as guidelines for ethical and socially responsible behavior. Regardless of the industry, most codes deal with quite similar issues. Patricia Breeding, integrity compliance officer for Covenant Health, in Knoxville, Tennessee, says, "They all address conflicts of interest, gifts and things like vendor relationships. They use the word 'customer' in one and 'patient' in another but they're all about doing the right thing."[38] Prohibition against bribery of government or corporate officials is being incorporated more frequently into ethical codes to combat potential major problems.

The Sarbanes–Oxley Act, triggered by the financial scandals around the year 2000, requires public companies to disclose whether they have adopted a code of ethics for senior financial officers. In some firms, workers at all levels are required to sign the code of conduct. A written code of conduct is more likely to influence behavior when both formal and informal leaders throughout the firm refer to it frequently. Furthermore, adherence to the code must be rewarded, and violation of the code should be punished.

## Developing Formal Mechanisms for Dealing with Ethical Problems

Many large employers have ethics programs of various types. Large organizations frequently establish ethics committees to help ensure ethical and socially responsible behavior. Top-level leadership participation in these formal mechanisms gives them more clout. Committee members include a top-management representative, plus other managers throughout the organization. An ethics and social responsibility specialist from the human resources department might also join the group. The committee establishes policies for ethics and social responsibility and may conduct an ethical audit of the firm's activities. In addition, committee members might review complaints about ethical problems.

Company ethics teams often establish an ethics hotline that enables workers who have questions about ethical behavior or want to report an ethics violation speak with a company official. Hotlines of this nature are more likely to be used when employees throughout the organization do not fear retaliation for reporting an ethical violation.

## Accepting Whistleblowers

A **whistleblower** is an employee who discloses organizational wrongdoing to parties who can take action. Whistleblowers often go directly to a federal government bureau to report what they consider to be fraud and poor ethics by their employer. Whistleblowers are often ostracized and humiliated by the companies they hope to improve. For example, they may receive no further promotions or poor performance evaluations. Also, many whistleblowers are fired or demoted, even for high-profile tips that proved true. A case in point is Julie Tishkoff, an administrative assistant at Wells-Fargo, who blew the whistle on Wells-Fargo top management in 2005, eleven years before the bank was fined $185 million. Tishkoff wrote to the bank's human resources department about such ethical violations as employees opening sham accounts, forging customer signatures, and mailing out unsolicited credit cards. At least two supervisors ignored her complaints. She kept complaining for four years before being fired.[39]

The Sarbanes–Oxley Act includes some protection for whistleblowers. Employees who report fraud related to corporate accounting, internal accounting controls, and auditing have a way of gaining reinstatement, as well as back pay and legal expenses. More than half of the pleas of whistleblowers are ignored.

Because the pleas of whistleblowers are often dismissed, it is important for leaders at all levels to create a comfortable climate for legitimate whistleblowing. The leader needs to sort out the difference between a troublemaker and a true whistleblower. Being a whistleblower requires a small act of leadership, in the sense of taking the initiative to bring about change. However, leaders of the organization that is turned in might not perceive the change as constructive.

Closely related to encouraging whistleblowers is for leadership to make it safe for people to speak up about even minor ethical violations. Elizabeth Morrison of New York University says that there are two fundamental challenges that prevent employees from speaking up about ethical violations. First is the feeling of futility that it isn't worth the effort because higher ups do not want to hear about problems. Second is the prevalent fear that speaking up will trigger anger by management or retribution (such as being fired). The leader should therefore avoid acting annoyed when a subordinate brings up an ethical violation.[40]

## Providing Training in Ethics and Social Responsibility

Forms of ethics training include messages about ethics and social responsibility from company leadership, classes on ethics at colleges, and exercises in ethics. These training programs reinforce the idea that ethical and socially responsible behavior is both morally right and good for business. Much of the content of this chapter reflects the type of information communicated in such programs. Training programs in ethics and social responsibility are most likely to be effective when the organizational culture encourages ethical behavior.

The Ethics Awareness Training at Lockheed Martin is frequently cited as a positive model of an ethics training program. The training provides an overview of Lockheed Martin's standards of business conduct and sensitizes employees to recognize and react to business situation that may require critical thinking about ethical issues. For example, should a proposed act of generosity by a supplier representative be considered excessive influence?

The annual training begins when Lockheed martin's Chairman, President, and CEO Marilyn Hewson trains her staff in ethics. The leaders trained by Hewson then train their respective teams. The format of training down the line continues until all employees have participated in a training sessions facilitated by their direct manager.

## LEADERSHIP SKILL-BUILDING EXERCISE 6-3

### Collecting Examples of Socially Responsible Behavior

Each class member contacts three currently employed people, and asks them "Tell me what your employer does that you think is socially responsible?" It may be helpful to explain what you mean by *socially responsible* because the term might not be generally understood. Perhaps class members can share their findings on a common platform, even a group e-mail. When all the data have been collected, see if you can reach a conclusion about what constitutes a common socially responsible practice. For example, "giving money to charity" or "paying decent wages" might be two frequent socially responsible practices.

The training includes observing several video scenarios that are based on real cases from the Ethics office. Group discussions follow the viewing that includes comments about how to apply company ethical techniques, and ask questions. As a result of the training, participants are more alert to reporting report ethical violations they see on the job.[41]

Leadership Skill-Building Exercise 6-3 gives you the opportunity to engage in a small amount of ethics training.

## Minimizing Abusive Supervision Throughout the Organization

Part of being an ethical workplace is fair and considerate treatment of employees by supervisors and managers. Despite this obvious truth, an unknown number of managers engage in the dark side of leadership referred to as **abusive supervision**, defined as "a dysfunctional leadership behavior that adversely affects its targets and the organization as a whole." Abusive supervision can take the form of hostile behaviors such as angry tantrums, public criticisms, and inappropriately assigned blame.[42]

Several abusive leadership behaviors as self- perceived by leaders are as follows:

- "I gave an employee the silent treatment."
- "I ridiculed an employee."
- "I told an employee that she or she is incompetent."[43]

Minimizing abusive supervision throughout the organization would include a variety of top-level leadership actions such as frequent communication about the topic, and coaching managers known to be abusive. Listening carefully to employee complaints about being abused would also be helpful.

In attempting to minimize abusive supervision, it is important for organizational leadership to recognize that what constitutes abuse partially depends on employee perceptions. One factor influencing perceptions of abuse is psychological entitlement. Such entitlement refers to a stable and overall tendency toward favorable self-perceptions and expectations of rewards even when there is little justification for such beliefs. The psychologically entitled employee is also reluctant to accept criticisms that conflicts with self-views and a tendency toward high expectations concerning rewards and praise. A set of studies showed that psychologically entitled employees are more likely than their counterparts to feel that they are victims of abuse. Feeling abused, entitled employees will often retaliate against their supervisor by undermining him or her, and the organization.[44] Undermining the organization would include purposely making errors at work and being rude toward customers.

## ical and Socially Responsible Behavior and ganizational Performance

High ethics and social responsibility are sometimes related to good financial performance, as suggested by a comprehensive analysis of the subject. Thomas W. H. Ng and Daniel C. Feldman conducted a meta-analysis of 101 samples published over a fifteen-year period, involving 29,620 study participants. Ethical leadership in the studies was usually measured by subordinate evaluations of their supervisor or manager. A major result of the analysis was that ethical leadership was positively related to job attitudes, job performance, and overall evaluation of the leaders. Another key finding of the meta-analysis was that ethical leadership was slightly related to task performance and good organizational citizenship behavior and was also helpful in reducing counterproductive work behavior. A contributing factor to the findings of the study was that ethical leaders are more trusted by employees, and trust often results in positive job attitudes and behaviors.[45]

According to a study conducted by the Ethics Resource Center, employees who work in an ethical environment tend to be better motivated. The study concluded that the chance to contribute to something larger than themselves and be recognized for it is a strong incentive to employees for delivering superior performance.[46] Using this approach, it is helpful if company leaders explain why the work is larger than oneself, such as a cement manufacturer explaining to employees that the cement is vital for building infrastructure that serves the needs of many people.

Another key payoff from high corporate social responsibility is the ability to attract high-quality employees. An experiment conducted at a career fair suggested that job seekers were more likely to apply for a job when the CEO of the company was ethical. The job seekers were less likely to apply when the CEO was morally questionable, or when his or her level of ethical behavior was unknown.[47] Two related experiments attempted to understand why an employer with high corporate social responsibility tends to attract so many job applicants. The conclusion reached was that corporate social responsibility sends out signals about organizational prestige that appeal to the pride that job seekers anticipate from being affiliated with the company. The studies also found that corporate social responsibility (CSR) sends out signals about organizational values that suggest whether the candidate will have a good values fit with the organization. The level of CSR also sends out signals about how well employees are treated.[48]

A study conducted with 1,084 employees from 17 countries suggests that when workers perceive their employer to have high corporate social responsibility, they tend to be more emotionally committed to the company. Perceptions of corporate social responsibility were measured by responses to statements such as, "Does our company do enough towards protecting the environment," and "How satisfied are you with the way your company is taking responsibility for its employees?" An example of a statement measuring commitment was, "Overall, how strong is your sense of loyalty to the company."[49] Employee commitment often improves organizational performance because turnover decreases, and workers invest more effort into their jobs.

The relationship between social responsibility and profits can also work in two directions: More profitable firms can better afford to invest in social responsibility initiatives, and these initiatives can lead to more profits. The relationship between social and financial performance may be a **virtuous circle**, meaning that corporate social performance and corporate financial performance feed and reinforce each other.[50]

In short, a leader who is successful at establishing a climate of high ethics and social responsibility can earn and save the company a lot of money. Yet, there are times when being socially responsible can eat into profits. For example, installing solar panels in a geographic area with limited sunshine might create a long payback from the panels.

## READER'S ROADMAP

So far in this book, we have examined the nature of leadership; the inner qualities of leaders; and leadership styles, contingency leadership, and the leader's ethical behavior and social responsibility. In the next chapter, we focus on how leaders acquire and maintain power and their use of organizational politics.

## SUMMARY

Principles of ethical and moral leadership all center on the idea that a leader should do the right thing, as perceived by a consensus of reasonable people. Key principles of ethical and moral leadership are as follows: (1) be honest and trustworthy and have integrity in dealing with others, (2) pay attention to all stakeholders, (3) build community, and (4) respect the individual.

Differences in ethics and morality can be traced to eight factors: (1) leader moral identity; (2) the leader's level of greed, gluttony, and avarice; (3) rationalization and implied permission to engage in unethical acts; (4) the leader's level of moral development; (5) a sense of entitlement; (6) situational influences; (7) a person's character; and (8) motivated blindness.

It has been proposed that to stay ethical, a leader must develop an ethical mind focused on good work.

Before reaching a decision about an issue that is not obviously ethical or blatantly unethical, a leader or manager should seek answers to questions such as: Is it right? Is it fair? Who gets hurt? Unethical behavior has brought companies into bankruptcy, led to layoffs of thousands of workers, diminished trust in stock investments, and discouraged many talented young people from embarking on a business career.

Another way a leader can be ethical and moral is to spearhead the firm, or a unit within it, toward doing good deeds—toward being socially responsible and creating an ethical organizational culture. Among the many possible socially responsible and ethical acts are (1) providing strategic leadership of social responsibility and ethics, (2) creating a pleasant workplace, (3) helping build a sustainable environment, (4) engaging in social entrepreneurship, (5) engaging in philanthropy, (6) working with suppliers to improve working conditions, (7) establishing written codes of conduct, (8) developing formal mechanisms for dealing with ethical problems, (9) accepting whistleblowers, (10) providing training in ethics, and (11) minimizing abusive supervision through the organization.

High ethics and social responsibility are sometimes related to good financial performance, according to research evidence and opinion. A meta-analysis revealed that ethical leadership was positively related to job attitudes, job performance, and overall evaluation of the leaders. Employees who work in an ethical environment tend to be better motivated. Corporate social responsibility can help in recruiting talented employees, and can lead to higher commitment to the company. Corporate social performance and corporate financial performance often feed and reinforce each other.

## KEY TERMS

Ethics 144
morals 144
integrity 146
entitlement 148

ethical mind 150
corporate social
  responsibility 152
social entrepreneurship 157

whistleblower 159
abusive supervision 160
virtuous circle 161

## GUIDELINES FOR ACTIONS AND SKILL DEVELOPMENT

A solid foundation for developing a leadership career is to establish a personal ethical code. An ethical code determines what behavior is right or wrong, good or bad, based on values. The values stem from cultural upbringing, religious teachings, peer influences, and professional or industry standards. A code of professional ethics helps a leader deal with such issues as accepting bribes, backstabbing coworkers, and sexually harassing a work associate.

A provocative explanation of the causes of unethical behavior emphasizes the strength of relationships among people. Assume that two people have close ties to each other—they may have worked together for a long time or have known each other both on and off the job. As a consequence, they are likely to behave ethically toward one another on the job. In contrast, if a weak relationship exists between two individuals, either party is more likely to treat the other badly. In the work environment, the people involved may be your work associates, your contacts, or your internal and external customers.[51] The message is for you as a leader to build strong relationships with others in order to increase the frequency of ethical behavior.

A set of experiments with supervisors suggests that abusive supervision is often triggered by poor-performing employees who may trigger a sense of hostility in the supervisor.[52] As a leader, it is therefore important to be on the alert that poor performance by a subordinate does prompt you to supervise abusively. You must exercise self-control to deal with poor performance professionally.

### Discussion Questions and Activities

1. If several reputable well-known companies have been charged with using bribes to obtain sales, why should you worry about being ethical?

2. The majority of business executives accused of unethical behavior have studied ethics either as a subject in a business course or as an entire course. So what do you think went wrong?

3. Suppose you had inside information that your employer was thinking about declaring bankruptcy, and you find out that a family member was about to purchase $20,000 in the stock of your employer. To what extent would it be unethical for you to dissuade the family member from making the investment?

4. How can consumers use the Internet to help control the ethical behavior of business leaders?

5. What responsibility should the major online retailers take to combat "porch pirates"? The latter are people who steal packages left at people's homes.

6. Should leaders of companies that produce fattening food that can lead to cardiac problems and obesity be targeted for being socially irresponsible?

7. How fair do you think it is to deny an executive a CEO position he or she had been promised because of a romantic relationship with a subordinate? Explain your reasoning.

8. As a present or future organizational leader, what can you do to be an ethical role model for others?

9. Provide an example of a company you consider to be highly ethical and socially responsible. What is the basis for your answer?

10. In this chapter, we have discussed ethical problems mostly in business. For sake of fairness and balance, identify a few ethical problems you have observed among lawyers, physicians, politicians, or sports figures.

## LEADERSHIP CASE PROBLEM A

### Salary Advance United Ponders Its Future

Max is the CEO of Salary Advance United, a payday lender with twenty-five locations. The core business of Salary Advance is to lend consumers advances of between $100 and $500 against their paycheck for short periods of time, usually about one week to ten days. Salary Advance also offers other financial services such as check cashing and wiring money. Similar to other payday lenders, Urban charges approximately $15 for a 2-week loan to their borrowers who tend to be high risk. If the loan interest were calculated on an annual basis, the rate would be 390 percent. Some states, including New York, cap interest rates at 16 percent for loans, even though store credit cards often charge over 20 percent for their loans. (Both 16 and 20 refer to annual rates.)

Max informs his management team during a meeting quite that he, along with them, is worried about the future of the business. He notes that fifteen states have already banned payday loans, and that more and more politicians are condemning the business, including the president of the United States. He reminds the team that some of the accusations against the industry are preposterous.

"My favorite example is that renting a full-size sedan costs about $75 before taxes," said Max. "If somebody rented the care for the entire year, or 365 days, the annual fee would be $27, 375 plus taxes. Yet no politician complains about the exorbitant rates charged by car-rental agencies. My biggest concern right now is that the state is going to shut us down."

Max then had a problem-solving session with the group, exploring alternatives that could be pursued to stay in business. One alternative that emerged was to set up online operations overseas in a country that welcomed such businesses (e.g., Malta or the West Indies). The suggestion was to still keep a few offices open to catch street traffic and offer services for wiring money. In this way, state regulations could be avoided.

Another alternative that the group formulated was to base the business on a Native American reservation, again to avoid state regulations. A handful of payday lenders have successfully made this transition.

Max concluded the meeting by saying, "We cannot forget that our mission is to help financially troubled people in need. Without our loans, many of our potential customers would have their cars repossessed of their homes foreclosed. Equally bad, they would have to use loan sharks to get money. Our interest rates may seem high to the outside world, but we have to charge enough to cover our risks and earn a small profit."

The team nodded in agreement with Max.

### Questions

1. What is your evaluation of the ethics of Salary Advance United making payday loans?
2. What do you think of the ethics of the two alternatives mentioned to avoid state regulations: locating offshore or on a Native American reservation?
3. What do you recommend to Max to make the business model of Salary Advance ethical enough to avoid being attacked by politicians?

## ASSOCIATED ROLE PLAY

One student plays the role of Max who is attempting to provide leadership to the group with respect to pondering the future of Salary Advance United. Several other students play the roles of member of the top-management team at the company. A group discussion ensues, with some attention paid to the ethics of Salary Advance United. Feedback can be provided about how well the ethical issues were handled.

## LEADERSHIP CASE PROBLEM B

### Are Drivers or Smartphones to Blame?

Top-level leaders at a company that manufactures smartphones, tablet computers, and portable music players, among other electronic devices held a one-day retreat. The purpose was to think though how well the company was contributing to society. Technology chief, Olivia, commented, "I am very proud of us as a company. Think of what we have done for the world. Because of our products, people are more productive, smarter, and happier. At any time of the day, millions of users can access the information they need, and get in touch with whoever they want. Furthermore, they don't have to clutter their minds with facts, or even know how to spell correctly, or do basic math. With the tap of a few buttons, or touching a screen, they get all the information they need."

CEO Raphael added, "You are so right Olivia. Also, people don't even have to pay for landline telephones any longer. And think of how hundreds of companies can hire fewer people because of our devices. I learned recently that many car dealerships have laid off many of their in-store sales reps because a good deal of car purchasing is now done over the Internet. And people don't have to purchase those ink-laden newspapers because they can get all the information they need on a hand-held device."

Derek, the marketing manager, with a worried look said to the group. "We all make a great living from the electronic devices we make and sell, and so do our competitors. The information technology industry has created millions of jobs. And maybe we have also eliminated millions of jobs. However, I want us as industry leaders to focus on one issue right now.

The accidents and deaths our devices are facilitating are getting out of hand. At first it was people sending and receiving calls on their cell phones that was creating driving hazards. Then along came texting which is even a bigger problem. Now we have data that the number of people who surf the Internet while driving is surging.

I know that states, provinces, and municipalities forbid texting or handheld phone use while driving, but the laws are largely ignored, and the carnage continues. I am asking us to consider what role we should play as an industry leader in getting consumers to use our products in a way that does not harm or kill other people on the streets and highways."

Raphael replied, "I think that local governments, Internet service providers, and perhaps schools have more responsibility for minimizing accidents with smartphone users." If we were making kitchen knives instead of electronic devices would we be responsible for the occasional deaths and injuries caused by these knives?

"In our situation, we have to ask whether the drivers or the smartphones are to blame for the accidents of distracted drivers."

### Questions

1. What role do you think this industry leader should play in encouraging safer use of their smartphones?
2. With the negative perspective Derek has about the use of smartphones while driving, should he be released from his position as the marketing manager?
3. How ethical and socially responsible are the opinions of Olivia and Raphael about the advantages of smartphones to society?

## ASSOCIATED ROLE PLAY

One student plays the role of Derek, who later in the meeting tells a story about a neighbor whose teenage daughter and two companions died in an auto accident because the daughter was texting while driving. Derek is purposely being dramatic because he wants the team to be more socially responsible. Two other students play the roles of Olivia and Raphael who sympathize with Derek's neighbor, yet want Derek to be more realistic about the company's social responsibility with respect to smartphones.

**LEADERSHIP** SKILL-BUILDING **EXERCISE 6-4**

**My Leadership Portfolio**

For this chapter's entry into your leadership journal, reflect on any scenario you have encountered recently that would have given you the opportunity to practice ethical or socially responsible behavior. The scenario could have taken place in relation to employment, an interaction with fellow students, or being a customer of some type. Write down the scenario, and how you responded to it. Indicate what you learned about yourself. An example follows:

> I had been thinking of purchasing advanced software to manage and edit photos on my computer. The software I needed would cost several hundred dollars. The other day, while going through my e-mail, I came upon an advertisement offering

the exact photo software I wanted for $50. At first, I thought this would be a real money saver. After thinking through the ethical issues, I came to realize that the person selling this software was probably a pirate. If I purchased from this character, I would be supporting a software pirate. Besides, buying stolen goods might even be a crime. I learned from this incident that there are many opportunities in everyday life to practice good—or bad—ethics. I want to become a moral leader, so practicing good ethics will help me.

> P.S.: By being ethical, I probably avoided buying virus-infected software that could have played havoc with my computer.

 **LEADERSHIP** SKILL-BUILDING **EXERCISE 6-5**

**Company Policy for Employee Recycling of Electronic Products**

Assume that you are in a leadership position within your company. You and several other managers are concerned about the physical environment becoming cluttered with discarded electronic products, including personal computers, laptop computers, smartphones, and television sets. You know that there are appropriate channels for discarding and recycling these products responsibly, yet these channels are often neglected. Your company has environmentally conscious procedures for getting rid of electronic

devices. You are concerned, however, that employees are not doing enough at home to safely discard used electronic products.

Work individually or with other students to develop a company policy that will facilitate employees being socially responsible when discarding electronic devices no longer in use. Recognize that the company has limited direct control over how employees conduct their personal life. A suggested guideline is to create a company policy about one hundred words long.

# NOTES

1. Original story based on facts and observations in the following sources: "Meet the Game Changer: Leila Janah, Fond and CEO of SAMA Group," *TOMS* (www.toms.com), September 11, 2015, pp. 1–9; "Ten Extraordinary Women Entrepreneurs," *Faction Studio NYC* (www.factoionstudio.com), 2016, pp. 3–4; Heather Wood Rudulph, "Get That Life: How I Started My Own Company at 25," *Cosmopolitan* (www.cosmopolitan.com), May 9, 2016, pp. 1–9; "About Leila," www.sama.com, 2016, p. 1; Sara Kessler, "For Redefining What It Means to Be as Not-for-Profit Business: The SAMA Group," *Fast Company*, March 2016, pp. 86–89; "Leila Janah: Co-Founder and CEO of LXMI," *LinkedIn* (www.linkedin.com), pp. 1–6.

2. James G. Clawson, *Level Three Leadership: Getting below the Surface*, Second Edition (Upper Saddle River, NJ: Prentice Hall, 2002), p. 54.

3. Cited in Joanne B. Ciulla, ed., *Ethics: The Heart of Leadership*, Second Edition (Westport, CO: Praeger, 2004), p. 119.

4. *National Business Ethics Survey* (Arlington, VA: Ethics Resource Center, 2013) (www.ethics.org).

5. Thomas E. Becker, "Integrity in Organizations: Beyond Honesty and Conscientiousness," *Academy of Management Review*, January 1998, pp. 154–161.

6. "A Conversation with Ron Wallace: From UPS Driver to President," *Executive Leadership*, September 2016, p. 3.

7. Tricia Bisoux, "Corporate Counter Culture," *BizEd*, November/December 2004, p. 18; "Jim Goodnight: Co-Founder & Chief Executive Office," *SAS* (www.sas.com), 2016.

8. Douglas R. May, Adrian Y. L. Chan, Timothy D. Hodges, and Bruce J. Avolio, "Developing the Moral Component of Authentic Leadership," *Organizational Dynamics*, no. 3, 2003, p. 248.

9. Peter G. Northouse, *Leadership: Theory and Practice*, Second Edition (Thousand Oaks, CA: Sage Publications, 2001), p. 263.

10. Clawson, *Level Three Leadership*, p. 57.

11. David M. Mayer, Karl Aquino, Rebecca L. Greenbaum, and Maribeth Kuenzi, "Who Displays Ethical Leadership, and Why Does It Matter?" *Academy of Management Journal*, February 2012, pp. 151–171.

12. "200 Highest-paid CEOs 2016," *Equilar/The New York Times* (www.equilar.com), May 27, 2015.

13. "KPMG's Timothy Flynn: Restoring Credibility and Not Looking Back," *Knowledge @ Wharton*, December 12, 2007, p. 1.

14. Lawrence Kohlberg, *Essays on Moral Development* (New York: Harper & Row, 1984).

15. Aaron Lucchetti and Monica Langley, "Perform-or-Die Culture Leaves Thin Talent Pool for Top Wall Street Jobs," *The Wall Street Journal*, November 5, 2007, p. A1.

16. Quoted in Marcy C. Gentile, "Talking About Ethics Across Cultures," *Harvard Business Review* (https:hbr.org), December 23, 2016, p. 2.

17. Max H. Bazerman and Ann E. Tenbrunsel, "Ethical Breakdowns," *Harvard Business Review*, April 2011, pp. 61–62.

18. H. Gardner, "The Ethical Mind: A Conversation with Psychologist Howard Gardner," *Harvard Business Review*, March 2007, pp. 51–56.

19. James L. Bowditch and Anthony F. Buono, *A Primer on Organizational Behavior*, Fifth edition (New York: Wiley, 2001), p. 4.

20. Keith Naughton, "U.S. Automakers Cut Retirees Loose," *Bloomberg Businessweek*, July 2–July 8, 2012, pp. 14–16.

21. John Browne and Robin Nuttail, "Beyond Corporate Social Responsibility: Integrated External Engagement," *McKinsey Quarterly* (www.mckinseyquarterly.com), March 2013, p. 1.

22. Richard L. Schmalensee, "The 'Thou Shalt' School of Business," *The Wall Street Journal*, December 30, 2003, p. B4.

23. Christine Arena, "'Corporate Social Responsibility': A Wobbly Concept," *The Christian Science Monitor* (CSMonitor.com), October 22, 2010, p. 2.

24. Milton Moskowitz and Robert Levering, "The 100 Best Companies to Work For," *Fortune*, March 15, 2915, pp. 141–154; Robert Levering and Milton Moskowitz, "The 2008 List," *Fortune*, February 4, 2008, p. 75.

25. "Sustainable Strides at Nike, Inc.," *News-Harvard Business School* (www.hbs.edu), April 16, 2015, p. 1.

26. Peter Carter, "UPS Offers Keys to Fuel Efficiency," www.truckinginfo.com, August 14, 2014, pp. 1–3.

27. Erika Brown, "Rehab, Reuse, Recycle," *Forbes*, April 21, 2008, pp. 70, 72; "Going All-In On Electronics Recycling with John Shegerian" *Conscious Company Magazine* (www.consciouscompanymagazine.com), Fall 2015, pp. 1–8.

28. Magali A. Delmas, Dror Etzion, and Nicholas Nairn-Birch, "Triangulating Environmental Performance: What Do Corporate Social Responsibility Ratings Really Capture?" *Academy of Management Perspectives*, August 2013, pp. 255–267.

29. Matt Smith, "Cheap Oil Is Shutting Down California Recycling Centers," *VICE News* (https://news.vice.com), June 30, 2016, pp. 1–9.

30. Matthew G. Grimes, Jeffery S. McMullen, and Toyah L. Miller, "Dialogue," *Academy of Management Review*, July 2013, p. 460.

31. BetterWorldBooks.com. Accessed October 15, 2016.

32. Toyah L. Miller, Matthew G. Grimes, Jeffery S. McMullen, and Timothy J. Vogus, "Venturing for Others with Heart and Head: How Compassion Encourages Social Entrepreneurship," *Academy of Management Review*, October 2012, pp. 616–640.

33. Farley Elliott, "Gang Indictment Leads Police to Several Homeboy Industries Employees," http://la.easter.com, June 22, 2015, p. 2; Melinda Newman, "Off the Streets and into Business," *Entrepreneur*, November 2013, pp. 34–38.

34. For details, see www.gatesfoundation.org.

35. Robert J. Bies, Jean M. Bartunek, Timothy L. Fort, and Mayer N. Zald, "Corporations as Social Change Agents: Individual, Interpersonal, Institutional, and Environmental Dynamics," *Academy of Management Review*, July 2007, pp. 788–793.

36. Charles Duhigg and David Barboza, "In China, Human Costs Are Built into an iPad," *The New York Times* (www.nytimes.com), January 25, 2012.

37. Jonny Evans, "Apple Has 'Work to Do' to Improve Factory Conditions," *Computerworld* (www.computerworld.com), February 12, 2015, pp. 1–4.

38. Quoted in Joanne Lozar Glenn, "Making Sense of Ethics," *Business Education Forum*, October 2004, p. 10.

39. Stacy Cowley, "At Wells Fargo, Complaints About Fraudulent Accounts Since 2005," *The New York Times* (www.nytimes.com), October 16, 2016, pp. 1–2.

40. Cited in Ron Carucci, "Why Ethical People Make Unethical Choices," *Harvard Business Review* (https://hbr.org), December 16, 2016, p. 3.

41. "Ethics Awareness Training," http://www.lockheedmartin.com/us/who-we-are/ethics/training.html, 2016.

42. Angela J. Xu, Raymond Loi, and Long W. Lam, "The Bad Boss Takes All: How Abusive Supervision and Leader-Member Exchange Interact to Influence Employee Silence," *The Leadership Quarterly*, October 2015, p. 763.

43. Szu-Han (Joanna) Lin, Hingjing Ma, and Russell E. Johnson, "When Ethical Leader Behavior Breaks Bad: How Ethical Leader Behavior Can Turn Abusive via Ego Depletion and Moral Licensing," *Journal of Applied Psychology*, June 2016, p. 820.

44. Paul Harvey, Kenneth J. Harris, William E. Gillis, and Mark J. Martinko, "Abusive Supervision and the Entitled Employee," *The Leadership Quarterly*, April 2014, pp. 204–217.

45. Thomas W. H. Ng and Daniel C. Feldman, "Ethical Leadership: Meta-Analytic Evidence of Criterion-Related and Incremental Validity," *Journal of Applied Psychology*, May 2015, pp. 948–965.

46. "Employees Who Work in an Ethical Environment Are More Inclined to Go the Extra Mile for the Boss," *Ethics Resource Center* (www.ethics.org), July 8, 2010.

47. Babatunde Ogunfowora, "The Impact of Ethical Leadership with the Recruitment Context: The Roles of Organizational Reputation, Applicant Personality, and Value Congruence," *The Leadership Quarterly*, June 2014, pp. 528–543.

48. David A. Jones, Chelsea R. Willness, and Sarah Madey, "Why Are Job Seekers Attracted by Corporate Social performance? Experimental and Field Tests of Three Signal-Based Mechanisms," *Academy of Management Journal*, April 2014, pp. 383–404.

49. Karsten Mueller, Kate Hattrup, Sven-Oliver Spiess, and Nick Lin-Hi, "The Effects of Social Responsibility on Employees' Affective Commitment: A Cross-Cultural Investigation," *Journal of Applied Psychology*, November 2012, pp. 1186–1200.

50. Sandra A. Waddock and Samuel B. Graves, "The Corporate Social Performance-Financial Performance Link," *Strategic Management Journal*, Spring 1997, pp. 303–319.

51. Daniel J. Brass, Kenneth D. Butterfield, and Bruce C. Skaggs, "Relationships and Unethical Behavior: A Social Network Perspective," *Academy of Management Review*, January 1998, pp. 14–31.

52. Lindie H. Liang et al., "Why Are Abusive Supervisors Abusive? A Dual-System Self-Control Model," *Academy of Management Journal*, August 2016, pp. 1385–1406.

# Power, Politics, and Leadership

S alesforce Chairman and Chief Executive Officer (CEO) Marc Benioff is widely regarded as one of the most powerful leaders in Silicon Valley. Salesforce specializes in customer relationship software and was the first company to offer software on demand, now known as the cloud. Salesforce products help their customers generate more sales leads and obtain a deeper understanding of their consumers. The company has close to one-half of the sales software market.

Larry Ellison, the CEO and co-founder of Oracle Corporation, the enterprise software giant, invested in Salesforce when it was launched in 1999. Benioff was 23 years old when he won the Rookie of the Year award at Oracle. By age 26, he was a key executive at the company. Ellison and Benioff are recognized as having transformed the database and software industry, respectively. Benioff has high self-confidence and has been known to trash talk his competitors in public. One of his guiding principles is "Think of it as you want it, not as it is." Another principle is to never give others your power. An example is that Benioff has expressed no interest in selling Salesforce, which generates over $50 billion in annual revenues.

As part of his powerful image, Benioff enjoys being confrontational and will pick fights, such as making negative comments about executives in competitive companies. Although Benioff is an innovator, he is also an imitator when closely following a product or service will help his firm. For example, his service called Chatter closely resembles Facebook, except that it is designed for intracompany use.

Another Benioff achievement is the invention of the App store, and later gifted the name to Steve Jobs at Apple. Salesforce then used the name App Exchange to provide apps for business. A recent company product is Salesforce Einstein that will integrate artificial intelligence (AI) into almost all Salesforce products. AI will insert predictive suggestions and insights into service, marketing, and sales. Benioff boasts that Einstein will serve as a new nerve system across the entire business and catch competitors by surprise.

Benioff enjoys symbols of power and influence. He has invested in 130 startups and the new Salesforce's new 1000-foot-tall skyscraper will be the tallest building west of the Mississippi. A tall building in Manhattan displays a large, sky-blue Salesforce sign, as do skyscrapers in Indianapolis and London. Benioff also sets powerful goals, such as doubling the company's annual revenues.

Benioff says, "I strongly believe the business of a business is to improve the world." In line with this belief, he and his wife have pledged millions of dollars in low-income housing to help deal with the housing crisis in Silicon Valley. Benioff and his wife have also funded two major children's hospitals in San Francisco and Oakland that include educational support in addition to health services. Both hospitals bear their name. The 1-1-1 Salesforce plan is a commitment to donate 1 percent of Salesforce's employee time, technology, and resources to nonprofits and charitable causes.

Benioff's primary nonwork activity is helping charitable causes and supporting candidates for political office. He graduated with a B.S. degree in business administration from the University of Southern California.[1]

This powerful and influential e-commerce executive's story illustrates several sources of power held by leaders, including expertise and the power of ownership. This chapter covers the nature of power, the ways leaders acquire power and empower others, and the use and control of organizational politics. Chapter 8 continues the discussion of organizational (or office) politics by examining influence tactics. An encouraging note for the student of power and organizational politics is that despite all the advances in technology and organizational theory, the basic principles of power, politics, and influence remain constant. For example, from cave people to the modern business executive, self-enhancement remains a basic motive.[2]

## Sources and Types of Power

To exercise influence, a leader must have **power**, potential, or ability to influence decisions and control resources. A recent analysis of power suggests that it consists of two broad types, the old and the new. *Old power* is held by few, and once it is acquired, it is jealously guarded. Powerful people have a substantial store of power which they can use as needed. Such power is inaccessible to most people, and it is leader driven. *New power* is created by many, is open, participatory, and is peer driven. Sharing knowledge on social media is an example of this new power, and so are consumers who provide input to the design of products they use.[3] Power in organizations is mostly about old power, but processes such as empowerment and shared leadership tend toward being the new power.

Organizational power can be derived from many sources. How people obtain power depends to a large extent on the type of power they seek. Therefore, to understand the mechanics of acquiring power, one must also understand what types of power exist and the sources and origins of these types of power. Seven types of power, including some of their subtypes, are described in the following sections.

# Position Power

Power is frequently classified according to whether it stems from the organization or the individual.[4] Three bases of power—legitimate power, reward power, and coercive power—stem from the person's position in the organization.

*Legitimate Power*    The lawful right to make a decision and expect compliance is called **legitimate power**. People at the highest levels in the organization have more power than do people below them. However, organizational culture helps establish the limits to anyone's power. Newly appointed executives, for example, are often frustrated with how long it takes to effect major change. A chief financial officer (CFO) recruited to improve the profitability of a telecommunications firm noted, "The company has been downsizing for three years. We have more office space and manufacturing capacity than we need. Yet whenever I introduce the topic of selling off real estate to cut costs, I get a cold reception."

At the top of the organization, a leader's legitimate power is strengthened when he or she carries the titles of both CEO and chairman or chairwoman. Executives who occupy the dual role show a unity of command and strong leadership to stakeholders. According to Lawrence A. Cunningham, a corporate governance professor at George Washington University, research indicates that the effectiveness of splitting the roles of chief and chairman can depend on the firm's prosperity. The split tends to improve the performance at struggling companies. In contrast, the split impairs the performance of prosperous firms.[5]

*Reward Power*    The authority to give employees rewards for compliance is **reward power**. If a vice president of operations can directly reward supervisors with cash bonuses for achieving productivity targets, this manager will exert considerable power. Almost any leader occupying a formal position has some reward power. Even the ability to give a subordinate a positive performance evaluation is a form of reward power.

*Coercive Power*    **Coercive power** is the power to punish for noncompliance; it is based on fear. A common coercive tactic is for an executive to demote a subordinate manager who does not comply with the executive's plans for change. Coercive power is limited, in that punishment and fear achieve mixed results as motivators. The leader who relies heavily on coercive power runs the constant threat of being ousted from power. Nevertheless, coercive power is widely practiced. At their worst, leaders who rely heavily on coercive power are considered to be power mongers in the sense that they will go to extremes to gain and retain power.[6] An example would be firing a capable subordinate because the person might be regarded by influential people as a possible replacement for the executive.

# Personal Power

Three sources of power stem from characteristics or behaviors of the power actor: expert power, referent power, and prestige power. All are classified as **personal power** because they are derived from the person rather than the organization. Expert power and referent power contribute to charisma. Referent power is the ability to influence others through one's desirable traits and characteristics. Expert power is the ability to influence others through specialized knowledge, skills, or abilities. A component of expert power is having information not widely possessed by others, such as being an accurate predictor of commodity prices.

An example of a leader with substantial expert power is Doug McMillon who became Wal-Mart's fifth CEO in company history, at age 47. He began his career with the company as a teenager unloading trucks at a Wal-Mart distribution center. McMillon then held positions in various aspects of purchasing and merchandising, which helped him develop expertise relevant to the company. His job knowledge combined with a friendly, charismatic image was key factor in choosing him to represent Walmart in television advertisements.[7]

Another important form of personal power is **prestige power**, the power stemming from a person's status and reputation.[8] A manager who has accumulated important business successes acquires prestige power. Managers acquire visibility based on their reputation—for example, a middle manager who has been successful at reducing turnover in the restaurant or hotel industry. Integrity is another contributor to prestige power because it enhances a leader's reputation. Executive recruiters identify executives who can readily be placed in senior positions because of their excellent track records (or prestige).

## Power Stemming from Ownership

Executive leaders accrue power in their capacity as agents acting on behalf of shareholders. The strength of ownership power depends on how closely the leader is linked to shareholders and board members. A leader's ownership power is also associated with how much money he or she has invested in the firm. An executive who is a major shareholder is much less likely to be fired by the board than one without an equity stake. The CEOs of high-technology firms are typically company founders who later convert the firm into a publicly held company by selling stock. After the public offering, many of these CEOs own stock worth several hundred million dollars, making their position quite secure. The New Golden Rule applies: The person who holds the gold rules.

## Power Stemming from Dependencies

According to the **dependence perspective**, people accrue power when others are dependent on them for things of value. Figure 7-1 depicts this basic model of sources of power. Because the things valued could be physical resources or a personal relationship, dependence power can be positional or personal. Richard M. Emerson noted that power resides implicitly in the other's dependence.[9] A leader–group member example would be that the group member who needs considerable recognition to survive becomes dependent on the leader, who is a regular source of such recognition. An organizational example is that the healthcare system in the United States has become heavily dependent on information technology to help streamline the system. Healthcare information technology specialists therefore have more power.

Should leaders lose some of their power to control resources, their power declines. For example, a real estate developer can lose power when several major properties lose money, or worse enter bankruptcy. (Part of the power lost is the ability to borrow money.) When business conditions improve, and the developer slowly rebuilds, he or she tends to regain power. Several key real estate developers lost fortunes in the real estate bust in south Florida around 2009, but then regained power with the rebirth of the real estate market in the same region four years later.

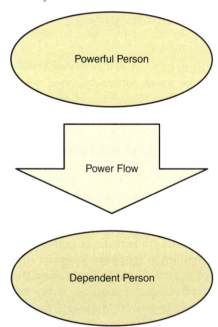

**FIGURE 7-1** The Dependence Theory of Power.

## Power Derived from Capitalizing on Opportunity

Power can be derived from being in the right place at the right time and taking the appropriate action. It pays to be where the action is. For example, the best opportunities in a diversified company lie in one of its growth divisions. Also, many small recycling firms moved from junkyard status to ecology firms as the interest in environmental sustainability surged in the mid-2000s. A person or a firm also needs to have the right resources to capitalize on an opportunity, such as having the capacity to recycle on a larger scale. As mentioned earlier, by around 2016, the demand for recycled materials had diminished. It therefore became more difficult for small recyclers to capitalize on the opportunity of the surge in demand for recycled.

## Power Stemming from Managing Critical Problems

The **strategic contingency theory** of power suggests that units best able to cope with the firm's critical problems and uncertainties acquire relatively large amounts of power.[10] The theory implies, for example, that when an organization faces substantial lawsuits, the legal department will gain power and influence over organizational decisions. Furthermore, the leader of the legal department gains power. The leaders of units directly involved with the organization's core purposes (such as product development) usually have more power than those leaders of departments not directly linked to the core purpose (such as maintenance).

## Power Stemming from Being Close to Power

The closer a person is to power, the greater the power he or she exerts. Likewise, the higher a unit reports in a firm's hierarchy, the more power it possesses. In practice, this means that a leader in charge of a department reporting to the CEO has more power than one in charge of a department reporting to a vice president. Leaders in search of more power typically maneuver toward a higher-reporting position in the organization.

## Power and Self-Serving Behavior

An obvious problem about leadership power is that it can be directed more toward self-serving behavior than the good of others including the organization and all stakeholders. A study conducted with working supervisors as well as a laboratory simulation investigated the influence of accountability on leader self-serving behavior. Accountability focused on the expectation that the leader may be called upon to justify his or her beliefs, feelings, and actions to others. Self-serving behavior in the study focused on the distribution of resources, such as the leader receiving a disproportional share of cash bonuses. The major finding of the study was that powerful leaders who were held accountable acted less self-servingly than their nonaccountable counterparts.[11]

Another set of studies helps explain why some people who attain power act out of self-interest, whereas others with power act in the interest of others. The influential (or moderating) variable studied was **moral identity**—the extent to which an individual holds morality as part of his or her self-concept. Trait power was measured both through a questionnaire about power, and subjective power was measured from study participants describing situations in which they experienced power. The study concluded that individuals with a strong moral identity were less likely to act in self-interest when they had strong trait power or subjective feelings of experiencing power. In contrast, individuals with a weak moral identity were more likely to act in self-interest under trait power or feelings of power.[12] If you are moral, you are less likely to use power for your own good.

To conclude our discussion of sources of power, historian Robert A. Caro reminds us that acquiring power alone does not make for great leadership. It takes an ambitious person to acquire power, and sometimes the approach to acquiring power may not be highly ethical, such as hoarding vital information or making others dependent on you. The person who then uses the accumulated power to create and implement a useful vision qualifies as an excellent leader.[13] The concept of who is an excellent leader could be based on a person's values. For example, many people believe that Mark Zuckerberg, the founder of Facebook, is a great leader because of the impact of Facebook on the world, and his philanthropy. Yet some people believe that Facebook wastes so much time and facilitates communication among evil doers that Zuckerberg should not be considered a great leader despite his power and influence.

The accompanying box Leader in Action describes a highly powerful business leader even though his name is not readily recognized outside his field.

## LEADER IN ACTION

### Google CEO Sundar Pichai, One of the World's Most Powerful Business Leaders

A few years ago Sundar Pichai became CEO of Google, the major division of Alphabet. He is an unassuming man of humble beginnings, growing up with his parents and a brother in a two-room apartment in the Chennai, India. Always brilliant, as shown in his ability to memorize hundreds of numbers dialed on a rotary phone, he was a reserved but fiercely competitive student.

Pichai has been described as the most powerful person in mobile. His rise to Google CEO took eleven years, based on his technical knowledge, team player attitudes, and astuteness about organizational politics. Today, Pichai's main responsibility is to assure that Google's core business and major source of revenue stay strong.

From his entry into Google as a product manager in 2004, Pichai has played a major role in the development of a series of key company products. His first assignment was to work on the Google toolbar which, in turn, lead to managing the team that developed the Chrome browser. The success of Chrome was the engine that powered Pichai through a rapid ascent to the CEO position. After the launch of Chrome, Pichai was promoted to vice president, and shortly thereafter to senior vice president.

Pichai took over the all-important Android division of Google in 2013. One of his accomplishments was to make sure that Android was carefully integrated into Google proper rather than be run as a separate division. His team was later responsible for developing the Chrome OS, operating systems used in Chrome laptops. Based on his success with these key products, Google cofounder Larry Page put him in charge of almost all the company's products and services including Google+ and advertising. In announcing the promotion, Page said, "Sundar has a tremendous ability to see what's ahead and mobilize teams around the super important stuff."

A former product manager at Google attributed part of Pichai's rise to power for having recruited, mentored, and retained a highly effective team. His team of product mangers has a reputation of being the best of the best. Furthermore, Pichai has avoided making enemies. He navigated organizational politics at Google to help his team be successful while not adversely affecting other teams. In terms of his focus on teams, Pichai says, "Nothing makes me happier than a product review in which I can sit with the team and they're showing me something they're building." People who work closely with Pichai comment favorably on his empathy, humor, and eagerness to encourage teamwork across Google.

Soft-spoken and polite, Pichai supported whatever team he led, and ensured that the efforts of every team member were recognized by outsiders to the team. When attending team meetings, Pichai would usually sit in the back, listen quietly, and then after everyone else had spoken, present a collaborative idea. Since he is at Google, Pichai has been well liked. He enjoys good rapport with Page, as well as with company outsiders. For example, he has visited South Korea to help forge a good relationship with Samsung executives. Because of his reputation of being enjoyable to work with many workers wanted to transfer to his organizational unit. It was therefore easier for Pichai to have built strong teams. (This observation was made prior to his CEO appointment, when he was directly in charge of teams.) A vice president who worked with Pichai for eight years said, "I would challenge you to find anyone at Google who doesn't like Sundar or who thinks he's a jerk."

## LEADER IN ACTION (continued)

Pichai is a graduate of the Indian Institute of Technology Kharagpur, with a major in metallurgical and materials engineering. He also holds a master's degree in science from Stanford University, and an MBA from the Wharton School of the University of Pennsylvania.

### QUESTIONS

1. What sources of power does Pichai appear to have acquired?

2. Google has loads of technically skilled, intelligent, and ambitious people. What do you think really gave Sundar Pichai an edge?

*Source:* Original story created from facts and observations in the following sources: Jillian D'Onfro, "The Incredible Rise of Sundar Pichai, One of the Most Powerful CEOs in the World," *Business Insider* (www.businessinsider.com), February 10, 2016, pp. 1–30; Harry McCraken, "At Our Scale, It's Important to Focus," *Fast* Company, December 2016/January 2017, pp. 72–74; D'Onfro, "Here's What Our Google Sources Are Saying About Sundar Pichai's Sudden Rise," *Business Insider* (www.businessinsider.com), October 28, 2014, pp. 1–2; Brad Stone, "How Google's Android Chief, Sunday Pichai, Became the Most Powerful Man in Mobile," *Bloomberg Businessweek*, June 30–July 6, 2014, pp. 46–51; Madhuvanti S. Krishnan, *The Hindu* (www.thehindu.com), August 20, 2015, pp. 1–5; "What Did Sundar Pichai Do That His Peers Didn't Do, to Get Promoted through the Ranks from an Entry Level PM to CEO of Google?" *www.quora.com,* October 28, 2014, pp. 1–6; Miguel Helft, "The Incredibly Fast Rise of Sundar Pichai," *Fortune* (http://fortune.com), pp. 1–11.

## ctics for Becoming an Empowering Leader

A leader's power and influence increase when he or she shares power with others. Empowerment is therefore the basic component of shared or distributed leadership. As team members receive more power, they can accomplish more—they become more productive. And because managers share credit for their accomplishments, they become more powerful. A truly powerful leader empowers team members to accomplish tasks on their own. Strategy theorist Gary Hamel believes that companies that empower and train people at all levels to lead can create competitive advantage. The inference is that talent from all levels should capitalized upon, not just the talents of those at the top of the organizational pyramid.[14]

Here we look briefly at the nature of empowerment before discussing a number of practices and two cautions about empowerment.

### The Nature of Empowerment

In its basic meaning, **empowerment** refers to passing decision-making authority and responsibility from managers to group members. Almost any form of participative management, shared decision making, and delegation can be regarded as empowerment. Gretchen M. Spreitzer conducted research in several work settings to develop a psychological definition of empowerment.[15] Four components were identified: meaning, competence, self-determination, and impact. Full-fledged empowerment includes all four dimensions, along with a fifth one, internal commitment.

*Meaning* is the value of a work goal, evaluated in relation to a person's ideals or standards. Work has meaning when there is a fit between the requirements of a work role and a person's beliefs, values, and behaviors. A person who is doing meaningful work is likely to feel empowered. *Competence,* or *self-efficacy,* is an individual's belief in his or her capability to perform a particular task well. People who feel competent believe that they have the capability to meet performance requirements in a given situation, such as a credit analyst saying, "I've been given the authority to evaluate credit risks up to $10,000 and I know I can do it well." A newer model of empowerment also features the key roles of self-efficacy and competence in helping a fellow group member feel that he or she has gained power.[16]

*Self-determination* is an individual's sense of having a choice in initiating and regulating actions. A high-level form of self-determination occurs when workers feel that they can choose the best method to solve a particular problem. Self-determination also involves such considerations as choosing the work pace and work site. A highly empowered worker might choose to perform the required work while on a cruise rather than remain in the office. *Impact* is the degree to which the worker can influence strategic, administrative,

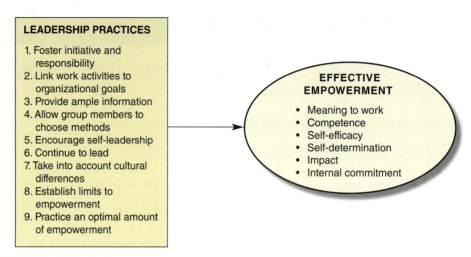

**LEADERSHIP PRACTICES**

1. Foster initiative and responsibility
2. Link work activities to organizational goals
3. Provide ample information
4. Allow group members to choose methods
5. Encourage self-leadership
6. Continue to lead
7. Take into account cultural differences
8. Establish limits to empowerment
9. Practice an optimal amount of empowerment

**EFFECTIVE EMPOWERMENT**

- Meaning to work
- Competence
- Self-efficacy
- Self-determination
- Impact
- Internal commitment

**FIGURE 7-2**   Effective Empowering Practices.

or operating outcomes on the job. Instead of feeling there is no choice but to follow the company's course, a worker might have a say in the future of the company. A middle manager might say, "Here's an opportunity for recruiting minority employees that we should exploit. And here's my action plan for doing so."

Another dimension of true empowerment is for the group member to develop an *internal commitment* toward work goals. Internal commitment takes place when workers are committed to a particular project, person, or program for individual motives. An example would be a production technician in a lawn mower plant who believes he or she is helping create a more beautiful world.

A good feel for what empower leadership means in practice can be derived from a questionnaire used to conduct research about such leadership. Three representative items used to measure empowering leadership are as follows:

1. My leader gives me power.
2. My leader is concerned that I reach my goals,
3. My leader shows me how I can improve my way of working.[17]

The focus of empowerment is usually on the changes taking place within the individual. However, groups can also be empowered in such a way that the group climate contributes to these attitudes and feelings. An example of a statement reflecting an empowering climate would be "People in our organization get information about the organization's performance in a timely fashion."[18] Being part of an empowered group can help a member commit to achieving shared goals.

## Empowering Practices

The practices that foster empowerment supplement the standard approaches to participative management, such as conferring with team members before reaching a decision. The practices, as outlined in Figure 7-2, are based on direct observations of successful leaders and experimental evidence. Before reading about these practices, do Leadership Self-Assessment Quiz 7-1.

# LEADERSHIP SELF-ASSESSMENT QUIZ 7-1

### Empowering Attitudes and Beliefs

**Instructions:** To empower employees successfully, the leader has to convey appropriate attitudes and have certain beliefs.

To the best of your ability, indicate which attitudes you now have and which ones require further development.

## QUIZ 7-1 (continued)

| Empowering Attitude or Belief | HAVE NOW | WOULD NEED TO DEVELOP |
|---|---|---|
| 1. Most workers have considerable unused talent that could be put to good use. | ☐ | ☐ |
| 2. Instead of demanding immediate results, the leader should give group members the time to develop the needed information or skill. | ☐ | ☐ |
| 3. It is productive for the leader to ask team members questions to help them develop a new perspective on problems. | ☐ | ☐ |
| 4. Responsible workers usually know what needs to be done without too much direction from the boss. | ☐ | ☐ |
| 5. It is ideal to let a professional worker figure out the best method for accomplishing a task. | ☐ | ☐ |
| 6. Even if workers are empowered, a little inspiration and encouragement from the leader is still useful. | ☐ | ☐ |
| 7. Feedback to workers is still useful even if they have considerable responsibility for a task or project. | ☐ | ☐ |
| 8. Quite frequently, workers have more knowledge of how to solve a particular problem than does the boss. | ☐ | ☐ |
| 9. I urge (or would urge) subordinates to think of problems as opportunities rather than as a burden. | ☐ | ☐ |
| 10. Good results come about when workers are encouraged to search for solutions without supervision. | ☐ | ☐ |

*Skill Development:* If, as a leader or manager, you already have most of these attitudes and have engaged in most of these behaviors, you will be good at empowerment. Most of these attitudes and practices can be developed without transforming your personality.

*Source:* Statements 9 and 10 are adapted from Robert P. Vecchio, Joseph E. Justin, and Craig L. Pearse, "Empowering Leadership: An Examination of Mediating Mechanisms Within a Hierarchical Structure," *The Leadership Quarterly*, June 2010, p. 540.

**Foster Initiative and Responsibility**    A leader can empower team members simply by fostering greater initiative and responsibility in their assignments. For example, a manufacturer of battery-powered construction tools might inform an information technology enthusiast in the company, "From now on, you are responsible for online sales. You have the product knowledge and the website smarts. I don't. The job is your baby."

Henry Mintzberg reminds us that many professional workers already have considerable initiative and responsibility. In his words: "Truly empowered workers, such as doctors in a hospital, even bees in a hive, do not await gifts from their managerial gods; they know what they are there to do, and just do it."[19]

**Link Work Activities to Organizational Goals**    Empowerment works better when the empowered activities are aligned with the strategic goals of the organization. Empowered workers who have responsibility to carry out activities that support the major goals of the organization will identify more with the company. At the same time, they will develop a feeling of being a partner in the business.[20] Imagine a scenario in which a company auditor is authorized to spend large sums of travel money to accomplish her job. She is given this authority because a strategic goal of top-level management is to become a company admired for its honest business practices.

***Provide Ample Information***   For empowerment to be effective, employees should have ample information about everything that affects their work. Especially important is for workers to fully understand the impact of their actions on the company's costs and profits. Armed with such information, employees are more likely to make decisions that have a positive influence on the bottom line. And they are more likely to use empowerment to make decisions that contribute to business success. For example, an empowered sales representative, armed with cost information, is less likely to grant discounts that lose money for the company.

***Allow Group Members to Choose Methods***   Under ideal conditions, the leader or manager explains to the individual or group what needs to be done (sets a direction) and lets the people involved choose the method. Explaining why the tasks need to be performed is also important. One of the roles of a true professional is to choose the method for accomplishing a task, such as a tax consultant deciding how to prepare the taxes for a business owner. Allowing people to determine the most efficient work technique is the essence of empowerment.

***Encourage Self-Leadership***   Encouraging team members to lead themselves is the heart of empowerment. The basic idea of **self-leadership** is that all organizational members are capable of leading themselves at least to some extent. Complete self-leadership would involve workers deciding what should be done, why it should be done, and how to accomplish the task. A trigger to self-leadership would be to give a handful of talented employees the general instructions, "Why not spend a few hours per week dreaming up something that can make us money?"

Workers who lead themselves to a meaningful extent feel more empowered because they assign more responsibility to themselves. As part of self-leadership, workers set their own goals and find their own rewards, thereby feeling more empowered. An example of this type of self-leadership would be a marketing specialist at an online pharmacy taking it on herself to see what could be done about so many customers dropping the service after about nine months. She decides to embark upon an e-mail and text-message campaign to discover why the service has so many dropouts. The process of contacting the customers winds up enhancing the retention rate, so the market rep feels rewarded. She then proposes her pilot program to company leadership.

***Continue to Lead***   Although leaders empower group members, they should still provide guidance, emotional support, and recognition. Mark Samuel helps companies organize into teams to enhance accountability for results, yet at the same time, he emphasizes the leader's role: "Empowerment often becomes an abdication of leadership. In other words, if I empower you, I don't have to guide you. People need guidance. Leadership cannot abdicate the role of providing guidance."[21] Because employees are empowered does not mean that they should be abandoned.

***Take into Account Cultural Differences***   All empowering practices can be influenced by cross-cultural factors. A group member's cultural values might lead to either an easy acceptance of empowerment or reluctance to be empowered. Americans are stereotyped as individualists. Nevertheless, they are so accustomed to working in teams (sports included) that being part of an empowered team would seem natural.

But not all cultures support empowerment. In one study, data from employees of a single firm with operations in the United States, Mexico, Poland, and India were used to test the fit of empowerment and continuous improvement practices with national culture. The company was engaged in light manufacturing, and data were collected from about forty sites. Empowerment was negatively associated with job satisfaction in the Indian plants but positively associated in the other three samples. The underlying cultural reason is that Indians (at least those working in India) expect the leader or manager to make most of the decisions.[22] Continuous improvement was positively related to satisfaction in all four samples.

*Establish Limits to Empowerment*    One of the major situations in which empowerment creates disharmony and dysfunction is when workers lack a clear perception of the boundaries of empowerment. Empowered group members may feel that they can now make decisions unilaterally, without conferring with managers, team leaders, or other team members.[23] Limits to empowerment might mean explaining to employees that they have more authority than before, but still they cannot engage in such activities as the following:

- Set their own wages and those of top management
- Make downsizing decisions
- Hire mostly friends and relatives
- Work fewer than forty hours for full pay
- Voicing their discontent about the company and its leadership on social media

Many employees justify dysfunctional actions by saying, "I'm empowered to do what I want." It is management's responsibility to guide employment activities that support the organization.

*Practice an Optimal Amount of Empowerment*    Empowerment, as with many approaches to leadership, should be practiced from a contingency perspective. The leader should size up the situation, and ask to what extent he or she should empower group members. A study conducted in eleven firms and six research centers investigated the optimal amount of empowerment. The researchers found that a certain amount of empowering leadership enhances the self-efficacy and performance of group members. Beyond this optimal amount, empowerment becomes a burdening amount that increases worker tension to the point that work performance is lowered. The problem is that too much empowerment can be overwhelming.[24]

Imagine a division head who empowers the industrial engineering group to find a way to reduce production costs by 10 percent. The industrial engineering group welcomes the challenges, and is happy to choose its own methods. The division head then empowers the group to reduce total costs in the division by 10 percent. An enormous empowered task of this nature quickly becomes a burden leading to job stress and lowered performance.

Another approach to exercising the right amount of empowerment is to take into account group member expectations about being empowered. A study with first-line manufacturing workers and their supervisory leaders explored the impact of supervisor matching the empowerment expectations of their subordinates, implying that some workers want more empowerment than others. Measures were taken of both how much empowerment subordinates wanted, and how well the supervisory leaders understood these expectations.

One study result was that workers experienced more role ambiguity (confusion about what was expected of them) when supervisors over-estimated how much empowerment they wanted. Another key result was that the less the leader is aware of the individual's demand for empowerment, the less the worker's level of intrinsic (internal) motivation. Conversely, intrinsic motivation of workers is higher when the leader has a more accurate perception of how much empowerment the workers really want.[25]

## Effective Delegation and Empowerment

A major contributor to empowerment is **delegation**, the assignment of formal authority and responsibility for accomplishing a specific task to another person. Without delegation, effective leadership and management cannot take place. Delegation becomes more important as more tasks need to be done, and those tasks are complex. To lead is to inspire and persuade others to accomplish tasks, not to accomplish everything by working alone.

Delegation is narrower than empowerment because it deals with a specific task, whereas empowerment covers a broad range of activities and a mental set about assuming more responsibility. Also, delegation often involves more checking on subordinates than does empowerment. Mark Hellerstein, the former CEO of a SM Energy Co., explains how he perceived the difference between delegation and empowerment: "When you delegate you are still in control. I empowered others to take control and responsibility."[26]

## LEADERSHIP SKILL-BUILDING EXERCISE 7-1

### Conducting an Empowerment Session

If you are already a manager, the description of empowering practices has given you some useful ideas about empowering others. The role-playing exercise described here gives you a chance to practice your empowering skills. One person plays the role of a leader, and six other people play the role of group members. You are meeting with your group today to get them started on the road toward empowerment. You will need to engage in dialogue with the group to begin the process. The following scenarios should be staffed by different groups of students:

### Information Technology Customer Service Center

You are in charge of an information technology call center whose primary activity is to respond to telephone inquiries from around the country from customers who are having problems using the company's software. The workers who answer the phone are full-time professionals, many of whom are recent college graduates. A major goal of yours is to empower your workers to do as much as they can to satisfy callers' demands. You want your staff to take more personal responsibility for customer problems.

### Debt-Collection Specialists

You are the manager of a regional office of a large debt-collection service. Most of your clients are business firms owed money by other firms. Your office is 25 percent below target for debt collection so far this fiscal year, with five months remaining. The standard methods of debt collection prescribed by the company do not appear to be effective enough. You meet with your staff today to empower them to go beyond the standard methods of debt collection, such as a series of letters, e-mail messages, and phone calls.

Doing this exercise is useful because it helps you develop the right mental set for a leader who empowers group members. Another advantage is that it sensitizes you to the importance of looking for signs of hesitation and ambivalence when you attempt to empower group members.

---

Delegation, like empowerment, is motivational because it gives group members a chance to develop their skills and demonstrate their competence. Instead of delegation being simply a method for the manager or leader to lighten the personal workload, it becomes a developmental opportunity for the recipient of the delegated task. When delegation is poor, conflict often erupts between the individual who thought he or she was responsible for a task and the delegator. An example is when a manager delegating a choice task to a subordinate and then taking it back as the task becomes more important to the organization.

A recommended way of making delegation effective is to specify how much accountability the person has for the delegated assignment. Delegation often fails because the person assigned the task does not know the amount of his or her responsibility. When the person assigned the task is an *issue owner*, the person has complete control over the task or decision.[27] Under such conditions, delegation and empowerment are equivalent.

You are invited to gain some practice in the realities of empowerment by doing Leadership Skill-Building Exercise 7-1. Keep in mind the importance of delegation when doing the exercise.

## Factors That Contribute to Organizational Politics

As used here, the term **organizational politics** refers to informal approaches to gaining power through means other than merit or luck. Politics are played to achieve power, either directly or indirectly. For example, a person seeking to enhance his or her legitimate power might use a variety of tactics to be favorably perceived by top-level decision makers in the company. Power may be achieved in such diverse ways as by being promoted, by receiving a larger budget or other resources, by obtaining more resources for one's work group, or by being exempt from undesirable assignments.

The meaning of *organizational politics* continues to shift in a positive, constructive direction. Politics are often used to advance the purposes of the leader's group such as obtaining valuable resources. A team of scholars have proposed the concept of leader political support that points to the contribution of political behavior. **Leader political support** refers to "political acts and influence behaviors performed by leaders to provide followers with valuable resources to advance individual, group, or organizational objectives."[28] Leaders need political skill for such purposes as building alliances and gaining resources for their constituents. Nevertheless, many writers still regard organizational politics as emphasizing self-interest at the expense of others, engaging in mysterious activities, or kissing up.

People want power for many different reasons, including having more prestige and income, which is why political behavior is so widespread in organizations. By definition, politics is used to acquire power. A number of individual and organizational factors contribute to political behavior, as described next.

## Pyramid-Shaped Organization Structure

The very shape of large organizations is the most fundamental reason why organizational members are motivated toward political behavior. A pyramid concentrates power at the top. Only so much power is therefore available to distribute among the many people who would like more of it. Each successive layer on the organization chart wields less power than the layer above. At the very bottom of the organization, workers have limited power except for their legal rights. Also, an entry-level worker with a valuable skill in a tight labor market has some usable power. Since most organizations today have fewer layers than they previously had, the competition for power has become more intense. Although empowerment may be motivational for many workers, it is unlikely to satisfy the quest to hold a formal position of power. Workers still struggle to obtain a corner office, a corner cubicle, or to sit closer to the boss in an open space arrangement.

## Subjective Standards of Performance

People often resort to organizational politics because they do not believe that the organization has an objective and fair way of judging their performance and suitability for promotion. Similarly, when managers have no objective way of differentiating effective people from less effective, they will resort to favoritism. The adage "It's not what you know but who you know" applies to organizations that lack clear-cut standards of performance.

## Environmental Uncertainty and Turbulence

When people operate in an unstable and unpredictable environment, they tend to behave politically. They rely on organizational politics to create a favorable impression because uncertainty makes it difficult to determine what they should really be accomplishing.

The uncertainty, turbulence, and insecurity created by corporate downsizings, or right-sizings, are a major contributor to office politics. Many people believe intuitively that favoritism plays a major role in deciding who will survive the downsizing. In response to this perception, organizational members attempt to ingratiate themselves with influential people.

## Emotional Insecurity

Some people resort to political maneuvers to ingratiate themselves with superiors because they lack confidence in their own talents and skills. A pension fund manager who has directed the firm toward investments with an annualized 8 percent return does not have to be overly political because he or she will have confidence in being capable. A person's choice of political strategy may indicate emotional insecurity. For instance, an insecure person might laugh loudly at every humorous comment the boss makes.

## Machiavellian Tendencies

Some people engage in political behavior because they want to manipulate others, sometimes for their own personal advantage. The term *Machiavellianism* traces back to Niccolo Machiavelli (1469–1527), an Italian political philosopher and statesman. His most famous work, *The Prince*, describes how a leader may acquire and maintain power. Machiavelli's ideal prince was an amoral, manipulating tyrant who would restore the Italian city-state of Florence to its former glory. Machiavelli has been described as charming, wicked, and disturbing,[29] which are also characteristics of the most extreme office politicians. Three hundred and sixty years later, a study by Gerald Biberman showed a positive relationship between Machiavellianism and political behavior, based on questionnaires that measured these two tendencies.[30]

## Encouraging Admiration from Subordinates

Most organizational leaders say they do not encourage kissing up and that they prefer honest feedback from subordinates. Yet, without meaning to, these same managers and leaders encourage flattery and servile praise. Managers, as well as other workers, send out subtle signals that they want to be praised, such as smiling after receiving a compliment and frowning when receiving negative feedback. Also, admirers are more likely to receive good assignments and high-performance evaluations. Executive coach Marshall Goldsmith explains that, without meaning to, many managers create an environment where people learn to reward others with accolades that are not completely warranted. People generally see this tendency in others but not in themselves.[31]

Communication technology, including social media, facilitates the admiration of superiors. A subordinate who might feel uncomfortable complimenting a superior in person or by phone can easily post a compliment online. For example, a status update on Facebook or a tweet might state: "Just received some dynamite feedback from Shana. She pointed me in right direction."

# Political Tactics and Strategies

To make effective use of organizational politics, leaders must be aware of specific political tactics and strategies. To identify and explain the majority of political tactics would require years of study and observation. Leaders so frequently need support for their programs that they search for innovative types of political behaviors. Furthermore, new tactics continue to emerge as the workplace becomes increasingly competitive.

The impact of political tactics and strategies by leaders on the behaviors of subordinates and colleagues depends to a large extent on perceptions of politics. When employees perceive that the environment is heavily political, particularly in the form of self-interest, they may be prompted to stand out from other workers rather than be good team players. For example, the employees might display more organizational citizenship behavior. Employees might believe that by demonstrating an interest in helping other workers, they will be more valued.[32] Later in the chapter, we will describe how excessive political behavior can have dysfunctional consequences to the organization, such as job stress.

## Ethical Political Tactics and Strategies

So far, we have discussed organizational politics without pinpointing specific tactics and strategies. This section describes a sampling of ethical political behaviors, divided into three related groups: tactics and strategies aimed at (1) gaining power, (2) building relationships with superiors and coworkers, and (3) avoiding political blunders.

All of these political approaches help the leader gain or retain power. Using them can also help the leader succeed in and manage stressful work environments. As defined by a group of researchers, **political skill** is a constructive force. It is an interpersonal style that manifests itself in being socially astute and engaging in behaviors that lead to feelings of confidence, trust, and sincerity.[33] For example, a middle manager with political skill might be able to defend his or her group against an angry CEO looking for a scapegoat. Despite the statements just made, political skill can be used for unethical purposes, as described in the following section.

Leadership Self-Assessment Quiz 7-2 gives you an opportunity to measure your tendencies toward engaging in positive political tactics and strategies.

# LEADERSHIP SELF-ASSESSMENT QUIZ 7-2

### The Positive Organizational Politics Questionnaire

**Instructions:** Answer each question "mostly agree" or "mostly disagree," even if it is difficult for you to decide which alternative best describes your opinion.

| | MOSTLY AGREE | MOSTLY DISAGREE |
|---|---|---|
| 1. Pleasing my boss is a major goal of mine. | ☐ | ☐ |
| 2. I go out of my way to flatter important people. | ☐ | ☐ |
| 3. I am most likely to do favors for people who can help me in return. | ☐ | ☐ |
| 4. I intend to, or already have, cultivated friendships with powerful people. | ☐ | ☐ |
| 5. I will compliment a coworker even if I have to think hard about what might be praiseworthy. | ☐ | ☐ |
| 6. If I thought my boss needed the help, and I had the expertise, I would show him or her how to use an electronic gadget for personal life. | ☐ | ☐ |
| 7. I laugh heartily at my boss's humor, so long as I think he or she is at least a little funny. | ☐ | ☐ |
| 8. I would not be too concerned about following a company dress code, so long as I looked neat. | ☐ | ☐ |
| 9. If a customer sent me a compliment through e-mail, I would forward a copy to my boss and another influential person. | ☐ | ☐ |
| 10. I smile only at people in the workplace whom I genuinely like. | ☐ | ☐ |
| 11. An effective way to impress people is to tell them what they want to hear. | ☐ | ☐ |
| 12. I would never publicly correct mistakes made by the boss. | ☐ | ☐ |
| 13. I would be willing to use my personal contacts to gain a promotion or desirable transfer. | ☐ | ☐ |
| 14. I think it is a good idea to send a congratulatory note to someone in the company who receives a promotion to an executive position. | ☐ | ☐ |
| 15. I think office politics is only for people who cannot succeed based on their talents. | ☐ | ☐ |
| 16. I have already started to develop a network of useful contacts. | ☐ | ☐ |
| 17. I am quite willing to make negative comments about my company on social media websites if the comments are deserved. | ☐ | ☐ |
| 18. I don't care if there are silly photos of me posted on the Internet because private life is separate from one's career. | ☐ | ☐ |
| 19. I have posted positive comments about my boss on the Internet. | ☐ | ☐ |
| 20. I have posted positive comments about my employer on the Internet. | ☐ | ☐ |

## QUIZ 7-2 (continued)

*Scoring and interpretation:* Give yourself a plus 1 for each answer that matches the answer key. Each question that receives a score of plus 1 shows a tendency toward playing positive organizational politics. The scoring key is as follows:

| | | |
|---|---|---|
| **1.** Mostly agree | **8.** Mostly disagree | **15.** Mostly disagree |
| **2.** Mostly agree | **9.** Mostly agree | **16.** Mostly agree |
| **3.** Mostly agree | **10.** Mostly disagree | **17.** Mostly disagree |
| **4.** Mostly agree | **11.** Mostly agree | **18.** Mostly disagree |
| **5.** Mostly agree | **12.** Mostly agree | **19.** Mostly agree |
| **6.** Mostly agree | **13.** Mostly agree | **20.** Mostly agree |
| **7.** Mostly agree | **14.** Mostly agree | |

- **1–9:** Below-average tendency to play office politics
- **10–14:** Average tendency to play office politics
- **15 and above:** Above-average tendency to play office politics; strong need for power

*Skill Development:* Thinking about your political tendencies in the workplace is important for your career because most successful leaders are moderately political. The ability to use politics effectively and ethically increases with importance in the executive suite. Most top players are effective office politicians. Yet being overly and blatantly political can lead to distrust, thereby damaging your career.

***Strategies Aimed at Gaining Power***   All political tactics are aimed at acquiring and maintaining power, even the power to avoid a difficult assignment. Tom Peters said years ago that although power can often be abused, it can also be used to benefit many people. "And as a career building tool, the slow and steady (and subtle) amassing of power is the surest road to success."[34] Here are nine techniques aimed directly at gaining power.

1.  ***Develop power contacts.*** Cultivating friendly, cooperative relationships with powerful organizational members and outsiders can make the leader's cause much easier to advance. Developing power contacts is a focused type of social networking. These contacts can benefit a person by supporting his or her ideas in meetings and other public forums. One way to develop these contacts is to be more social, for example, by throwing parties and inviting powerful people and their guests. Some organizations and some bosses frown on social familiarity, however. And power holders receive many invitations, so they might not be available.

Considerable networking for the development of power contacts takes place through social networking websites geared toward professionals, such as LinkedIn, and specialty sites such as those geared toward specific industry groups, such as sales and marketing, and information technology. Business writer Denise Campbell notes that the social media websites have become to business professionals and entrepreneurs what golf is to C-suite occupants—an opportunity to strategically network and execute business transactions. Also, social media can level the playing field by allowing more people access without restrictions on time, location, or social status.[35]

In order to develop power contacts, it is often necessary to understand the informal network, or who is in contact with influential people in the organization.[36] Mapping the informal social network in an organization can be complex and time-consuming yet here are sample questions you need to answer:

- Who is in regular contact with whom?
- Who appears to have ties to the most powerful players in the organization?
- Who appear to be among the most popular people in the organization?

A key aspect of networking is to find some way of reciprocating when a network member provides you a useful contact or helps you in some other way. Leadership Skill-Building Exercise 7-2 provides some insight into reciprocity when networking.

## LEADERSHIP SKILL-BUILDING EXERCISE 7-2

### Paying Back Favors from Network Members

Most readers are aware that effective networkers find some way to pay back those people in their network who have done them favors. For example, if a store owner refers you to a contact that leads to a job interview you might refer a customer to his or her store. However, finding useful ways to reciprocate favors by network members is not so easy. Your assignment is to brainstorm in groups to develop alternative solutions to the problem, *"How can we reciprocate when a network member does us a favor?"*

The network members can be those developed offline as well as those you have developed virtually, such as Facebook members. Aim for at least a dozen suggestions. After first compiling the suggestions, refine the list for duplication and precision. Perhaps reduce your list to the six most effective suggestions. If feasible, a team leader from each group presents the suggestions to the rest of the class.

Class members might then discuss answers to these questions: (1) Which several suggestions were the most frequently offered across the groups? (2) Which suggestions do I think are good enough to use now or in the future?

2. ***Have a compelling vision.*** Jeffrey Pfeffer, a noted professor of organizational behavior at Stanford University, writes that a compelling vision helps the leader exercise power. A compelling vision in this context is a socially valuable objective. A leader within a school system will often recommend a particular initiative, such as establishing rewards for good teachers, because it is in the best interests of the children. In a business organization, a leader might propose an initiative, such as acquiring another company, because it serves the interests of shareholders.[37]

3. ***Control vital information.*** Power accrues to those who control vital information. Many former government or military officials have found power niches for themselves in industry after leaving the public payroll. Frequently, such an individual will be hired as the Washington representative of a firm that does business with the government. They control the vital information of knowing whom to contact in order to sidestep some of the roadblocks to getting government contracts approved.

   Although the reflex answer for obtaining information is now "Google it," personal contacts are still important for nonrecorded information. To facilitate controlling vital information, it is politically important to stay informed. Successful leaders develop a pipeline to help them keep abreast, or even ahead, of developments within the firm. For this reason, a politically astute individual befriends the president's top aide. No other source offers the potential for obtaining as much information as the executive administrative assistant.

4. ***Do what the political environment demands.*** A high-level political strategy is to do whatever the political environment demands to attain your goals. In this way, you gain the support of decision makers. At Amazon.com, the focus of top-level management including Jeff Bezos is the highest possible customer satisfaction. A politically astute manager or professional looking to get in good graces with people in power would therefore frequently mention ways of taking customer satisfaction to an even higher level.

5. ***Remember that everyone expects to be paid back.*** According to the Law of Reciprocity, everybody in the world expects to be paid back.[38] If you do not find some way to reimburse people for the good deeds they have done for you, your supply of people to perform good deeds will run short. Because many of these good deeds bring you power, such as by supporting your initiative, your power base will soon erode. As a way of paying back the person who supported your initiative, you might mention publicly how the person in question provided you with expert advice on the technical aspects of your proposal.

6. *Be politically correct.* Political correctness involves being careful not to offend or slight anyone, and being extra civil and respectful.[39] The politically correct person therefore avoids creating some enemies who might erode his or her power. An effective use of political correctness would be to say that "we need a ladder in our department because we have workers of different heights who need access to the top shelves." It would be politically incorrect to say, "We need ladders because we have some short workers who cannot reach the top shelves."

7. *Be the first to accept reasonable changes.* A natural inclination for most people is to resist change, so the person who steps forward first to accept reasonable changes will acquire some political capital. The team member who welcomes the changes exerts a positive influence on group members who may be dragging their heels about the change. An example might be that the company is attempting to shift to an online system of performance evaluation, thereby eliminating paper filing. It is politically wise to be an early adopter of the new system.

8. *Inquire about improving your performance.* A useful tactic for developing a positive relationship with your manager is to ask about ways to improve your performance. Instead of implying that you want to become one of his or her in-group members, simply state that you are looking to make a stronger contribution to the group. Two recommended questions are "How am I doing?" and "What would you like to see from me?"[40]

9. *Develop positive psychological capital.* A comprehensive strategy for both gaining power and building relationships is to develop **positive psychological capital**. The term refers to an individual's positive psychological state of development, characterized by four psychological resources: self-efficacy, hope, optimism, and resilience. (Self-efficacy refers to confidence to take on and invest the necessary effort to succeed at challenging tasks.) Although a complex aspect of behavior, positive psychological capital can be developed over time, particularly if the individual focuses on one of the four resources at a time. A person with considerable positive psychological capital tends to be powerful.

   A study conducted with 79 police leaders and 264 sergeants indicated that leaders' psychological capital was positively related to the job performance of their team members. Performance was measured in terms of a straightforward scale developed for the study, with one of the items being, "How would you judge the overall competence of this individual?"[41] The link to power in this study is that strong job performance by subordinates accrues power to the leader.

**Strategies and Tactics Aimed at Building Relationships**  You would probably not be studying leadership if you did not think building relationships was a key part of success in the workplace. To reinforce this point, here is what Stephen I. Sadove, the former chairman and chief executive of Saks, Inc., and now a private equity investor, said were his biggest leadership lessons:

> I used opportunities to get involved and develop relationships with a diverse set of people, as opposed to the narrow group of people I was dealing with day-to-day, and that made a huge difference. It shaped my philosophy in terms of the importance of relationship building. It really underlies my entire philosophy of how to run a business.[42]

The lion's share of organizational politics involves building positive relationships with network members who can be helpful now or later. This network includes superiors, subordinates, other lower-ranking people, coworkers, external customers, and suppliers. Following are several representative strategies and tactics:

1. *Display loyalty.* A loyal worker is valued because organizations prosper more with loyal than with disloyal employees. Blind loyalty—the belief that the organization

cannot make a mistake—is not called for because most rational organizations welcome constructive criticism. A clear form of loyalty to the organization is longevity. Although job-hopping is more acceptable today than in the past, tenure with the company is still an asset for promotion. Tenure tends to contribute more to eligibility for promotion in a traditional industry, such as food processing, than in high-technology firms.

2. *Manage your impression.* Impression management includes behaviors directed at enhancing one's image by drawing attention to oneself. Often the attention of others is directed toward superficial aspects of the self, such as clothing and grooming. Yet, impression management also deals with deeper aspects of behavior, such as speaking well and presenting one's ideas coherently. Bad speech habits are recognized as a deterrent to advancement in organizations.[43] Impression management also makes a contribution because it makes you more visible to others, meaning that your presence in the organization is noticed.

   Another part of impression management is telling people about your success or implying that you are an insider. E-mail is used extensively today to send messages to others for the purpose of impressing them with one's good deeds. Displaying good business etiquette has received renewed attention as a key part of impression management, with companies sending staff members to etiquette classes to learn how to create favorable impressions on key people. Etiquette training for professionals and managers is in high demand because so many people have neglected to learn about etiquette earlier in life, and civility in the workplace has declined. Many management scholars take a dim view of impression management, yet the topic has been carefully researched.[44]

3. *Ask satisfied customers to contact your boss.* A favorable comment by a customer receives considerable weight because customer satisfaction is a top corporate priority. If a customer says something nice, the comment will carry more weight than one from a coworker or subordinate. The reason is that coworkers and subordinates might praise a person for political reasons. Customers' motivation is assumed to be pure because they have little concern about pleasing suppliers.

4. *Be courteous, pleasant, civil, and positive.* Courteous, pleasant, civil, and positive people are the first to be hired and the last to be fired (assuming they also have other important qualifications). Polite behavior provides an advantage because many people believe that civility has become a rare quality. Civility refers to behavior that includes politeness and regard for others in the workplace. A recent study conducted in a biotechnology firm found that workers who perceived a coworker as civil would be more likely to seek that person out for advice and to see that person as a leader.[45]

5. *Ask advice.* Asking advice on work-related topics builds relationships with other employees. Asking another person for advice—someone whose job does not require giving it—will usually be perceived as a compliment. Asking advice transmits a message of trust in the other person's judgment. Leadership Skill-Building Exercise 7-3 gives you the opportunity to practice asking advice in a sensible way.

6. *Send thank-you notes to large numbers of people.* One of the most basic political tactics, sending thank-you notes profusely, is simply an application of sound human relations. Many successful people take the time to send handwritten notes to employees and customers to help create a bond with those people. Handwritten notes have gained in currency because they are a refreshing change from electronic communication.

7. *Flatter others sensibly.* Flattery in the form of sincere praise can be an effective relationship builder. By being judicious in your praise, you can lower the defenses of work associates and make them more receptive to your ideas. A survey of 760 directors found that ingratiatory behavior toward the chief executive plays a bigger role in

# LEADERSHIP SKILL-BUILDING EXERCISE 7-3

### Asking Advice Role Play

One student plays the role of a team leader who wants to build constructive relationships with coworkers and superiors by asking advice. At the same time, the student does not want to generate the impression of being someone who needs considerable help in solving problems. The student therefore must think of a topic for asking advice that shows a legitimate interest in the other person's opinion, yet not appear clueless. It might therefore require a few minutes to think of an advice-asking topic. Another student plays the role of the advice-giver who might enjoy giving the advice, or be annoyed that he or she is being bothered. The rest of the class members will observe and provide some feedback on the effectiveness of the advice-asking techniques.

The potential contribution of this exercise is that it may help raise your awareness of the opportunity to engage in constructive political behavior. Recognizing opportunities to gain political advantage can be helpful to a leader's career.

The importance of praising others through flattery shows up in the leadership principles espoused by Dale Carnegie in his advice to be lavish in your praise about any improvement. Decades of research indicate that reinforcing the behavior you want can lead to behavioral change.[47] In the situation under discussion, the behavioral change the political actor wants is to be more valued by the object of the praise.

receiving a board appointment than does having attended an elite school or having elite social connections. James D. Westphal and Ithai Stern concluded that the most efficient way to get more board appointments is to engage in ingratiating behavior (a form of politics). The type of political behavior focused on flattery. Providing advice and information to CEOs frequently was advantageous. Furthermore, not monitoring the strategic decisions of board members too closely was also effective in receiving nominations to other boards.[46]

8. ***Reach  out to your boss's boss.*** Developing a working relationship with the manager of your immediate manager helps increase your power base at the same time. Your boss's boss is a key person in your network because he or she can have considerable influence over your career. Several approaches for developing a good relationship with your manager's manager, follow. First, connect with that individual on a personal level. Look for a common interest, such as both being a booster of Para Olympics. Second, if you receive a compliment for your good work from somewhere else in the organization or from a customer, pass that information along to your boss. The latter is likely to pass that information along to his or her boss. Third, volunteer for a cross-functional committee. You boss's boss is likely to quickly learn about this meritorious activity.[48]

An example of the research evidence about the contribution of political skill to relationship building comes from a study with 179 employees conducted in a retail service organization. Employees who scored higher on a test of political skill tended to overcome a challenging aspect of leader–member exchanges. Prior research had suggested that superiors and subordinates who were of the same race typically had better quality leader–member exchanges (or quality of the relationship). Correspondingly, racial dissimilarity was associated with a poorer quality leader–member exchange. The results of the study under consideration indicated that subordinates with good political skill were able to develop better relationships with superiors who were of a different race.[49]

A study with 1,600 headmasters and teachers in German state schools adds another perspective on how political skills contribute to leader effectiveness. The study found that political skills facilitated leaders being able to carry out both transformational and transactional leadership. For example, transformational leadership requires political skill because the leader needs to be able to size up the needs of stakeholders. Both transformational and transactional leadership enhanced their leadership effectiveness, as measured by teacher ratings of the headmaster.[50]

**Strategies Aimed at Avoiding Political Blunders**    A strategy for retaining power is to refrain from making power-eroding blunders. Committing these politically insensitive acts can also prevent one from attaining power. A pattern of committing political blunders could reflect low emotional intelligence, and even worse, self-defeating behavior. A serious blunder can be a swift path to derailing a person's career.[51] Take Leadership Self-Assessment Quiz 7-3 to examine your tendencies toward making blunders. Several leading blunders are described next.

1. *Criticizing the boss in a public forum.* The oldest saw in human relations is to "praise in public and criticize in private." Yet in the passion of the moment, we may still surrender to an irresistible impulse to criticize the boss publicly. Also, hundreds of people have lost their jobs because they make a vindictive statement about their boss on a social media website, particularly Facebook. Negative e-mail messages about the company can be political suicide also. An example would be a professional at a pharmaceutical company posting a statement that the company was being unethical in way over-pricing a new drug for lowering blood pressure.

2. *Bypassing the boss.* Protocol is still highly valued in a hierarchical organization. Going around the boss to resolve a problem is therefore hazardous. You might be able to accomplish the bypass, but your career could be damaged and recourses limited. Except in cases of outrageous misconduct such as blatant sexual harassment or criminal misconduct, your boss's boss will probably side with your boss. It was advised earlier to develop a good relationship with your boss's boss. This technique must be used with sensitivity to avoid the appearance of a boss bypass.

## LEADERSHIP SELF-ASSESSMENT QUIZ 7-3

### The Blunder Quiz

**Directions:** Indicate whether you agree or disagree with the following statements.

| | AGREE | DISAGREE |
|---|:---:|:---:|
| 1. It is acceptable to criticize your manager in a meeting as long as the criticism is valid. | ☐ | ☐ |
| 2. If your boss criticizes you, an effective way of getting revenge is to post a tweet making fun of him or her. | ☐ | ☐ |
| 3. If my boss showed me a photo of his or her dog, and I thought the dog was ugly, I would say so. | ☐ | ☐ |
| 4. If I worked for Microsoft, I would still use whatever search engine I thought was best instead of using Bing (the Microsoft search engine) while at the office. | ☐ | ☐ |
| 5. If I thought my company's product or service was not worth the price, I would openly express my opinion on the job. | ☐ | ☐ |
| 6. If I objected to a decision made by top management, I would send a company-wide e-mail, or make an intranet post, explaining my objection. | ☐ | ☐ |
| 7. I am willing to insult any coworker if the insult is deserved. | ☐ | ☐ |
| 8. If I am at a meeting, and the content becomes boring, I will take out my smartphone and check e-mail or surf the Web. | ☐ | ☐ |
| 9. If I thought that my company's stock was a poor investment, I would freely share my opinion with work associates. | ☐ | ☐ |

## QUIZ 7-3 (continued)

| | | |
|---|---|---|
| 10. | During a national election, I would place campaign banners for my favorite candidates outside my cubicle or office, or on my desk in an open work area. | ☐ ☐ |
| 11. | I see no problem in using competitors' products or services and letting my superiors know about it. | ☐ ☐ |
| 12. | If I thought the CEO of my company were way overpaid, I would send him or her an e-mail making my opinion known. | ☐ ☐ |
| 13. | During a company picnic, I would go on at length about my opinion on the effectiveness of a major political figure. | ☐ ☐ |
| 14. | I openly criticize most new ventures my company or department is contemplating, pointing out that most new ventures fail. | ☐ ☐ |
| 15. | I avoid any deliberate attempt to please or impress coworkers or superiors. | ☐ ☐ |

**Total: "Agree" _____ "Disagree" _____**

**Scoring and Interpretation:** The greater the number of statements you agree with, the more prone you are to political blunders that can damage your career. You need to raise your awareness level of workplace blunders.

3. **Declining an offer from top management.** Turning down top management, especially more than once, is a political blunder. You thus have to balance sensibly managing your time against the blunder of refusing a request from top management. Today, an increasing number of managers and corporate professionals decline opportunities for promotion when the new job requires geographic relocation. For these people, family and lifestyle preferences are more important than gaining political advantage on the job.

4. **Putting your foot in your mouth (being needlessly tactless).** To avoid hurting your career, it is important to avoid—or at least minimize—being blatantly tactless toward influential people. An example would be telling the CEO that he or she should delegate speech making to another person because he or she is such a poor speaker. When you feel you are on the verge of being critical, delay your response, and perhaps reword it for later delivery. Use your emotional intelligence! If you are needlessly tactless, compensate the best you can by offering a full apology later.

   Putting your foot in your mouth can also take the form of making a public statement that many people interpret to have a negative meaning or to reflect callousness. The Deepwater Horizon oil rig explosion in 2010 spewed hundreds of millions of gallons of oil into the Gulf of Mexico and killed eleven workers. BP chief executive at the time, Tony Hayward, made a series of public appearances explaining the company's recovery efforts. During one appearance, Hayward said he wanted his "life back," which angered many people because they thought he had not suffered much in comparison to the many victims of the disaster. This gaffe contributed to his inability to elicit much empathy from the U.S. public, and he was dismissed shortly thereafter.[52]

5. **Not conforming to the company dress code.** Although some degree of independence and free thinking is welcome in many organizations, violating the dress code can block you from acquiring more power. Conforming to the dress code suggests that you are part of the team and you understand what is expected. Dress codes can be violated by dressing too informally *or* formally, and by wearing clothing that symbolizes a cultural identity.[53]

6. **Being revengeful and hostile during an exit interview.** After a person resigns a position, many companies conduct an exit interview in which departing employees

are asked to discuss the reason for quitting. Under the best of circumstances, the employee who quits would offer constructive suggestions that would improve the working conditions and work climate for present and future employees. This would enhance a person's reputation and perhaps lead to a more positive employment reference in the future. The exiting employee is invited to be frank, but frankness to the point of getting revenge by saying hostile things about the company and the manager is a career-retarding error. Often the employee will receive a negative, or at best neutral, employment reference.

7. ***Indiscreet behavior in private life.*** Employees are representatives of the company, so their behavior off the job is considered to contribute to their performance—particularly in the case of managers. Embarrassing the company will often lead to dismissal, combined with a negative reputation that will be difficult to shake for purposes of future employment. Indiscreet behavior in private life that can lead to dismissal includes being caught for shoplifting, a citation for driving under the influence of alcohol, being arrested for drug offense, charges of using the services of a prostitute, and assault and battery against another person. Although sports and entertainment celebrities are well known for such indiscreet behavior, business and government officials have engaged in similar behavior.[54]

A useful skill of organizational politics is to be able to recover from blunders considered that such missteps can lead to embarrassment or even career retardation. Considering that the other side is most likely to be offended, it is best to appease that person. Appeasing might work because the primary intent of the blunderer is to attain forgiveness, rather than gain advantage. Assume that a person has been indiscreet in private life in the form of having spent one night in jail for drunken and disorderly conduct. An appeasement approach to higher ups might be to apologize and then ask to take on a community task on behalf of the company without pay as a form of retribution. An illustrative community task would be delivering gifts to children hospitalized for a serious illness.

## Unethical Political Tactics and Strategies

Any technique of gaining power can be devious if practiced in the extreme. A person who displays loyalty to a boss by feeding him or her insider information that could affect the price of company stock is being devious. Some approaches are unequivocally unethical, such as those described next. In the long run, they erode a leader's effectiveness by lowering credibility. Devious tactics might even result in lawsuits against the leader, the organization, or both.

*Backstabbing*   The ubiquitous backstab requires that you pretend to be nice but all the while plan someone's demise. A frequent form of backstabbing is to initiate a conversation with a rival about the weaknesses of a common boss, encouraging negative commentary and making careful mental notes of what the person says. When these comments are passed along to the boss, the rival appears disloyal and foolish. E-mail is a widely used medium for the backstab. The sender of the message documents a mistake made by another individual and includes key people on the distribution list. A sample message sent by one manager to a rival began as follows, "Hi, Ted. I'm sorry you couldn't make our important meeting. I guess you had some other important priorities. But we need your input on the following major agenda item we tackled...."

*Embrace or Demolish*   The ancient strategy of "embrace or demolish" suggests that you remove from the premises rivals who suffered past hurts through your efforts; otherwise, the wounded rivals might retaliate at a vulnerable moment. This kind of strategy is common after a hostile takeover; many executives lose their jobs because they opposed the takeover. A variation of embrace or demolish is to terminate managers from the acquired organization who oppose adapting to the culture of the new firm. For example, a free-wheeling manager who opposes the bureaucratic culture of the acquiring firm might be terminated as "not able to identify with our mission."

*Setting a Person Up for Failure* The object of a setup is to place a person in a position where he or she will either fail outright or look ineffective. For example, an executive whom the CEO dislikes might be given responsibility for a troubled division whose market is rapidly collapsing. The newly assigned division president cannot stop the decline and is then fired for poor performance.

*Playing Territorial Games* Also referred to as turf wars, **territorial games** involve protecting and hoarding resources that give one power, such as information, relationships, and decision-making authority. Territorial behavior, according to Annette Simmons, is based on a hidden force that limits peoples' desire to give full cooperation. People are biologically programmed to be greedy for whatever they think it takes to survive in the corporate environment.

The purpose of territorial games is to vie for the three kinds of *territory* in the modern corporate survival game: information, relationships, or authority. A relationship is hoarded through such tactics as discouraging others from visiting a key customer or blocking a high performer from getting a promotion or transfer.[55] For example, the manager might tell others that his star performer is mediocre to prevent the person from being considered for a valuable transfer possibility. Other examples of territorial games include monopolizing time with clients, scheduling meetings so someone cannot attend, and shutting out coworkers from joining you on an important assignment.

*Creating and Then Resolving a False Catastrophe* An advanced devious tactic for a manager is to pretend a catastrophe exists and then proceed to "rescue" others from the catastrophe, thereby appearing to be a superhero.[56] The political player rushes in and declares that everything is a mess and the situation is almost hopeless; shortly thereafter, he or she resolves the problem. An example would be for a newly appointed information technology manager to inform top management that the system he inherited is antiquated and approaching the point of severely damaging the company's operations. One week later, he claims to have miraculously overhauled the information system, such as by ordering new equipment and hiring a few key personnel.

*Abusing Power* Abusing power might be conceptualized as an unethical political tactic because the abuse often relates to behavior outside of formal responsibility. (Formal ways of abusing power might be for a CEO to close a plant overseen by a manager he or she disliked, or to use company funds to build an exorbitantly luxurious personal office.) Political abuse of power includes such acts as shouting and swearing at subordinates, sexually harassing them, and humiliating them in meetings. Several surveys have suggested that most rude and inappropriate behaviors, such as the shouting of profanities, stem from those people with the most formal authority.[57] Executive abuse of power of the nature just described is a special case of abusive supervision.

Leadership Skill-Building Exercise 7-4 gives you an opportunity to think through which aspects of organizational politics you find offensive, whether they be positive or negative techniques.

## LEADERSHIP SKILL-BUILDING EXERCISE 7-4

### Identifying the Most Annoying Political Behavior Tactics

Contact three people, including yourself, to identify the two most annoying tactics of political behavior you or they have observed in the workplace. Perhaps class members can share their findings on a common platform, even a group e-mail or shared website. After the data have been collected, look to identify which one or two annoying tactics are the most frequent, such as "Being nice to superiors and customers, but nasty to subordinates." Next, reach a conclusion as to how a successful leader might be able to curb a couple of these annoying political tactics.

## ercising Control over Dysfunctional Politics

Carried to excess, organizational politics can hurt an organization and its members. Too much politicking can result in wasted time and effort, thereby lowering productivity. A group of researchers conducted a meta-analysis of available studies of the relationship between the perception of organizational politics and certain important outcomes. The perception of political behavior refers to the recognition that organizational politics is present, as in "I can't take all the politics around here." The major outcomes related to the perception of politics were as follows: (1) more strain, or adverse effects of stress, (2) more intentions to quit, (3) less job satisfaction, (4) less emotional commitment to the employer, (5) lower task performance, and (6) less organizational citizenship behavior.[58]

In short, when a high degree of political behavior is perceived to exist, it can damage individuals and the organization. To avoid these negative consequences, leaders are advised to combat political behavior when it is excessive and dysfunctional.

In a comprehensive strategy to control politics, *organizational leaders must be aware of its causes and techniques.* For example, during a downsizing, the CEO can be on the alert for instances of backstabbing and transparent attempts to please. Open communication also can constrain the impact of political behavior. For instance, open communication can let everyone know the basis for allocating resources, thus reducing the amount of politicking. If people know in advance how resources are allocated, the effectiveness of attempting to curry favor with the boss will be reduced. When communication is open, it also makes it more difficult for some people to control information and pass along gossip as a political weapon.

*Avoiding favoritism and cronyism*—avoiding giving the best rewards to the group members you like the best or to old friends—is a potent way of minimizing politics within a work group. If group members believe that getting the boss to like them is much less important than good job performance in obtaining rewards, they will kiss up to the boss less frequently. In an attempt to minimize favoritism, managers must reward workers who impress them through task-related activities.

*Setting good examples at the top of the organization* can help reduce the frequency and intensity of organizational politics. When leaders are nonpolitical in their actions, they demonstrate in subtle ways that political behavior is not welcome. It may be helpful for the leader to announce during a staff meeting that devious political behavior is undesirable and unprofessional.

Another way of reducing the extent of political behavior is for *individuals and the organization to share the same goals*, a situation described as *goal congruence*. If political behavior will interfere with the company and individuals achieving their goals, workers with goal congruence are less likely to play office politics excessively. A project leader is less likely to falsely declare that the boss's idea is good just to please the boss if the project leader wants the company to succeed.

Politics can sometimes be constrained by a *threat to discuss questionable information in a public forum.* People who practice devious politics usually want to operate secretly and privately. They are willing to drop hints and innuendoes and make direct derogatory comments about someone else, provided they will not be identified as the source. An effective way of stopping the discrediting of others is to offer to discuss the topic publicly.[59] The person attempting to pass on the questionable information will usually back down and make a statement closer to the truth.

*Hiring people with integrity* will help reduce the number of dysfunctional political players. References should be checked carefully with respect to the candidate's integrity and honesty.[60] Say to the reference, "Tell me about ———'s approach to playing politics." The principle used at Facebook is to "Look for empire builders, self-servers, and whiners in the hiring process—and don't hire them,"

*Emphasize that success can mean a lateral move as well as a promotion.* Another Facebook initiative to reduce political behavior is to emphasize that moving into management

# LEADERSHIP SKILL-BUILDING EXERCISE 7-5

### Controlling Office Politics

One student plays the role of a corporate executive visiting one of the key divisions. Six other students play the roles of managers within the division, each of whom wants to impress the boss during their meeting. The corporate executive gets the meeting started by asking the managers, in turn, to discuss their recent activities and accomplishments. Each division-level manager will attempt to create a very positive impression on the corporate executive. After about nine minutes of observing them fawning over him or her, the executive decides to take action against such excessive politicking. Review the information on political tactics and their control before carrying out this role-assuming exercise.

is not necessarily a promotion, but a lateral move and a parallel track. The purpose of managers at the company is to support people and remove barriers to getting things done. If managerial positions are not so important, fewer people will use political tactics to get a vertical promotion.[61] (Yet it is difficult to overcome the strongly held belief in most cultures that a promotion brings power. Besides, top-level positions at Facebook pay much more than individual contribution positions.)

Leadership Skill-Building Exercise 7-5 provides an opportunity to practice the subtle art of discouraging excessive political behavior on the job.

## READER'S ROADMAP

So far in this book, we have examined the nature of leaders, their ethics, and how they acquire power. The next chapter explains influence tactics, or ways of converting power into action.

## SUMMARY

Organizational power is derived from many sources, including position power (legitimate, reward, and coercive) and personal power (expert, reference, and prestige). Power also stems from ownership, dependencies, capitalizing on opportunity, managing critical problems, and being close to power. A problem with leadership power is that it can be self-serving. People with a strong moral identity are less likely to use power for self-interest.

Full-fledged empowerment includes the dimensions of meaning, self-determination, competence, impact, and internal commitment. Actions that can be taken to become an empowering leader include the following: foster initiative and responsibility, link work activities to the goals of the organization, provide ample information, allow group members to choose methods, encourage self-leadership, and continue to lead. Also, take into account cultural differences in how empowerment is accepted, establish limits to empowerment, and practice an optimal amount of empowerment. Delegation is another important part of empowerment.

To acquire and retain power, a leader must skillfully use organizational politics. The meaning of *politics* continues to shift in a positive, constructive direction. Contributing factors to organizational politics include the pyramidal shape of organizations, subjective performance standards, environmental uncertainty, emotional insecurity, Machiavellian tendencies, and encouraging admiration from subordinates.

To make effective use of organizational politics, leaders must be aware of specific political tactics and strategies. Ethical methods can be divided into those aimed directly at gaining power, those aimed at building relationships, and those aimed at avoiding political blunders. Unethical and devious tactics, such as the embrace or demolish strategy, constitute another category of political behavior.

Carried to extremes, organizational politics can hurt an organization and its members. Being aware of the causes and types of political behavior can help leaders deal with the problem. Setting good examples of nonpolitical behavior is helpful, as is achieving goal congruence and threatening to publicly expose devious politicking. It is also good to hire people who have integrity. Emphasizing that success can mean a lateral move as well as a promotion *might* work.

## KEY TERMS

power  170
legitimate power  171
reward power  171
coercive power  171
personal power  171
prestige power  171
dependence perspective  172

strategic contingency theory
    173
moral identity  173
empowerment  175
self-leadership  178
delegation  179
organizational politics  180

leader political support  181
political skill  182
positive psychological capital
    186
territorial games  192

## GUIDELINES FOR ACTIONS AND SKILL DEVELOPMENT

Developing political skill is well worth the effort for almost anyone who wants to attain career success and personal satisfaction. A meta-analysis of 120 scientific articles found that the following outcomes were associated with political skill (as measured by a questionnaire): career success, self-efficacy, job satisfaction, organizational commitment, work productivity, organizational citizenship behavior, and personal reputation. Political skill was found to be negatively related to psychological strain (the byproduct of stress).[62]

A striking advantage of gaining power is that it helps you control your environment, which, in turn, leads to less stress and better physical and mental health—and therefore prolongs your life. In contrast, having so little power that you cannot control your job and environment creates stress, leading to poorer physical and mental health, and quite often a shorter life.[63] Finding ways to increase your power is therefore a vital life skill.

So much has been said and written about the importance of building your in-person and virtual network that it seems as if the more contacts you have the better. It is usually better to have a smaller network of useful, high-quality contacts. British anthropologist Robin Dunbar claims the average human can maintain only 150 close social connections. With information technology, that number can be stretched a bit, but mental capacity and available time set limits to the size of a useful network.[64]

### Discussion Questions and Activities

1. How might a person in a fashion clothing company (such as upscale suits and dresses) have a lot of power even if he or she does not hold an executive title?

2. Many business leaders today give up having a private office, and instead work at a desk or cubicle in the middle of the work area to be among other employees. What effect do you think this work area placement has on their power?

3. Contrary to popular opinion, CEOs of major U.S. companies come from a wide variety of private universities and state universities, not just a handful of well-publicized MBA programs. What does this fact tell you about sources of power and organizational politics?

4. What can you do this week to enhance your power?

5. To what extent do you think wearing the right type of clothing and accessories can really make a person appear more powerful?

6. Many business leaders say something to the effect of, "We practice empowerment because we don't expect our employees to leave their brains at the door." What are these leaders talking about?

7. Many people have asked the question "Isn't office politics just for incompetents?" What is your answer to this question?

8. How might emotional intelligence be related to committing political blunders?

9. A regular occurrence in business firms, and some government agencies, is for somebody to be fired because of a Facebook or Twitter post criticizing the employer or a specific manager. Why do you think so many people commit this career-threatening error?

10. Ask an experienced worker to give you an example of the successful application of organizational politics. Which tactic was used, and what was the outcome?

## LEADERSHIP CASE PROBLEM A

### Ray, the Empowered Athletic Club Director

Ray was moving along well in his career in sports administration, having graduated from college with a degree in sports and health administration five years ago. He spent the first two years after graduation working as a fitness instructor at one health and fitness club. Ray then found a position as an assistant manager at a chain of athletic clubs, Modern Fitness. The manager suddenly resigned to move to an athletic club in Las Vegas. Ray was then asked by the CEO of the chain to accept the position as manager of the local Modern Fitness. The CEO, Larry, said to Ray, "You've got the smarts and the charisma to do a great job as manager." Ray was flattered, and he saw the management position as a splendid opportunity to make a contribution in his chosen field.

Five months into the job, all was going well with the Modern Fitness staff. The group appeared to be well motivated, customer complaints were at a minimum, and only one person had quit voluntarily. Yet the local Modern Fitness was facing a problem of declining club enrollment, rather than experiencing growth. New club memberships enrollments were not coming in fast enough to make up for existing members not renewing their enrollment.

Larry, who carefully reviewed enrollment data each month, scheduled a meeting at Ray's club to discuss the enrollment picture. Larry told Ray that he was pleased with the operations of the club, but not with the enrollment figures. "I am empowering you to boost enrollment to a net gain," said Larry, "do what you need to do."

Ray replied, "Larry I am doing all I can. We send out flyers. We advertise on social media. We encourage word-of-mouth advertising. This town is saturated with athletic and fitness clubs. It's tough for our Modern Fitness club to get a bigger market share. What advice can you give me to boost enrollment?"

Larry responded, "Ray you are empowered as the manager to boost enrollment working within your advertising budget. Boosting enrollment is your responsibility, not mine. We'll talk about your enrollment figures again in thirty days."

### Questions

1. How effective is Larry's approach to empowering Ray to boost enrollment?
2. Which political tactic or tactics do you recommend Ray use to deal effectively with his empowering boss?
3. What might Larry do to help Ray boost enrollment, within the limits of empowerment?

## ASSOCIATED ROLE PLAY

One person plays the role of Ray who wants to be an effective Modern Fitness manager and leader, but he knows that he needs help. Three days after the meeting, he gets on the phone with Larry asking him for whatever guidance he can offer. Another person plays the role of Larry who believes that the most effective way to being an empowering manager is to turn over total control of a problem to a subordinate.

# LEADERSHIP CASE PROBLEM B

## Team Leader Tanya Wants to Be Truthful

Tanya is the team leader of a cross-functional product-development group in a consumer products company. The group meets from time to time to discuss new ideas for products. Another of its key activities is to help develop a product after agreement is reached by higher-level management that a product idea is worth pursuing. Tanya enjoys her role as the leader of a cross-functional team, and she hopes to use the experience as a springboard to a marketing executive position.

Tanya prides herself in being candid and direct in her interactions with coworkers in marketing department in which she works as a senior marketing analyst and assistant to the department head. Tanya is also proud of how she is candid in her interactions with members of the product-development team.

Two weeks ago, the team was meeting to discuss the merits of introducing a multifruit flavored energy drink to the market. The CEO was attending this particular meeting to get a direct feel for how the product-development team operates. Ten minutes into the meeting Tanya said, "We have to carefully evaluate whether an energy drink has any chances of success. As we all know, our company has had far too many flops. I remember we once introduced an instant-spaghetti product to the market that was a total bomb. I think we lost $10 million on that idea, and we were ridiculed by food critics." In response to Tanya's comment, the CEO shook his head from side to side but made no spoken response.

One week ago, Tanya posted the following comment on Facebook, Twitter, and Instagram: "<u>Name of company</u> is getting ravaged by house brands. But not to worry, we make a lot of those house brands for large supermarket chains and bog box discounters." The vice president of marketing, asked a staff member to investigate whether Tanya was really the person responsible for this post, and to report back to her with the answer.

At a product-development meeting today, a food-packaging scientist named Obdu Wobegun attended because there would be some key issues about package design likely to surface. Tanya welcomed Obdu to the meeting, and then asked, "Obdu are you sure you are a United States citizen? We can't afford to have any foreign spies at our meeting."

Later today, Tanya received a text message from her immediate manager Gus that read: "We must talk in person. You are out of control."

### Questions

1. In what ways might Tanya be committing political blunders?
2. If Tanya is committing political blunders, to what extent might they hinder her chances of becoming a vice president of marketing?
3. How should Tanya's boss deal with her with respect to the type of political blunders she has committed?

# ASSOCIATED ROLE PLAY

One student plays the role of Tanya's boss, Gus, who wants to have a frank discussion with Tanya with respect to the type of political blunders it has been rumored that she is committing. Tanya perceives herself to have the positive leadership qualities of candor and truthfulness. Gus wants to explain to Tanya that her insensitivity could block her career and might even adversely affect her performance evaluation. Run the role play for about eight minutes, and have observers provide feedback.

## LEADERSHIP SKILL-BUILDING **EXERCISE 7-6**

### My Leadership Portfolio

For this insert into your leadership portfolio, think through all the recent opportunities you might have had to use political tactics. How did you deal with the situation? Did you capitalize on any opportunities? Did you use an ethical approach? Did you use any unethical tactics? Did you commit any political blunders? Here would be an example:

> I saw a flyer indicating that our Business Management Association was having a guest speaker, an executive from Merrill Lynch. I had been pretty busy with studies, my job, and social life, yet I decided to invest the time and attend. As it worked out, the meeting was a wonderful opportunity to make a couple of good contacts. After the talk, I spoke to the speaker and complimented her. We had a brief conversation about how I was looking for a career in investment banking, and she gave me her business card. I sent her an e-mail message the next day, thanking her for the time she gave me. I also met a couple of important people at the meeting and got their cards also.

## NOTES

1. Original story based on facts and observations in the following sources: Alex Konrad, "Nonstop Benioff," *Forbes*, September 13, 2016, pp. 84, 88–98; Ray Bennett, "How Salesforce CEO Marc Benioff Is Changing the World: 10 Facts You Didn't Know," *Better World International* (www.betterworldinternational .org), July 29, 2016, pp. 1–5; Eugene Kim, "Salesforce CEO Marc Benioff Built a $50 Billion Empire by Following 7 Lessons from His Mentor Turned Nemesis Larry Ellison," *Business Insider* (www .businessinsider.com), September 5, 2015, pp. 1–14; Rachel King, "Salesforce's Ambitions Face Test," *The Wall Street Journal*, December 10, 2016, p. B3.
2. Jeffrey Pfeffer, "You're Still the Same: Why Theories of Power Hold over Time and Across Contexts," *The Academy of Management Perspective*, November 2013, pp. 269–280.
3. Jeremy Helmans and Henry Timms, "Understanding 'New Power'," *Harvard Business Review*, December 2014, p. 50.
4. John R. French and Bertram Raven, "The Basis of Social Power," in Dorwin Cartwright, ed., *Studies in Social Power* (Ann Arbor, MI: Institute for Social Research, 1969); Timothy R. Hinkin and Chester A. Schrieschheim, "Power and Influence: The View from Below," *Personnel*, May 1988, pp. 47–50.
5. Lawrence A. Cunningham, "The Secret Sauce of Corporate Leadership," *The Wall Street Journal*, January 26, 2015, p. A13.
6. Bryant Urstadt, "The Sociopath Network," *Bloomberg Businessweek*, July 28–July 31, 2011, pp. 82–83.
7. Max Nisen, "How Doug McMillon Went from Unloading Trucks at Wal-Mart to Its Next CEO," (http://finance.yahoo.com), November 27, 2013, pp. 1–3; Brian Sozzi, "Why Doug McMillon Is the First-Ever Walmart CEO to Star in a TV Commercial," *The Street* (www.thestreet.com), August 23, 2016, pp. 1–2.
8. Sydney Finkelstein, "Power in Top Management Teams: Dimensions, Measurement, and Validation," *Academy of Management Journal*, August 1992, p. 510.
9. Richard M. Emerson, "Power-Dependence Relations," *American Sociological Review*, Vol. 27, 1962, p. 32.
10. C. R. Hinings, D. J. Hickson, C. A. Lee, R. E. Schenck, and J. W. Pennings, "Strategic Contingencies Theory of Intraorganizational Power," *Administrative Science Quarterly*, 1971, pp. 216–229.
11. Diana Rus, Daan van Kippenberg, and Barbara Wisse, "Leader Power and Self-Serving Behavior: The Moderating Role of Accountability," *The Leadership Quarterly*, February 2012, pp. 13–26.
12. Katherine A. DeCelles, D. Scott DeRue, Joshua D. Margolis, and Tara L. Ceranic, "Does Power Corrupt or Enable? When and Why Power Facilitates Self-Interested Behavior," *Journal of Applied Psychology*, May 2012, pp. 681–689.
13. "Lessons in Power: Lyndon Johnson Revealed: A Conversation with Historian Robert A. Caro," *Harvard Business Review*, April 2006, pp. 47–52.
14. "Leaders Everywhere: A Conversation with Gary Hamel," *McKinsey & Company* (www.mckinsey .com), May 2013, p. 1.

15. Gretchen M. Spreitzer, "Psychological Empowerment in the Workplace: Dimensions, Measurement, and Validation," *Academy of Management Journal*, October 1995, pp. 1442–1465.

16. Lauren Bennett Cattaneo and Aliya R. Chapman, "The Process of Empowerment: A Model for Use in Research and Practice," *American Psychologist*, October 2010, pp. 646–659.

17. Stein Amundsen and Øyvind L. Martinsen, "Empowering Leadership: Construct Clarification, Conceptualization, and Validation of a New Scale," *The Leadership Quarterly*, June 2014, p. 493.

18. Scott E. Seibert, Seth R. Silver, and W. Alan Randolph, "Taking Empowerment to the Next Level: A Multiple-Level Model of Empowerment, Performance, and Satisfaction," *Academy of Management Journal*, June 2004, pp. 332–349.

19. Henry Mintzberg, *Managing* (San Francisco, CA: Berrett-Koehler, 2009), p. 64.

20. Barbara Ettorre, "The Empowerment Gap: Hype vs. Reality," *HR Focus*, July 1997, p. 5.

21. Dimitry Elias Léger, "Tell Me Your Problem, and I'll Tell You Mine," *Fortune*, October 6, 2000, p. 408.

22. Christopher Robert et al., "Empowerment and Continuous Improvement in the United States, Mexico, Poland, and India: Predicting Fit on the Basis of the Dimensions of Power Distance and Individualism," *Journal of Applied Psychology*, October 2000, pp. 751–765.

23. Kyle Dover, "Avoiding Empowerment Traps," *Management Review*, January 1999, p. 52.

24. Minyoung Cheong, Seth M. Spaid, Francis J. Yammarino, and Seokhwa, "Two Faces of Empowering Leadership: Enabling and Burdening," *The Leadership Quarterly*, August 2016, pp. 602–616.

25. Sut I. Wong Humborstad and Bârd Kuvas, "Mutuality in Leader–Subordinate Empowerment Expectation: Its Impact on Role Ambiguity and Intrinsic Motivation," *The Leadership Quarterly*, Vol. 24, no. 2, April 2013, pp. 363–377.

26. "Mark Hellerstein, "Learn to Empower Others," *Executive Leadership*, April 2013, p. 3.

27. Bob Frisch and Cary Greene, "To Hold Someone Accountable, First Define What Accountable Means," *Harvard Business Review* (https://hbr.org), June 28, 2016, pp. 1–4.

28. B. Parker Ellen III, Gerald R. Ferris, and M. Ronald Buckley, "Leader Political Support: Reconsidering Leader Political Behavior," *The Leadership Quarterly*, December 2013, p. 845.

29. David Polansky, "Counsel to Tyrants," *The Wall Street Journal*, November 12, 2013. Comment contained in book review of Joseph Markulin, *Machiavelli* (Amherst, NY: Prometheus, 2013).

30. Gerald Biberman, "Personality Characteristics and Work Attitudes of Persons with High, Moderate, and Low Political Tendencies," *Psychological Reports*, Vol. 57, 1985, p. 1309.

31. Marshall Goldsmith, "All of Us Are Stuck on Suck-Ups," *Fast Company*, December 2003, p. 117.

32. K. Michele Kacmar, Daniel G. Bachrach, Kenneth J. Harris, and Sizanne Zivnuska, "Fostering Good Citizenship Through Ethical Leadership: Exploring the Moderating Role of Gender and Organizational Politics," *Journal of Applied Psychology*, May 2011, p. 635.

33. Pamela L. Perrewé et al., "Political Skill: An Antidote for Workplace Stressors," *Academy of Management Executive*, August 2000, p. 115.

34. Tom Peters, "Power," *Success*, November 1994, p. 34.

35. Denise Campbell Laidler, "What's Your Social Media Strategy?" *Black Enterprise*, November 2010, p. 75.

36. "Dealing with Office Politics: Navigating the Minefield," *Mind Tools*, p. 2. Retrieved October 24, 2016, from https://www.mindtools.com/pages/article/newCDV_85.htm.

37. Jeffrey Pfeffer, "Power Play," *Harvard Business Review*, July–August 2010, p. 92.

38. Michael Warshaw, "The Good Guy's (and Gal's) Guide to Office Politics," *Fast Company*, April 1998, p. 160.

39. Robin J. Ely, Debra Meyerson, and Martin N. Davidson, "Rethinking Political Correctness," *Harvard Business Review*, September 2006, p. 80.

40. Rebecca Knight, "What to Do When Your Boss Has a Favorite (and It's Not You)," *Harvard Business Review* (hbr.org), June 16, 2016, p. 4.

41. The definition of psychological capital and the research findings are from Fred O. Walumbwa, Suzanne J. Peterson, Bruce J. Avolio, and Chad A. Hartnell, "An Investigation of the Relationships among Leader and Follower Psychological Capital, Service Climate, and Job Performance," *Personnel Psychology*, Winter 2010, pp. 937–963.

42. Cited in Adam Bryant, "For the Chief of Saks, It's Culture That Drives Results," *The New York Times* (www.nytimes.com), May 28, 2010.

43. Joann S. Lublin, "To Win Advancement, You Need to Clean Up Any Bad Speech Habits," *The Wall Street Journal*, October 3, 2004, p. B1.

44. Much of the scholarly impression management research is reviewed in Andrew J. DuBrin, *Impression Management in the Workplace: Research, Theory, and Practice* (New York and London: Routledge, 2011).

45. Christine L. Porath, Alexandra Gerbasi, and Sebastian L. Schorch, "The Effects of Civility and

Advice, Leadership, and Performance," *Journal of Applied Psychology*, September 2015, pp. 1527–1541.

46. James D. Westphal and Ithai Stern, "Flattery Will Get You Everywhere (Especially If You Are a Male Caucasian): How Ingratiation, Boardroom Behavior, and Demographic Minority Status Affect Additional Board Appointments at U.S. Companies," *Academy of Management Journal*, April 2007, pp. 267–288.

47. Tessa E. Basford and Andrea Molberg, "Dale Carnegie's Leadership Principles: Examining the Theoretical and Empirical Support," *Journal of Leadership Studies*, Vol. 6, no. 4, 2013, pp. 34–35.

48. "How to Develop a Good Relationship with Your Boss's Boss," *The Management Tip of the Day from Harvard Business Review*, September 15, 2016. p. 1.

49. Robyn L. Brouer, Allison Duke, Darren C. Treadway, and Gerald R. Ferris, "The Moderating Effect of Political Skill on the Demographic Dissimilarity—Leader–Member Exchange Quality Relationship," *The Leadership Quarterly*, April 2009, pp. 61–69.

50. Christian Ewen et al., "Further Specification of the Leader Political Skill-Leadership Effectiveness Relationships: Transformational and Transactional Leader Behavior as Mediators," *The Leadership Quarterly*, August 2013, pp. 516–533.

51. Andrew J. DuBrin, "Political Blunders within Organizations," in Eran Vigoda-Gadot and Amos Drory, eds., *Handbook of Organizational Politics: Looking Back and Into the Future*, Second Edition (Cheltenham, UK: Edward Elgar, 2016), pp. 172–192.

52. Paul Sonne, "Hayward Fell Short of Modern CEO Demands," *The Wall Street Journal*, July 26, 2010, p. A7.

53. Tracy Minor, "Office Politics: Master the Game by Making Connections," *Monster: Diversity & Inclusion* (monster.com), October 30, 2002.

54. DuBrin, "Political Blunders within Organizations," pp. 181–182.

55. Annette Simmons, *Territorial Games: Understanding & Ending Turf Wars at Work* (New York: AMACOM, 1998); Robert J. Herbold, *The Fiefdom Syndrome* (New York: Currency Doubleday, 2004).

56. Jared Sandberg, "Office Superheroes: Saving the Rest of Us from Unseen Dangers," *The Wall Street Journal*, December 10, 2003, p. B1.

57. Jonah Lehr, "The Power Trip," *The Wall Street Journal*, August 14–15, 2010, p. W1; Anne Kreamer, "Go Ahead—Cry at Work," *Time*, April 4, 2011, p. 52.

58. Chu-Hsiang Chang, Christopher C. Rosen, and Paul E. Levy, "The Relationship between Perceptions of Organizational Politics and Employee Attitudes, Strain, and Behavior: A Meta-Analytic Examination," *Academy of Management Journal*, August 2009, pp. 779–801.

59. Robert P. Vecchio, *Organizational Behavior*, Fourth Edition (Fort Worth, TX: The Dryden Press, 2000), p. 136.

60. "Throw Politics Out of Your Office," *Manager's Edge*, July 2001, p. 8.

61. The two comments about Facebook are from Jay Parikh, "How Facebook Tries to Prevent Office Politics," *Harvard Business Review* (hbr.org), June 29, 2016, pp. 2–3.

62. Timothy P. Munyon, James K. Summers, Katrina M. Thompson, and Gerald R. Ferris, "Political Skill and Work Outcomes: A Theoretical Extension, Meta-Analytic Investigation, and Agenda for the Future," *Personnel Psychology*, no. 1, 2015, pp. 143–184.

63. Research synthesized in Pfeffer, "Power Play," p. 90.

64. Research cited in Drake Bennett, "The Dunbar Number," *Bloomberg Businessweek*, January 14–January 20, 2013, pp. 52–56.

# Influence Tactics of Leaders

Tim Cook became the chief executive officer (CEO) of Apple Inc. in 2011, shortly before the death of the legendary cofounder Steve Jobs. Before becoming CEO, he had distinguished himself as an exceptional leader of company operations and was considered a master at managing supply chains. As CEO, Cook has continued to function as an influential leader and manager. In place of the innovation machine of Apple past, Cook has created a corporate juggernaut that offers incremental upgrades on existing successful products. For example, the Apple Watch can be considered an expansion of the iPhone, rather than an entirely new product.

Cook emphasizes thinking of the long-term greatness of Apple. He wants the company to have a bigger and broader future than anything cofounder Jobs could effect during his relatively short life. In response to analysts who grade the company quarterly, Cook said, "We try to be very clear that we are making our decisions based on the long term." Despite a flattening of sales of the iPhone recently somewhat due to market saturation, Apple has continued it phenomenal success under Cook's leadership. During the first five years of Cook's rein, company revenues tripled, the work force doubled, and its global reach has expanded.

A key part of Cook's leadership approach is to emphasize transparency and teamwork within the company. Cook has a calm demeanor, listens carefully to people, and is much more approachable than the volatile Steve Jobs. With Cook in charge, management team members worry less about attempting to please an unpredictable boss. One of the ways in which Cook listens to employees is through an open-door policy, meaning that workers throughout Apple contact him directly with their concerns. Cook behaves as a coach who trusts his team members rather than a mastermind who calls all the shots. When Cook does micromanage, the activity that receives close scrutiny is supply-chain management.

Cook has been known to depart from his calm approach when his core beliefs about running the enterprise are questioned. At a shareholder's meeting, Cook was challenged about his commitment to making factories carbon-neutral and removing harmful chemicals from its products. Cook said angrily, "I don't consider the bloody ROI [return on investment]. If you want me to do things only for ROI reasons, you should get out of the stock."

Cook also exerts influence in social responsibility. Because Apple makes so many physical products, he ensures that the company looks for ways to minimize polluting the environment. He is also an advocate of human rights, including gay and transgender rights in the workplace, as well as looking for ways to forward education at all levels. Cook says, "And so our culture is to leave the world better than we found it. And we try really hard to do that."

Cook graduated from Auburn University with a BS degree in industrial engineering and holds an MBA from Fuqua School of Business at Duke University.[1]

In his leadership role, Tim Cook is working hard to influence employees to collaborate in his quest to keep Apple a great company for the long term. He emphasizes teamwork, collaboration, and looking at the big picture. Without effective influence tactics, a leader is similar to a soccer player who has not learned to kick a soccer ball, or a newscaster who is unable to speak. Leadership, as oft repeated, is an influence process.

To become an effective leader, a person must be aware of the specific tactics leaders use to influence others. Here, we discuss a number of specific influence tactics, but other aspects of leadership also concern influence. Being charismatic, as described in Chapter 3, influences many people. Leaders influence others through power and politics, as described in Chapter 7. Furthermore, motivating and coaching skills, as described in Chapter 10, involve influencing others toward worthwhile ends.

The terms *influence* and *power* are sometimes used interchangeably, whereas at other times, power is said to create influence and vice versa. In this book, we distinguish between power and influence as follows: **Influence** is the ability to affect the behavior of others in a particular direction, whereas **power** is the potential or capacity to influence. Leaders are influential only when they exercise power. A leader, therefore, must acquire power in order to influence others.

Influence tactics have grown in importance because so often a leader or corporate professional has to influence others without having formal authority over them. Judy Vredenburgh, the CEO of Girls Inc., provides a good example. (Girls Inc. is a nonprofit organization that provides educational programs and scholarship for girls.) She says that "in nonprofits, decision have to be very participative. You don't have as much formal authority and resources; you have to use informal influence to create change."[2] In business organizations also, it is often necessary to obtain the cooperation of workers who do not report to you, such as going outside your department to borrow expertise.

This chapter presents a model of power and influence, a description and explanation of influence tactics (both ethical and less ethical), a description of how leaders influence large-scale change, and the sequencing of influence tactics. We also present a theory about the characteristics group members expect in a leader in order to be influenced by him or her.

# A Model of Power and Influence

The model shown in Figure 8-1 illustrates that the end results of a leader's influence (the outcomes) are a function of the tactics he or she uses. The influence tactics are, in turn, moderated, or affected, by the leader's traits, the leader's behaviors, and the situation.

Looking at the right side of the model, the three possible outcomes are commitment, compliance, and resistance. **Commitment** is the most successful outcome: The target of the influence attempt is enthusiastic about carrying out the request and makes a full effort, and is therefore fully engaged. Commitment is particularly important for complex, difficult tasks because these require full concentration and effort. If you were influencing a technician to upgrade your operating system software, you would need his or her commitment. **Compliance** means that the influence attempt is partially successful: The target person is apathetic (not overjoyed) about carrying out the request and makes only a modest effort. The influence agent has changed the person's behavior but not his or her attitude. A long-distance truck driver might comply with demands that he sleep certain hours between hauls, but he is not enthusiastic about losing road time. Compliance for routine tasks—such as wearing a hard hat on a construction site—is usually good enough. Resistance is an unsuccessful influence attempt: The target is opposed to carrying out the request and finds ways to either not comply or do a poor job. **Resistance** includes making excuses for why the task cannot be carried out, procrastinating, and outright refusing to do the task.[3]

Going to the left side of the model, the leader's personality traits affect the outcome of influence tactics. An extroverted and warm leader who has charisma can more readily use some influence tactics than a leader who is introverted and cold. For example, he or she can make an inspirational appeal. A highly intelligent leader would be able to influence others because he or she has built a reputation as a subject matter expert (SME). Whichever influence tactics leaders choose, the goal is to get group members on their side.

The leader's behaviors also affect the outcome of influence tactics in a variety of ways. For example, setting high standards facilitates making an inspirational appeal. Additionally, leaders who perform well consistently are better able to lead by example because they are good role models. Finally, the situation partly determines which influence tactic will be effective. The organizational culture or subculture is one such key situational factor. For example, in a high-technology environment, inspirational appeal and emotional display are less likely to be effective than rational persuasion and being an SME, because high-tech workers are more likely to be impressed by facts than by feelings.

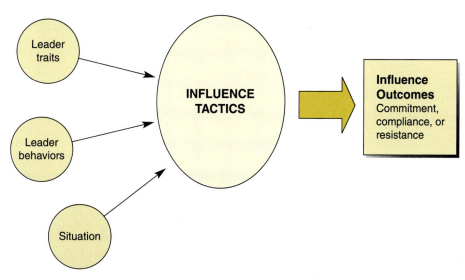

**FIGURE 8-1**   A Model of Power and Influence.

# LEADERSHIP SELF-ASSESSMENT QUIZ 8-1

**Survey of Influence Tactics**

**Instructions:** Indicate how frequently you use the influence tactics listed here: VI = very infrequently or never; I = infrequently; S = sometimes; F = frequently; VF = very frequently. The VI to VF categories correspond to a 1-to-5 scale.

|  | | 1<br>VI | 2<br>I | 3<br>S | 4<br>F | 5<br>VF |
|---|---|---|---|---|---|---|
| 1. | I lead by demonstrating the right behavior myself. | ☐ | ☐ | ☐ | ☐ | ☐ |
| 2. | I rely on facts and logic to persuade others. | ☐ | ☐ | ☐ | ☐ | ☐ |
| 3. | People often listen to me because of my expertise. | ☐ | ☐ | ☐ | ☐ | ☐ |
| 4. | If I want something done, I stand ready to do a favor in return. | ☐ | ☐ | ☐ | ☐ | ☐ |
| 5. | I enjoy negotiating a price or an offer. | ☐ | ☐ | ☐ | ☐ | ☐ |
| 6. | I am assertive (open and forthright in my demands). | ☐ | ☐ | ☐ | ☐ | ☐ |
| 7. | I joke with or kid other people to make a point. | ☐ | ☐ | ☐ | ☐ | ☐ |
| 8. | I sometimes get quite emotional to make a point. | ☐ | ☐ | ☐ | ☐ | ☐ |
| 9. | I promise to reward the person to get what I want. | ☐ | ☐ | ☐ | ☐ | ☐ |
| 10. | I attempt to get other people on my side in order to win my point. | ☐ | ☐ | ☐ | ☐ | ☐ |
| 11. | I cooperate with others in order to influence them. | ☐ | ☐ | ☐ | ☐ | ☐ |
| 12. | As a leader, I participate heavily in the task of the group. | ☐ | ☐ | ☐ | ☐ | ☐ |
| 13. | I form an alliance with the other person. | ☐ | ☐ | ☐ | ☐ | ☐ |
| 14. | I threaten to go over the person's head to the boss. | ☐ | ☐ | ☐ | ☐ | ☐ |
| 15. | I compliment the other person. | ☐ | ☐ | ☐ | ☐ | ☐ |
| 16. | I use as much charm as possible to get my way. | ☐ | ☐ | ☐ | ☐ | ☐ |
| 17. | I will post a positive comment about a work associate on a social media site if he or she has done something I particularly like. | ☐ | ☐ | ☐ | ☐ | ☐ |
| 18. | I will make a comment pointing out that I am not much good at what I want the other person to do. | ☐ | ☐ | ☐ | ☐ | ☐ |
| 19. | I would bring the person a little gift, such as a beverage he or she likes or an attractive ballpoint pen. | ☐ | ☐ | ☐ | ☐ | ☐ |
| 20. | I refer to the importance of doing a particular task for the overall good of the organization. | ☐ | ☐ | ☐ | ☐ | ☐ |

**Scoring and Interpretation:** The more of these tactics you use frequently or very frequently, the more influential you probably are. Experience is a factor because you could be potentially influential but have not yet had the opportunity to use many of these tactics.

**Skill Development:** The survey of influence tactics might give you some clues for development. Look for influence tactics that appear to represent a good idea, but where you need skill development. Next, take the opportunity to practice the tactic. For example, take Statement 15, "I compliment the other person." Perhaps you neglect to compliment others when you want to influence them. Use the guidelines for flattery given in the previous chapter practice to compliment another person when you want to influence him or her.

The rest of this chapter identifies and describes influence tactics, including some mention of situational variables. Leader traits and power have been described in previous chapters. Leadership Self-Assessment Quiz 8-1 will give you an opportunity to think about which influence tactics you tend to use.

## Description and Explanation of Influence Tactics

Influence tactics are often viewed from an ethical perspective. Following this perspective, the influence tactics described here are classified into three categories: (a) Those that are essentially ethical and honest, (b) those that are essentially neutral with respect to ethics and honesty, and (c) those that are essentially manipulative and dishonest. The categorization presented here is far from absolute. Except for the extremes, most of the tactics could conceivably be placed in any of the three categories, depending on how they are used. For example, one can use the tactic "joking and kidding" in either a well-meaning or mean-spirited way. Joking and kidding could therefore be classified as "essentially ethical," "essentially neutral," or "essentially dishonest and unethical."

### Essentially Ethical and Honest Tactics

This section describes essentially ethical and honest tactics and strategies for influencing others, as outlined in Table 8-1. Used with tact, diplomacy, and good intent, these strategies can help you get others to join you in accomplishing a worthwhile objective. Because these influence tactics vary in complexity, they also vary with respect to how much time is required to develop them.

*Leading by Example, Respect, and Trust*    A simple but effective way of influencing group members is by **leading by example** or acting as a positive role model. The ideal approach is to be a "do as I say and do" manager—that is, one whose actions and words are consistent. Actions and words confirm, support, and often clarify each other. Being respected facilitates leading by example because group members are more likely to follow the example of leaders they respect. A major way in which a leader obtains respect is by being trusted. Part of the respect Tim Cook has received is that she can be trusted to follow through on his plans such as acquiring companies to help Apple grow and paying dividends to investors to provide an additional reward for investing in the company.

**TABLE 8-1**  Essentially Ethical and Honest Influence Tactics

| | |
|---|---|
| **1.** | Leading by example and respect |
| **2.** | Using rational persuasion |
| **3.** | Telling true stories |
| **4.** | Explaining the benefits to the target |
| **5.** | Making a personal appeal |
| **6.** | Developing a reputation as a subject matter expert |
| **7.** | Exchanging favors and bargaining |
| **8.** | Legitimating a request |
| **9.** | Making an inspirational appeal, being charming, and emotional display |
| **10.** | Consultation with others |
| **11.** | Forming coalitions |
| **12.** | Being a team player |
| **13.** | Practicing hands-on leadership |

Leading by example is often interpreted to mean that the leader works long and hard, and expects others to do the same, with this type of behavior being prevalent among entrepreneurs who hire a staff. During the startup phase of a company, the entrepreneur will often work over sixty hours per week and expect the new hires to follow a similar work schedule.

Research conducted with 683 workers and managers in a large communication organization indicated that a leader who demonstrates organizational citizenship behavior (OCB) is likely to influence subordinates to behave in a similar manner. Leader OCB was measured by area managers rating their subordinate managers. One dimension of citizenship behavior measured was performance above and beyond the call of duty and high attention to quality. Group managers rated the OCB of their groups as a whole. The result showed that managers who received high ratings on OCB tended to have subordinate groups that exhibited strong OCB. Leading by example may therefore promote group-level behaviors that enhance organization effectiveness.[4]

**Using Rational Persuasion**    Rational persuasion is an important tactic for influencing people. It involves using logical arguments and factual evidence to convince another person that a proposal or request is workable and likely to achieve the goal. Assertiveness combined with careful research is necessary to make rational persuasion an effective tactic. It is likely to be most effective with people who are intelligent and rational. CEOs typically use rational persuasion to convince their boards that an undertaking, such as product diversification, is mandatory. A major moderating variable in rational persuasion is the credibility of the influence agent. Credibility helps an individual be more persuasive in two ways. First, it makes a person more convincing. Second, it contributes to a person's perceived power, and the more power one is perceived to have, the more targets will be influenced.[5]

The following two statements are samples of how rational persuasion is measured as perceived by subordinates in research about influence processes.

- Explains clearly why a request or proposed change is necessary to attain a task objective
- Provides information or evidence to show that a proposed activity or change is likely to be successful[6]

Leaders who emphasize the rational decision-making model favor rational persuasion. For example, a leader favoring this model might say, "Don't tell me what you feel, give me the facts," in response to a subordinate who said, "I have the feeling that morale is down." Leaders at Google heavily emphasize such data-based decision making. A Google professional in a meeting would be rejected if he or she said, "I think there are too many random photos appearing in Google Images." In contrast, he or she would be accepted if the statement were, "I sampled one hundred Google Images, and found that eight of them had random images."

**Telling True Stories**    In Chapter 3, storytelling was mentioned as part of the communication style of charismatic leaders. Storytelling has become accepted also an effective method for most leaders when attempting to influence workers. Leadership at Amazon.com attempts to influence warehouse workers not to steal by telling stories about Amazon workers who were fired for theft. In the warehouses, the company puts on flat-screen TVs that display examples of alleged on-the-job theft, and the fact that the employees were terminated. The images are accompanied by details such as when and what the workers stole, the value of the stolen merchandise. Also depicted is the method of stealing such as changing an address label or stuffing merchandise in their socks, and the fact that many of these workers are arrested. The stories influence many employees by reminding them there is a high probability of thieves will be caught.[7] (It is possible that many readers would classify this use of storytelling as less than an ethical influence tactic.)

A major concern about the widespread use of PowerPoint in organizations is that many presenters rely so heavily on facts, figures, fancy graphics, and clipart that they neglect the art of storytelling.[8] A way for the leader to use PowerPoint slides and still capitalize on the influential of storytelling is to supplement the slides with appropriate anecdotes. For example, a marketing manager of a hotel chain might be making a PowerPoint presentation of how the company was gaining market share in a particular region of the country. The manager might pause to share an anecdote of how a family sent the company and e-mail expressing gratitude that their favorite hotel was coming to town.

### Explaining Benefits to the Target

A strongly effective way of influencing another person is to explain what's in it for him or her if that individual honors your request. **Apprising** means that the influence agent explains how carrying out a request or supporting a proposal will benefit the target personally, including advancing the target's career.[9] An example of apprising would be for the manager to tell a subordinate, "Perhaps two weeks helping out for one month on the company's oil rig in the Arctic Circle may seem like a tough assignment. But you will seem like a hero to top management, and you will make great contacts." Two apprising behaviors on the part of the leader are as follows:

- Describes benefits you could gain from doing a task or activity (e.g., learn new skills, meet important people, and enhance your reputation)
- Explains how the task he or she wants you to do could help your career

### Making a Personal Appeal

A personal appeal in the context of influence theory is the same as it is in everyday life. The agent asks the target to implement a request or support a proposal out of friendship.[10] Another form of personal appeal is to ask for a personal favor before specifying the nature of the favor, as in "How would you like to do something important for me?" Asking for a favor without specifying its nature would likely be interpreted as unprofessional in a work environment. Two behaviors reflecting a personal appeal by a leader are as follows:

- Appeals to your friendship when asking you to do something
- Asks for your help as a personal favor

### Developing a Reputation as a Subject Matter Expert

Becoming an SME on a topic of importance to the organization is an effective strategy for gaining influence. Being an SME can be considered a subset of rational persuasion. Managers who possess expert knowledge in a relevant field and who continually build on that knowledge can get others to help them get work accomplished. Many of the leaders described throughout this text use expert knowledge to influence others. The leaders of Internet and social media companies such as Google and Foursquare are usually SMEs.

In recent years, General Electric Co. (GE) has emphasized the importance of industry expertise for business unit managers. GE is now keeping its senior leaders in place longer with the expectation that deeper understanding of the products and customers will enhance sales. In the past, business unit leaders relocated every few years to give them a broader understanding of the company. David Joyce, the CEO for GE Aviation, operation, represents the subject matter expertise approach. He has spent his entire thirty-six years with GE working his way up the aviation unit.[11]

Small business owners, in particular, rely on being SMEs because they founded the business on the basis of their product or technical knowledge. (Also, the major high-tech companies usually began small.) For example, the leader of a software company is usually an expert in software development.

### Exchanging Favors and Bargaining

Offering to exchange favors if another person will help you achieve a work goal is another standard influence tactic. By making an exchange, you strike a bargain with the other party. The exchange often translates into being willing to reciprocate at a later date. It might also be promising a share of the benefits if the other person helps you accomplish a task. For example, you might promise to place a person's name on a report to top management if that person will help you analyze the data and prepare the tables.

A recommended approach to asking for a favor is to give the other person as much time as feasible to accomplish the task, such as by saying, "Could you find ten minutes between now and the end of the month to help me?" Not pressing for immediate assistance will tend to lower resistance to the request. Giving a menu of options for different levels of assistance also helps lower resistance. For example, you might ask another manager if you can borrow a technician for a one-month assignment; then, as a second option, you might ask if the technician could work ten hours per week on the project.[12] To ensure that the request is perceived as an exchange, you might explain what reciprocity you have in mind: That you will mention your coworker's helpfulness to his or her manager.

Two behavior specifics for exchanging favors and bargaining are as follows:

- Offers to do a specific task for you in return for your help and support
- Offers to do something for you in the future for your help now

### Legitimating a Request

To legitimate is to verify that an influence attempt is within your scope of authority. Another aspect of legitimating is showing that your request is consistent with the organizational policies, practices, and expectations of professional people. Making legitimate requests is an effective influence tactic because most workers are willing to comply with regulations. A team leader can thus exert influence with a statement such as this one: "Top management wants a 25 percent reduction in customer complaints by next year. I'm therefore urging everybody to patch up any customer problems he or she can find."

Legitimating sometimes takes the form of subtle organizational politics. A worker might push for the acceptance of his or her initiative because it conforms to the philosophy or strategy of higher management. At Amazon.com, for example, it is well known that CEO Jeff Bezos likes to keep costs to a minimum. A distribution center manager might then encourage workers to be careful about wasting energy because "It's something Jeff would want us to do."

Two leadership behaviors that reflect legitimating are as follows:

- Says that his or her request is consistent with official rules and policies
- Verifies that a request is legitimate by referring to a document such as a work order, policy manual, charter, bylaws, or formal contract

### Making an Inspirational Appeal, Being Charming, and Emotional Display

A leader is supposed to inspire others, so it follows that making an inspirational appeal is an important influence tactic. As Jeffrey Pfeffer notes, "Executives and others seeking to exercise influence in organizations often develop skill in displaying, or not displaying, their feelings in a strategic fashion."[13] An inspirational appeal usually involves displaying emotion and appealing to group members' emotions. A moderating variable in the effectiveness of an inspirational appeal or emotional display is the influence of agent's **personal magnetism**, or the quality of being captivating, charming, and charismatic. Possessing personal magnetism makes it easier for the leader to inspire people.

The relevance of inspiration to influence is emphasized by the research of John H. Zenger and his associates. Based on results from 150,000 360-degree feedback assessments of 11,000 leaders, it was found that the key leadership behavior was, "Inspires and motivates to high performance." A key component of inspiring and motivation was found to be understanding the role of emotion in the workplace as well as being able to use his or her emotions comfortably.[14]

A useful component of inspirational appeal for leaders is to provide meaning to the work, showing that it has significance to the entire organization or the outside world. Most people like to be involved with projects that matter, and sometimes the leader might have to explain why the work matters.[15] For example, the leader of a company that specializes in subprime mortgages might have to explain, "Without our type of work, loads of people with modest incomes would not be able to become homeowners."

Another approach to inspiring workers is to create a vision that surpasses the wants and needs of most people.[16] One of the ways in which leaders at both Apple and Google have inspired workers is to involve them in a vision of "changing the world" with their products and services.

Two recorded behaviors of leaders who make an inspirational appeal are as follows:

- Says a proposed activity or change is an opportunity to do something really exciting and worthwhile
- Makes an inspiring speech or presentation to arouse enthusiasm for a proposed activity or change

**Consultation with Others**    Consultation with others before making a decision is both a leadership style and an influence technique. The influence target becomes more motivated to follow the agent's request because the target is involved in the decision-making process. Consultation is most effective as an influence tactic when the objectives of the person being influenced are consistent with those of the leader.[17] An example of such goal congruity took place in a major corporation. The company had decided to shrink its pool of suppliers to form closer partnerships with a smaller number of high-quality vendors. As a way of influencing others to follow this direction, a manufacturing vice president told his staff, "Our strategy is to reduce dealing with so many suppliers to improve quality and reduce costs. Let me know how we should implement this strategy." The vice president's influence attempt met with excellent reception, partially because the staff members also wanted a more streamlined set of vendor relationships. Two specific leadership behaviors reflecting consultation are as follows:

- Asks you to suggest things you could do to help him or her achieve a task objective or resolve a problem
- Invites you to suggest ways to improve a preliminary plan or proposal that he or she wants you to support or help implement

**Forming Coalitions**    At times, it is difficult to influence an individual or group by acting alone. A leader will then have to form coalitions, or alliances, with others to create the necessary clout. A **coalition** is a specific arrangement of parties working together to combine their power. Coalition formation works as an influence tactic because, to quote an old adage, "there is power in numbers." Coalitions in business are a numbers game—the more people you can get on your side, the better. However, the more powerful leaders are, the less they need to create a coalition.

Having a network of powerful people facilitates forming a coalition. If you need something done, you can get these other influential people to agree that it is a good idea. An example of getting something done might be getting permission to erect an office building close to a park. Simply having a large number of followers, friends, and links on social media is not sufficient for building a network of powerful people. You need to see occasionally or talk on the phone to build a relationship strong enough to form a coalition.

Two specific leadership behaviors that reflect coalition formation are as follows:

- Mentions the names of other people who endorse a proposal when asking you to support it
- Brings someone along for support when meeting with you to make a request or proposal

**Being a Team Player**    Influencing others by being a good team player is an important strategy for getting work accomplished. A leader might be a team player by doing such things as pitching in during peak workloads. An example would be an information technology team leader working through the night with team members to combat a virus attack on the company's computer network.

Being a team player is a more effective influence tactic in an organizational culture that emphasizes collaboration than one in which being tough-minded and decisive is more in vogue. For example, leaders at hedge funds typically spend a lot of time doing analytical work, such as selecting stocks and porting over data. Collaborating with others in a team-work mode is less important for their success as measured by the return on investment.

*Practicing Hands-On Leadership* A **hands-on leader** is one who gets directly involved in the details and processes of operations. Such a leader has expertise, is task oriented, and leads by example. By getting directly involved in the group's work activities, the leader influences subordinates to hold certain beliefs and to follow certain procedures and processes. For example, managers who get directly involved in fixing customer problems demonstrate to other workers how they think such problems should be resolved.

Hands-on leadership is usually expected at levels below the executive suite, yet many high-level executives are also hands-on leaders. A strong example is Sergio Marchionne, the Fiat Chrysler CEO, who intervenes in such matters as a leaking car door handle. The downside of being a hands-on leader is that if you do it to excess, you become a micro-manager. Despite the extraordinary empire Jeff Bezos of Amazon controls, he is an intense hands-on leader. A few years ago, Bezos bought the *Washington Post* with his own money. At one point Bezos received an e-mail from a reader complaining about the time it took to download the *Post* mobile app. Bezos proceeded to tell the newspaper's chief information officer how long the download must be in milliseconds.[18]

## Essentially Neutral Influence Tactics

The four influence tactics described in this section and listed in Table 8-2 might best be regarded as neutral with respect to ethics and honesty. If implemented with good intent, they tend to be positive, but if implemented with the intent of duping another person, they tend to be negative.

*Ingratiation* Ingratiation is pervasive in organizations because being liked is quite important to many people.[19] When ingratiation takes the form of well-deserved flattery or compliments, it is a positive tactic. Yet, getting somebody else to like you can be considered a mildly manipulative influence tactic if you do not like the other person.

Ingratiation is often directed upward, in the sense of a subordinate attempting to get the superior to like him or her, as in organizational politics. Ingratiation also works in a downward direction, when leaders attempt to get their subordinates to like them. Typical ingratiating techniques directed toward subordinates include luncheon invitations, compliments, giving a plum work assignment, and feeding a subordinate's hobby, such as contributing a rare stamp to an employee's collection.

Leaders who ordinarily are quite the opposite of ingratiating will sometimes go out of their way to be humble and agreeable to fit an important purpose. An example is the CEO of a large fast-food franchise operation. She might be cutting and sarcastic when at company headquarters. Yet when on a goodwill tour to visit franchisees, she is ingratiating. For example, she compliments the quality of the food of one of the chain restaurants, and asks to be photographed with the franchisee.

Ingratiating tactics identified in a study about influence tactics included the following:

- Says you have the special skills or knowledge needed to carry out a request
- Praises your skill or knowledge when asking you to do something

Leadership Self-Assessment Quiz 8-2 provides you an opportunity to measure your own ingratiating tendencies and to think through further what ingratiating yourself to work associates means in practice. Remember that being liked helps you get promoted, receive more compensation, and avoid being downsized, yet you should avoid being dishonest.

**TABLE 8-2** Essentially Neutral Influence Tactics

| | |
|---|---|
| **1.** | Ingratiation |
| **2.** | Joking and kidding |
| **3.** | Upward appeal |
| **4.** | Co-opting antagonists |

# LEADERSHIP SELF-ASSESSMENT QUIZ 8-2

### The Leader Ingratiating Checklist

As a leader in the present, past, or future, which of the following behaviors is something you have done or would do?

| | LEADER BEHAVIOR | YES | NO |
|---|---|---|---|
| 1. | Say "you look great" to work associates whether or not I thought it was true. | ☐ | ☐ |
| 2. | Laugh and smile when I hear almost any joke. | ☐ | ☐ |
| 3. | Say I was a big fan of the other person's sports team. | ☐ | ☐ |
| 4. | Express admiration for the experience of my manager. | ☐ | ☐ |
| 5. | Tell subordinates how proud I am to have them on my team. | ☐ | ☐ |
| 6. | Look at a photo of a newborn of someone else and say something like, "He (or she) is one of the cutest babies I have ever seen." | ☐ | ☐ |
| 7. | Tell a group member that he or she has unusually good taste in clothing. | ☐ | ☐ |
| 8. | As for technical advice from a work associate even if I did not need the information. | ☐ | ☐ |
| 9. | Acknowledge the birthdays of others whenever possible. | ☐ | ☐ |
| 10. | Compliment my manager regularly. | ☐ | ☐ |
| 11. | Compliment my group members regularly. | ☐ | ☐ |
| 12. | Send congratulatory notes to executives when the organization has achieved good results. | ☐ | ☐ |
| 13. | After seeing a photo of someone's pet, say something to the effect, "one of the cutest I have ever seen." | ☐ | ☐ |
| 14. | Compliment strongly the work ethic of a group member even when he or she is an average performer. | ☐ | ☐ |
| 15. | Tell your manager that you are pleased that you and he (or she) on one the same "wave length " or "page." | ☐ | ☐ |

*Scoring and Interpretation:* The more of these behaviors you use or have used, especially if used frequently, the more ingratiating you are. A caution is that if you use 13 or more of these behaviors frequently, you might be perceived as insincere.

*Skill Development:* Leaders or future leaders should remember that a moderate amount of ingratiating behavior is the norm in relationships with superiors and subordinates. Ingratiation is frequently an effective influence tactic, and should therefore be part of your leadership tool kit.

Leadership Skill-Building Exercise 8-1 provides an opportunity to practice ingratiation in a simulated work setting.

# LEADERSHIP SKILL-BUILDING EXERCISE 8-1

### The Ingratiating New Division Manager

One student plays the role of a division manager who has been appointed to the position only two weeks ago. The division manufactures tires for large vehicles such as trucks, busses, and tractors, and has been losing money for several years because of overseas competition. Nobody on the management team has received a salary increase or bonus in three years. Today the new division manager is meeting with management team, role played by several other students. To increase his or her leadership effectiveness, the division manager decides to be ingratiating toward the team. Run the role play for about ten minutes, and observers might provide feedback on the effectiveness of the ingratiating tactics.

*Joking and Kidding*    Good-natured kidding is especially effective when a straightforward statement might be interpreted as harsh criticism. Joking or kidding can thus get the message across and lower the risk that the influence target will be angry with the influence agent. Joking and kidding might be interpreted either as dishonest or as extraordinarily tactful because the criticizer softens the full blow of the criticism. A small business owner successfully used joking and kidding to help the receptionist wear clothing more appropriate for the position. As the owner entered the office, he noticed that the receptionist was wearing a tank top and very large hoop earrings. The owner said, "Melissa, you look great, but I think you have your dates confused. You are dressed for the company picnic, and it takes place tomorrow." Melissa smiled, and then dressed more professionally in the future.

*Upward Appeal*    In **upward appeal**, the leader exerts influence on a team member by getting a person with more formal authority to do the influencing. Some managers and researchers regard upward appeal as an ethical and standard practice, yet it does contain an element of manipulation and heavy-handedness. An example: "I sent the guy to my boss when he wouldn't listen to me. That fixed him." More than occasional use of upward appeal weakens the leader's stature in the eyes of group members and superiors, eroding effectiveness. Leaders can apply upward appeal in other ways. A leader might attempt to persuade another staff member that higher management approved his or her request. The target of the influence event is thus supposed to grant acceptance automatically. Or, the leader can request higher management's assistance in gaining another person's compliance with the request. The influence target thus feels pressured.[20]

*Co-Opting Antagonists*    A potentially effective influence tactic, as well as a method of conflict resolution, is to find a clever way to get the other person or group of persons to join forces with you. In this sense, to **co-opt** is to win over opponents by making them part of your team or giving them a stake in the system.[21] Assume that the director of human resources is receiving considerable opposition to some of her initiatives from the chief financial officer (CFO). For example, the CFO is opposed to her proposed program of cross-cultural training. To soften the opposition, and perhaps even make him an ally, the director of human resources invites the CFO to become a member of the "human resources advisory board" composed of company executives and distinguished citizens from the community.

## Essentially Dishonest and Unethical Tactics

The tactics described in this section are less than forthright and ethical, yet they vary in intensity with respect to dishonesty. Most people would consider the first two strategies presented here as unethical and devious, yet they might regard the second two tactics as still within the bounds of acceptable ethics, even though less than fully candid. The tactics in question are outlined in Table 8-3.

*Deliberate Machiavellianism*    Niccolò Machiavelli advised that princes must be strong, ruthless, and cynical leaders because people are self-centered and self-serving. As implied in Chapter 7, people in the workplace who ruthlessly manipulate others have therefore come to be called **Machiavellians**. They tend to initiate actions with others and control the interactions. Machiavellians regularly practice deception, bluffing, and other manipulative tactics.[22] A modern example of deliberate Machiavellianism is the practice of forcing managerial and professional employees into working many extra hours of uncompensated overtime. The employees are told that if they refuse to work extra hours, they will not be considered worthy of promotion or as good team players. Even when

TABLE 8-3 Essentially Dishonest and Unethical Influence Tactics

| |
| --- |
| **1.** Deliberate Machiavellianism |
| **2.** Gentle manipulation of people and situations |
| **3.** Undue pressure |
| **4.** Debasement |

positions in other companies are readily available, most career-minded people will stay because they want to preserve a good reputation.

**Gentle Manipulation of People and Situations**    Some people who attempt to influence others are manipulative, but to a lesser extent than an outright Machiavellian. They gain the compliance of another person by making untrue statements or faking certain behaviors. For example, a leader might imply that if a colleague supports his position in an intergroup conflict, the person might be recommended for promotion. Another manipulative approach is to imply dire consequences to innocent people if the influence target does not comply with demands of the influence agent, such as "Even if you don't want to put in extra effort for me, think of the people with families who will be laid off if we don't make our targets."

A widely used manipulative approach is to tap into social norms in order to gain consensus. According to Steve Martin, behavior specialist at the consulting firm Influence at Work, this technique can move people to model their behavior after others. He gives the example of working with the U.K. tax collecting service. Martin witnessed an increase in the return rate after enclosing messages such as "nine out of ten people pay their tax on time." The rate of returns increased even more when the tax collection service presented messages referring to the number of people who field returns with the individual's own town or postal code.[23] A workplace example is a manager who informs the vice president that she wants an enlarged budget for attendance at the latest social networking seminars because "all other companies are doing it."

The technique of tapping into social norms can be combined with peer pressure to influence a group member. If one person is not stepping forward to work well as a team member, the manager will say, "Bob, everyone in the department is committed to developing a team atmosphere, and we'd like you to be a part of it."[24]

**Undue Pressure**    Effective leaders regularly use motivational techniques such as rewards and mild punishments. Yet, when rewards become bribes for compliance and threats of punishment become severe, the target person is subjected to undue pressure or coercion. An example of a bribe by a manager might be, "If you can work eighty hours on this project this week, I'll recommend you for the highest pay grade." Another approach to pressure is for the manager to scream and swear at the subordinate as a form of intimidation. As one manager under pressure of his own shouted to a subordinate: "Get some of these ____ receivables paid by the end of the week or find another job."

Two specific behaviors labeled pressure in a research study were as follows:

- Uses threats or warnings when trying to get you to do something
- Tries to pressure you to carry out a request

**Debasement**    A subtle manipulative tactic is **debasement**, demeaning or insulting oneself to control the behavior of another person. The CEO of an upscale clothing company believed that the designer of a man's suit had gone too far in creating a snug fit. To influence the designer to modify the style of the suit, the CEO said, "You are the expert, and I don't know a lot about suit design. But why would anybody buy a suit that looks like it fit him when he was 20 pounds thinner?" Specific debasing tactics revealed by research include the following: "I lower myself so she'll do it," and "I act humble so she'll do it."[25]

In studying the most severe unethical influence (and political) tactics, it is important to recognize that the use of these influence approaches can bring about human suffering. For example, bullying and intimidating tactics may not be illegal, but they are unethical. Cruelty in the organization creates many problems. As one observer notes, "Cruelty is blatantly unethical and erodes the organizational character through intellectual, emotional, moral, and social vices that reduce the readiness of groups to act ethically."[26] Examples of cruelty include insulting a group member's physical appearance or belittling him or her.

The type of influence tactics described in this chapter are apparently effective in attaining positive task and relations outcome. Task outcomes generally refer to job performance, whereas relations outcomes refer to behavior such as gaining the cooperation of others.

A team of researchers headed Soojin Lee of the College of Business Administration at the Chonnam University in South Korea, conducted a meta-analysis of the relationship between influence tactics and task and relations outcomes. Forty-nine independent samples, comprising almost 9,000 participants were investigated.

Positive relationships were found between outcomes and rational persuasion, inspirational appeal, explaining benefits, collaboration, ingratiation, and consultation. A negative relationship was found between pressure and outcomes. (Note that these seven influence tactics have been described in this chapter.) Rational persuasion was found to be the most consistently effective influence tactic under a variety of conditions, such as the setting of the study.[27] The accompanying box Leader in Action describes a leader who uses a variety of influence tactics to keep his enterprise going.

## LEADER IN ACTION

### SolarCity CEO Lyndon Rive Wants Solar Panels to Become the Dominant Energy

#### Source

Lyndon Rive and his brother Peter cofounded SolarCity in 2006. The company designs, finances, and installs photovoltaic systems, performs energy audits, and builds charging stations for electric vehicles. Most of SolarCity's work centers on installing solar panels in homes, followed by financing the system, and leasing it back to the homeowner. The founding value proposition of SolarCity was to both manufacture and install solar panels for the home.

Rive is the cousin of the famous entrepreneur Elon Musk, who is the chairman of SolarCity, and the CEO and founder of Tesla Motors, as well as SpaceCity. As a seventeen-year-old, Rive ran a homeopathic-medicine business, and has a reputation for exaggerating the positive side of his claims.

Rive says "The core mission of the company is selling clean energy at a lower cost than fossil fuel. Period." Rive's vision is that American homes will someday generate their own clean electricity, and also have a Tesla that draws electricity from a solar-powered charger in the garage. He hopes that someday solar energy will no longer be a niche. He says, "In that scenario, humanity wins. Right now it isn't winning."

Rive and his counterparts in competitive companies continuously attempt to convince fossil energy users in the United States to convert to solar-powered electricity. Approximately .39 percent of homes in the United States currently use solar power for their source of electricity. Yet Rive and his colleagues say that solar energy sources are going to gain traction in the upcoming years. Rive predicts that in thirteen years, one half of our electricity will be solar. Once the price of solar becomes more competitive, the use of fossil fuel will plunge. (Installing a

solar panel system on the rooftop of a home now costs approximately $30,000 minus tax credits.) Many financial analysts question whether SolarCity has a business model that will generate profits in the future.

Another approach SolarCity leadership is using to influence the conversion to solar tiles is to use Uber and Lyft drivers to sell panels to riders. Commissions for the drivers run about $1,000 per sale of solar systems. To help explain why solar energy will definitely gain momentum, Rive points to the success of the launch of the Model 3 Tesla electrical vehicle. The link between electrical vehicles and solar energy is that companies SolarCity and competitors will be building effective battery technology for the home. As more and more cities and countries plan to convert to 100 percent renewable energy in the next few years, the emphasis on storing electricity in batteries will increase.

In 2016, Elon Musk, Lyndon Rive and Peter Rive bought $100 million of solar bonds from SolarCity. An analyst explained that this huge purchase was necessary because the rooftop solar company was burning through a lot of cash. ("Burning cash" refers to a company not generating enough revenue to cover expenses, and therefore going through investor money.) The bond purchase took place as Musk's electric car company Tesla Motors Inc. was in the process of acquiring SolarCity.

Shortly thereafter, Elon Musk proposed that Tesla and SolarCity merge because the two companies share the same goal of accelerating the advent of sustainable energy. The merged companies would help make solar roofs more physically attractive than a traditional roof, generate electricity, and last longer. The solar panel roof would also cost less to install, and save on the

## LEADER IN ACTION (continued)

cost of electricity. According to Musk, consumers who owned a Tesla vehicle and batteries for household electricity, plus a SolarCity roof could generate enough clean energy to reduce greenhouse gasses, and would also be admired by neighbors.

### QUESTIONS

1. Which influence tactics does it appear that Lyndon Rive is using to lead his company toward success?

2. What about you? Has Rive convinced you having solar panels installed at a home would be good for the homeowner and society?

*Source:* Original story based on facts and observations in the following sources: Danielle Mugio, "SolarCity's CEO Told Us Solar Energy Will Reach a Tipping Point in Just 5 Years—Here's Why," *Tech Insider,* (www.techinsider.io), June 14, 2016. pp. 1–5; Brian Eckhouse, "Musk and Rive Brothers Buying $100 Million of SolarCity Bonds," (www.bloomberg.com), August 23, 2016, p. 1. Brian Dumaine, "Mr. Sunshine," *Fortune,* October 27, 2014, pp. 96–104; "Lyndon Rive: C-Founder, Chief Executive Officer," *SolarCity Executive Management,* 2016. p. 1, 3; Cassandra Sweet and Tim Higgins, "Tesla's Chief Offers Merger Vision," *The Wall street Journal,* October 31, 2016, p. B; Cassandra Sweet, "SolarCity Is Cutting Costs," *The Wall Street journal,* September 23, 2016, p. B5.

Leadership Skill-Building Exercise 8-2 gives you an opportunity to practice influence tactics in a high-stakes business situation.

## LEADERSHIP SKILL-BUILDING EXERCISE 8-2

### Influence Tactics

One student plays the role of a CFO of a large company. After months of analysis, the CFO decides that a key step the company can take to be profitable during the next several years is to get about 5,000 employees to accept voluntary retirement. As severance pay, the workers who accept the retirement package will receive one year's salary, depending on the length of service. The buyout could cost the company around $5 million in payouts plus some liability for future health benefits and retirement pay. Four other students will play the role of the top-management team, several of whom might be skeptical about the soundness of the plan offered by the CFO. Observers will pay close attention to the influence tactics used by the CFO, and perhaps by the other members of the top-management team.

Leadership Skill-Building Exercise 8-3 will help you recognize several of the influence tactics described in this chapter. Another tactic mentioned in the exercise, assertiveness, was described in Chapter 2.

## LEADERSHIP SKILL-BUILDING EXERCISE 8-3

### Identifying Influence Tactics

***Instructions:*** After reading the following passage, identify which influence tactics the leader is using, and explain your reasoning.

Gina is the director of human resources in a diversified company with approximately 50,000 workers. She has assembled her five direct reports in a hotel conference room for a Saturday morning meeting. With an intense facial expression, Gina launched directly into her presentation, supported by PowerPoint slides on a large screen.

"Enjoy your coffee, tea, juice, donuts, bagels, and pastries because I can offer you no other goodies this morning. As HR professionals, you know we are in trouble. As hard as we all work, and as much good as we do, our jobs are in peril. The trend is clear. Our corporation, similar to many others, might be outsourcing our work to HR vendors. The movement has already begun with payroll being outsourced last year and health insurance this year.

## EXERCISE 8-3 (continued)

"Even worse, the corporate group is planning to purchase HR software that will enable line managers throughout the company to take care of their own HR responsibilities, such as recruiting and selection.

"I want to work with all of you to develop strategies and tactics so vital that the top-management team will decide to keep our group intact, and not join the outsourcing movement. We need also to discourage line managers from being performing HR on their own without our help. Think of HR activities so vital that we become indispensable. Maybe we should be coordinating a flu-shot program. Maybe we should beef up our wellness program so much that absenteeism and insurance costs are reduced to an extent that our contribution to the bottom line is obvious even to our CFO.

"Now that I've told you the truth, let's get started having a true dialogue about the challenges facing us."

## Leadership Influence for Organizational Change

Most of the discussion so far relates to the leader/manager influencing people one at a time or in small groups. Top-level leaders exert many of their influence attempts in the direction of bringing about changes throughout the entire organization, often by attempting to overhaul the organizational culture. One such change would be attempting to influence a culture that was too collaborative to make decisions more quickly and independently, or the reverse. Another change would be to make the culture more focused on products the market wanted and less focused on innovation for its own sake. Yet another cultural change facing a CEO would be to make a risk-averse workforce more entrepreneurial and risk taking.

Before plunging ahead with attempts at massive cultural change, the leader needs to study the old culture and understand why it contributed to the prosperity and growth of the organization. When Mary Barra was appointed CEO of General Motors (GM), she saw the need to shift the culture in the direction of a less bureaucratic, more innovative, and fast-moving organization. Yet Barra had worked her way up the organization from an entry-level engineer. She therefore understood that GM had become one of the world's most successful and well-known companies, relying on a classic bureaucratic structure. Consequently, Barra treaded lightly in terms of insulting people who felt part of the "Old GM."

After a new CEO is appointed, the person typically makes a public statement to the effect that: "My number-one job is to change the culture." A leader might do the following to bring about change as well as ensuring that a healthy corporate culture is maintained.

- Serve as a role model for the desired attitudes and behaviors. Leaders must behave in ways consistent with the values and practices they wish to see imitated throughout the organization. If the change the leader wants is a stronger focus on customer service, leaders must treat employees as customers, thereby acting as role models for the way customers should be treated. The leaders must also talk in positive terms about customer service, with a statement such as "The real joy in our work is helping customers solve their problems." Another frequently used method of bringing about change by acting as a role model is for the newly appointed leader to be frugal to encourage frugality throughout the organization. The frugal CEO, for example, might fly on commercial airlines and not by corporate jet, have one instead of several administrative assistants, and eat lunch in the company cafeteria.

- Impose a new approach through executive edict. From the time, he started his position as chairman and CEO of General Electric, Jeff Immelt was on a mission to transform the hard-driving process-oriented company into an organization steeped in creativity and wired for business growth. In addition to outstanding efficiency in operations, Immelt presented new imperatives for risk taking, sophisticated marketing, and, of utmost importance, innovation.[28] Fifteen years later, his approach to culture change was still bringing about positive, but not spectacular, results. Immelt now refers to GE as "the digital industrial" company. One reason is that GE now has a fast-growing software business that is a dominant play in the market for digital tools to control major industrial operations. Another reason is that under the leadership of Immelt, the company's own software is helping streamline its own manufacturing and design pro processes.[29] (Immelt resigned in 2017.)

- Establish a reward system that reinforces the culture, such as giving huge suggestion awards to promote an innovative culture. Jeff Bezos at Amazon.com is so committed to innovation that being imaginative is almost a requirement for being promoted into a key position at the company.

- Foster understanding and conviction by helping people throughout the organization understand why the change is necessary. The reasons the change is  necessary  may be abundantly clear to the company leadership, but these reasons have to be broadly communicated. Two consultants at McKinsey & Company recommend that leaders develop a change story that helps all stakeholders understand where the company is headed, why it is changing, and why this change is important.[30] In recent years, top-level leadership at McDonalds' Corporation has had to work diligently with corporate managers to explain that the market for rapid-service restaurants has become highly competitive. More people were eating at home, and trying other fast-food restaurants. The changes made innovation in McDonald's offering essential. (Serving breakfast all day was one such innovation.)

- Hold people accountable for the changes in behavior that support the cultural shift. If company leadership decides that customer service should receive top priority, employees at all levels should be measured on customer service in their performance reviews. If not, the cultural shift to place a higher value on customer service will not take place.[31]

- Select candidates for positions at all levels whose values mesh with the values of the desired culture. Many firms hire only those candidates whose work and school experience suggest that they might be good team players—a cultural value.

- Sponsor new training and development programs that support the desired cultural values. Among many examples, top management might sponsor diversity training to support the importance of cultural diversity, or training in quality to support the value of quality.

A leader who exhibited all of these behaviors would qualify as a transformational leader because of all the positive changes.

## equencing of Influence Tactics

An important consideration in using influence tactics is the sequence or order in which they should be applied. In general, you should begin with the most positive, or least abrasive, tactic. If you do not gain the advantage you seek, proceed to a stronger tactic. For example, if you want a larger salary increase than that initially assigned to you, try rational persuasion. If persuasion does not work, move on to exchanging favors. Use a more abrasive tactic such as upward appeal only as a last resort. The reason is that abrasive tactics trigger revenge and retaliation. Many people who have taken their complaints to an outside agency, such as a governmental office, have found themselves with a limited future in their organization. Although the appeal is legally justified, it is politically unwise.

The sequencing of tactics can also be considered in terms of cost and risk. A sensible approach is to begin with low-cost, low-risk tactics. If the outcome is important enough to the influence agent, he or she can then proceed to higher-cost and higher-risk influence tactics. An example of a low-cost, low-risk tactic would be joking and kidding. An accounting manager who was disappointed with the budget offered to her group might

## LEADERSHIP SKILL-BUILDING EXERCISE 8-4

### Applying Influence Tactics

Divide the class into small teams. Each group assigns one leadership influence tactic to each team member. During the next week or so, each team member takes the opportunity to practice the assigned influence tactic in a work or personal setting. Hold a group discussion with the same class teams after the influence attempts have been practiced. Report the following information: (1) Under what circumstances the influence tactic was attempted; (2) how the influence target reacted; and (3) what results, both positive and negative, were achieved.

Practicing influence tactics directly contributes to your leadership effectiveness because leadership centers on influence. If you want to exert leadership as an individual contributor, you will have to be particularly adept at using influence tactics because your formal authority will be quite limited.

say to her boss, "Does the new budget mean that our group will have to pay for our own laser cartridges and green eyeshades?" It would be much more costly in terms of time and potential retaliation to form a coalition with another under-budgeted group to ask for an enlarged budget.

In addition to the sequencing of tactics, the influence agent must also consider the direction of the influence attempt as a contingency factor. In general, the more position power an individual exerts over another, the less the need for being cautious in the use of influence tactics. For example, a vice president can more readily use undue pressure against a supervisor than vice versa. When you have more power, there are likely to be fewer negative consequences from using more powerful tactics.

Leadership Skill-Building Exercise 8-4 provides an opportunity to practice implementing various influence tactics. As with any other skill, influence skills need to be practiced under field conditions.

## Implicit Leadership Theories and Leadership Influence

A final perspective on influence tactics is that people are more likely to be influenced by leaders who match their expectations of what a leader should be. **Implicit leadership theories** are personal assumptions about the traits and abilities that characterize an ideal organizational leader. These assumptions, both stated and unstated, develop through socialization and past experiences with leaders. The assumptions are stored in memory and activated when group members interact with a person in a leadership position. Our assumptions about leaders help us make sense of what takes place on the job. Assume that Reggie was raised in a household and neighborhood in which business leaders are highly respected and thought to be dedicated and intelligent. When Reggie later works in a full-time professional job, he is most likely to be influenced by a supervisor he perceives to be dedicated and intelligent because this person fits Reggie's preconceived notion of how a leader should behave.

According to implicit leadership theory, as part of making assumptions and expectations of leader traits and behaviors, people develop leadership prototypes and antiprototypes. *Prototypes* are positive characterizations of a leader, whereas *antiprototypes* are traits and behaviors that people do not want to see in a leader. People have different expectations of what they want in a leader, yet research conducted with 939 subordinates in 2 different samples in British companies shows there is some consistency in implicit leadership theories. The study showed that these theories are consistent across different employee groups and are also stable, trait-based stereotypes of leadership.[32] Another study in England showed that if the leader matches employee assumptions about having the

**TABLE 8-4** Implicit Leadership Theory Dimensions

| LEADERSHIP PROTOTYPE | LEADERSHIP ANTIPROTOTYPE |
|---|---|
| **1.** Sensitivity (compassion, sensitive) | **1.** Tyranny (dominant, selfish, manipulative) |
| **2.** Intelligence (intelligent, clever) | **2.** Masculinity (male, masculine) |
| **3.** Dedication (dedicated, motivated) | |
| **4.** Charisma (charismatic, dynamic) | |
| **5.** Strength (strong, bold) | |
| **6.** Attractiveness (well dressed, classy) | |
| **7.** Trustworthiness (honesty, integrity) | |

*Source:* Gathered from information in Olga Epitropaki and Robin Martin, "Implicit Leadership Theories in Applied Settings: Factor Structure, Generalizability, and Stability over Time," *Journal of Applied Psychology*, April 2004, pp. 297–299. Olga Epitropaki and Robin Martin, "Implicit Leadership Theories in Applied Settings: Factor Structure, Generalizability, and Stability over Time," *Journal of Applied Psychology*, April 2004, pp. 297–299; Austin lee Nichols and Catherine A. Cottrell, "What do People Desire in Their Leaders? The Role of Leadership Level on Trait Desirability," *The Leadership Quarterly*, August 2014, pp. 711–729

right traits, the leader–member exchange (LMX) will be more positive. In turn, the group member will be more readily influenced by the leader.[33]

A study with workers about implicit leadership indicated that people's perceptions of which characteristics they desire in a leader is associated with the level of the position. It was found that workers desire (a) dominant traits more in high-level, than in low-level leaders, a(b) interpersonal traits more in low-level leaders than in high-level leaders.[34]

Table 8-4 lists the six traits group members want to see in a leader (prototypes), as well as the two traits they do not want to see in a leader (antiprototypes). Your study of leadership traits in Chapters 2 and 3 will reinforce these leadership attributes. The antiprototype of *masculinity* suggests that followers prefer a compassionate and relationship-oriented leader to a command-and-control leader. An implication of these data is that a leader who fits group members' prototypes is more likely to influence them than a leader who fits their antiprototype.

A potential problem with leadership prototypes is that superiors and subordinates might rate leaders favorably who fit these prototypes, even if the leader's performance is not so strong. For example, Sam might be an intelligent and dedicated leader of a call center but in reality accomplish very little.[35]

## READER'S ROADMAP

So far we have studied considerable information about the nature of leadership; the attributes, behaviors, and styles of leaders; the ethics and social responsibility of leaders; and how leaders exert power and use politics and influence. The next chapter explains a variety of techniques for developing teamwork.

## SUMMARY

To become an effective leader, a person must be aware of specific influence tactics. Influence is the ability to affect the behaviors of others in a particular direction. Power, in contrast, is the potential or capacity to influence. A model presented here indicates that a leader's influence outcomes are a function of the influence tactics he or she uses. The influence tactics are, in turn, moderated, or affected, by the leader's traits and

behaviors and also by the situation. The outcomes of influence attempts are commitment, compliance, or resistance, all of which influence end results such as group success or failure.

Influence tactics are often viewed from an ethical perspective. Some tactics are clearly ethical, some are neutral, but others are clearly unethical. Used with tact, diplomacy, and good intent, ethical influence tactics can be quite effective. The essentially ethical tactics described here are leading by example and respect; using rational persuasion; telling true stories; explaining the benefits to the target; personal appeal; being an SME; exchanging favors and bargaining; legitimating a request; making an inspirational appeal; being charming, and emotional display; consulting with others; forming coalitions, being a team player; and practicing hands-on leadership.

Influence tactics essentially neutral with respect to ethics are ingratiation, joking and kidding, upward appeal, and co-opting antagonists. Essentially dishonest and unethical tactics presented here were deliberate Machiavellianism, gentle manipulation of people and situations, undue pressure, and debasement.

Top-level leaders exert many of their influence attempts toward bringing about changes throughout the entire organization, often by attempting to overhaul the organizational culture. The leader should first study the old culture to search for its merits. Tactics for cultural change by the leader include serving as a role model;

executive edict; giving rewards to reinforce the culture; helping people understand why change is necessary; holding people accountable for necessary changes; selecting candidates who fit the culture; and establishing training and development programs to support the culture.

Sequencing of influence tactics is an important consideration. In general, begin with the most positive, or least abrasive, tactic. If you do not gain the advantage you seek, proceed to a stronger tactic. Also, begin with low-cost, low-risk tactics.

Implicit leadership theories are personal assumptions about the traits and abilities that characterize an ideal organizational leader. Prototypes are positive characterizations of a leader, whereas antiprototypes are negative. Subordinates are more likely to be influenced by leaders who fit their prototype, and do not fit their antiprototype, of a leader. Dominant traits are more desired in top-level leaders, whereas interpersonal traits are more desirable in lower-level leadership roles.

## KEY TERMS

## GUIDELINES FOR ACTIONS AND SKILL DEVELOPMENT

To become an effective leader, learning to use influence tactics comfortably is inevitable. If you use influence tactics naturally, without giving them much thought, there is still more to learn. For example, even a great leader such as Elton Musk might be even more effective with employees if he were more conciliatory toward those people he perceived to be of average intelligence. Being conciliatory fits the influence tactics of being charming and consulting with others.

In order for many influence tactics to work well, such as being a hands-on leader or joking and kidding, the regular physical presence of a leader is valuable. Some CEOs today attempt to conduct much of their work digitally, and perhaps even live in a city 3,000 miles away from company headquarters. The lowly visible leader not only loses influence but also might be dismissed. A case in point is Federica Marchionni was forced out as CEO of Land's End Inc. She had attempted to bring about broad changes at the catalog retailer that

annoyed employee and turned away shoppers. The former Ferrari executive was never able to influence employees to accept her vision of a more fashionable Land's End. A point of contention was that Marchionni spent about one week a month at the company's Wisconsin's headquarters, preferring instead to work out of an office in the garment district of New York.[36]

### Discussion Questions and Activities

1. Explain the following analogy: Influence is to leadership as eggs are to an omelet.
2. Which influence tactic described in this chapter do you think would work the best for you? Why?
3. Which of the influence tactics described in this chapter do you think are the most important for a person in his or her first leadership assignment? Explain your reasoning.
4. With so many workers habituated to using mobile devices for so much of their work, should

company management develop apps for influencing subordinates? Explain your reasoning.

5. Assume that as their leader, you wanted to influence minimum wage earners in an order-fulfillment center to work faster. Which one or two influence tactics are likely to be effective?

6. How should an ambitious person draw the line between being an effective at ingratiation and being obnoxious?

7. Why is developing a reputation as an SME important for a leader if leadership deals so heavily with interpersonal skills?

8. How might a business owner use tapping into the social norms to get his or her employees to lead a healthier lifestyle?

9. Over a long period of time, Sears has slipped from being America's largest retailer to struggling for survival in recent years. What cultural change can you suggest to help company leadership at Sears restore some of the retailer's past glory?

10. Get the opinion of an experienced leader as to the most effective influence tactics. Share your findings with class members.

## LEADERSHIP CASE PROBLEM A

### Steve Tackles Mall World

Thirty-nine year-old Steve was ecstatic. Ever since he earned an MBA a few years ago, he set his sights on becoming a CEO, somewhere, somehow. If need be, he would purchase an existing small company if he could figure out a scheme to raise enough cash and borrowing power. Steve was moving along well in his career as a marketing manager in a real estate development company when he received the opportunity to become a CEO. The CEO of an affiliated company, Mall World, suddenly resigned because of all the pressures associated with the position.

The board explained to Steve that he was offered the position because of his drive, leadership skills, incisive thinking, and educational qualifications. Steve was told that the job would be tough, but that he would be given two years to improve occupancy rates at the five malls the company owned and operated in the United States and Canada. During his first couple of weeks as CEO of Mall World, Steve went on a listening tour, speaking with members of the top-management team, mall managers, and a few anchor tenants. In addition to more general discussions, Steve asked each person he spoke with what he or she thought of the future of shopping malls. Among the comments he heard are as follows:

*Leasing Manager, Home Office:* The lower occupancy rates are hardly a problem. Americans love their malls. Our malls are still the most comfortable place to shop, dine, and interact with strangers and store associates. As the economy picks up, we once again have more demand for our space than we can provide.

*Mall Manager in Boston Area:* Anyone who thinks that online shopping will take a permanent bite out of mall shopping is just plain stupid. It is natural for people to want to touch, feel, smell, and experience goods in person. "Have you ever attempted to try on a sweater over the Internet?" [Said with a grin and laugh.]

*Mall Manager in Toronto Area:* You may not be old enough to recognize it Steve, but mall occupancy rates run in cycles. When gas prices and unemployment are relatively high, few consumers visit the mall. As a result, a few of the weaker stores close in panic. And cold weather will always contribute to mall traffic. When the conditions outside are uncomfortable, people love to flock to the malls to walk around comfortably, shop, and dine. Our future is as secure as the bricks and mortar encasing us.

*Marketing Manager, Home Office:* I wouldn't worry too much about the relatively high number of vacancies in our malls. We have some attractive new leasing programs coming along that will have tenants flocking to the mall. Online shopping will taper off as the novelty wears thin. Having packages stolen from your front door will also cool down some of the interest in online shopping.

*Small Store Manager in Chicago Area Mall:* I am starting to think why bother with having a bricks and mortar store. Mall traffic has been slowing down for a couple of years. With an online store, I wouldn't have the huge overhead of renting space in a mall.

As Steve attempted to synthesize the feedback, he thought that unfortunately the store manager might be close to telling the true story. He also thought that most of the opinions he heard suggested the need for a quick attitude change in order to help Mall World survive.

### Questions

1. In what way does this case suggest that a culture change might be necessary at Mall World?

2. What steps might Steve take to influence his managers that they need to worry more about the future of Mall World, as well as taking action steps to improve occupancy rates?

3. Which specific influence tactics do you recommend Steve use with his managers?

## ASSOCIATED ROLE PLAY

One student plays the role of Steve, who decides to attempt to influence mall manager in the Boston Area to think more competitively about mall occupancy rates. (Or the other student can select one of the other managers that Steve interviewed.) The other student plays the role of the mall manager who thinks that CEO Steve is worrying needlessly. Run the role play for about eight minutes. Observers can provide feedback on how well the influence attempt went.

## LEADERSHIP CASE PROBLEM B

### Katerina Demands Results

Katerina is the regional manager of an international chain of luxury goods boutiques, Florentine Bravado. Each boutique, or store, is about 4,000 square feet, and features expensive watches, handbags, men's and women's suits, and jewelry. Michael Kors would be a direct competitor of Florentine Bravado. All twelve store managers in Katerina's region report directly to her, along with a small administrative staff at regional headquarters. Florentine Bravado stores are located in upscale malls, and the company also sells merchandise online from the corporate location.

Katerina's goal for the upcoming year is to stabilize or enhance sales at her twelve stores. Store revenues have been declining about 4 percent per year for the last five years, in both her region and the entire company. Katerina wants her region to standout by reversing this trend. Before holding in-person discussions with her store managers, Katerina sent out an e-mail to all the managers. The e-mail read as follows:

"What is happening to our cultural icon, Florentine Bravado? Are we falling prey to the same misery encroaching upon the many mundane retailers? Are our formerly loyal customers buying trinkets at discount stores instead of shopping at Bravado? Are our customers now purchasing knock-offs from overseas imitators?"

Three days later, Katerina met with Garth, the store manager located in the region's most upscale mall. She said, "Garth what is wrong with you? We give you all the advertising support you need, and your results for the last quarter are putrid. I want to see a 3 percent improvement in your sales for next quarter. No moaning, no groaning, no excuses."

Garth replied, "I would like to see a 3 percent or more sales increase next quarter also. Yet you are expecting too much. The holiday shopping season is behind us, and we can expect a normal sales decrease. Neither I nor my sales associates have found a way to drag people in the mall into our store and force them to buy a $9,000 watch or a $1,200 handbag. We have to deal with the realities of the economy."

Katerina responded, "Garth, I told you at the outset. No moaning, no groaning, no excuses. Your goal is a 3 percent sales increase, and it's not negotiable."

Five days later, Katerina met with Sonya, the manager of a low-performing store. Katerina said forcibly, "Sonya I want you to understand clearly that your days of operating a low-performing store are over. Forget your European charm. Persuade the people who visit the store to walk away with a purchase. Get on the backs of those laid-back sales associates, and make them sell, sell, sell. The corporate group and I need you to boost sales. Do you understand my message?"

Sonya rebutted, "Katerina, I thought that you understood the luxury goods business. We are not selling kegs of beer to bar owners. Luxury consumers have to be gently coaxed to make a purchase like an $800 pair of cufflinks. He could easily purchase a pair of cufflinks for $15 that would get the job done."

Katerina responded, "Nice try Sonya, but Florentine Bravado looks at the bottom line, not excuses. Show me some good sales results real soon."

### Questions

1. Which influence tactics does Katerina appear to be using, and how effective do they appear to be?
2. What other approach might Katerina take to getting her store managers to enhance sales?
3. To what extent do you think that Katerina is too abrasive in her role as regional manager?

## ASSOCIATED ROLE PLAY

One student plays the role of Katerina who is delivering a kinder, gentler message to store manager about the need to boost sales by 3 percent for the next quarter. Another student plays the role of a store manager who likes the tone of Katerina's message and wants to cooperate. Other students will provide feedback about the extent to which Katerina has most likely influenced the store manager.

 LEADERSHIP SKILL-BUILDING EXERCISE 8-5

### My Leadership Portfolio

Influence is necessary for leaders, so you need to practice your influence tactics to enhance your leadership effectiveness. In this chapter's entry to your leadership journal, describe any influence tactic you implemented recently. Describe what you did and how the influence target reacted. Comment on how you might use the tactic differently in your next influence attempt. Also describe which influence tactic or combination of tactics you plan to use in the upcoming week. Here is a possible example:

> I coach a youth basketball team called the West Side Chiefs. The kids are great, and I am enjoying the experience. Yet the name Chiefs really bothers me because it is so behind the times, and a lot of people think using the term *Chief* for sport is racist. So I tried to influence the league director that we needed a name change. I presented my argument using a bunch of facts about how Chief has become passé for sports teams. (My technique was rational persuasion.) I did get a listen, but I didn't get approval for the name change. So next, I combined my logical argument with an inspirational appeal. I asked the league directors how they would like it if our team were called The West Side Chinese or the West Side Jews. Finally, my influence tactics worked, and for next season my team will be the West Side Rattlers.

## NOTES

1. Original story based on facts and observations in the following sources: Rick Tetzell, "A Whole New Apple," *Fast Company*, September 2016, pp. 66–74, 96–97; Jon Swartz and Marco della Cava, "Incremental Apple Should 'Swing for the Fences'," *USA Today Money*, September 7, 2016, p. 4B; "How Does Tim Cook's Management Style Differ from Steve Jobs? (AAPL)," (www.investopedia.com), October 28, 2015, pp. 1–4; Adam Lashinsky, *Fortune*, April 5, 2015, pp. 60–63; Brad Stone and Adam Satariano, "Tim Cook's Reboot: The New Products and Apple Pay Are Only Half the Story," *Bloomberg Businessweek*, September 22–28, 2014, pp. 64–71; Gerard Baker, "Tim Cook: TV, Cars, Watches and More," *The Wall Street Journal*, October 27, 2015, p. R1; Steve Tobak, "Leadership Lessons from Apple CEO Tim Cook," (www.entrepreneur.com), September 10, 2014, pp. 1–7.
2. "Judy Vredenburgh: Chief Executive Officer, Girls, Inc." *Bloomberg Businessweek*, October 19–October 28, 2015, p. 80.
3. Tal Yaffe and Ronit Kark, "Leading by Example: The Case of Leader OCB," *Journal of Applied Psychology*, July 2011, pp. 806–826.
4. Yaffe and Kark, "Leading by Example," pp. 806–826.
5. Mitchell S. Nesler, Herman Aguinis, Brian M. Quigley, and James T. Tedeschi, "The Effect of Credibility on Perceived Power," *Journal of Applied Social Psychology*, Vol. 23, no. 17, 1993, pp. 1407–1425.
6. The sample statements indicating the influence tactic in question here and at the other places in the chapter where they are presented are from Gary Yukl, Charles F. Seifert, and Carolyn Chavez, "Validation of the Extended Influence Behavior Questionnaire," *The Leadership Quarterly*, October 2008, pp. 618–620 (© Gary Yukl).
7. Josh Eidelson, "Amazon's Story is Kind of a Bummer," *Bloomberg Businessweek.com*, March 14–20, 2016, pp. 40–41.
8. Patrick Burke, "Let's Trade PowerPoint for Good Stories," *Democrat and Chronicle*, November 15, 2015, p. 1E.

9. Yukl, Siefert, and Chavez, "Validation of the Extended Influence Behavior Questionnaire," p. 610.

10. Ibid. (For both endnotes 9 and 10 the definitions are credited as Copyright © 2001 by Gary Yukl.)

11. Kate Linebaugh, "The New GE Way: Go Deep, Not Wide," *The Wall Street Journal*, March 7, 2012, p. B; "David L. Joyce," ge.com, 2016.

12. "You Scratch My Back … Tips on Winning Your Colleague's Cooperation," *Working Smart*, October 1999, p. 1.

13. Jeffrey Pfeffer, *Managing with Power: Power and Influence in Organizations* (Boston, MA: Harvard Business School Press, 1992), p. 224.

14. John H. (Jack) Zenger, "Leadership's Silver Bullet: The Magic of Inspiration," in Marshall Goldsmith, John Baldoni, and Sarah McArthur, eds., *The AMA Handbook of Leadership* (New York: AMACOM, 2010), pp. 103–109.

15. Alan Murray, *The Wall Street Journal Essential Guide to Management* (New York: Harper Business, 2010), p. 90.

16. Carlin Flora, "The Art of Influence," *Psychology Today*, September/October 2011, pp. 68–69.

17. Gary Yukl, *Skills for Managers and Leaders: Text, Cases, and Exercises* (Upper Saddle River, NJ: Prentice Hall, 1990), p. 65.

18. Lukas I. Alpert and Jack Marshall, "Bezos Has Hands-On Role at Newspaper," *The Wall Street Journal*, December 21, 2015, p. B1.

19. Trevor A. Foulk and David M. Long, "Impressed by Impression Management: Newcomer Reactions to Ingratiated Supervisors," *Journal of Applied Psychology*, October 2016, p. 1493.

20. Gary Yukl and Cecilia M. Falbe, "Influence Tactics and Objectives in Upward, Downward, and Lateral Influence Attempts," *Journal of Applied Psychology*, April 1990, p. 133.

21. Jeffrey Pfeffer, "Power Play," *Harvard Business Review*, July–August 2010, p. 90.

22. Bernard M. Bass (with Ruth Bass), *The Bass Handbook of Leadership: Theory, Research, & Managerial Applications*, Fourth Edition (New York: The Free Press, 2008), p. 160.

23. Cited in Heidi Grant Halvorson, "How to Be a Better Boss," *The Wall Street Journal*, January 2, 2013, p. B6.

24. "Create an Arsenal of Influence Strategies," *Manager's Edge*, March 2003, p. 1.

25. David M. Buss, Mary Gomes, Dolly S. Higgins, and Karen Lauterbach, "Tactics of Manipulation," *Journal of Personality and Social Psychology*, December 1987, p. 1222.

26. Comment contributed anonymously to author by a professor of organizational behavior.

27. Soojin Lee et al., "How Do I Get My Way? A Meta-Analytic Review of Research on Influence Tactics," *The Leadership Quarterly*, February 2017, pp. 210–228.

28. Diane Brady, "The Immelt Revolution: He's Turning GE's Culture Upside Down, Demanding Far More Risk and Innovation," *BusinessWeek*, March 28, 2005, pp. 64–66, 71–73.

29. Ted Mann, "GE Will Invest In Expanding Software Business," *The Wall Street Journal*, June 24, 2016, p. B6.

30. Tesa Basford and Bill Schaninger, "The Four Building Blocks of Change," *McKinsey Quarterly* (www.mckinsey.com), April 2016, pp. 2–3.

31. Beth Sears, "Strategic Cultural Change," *Democrat and Chronicle*, July 5, 2015, p. 5E.

32. Olga Epitropaki and Robert Martin, "Implicit Leadership Theories in Applied Settings: Factor Structure, Generalizability, and Stability over Time," *Journal of Applied Psychology*, April 2004, pp. 297–299.

33. Olga Epitropaki and Robert Martin, "From Real to Ideal: A Longitudinal Study of Implicit Leadership Theories in Leader–Member Exchanges and Employee Outcomes," *Journal of Applied Psychology*, July 2005, pp. 659–676.

34. Austin Lee Nichols and Catherine A. Cottrell, "What Do People Desire in their Leaders? The Role of Leadership Level on Trait Desirability," *The Leadership Quarterly*, August 2014, pp. 711–729.

35. Nina Maureen Junker and Rolf van Dick, "Implicit Theories in Organizational Settings: A Systematic Review and Research Agenda of Implicit Leadership," *The Leadership Quarterly*, December 2014, p. 1188.

36. Suzanne Kapner and Joann S. Lublin, "Land's End CEO Is Pushed Out After 19 Months," *The Wall Street Journal*, September 27, 2016, p. B1.

# Developing Teamwork

After studying this chapter and doing the exercises, you should be able to

- Understand the leader's role in a team-based organization.
- Describe leader actions that foster teamwork.

- Explain the potential contribution of outdoor training to the development of team leadership.
- Describe how the leader–member exchange model contributes to an understanding of leadership.

By job title, Sheryl Sandberg is chief operating officer (COO) at Facebook, placing her in charge of business operations that encompass sales, marketing, business development, human resources, public policy, and communication. Beyond her job title, Sandberg has been a driving force behind the phenomenal success of Facebook, the best-selling author of *Lean-in: Women, Work, and the Will to Succeed,* and regarded as one of the most powerful women in the world. She is also a mentor to her boss, company cofounder, Mark Zuckerberg.

Jim Breyer, a member of the Facebook board, said about Sandberg, "I have never met anyone with her combination of infectious, enthusiastic spirit, combined with extraordinary intelligence." As Zuckerberg sees it, Sandberg "…is unique in that she has a high IQ and EQ [emotional intelligence quotient], and it's just really rare to get than in any single person."

An emphasis on teamwork and developing strong teams is a key component of Sandberg's leadership within Facebook. She believes that a leader must win both the minds and the hearts of team members in order to have highly productive teams. Sandberg says, "If the people who work for you believe in you and believe in your mission, they will not just do their daily tasks well but they will do it with true passion."

Sandberg believes that teamwork is facilitated when team members interact in an informal and flexible manner. In her early days at Facebook, she would encourage her subordinates not to use PowerPoint presentations when they met as a team, so the meetings did not have a formal and rigid atmosphere. Yet she did not mean to discourage PowerPoint presentations with clients, as a few team members interpreted her suggestions. After Sandberg heard about the misinterpretation of her PowerPoint rule she told the team, "The next time you hear a bad idea—like not doing proper client presentations—speak up. Even if you think it is what I have asked for, tell me I am wrong."

Being an attentive listener, and making careful observations about how people feel is another way in which Sandberg develops teamwork. She believes that when people feel understood, they are more likely to work smoothly with each other. For example, she might say during a meeting, "Chad is very happy today because he simplified a Facebook feature that was baffling too many users."

Before joining Facebook in 2001, Sandberg was vice president (VP) of global online sales & operations at Google, Chief of Staff to the United States Secretary of the Treasury, and a management consultant at McKinsey & Company. Sandberg graduated from Harvard College, with a major in economics, and an MBA from Harvard University.[1]

The comments by a major high-technology executive illustrate the importance business firms attach to building better teamwork. Developing teamwork is such an important leadership role that team building is said to differentiate successful from unsuccessful leaders.[2] Furthermore, leaders with a reputation as teamwork builders are often in demand, such as Tim Cook, the *chief executive officer* (CEO) of Apple Inc. His ability to work smoothly with managers from different disciplines at the company has contributed to him being chosen as the CEO of Apple to replace the late Steve Jobs.

A difficulty in understanding teams is that the words *teams* and *teamwork* are often overused and applied loosely. For some people, *team* is simply another term for *group*. As used here, a **team** is a work group that must rely on collaboration if each member is to experience the optimum success and achievement. **Teamwork** is work done with an understanding and commitment to group goals on the part of all team members.

All teams are groups, but not all groups are teams. Jon R. Katzenbach and Douglas K. Smith, on the basis of extensive research in the workplace, make a clear differentiation between teams and groups.[3] A team is characterized by a common commitment, whereas the commitment within a group might not be as strong. A team accomplishes many collective work products, whereas group members sometimes work slightly more independently. A team has shared leadership roles, whereas members of a group have a strong leader.

Although the distinction between a group and a team may be valid, it is difficult to cast aside the practice of using the terms *group* and *team* interchangeably. For example, a customer service team is still a team even if its teamwork is poor.

The concepts of teams and teamwork apply throughout the organization, as well to a wide variety of organizations. A basic example is that a veterinary assistant at an animal care hospital explains that a lot of teamwork is required in his post. He works with veterinarians, technicians, customer service representatives, and kennel staff daily.[4] Teamwork facilitates the domestic animals receiving the care they need.

The central focus of this chapter is a description of specific leader actions that foster teamwork. We also describe outdoor training, a widely used method of teamwork development. In addition, we summarize a leadership theory that provides insight into how teamwork emerges within a work group.

## Leader's Role in the Team-Based Organization

Although an important goal of a team-based organization is for group members to participate in leadership and management activities, leaders still play an important role. In fact, they learn to lead in new ways. Team-based organizations need leaders who are knowledgeable in the team process and can help with the interpersonal demands of teams, for example, by giving feedback and resolving conflict. Quite often the leader is a facilitator who works with two or three teams at a time. He or she helps them stay focused when personality and work style differences create problems. John Mackey, the co-CEO of Whole Foods Market, has built an organization structure based on interlocking teams. Each Whole Foods store is organized around eight to ten teams for traditional departments such as produce and checkout. Part of his leadership of these teams is to engage them in friendly competition to earn rewards.[5]

Without effective leadership, teams can get off course, go too far or not far enough, lose sight of their mission, and become blocked by interpersonal conflict. Effective leadership is particularly important early in the history of a group to help it reach its potential. Key roles of a leader in a team-based organization include the following:

- Building trust and inspiring teamwork
- Coaching team members and group members toward higher levels of performance, even to the point of being a high-performing transformational team (one that brings about major constructive changes)
- Facilitating and supporting the team's decisions
- Expanding the team's capabilities
- Creating a team identity
- Anticipating and influencing change
- Inspiring the team toward higher levels of performance
- Enabling and empowering group members to accomplish their work
- Encouraging team members to eliminate low-value work[6]

Several of these roles have already been noted in this book, and several others, such as building trust and coaching, are described later. All of these roles contribute to effective leadership in general. The enabling role, for example, centers on empowerment. Yet properly motivating team members also enables, or facilitates, work accomplishment. The leader behavior and attitudes that foster teamwork, described in the next section, might also be interpreted as part of the leader's role in a team-based organization.

A role for executive-level leaders requiring separate mention is that of leading a number of teams within the organization, referred to as **intergroup leadership**. A basic example is that the CEO needs to coordinate the efforts of large teams, such as marketing, finance, information technology, and operations. An even broader challenge is for the executive to lead groups and teams in different organizations, such as a joint venture between two companies working together to build a petroleum pipeline across the United States and Canada.

To carry out the role successfully of building teamwork among various teams, a starting point is for the leader to frequently talk about the identity of the team composed of teams. Three researchers on the topic argue that the leader must work at building a shared collective identity across the teams.[7] For example, the leader of the collection of teams building the pipeline might occasionally communicate the message, "Through our collective effort we have become a team bringing North American energy to North Americans."

Intergroup leadership can also take place at middle levels within the organization. When the leader is not a member of the team, he or she is classified as an *external leader*. A study conducted in three different industrial workplaces with self-managing teams offers some understanding of the external leader's role. (A self-managing team has considerable autonomy.) It was found that under ordinary work conditions, when the leaders were too actively involved in coaching the team and in sense making, satisfaction with leadership declined. An example of sense making here would be identifying increases in the price of natural gas, and then explaining to the facilities maintenance team how price increases will affect their work. When the team faced disruptive conditions, such as an unusually heavy work overload or a rapid change in technology, coaching and sense making by the leader increased satisfaction with leadership.[8]

A notable challenge for the manager who leads a variety of teams is that different teams within the organization might have a culture of their won, referred to as a subculture. Leading effectively across the organization requires skill in working across the different subcultures.[9] At Whole Foods, for example, the finance group might have a subculture quite different from the team that receives goods from delivery trucks.

We emphasize again that an important role for the leader in a team-based organization is often to lead a group of people who do not report directly to him or her. As a consequence, many of the teamwork development tactics described in this chapter become all the more important for accomplishing results.

# Leader Actions That Foster Teamwork

Fostering teamwork is well worth the leader's attention because teamwork is a major contributor to team success. Sometimes a leader's inspiring personality alone can foster teamwork. An experiment with Dutch business students showed that leaders who were perceived as charismatic and fair facilitated cooperation among group members.[10] Yet, inspirational leaders, as well as less charismatic ones, can also encourage teamwork through their attitudes and what they do. Table 9-1 lists the teamwork-enhancing actions that are described in the following pages. For convenience, the actions are divided into two types: actions that leaders can take using their own resources (informal techniques) and actions that generally require organization structure or policy (formal techniques).

**TABLE 9-1** Leader Actions That Foster Teamwork

| ACTIONS LEADERS CAN TAKE USING THEIR OWN RESOURCES | ACTIONS GENERALLY REQUIRING ORGANIZATION STRUCTURE OR POLICY |
|---|---|
| 1. Defining the team's mission and tasks | 1. Designing physical structures that facilitate communication |
| 2. Establishing a climate of trust | 2. Emphasizing group recognition and rewards |
| 3. Developing a norm of teamwork, based on cooperation theory | 3. Initiating ritual and ceremony |
| 4. Developing group emotional intelligence | 4. Practicing open-book management |
| 5. Emphasizing pride in being outstanding | 5. Selecting team-oriented members |
| 6. Serving as a model of teamwork, including power sharing and collective leadership | 6. Using technology that facilitates teamwork including social media |
| 7. Using a consensus leadership style | 7. Blending representatives from the domestic company and foreign nationals on the team |
| 8. Establishing urgency, demanding performance standards, and providing direction | |
| 9. Encouraging competition with another group | |
| 10. Engaging in ample interaction with the team and providing positive feedback | |
| 11. Minimizing micromanagement | |
| 12. Practicing e-leadership for virtual teams | |

# Actions Leaders Can Take Using Their Own Resources

***Defining the Team's Mission***    A starting point in developing teamwork is to specify the team's mission. Commitment to a clear mission is a key practice of a highly effective team. The mission statement for the group helps answer the questions, "Why are we doing this?" and "What are we trying to accomplish?" To answer these questions, the mission statement should set out a specific goal, purpose, and philosophical tone. Any goal contained within the mission statement should be congruent with organizational objectives. If a team wants to cut back on its number of suppliers, the organization should have the same intent as well. Here are two examples of team mission statements:

- To plan and implement new manufacturing approaches to enhance our high-performance image and bolster our competitive edge
- To enhance our website development capability, so we can provide decision makers throughout the organization with assistance in developing websites that exceed the state of the art

The leader can specify the mission when the team is formed or at any other time. Developing a mission for a long-standing team breathes new life into its activities. Being committed to a mission improves teamwork, as does the process of formulating a mission. The dialogue necessary for developing a clearly articulated mission establishes a climate in which team members can express feelings, ideas, and opinions. Shared leadership is required in developing a mission, as in most other ways of enhancing teamwork.

To help implement the mission, it is useful for the leader to define the team tasks, or to work with the group in defining these tasks. Team members can then identify the subtasks for which each member has responsibility. Each team member needs to know how he or she is responsible for attaining the mission and goals.[11] For example, a dental office might want to understand why so many patients have left the practice. One team member might be assigned the task of contacting former patients, and another team member might be assigned the task of asking current patients if they are experiencing any problems with the dental practice.

***Establishing a Climate of Trust***    If team members do not trust each other or the leader, it is unlikely that they will work cooperatively together. Trust is at the heart of collaboration. Unless team members trust each other, they will not be dependent on each other and therefore will not work well as a team.[12] A starting point in establishing a climate of trust is for the leader to be credible and engage in the many other trustworthy behaviors described in Chapter 2. Encouraging open communication about problems and sharing information are two specific ways the leader can help promote a climate of trust. Being open about problems facing the group and being candid in expressing opinions is often referred to as the leader being *transparent*.

***Developing a Norm of Teamwork Based on Cooperation Theory***    A major strategy of teamwork development is to promote the attitude among group members that working together effectively is expected. Most profit as well as not-for-profit organizations emphasize that teamwork is important. A representative example is HP Financial Services, a unit of Hewlett-Packard Co. Irv Rothman, president and chief executive of this 1,500 employee division, says he maximizes performance by organizing into small, manageable teams. Employees are expected to manage themselves to make decisions on behalf of the customer. Teams are asked to behave like they are business owners.[13] (Both of these points carry the message that teamwork is the expected behavior.)

Another approach to developing a norm of teamwork is to discourage excessive politicking in which employees attempt to appear more capable than teammates, and might even discredit the contribution of others to the team. Gary Rankin and Colin Gautrey recommend that the political infighting can be decreased through encouraging teamwork. A specific technique is for the team leader to incorporate into his or her dialogue the terms "working together," and "winning team."[14]

A norm of teamwork is based on **cooperation theory**, a belief in cooperation and collaboration rather than competitiveness as a strategy for building teamwork.[15] Individuals who are accustomed to competing with one another for recognition, salary increases, and resources must now collaborate. Despite the challenge of making a culture shift, the leader can make progress toward establishing a teamwork norm by doing the following:

- Encourage team members to treat one another as if they were customers, thus fostering cooperative behavior and politeness.
- Explicitly state the desirability of teamwork on a regular basis both orally and in writing.
- Communicate the norm of teamwork by frequently using words and phrases that support teamwork. Emphasizing the words *team members* or *teammate* and deemphasizing the words *subordinates* and *employees* helps communicate the norm of teamwork.
- Work with the group to establish a code of conduct that everyone agrees to follow. Aspects of the code might include "never abandon a teammate," "never humiliate anyone," and "keep all agreements." Also helpful is to facilitate productive conversation by prohibiting unfair interruptions, and encouraging participation by all team members during physical or virtual meetings.[16]

Normative statements about teamwork by influential team members are also useful in reinforcing the norm of teamwork. A team member might assume a leadership role by saying to coworkers: "I'm glad this project is a joint effort. I know that's what earns us merit points here."

Research reported by Adam Grant reinforces the importance of cooperation within teams for attaining high team performance. A team of researchers investigated what made U.S. intelligence units effective. Hundreds of analysts from sixty-four different intelligence groups were surveyed, interviewed, and observed, and the researchers ranked those units from best to worst. The single strongest predictor of group effectiveness was the amount of help the analysts gave each other. It was found that in the highest performing teams, analysts invested extensive time and energy in coaching, teaching, and consulting with colleagues. The cooperative behavior assisted analysts in such ways as filling in gaps in their knowledge and recognizing patterns in seemingly disconnected pieces of information. In the units related the lowest by the researchers, the analysts exchanged small amounts of mutual help and struggled to make sense of considerable data.[17]

A robust approach to establishing a norm of teamwork is to encourage prosocial motivation among team members. Team members are coached to understand that the motivation to help each other should be as strong as the motivation to attain individual and group goals. A combination of field and laboratory studies found that when prosocial motivation in the team was high, team processes such as citizenship behavior increased, and so did team effectiveness. Furthermore, team cooperation also increased.[18]

***Develop Group Emotional Intelligence***   The leader's role in developing teamwork can also be described as helping the group develop emotional intelligence. The leader contributes to the group's emotional intelligence by creating norms that establish mutual trust among members. It is also important for members to have a sense of group identity as defined in their mission statement. Group efficacy, or feeling competent to complete the group task, also contributes to emotional intelligence. Ensuring that the group has the right skills can enhance such efficacy. These three conditions—mutual trust, group identity, and group efficacy—are the foundation of cooperation and collaboration.

The leader can also promote group emotional intelligence by bringing emotions to the surface in both group and one-on-one meetings. The leader then discusses how these emotions might be affecting the group's work.[19] For example, team members might discuss how they feel about their perceived importance to the organization. One maintenance group said that they felt entirely unappreciated until a key piece of equipment broke down, and this underappreciation was adversely affecting their morale. The team leader helped the group develop an internal public relations campaign about their contribution to productivity.

# LEADERSHIP SKILL-BUILDING EXERCISE 9-1

## Shelters for the Homeless

This exercise should take about thirty-five minutes; it can be done inside or outside class. Organize the class into teams of about six people. Each team takes on the assignment of formulating plans for building temporary shelters for the homeless. The dwellings you plan to build, for example, might be two-room cottages with electricity and indoor plumbing. During the time allotted to the task, formulate plans for going ahead with Shelters for the Homeless. Consider dividing up work by assigning certain roles to each team member. Sketch out tentative answers to the following questions: (1) How will you obtain funding for your venture? (2) Which homeless people will you help? (3) Where will your shelters be? (4) Who will do the construction? After your plan is completed, evaluate the quality of the teamwork that took place within the group. Review the chapter for techniques you might have used to improve it.

The same kind of teamwork skills you use in this exercise can be readily applied to most teamwork assignments on the job. Note carefully that although some types of teams call for members to be generalists, dividing up the tasks is still a basic principle of collective effort.

*Emphasizing Pride in Being Outstanding*   A standard way to build team spirit, if not teamwork, is to help the group realize why it should be proud of its accomplishments. Most groups are particularly good at some task. The leader should help the group identify that task or characteristic and promote it as a key strength. An order-fulfillment department, for example, might have the best on-time shipping record in the region. Or, a claims-processing unit might have the fewest overpayments in an insurance company.

To try your hand at being part of an outstanding team, do Leadership Skill-Building Exercise 9-1.

*Serving as a Model of Teamwork, Including Power Sharing and Collective Leadership*
A powerful way for a leader to foster teamwork is to be a positive model of team play. And one way to exemplify teamwork is to reveal important information about ideas and attitudes relevant to the group's work. As a result of this behavior, team members may follow suit. A leader's self-disclosure fosters teamwork because it leads to shared perceptions and concerns.[20] Self-disclosure is an element of leader transparency. Interacting extensively with team members serves as a model of teamwork because it illustrates the mechanism by which team development takes place—frequent informal communication. While interacting with team members, the team leader can emphasize that he or she is a team member. For example, it is better to say "We have to get this done by Friday," than "You have to…"

Another way of being a model of teamwork is to share power with group members because a good team player avoids hogging power and making all of the decisions. As each team member takes the opportunity to exert power, he or she feels more like a major contributor to team effort. We are referring here yet again to shared or collective leadership. Peter Pronovost, an anesthesiologist and critical-care specialist at Johns Hopkins Hospital, believes that hospitals would be safer for patients with more power sharing among physicians and other medical personnel. (The mistakes in hospitals he refers to include ordering the wrong drug or operating on the wrong limb.) Pronovost believes that nurses should have the power to challenge doctors, and members of the medical team need to work like flight crews in terms of power sharing to help minimize medical mistakes.[21]

Power sharing can also take the form of team members feeling free to offer constructive the organization providing constructive feedback to the team leader. Sheryl Sandberg asking for team members to provide her feedback on a bad idea she suggests (as described in the chapter opener) illustrates this approach.

To be a model of team play as a leader, you need the attitudes of a team player. Leadership Self-Assessment Quiz 9-1 gives you an opportunity to measure such attitudes.

# LEADERSHIP SELF-ASSESSMENT QUIZ 9-1

## Team Player Attitudes

***Instructions:*** Describe how well you agree with each of the following statements, using the following scale: disagree strongly (DS); disagree (D); neutral (N); agree (A); agree strongly (AS).

|     |                                                                                                      | DS | D | N | A | AS |
| --- | ---------------------------------------------------------------------------------------------------- | -- | - | - | - | -- |
| **1.**  | I am at my best when working alone.                                                              | 5  | 4 | 3 | 2 | 1  |
| **2.**  | I have belonged to clubs and teams since I was a child.                                          | 1  | 2 | 3 | 4 | 5  |
| **3.**  | It takes far too long to get work accomplished with a group.                                     | 5  | 4 | 3 | 2 | 1  |
| **4.**  | I like the friendship of working in a group.                                                     | 1  | 2 | 3 | 4 | 5  |
| **5.**  | I would prefer to run a one-person business than to be a member of a large firm.                 | 5  | 4 | 3 | 2 | 1  |
| **6.**  | It is difficult to trust others in the group on key assignments.                                 | 5  | 4 | 3 | 2 | 1  |
| **7.**  | Encouraging others comes to me naturally.                                                        | 1  | 2 | 3 | 4 | 5  |
| **8.**  | I like the give-and-take of ideas that is possible in a group.                                   | 1  | 2 | 3 | 4 | 5  |
| **9.**  | It is fun to share responsibility with others in the group.                                      | 1  | 2 | 3 | 4 | 5  |
| **10.** | Much more can be accomplished by a team than by the same number of people working alone.         | 1  | 2 | 3 | 4 | 5  |
| **11.** | I will often poke fun at my other members of my work group through a social media post.          | 5  | 4 | 3 | 2 | 1  |
| **12.** | I would pay a deserving compliment to a team member through a social media post.                 | 1  | 2 | 3 | 4 | 5  |
|     | **Total score:**                                                                                 |    |   |   |   |    |

***Scoring and Interpretation:*** Add the numbers you circled to obtain your total score.

- **46–60:** You have strong positive attitudes toward being a team member and working cooperatively with other members.
- **35–46:** You have moderately favorable attitudes toward being a team member and working cooperatively with other members.
- **15–34:** You much prefer working by yourself to being a team member. To work effectively in a company that emphasizes teamwork, you may need to develop more positive attitudes toward working jointly with others.

***Using a Consensus Leadership Style*** Teamwork is enhanced when a leader practices consensus decision making. Contributing to important decisions helps group members feel that they are valuable to the team. Consensus decision making also leads to an exchange of ideas within the group, with group members supporting and refining each other's suggestions. As a result, the feeling of working jointly on problems is enhanced. Generation X managers (born between 1965 and 1980) and Generation Y managers (born between 1981 and 2002) are likely to practice consensus leadership. Of course, it is the older members of Generation Y who would hold managerial positions. Part of the reason is that many of these people have taken leadership courses.

Striving for consensus does not mean that all conflict is submerged to make people agree. Disagreements over issues are healthy, and team members are more likely to be committed to the consensus decision if their voice has been heard. When voices are heard, some power is shared. An example of a conflict over an issue would be the marketing team of an automotive company debating whether dealer discounts improve sales in the long run.

***Establishing Urgency, Demanding Performance Standards, and Providing Direction***    Team members need to believe that the team has urgent, constructive purposes. They also want a list of explicit expectations. The more urgent and relevant the rationale is, the more likely it is that the team will achieve its potential. A customer service team was told that further growth for the corporation would be impossible without major improvements in providing service to customers. Energized by this information, the team met the challenge.

To help establish urgency, it is helpful for the leader to challenge the group regularly. Teamwork is enhanced when the leader provides the team valid facts and information that motivate them to work together to modify the status quo. New information prompts the team to redefine and enrich its understanding of the challenge it is facing. As a result, the team is likely to focus on a common purpose, set clearer goals, and work together more smoothly.[22]

Studies in several industry settings, including the development of the Boeing 777 mid-size airliner, suggest that urgent, demanding tasks also contribute to the teamwork effectiveness of teams composed of top talent. The researchers in question raise the caution that leader should prune anybody from the group who is not a good team player, regardless of the person's capability.[23]

Demanding tasks also facilitate good performance because reasonably high demands act as healthy stressors that boost performance. For example, imagine that a sales manager has rolled out new sales management software, but just a few sales representatives have inputted their activity as required by the software. The sales manager might try direct feedback such as, "It's Wednesday and so far only three reps have provided data. When is everybody going to participate?"[24]

***Encouraging Competition with Another Group***    One of the best-known methods of encouraging teamwork is rallying the support of the group against a real or imagined threat from the outside. Beating the competition makes more sense when the competition is outside your organization. When the enemy is within, the team spirit within may become detrimental to the overall organization, and we–they problems may arise. While encouraging competition with another group, the leader should encourage rivalry, not intense competition that might lead to unethical business practices, such as making false charges against them. An example of ethical competition against another group would be a product development group at Dodge Ram competing to produce a pickup truck that outperformed the Ford 150 series of pickups.

***Engaging in Ample Interaction with the Team and Provide Positive Feedback***    A helpful tactic for building teamwork is to build positive relationships with team members, and relationships are built on conversations.[25] The conversations should go beyond superficialities such as discussing weekend plans or how busy the team member is. Meaningful topics would include the team member's perception of potential problems, his or her job satisfaction, and suggestions for improvement.

An effective way of interacting with team members is to hold question-and-answer sessions. The same approach demonstrates participative leadership. Both leader and members ask and answer questions, such as "How can we make an even bigger contribution to the company?" When Kevin Johnson became CEO of Juniper Networks, he met with all his direct reports as a group. He told them that their input was very important. Two of the questions he asked were "What needs to change, and why?" and "What do you hope I do as CEO?" The group question-and-answer sessions appeared to have a positive impact on creating a cohesive top-management team.[26]

A motivational form of interacting with the team is to provide positive feedback about recent activities. Giving team members regular updates on personal performance as well as company performance helps workers feel valued.[27] The sales manager for software above might say to the group, "I know that I was nagging you about providing the input for the new software to operate. But you've done a fine job, and now our team has helped boost company revenue three percent this past quarter."

*Minimizing Micromanagement*   A strategic perspective on encouraging teamwork is for the leader to minimize **micromanagement**, the close monitoring of most aspects of group member activities (as mentioned in Chapter 4 in relation to leadership behaviors). To be a good team leader, the manager must give group members ample opportunity to manage their own activities. Avoiding micromanagement is a core ingredient of employee empowerment because empowered workers are given considerable latitude to manage their own activities. Not stepping in to make suggestions or corrections helps team members develop, and the feeling of growing professionally will often translate into workers developing a stronger team spirit.

An effective way of avoiding micromanagement is for the leader to learn to ignore minor actions that he or she does not like, yet are not real problems. Suppose a manager has a preference for certain fonts used in PowerPoint presentations. To avoid being a micromanager, he or she should not insist that team members use only the favored fonts in PowerPoint slides.

A micromanager is also referred to as a *control freak*, because he or she wants to maintain so much control. When a micromanager is particularly talented, and also well liked, micromanagement is less of a detriment to teamwork, as implied by the accompanying Leader-In-Action insert.

The contingency leader recognizes the fine line between avoiding micromanagement and not providing the guidance and accountability that team members may need to function well as a unit. Consultant Bruce Tulgan reports, "When we asked employees what they want from the people above them, the first thing they mention is never a raise. It's always more coaching, more guidance, clearer goals, more constructive criticism, and more recognition for achievement."[28] An implication is that a manager tinged with a little micromanagement is likely to engage in these constructive behaviors.

*Practicing E-Leadership for Virtual Teams*   The heavy presence of communication technology has had a significant impact on team leadership, especially when team members do not work in the same physical location.

If team leader Jennifer, based in Seattle, sends a note of congratulations to team member Surinda, based in Mumbai, she is practicing e-leadership. Jennifer and Surinda are part of a virtual team: They work with each other, yet they do not share the same physical facility. **E-leadership** is a form of leadership practiced in a context where work is mediated by information technology. The leadership focus shifts from individuals to networks of relationships because the Internet facilitates connecting so many people.[29] E-leadership could, therefore, encompass any activity undertaken by a leader when the Internet connects people. Our concern here is how e-leadership facilitates building teamwork, especially in a virtual team.

When team members are geographically dispersed, a leader's communication with team members takes place using information technology, including the dissemination of information needed for task accomplishment. The original virtual teams were established to facilitate innovation among experts around the world who did not have the time to travel. A participative leader may establish chat rooms to solicit opinions from members of a cross-border virtual team before reaching a final decision. Videoconferencing is ideal for virtual teams because it allows members to see and interact with other from remote locations at the same time.

The trend toward forming cross-cultural teams from geographically dispersed units of a firm increases the application of virtual teams. Strategic alliances in which geographically dispersed companies work with each other depend on virtual teams in many ways. IBM makes some use of virtual teams in selling information technology systems, partially because so many IBM field personnel work remotely. Meeting electronically does not cure all of the problems of geographically dispersed teams from different cultures. For example, the team leader or manager must often confront the problem of different attitudes toward hierarchy and authority, such as workers from many cultures not feeling comfortable with the flat structure of a team.[30]

## LEADER IN ACTION

### J. Crew CEO and Madewell Founder Mickey Drexler, the World Class Micromanager

Mickey Drexler was the chief executive of the J. Crew Group through 2017, a long-time Gap CEO, and the founder of Madewell, a retail chain catering to city women who prefer a hint of a tomboy style. Not too long ago, Drexler took three steps into a Madewell store in downtown New York, and he was visibly annoyed. Eight umbrellas scattered on the hardwood floor, and dripping rain, caught his eye. "This is a mess. This looks bad to customers. Doesn't it?"

A few minutes later, a woman customer walked by wearing a long jacket and knee-high boots, with a pair of sunglasses perched on top of her head. Drexler suddenly developed a brighter mood. He said he loved her look, and he loved it more because she was carrying a Madewell bag. He saw another woman trying on skinny jeans and wearing a red plaid shirt. Pointing to the woman, Drexler said, "That is our bread and butter."

Drexler is credited with being one of several fashion merchants who have defined affordable American style. He is also known for focusing in so carefully on fashion details that he is perceived by many work associates to be hands-on manager to the point of micromanaging. At his own admission, Drexler is a control freak. He says that he is a very proud micromanager. "If you don't care about the lapel or the buttons or the fit, then you are doing a disservice to the consumer. We're all inside the tunnel, speaking the language of business, but we need to speak the language of customers." Drexler's job satisfaction is the highest when he is involved in every facet of merchandising, even button selection. He also personally responds to shopper e-mails and telephone calls.

Drexler cares about company performance as well as fashion details. In 2016, J. Crew made a bold move to boost sales by selling some of its apparel on Nordstrom's website and at 16 Nordstrom stores. Drexel said that Nordstrom would be perfect partner because both J. Crew and Nordstrom share the same high standards of service and store experience. Nordstrom was already selling closed from Madewell on line and at 76 of its stores.

Drexler owns several homes and travels by private plane. He graduated from the University of Buffalo with an undergraduate degree in business administration. Later he earned an MBA from the Graduate School of Management at Boston University.

### QUESTIONS

1. Why might Drexler's micromanagement be acceptable in his role as a fashion-industry executive?

2. It has been reported that when Drexler is talking to other people he multitasks such as consulting his smartphone, writes e-mails, and tosses out a few murmuring sounds to indicate he is following the other person. How does this behavior fit a micromanager?

*Source:* Original story based on facts and observations in the following sources: Mallory Schlossberg, "J. Crew Just Made a Desperate Move to Save Itself," (https://finance.yahoo.com), August 30, 2016, pp. 1–3; Danielle Sacks, "10 Creativity Tips From J. Crew CEO Mickey Drexler," (www.fastcompany.com), April 15, 2013, pp. 1–3; Laura M. Holson, "At Madewell, Mickey Drexler's Third Act," *The New York Times* (www.nytimes.com), February 4, 2015, pp. 1–5; Aimee Groth, "If You Ever Have a Meeting With Mickey Drexler, You Should Be Prepared for This," *Business Insider* (www.businessinsider.com), April 12, 2012, pp. 1–2; Tina Gaudoin, "Mickey Drexler: Retail Therapist," *The Wall Street Journal* (http://magazine.wsj.com), June 10, 2010, p. 3.

---

The leader can foster team spirit (and therefore teamwork) by sending congratulatory e-mail messages for a job well done. In short, the e-leader improves teamwork by staying connected electronically to team members—although not to the point of blitzing them with so many messages that he or she becomes an annoyance.

Another driving force for the use of virtual teams has been the **gig economy**—workers who are involved in some form of freelancing or contracting, often based on outsourcing. A person accepting a gig works on demand, often through a digital marketplace.[31] The freelancers are typically working part time, but make a contribution to the efforts of the total team. Visualize a mineral exploration team working for a mining company. The team makes occasional use of a specialist who uses drones to take videos and still photos of difficult-to-reach locations. The "drone-guy" or "drone gal" is part of the team, even though he or she does not receive a fulltime salary.

Based on observations, interviews, and survey data, two intensive studies have identified leadership practices of effective leaders of virtual teams. The purpose of these practices is to overcome the unique challenges of managing virtual teams, such as not being able to see in-person when the team needs focus and direction. The conclusions of the researchers along with a few other studies dealing mostly with building teamwork are presented next.[32]

1. *Establish and maintain trust through the use of communication technology.* A major hurdle in working with a virtual team is deciding on what information gets communicated and to whom. In some instances, a norm might be established that restricts members from conveying negative information to anyone outside the team. It is also useful to ensure that all team members are equally inconvenienced by time zone differences, such as having a meeting at 3 A.M. their time. Meeting times would be rotated, so team members in one time zone would not suffer.

2. *Ensure that diversity in the team is understood, appreciated, and leveraged.* Diversity within the team can take many forms, such as experience, skills, and interests. To ensure that diversity is understood and appreciated, leaders frequently develop an expertise directory when the team first forms. The directory can include a photo of each member along with details about his or her training, experience, and previous assignments. A skills matrix of team members can serve the same purpose.

3. *Maintain frequent communications, including virtual meetings.* The majority of team leaders in the study reported that regular videoconferences involving all members were the lifeblood of the team, even when tasks were distributed among the team members. The virtual meetings are used to keep members engaged, excited about the work, and aligned with each other. At the beginning of the meeting, it is helpful to have the team member reconnect with the human side of each team member. Exchanging personal stories helps build closeness. A couple of minutes of warmup are recommended, such as commenting on extreme weather in one region, or an outstanding athletic team victory.

   Other forms of communication besides videoconferences can serve the function of developing teamwork. At Nokia, for example, the favored communication tool is text messaging, while at other companies e-mail or voice mail was more effective. Many companies use internal social media websites to encourage frequent shared interaction among team members. Most importantly, communication should be frequent and rapid.

4. *Monitor team progress through the use of technology.* An example of monitoring would be checking to see who is using the team's online knowledge repository regularly and who is not. The leader can also check to see if some members are not doing their fair share of work, and then coach the underperformer. This approach might improve teamwork because loafers drag down a team.

5. *Enhance external visibility of the team and its members.* Virtual team members may have at least two bosses (the virtual team leader and the on-site boss), so it is important that the work of the virtual team gets reported externally. A virtual team in the electronics testing industry was required to report the team's results to a steering committee. The link to teamwork is that receiving rewards and recognition helps build team spirit.

6. *Ensure that individuals benefit from participating in virtual teams.* Even if the members are good team players, they need personal benefits to experience team spirit. One approach is to have virtual reward ceremonies, such as having gifts delivered to each team member and then having a virtual party. (No need for designated drivers here because the party takes place at the homes of team members!) The team leader can also encourage executives at the team members' work environment to thank the team members. Offering opportunities for personal growth, such as mini-lectures by an expert, can also be helpful.

7. **To maintain a high-touch environment, conduct one or two face-to-face meetings per year.** Electronic technology is not a perfect substitute for human interaction. Lack of attention during virtual meetings is a warning sign to look for. Virtual teams that invest in one or two face-to-face meetings annually tend to perform better than those who skip such meetings.[33] Even the use of the most advanced videoconferencing equipment or Skype lacks the feel of interacting with a colleague face to face.

You will observe that the seven suggestions for leading virtual teams include both actions leaders can take on their own, plus the use of company technology.

## Actions Generally Requiring Organization Structure or Policy

**Designing Physical Structures That Facilitate Communication**   Group cohesiveness, and therefore teamwork, is fostered when team members are located close together and can interact frequently and easily. In contrast, people who spend most of their time in their private offices or cubicles are less likely to interact. Frequent interaction often leads to camaraderie and a feeling of belongingness. A useful tactic for achieving physical proximity is to establish a shared physical facility, such as a conference room, research library, or beverage lounge. This area should be decorated differently from other areas in the building, and a few amenities should be added, such as a coffeepot, microwave oven, and refrigerator. Team members can then use this area for refreshments and group interaction.

Recognizing the contribution of a shared physical facility to promoting teamwork, many organizations have incorporated more open working space into the workplace, often eliminating private offices and cubicles.

The use of open office space to enhance collaboration and creativity is frequently accepted uncritically by CEOs and company owners. The noisy, open-floor plans that have become a staple of office life have received many employee complaints. A major problem is the assault on privacy and quiet reflection of open offices. To counter the potential negative effect on employees and productivity, some companies are taking the following measures: adding soundproof rooms; creating quiet zones; and rearranging floor plans to aid employees eager to escape disruptions at their desk or table.[34]

**Emphasizing Group Recognition and Rewards**   Giving rewards for group accomplishment reinforces teamwork because people receive rewards for what they have achieved collaboratively. Also, much of work that is accomplished in organizations requires collaboration, so group rewards are justifiable and sensible. A warning, however, is that many employees may view switching to a team-based pay plan that places much of their pay at risk as an unnerving proposition. Quite often a mix of individual rewards and team rewards is the most effective in terms of morale.

The recognition accompanying the reward should emphasize the team's value to the organization rather than that of the individual. Recognition promotes team identity by enabling the team to take pride in its contributions and progress. The following are examples of team recognition:

- A display wall for team activities such as certificates of accomplishment, schedules, and miscellaneous announcements
- Celebrations to mark milestones such as first-time activities, cost savings, and safety records
- Team-of-the-Month award, with gifts from the organization to team members or to the entire team

Another aspect of rewarding team performance is to avoid disincentives for teamwork. An example would be a stack-ranking system in which a fixed percentage of workers must be classified as bottom or poor performers, regardless of the team's overall performance.[35]

**Initiating Ritual and Ceremony**   Another way to enhance teamwork is to initiate ritual and ceremony.[36] Ritual and ceremony afford opportunities for reinforcing values, revitalizing spirit, and bonding workers to one another and to the team. An example is holding a team dinner whenever the group achieves a major milestone, such as making a winning bid on a major contract. Another formal ritual is to send a team on a retreat to develop its mission and goals and to build camaraderie. When the team is working and socializing closely together during the retreat—even one long day—teamwork is reinforced.

*Practicing Open-Book Management*   A method of getting the company working together as a team is to share information about company finances and strategy with large numbers of employees. In **open-book management**, every employee is trained, empowered, and motivated to understand and pursue the company's business goals. In this way, employees become business partners and perceive themselves to be members of the same team.

In a full form of open-book management, workers share strategic and financial information as well as responsibility. The company also shares risks and rewards based on results, so workers are likely to pull together as a team so that the company can succeed.[37] The idea is to have a well-informed, partner-oriented, high-performance company. Part of keeping workers well informed is for company leaders to host roundtable discussions about company financial information. Another approach is to regularly disseminate, by e-mail, information about the company's financial progress.

President and CEO of Monroe Wheelchair, a company that sells motorized, customizable wheelchairs, explains how and why the company practices open-book management: "We share all our financials with every employee every month. We track key performance indicators, trend them and share with employees. It helps them feel comfortable that the company is successful."[38]

*Selecting Team-Oriented Members*   A foundation strategy for achieving good teamwork is to select members for the team with aptitude, skill, and interest in teamwork. (Selecting team-oriented members is often a company policy, but it is also an action managers can take operating on their own.) A starting point is self-selection. It is best for the team leader to choose workers who ask to be members of a team. A person's record of past team activity can also help one determine whether that person is an effective team player (as suggested in the opening case to this chapter). Many managers believe that those who participate in team sports now or in the past are likely to be good team players on the job.

At times, workers will be assigned to the team rather than selected by the team leader or team members, so selecting team-oriented members is not possible. Among the key criteria for selecting teamwork-oriented members would be teamwork experience, prior success as a team player, and favorable personality traits such as agreeableness and extraversion.

Todd Carlisle is now the VP of Human Resources at Twitter. When he was the Google staffing manager, he looked carefully for teamwork preferences and skills when selecting new employees for the company. One of Carlisle's criteria is simply how likeable the candidates are: "You have to want to take them to lunch after the interview. It's important to hire leaders who play well with others, so ask about their experiences working on a team. Their bragging that they convinced everybody else that they were right or taking credit for everything are red flags."[39]

*Using Technology That Enhances Teamwork*   Workers can collaborate better when they use information technology that fosters collaboration, often referred to as *collaborative* software. For example, the straightforward act of exchanging frequent e-mail messages and instant messages can facilitate cooperation. Electronic brainstorming is another example of groupware. Virtual teams by their nature rely on information technology to enhance teamwork.

Videoconferencing as mentioned in relation to virtual teams facilitates teamwork. Geographically separated workers can participate in a virtual conference and exchange ideas *almost* as effectively as in a face-to-face meeting. An example is TelePresence, an advanced conferencing system installed in its own offices, customer offices, and in the homes of company executives. Meetings can be called spontaneously and group decisions made rapidly without traveling.

Social networking might be regarded as the most far-reaching technology for enhancing teamwork because so many workers can exchange information with each other and thereby collaborate more extensively. Also, when groups of people can readily see what information others are exchanging, a spirit of cooperation might develop. Even the exchange of jokes and interesting YouTube and Hulu videos might improve team spirit.

***Blending Representatives from the Domestic Company and Foreign Nationals on the Team***   Cross-cultural considerations enter into enhancing teamwork as well as in most aspects of leadership. The fact of working with people from your own country as well as a representative from the country of company headquarters often enhances teamwork. Perhaps having a representative from the parent company, yet still respecting local talent, creates a spirit of cooperation. Also, blending cultural differences is appealing to some workers and might make them more interested in performing as a team.

A case in point is the experience of Jessica C. Isaacs, senior vice president of field operations for a reinsurance division of AIG. She notes: "Every time we've opened in a new country, instead of shipping expats in we've seen a transition from that and we've started to hire more local talent. My best performing teams are teams where I have lots of local talent sprinkled with some expat or foreign talent. Having the balance really optimizes everyone's skill set and opens new opportunities."[40]

## fsite Training and Team Development

Cognitive information about strategies and tactics for improving teamwork is potentially valuable. People reading such information can selectively apply the concepts, observe the consequences, and then fine-tune an approach. Another approach to developing teamwork is to participate in experiential activities (several are presented throughout this text).

The most popular experiential approach to building teamwork and leadership skills is offsite training, also referred to as outdoor training. Wilderness training is closely associated with outdoor training, except that the setting is likely to be much rougher—perhaps in the frozen plains of northernmost Minnesota. Some forms of outdoor training take place in city parks, as well as in the city itself in order to rehabilitate or build a house.

Both outdoor and wilderness training are forms of learning by doing. Participants are supposed to acquire leadership and teamwork skills by confronting physical challenges and exceeding their self-imposed limitations. The goals of offsite training are reasonably consistent across different training groups, including the following:

- Discover your strengths and weaknesses
- Test your limits (they are far broader than you imagine)
- Work together as a team
- Have fun
- Face the essence of who you are and what you are made of

## Features of Outdoor and Offsite Training Programs

Program participants are placed in a demanding outdoor environment, where they rely on skills they did not realize they had and on one another to complete the program. The emphasis is on building not only teamwork but also self-confidence for leadership. Sometimes lectures on leadership, self-confidence, and teamwork precede the activity. The list of what constitutes a team-building activity continues to grow and now includes tightrope walking, gourmet cooking as a team, paintballing, and scavenger hunts. Building or repairing houses for people in need is popular. Some corporate team-building activities required specialized skills, two of which are NASCAR racing and sailboat and regatta racing.

Another novel approach is for participants to perform stand-up comedy in front of work associates. Participants attend a Comedy Experience workshop in which they learn about the importance of humor on the job and develop their own three-to-four minute comedy routines. The potential payoff to the company from staff members taking a turn at stand-up comedy is that the experience brings them closer together. As you would imagine, some participants are so frightened by having to do stand-up comedy that they derive no benefit from the program.[41]

Outward Bound is the best-known and largest outdoor training program. It offers more than 500 courses in wilderness areas in twenty states and provinces. The courses typically run from three days to four weeks. Worldwide, Outward Bound runs about forty-eight schools on five continents. The Outward Bound Professional Development Program, geared toward organizational leaders, emphasizes teamwork, leadership, and risk taking. The wilderness is the classroom, and the instructors draw analogies between each outdoor activity and the workplace. Among the courses offered are dog-sledding, skiing and winter camping, desert backpacking, canoe expeditions, sailing, sea kayaking, alpine mountaineering, mountain backpacking and horse-trailing, and cycling.

Rope activities are typical of outdoor training. Participants are attached to a secure pulley with ropes; then they climb up a ladder and jump off to another spot. Sometimes, the rope is extended between two trees. Another activity is a trust fall, in which each person takes a turn standing on a platform and falling backward into the arms of coworkers. The trust fall can also be done on ground level. Many readers of this book have already participated in a trust fall. Leadership Skill-Building Exercises 9-2 and 9-3 present offsite activities, with 9-2 being rare, and 9-3 quite frequent.

Outdoor training enhances teamwork by helping participants examine the process of getting things done through working with people. Participants practice their communication skills in exercises such as rappelling down a cliff by issuing precise instructions to one another about how to scale the cliff safely. At the same time, they have to learn to trust one another because their survival appears to depend on trust.

# LEADERSHIP SKILL-BUILDING EXERCISE 9-2

## The Team Leader Candidates

Gather in a group of about six people, on your own or in front of the class. Your group is to carry out a mission that all members can visualize, such as the product development team for a pet food manufacturer. Management has empowered you to select your own team leader, and each of you would like to be chosen for the position. After being given about fifteen minutes to prepare, each person will address the rest of the team explaining why he or she should be chosen as the team leader. After the presentations are completed, hold a brief group discussion about the effectiveness of the presentations. Attempt to reach consensus about which candidate should be chosen as team leader. Also, reflect on what this exercise demonstrated about team leadership and teamwork.

# LEADERSHIP SKILL-BUILDING EXERCISE 9-3

## The Scavenger Hunt

The purpose of this standard teamwork exercise is to demonstrate the importance of cooperation and collaboration in accomplishing a task under pressure. The class is divided into teams of approximately five students. How much time you can devote to the task depends upon your particular class schedule. The instructor will supply each team with a list of items to find with a prescribed period of time—usually about forty-five minutes. Given the time constraints, the group will usually have to conduct the hunt on campus. The following is a representative list of items to find in an on-campus scavenger hunt:

- A fountain pen
- A piece of chalk
- A CD disk
- A man's tie
- A woman's hat

When the group returns after the forty-five minutes have expired, hold a public discussion about what you learned about teamwork and what insights your acquired to help a leader develop teamwork.

## Evaluation of Offsite Training for Team Development

The merits and drawbacks of office site or outdoor training lack scientific verification. Many outdoor trainers and participants believe strongly that they derive substantial personal benefits from outdoor training. Among the most important are greater self-confidence, appreciating hidden strengths, and learning to work better with others. Strong proponents of outdoor training believe that those who do not appreciate the training simply do not understand it. Many training directors also have positive attitudes toward outdoor training. They believe that a work team that experiences outdoor training will work more cooperatively back at the office.

Many people, however, have legitimate reservations about outdoor training. Although outdoor trainers claim that almost no accidents occur, a threat to health and life does exist, and groin injuries are frequent. (To help minimize casualties, participants usually need medical clearance.) Another concern is that the teamwork learned in outdoor training does not spill over into the job environment.

A major concern about offsite training is that some participants or potential participants find it repellent. Not every worker wants to play games, climb rocks, or prepare a gourmet meal with coworkers after hours. They would prefer a more natural, relaxing environment in which to build teamwork, such as doing volunteer work or having a family day at the workplace.[42]

One way to facilitate the transfer of training from outdoors to the office is to hold debriefing and follow-up sessions. Debriefing takes place at the end of outdoor training. The participants review what they learned and discuss how they will apply their lessons to the job. Follow-up sessions can then be held periodically to describe progress in applying the insights learned during outdoor training.

## e Leader–Member Exchange Model and Teamwork

Research and theory about the development of teamwork lag research and theory about many other aspects of leadership. Nevertheless, the leader–member exchange model, developed by George Graen and associates, helps explain why one subgroup in a unit is part of a cohesive team but another group is excluded.[43] The theory, already mentioned several times in this text, deals with the relationship between a leader and a team member. However, the same theory tells us a lot about teamwork.

The **leader–member exchange (LMX) model** proposes that leaders develop unique working relationships with group members. One subset of employees, the in-group, is given additional rewards, responsibility, and trust in exchange for their loyalty and performance. The in-group becomes part of a smoothly functioning team headed by the formal leader. In contrast, the out-group employees are treated in accordance with a more formal understanding of leader–group member relations. Out-group members are less likely to experience good teamwork.

Figure 9-1 depicts the major concept of the LMX model. Here we look at several aspects of LMX as it relates most closely to teamwork. LMX has also been researched in relationship to many other aspects of workplace behavior, and published research about LMX continues to expand.

## Different Quality Relationships

Leaders do not typically use the same leadership style in dealing with all group members. Instead, they treat each member somewhat differently. The linkages (relationships) that exist between the leader and each individual team member probably differ in quality. In theory, the differences lie on a continuum of low quality to high quality. With group members on the top half of the continuum, the leader has a good relationship; with those on the lower half of the continuum, the leader has a poor relationship. Each of these pairs

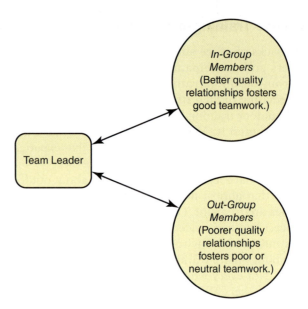

**FIGURE 9-1**   The Leader–Member Exchange Model.

of relationships, or dyads, must be judged in terms of whether a group member is in or out with the leader. The positive regard that leaders and members have for each other is a major contributor to the quality of their relationship.[44]

A note of caution about LMXs is that evidence suggests that the leader and the group members may perceive the quality of the exchange differently.[45] For example, the leader might think the exchange is positive, whereas the subordinate might think the exchange is neutral or negative. Because of this difference in perception, the leader should look carefully for evidence of the quality of a relationship with a given subordinate.

***Treatment of In-Group Versus Out-Group Members***   In-group members are invited to participate in important decision making, are given added responsibility, and are privy to interesting gossip. Members of the out-group are managed according to the requirements of their employment contract. They receive little warmth, inspiration, or encouragement. In-group members tend to achieve a higher level of performance, commitment, and satisfaction than do out-group members. Furthermore, they are less likely to quit. A study conducted in a retail setting found that when the quality of the LMX is high, group members are more strongly committed to company goals.[46] In turn, this commitment leads to stronger teamwork because the workers pull together to pursue goals.

***Reciprocity Between Leader and Members***   The in-group versus out-group status also includes an element of reciprocity or exchange. The leader grants more favors to the in-group member, who in response works harder to please the leader, a contributor to being a good team player. Two studies provide more specific information about the consequences of a positive exchange between a supervisor and group members. In a hospital setting, positive exchanges involved group members' engaging in increased good citizenship behavior and in-group role behaviors such as putting extra effort into performing their duties.[47] As a result, the leader would feel justified in granting the in-group members more resources, such as a larger salary increase or a larger budget.

***Satisfaction with Teamwork***   A study conducted with both public-sector and private-sector nurses in Iran provides direct support for the idea that LMX is related to teamwork. The findings suggested that the higher the satisfaction with relationships with the supervisor, the higher the level of satisfaction with teamwork. A secondary finding was that nurses who were more satisfied with teamwork experience better clarity about their roles in dealing with patients. Expressed differently, lower satisfaction with teamwork was associated with more role ambiguity in dealing with patients.[48]

**Extra-Role Behavior**    A study conducted in diverse industrial settings also found that high-quality exchanges between supervisors and employees contribute to employees' engaging in extra-role behavior, or being cooperative in ways that were not expected of them. Supervisory ratings of employee altruism were used to measure helping behaviors, as when an accountant helps a sales representative prepare a sales forecast. The researchers concluded that through the development of high-quality relationships with group members, supervisors are able to motivate the group members and enable them to engage in helping behaviors that benefit them as well as their coworkers.[49]

**Safety Performance**    Another contribution of positive LMXs is that they facilitate good safety performance, an important aspect of teamwork in many work environments. Sixty-four group leaders in a manufacturing plant participated in a study. A major finding of the study was that positive LMXs were associated with more communication about safety. The enhanced communication led to more commitment to safety, which in turn led to fewer accidents on the job.[50]

**Transformational Effects**    Another of the many consequences of positive LMXs is that they may facilitate the leader having a transformational effect. A study of 283 individuals from a broad cross section of job types indicated that transformational relationships were significantly stronger for followers who perceived high-quality relationships with their supervisors. An example of a transformational relationship would be inspiring the subordinate to seek different perspectives when solving problems or bringing about change. Transformational effects also tie in with teamwork because the workers become energized to jointly accomplish goals.[51]

**Leader Status**    When group members perceive leaders to have high status, it is easier for the leader to form the type of high-quality relationships that contribute to good teamwork. A study of 184 bank employees and 42 managers found that leaders who were perceived to have higher quality relationships with their bosses and who were strongly connected to network members were regarded as having relatively high status. As a result, the leaders were able to have higher quality exchanges with their subordinates.[52]

## First Impressions

The leader's first impression of a group member's competency plays an important role in placing the group member in the in-group or in the out-group. Another key linking factor is whether the leader and team member have positive or negative chemistry. We can assume that group members who make effective use of influence and political tactics increase their chances of becoming members of the in-group.

A field study seems to confirm that first impressions make a difference. The researchers gathered ratings of six aspects of the manager–group member dyad. Results showed that the initial leader expectations of members and member expectations of the leader were good predictors of the LMXs at two weeks and at six weeks. Member expectations of the leader also accurately predicted member assessments of the quality of the LMX at six months. An important interpretation of these results is that the LMX is formed in the first days of the relationship.[53] As the adage states, "You have only one chance to make a good first impression."

In summary, the LMX model provides a partial explanation of teamwork development. Members of the in-group work smoothly together and with the leader because they feel privileged. Being a member of the out-group may not diminish teamwork, but it certainly does not make a positive contribution.

## READER'S ROADMAP

So far we have studied considerable information about the nature of leadership; the attributes, behaviors, and styles of leaders; the ethics and social responsibility of leaders; and how leaders exert power and use politics and influence. The techniques for developing teamwork are part of a leader's relationship with the group, as is the subject of the next chapter, motivational skills.

## SUMMARY

Developing teamwork is a key leadership role. Teamwork is an understanding of and commitment to group goals on the part of all group members.

Leaders still play an important role in a team-based organization, such as being expert in the team process, being facilitators, building trust and inspiring teamwork, and enabling and empowering group members to accomplish their work. The enabling role centers on empowerment. It is important for top-level leaders to build a shared collective identity among the teams reporting to them. The external leader of a self-managing team plays a key role when the team faces disruptive conditions.

A wide range of leader actions fosters teamwork. Measures leaders can take using their own resources include the following: (1) defining the team's mission and tasks; (2) establishing a climate of trust; (3) developing a norm of teamwork based on cooperation theory; (4) developing group emotional intelligence; (5) emphasizing pride in being outstanding; (6) serving as a model of teamwork, including power sharing and collective leadership; (7) using a consensus leadership style; (8) establishing urgency, demanding performance standards, and providing direction; (9) encouraging competition with another group; (10) engaging in ample interaction with the team and providing positive feedback; (11) minimizing micromanagement; and (12) practicing e-leadership for virtual teams.

Techniques to foster teamwork that require relying on organization structure or policy include the following: (1) designing physical structures that facilitate communication; (2) emphasizing group recognition and rewards; (3) initiating ritual and ceremony; (4) practicing open-book management; (5) selecting team-oriented members; (6) using technology that facilitates teamwork; and (7) blending representatives from the domestic company and foreign nationals on the team.

In offsite training, a popular experiential approach to building teamwork and leadership skills, building self-confidence is the focus. Outdoor training enhances teamwork by helping participants examine the process of collaboration. The Outward Bound Professional Development Program is geared toward organization leaders. Opinion about the effectiveness of outdoor training for developing teamwork and leadership skills is mixed. Concern has been expressed that the skills learned in the field do not carry over to the workplace.

The LMX model helps explain why one subgroup in a work unit is part of a cohesive team and another unit is excluded. According to the model, leaders develop unique working relationships with subordinates. As a result, in-groups and out-groups are created. Members of the in-group tend to perform better, have higher satisfaction, and exhibit more teamwork than members of the out-group. LMX has effects on reciprocity between leaders and members, satisfaction with teamwork, extra-role behavior' safety performance, and transformational leadership. The leader's first impression of a group member's competency plays an important role in placing that person into the in-group or the out-group.

## KEY TERMS

team  226
teamwork  226
cooperation theory  230

micromanagement  234
e-leadership  234
open-book management  238

leader–member exchange (LMX) model  241

# GUIDELINES FOR ACTION AND SKILL DEVELOPMENT

When attempting to develop teamwork, the leader would ordinarily be thinking of coaching individual team members to be more effective team players. Some research, however, suggests that teamwork is more likely to be enhanced when the team leader coaches the team as an entity.[54] For example, the team leader might meet with the group physically or through an internal website, and say, "I don't notice you folks offering each other enough constructive feedback. In an effective team, the members learn from each other."

Organizations are based on collaboration, and most leaders and many leadership researchers are so enamored with collaboration that they neglect its potential negative side effects. From the organizational standpoint, too much collaboration can drain time from independent thought and action. A small example is the time required to respond to every alert from collaborative software, such as a team member somewhere making a tiny input to the project.

From the individual perspective, recent research suggests that collaborative work has become highly time consuming, At many companies, workers spend about 80 percent of the their time in meetings or answering requests from work associates. All this collaborative work can lead to bottlenecks in work and burnout for individuals. As a leader you might need to decrease collaboration where it is not necessary, and make collaboration more efficient when it is needed.[55] For example, no need to inform fifty people that you resolved a customer complaint about merchandise that was damaged upon shipment.

## Discussion Questions and Activities

1. What would be the potential disadvantages of selecting a team leader who is highly charismatic and visionary?

2. Some top-level managers prohibit or discourage workers from telecommuting (including working from home and other remote locations) because they think such activity interferes with teamwork. What is your opinion on this issue?

3. Imagine yourself as the team leader, and the gang invites you to join them for an after-hours drink at a bar. From the standpoint of enhancing teamwork, explain whether joining the team would be effective.

4. Is there a role for independent-thinking, decisive, and creative leaders in a team-based organization? Explain.

5. When evaluating candidates, some hiring managers draw the distinction between a "team player" versus an "independent thinker." What is your opinion of the validity of this distinction?

6. At the hamburger chain, Five Guys, each member of the top-management team wears khaki pants and a polo shirt with the Five Guys logo. What impact do you think this practice has on teamwork?

7. As the team leader, should you make an effort to speak more clearly and use better grammar that the team members? Explain your reasoning.

8. What is your opinion of the value of experience in team sports for becoming a good team player in the workplace?

9. One of the character-building exercises in the Tough Mudder obstacle course is "electro-shock therapy" in which participants pass through a dangling curtain of electrical wires, some carrying 10,000 volts of electric shock. Any thoughts on the leadership-skill value of this exercise, along with the ethics of the task?

10. How can political skill help a person avoid being adversely affected by the leader–member exchange model?

# LEADERSHIP CASE PROBLEM A

### Ashley Wants to Boost Teamwork

Ashley considered herself fortunate to be chosen as the team leader for one of the newly formed teams at the insurance company where she worked. The purpose of forming teams was to improve customer service. Each team now had the authority to issue policies and settle claims, within limits, for specific geographic regions. Before the shift into teams, separate departments existed for sales, underwriting, and claims.

Although the company was profitable, it received too many criticisms about poor service, particularly in the time required to process a claim. Sales representatives within the company contended that the underwriting department took too long to approve and issue policies.

One of Ashley's first initiatives was to hold frequent in-person meetings to discuss how service was going to be improved. She emphasized to the team that the company had adopted the popular team concept and that teams were empowered to look for ways to improve efficiency. Ashley also emphasized that each team member had more responsibility than under the department structure. Each team member would be doing some sales, underwriting, and claims.

Team member George commented during one of the meetings, "Just think of it, three jobs in one and being paid just the same as before." During the same meeting, team member Roz asked, "What's so special about calling us a team? I had a nice job in the underwriting department before these teams were formed. I enjoyed that work. Now my job is more confusing."

Ashley responded, "The company decided this was the way to go. Trust me, everything will work out fine. Just go along with the team idea for now."

Four months after the teams were formed, Ashley's boss, James, met with her to discuss progress. James said, "Your team isn't making as much progress as I would like. Policies are not being issued any faster. Customer complaints about slow claims settlements are at the same level as before we converted into teams.

The other teams are making more progress. Does your team have a problem?"

"We do have a problem," said Ashley. "Everyone comes to work just as in the days before teams. They do most of the work alone, but they send e-mail messages to each other as needed. It just seems to be business as usual. So far, the idea of a high-producing team hasn't caught on."

"Are you an effective team leader?" asked James.

"I think I am," said Ashley. "I do everything I'm supposed to. I hold meetings, I post messages. I answer all questions asked of me. I try to settle problems."

"I'll be back to you in two months to discuss your team's progress. I want to see some improved results in terms of better customer service."

### Case Questions

1. How can Ashley be a more effective team leader?
2. What can Ashley do to get her team more interested in functioning as a team?
3. Based on whatever information you have found in the case, what is your evaluation of Ashley's charisma?

## ASSOCIATED ROLE PLAY

In this group role play, one student plays the role of Ashley who holds a team meeting designed to get her group more oriented toward teamwork. The e-mail she sent a few days before the meeting just alluded to a team meeting to discuss items relevant to the team progress. During the meeting, Ashley attempts to implement a few ideas for developing strong teamwork. Several other students play the role of team members, not all of whom see much value in the team structure. Run the role play for about eight minutes. Observers will look to see if Ashley uses any technique, or says anything, that will most likely inspire this team to higher levels of performance. Observe the reactions of team members to see if they appear to be inspired. Check to see if Ashley uses any specific technique of teamwork development, rather than simply using common sense.

# LEADERSHIP CASE PROBLEM B

## Should We Dump the Open-Plan Office?

Jason is the CEO of an advertising agency with 125 employees. The agency helps its client develop advertising and marketing themes and place ads in all media including print, the Internet, and mobile apps. Jason is pleased with productivity at the agency, yet he believes with stronger teamwork in all departments productivity would be enhanced. Jason has read and heard a lot in recent years about the teamwork benefits of an open-plan office or an open-office space. An online comment made by Mark D. Okerstrom, the chief financial officer (CFO) of Expedia, particularly impressed him: "Modern tech workers want an office that puts collaboration opportunities front and center."*

Jason thought that his advertising firm required perhaps even more collaboration than an online travel agency, such as Expedia. He then carefully evaluated the openness of the agency's office space, working with Baxter, her director of administration. Jason noted that about two-thirds of the agency employees were assigned to cubicles, and a few to private offices. He decided to make a major structural change to the office layout, enlisting the help of Baxter, and an outside office-design specialist, Kaitlin. The new open-plan office was installed over a four-day period, including a Saturday and Sunday. Jason himself moved from his private office to a desk in the center of the open-work area.

Before making the changes, Jason sent an e-mail to the entire staff with the explanation that the purpose of the new office layout was to enhance teamwork, collaboration and creativity. He welcomed feedback on the new plan, and also stated that the new office layout would be tried for one year before becoming permanent. Jason received back a handful of comments. A few of the comments welcomed the opportunity to become a more modern office, whereas a few others expressed concern about a potential negative impact on creativity and morale.

As the weeks passed under the new plan, a few workers casually mentioned that they enjoyed the opportunity to have more frequent face-to-face interaction with colleagues. In contrast, many more negative comments about the new open-plan office space surfaced.

Sarah, the supervisor of media placements told Jason, "The open-office plan is driving out some of older workers. Three people over fifty have quit in the last month. They say that listening to constant chatter and smartphones beeping may be okay for millennials, but they find it to be overwhelming. I guess that some of our older workers prefer tranquility to noise when it comes to doing serious work."

Tony, the highest paid advertising copywriter told Jason directly, "You have got to stop this insanity of open-office space. It might work for office routine, but it's a disaster for creative output. How can you expect me to be creative in the midst of people talking, phones ringing, and people stopping by my table to discuss sports and TV shows? When I'm trying to develop an advertising or marketing theme for a client, I try to use one of our two conference rooms. The rooms are usually filled with somebody else trying to escape the open space, so I might have to go to my car or work from home. We don't have a telecommuting program so coming to the office late is a little awkward."

Konrad, a specialist in purchasing advertising space for clients, wrote an e-mail to Jason, that included these comments: "Working in an open-plan office space has actually alienated me a little from my colleagues. It's like we all working together in a subway. Even smelling the cologne and perfume of my coworkers is a little annoying. Talking on the phone to a media person can be difficult also because of all the buzzing around me. When is this experiment going to end?"

### Questions

1. How might CEO Jason make better use of office space to promote teamwork?
2. To what extent are the workers opposed to the open-plan office simply being inflexible?
3. Identify several rules Jason might introduce that would make the open-plan office more conducive to effective teamwork.

*Quoted in "View from the Top," *The Wall Street Journal*, May 31, 2016, p. B1.

## ASSOCIATED ROLE PLAY

In this group role play, six students are sitting at the same table at the advertising agency described in the case. The group task is to develop a catchy advertising theme for a client who wants to promote a new type of dog biscuit that removes plaque from the teeth of dogs. Time is short because the client wants the theme by late this afternoon. The role players want to collaborate as much as possible but an advertising theme for the biscuits must be found. Run the role play for about ten minutes, and other class members will provide feedback about the teamwork and creativity.

 **LEADERSHIP** SKILL-BUILDING **EXERCISE 9-4**

### My Leadership Portfolio

Now that you have studied a basketful of ideas about enhancing teamwork, you can add to your skill repertoire by implementing a few of these tactics. The next time you are involved in group activity, either as the leader or as a group member, attempt to enhance cooperation and teamwork within the group. Make specific use of at least two of the recommended tactics for improving teamwork. Make an entry in your journal after your first attempts to enhance teamwork. Here is an example:

> I am the head of the Latino Business Club at our college. Attendance hasn't been too great in recent meetings, and the club seems headed nowhere. So at our last meeting, I suggested that we devote the entire meeting to building a mission statement. I explained that if we knew what our purpose was, maybe we would pull together better. We are still working on the mission, but so far it has to do with enhancing the impact and reputation of Hispanic business leaders. I also suggested that we invest in T-shirts with a logo we could be proud of. This idea may sound hokey, but the group really rallied around the idea of building unity through new T-shirts.

 **LEADERSHIP** SKILL-BUILDING **EXERCISE 9-5**

### The Trust Fall

Perhaps the most widely used team-building activity is the trust fall, which may be familiar to many readers. Nevertheless, each application of this exercise is likely to produce new and informative results. The class organizes itself into teams. In each team, each willing member stands on a chair and falls back into the arms of teammates. A less frightening alternative to falling off a chair is to simply fall backward standing up. Team members who, for whatever physical or mental reason, would prefer not to fall back into others or participate in catching others are unconditionally excluded. However, they can serve as observers. After the trust falls have been completed, a team leader gathers answers to the following questions and then shares the answers with the rest of the class.

1. How does this exercise develop teamwork?
2. How does the exercise develop leadership skills?
3. What did the participants learn about themselves?

## NOTES

1. Original story based on facts and observations in the following sources: John A. Byrne, "Sheryl Sandberg On Leadership: 'It's Better to Inspire than Direct'," *www.poetsandquants.com*, June 29, 2015, pp. 1–2; Tren Griffin, "A Dozen Things I've Learned from Sheryl Sandberg About Management, Careers, and Business," *25iq* (https://25iq.com), February 7, 2015, pp. 1–4; Richard Feloni, "Sheryl Sandberg Explains the Most Valuable Aspect of Her Relationship with Her Boss, Mark Zuckerberg," *Business Insider* (www.busienssinsider.com), June 28, 2015, pp. 1–2; "Learn the Art of Leadership from Sheryl Sandberg," *Right Management* (www.right.com), March 4, 2015, pp. 1–3; Allison Pearson, "Waiting

for Superwoman," *Bloomberg Businessweek*, March 11–17, 2013, pp. 6–7.

2. Edwin A. Locke and Associates, *The Essence of Leadership: The Four Keys to Leading Successfully* (New York: Lexington/Macmillan, 1991), p. 94.

3. Jon R. Katzenbach and Douglas K. Smith, "The Discipline of Teams," *Harvard Business Review*, March–April 1993, p. 112.

4. Robin L. Flanigan, "Teamwork, Says Veterinary Assistant, Always Saves the Day," *Democrat and Chronicle*, March 6, 2016, p. 2E.

5. David Burkus, "Why Whole Foods Builds It Entire Business On Teams," *Forbes* (www.forbes.com), June 8, 2016, pp. 1–2.

6. Peter Hawkins, *Leadership Team Coaching: Collective Transformational Leadership* (London and Philadelphia, PA: Kogan Page Limited, 2011); Andrew J. DuBrin, *The Reengineering Survival Guide: Managing and Succeeding in the Changing Workplace* (Mason, OH: Thomson Executive Press, 1996), pp. 129–144.

7. Michael A. Hogg, Daan Van Knippenberg, and David E. Rast III, "Intergroup Leadership in Organizations: Leading Across Group and Organizational Boundaries," *Academy of Management Review*, April 2012, pp. 232–255.

8. Frederick P. Morgeson, "The External Leadership of Self-Managing Teams: Intervening in the Context of Novel and Disruptive Events," *Journal of Applied Psychology*, May 2005, pp. 497–508.

9. Roger Schwarz, "Getting Teams with Different Subcultures to Collaborate," *Harvard Business Review* (https://hbr.org), July 22, 2016, pp. 1–6.

10. David De Cremer and Daan van Knippenberg, "How Do Leaders Promote Cooperation? The Effects of Charisma and Procedural Fairness," *Journal of Applied Psychology*, October 2002, pp. 858–866.

11. Christopher Hann, "Better Together," *Entrepreneur*, September 2016, p. 16.

12. James M. Kouzes and Barry Z. Posner, *The Leadership Challenge*, third Edition (San Francisco: Jossey-Bass, 2002), p. 244.

13. "A Conversation with Irv Rothman: Teamwork at Its Best," *Executive Leadership*, December 2013, p. 3; "Irv Rothman: President/CEO HP Financial Services," *Lateral Investment Management* (http://lateralim.com), 2015.

14. Gary Ranker and Colin Gautrey, "Adjusting the Political Temperature of Your Team," in Marshall Goldsmith, John Baldoni, and Sarah McArthur (eds.), *The AMA Handbook of Leadership* (New York: AMACOM, 2010), p. 185.

15. Dean Tjosvold and Mary M. Tjosvold, *The Emerging Leader: Ways to a Stronger Team* (New York: Lexington Books, 1993); "Improve Teamwork with a 'Code of Conduct'," *Manager's Edge*, February 2005, p. 1.

16. David Spungin, "Google's Surprising Insights on Team Effectiveness," *www.linkedin.com*, April 1, 2016, p. 3.

17. Adam Grant, "Givers Take All: The Hidden Dimension of Corporate Culture," *McKinsey Quarterly*, April 2013, pp. 1–10.

18. Ha Hu and Robert C. Liden, "Making a Difference in Teamwork: Linking Team Prosocial Motivation to Team Processes and Effectiveness," *Academy of Management Journal*, August 2015, pp. 1102–1127.

19. Vanessa Urch Druskat and Steven B. Wolff, "Building the Emotional Intelligence of Groups," *Harvard Business Review*, March 2001, pp. 80–90.

20. Paul S. George, "Teamwork Without Tears," *Personnel Journal*, November 1987, p. 129.

21. Peter Pronovost and Eric Vohr, *Safe Patients, Smart Hospitals* (New York: Hudson Street Press, 2010).

22. Jon R. Katzenbach and Douglas K. Smith, "The Discipline of Teams," pp. 118–119.

23. Michael Mankins, Alan Bird, and James Root, "Making Star Teams Out of Star Players," *Harvard Business Review*, January–February 2013, pp. 77–78.

24. "Improve Your Team's Performance by Turning Up the Stress," *The Management Tip of the Day from Harvard Business Review*, September 20, 2016, p. 1.

25. Amy C. Edmonson, "Teamwork on the Fly," *Harvard Business Review*, April 2012, p. 78.

26. "A New CEO Asked Just 4 Questions," *Executive Leadership*, May 2013, p. 5.

27. Christine Porath, "Give Your Team More Effective Positive Feedback," *Harvard Business Review* (hbr.org), October 25, 2016, pp. 1–9.

28. Anne Fisher, "In Praise of Micromanaging," *Fortune*, August 23, 2004, p. 40.

29. Bruce J. Avolio and Surinder S. Kahai, "Adding 'E' to E-Leadership: How It May Impact Your Leadership," *Organizational Dynamics*, Vol. 31, no. 4, 2003, p. 325.

30. Jeanne Brett, Kristen Belfar, and Mary C. Kern, "Managing Multicultural Teams," *Harvard Business Review*, November 2006, pp. 87–88.

31. Elka Torpey and Andrew Hogan, "Working in a Gig Economy," *Career Outlook*, U. S. Bureau of Labor Statistics (www.bls.gov), May 2016, p. 1.

32. Arvind Malhotra, Ann Majchzak, and Benson Rosen, "Leading Virtual Teams," Academy of Management Perspectives, February 2007, pp. 60–70; study reported in Lynda Gratton, "Working Together ... When Apart," *The Wall Street Journal*, June 16–17, 2007, p. R4; Keith Ferrazzi, "Getting Virtual Teams Right," *Harvard Business Review*,

December 2014, pp. 120–123; Bill Leonard, "Managing Virtual Teams," *HR Magazine*, June 2011, pp. 38–42.

33. Richard Lepsinger, "Virtual Team Failure: 6 Common Missteps That Threaten Your Team's Success," *Communication Briefings*, February 2011, p. 6.

34. Alina Dizik, "Open Offices Lose Some of Their Openness," *The Wall Street Journal*, October 3, 2016, p. R7.

35. Michael Mankins, Alan Bird, and James Root, "Making Star Teams Out of Star Players," *Harvard Business Review*, January–February 2013, p. 77.

36. Lee G. Bolman and Terrence E. Deal, "What Makes a Team Work?" pp. 41–42.

37 Thomas J. McCoy, Creating an "Open Book" *Organization ... Where Employees Think & Act Like Business Partners* (New York: AMACOM, 1999); John Case, "HR Learns How to Open the Books," *HR Magazine*, May 1998, pp. 71–76.

38. Todd Clausen, "Open Book Management Helps Monroe Wheelchair Thrive," *Democrat and Chronicle*, March 27, 2016, p. 161.

39. Quoted in Jennifer Wang, "Unbeatable," *Entrepreneur*, February 2011, p. 16.

40. Quoted in Sonia Alleyne, "Rallying the Troops," *Black Enterprise*, February 2011, p. 75.

41. Max Mihelich, "Bit by Bit: Stand-Up Comedy as a Team-Building Exercise," *Workforce Management*, February 2013, p. 16.

42. "Avoid 'Cringe Factor' in Team Building," *Manager's Edge*, May 2009, p. 8.

43. George Graen and J. E. Cashman, "A Role-Making Model of Leadership in Formal Organizations: A Developmental Approach," in J. G. Hunt and L. L. Larson (eds.), *Leadership Frontiers* (Kent, OH: Kent State University Press, 1975), pp. 143–165; Robert P. Vecchio, "Leader–Member Exchange, Objective Performance, Employment Duration, and Supervisor Ratings: Testing for Moderation and Mediation," *Journal of Business and Psychology*, Spring 1998, p. 328.

44. Elaine M. Engle and Robert G. Lord, "Implicit Theories, Self-Schemas, and Leader–Member Exchange," *Academy of Management Journal*, August 1997, pp. 988–1010.

45. Xiaohua (Tracy) Zhou and Chester A. Schriesheim, "Supervisor–Subordinate Convergence in Descriptions of Leader–Member Exchange (LMX) Quality: Review and Testable Propositions," *The Leadership Quarterly*, December 2009, pp. 920–932.

46. Howard J. Klein and Jay S. Kim, "A Field Study of the Influences of Situational Constraints, Leader–Member Exchange, and Goal Commitment on Performance," *Academy of Management Journal*, February 1998, pp. 88–95.

47. Randall P. Settoon, Nathan Bennett, and Robert C. Liden, "Social Exchange in Organizations: Perceived Organizational Support, Leader–Member Exchange, and Employee Reciprocity," *Journal of Applied Psychology*, June 1995, pp. 219–227.

48. Hoisein Vazifehdost and Mahmood Rahmani, "The Relationship Between Teamwork, Role Ambiguity, Supervisor–Nurse and Well-Being: Public against Private Sector Nurse," *International Journal of Research in Social Sciences*, no. 4, 2013, pp. 18–31.

49 Pamela Tierney and Talya N. Bauer, "A Longitudinal Assessment of LMX on Extra-Role Behavior," *Academy of Management Best Papers Proceedings*, 1996, pp. 298–302.

50. David A. Hofman and Frederick P. Morgeson, "Safety-Related Behavior as a Social Exchange: The Role of Perceived Organizational Support and Leader–Member Exchange," *Journal of Applied Psychology*, April 1999, pp. 286–296.

51. Ronald F. Piccolo and Jason A. Colquitt, "Transformational Leadership and Job Behaviors: The Mediating Role of Core Job Characteristics," *Academy of Management Journal*, April 2006, pp. 327–340.

52. Vijaya Venkataramani, Stephen G. Green, and Deidra J. Schleicher, "Well-Connected Leaders: The Impact of Leaders' Social Network Ties on LMX and Members' Work Attitudes," *Journal of Applied Psychology*, November 2010, pp. 1071–1084.

53. Robert C. Liden, Sandy J. Wayne, and Deal Stilwell, "A Longitudinal Study on the Early Development of Leader–Member Exchanges," *Journal of Applied Psychology*, August 1993, pp. 662–674.

54. Ruth Wageman, Colin M Fisher, and J. Richard Hackman, "Leading Teams When the Time Is Right: Finding the Best Moments to Act," *Organizational Dynamics*, July–September 2009, p. 193.

55. Rob Cross, Reb Rebele, and Adam Grant, "Collaborative Overload," *Harvard Business Review*, January–February 2016, pp. 74–79.

## CHAPTER 1

# Motivation and Coaching Skills

CHAPTER 10

## LEARNING OBJECTIVES

After studying this chapter and doing the exercises, you should be able to

- Explain the leader's role in employee engagement.
- Identify and describe leadership skills linked to expectancy theory.
- Describe goal theory.
- Describe how leaders can motivate others through recognition.

- Describe coaching as an approach to motivation. Understand the characteristics of coaching and how to practice coaching skills and techniques.
- Describe how executive coaches help enhance leadership skills.

## CHAPTER OUTLINE

**Leadership and Employee Engagement**

The Impact of Worker Engagement on Productivity

Meaningful Work for Employee Engagement

Relationship with Leader and Employee Engagement

**Expectancy Theory and Motivational Skills**

Basic Components of Expectancy Theory

Leadership Skills and Behaviors Associated with Expectancy Theory

**Goal Theory**

Basic Findings of Goal Theory

The Importance of How Goals Are Attained and Other Concerns

**Using Recognition and Pride to Motivate Others**

Appealing to the Recognition Need of Others

Appealing to Pride

**Coaching as an Approach to Motivation**

Key Characteristics of Coaching

**Coaching Skills and Techniques**

**Executive Coaching and Leadership Effectiveness**

Specific Forms of Assistance Provided by Executive Coaches

Contributions of and Concerns About Executive Coaching

**Summary**

**Key Terms**

**Guidelines for Action and Skill Development**

**Leadership Case Problem A**

**Leadership Case Problem B**

**Notes**

K im Jordan is the co-founder and Executive Chair of New Belgian Brewing, the third-largest crafter brewer in the United States, with Fat Tire being its flagship beer. Jordan's present responsibilities focus on developing business strategy and creating visions. She was previously the chief executive officer (CEO) of New Belgian for six years. Jordan attributes much of the success of the company to a loyal group of employees, most of whom have an ownership stake in the company. Stock ownership along with other humanistic approaches has contributed to high employee engagement. Jordan believes that the New Belgian has a "high-involvement culture" of engaged, enthusiastic workers.

By early 2103 more than 500 company employees, assumed 100 percent ownership of the company. High morale is indicated by an employee turnover rate of less than 5 percent. A related observation is that employees contribute many ideas about improving company operations as well as the beer.

Jordan also believes in corporate transparency as a way of involving employee. All New Belgian employees have access can access the company intranet and review the company financials to see how corporate money is spent. Sales and performance figures are also reviewed at monthly meetings with employees.

Jordan began her career in social work, which has influenced her humanistic approach to leadership, and her lifelong commitment to building healthy communities. She also emphasizes protecting the external environment (environmental stewardship), and philanthropic giving. Jordan has spoken to thousands of people in business, the nonprofit sector, and academia about how to create a vibrant and rewarding organization culture that enhances profits and as well as her coworker's and customer lives.

Three of the company's core values and beliefs are as follows: (1) Promoting beer culture and the responsible enjoyment of beer; (2) environmental stewardship by honoring nature at every turn of the business; and (3) cultivating potential through learning, high involvement culture, and the pursuit of opportunities. Jordan's beliefs about leadership include the ideas that the vast majority of people want to do the right thing, and people want to be connected to something bigger than them.

Jordan attended Colorado State University, presumably with a major in social work. Previously she attended a Quaker high school.[1]

This story about a well-known brewery executive illustrates the importance of leaders engaging and motivating employees. In this chapter, we approach motivation and coaching skills from various perspectives. First, we take an overview of motivation by explaining the leader's role in employee engagement. We then examine first how leaders make effective use of expectancy theory, recognition, and goal setting to motivate group members. Second, we describe coaching, including a description of specific coaching skills and the role of the executive coach. Most readers of this book have already studied motivation, so here we describe how it is possible to apply a few popular motivation theories rather than repeat a discussion of theories you have already studied, such as reinforcement theory or Maslow's need hierarchy.

## Leadership and Employee Engagement

A broad purpose of leaders applying motivation and coaching techniques is to get employees involved in their work and excited about working for the organization. **Engagement** is the current buzz word for the commitment workers make to their employer. The term generally refers to high levels of personal investment in the tasks performed on a job.[2] Engagement is reflected in employee willingness to stay with the firm and go beyond the call of duty.

Later in this section, we describe how leaders can enhance employee engagement through making work more meaningful. A preliminary observation about the impact of leadership on employee engagement comes from a study of industrial consultants in the Netherlands. Using both surveys and individual diaries, it was found that leaders perceived to be transformational had a positive impact on worker optimism, resulting in workers experiencing engagement on a daily basis.[3]

Gaining employee commitment is especially important in the current era because a study conducted in 142 countries found that about 63 percent of workers are not fully engaged in their work. They do what is expected of them but do not contribute extra mental and physical effort to be outstanding. Furthermore, their motivation is low and they are less likely to invest discretionary effort in important organizational outcomes. The same study found that 13 percent of employees are engaged, and 24 percent actively disengaged.[4] More recent data suggest that two out of three millennials plan to leave their current role by 2020, presumably because many of them feel disengaged.[5]

Leadership Self-Assessment Quiz 10-1 provides you an opportunity to think about your own level of engagement in a present or past position.

# LEADERSHIP SELF-ASSESSMENT QUIZ 10-1

## My Work Engagement Tendencies

Indicate the extent to which each of the following statements describes your behavior or attitude by circling one number. The numbers refer to disagree strongly (DS), disagree (D), neither agree nor disagree (N), agree (A), and agree strongly (AS). Consider enlisting the help of someone who knows your behavior and attitudes well to help you respond accurately to the statements.

| | STATEMENT ABOUT JOB AND WORK | DS | D | N | A | AS |
|---|---|---|---|---|---|---|
| 1. | I feel filled with energy while at work. | 1 | 2 | 3 | 4 | 5 |
| 2. | My work usually starts to get a little dull after the first couple of hours on the job. | 5 | 4 | 3 | 2 | 1 |
| 3. | I am very proud of my work. | 1 | 2 | 3 | 4 | 5 |
| 4. | I plan to quit my job as soon as a better one comes along. | 5 | 4 | 3 | 2 | 1 |
| 5. | While at work I often daydream about how nice it would be to be retired. | 5 | 4 | 3 | 2 | 1 |
| 6. | My job is a key part of who I am. | 1 | 2 | 3 | 4 | 5 |
| 7. | I think that helping my coworkers is an important part of my job. | 1 | 2 | 3 | 4 | 5 |
| 8. | I feel an emotional attachment toward my company. | 1 | 2 | 3 | 4 | 5 |
| 9. | I look forward to each work day with loads of excitement. | 1 | 2 | 3 | 4 | 5 |
| 10. | I should really find a different line of work. | 5 | 4 | 3 | 2 | 1 |
| 11. | The most exciting thing about my job is the fact that I get paid. | 5 | 4 | 3 | 2 | 1 |
| 12. | I really care about the welfare of my company. | 1 | 2 | 3 | 4 | 5 |
| 13. | It is really boring answering these questions about my job and work. | 5 | 4 | 3 | 2 | 1 |
| 14. | Almost every detail of my job interests me. | 1 | 2 | 3 | 4 | 5 |
| 15. | My job inspires me. | 1 | 2 | 3 | 4 | 5 |

*Scoring and Interpretation:* Calculate your score by adding up the numbers circled:

- **60–75:** You are intensely engaged and involved in your work and job which should contribute substantially to your job satisfaction as well as your job performance.
- **30–59:** You have an average degree of engagement and commitment in your work and job.
- **15–29:** You are below average in work engagement and commitment. Solicit feedback from others to see if this low score is warranted. If the score is accurate, exercise self-discipline to look for aspects of your work that you find interesting, and build on these as a foundation to become more engaged in your work.

*Source:* A few of the statements in the quiz are based on questionnaire items presented in Wilmar B. Schaufeli, Arnold B. Baker, and Marisa Salanova, "The Measurement of Work Engagement with a Short Questionnaire: A Cross-National Study," *Educational and Psychological Measurement,* August 2006, p. 714.

# The Impact of Worker Engagement on Productivity

According to Jim Harter, a Gallup research scientist, engagement—or the lack of it—has substantial implications for how well business organizations achieve their goals.[6] Quantitative evidence points toward the impact of employee engagement. The State of the American Workplace report shows that companies with a 9-to-1 ratio of engaged to actively disengaged employees experience 147 percent higher earnings per share, on average, in comparison to their competitors.[7]

A key link between leadership, motivation and coaching techniques, and engagement is that leaders need to use motivation and coaching techniques to help keep employees engaged. An example of the value of a coaching technique is that a survey of 1,000 employees revealed that leaders who give positive feedback to employees foster engagement. Furthermore, giving mostly negative feedback is better than no feedback or being ignored. A total of 5 percent of employees were engaged who believed that supervisors focused on their weaknesses (11 percent of employees fell into this category).[8]

Skill-Building Exercise 10-1 provides you an opportunity to develop fresh insights into employee engagement.

## LEADERSHIP SKILL-BUILDING EXERCISE 10-1

### Collecting Live Data on Worker Engagement

The purpose of this exercise is to obtain some first-hand data about worker engagement, and then think through the leadership implications of your findings. Conduct interviews of about seven minutes in length with the next five working people you can find, doing any kind of work, at any job level. In-person or telephone interviews would be best, but if necessary use e-mail, text messaging, chat, or social media. Ask each interviewee how much he or she feels engaged in or committed to his or her present job. Also, ask why the person feels that way.

After you have collected your interview data, think through the leadership implications, such as the following:

1. What could I do as a leader to facilitate group members getting more engaged in their work?

2. What role did leaders play in helping my interviewees get engaged in their work?

If class time permits, it could prove insightful for class members to share some of their findings.

## Meaningful Work for Employee Engagement

Engagement and meaningfulness of work are closely related. Recent research suggests that engagement is a positive motivational state directed toward obtaining meaningfulness at work.[9] A key driver of worker engagement therefore is the opportunity to perform **meaningful work**, the feeling of doing work that matters or makes a difference. Engagement is facilitated when employees understand how their output makes a contribution to the organization and the larger world.[10] Research by McKinsey and company indicates that the opportunity to make an impact in the following four areas is the most likely to increase the meaningfulness of work for employees:

- *On society*—including making a better society, building the community, or managing resources carefully. Millennials, for example, are known to care about social issues and find it easier to be engaged when their employer is helping address problems across the globe.[11]
- *On the customer*—for example, making life easier for customers and providing a superior service or product.
- *On the workgroup or team*—for example, having a sense of belonging, a caring environment, or working collectively in an efficient and effective manner.
- *On themselves*—including personal development, higher financial compensation, and a sense of empowerment.

A management team at an American financial services firm worked to create stories related to these four sources of impact in order to enhance worker engagement in reducing costs. The society source of impact was told in terms of more affordable housing. The impact on customers was described in relation to increased simplicity and flexibility, fewer errors, and more competitive prices. The team impact story was told in terms of less duplication of effort, more delegation, increased accountability, and a faster pace. Finally, the story about individual impact was related to bigger and more attractive jobs, an opportunity to build turn-around skills, and creating one's own institution. Within one month, the number of employees reporting that they were motivated to bring about cost reductions surged to 57 percent from 55 percent, based on morale surveys.[12]

A major way in which leaders can make work highly meaningful for subordinates is to provide them with the opportunity to lead projects or task forces. Such leadership opportunities enhance engagement of the heads of the projects or task forces. According to a McKinsey global survey of 1,047 executives, other managers, and employees, the opportunity to lead projects or tasks forces was an extremely or highly effective incentive. (A comparable percentage responded that performance-based cash incentives had the same effect.)[13]

Leadership Self-Assessment Quiz 10-2 gives you an opportunity to personalize the concept of meaningful work and employee engagement.

## LEADERSHIP SELF-ASSESSMENT QUIZ 10-2

### How Meaningful Is My Work?

**Instructions:** Indicate whether you mostly agree or mostly disagree as to how well each of the following statements applies to your present, or a previous, position. If relating to a job you hold or have held is not sensible, relate each of the statements to school or volunteer work.

| STATEMENT ABOUT THE WORK AND/OR JOB | MOSTLY AGREE | MOSTLY DISAGREE |
|---|---|---|
| **1.** When I am at work, the time flies by quickly. | ☐ | ☐ |
| **2.** My job gives me as much pleasure as participating in my favorite pastime. | ☐ | ☐ |
| **3.** The work I do really helps other people. | ☐ | ☐ |
| **4.** The work I do really has an impact on society. | ☐ | ☐ |
| **5.** I feel totally absorbed in my work. | ☐ | ☐ |
| **6.** I am so excited about my job. | ☐ | ☐ |
| **7.** I discover something new and interesting about my job almost every week. | ☐ | ☐ |
| **8.** My job fills me with energy because it is so exciting. | ☐ | ☐ |
| **9.** It would make me sad to let my coworkers down. | ☐ | ☐ |
| **10.** I put a lot of mental energy into my job. | ☐ | ☐ |
| **11.** I put a lot of physical energy into my job. | ☐ | ☐ |
| **12.** I would feel guilty if I was too sick to come to work. | ☐ | ☐ |
| **13.** I don't care if many celebrities earn much more money than I because my work is very important. | ☐ | ☐ |
| **14.** I throw myself into my job. | ☐ | ☐ |
| **15.** My work helps give me a purpose in life. | ☐ | ☐ |

## LEADERSHIP SELF-ASSESSMENT QUIZ 10-2 (continued)

**Scoring and Interpretation:** The more of the above statements you agree with, the more meaning you have in your work and your job.

- **12–15:** Your work is quite meaningful, and if your attitudes persist, you should have a long and rewarding career.

- **5–11:** You have an average degree of meaningfulness in your work and job.

- **1–4:** Your work may not be meaningful enough to bring you long-term satisfaction. You are advised to look for ways to make your work more meaningful, such as looking for new tasks that you perceive as more meaningful.

*Source*: A few of the statements in the quiz are based on questionnaire items presented in a review of the literature found in Michael S. Christian, Adela S. Garza, and Jerel E. Slaughter, "Work Engagement: A Quantitative Review and Test of Its Relation with Task Performance," *Personnel Psychology*, no. 1, 2011, pp. 108–109.

## Relationship with the Leader and Employee Engagement

Looking at the leader's role in enhancing motivation more broadly, Jean Houston, an Atlanta-based human resources consultant, says that managers can engage their workers by seeing them as whole people and having courageous conversations that will build trust and see what is really going on. Houston also encourages managers to learn and use soft skills such as communication, recognition, mentoring, and caring because soft skills can have a hard impact.[14] (Such is the thrust of this chapter and this book.) According to a survey conducted by BlessingWhite Inc., 20 percent of respondents cited career advancement as a key driver of engagement. A specific technique for leaders to engage employees is therefore to initiate career discussions.[15]

A study conducted in a large multinational technology firm in Brazil found that the employee's unique relationship with their leader creates follower engagement. Having a high-quality relationship with the leader was found to be a more important driver of work engagement than was inspirational leadership behavior. A key finding of the study was that **leader–member exchange (LMX)** contributed more to worker engagement than did transformational leadership. A conclusion reached in the study was that a better relationship with the leader will cause followers to reciprocate with higher levels of emotional investment in the job.[16]

Another illustrative way in which leaders can facilitate engagement among employees is to provide them feedback on the progress they are making with their work. (Providing feedback can be considered part of a leader–member relationship.) Teresa Amabile and Steven Kramer gathered and analyzed diary reports from 238 professional-level workers in twenty-six project teams from seven companies across three different industries. The diaries were e-mailed to participants, and asked a few questions about the day, including what stood out in relation to work. Based on 12,000 diary entries, the authors discovered that a feeling of making progress was the key to employee engagement among these workers.[17] An example of a leader providing feedback on worker of progress would be to say, "It looks like you found a way to reduce energy costs another one percent toward our goal of a 25 percent reduction."

Leaders can also enhance employee engagement by discussing career advancement opportunities with them. The perception of advancement opportunities is an accepted way of facilitating worker engagement including loyalty to the company.

A promising new understanding of how leaders influence subordinates to become engaged is through the energy people derive from a positive relationship with their leader. To personalize this concept, think about people in your network who energize you to engage in constructive activity. A series of three studies showed that the *relational energy* workers derive from their relationship with their leader prompts them to become more work engaged. Both energy and engagement in the study were measured by questionnaires. Two examples of "energy" statements were (1) I feel invigorated when I interact with this person, and (2) I would go to this person when I feel the need to be "pepped up." The engagement statements were quite similar to those found in Leadership Self-Assessment Quiz 10-1.[18]

## Expectancy Theory and Motivational Skills

Expectancy theory is a good starting point in learning how leaders can apply systematic explanations of motivation, for two major reasons. First, the theory is comprehensive: It incorporates and integrates features of other motivation theories, including goal theory and positive reinforcement. Second, it offers the leader many guidelines for triggering and sustaining constructive effort from group members. Although not much research is conducted about expectancy theory nowadays, it remains a stable approach to understanding work motivation.

The **expectancy theory** of motivation is based on the premise that the amount of effort people expend depends on how much reward they expect to get in return. In addition to being broad, the theory deals with cognition and process. Expectancy theory is cognitive because it emphasizes the thoughts, judgments, and desires of the person being motivated. It is a process theory because it attempts to explain how motivation takes place.

The theory is really a group of theories based on a rational, economic view of people.[19] In any given situation, people want to maximize gain and minimize loss. The theory assumes that they choose among alternatives by selecting one they think they have the best chance of attaining. Furthermore, they choose the alternative that appears to have the biggest personal payoff. Given a choice, people will select the assignment they think they can handle the best and will benefit them the most.

### Basic Components of Expectancy Theory

Expectancy theory contains three basic components: valence, instrumentality, and expectancy. Because of these three components, the theory is often referred to as VIE theory. Figure 10-1 presents a basic version of expectancy theory. All three elements must be present for motivation to take place. To be motivated, people must value the reward, think they can perform, and have reasonable assurance that their performance will lead to a reward.

*Valence*    The worth or attractiveness of an outcome is referred to as **valence**. As shown in Figure 10-1, each work situation has multiple outcomes. An **outcome** is anything that might stem from performance, such as a reward. Each outcome has a valence of its own. And each outcome can lead to other outcomes or consequences, referred to as *second-level*

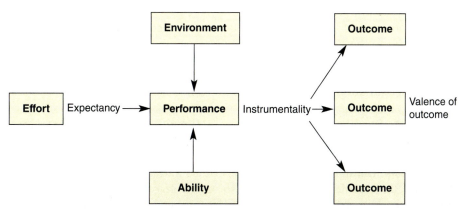

**FIGURE 10-1**    The Expectancy Theory of Motivation.

*outcomes*. A person who receives an outstanding performance evaluation (a first-level outcome) becomes eligible for a promotion (a second-level outcome). Second-level outcomes also have valences. The sum of all the valences must be positive if the person is to work hard. If the sum of all of the valences is negative, the person might work hard to avoid the outcome.

Valences range from -100 to +100 in the version of expectancy theory presented here. (The usual method of placing valences on a -1.00 to +1.00 scale does not do justice to the true differences in preferences.) A valence of +100 means that a person intensely desires an outcome. A valence of -100 means that a person is strongly motivated to avoid an outcome such as being fired or declaring bankruptcy. A valence of zero signifies indifference to an outcome and is therefore of no use as a motivator.

An example of using negative and positive valence at the same time would be for the CEO to use data to point out how bleak the company will become if it does not change, and how wonderful the company will become if it does change.

*Instrumentality*   An individual's assessment of the probability that performance will lead to certain outcomes is referred to as **instrumentality**. (An instrumentality is also referred to as a *performance-to-outcome expectancy* because it relates to the outcome people expect from performing in a certain way.) When people engage in a particular behavior, they do so with the intention of achieving a desired outcome or reward. Instrumentalities range from 0 to 1.0, where 0 is no chance of receiving the desired reward and 1.0 is a belief that the reward is certain to follow. For example, a whose job category makes him or he eligible for overtime pay, might say, "I know for sure that if I work overtime, I will receive overtime pay."

*Expectancy*   An individual's assessment of the probability that effort will lead to correct performance of the task is referred to as **expectancy**. (The same concept is also referred to as *effort-to-performance expectancy*.) An important question people ask themselves before putting forth effort to accomplish a task is, "If I put in all this work, will I really get the job done properly?" Expectancies range from 0 to 1.0, where 0 is no expectation of performing the tasks correctly, and 1.0 signifies absolute faith in being able to perform the task properly. Expectancies thus influence whether a person will even strive to earn a reward. Self-confident people have higher expectancies than do less self-confident people. Being well trained increases a person's subjective sense that he or she can perform the task.

The importance of having high expectancies for motivation meshes well with the contribution of **self-efficacy**, the confidence in your ability to carry out a specific task. If you have high self-efficacy about the task, your motivation will be high. Low self-efficacy leads to low motivation. Some people are poorly motivated to skydive because they doubt they will be able to pull the rip cord while free falling at 120 mph.

In short, if you are confident about your task-related skills, you will get your act together to do the task. This is one reason that you should give people the skills and confidence they need to put forth effort.

An apparent contradiction in expectancy theory requires explanation. Some people will engage in behaviors with low expectancies, such as trying to invent a successful new product or become the CEO of a major corporation. The compensating factor is the large valences attached to the second-level outcomes associated with these accomplishments. The payoffs from introducing a successful new product or becoming a CEO are so great that people are willing to take a long shot that helps verify the justification for leaders' and managers' concern about motivating employees: People who try harder perform better.

## Leadership Skills and Behaviors Associated with Expectancy Theory

Expectancy theory has many implications for leaders and managers with respect to motivating others.[20] Some of these implications also stem from other motivational theories, and they fit good management and leadership practice in general. As you read each implication, reflect on how you might apply the skill or behavior during a leadership assignment.

1. ***Determine what levels and kinds of performance are needed to achieve organizational goals.*** Motivating others proceeds best when workers have a clear understanding of what needs to be accomplished. At the same time, the leader should make sure that the desired levels of performance are possible. For example, sales quotas might be set too high because the market is already saturated with a particular product or service.

2. ***Make the performance level attainable by the individuals being motivated.*** If the group members believe that they are being asked to perform extraordinarily difficult tasks, most of them will suffer from low motivation. A task must generally be perceived as attainable to be motivational.

3. ***Train and encourage people.*** Leaders should give group members the necessary training and encouragement to be confident they can perform the required task. Some group members who appear to be poorly motivated simply lack the right skills and self-confidence.

4. ***Make explicit the link between rewards and performance.*** Group members should be reassured that if they perform the job to standard, they will receive the promised reward.

5. ***Make sure the rewards are large enough.*** Some rewards that are the right kind fail to motivate people because they are not in the right amount. The promise of a large salary increase might be motivational, but a 1 percent increase will probably have little motivational thrust for most workers.

6. ***Analyze what factors work in opposition to the effectiveness of the reward.*** Conflicts between the leader's package of rewards and other influences in the work group may require the leader to modify the reward. For example, if the work group favors the status quo, a large reward may be required to encourage innovative thinking.

7. ***Explain the meaning and implications of second-level outcomes.*** It is helpful for employees to understand the value of certain outcomes, such as receiving a favorable performance evaluation. (For example, it could lead to a salary increase, assignment to a high-status task force, or promotion.)

8. ***Understand individual differences in valences.*** To motivate group members effectively, leaders must recognize individual differences or preferences for rewards. An attempt should be made to offer workers rewards to which they attach a high valence. One employee might value a high-adventure assignment; another might attach a high valence to a routine, tranquil assignment. Cross-cultural differences in valences may also occur. For example, many (but not all) Asian workers prefer not to be singled out for recognition in front of the group. According to their cultural values, receiving recognition in front of the group is insensitive and embarrassing. Another example is that a $1,000 watch have more valence in the United States than in countries that downplay a flamboyant display of wealth. Leadership Skill-Building Exercise 10-2 deals with the challenge of estimating valences.

## Goal Theory

Goal setting is a basic process that is directly or indirectly part of all major theories of work motivation. Leaders and managers widely accept goal setting as a means to improve and sustain performance. A vision, for example, is really an exalted goal. One example is that Yang Yuanqing, the CEO of Lenovo, motivates his team with his aggressive vision for the computer manufacturer's global growth. To develop goals to support the vision, an annual meeting is held at his home for senior executives. Wineglass in hand, each executive shares an ambitious goal, which is then toasted by the group. An example: "We'll sell more PCs than Hewlett Packard next year." At another kickoff meeting, Yang established

# LEADERSHIP SKILL-BUILDING EXERCISE 10-2

## Estimating Valences for Applying Expectancy Theory

**Instructions:** A major challenge in applying expectancy theory is estimating what valence attaches to possible outcomes. A leader or manager also has to be aware of the potential rewards or punishment in a given work situation. Listed are a group of rewards and punishments, along with a space for rating the reward or punishment on a scale of -100 to +100. Work with about six teammates, with each person rating all of the rewards and punishments.

| POTENTIAL OUTCOME | RATING (−100 TO +100) |
| --- | --- |
| 1. Promotion to vice president | _____ |
| 2. One-step promotion | _____ |
| 3. Above-average performance evaluation | _____ |
| 4. Top-category performance evaluation | _____ |
| 5. $10,000 performance bonus | _____ |
| 6. $5,000 performance bonus | _____ |
| 7. $150 gift certificate | _____ |
| 8. Employee-of-the-month plaque | _____ |
| 9. Note of appreciation sent by e-mail or posted on social media website, and placed in file | _____ |
| 10. Lunch with boss at good restaurant | _____ |
| 11. Lunch with boss in company cafeteria | _____ |
| 12. Challenging new assignment | _____ |
| 13. Allowed to accumulate frequent flyer miles for own use | _____ |
| 14. Allowed to ride in company-owned jet for business travel | _____ |
| 15. Assigned latest wearable technology for own use | _____ |
| 16. Private corner office with great view | _____ |
| 17. Assigned a full-time administrative assistant | _____ |
| 18. Documentation of poor performance | _____ |
| 19. Being fired | _____ |
| 20. Being fired and put on industry bad list | _____ |
| 21. Demoted one step | _____ |
| 22. Demoted to entry-level position | _____ |
| 23. Being ridiculed in front of others | _____ |
| 24. Being suspended without pay | _____ |
| 25. Being transferred to undesirable geographic location | _____ |

After completing the ratings, discuss the following issues:

1. Which rewards and punishments received the most varied ratings?

2. Which rewards and punishments received similar ratings?

Another analytical approach would be to compute the means and standard deviations of the valences for each outcome. Each class member could then compare his or her own valence ratings with the class norm. To add to the database, each student might bring back two sets of ratings from employed people who are not in the class.

To apply this technique to the job, modify this form to fit the outcomes available in your situation. Explain to team members that you are attempting to do a better job of rewarding and disciplining and that you need their thoughts. The ratings made by team members might provide fruitful discussion for a staff meeting.

an even broader goal for his team: "We either take the opportunity to transform ourselves or be disrupted and become a loser."[21]

The core finding of goal theory is that individuals who are provided with specific hard goals perform better than those who are given easy, nonspecific, "do your best" goals or no goals. At the same time, however, the individuals must have sufficient ability, accept the goals, and receive feedback related to the task.[22] Our overview of goal theory elaborates on this basic finding.

## Basic Findings of Goal Theory

The premise underlying goal theory (or goal-setting theory) is that behavior is regulated by values and goals. A **goal** is what a person is trying to accomplish. Our values create within us a desire to behave in a way that is consistent with them. For example, a leader who values honesty will establish a goal of hiring only honest employees. The leader would therefore have to make extensive use of reference checks and honesty testing. Edwin A. Locke and Gary P. Latham have incorporated hundreds of studies about goals into a theory of goal setting and task performance.[23] Figure 10-2 summarizes some of the more consistent findings, and the information that follows describes them. A leader should keep these points in mind when motivating people through goal setting.

To begin, remember that *specific goals lead to higher performance than do generalized goals*. Telling someone, "Do your best" is a generalized goal. A specific goal would be, "Increase the number of new hires to our management training program to fifteen for this summer." Another key point is that *performance generally improves in direct proportion to goal difficulty*. The harder one's goal is, the more one accomplishes. An important exception is that when goals are too difficult, they may lower performance. Difficulty in reaching the goal leads to frustration, which in turn leads to lowered performance (as explained in relation to expectancy theory).

The finding about effective goals being realistic has an important exception for the accomplishment of high-level complex tasks. Effective leaders often inspire constituents by framing goals in terms of a noble cause or something heroic.[24] The manager of a group that made photo printers, for example, might explain that making high-quality printers enables people to preserve their memories. Here are two suggestions for developing noble powerful goals:

- Create a big, comprehensive goal: an ideal accomplishment for your group.
- Break the goal down into smaller steps, such as hiring two top-notch workers for the group. Regard each step (or subgoal) as a project designed to get you to your destination. The same approach has been referred to as "running sprints rather than marathons."

*For goals to improve performance, the group member must accept them.* If a group member rejects a goal, he or she will not incorporate it into planning. This is why it is often helpful to discuss goals with group members rather than impose goals on them. Other research, however, suggests that the importance of goal commitment may be overrated.

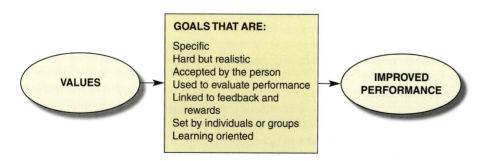

**FIGURE 10-2**    Goal Theory.

Goals appeared to improve performance whether or not people participating in the studies felt committed to them.[25] Despite these recent findings, many managers and leaders think employee commitment to goals is important.

Participating in goal setting has no major effect on the level of job performance except when it improves goal acceptance. Yet the leader should recognize that participation is valuable because it can lead to higher satisfaction with the goal-setting process. *Goals are more effective when they are used to evaluate performance.* When workers know that their performance will be evaluated in terms of how well they attain their goals, the impact of goals increases.

A key principle is that *goals should be linked to feedback and rewards.* Rewarding people for reaching goals is the most widely accepted principle of management. Another goal-setting principle is that *group goal setting is as important as individual goal setting.* Having employees work as teams with a specific team goal, rather than as individuals with only individual goals, increases productivity. Furthermore, a combination of compatible group and individual goals is more effective than either individual or group goals alone.

A final goal-setting principle is that a *learning goal orientation* improves performance more than a *performing goal orientation* does. A person with a learning (or mastery) goal orientation wants to develop competence by acquiring new skills and mastering new situations. In contrast, the person with a performing goal orientation wants to demonstrate and validate his or her competence by seeking favorable judgments and avoiding negative judgments.

A meta-analysis of seventy-six different results with the impact of goals on group performance also supported several of the conclusions just presented. The major findings of the study of studies included the following:

1. Specific difficult goals yield higher group performance than do nonspecific goals.
2. Moderately difficult and easy goals also enhance group performance but to a lesser extent than do difficult goals.
3. Participation did not have much of an influence on the effectiveness of goals.
4. Egocentric goals aimed at maximizing individual performance had a negative impact on group performance.[26]

Encouraging support for the contribution of goals to organizational success comes also from an international research effort conducted over a decade with 8,000 manufacturers in twenty countries. The general finding was that following good management practices enhances organizational success. A specific finding relevant to the present discussion is that when company management supports long-term goals with tough, but achievable short-term performance benchmarks (or goals), the organization is more likely to be profitable.[27]

## The Importance of How Goals Are Attained and Other Concerns

A major concern about using goals to motivate performance is that leaders, as well as other workers, will take unethical and dysfunctional shortcuts to attain their goals. For example, a CEO might drastically reduce investment in research and development and lay off too many valuable workers to meet a profit goal such as earnings per share. Also, managers have been known to engage in unethical behavior such as shipping unfinished products to reach sales goals.[28] To implement goal setting without creating dysfunctions, it is therefore essential to specify *how* the goals will be attained with a particular focus on ethical behavior.

The use of financial incentives for attaining goals often encourages unethical behavior. A striking example of this potential problem was described in Chapter 6 in relation to business ethics. Wells Fargo CEO John Stumpf (now replaced) emphasized cross selling, or pushing account holders to open new accounts with the bank. Bank employees were put under exceptionally high pressure to boost the number of customer accounts. Regional bosses established daily quotas for tellers and bankers, demanding that they stay late or work on weekends or be fired. A negative result of these sales goals was that Wells Fargo representatives opened many accounts for customers without their consent. Federal regulators ultimately imposed heavy fines on the bank, and the Wells Fargo reputation was tarnished. Furthermore, the bank has disbanded sales goals.[29]

A heavy emphasis on goals can also create such problems as workers focusing so much on attaining their goals that they neglect emergencies and new opportunities. For example, a recruiter might ignore an inquiry from an excellent prospect because he or she had to finish a quota of processing job inquiries to the company website. A related problem with goals, such as working to earn large commissions, is that other aspects of a sales representative's position might be ignored. For example, Susan Parker, the owner of the dressmaker Bari Jay, observed that her commissioned sales representative tended to ignore some accounts where they didn't see a big commission opportunity. Parker's antidote to the problem was to give year-end bonuses and profit sharing to employees rather than commissions.[30]

The potential pitfalls of over-reliance on goals have been humorously condensed by group of researchers suggesting the following "warning label" for setting goals:[31]

Goal setting is widely practiced by leaders and managers, but they typically do not give careful consideration to goal theory. Leadership Skill-Building Exercise 10-3 gives you an opportunity to apply what you have learned about goal setting.

## WARNING

Goals may cause systematic problems in organizations due to narrowed focus, increased risk taking, unethical behavior, inhibited learning, decreased cooperation, and decreased intrinsic motivation.

Use care when applying goals in your organization.

## LEADERSHIP SKILL-BUILDING EXERCISE 10-3

### The Application of Goal Theory

In a group of about five to six people, visualize yourself as a task force leader whose mission is to enhance the productivity of individual workers throughout the company. (Productivity in this context refers to the ratio of outputs to inputs, or efficiency.) The company manufactures sports clothing such as athletic shoes, swimsuits, running suits, and soccer outfits. One of the group members plays the role of the task force leader. The leader must help the group establish goals that are likely to be motivational, following the principles of goal theory.

The goal of today's meeting is to establish four goals that are likely to lead to a more productive organization without creating excessive strain on workers. After each team has established it goals, present them to other class members. Students listening to the goals of the other groups might offer constructive feedback.

Practice in setting effective goals is useful because leaders and managers are frequently expected to set goals. When the goal follows at least some of the major findings of goal theory, there is a greater likelihood that productivity will increase.

## Using Recognition and Pride to Motivate Others

Motivating others by giving them recognition and praise can be considered a direct application of positive reinforcement, or reinforcing the right behavior by giving a reward. Recognition programs to reward and motivate employees are a standard practice in business and nonprofit firms. An example is rewarding high-performing employees with a wristwatch inscribed with the company logo or designating them as employee of the month. Pride, as described next, is related to recognition. People who are proud of their work want to be recognized for their good deeds.

Recognition is a strong motivator because it is a normal human need. Tony Schwartz, head of the Energy Project, reminds us that nothing influences employees' engagement as the feeling that they are genuinely cared for and valued by their leaders.[32] (Both being cared for and valued are strong forms of recognition.) Recognition is also effective because most workers feel they do not receive enough recognition. As indicated by Stress in America survey conducted by the American Psychological Association a few years ago, only 46 percent of the employees are satisfied with the recognition practices of their employer.[33]

David Novak, the Yum Brands' former CEO, has received the most recognition of any business executive for emphasizing the motivational impact of recognition. Under Novak's tenure, Yum Brands became a multibillion dollar player in the fast food industry. (Three key brands are KFC, Pizza Hut, and Taco Bell.) Novak believed that he helped turn the company's fortunes around by emphasizing recognition. His formal program of recognition began by rewarding employees for good work by tossing them a rubber chicken. Today, Novak is an evangelist of employee recognition, including a simple "thank you" for a job well done.[34]

To think through the strength of your own need for recognition, take Leadership Self-Assessment Quiz 10-3.

### Appealing to the Recognition Need of Others

To appeal to the recognition need of others, identify a meritorious behavior, and then recognize that behavior with an oral, written, or material reward. Two examples of using recognition to sustain desired behavior (a key aspect of motivation) follow:

- As the team leader, you receive a glowing letter from a customer about Kate, one of your team members, who solved the customer's problem. You have the letter laminated and present it as a gift to Kate. (The behavior you are reinforcing is good customer service.)
- As the manager of IT, one of your software engineers, Evan, suggests that you post an ad on craigslist to fill two vacancies for software technicians. You are skeptical at first, but you give it a try, and your recruiting goals are met. You warmly congratulate Evan. You are rewarding his proactive behavior.

An outstanding advantage of recognition, including praise, as a motivator is that it is no cost or low cost yet powerful. Reward expert Bob Nelson reminds us that while money is important to employees, thoughtful recognition motivates them to elevate their performance.[35] Furthermore, one of the Dale Carnegie principles of leadership states: "Praise the slightest improvement and praise every improvement; be hearty in your approbation and lavish in your praise." This basic principle is strongly supported by decades of research on operant conditioning, including positive reinforcement.[36]

Recognition thus has an enormous return on investment in comparison to a cash bonus. Following are a few suggestions for the motivational use of recognition and praise:

1. To maximize its motivational impact, recognition should be linked to corporate values and should also help workers attain personal goals. Visualize a security guard whose outside passion is sustaining the environment and who becomes recognized

## LEADERSHIP SELF-ASSESSMENT QUIZ 10-3

### How Much Do I Crave Recognition?

*Instructions:* Respond to the following statements on the following scale: disagree strongly (DS), disagree (D), neutral (N), agree (A), and agree strongly (AS).

| | | DS | D | N | A | AS |
|---|---|---|---|---|---|---|
| 1. | I keep (or would keep) almost every plaque, medal, or trophy I have ever received on display in my living quarters. | 1 | 2 | 3 | 4 | 5 |
| 2. | I feel a nice warm glow each time somebody praises my efforts. | 1 | 2 | 3 | 4 | 5 |
| 3. | When somebody tells me "nice job," it makes my day. | 1 | 2 | 3 | 4 | 5 |
| 4. | When I compliment someone, I am really looking for a compliment in return. | 1 | 2 | 3 | 4 | 5 |
| 5. | I would rather win an employee-of-the-month award than receive a $100 bonus for my good work. | 1 | 2 | 3 | 4 | 5 |
| 6. | If I had the resources to make a large donation to charity, I would never make the donation anonymously. | 1 | 2 | 3 | 4 | 5 |
| 7. | Thinking back to my childhood, I adored receiving a gold star or similar acknowledgment from my teacher for my good work. | 1 | 2 | 3 | 4 | 5 |
| 8. | I would rather be designated as *Time* magazine's Person of the Year than be one of the world's richest people. | 1 | 2 | 3 | 4 | 5 |
| 9. | I love to see my name in print or electronically. | 1 | 2 | 3 | 4 | 5 |
| 10. | I do not receive all the respect I deserve. | 1 | 2 | 3 | 4 | 5 |
| 11. | I regularly check to see how many times my name shows up on an Internet search (such as Google or Bing). | 1 | 2 | 3 | 4 | 5 |
| | Total score | | | | | _____ |

*Scoring and Interpretation:* Add the circled numbers to obtain your total score.

- **50–55:** You have an above-average recognition need. Recognition is therefore a strong motivator for you. You will be happiest in a job where you can be recognized for your good deeds.
- **30–49:** You have an average need for recognition and do not require constant reminders that you have done a good job.
- **11–29:** You have a below-average need for recognition and like to have your good deeds speak for themselves. When you do receive recognition, you would prefer that it be quite specific to what you have done, and not too lavish. You would feel comfortable in a work setting with mostly technical people.

with the new title of Security and Energy Conservation Monitor. The title combines his interest in saving energy with the company's interest in keeping outside doors closed and unusual lights turned off.[37]

2. Inform others in the group and organization about the meritorious behavior, such as via a mention in a staff meeting or a posting on the intranet. Also, praise related to specific tasks is usually more effective than general praise. Workers may appreciate praise, but they also prefer to know what specifically they are being praised for, such as, "Your forecast for the sale of our cutting gear to factories in Poland was right on target. Congratulations."

3. Do not use praise to set employees in competition against one another. Praise the employee who merits the praise, but do not suggest that other employees are less praiseworthy, such as: "Great job, José. I wish the rest of the group had put in the same kind of effort."[38]

4. Take into account the individual's preference for the type of praise. A challenge in using recognition effectively is that not everyone responds well to the same form of recognition. An example is that highly technical people tend not to like general praise like "Great job" or "Awesome, baby." Instead, they prefer a laid-back, factual statement of how their work made a contribution. According to one study, the more highly a person sees himself or herself as having a technical orientation, the more the person wants praise to be quite specific and task oriented.[39] The tech center worker who just conquered a virus on your desktop would prefer a compliment such as, "I appreciated you having disabled the virus and restored my computer to full functioning." This type of compliment would be preferable to, "Fantastic, you are a world-class virus fighter."

## Appealing to Pride

Wanting to feel proud motivates many workers, and giving recognition for a job well done helps satisfy this desire to feel proud. Being proud of what you accomplish is more of an internal (intrinsic) motivator than an external (extrinsic) motivator, such as receiving a gift. Giving workers an opportunity to experience pride can therefore be a strong internal motivator, yet they simultaneously receive recognition.

Imagine that you are the assistant service manager at a company that customizes recreational vehicles to meet the requirements of individual clients. Your manager asks you to prepare a PowerPoint presentation of trends in customization for people who live most of the year in their recreational vehicles RVs. You make your presentation to top management, the group applauds, executives shake your hand, and later you receive several congratulatory e-mail messages. One of the many emotions you experience is likely to be pride in having performed well. You are motivated to keep up the good work.

Workers can also experience pride in relation to recognition symbols. For example, a worker might receive a floor clock for having saved the company thousands of dollars in shipping costs. The clock might be more valuable to the worker as a symbol of accomplishment than as a household decoration. The feeling of pride stems from having accomplished a worthwhile activity (saving the company money) rather than from being awarded a floor clock.

According to consultant Jon R. Katzenbach, managers and leaders can take steps to motivate through pride. A key tactic is for the manager to set his or her compass on pride, not money. It is more important for workers to be proud of what they are doing day by day than for them to be proud of reaching a major goal. The manager should celebrate steps (or attaining small goals) equally as much as landings (major goals). (As described earlier, the feeling of making progress contributes to the meaningfulness of work.) The most effective pride builders are masters at identifying and recognizing the small achievements that will instill pride in their people.[40]

## Coaching as an Approach to Motivation

Effective leaders are good coaches, and good coaches are effective motivators. The coaching demands are much less rigorous for leaders who have little face-to-face contact with organization members, such as financial deal makers, CEOs, and chairpersons of the board. Nevertheless, coaching plays an important role in the organization, as expressed by John Russell, managing director of Harley-Davidson Ltd: "I never cease to be amazed at the power of the coaching process to draw out the skills or talent that was previously hidden within an individual, and which invariably finds a way to solve a problem previously thought insolvable."[41]

Coaching is a way of enabling others to act and build on their strengths. The major purpose of coaching is to bring about constructive change in performance and/or behavior. To coach is to care enough about people to invest time in building personal relationships with them. The organization also benefits from coaching because of the elevated productivity of many of the workers who are coached. Coaching is also seen as a key vehicle for engaging (or motivating) workers. A survey-based report found that organizations have less money to compensate employees, so they look to coaching and development as a method to boost engagement and retention.[42]

## Key Characteristics of Coaching

Coaching in the workplace might ordinarily be explained as the art of management. Because a coaching relationship is unique, the person being coached is better motivated to accomplish goals for the good of the organization. Coaching is an interaction between two people, usually the manager and an employee. The purpose of the interaction is to help the employee learn from the job in order to help his or her development. The interaction of the two personalities influences the coaching outcome. Some leaders, for example, can successfully coach certain people but not others.

Coaching requires a moderate degree of interpersonal risk and trust on the part of both people in the relationship. The coach might give the person being coached wrong advice. Or the person being coached might reject the coach's encouragement. Think of the risk involved when a basketball player asks the coach for advice on how to correct a shot that is not working well. As a result of the coaching, the player might shoot more poorly, to the embarrassment of both. Similarly, an organizational leader might coach a team member in a direction that backfires—for example, that results in even fewer sales than before.

Effective coaching focuses on the growth and development of individuals rather than telling them what to do in a given situation. To help subordinates grow and develop, the leader as coach should give subordinates the resources they need to make their own decisions. The people being coached should be challenged to find the right solution, and then should be provided feedback on how well they have performed.[43]

Assume that a manager wants the accident rate on the construction of skyscrapers reduced substantially. Instead of telling a direct report exactly how to accomplish this goal, the manager might point to new sources of help for accident reduction. In the process, the direct report might find solutions the manager did not already know about.

At its best, coaching offers concrete contributions, including higher motivation. An effective coach keeps spirits up and offers praise and recognition frequently. Good coaching also leads to personal development. Group members are encouraged to cross-train and serve as backups for each other. Good coaching also improves group performance. The effective coach makes team members aware of one another's skills, and how these skills can contribute to attaining the group's goals.[44]

The accompanying Leader in Action profile illustrates how effective coaching might contribute to an organization.

 **LEADER IN ACTION**

### Accounting Firm Partner Gary Coaches Tax Accountant Vanessa

Gary is a partner in a public accounting firm located in a medium-size city. The firm provides a full range of accounting services to small business and individuals, including basic accounting, tax accounting, estate planning, and financial counseling. The firm has a staff of approximately 90 employees. Although the accounting firm is still profitable, Gary has concerns about the volume of activity in the tax accounting department. Today Gary meets with Vanessa, the tax accounting supervisor to discuss his concerns. A partial transcript of their meeting follows:

*Gary:* How are you doing these days, Vanessa?

*Vanessa:* Thanks for asking, Gary. I'm doing pretty well, and my tax accountants remain a loyal, hardworking group.

*Gary:* I agree that your group including you is hardworking and loyal. But as we've exchanged information about in

## LEADER IN ACTION (continued)

e-mails, the revenues from tax accounting have been sliding a little for the past five quarters.

*Vanessa:* The way the world is going, that's inevitable.

*Gary:* What do you mean by "The way the world is going"?

*Vanessa:* One problem is that small businesses are on the decline in our area, and the population is shrinking a bit. Yet the monster problem is that so many of our former clients are using accounting software to prepare their own taxes. This is true, especially for uncomplicated tax returns.

*Gary:* What you say is true, but what are you doing to counteract these trends?

*Vanessa:* My group and I have out extra effort into providing outstanding service to clients. We do our best to search for ways to lower taxes, and to explain any errors in the data they present us.

*Gary:* Exceptional customer service is always a winning proposition, but what other creative suggestions can you make for bringing in more clients?

*Vanessa:* Maybe our firm should do more marketing through television, radio, the social media, and print ads.

*Gary:* Your suggestion is sensible, Vanessa, but our firm has found that advertising has not been cost effective for us.

Besides, the principals think that advertising is undignified for an accounting firm. What other suggestions can you shake loose.

*Vanessa:* Gary, here is my last and final offer (said with a smile). I have heard that community outreach by tax accountants can bring in clients. Whenever we can create the opportunity, or the opportunity presents itself, we can talk to groups about tax preparation and planning. For example, I have heard that many assisted-living residences enjoy having an outside speaker. And seniors in these residences usually need help in preparing their taxes. Although they do not have active income, their investments complicate tax preparation.

*Gary:* Vanessa, I think your last and final offer is a winner. How about sending me a written description of your community outreach program? Our firm will support you in any way we can,

### QUESTIONS

1. How effective does Gary appear to be in his coaching role?
2. What suggestions can you offer Gary so he could be more effective in his coaching role?

## Coaching Skills and Techniques

Leaders and managers have varied aptitudes for coaching. One way to acquire coaching skill is to study basic principles and suggestions and then practice them. Another is to attend a training program for coaching that involves modeling (learning by imitation) and role playing. Here we examine a number of suggestions for coaching, all of which might also apply to coaching a group or a team as well as an individual. The typical scenario for a leader to coach a team would take place in a meeting with all or most of the group. If implemented with skill, the suggestions will improve the chances that coaching will lead to improved performance of individuals and groups.

1. ***Define the issues and communicate clear expectations to group members.*** A logical first step in coaching a subordinate is to explain why you are coaching that person in the first place.[45] For example, you might want a team member to produce a higher number of creative ideas. For people to perform well and to continue to learn and grow, they need a clear perception of what is expected of them. The expectations of a position become the standards by which performance will be judged, thus serving as a base point for coaching. If a team member is supposed to contribute three new ideas each month for improving operations, coaching is justified when an average of only one idea per month is forthcoming.

2. ***Build relationships.*** Effective coaches build personal relationships with team members and work to improve their interpersonal skills.[46] Having established rapport with

team members facilitates entering into a coaching relationship with them. The suggestions that follow about active listening and giving emotional support are part of relationship building.

3. *Give feedback on areas that require specific improvement.* To coach a group member toward higher levels of performance, the leader pinpoints what specific behavior, attitude, or kills require improvement. An effective coach might say, "I read the product-expansion proposal you submitted. It's OK, but it falls short of your usual level of creativity. Our competitors are already carrying each product you mentioned. Have you thought about …?" Another important factor in giving specific feedback is to avoid generalities and exaggerations, such as, "You never come up with a good product idea" or "You are the most unimaginative product development specialist I have ever known." To give good feedback, the leader or manager has to observe performance and behavior directly and frequently, such as by watching a supervisor dealing with a safety problem.

A major challenge in giving feedback is that many people find negative feedback to be uncomfortable. It is therefore helpful to get the person's buy-in, or at least acceptance, to receive the feedback. For example, if coaching on the fly, the leader might ask, "Chris, I'd like to offer some quick feedback because I want to help you. Is this a good time?"[47]

Feedback is also likely to be less intimidating when the coach explains which behaviors should decrease and which should increase. This approach is a variation of combining compliments with criticism to avoid insulting the person being coached. You might say, "Tanya, I need you to place more emphasis on quality and less on speed."

Feedback can also be made less intimidating when the coach begins with a question, such as *How do you think you're doing?*" The question helps give the person being coached joint ownership of the problem, and helps him or her feel included rather than excluded.[48]

Should the coach be dealing with a person who is highly sensitive to criticism, it can be helpful to convert the criticism into a positive suggestion to avoid intimidating the person being coached. Replace "A few of your facts were way off in your last report" with "You could improve your accuracy by double checking your facts."

Inside or outside of a formal coaching session, feedback is a vital aspect of the leadership role. Tiffany Cooper Gueye, chief executive officer of BELL, a nonprofit organization that assists urban children, explains: "Assuming I have all the right people in the right positions, I think the most important thing I can do for them is provide direct, honest, clear feedback. And I get a lot of feedback in return from my direct reports that they really value that."[49]

4. *Listen actively.* Listening is an essential ingredient in any coaching session. An active listener tries to grasp both facts and feelings. Observing the group member's nonverbal communication is another part of active listening. The leader must also be patient and not poised for a rebuttal of any difference of opinion between him or her and the group member. Beginning each coaching session with a question helps set the stage for active listening. The question will also spark the employee's thinking and frame the discussion: For example, "How might we use the new database of customers who have purchased similar products help our staff generate more sales?"

Part of being a good listener is encouraging the person being coached to talk about his or her performance. Asking open-ended questions facilitates a flow of conversation: For example, ask, "How did you feel about the way you handled conflict with the marketing group yesterday?" A close-ended question covering the same issue would be, "Do you think you could have done a better job of handling conflict with the marketing group yesterday?"

Listening often begins by asking powerful questions, and then engaging in dialogue to arrive at new ideas, insights, and action steps together. A powerful question might be, "You have so much talent. What aren't you living up to your potential?"[50]

5. *Help remove obstacles.* To perform at anywhere near top capacity, individuals may need help in removing obstacles such as a maze of rules and regulations and rigid budgeting. An important role for the leader of an organizational unit is thus to be a

barrier buster. A leader or manager is often in a better position than a group member to gain approval from a higher level manager, find money from another budget line, expedite a purchase order, or authorize hiring a temporary worker to provide assistance. Yet, if the coach is too quick to remove obstacles for the group member, the latter may not develop enough self-reliance.

6. *Give emotional support and empathy.* By being helpful and constructive, the leader provides much-needed emotional support to the group member who is not performing at his or her best. A coaching session should not be an interrogation. An effective way of giving emotional support is to use positive rather than negative motivators. For example, the leader might say, "I liked some things you did yesterday, and I have a few suggestions that might bring you closer to peak performance."

Displaying empathy is an effective way to give emotional support. Indicate with words that you understand the challenge the group member faces with a statement such as, "I understand that working with a reduced staff has placed you under heavy time pressures." The genuine concern you show will help establish the rapport useful in working out the problem together.

7. *Reflect content or meaning.* An effective way of reflecting meaning is to rephrase and summarize concisely what the group member is saying. A substandard performer might say, "The reason I've fallen so far behind is that our company has turned into a bureaucratic nightmare. We're being hit right and left with forms to fill out for customer satisfaction. I have fifty e-mail messages that I haven't read yet." You might respond, "You're falling so far behind because you have so many forms and messages that require attention." The group member might then respond with something like, "That's exactly what I mean. I'm glad you understand my problem." (Notice that the leader is also giving the group member an opportunity to express the feelings behind his or her problem.)

8. *Give some gentle advice and guidance.* Too much advice giving interferes with two-way communication, yet some advice can elevate performance. Also, workers being coached usually expect to receive some advice. The manager should assist the group member in answering the question "What can I do about this problem?" Advice in the form of a question or suppositional statement is often effective. One example is, "Could the root of your problem be insufficient planning?" A direct statement such as, "The root of your problem is probably insufficient planning," often makes people resentful and defensive. By responding to a question, the person being coached is likely to feel more involved in making improvements.

Part of giving gentle guidance for improvement is to use the word *could* instead of *should*. To say, "You should do this," implies that the person is currently doing something wrong, which can trigger defensiveness. Saying, "You could do this," leaves the person with a choice: Accept or reject your input, and weigh the consequences.[51] (You *could* accept this advice to become a better coach!)

9. *Allow for modeling of desired performance and behavior.* An effective coaching technique is to show the group member, by example, what constitutes the desired behavior. Assume that a manager has been making statements to customers that stretch the truth, such as falsely saying that the product met a zero-defects standard. In coaching him, the manager's boss might allow the manager to observe how she handles a similar situation with a customer. The manager's boss might telephone a customer and say, "You have been inquiring about whether we have adopted a zero-defects standard for our laser printers. Right now, we are doing our best to produce error-free products. Yet so far we do not have a formal zero-defects program. We stand by our printers and will fix any defect at no cost to you."

10. *Gain a commitment to change.* Unless the leader receives a commitment from the team member to carry through with the proposed solution to a problem, the team member may not attain higher performance. An experienced manager develops an intuitive sense for when employees are serious about performance improvement. Two clues that commitment to change is lacking are (1) over-agreeing about the need for change and (2) agreeing to change without display of emotion.

11. **Applaud good results.** Effective coaches on the playing field and in the workplace are cheerleaders. They give encouragement and positive reinforcement by applauding good results. Some effective coaches shout with joy when an individual or team achieves outstanding results; others applaud. Good results, of course, can only be applauded if results are measured.

The scientifically minded reader might be wondering if there is evidence that coaching by leaders and managers has a tangible effect on performance. A positive answer is furnished by a recent study of conducted with 1,246 sales representatives in 136 teams within a pharmaceutical company over a year. Manager's coaching skill was evaluated in the context of a training exercise that simulated pharmaceutical representative interactions with physicians. Coaching skill was rated by both the managers' direct bosses and their regional supervisors. The study found that the managers' coaching skill was directly related to the annual sales goal attainment of the sales representatives that they supervised. Part of the good results attained by coaching was attributed to the managers providing clarity about job expectations.[52]

Leadership Self-Assessment Quiz 10-4 will help you think through the development you need to be an effective coach. If you are already an effective coach, look for ways to improve. Leadership Skill-Building Exercise 10-4 gives you a chance to practice coaching.

# LEADERSHIP SELF-ASSESSMENT QUIZ 10-4

### Characteristics of an Effective Coach

*Instructions:* Following is a list of traits, attitudes, and behaviors characteristic of effective coaches. Place a check mark next to each trait, attitude, or behavior that you need to develop along those lines (for example, whether you need to become more patient). On a separate sheet of paper, design an action plan for improvement for each trait, attitude, or behavior that you need to develop. An example of an action plan for improving patience might be, "I'll ask people to tell me when I appear too impatient. I'll also try to develop self-control about my impatience."

| TRAIT, ATTITUDE, OR BEHAVIOR | |
|---|---|
| 1. Empathy (putting self in other person's shoes) | ☐ |
| 2. Listening skill | ☐ |
| 3. Insight into people | ☐ |
| 4. Diplomacy and tact | ☐ |
| 5. Patience toward people | ☐ |
| 6. Concern for welfare of people | ☐ |
| 7. Low hostility toward people | ☐ |
| 8. Self-confidence and emotional security | ☐ |
| 9. Noncompetitiveness with group members | ☐ |
| 10. Enthusiasm for people | ☐ |
| 11. Satisfaction in helping others grow | ☐ |
| 12. Interest in development of group members | ☐ |
| 13. High expectations for each group member | ☐ |
| 14. Ability to give authentic feedback | ☐ |
| 15. Interest in people's potential | ☐ |
| 16. Honesty and integrity (or trustworthiness) | ☐ |
| 17. Friendliness | ☐ |
| 18. Develops trust and respect | ☐ |

*Source:* Items 11–15 gathered from information in William D. Hitt, *The Leader-Manager: Guidelines for Action* (Columbus, OH: Battelle Press, 1988), pp. 183–186.William D. Hitt, *The Leader-Manager: Guidelines for Action* (Columbus, OH: Battelle Press, 1988), pp. 183–186.

## LEADERSHIP SKILL-BUILDING EXERCISE 10-4

### Coaching for Improved Performance

Clayton is a financial consultant (stockbroker) at a branch office of an established financial services firm. His manager, Marlene, is concerned that Clayton is 25 percent below quota in sales of a new gold mutual fund offered by the company. Marlene schedules a late afternoon meeting in her office to attempt to help Clayton make quota. She has told Clayton, "I want to talk about your sales performance on the new gold fund and see if I can be helpful." Clayton is concerned that the meeting might be a discipline session in disguise.

Have one member of the class assume the role of Marlene, and another the role of Clayton. Marlene will attempt to implement recommended coaching techniques. Other class members will watch and then provide constructive feedback.

This exercise is a key skill builder because so much of face-to-face leadership involves working out performance problems with group members. If every employee were an outstanding, independent performer, we would have less need for managers and leaders.

## Executive Coaching and Leadership Effectiveness

A form of coaching in vogue is for managers to consult professional coaches to help them become more effective leaders and to guide them in their careers. **Executive coaching** is "a one-on-one development process formally contracted between a coach and a management-level client to help achieve goals related to professional development and/or business performance."[53]

In the past, business psychologists were typically hired as outside coaches to help managers become more effective leaders. Today, people from a wide variety of backgrounds become executive coaches, as well as career coaches and life coaches. Many executive coaches are former executives themselves.

### Specific Forms of Assistance Provided by Executive Coaches

Executive coaches help managers become more effective leaders by helping them in a variety of ways. A variety of reasons for hiring coaches are described next. However, it is unlikely that one coach would provide all these services, or that one manager would want or need all of them.

- Helping corporate stars attain peak performance, similar to an athletic coach working with an outstanding athlete. One approach to heightened performance is to help the leader uncover personal assets and strengths he or she may not have known existed. An example would be discovering that the leader has untapped creativity and imagination.[54]
- Counseling the leader about weaknesses that could interfere with effectiveness, such as being too hostile and impatient. The coach will also solicit feedback by interviewing coworkers and subordinates, and then distilling the feedback to help the executive.
- Serving as a sounding board when the leader faces a complex decision about strategy, operations, or human resource issues. Closely related to being a sounding board is a coach's ability to ask tough questions, such as asking why the executive is pursuing a particular strategy.[55]
- Making specific suggestions about self-promotion and image enhancement, including suggestions about appearance and mannerisms.
- Helping the leader achieve a better balance between work and family life, thereby having more focused energy for the leadership role.

- Serving as a trusted confidante to discuss issues the leader might feel uncomfortable talking about with others: for example, talking about feeling insecure in his or her position.
- Giving advice about career management, such as developing a career path.
- Strengthening the executive's strategic decision-making skills by helping him or her think more broadly about issues and appreciate how his or her actions will affect the organizational system. The coach might point out a blind spot in the leader's decision making, such as neglecting part of the human consequences of a decision.
- Serving as a coach to the entire team to help guide the team to insights into their behavior as it affects performance, and to help improve the teamwork.[56]

Note that the coach works as an adviser about behavior but does not explicitly help the leader with functional details of the job, such as how to develop a new product strategy or design an organization.

The leader/manager's employer usually hires the executive coach. The purpose of engaging the coach could be to accelerate the development of a star player or assist an executive who is having soft-skill problems. For example, the direct reports of a manager at a consulting firm referred to her as a "weed whacker," so an executive coach was hired to help the executive develop more emotional intelligence. The executive soon learned that employees perceived in her tone and body language that she was attacking them. Coaching helped her soften her approach and work better with others.[57]

A refinement of individual coaching is for the coach to work with both the individual and his or her work associates. The coach solicits feedback from the group members and involves them in helping the manager improve. For example, the coach might tell team members to assert their rights when the manager throws a temper tantrum or makes unreasonable demands. The coach might also work with the superiors or peers of the person being coached to obtain useful feedback about the leader's behavior.

## Contributions of and Concerns About Executive Coaching

Executive coaching may frequently accomplish several of the ends specified in the previous list. Executive coaching, however, has some potential drawbacks for the leader. A major problem is that a coach may give advice that backfires because he or she does not understand the particular work setting. One outside coach told a manager in an information technology firm that she should become more decisive in her decision making and less dependent on consensus. The advice backfired because the culture of the firm emphasized consensus decision making. Furthermore, many people who present themselves as executive coaches may not be professionally qualified or may not have much knowledge about business.[58]

An ethical problem is that many coaches delve into personal and emotional issues that should be reserved for mental health professionals. The leader who is performing poorly because of a deep-rooted problem, such as hostility toward others, is given superficial advice about making nice. (The opposite ethical problem occurs when a relationship coach offer business advice, without having the experience or qualifications to offer such advice.) Another potential ethical problem is that the leader/manager may become too dependent on the coach, checking with him or her before making any consequential decision.[59]

## READER'S ROADMAP

So far, we have studied considerable information about the nature of leadership; the attributes, behaviors, and styles of leaders; the ethics and social responsibility of leaders; and how leaders exert power and use politics and influence. The techniques for developing teamwork are part of a leader's relationship with the group, as is the subject of this chapter: motivation and coaching skills. In the next chapter, we describe creativity and innovation as part of leadership.

## SUMMARY

Effective leaders are outstanding motivators and coaches, and the role of the leader and manager today emphasizes coaching. A broad purpose of leaders applying motivation and coaching techniques is getting employees involved in their work and excited about working for the organization. Engagement is reflected in employee willingness to stay with the firm and go beyond the call of duty. Leaders use motivation and coaching techniques to help keep employees engaged. Employee engagement has a positive impact on productivity. Meaningful work is a key driver of worker engagement. The opportunity to lead projects or task forces makes work meaningful, as does having a good relationship with the leader, and the feeling of making daily progress in one's work.

The expectancy theory of motivation is useful for developing motivational skills because it is comprehensive, building on other explanations of motivation. Expectancy theory has three major components: valence, instrumentality, and expectancy. *Valence* is the worth or attractiveness of an outcome. Each work situation has multiple outcomes, and each outcome has a valence of its own. Valences range from −100 to +100 in the version of expectancy theory presented here. Zero valences reflect indifference and therefore are not motivational. Very high valences help explain why some people persist in efforts despite a low probability of payoff. *Instrumentality* is the individual's assessment of the probability that performance will lead to certain outcomes. (An outcome is anything that might stem from performance, such as a reward.) *Expectancy* is an individual's assessment of the probability that effort will lead to performing the task correctly.

Expectancy theory has implications and provides guidelines for leaders, including the following: (1) determine necessary performance levels; (2) make the performance level attainable; (3) train and encourage people; (4) make explicit the link between rewards and performance; (5) make sure the rewards are large enough; (6) analyze factors that oppose the effectiveness of the reward; (7) explain the meaning and implications of second-level outcomes; and (8) understand individual differences in valences.

Goal setting is a basic process that is directly or indirectly part of all major theories of motivation. Goal theory includes the following ideas: (1) specific and difficult goals result in high performance (yet outrageous goals can inspire); (2) goals must be accepted by group members; (3) goals are more effective when they are linked to feedback and rewards; (4) the combination of individual and group goals is very effective; and (5) a learning goal orientation is more effective than a performance goal orientation. A meta-analysis of many studies supports the conclusions just presented about the effectiveness of goals.

A major concern about using goals to motivate performance is that leaders, as well as other workers, will take unethical and dysfunctional shortcuts to attain their goals. A heavy emphasis on goals can also create problems such as workers focusing so much on attaining their goals that they neglect emergencies and new opportunities.

Motivating others by giving them recognition and praise can be considered a direct application of positive reinforcement. Recognition programs to reward and motivate employees are standard practice. Recognition is a strong motivator because it is a normal human need to crave recognition, and workers often do not feel they receive enough recognition. To appeal to the recognition need, identify a meritorious behavior and then recognize that behavior with an oral, written, or material reward. To maximize its motivational impact, recognition should be linked to corporate values and personal goals. Recognition and praise are no-cost or low-cost motivators that are powerful.

Giving workers an opportunity to experience pride can be a strong internal motivator, yet workers still receive recognition. To motivate through pride, it is best for the manager to set the compass on pride, not money, and for workers to be proud of daily accomplishments.

A major purpose of coaching is to achieve enthusiasm and high performance in a team setting. Several characteristics of coaching contribute to its close relationship with leadership. Coaching is a two-way process, suggesting that being a great coach requires having a talented team. Coaching requires a moderate degree of interpersonal risk and trust on the part of both sides in the relationship. Effective coaching focuses on the growth and development of people rather than telling them how to deal with a given situation.

Suggestions for improving coaching are as follows: (1) define the communicate clear expectations, (2) build relationships, (3) give feedback on areas that require specific improvement, (4) listen actively, (5) help remove obstacles, (6) give emotional support and empathy, (7) reflect content or meaning, (8) give gentle advice and guidance, (9) allow for modeling of desired performance and behavior, (10) gain a commitment to change, and (11) applaud good results.

Managers frequently consult executive coaches to help them be more effective leaders. Such coaches provide a variety of services, including helping attain peak performance, counseling about weaknesses, helping achieve balance in life, helping the leader uncover hidden assets, and giving career advice. Executive coaching often achieves its purposes, yet there are potential problems: Executive coaches can give bad advice, the coach might be unqualified in general or to deal with mental health issues, and the leader may become too dependent on the coach.

## KEY TERMS

engagement  252
meaningful work  254
expectancy theory  257
valence  257

outcome  257
instrumentality  258
expectancy  258
self-efficacy  258

goal  261
executive coaching  272

## GUIDELINES FOR ACTION AND SKILL DEVELOPMENT

A positive picture of worker engagement is usually painted by management researchers and management consultants. Nevertheless, there appears to be an optimum amount of engagement for leaders and their subordinates. It is possible for highly engaged employees to become so involved in their job that they become too little concerned about other important parts of their life. Studies have found that highly engaged workers tend to suffer from work interfering with personal life, including the development of health problems. Highly engaged workers are also at risk for burnout, leading to poor job performance.[60]

Given that recognition can be such a relatively low-cost, yet highly effective motivator, the leader/manager should keep in mind available forms of recognition. In addition to considering those in the following list, use your imagination to think of other forms of recognition. For the recognition technique to work well, it should have high valence for the person or group under consideration.

- Compliments, such as *"You help us accomplish our mission,"* or *"Our customers love what you are doing for them"* to give encouragement for a job well done
- Comradeship with the boss
- A pat on the back or a handshake
- Public expression of appreciation such as on an intranet or social media website (company exclusive or public), including a note of thanks to the individual (handwritten, e-mail, or text message)
- A flattering letter from a customer distributed over e-mail
- Employee of the month award
- A gift from the company recognition program, such as a watch, a clock, or a pin

Approaches to recognition may pack an extra punch when they do not take the same form every time. For a job well done, the worker might receive a warm e-mail one week, a gift certificate the next, and perhaps an employee of the month designation in the future.

### Discussion Questions and Activities

1. Kim Jordan, the executive chair of New Belgian Brewery, emphasizes her high level of humanism. What is your opinion about a company that produces beer still being humanistic?
2. Why should a leader be concerned about employee engagement when almost all of his or her direct reports are corporate professionals?
3. To what extent would the amount of financial compensation you receive in a position influence your level of engagement?
4. Identify several outcomes you expect from occupying a leadership position. What valences do you attach to them?
5. How can the influence exerted by a charismatic leader tie in with expectancy theory?
6. What is an example of a noble cause the plant manager of a division that manufactures paper-clips might use to motivate workers?
7. For purposes of recognition, many companies give out watches, clocks, sport shirts, and crystal vases with a company logo embedded. What do you think of the effectiveness of this form of recognition?
8. Imagine that you are a hospital administrator, and you are told that a custodial worker just saved the life of a patient who was choking on a pretzel. What type of recognition would you give this custodial worker?
9. Imagine that you have a couple of extra high performers reporting to you, who are carrying out all their job responsibilities in a superior manner. What kind of coaching might you conduct with these people?
10. Ask a manager or coach to describe the amount of coaching he or she does on the job. Be prepared to bring your findings back to class.

## LEADERSHIP CASE PROBLEM A

### Firing Up the Commercial Uniform Team

Derrick is the regional manager for Commercial Uniform Inc. (CUI), a large company that provides uniforms for organizations such as hotels, car rental agencies, and banks that provide uniforms for their employees. CUI also provides dry cleaning for the uniforms. Derrick is responsible for the operations of providing the uniforms and associated dry cleaning. His other responsibilities also include running the office and making sure that the company fleet of delivery vans is running smoothly.

The van drivers are the heart of the commercial laundry business because they pick up and deliver the uniforms that require dry cleaning. The drivers also deliver new uniforms to customers. Wages of the van drivers have been flat for several years because competition makes it difficult to increase prices for services. Also, there has been a slight decline in the sale of uniforms because more workplaces, such as hotels have shifted toward more informal business attire. Derrick recognizes also that other workers at CUI are experiencing similar problems about flat wages, and a business in slight decline.

Derrick notes, "Uniforms help provide discipline to a business but they are losing a little of their past popularity. It is much cheaper for a hotel, bank, or large automobile service center to allow employees to wear their own clothing to work. Derrick has been in contact with HR director Madison to discuss the challenges of keeping the van drivers charged up when raises and bonuses will be almost nonexistent for the foreseeable future. Madison says she and the CEO believe that recognition in the form of praise should be an effective way to motivate almost any van driver. Madison said she would be sending instructions to Derrick about praising drivers by both e-mail and the company intranet. Derrick believes that he does use praise, but would now do it more systematically, following some of the ideas in the information disseminated by Madison.

Two days later, Derrick dropped by the cubicle of Courtney, the supervisor of customer billing. After a couple of minutes of talk about her work, Derrick said, "Courtney, it's just great how you keep the money flowing into the company bank account. Without your efforts CUI would have to shut down." Courtney replied, "Thanks Derrick, have a great day."

Laster that day, Derrick visited a nearby company warehouse where the drivers load their vans before taking off on their route. Derrick said to Hector a van driver, "Top job. Without you making timely stops at your customers, we have no business." Hector smiled and said, "Thanks Derrick. It feels great to make a contribution."

Derrick liked the way her praise was going, so when she ran into Kaitlin, the sales manager, in the office, he said, "You're doing great. It's so much fun to be working with a cool and talented woman." Kaitlin replied with a quizzical look, "Good enough Derrick, whatever you think."

During a visit to the field, Derrick commented to Boris, a supervisor of van drivers, "I like how hard and fast your drivers work. You set a high standard for our operations." Boris replied, "Right on, Derrick."

### Case Questions

1. How well is Derrick praising his workers? What advice can you offer him to be more effective in her praise?
2. Which statement of praise do you think was the most effective, and why?
3. Which statement of praise do you think was the least effective, and why?

## ASSOCIATED ROLE PLAY

One student plays the role of Derrick who wants to use recognition to fire up several members of the uniform delivery team. One student plays the role of Clyde, a van driver who thinks he has been doing a mediocre job, and because of it worries about his job security. He is therefore somewhat surprised to receive recognition from Derrick. Another student plays the role of Vanessa, a van driver who thinks she is the best driver in the company. When Derrick drops by Vanessa is expecting effusive praise. Run the role play for about nine minutes with observers providing feedback on the effectiveness of the recognition Derrick provides.

## LEADERSHIP CASE PROBLEM B

### Tyler Faces a Feedback Challenge

Tyler is the chief operations officer (COO) of Mining and Drilling Co., a company that manufactures equipment for the mining industry. With the CEO being heavily involved in strategy formulation, mergers and acquisitions, and company finances, Tyler is essentially in charge of running the company. With all the exploration for resources in recent years, the company is prospering.

Tyler sees a major part of his role at Mining and Drilling to be that of a leader who inspires, guides, and monitors the behavior of subordinates. At the moment, Tyler is facing what he considers to be a delicate issue. He wants to provide constructive feedback to one of his direct reports, Gus, the director of materials management. The feedback has to do with incidents he heard about Gus's relationships with staff members. Although none of these incidents or reported incidents rumors deals with behavior that violates the code of conduct at Mining and Drilling, they suggest poor professionalism.

Sherry, an office manager, once told Tyler that Gus often stares at her in a lecherous manner. Sherry also said that Gus tends to stand about five inches from her when they have a conversation about work-related matters.

A few weeks ago, Tyler heard Garth, the IT manager, joke about how much advice and help Gus wants with his off-the-job communication technology pursuits,

such as setting up a smart house and interconnecting the electronic devices in his home.

Last week Tyler asked Kaitlin, his administrative assistant, how she and her family planned to spend the weekend. Kaitlin said with a sarcastic expression on her face, "As usual, I will have to put a lot of time into deleting the dozens of text messages Gus sends me. I don't do anything to encourage Gus, but he keeps bombarding me with silly messages. Last night he sent me five texts about cute things his dog did recently."

Tyler was wondering how he should approach Gus about his behavior unbecoming to a company executive, yet still not in violation of company policy. "I should give Gus some feedback about these problems," thought Tyler. "Yet I don't want to damage my relationship with one of the key leaders at Mining and Drilling."

### Questions

1. Are the reported incidents in relation to Gus even worth the attention of a COO?
2. If you think the case describes a problem worthy of his attention, how should Tyler coach Gus about the reported incidents?
3. What opening line do you recommend for Tyler if he does hold a coaching session with Gus about the incidents reported in the case?

## ASSOCIATED ROLE PLAY

You guessed it. One person plays the role of CEO Tyler who decides to hold a coaching session with COO Gus about the latter's unprofessional behavior. Tyler feels awkward because he is not even certain that he should be providing feedback to Gus about the incidents. Gus

assumes that the session will be about a key operations or strategy issue. Furthermore, Gus doesn't think he has a problem about behaving professionally. Observers will provide feedback on how well the coaching and feedback session went.

## LEADERSHIP SKILL-BUILDING EXERCISE 10-5

### My Leadership Portfolio

One of the easiest and most powerful ways of motivating people is to recognize their efforts, as described in this chapter. Like any other interpersonal skill, being effective at giving recognition takes practice. During the next week, find three people to recognize, and observe how they react to your recognition. For example, if a server gives you fine service, explain after the meal how much you enjoyed the service and leave a larger-than-average tip. If your hair stylist does a fine job,

similarly provide a compliment and a generous tip. Or find some helper to recognize with a compliment but without a tip. Observe the responses of these people—both their facial expressions and what they say. Of even more importance, observe if any of these people appear eager to serve you the next time you interact with them.

As with other parts of your leadership portfolio, keep a written record of what happened to you and how much skill you think you have developed.

# NOTES

1. Original story based on facts and observations in the following sources: Michelle Goodman, "Skin In the Game: How to Build an Employee-Owned Business," *Entrepreneur*, February 2015, pp. 64–69; "New Belgium President and COO Christine Perich to Assume CEO Position," *www.newbelgium.com*, August 10, 2015, pp. 3–4; Kim Jordan, "Our Team," *New Belgium Family Foundation* (www.nbfamilyfoundation .org), pp. 1–2. Retrieved August 4, 2016; "History and Core Values and Beliefs," *www.newbelgium.com*, pp. 1–3. Retrieved August 4, 2016. Michael Zakaras, "New Belgium Brewing's Kim Jordan on How to Get Your Team to Own It," *Forbes* (www.forbes.com), March 25, 2016, pp. 1–7.

2. Michael S. Christian, Adela S. Garza, and Jerel E. Slaughter, "Work Engagement: A Quantitative Review and Test of Its Relation with Task Performance," *Personnel Psychology*, no. 1, 2011, p. 89.

3. Maria Tims, Arnbold B. Bakker, and Desponia Xanthopoulou, "Do Transformational Leaders Enhance Their Followers' Daily Work Engagement?" *The Leadership Quarterly*, February 2011, pp. 121–131.

4. Steve Crabtree, "Worldwide, 13% of Employees Are Engaged at Work," *Gallup.com* (http://www.gallup .com), October 8, 2013, pp. 1–6.

5. *Deloitte Millennial Survey* cited in Christie Mann, "3 Unconscious Habits Eroding Employee Engagement," *www.clomedia.com*, August 10, 2016, p. 1.

6. Cited in Gary Kranz, "Employees Want Feedback, Even If It's Negative," *Workforce Management*, February 2010, p. 11.

7. Susan Sorenson and Keri Garman, "How to Tackle U.S. Employees' Stagnating Engagement," *Gallup Business Journal* (http://businessjournal.gallup .com/), June 11, 2013, pp. 1–2.

8. Garry Kraus, "Employees Want Feedback—Even If It's Negative," *Workforce Management*, February 2010, pp. 10–11.

9. Zinta S. Byrne, Janet M. Peters, and James W. Weston, "The Struggle With Employee Engagement: Measures and Construct Clarification Using Five Samples," *The Journal of Applied Psychology*, September 2016, p. 1222.

10. Christie Mann, "3 Unconscious Habits Eroding Employee Engagement," p. 2.

11. Beth Sears, "Engage Workers, Help Bottom Line," *Democrat and Chronicle*, February 21, 2016, p. 4E.

12. Susie Cranston and Scott Keller, "Increasing the 'Meaning Quotient' of Work," *McKinsey Quarterly* (www.mckinseyquarterly.com), January 2013, pp. 4–5.

13. Martin Dewhurst, Matthew Guthridge, and Elizabeth Mohr, "Motivating People: Getting Beyond Money," *McKinsey Quarterly* (www.mckinseyquarterly.com), November 2009, pp. 1–2.

14. Cited in Laura Raines, "Re-engaging Workers Is a Big Hurdle for HR," *AJC* (www.ajc.com/jobs), March 17, 2011, p. 2.

15. Survey cited in "Special Report: Employee Engagement," *Workforce Management*, July 11, 2011, p. 26.

16. Tyler C. Burch and Cristiano L. Guarana, "The Comparative Influences of Transformational Leadership and Leader-Member Exchange on Follower Engagement," *Journal of Leadership Studies*, no. 3, 2014, pp. 6–25.

17. Tersa Amabile and Steven Kramer, *The Progress Principle Using Small Wins to Ignite Joy, Engagement, and Creativity at Work* (Boston, MA: Harvard Business School Press, 2011).

18. Bradley P. Owens, Wayne E. Baker, Dana McDaniel Sumpter, and Kim S. Cameron, "Relational Energy at Work: Implications for Job Engagement and Job Performance," *Journal of Applied Psychology*, January 2016, pp. 35–49.

19. Thad Green, *Motivation Management: Fueling Performance by Discovering What People Believe About Themselves and Their Organizations* (Palo Alto, CA: Davies-Black Publishing, 2000). An original version of expectancy theory applied to work motivation is Victor H. Vroom, *Work and Motivation* (New York: Wiley, 1964).

20. David A. Nadler and Edward E. Lawler III, "Motivation: A Diagnostic Approach," in Richard Hackman, Edward E. Lawler III, and Lyman W. Porter (eds.), *Perspectives on Behavior in Organizations*, Second Edition (New York: McGraw-Hill, 1983), pp. 67–78; James A. F. Stoner and R. Edward Freeman, *Management*, Fourth Edition (Upper Saddle River, NJ: Prentice Hall, 1989), p. 448.

21. Miquel Helft, "Can Lenovo Do It?" *Fortune*, May 23, 2013. *CNN Money* (http://money.com), May 23, 2013, pp. 1–2; John West, "Lenovo CEO Yuanquing Yang, "Transform or Be a Loser," *www.bizjournals .com*, April 14, 2015, p. 1.

22. Literature reviewed in Gerard H. Seitjts, Gary P. Latham, Kevin Tasa, and Bradon W. Latham, "Goal Setting and Goal Orientation: An Integration of 'Two Different Yet Related Literatures'," *Academy of Management Journal*, April 2004, pp. 227–228.

23. Edwin A. Locke and Gary P. Latham, *A Theory of Goal Setting and Task Performance* (Upper Saddle River, NJ: Prentice Hall, 1990); Latham, *Work*

Motivation: History, Theory, Research, and Practice (Thousand Oaks, CA: Sage Publications, 2007; Locke and Latham, eds., New Developments in Goal Setting and Task Performance (New York, NY: Routledge, 2013).

24. "Motivate Staff with Noble Cause," Manager's Edge, June 2005, p. 1.

25. John J. Donavan and David J. Radosevich, "The Moderating Role of Goal Commitment on the Goal Difficulty–Performance Relationship: A Meta-Analytic Review and Critical Reanalysis," Journal of Applied Psychology, April 1998, pp. 308–315.

26. Ad Kleingeld, Heleen van Mierlo, and Lidia Arends, "The Effect of Goal Setting on Group Performance: A Meta-Analysis," Journal of Applied Psychology, November 2011, pp. 1289–1304.

27. Nicholas Bloom, Raffela Sadun, and John Van Reenen, "How Three Essential Practices Can Address Even the Most Complex Global Problems," Harvard Business Review, November 2012, pp. 76–82.

28. Maurcie E. Schweitzer, Lisa Ordoñez, and Bambi Douma, "Goal Setting as a Moderator of Unethical Behavior," The Academy of Management Journal, June 2004, p. 430.

29. Massimo Calabresi, "Wells Fargo Customer Fraud Deals Political Setback to Banks," Time, October 3, 2016, p. 14; Rachel Louise Ensign, Yuka Hayasi, and Emily Glazer, "Wells CEO Placed on Hot Seat Again," The Wall Street Journal, September 30, 2016, p. C2.

30 Cited in Adriana Gardella, "Owner Gets Lesson in Managing Sales Reps," The New York Times, February 4, 2013, p. 1.

31. Lisa D. Ordóñez, Maurice E. Schweitzer, Adam D. Galinksy, and Max H. Bazerman, "Goals Gone Wild: The Systematic Side Effects of Overprescribing Goal Setting," Academy of Management Perspective, February 2009, p. 14.

32. Tony Schwartz, "Powering Employees with More Than a Paycheck," The New York Times Dealbook (http://dealbook.nytimes.com/), November 10, 2013, p. 2.

33. "Employees Want More Recognition, Growth Opportunity," American Psychological Association (www.phwa.org/media), 2011.

34. Rita Pyrilis, "Finger Lickin' Meets Rubber Chicken," Workforce, May 2016, pp. 40–42.

35. Leslie Gross Klaff, "Getting Happy with the Rewards King," Workforce, April 2003, p. 47.

36. Analysis presented in Tessa E. Basford and Andrea Molberg, "Dale Carnegie's Leadership Principles: Examining the Theoretical and Empirical Support," Journal of Leadership Studies, no. 4, 2013, p. 34.

37. Adrian Gostick and Chester Elton, The Carrot Principle: How the Best Managers Use Recognition to Engage Their People, Retain Talent, and Accelerate Performance (New York: The Free Press, 2007).

38. "Raise Workplace Morale without Spending a Dime," Communication Briefings, April 2010, p. 5.

39 Andrew J. DuBrin, "Self-Perceived Technical Orientation and Attitudes toward Being Flattered," Psychological Reports, vol. 96, 2005, pp. 852–854.

40 Cited in John A. Byrne, "How to Lead Now," Fast Company, August 2003, p. 66.

41 Quoted in Sally Ward, "Coach Employees for Peak Performance," Democrat and Chronicle, November 12, 2013, p. 7A.

42 Survey cited in Garry Kranz, "Companies Draw Coaching Plays but Managers' Skills Could Be Technically Foul," Workforce Management, August 2011, p. 6.

43 Douglas Riddle, "Prepping Tomorrow's Leaders Today," Leading Effectively (www.ccl.org), September 2006.

44 Robert D. Evered and James E. Selman, "Coaching and the Art of Management," Organizational Dynamics, Autumn 1989, p. 15.

45 "Coaching's 3 Critical Steps," Executive Leadership, October 2016, p. 4.

46 "Coaching—One Solution to a Tight Training Budget," HRfocus, August 2002, p. 7.

47 Tina Smagala, "Giving Effective Feedback on the Fly," Democrat and Chronicle, May 28, 2013, p. 5B.

48 Karen Wright, "A Chic Critique," Psychology Today, March/April 2011, p. 59.

49 Quoted in Adam Bryant, "Want to Inspire? Don't Sugarcoat Your Feedback," The New York Times (www.nytimes.com), September 10, 2011, p. 2.

50 Andrew Neitlich, "Coaching vs. Consulting: Find the Perfect Balance to Get Buy-in and Results," www.clomedia.com, August 4, 2016, p. 2.

51 "Fast Tips for Savvy Managers," Executive Strategies, April 1998, p. 1.

52 Jason J. Dahling, Smantha Ritchie Taylor, Samantha L. Chau, and Stephen A. Dwight, "Does Coaching Matter? A Multilevel Model Linking Managerial Coaching Skill and Frequency to Sales Goal Attainment," Personnel Psychology, no. 4, 2016, pp. 863–894.

53 Anna Marie Valerio and Robert J. Lee, Executive Coaching: A Guide for the HR Professional (San Francisco: Pfeiffer, 2005).

54 Douglas P. Shuit, "Huddling with the Coach," Workforce Management, February 2005, pp. 53–57.

55 Diane Brady, "The Unknown Guru," Bloomberg Business Week, November 29–December 5, 2010, p. 86.

**56** "8th Annual Survey: Executive Coaching at the Summit," *The Executive Coaching Survey 2013*, © Sherpa Coaching, p. 8.

**57** Michael Maccoby, "The Dangers of Dependence on Coaches," *Harvard Business Review*, January 2009, p. 95.

**58** Amy Joyce, "Career Coaches Nurture Executives," *Washington Post* (syndicated story), August 16, 2004.

**59** Stratford Sherman and Alyssa Freas, "The Wild West of Executive Coaching," *Harvard Business Review*, November 2004, pp. 86–88; Diane Brady, "The Unknown Guru," *Bloomberg Business Week*, November 29–December 5, 2010, p. 86.

**60** Lewis Garrad and Tomas Chamorro-Premuzic, "The Dark Side of High Employee Engagement," *Harvard Business Review* (https://hbr.org), August 16, 2016, p. 3.

# Creativity, Innovation, and Leadership

## LEARNING OBJECTIVES

After studying this chapter and doing the exercises, you should be able to

- Identify the steps in the creative process.
- Identify characteristics of creative problem solvers.
- Be prepared to overcome traditional thinking in order to become more creative.

- Describe both organizational and individual approaches to enhance creative problem solving.
- Explain how the leader and the organization can establish a climate that fosters creativity.
- Identify several leadership practices that contribute to organizational innovation.

## CHAPTER OUTLINE

A couple of years ago the Google division of Alphabet Inc. was seeking to dramatically grow its cloud computing business. To accomplish this major thrust, Google turned to Diane Greene, a board member with a successful track record in entrepreneurship, innovation, and dealing with enterprises (business organizations). She now holds the job title, executive vice president of Google Cloud Enterprise. Greene had founded VMware, and built it into a major player in corporate computing. Google had traditionally served individuals rather than enterprises. Google chief executive officer (CEO) Sundar Pichai posted about Greene, "As a long-time industry veteran and co-found of and CEO of VMware, Diane needs no introduction. Cloud computing is revolutionizing the way people live and work and there is no better person to lead this important area." The first company Greene cofounded was a five-person business that provided streaming videos.

At the outset of her Google position, she was given broad authority over the company's cloud offerings, including leadership of engineering, sales support, and marketing. A former Google engineer said about Greene, "She clearly has a passion for enterprise customers. This will be great from a DNA injection point of view for Google." A former Chief technology officer at VMware said about Greene when she joined Google: "She is awesome and immediately changes the game for Google's cloud efforts. The engineering team at bebop was outstanding as well and they'll bring a ton of enterprise DNA to Google."

To get Greene on the Google leadership team, the company acquired bebop Technologies Inc., a company she founded in 2012 that was working on human resources, benefits and training management software services. Most of bebop's 29 employees joined Google. The chairman of a cloud computing firms that works closely with Google said that Greene's experience at VMware developed her knowhow in building products that are flexible enough to appeal to enterprises with different budgets, capabilities, and technology.[1]

The story about Google illustrate the importance of having leaders who are creative themselves, and also know how to lead creative people. An IBM survey of 1,500 CEOs across 33 industries and 60 countries also emphasizes the relevance of creativity in organizations. It was found that the number one attribute CEOs look for in their new hires is not discipline, integrity, cognitive intelligence, or emotional intelligence. It is creativity.[2] (The other attributes, however, often contribute to creativity.)

By thinking creatively, a person can form a new enterprise or enlarge an existing one that can keep many people engaged in productive activity. However, the creative idea has to be executed properly for innovation to take place. Although the terms *creativity* and *innovation* are often used interchangeably, **innovation** refers to the creation of new ideas and their *implementation* or *commercialization*. True innovation involves a breakthrough development, and is regarded by some management thinkers as the only sustainable source of competitive advantage.[3]

The late long-time leadership authority Warren Bennis regards creativity as an essential characteristic of leaders.[4] The role of a creative leader is to bring into existence ideas and things that did not exist previously or that existed in a different form. Leaders are not bound by current solutions to problems. Instead, they create images of other possibilities. Leaders often move a firm into an additional business or start a new department that offers another service.

This chapter emphasizes the development of creativity in the leader. It also explains the nature of creativity and creative people and examines the leader's role in establishing an atmosphere that helps group members become more creative, along with leadership practices conducive to innovation.

## Steps in the Creative Process

An important part of becoming more creative involves understanding the stages involved in **creativity**, which is generally defined as the production of novel and useful ideas. A still well-accepted model of creativity developed almost ninety years ago can be applied to

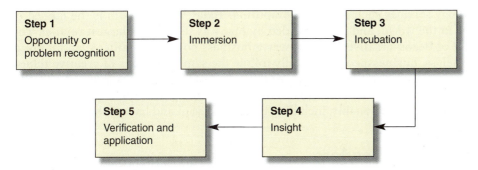

**FIGURE 11-1** Steps in the Creative Process.

organizations. This model divides creative thinking into five stages,[5] as shown in Figure 11-1. Step 1 is *opportunity* or *problem recognition*: A person discovers that a new opportunity exists or a problem needs to be resolved. One day in 1994, a financial analyst named Jeff Bezos was seated at his desk at the New York hedge fund, D. E. Shaw, when he noticed an astonishing statistic: The number of Internet users was growing by 2,300 percent per year. Bezos thought that there must be some good way to commercialize this development. Bezos was concerned that he or his company had not yet capitalized on the revolutionary development called the Internet. He detected an opportunity for some kind of business, but he did not yet know which one.[6]

Step 2 is *immersion*: The individual concentrates on the problem and becomes immersed in it. He or she will recall and collect information that seems relevant, dreaming up alternatives without refining or evaluating them. Bezos grabbed every fact he could about mail order businesses and thought about which ones could be conducted more efficiently over the Internet than by the traditional means, such as phoning in or writing for orders.

Step 3 is *incubation*: The person keeps the assembled information in mind for a while. He or she does not appear to be working on the problem actively, but the subconscious mind is still engaged. While the information is simmering, it is being arranged into meaningful new patterns. Bezos kept thinking about using the Internet for a mail order business while performing his regular work.

Step 4 is *insight*: The problem-conquering solution flashes into the person's mind at an unexpected time, such as on the verge of sleep, during a shower, or while running. Insight is also called the *Aha!* experience: All of a sudden, something clicks. At some point it clicked in Bezos's mind that books were the commodity for which no comprehensive mail order catalog existed because a catalogue of this nature would be much too large to mail profitably. A catalogue of this type would be ideally suited to the Internet because a vast database could be shared with an almost unlimited number of users. The aha! experience usually arrives after hours of thought and study, as indicated by Step 2, immersion.

Step 5 is *verification and application*: The individual sets out to prove that the creative solution has merit. Verification procedures include gathering supporting evidence, using logical persuasion, and experimenting with new ideas. Application requires tenacity because most novel ideas are first rejected as being impractical. The day after his insight experience, Bezos flew to Los Angeles to the American Booksellers' Convention to learn all he could about the book business. One key fact he found was that the major book wholesalers had already assembled electronic lists of their inventory. Bezos reasoned that the potential new venture only needed one Internet location where the book-buying public could search through the stock and place orders directly.

Because his employer wasn't interested in jumping into the Internet bookselling business, Bezos decided to go into business for himself, founding Amazon.com. He and his wife then drove to Seattle, Washington, to set up the new business, drawing up the business plan as they rolled down the highway in a 1988 Chevy Blazer.

Bezos' opportunity spotting has evolved into a major business corporation that now sells all kinds of merchandise in addition to books and music, as well as information technology services such as cloud computing. Today, Amazon.com is the largest online retailer in the world, and also regarded by many as the world's largest retailer. The end product of Bezos' creative thinking was a business possibility rather than an invention. Nevertheless, businesspeople typically follow the same five steps of creative thought as do inventors. Even though creativity usually follows the same steps, it is not a mechanical process that can be turned on and off. Much of creativity is intricately woven into a person's intellect and personality, including being observant and having sharp intuition.

## Characteristics of Creative Leaders

Creative leaders, like creative workers of all types, are different in many ways from their less creative counterparts. They are devoted to their fields and enjoy intellectual stimulation, and they challenge the status quo, which leads them to seek improvements. Above all, creative people are mentally flexible and can see past the traditional ways of looking at problems.

As described next, the specific characteristics of creative people, including creative leaders, can be grouped into four areas: knowledge, cognitive abilities, personality, and passion for the task and the experience of flow.[7] These characteristics are highlighted in Figure 11-2. Before studying this information, compare your thinking to that of a creative person by doing Leadership Self-Assessment Quiz 11-1.

### Knowledge

Creative problem solving requires a broad background of information, including facts and observations. Knowledge provides the building blocks for generating and combining ideas. Most creative leaders are knowledgeable, and their knowledge contributes to their charisma. A well-known case in point is Steven P. Jobs, the late chief executive of Apple Inc. He contributed design and marketing decisions to most of Apple's key products, and he played a major role in the development of the popular iPhone and iPad. A contributor to Jobs' creativity is his in-depth technical knowledge of computer hardware and software. He was also fascinated with calligraphy in college that helped him sharpen his sense of design. Jobs said at the peak of his career something to the effect that creativity is the result of having enough dots to connect. (The dots are bits of knowledge.)

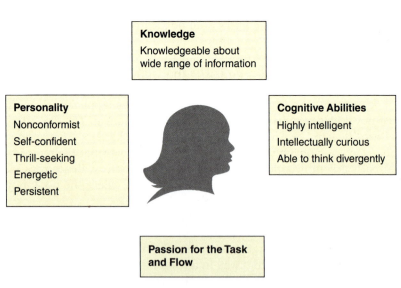

**FIGURE 11-2** Characteristics of Creative Leaders.

# LEADERSHIP SELF-ASSESSMENT QUIZ 11-1

## The Creative Personality Test

**Instructions:** Describe each of the following statements as "mostly true" or "mostly false."

| | | MOSTLY TRUE | MOSTLY FALSE |
|---|---|---|---|
| 1. | It is generally a waste of time to read magazine articles, Internet articles, and books outside my immediate field of interest. | ☐ | ☐ |
| 2. | I frequently have the urge to suggest ways of improving products and services I use. | ☐ | ☐ |
| 3. | Taking an elective course outside of my major is (or was, or would be) a time waster. | ☐ | ☐ |
| 4. | I am a person of very strong convictions. What is right is right; what is wrong is wrong. | ☐ | ☐ |
| 5. | I enjoy it when my boss hands me vague instructions. | ☐ | ☐ |
| 6. | Making order out of chaos is actually fun. | ☐ | ☐ |
| 7. | Only under extraordinary circumstances would I deviate from my To Do list (or other ways in which I plan my day). | ☐ | ☐ |
| 8. | I sometimes use search engines other than Google just to explore something different. | ☐ | ☐ |
| 9. | Rules and regulations should not be taken too seriously. Most rules can be broken under unusual circumstances. | ☐ | ☐ |
| 10. | Playing with a new idea is fun even if it does not benefit me in the end. | ☐ | ☐ |
| 11. | Some of my best ideas have come from building on the ideas of others. | ☐ | ☐ |
| 12. | In writing, I try to avoid the use of unusual words and word combinations. | ☐ | ☐ |
| 13. | I frequently jot down improvements in the job I would like to make in the future. | ☐ | ☐ |
| 14. | I prefer to stay with technology devices I know well rather than frequently updating my equipment or software. | ☐ | ☐ |
| 15. | I prefer writing personal notes or poems to loved ones rather than relying on greeting cards. | ☐ | ☐ |
| 16. | At one time or another in my life, I have enjoyed doing puzzles. | ☐ | ☐ |
| 17. | If your thinking is clear, you will find the one best solution to a problem. | ☐ | ☐ |
| 18. | It is best to interact with coworkers who think much like you. | ☐ | ☐ |
| 19. | I would readily accept an assignment to a new product development committee. | ☐ | ☐ |
| 20. | Tight controls over people and money are necessary to run a successful organization. | ☐ | ☐ |

**Scoring and Interpretation:** Give yourself a score of 1 for each answer that matches the answer key:

| | | |
|---|---|---|
| 1. Mostly false | 8. Mostly true | 15. Mostly true |
| 2. Mostly true | 9. Mostly true | 16. Mostly true |
| 3. Mostly false | 10. Mostly true | 17. Mostly false |
| 4. Mostly false | 11. Mostly true | 18. Mostly false |
| 5. Mostly true | 12. Mostly false | 19. Mostly true |
| 6. Mostly true | 13. Mostly true | 20. Mostly false |
| 7. Mostly false | 14. Mostly false | |

**Total score:** _____

## QUIZ 11-1 (continued)

Extremely high or low scores are the most meaningful. A score of 15 or more suggests that your personality and attitudes are similar to those of creative people, including creative leaders. A score of 8 or less suggests that you are more of an intellectual conformist at present. Do not be discouraged. Most people can develop in the direction of becoming more creative.

How does your score compare to your self-evaluation of your creativity? We suggest you also obtain feedback on your creativity from somebody familiar with your thinking and your work.

An example of connecting dots is the development of high-tech activity monitors that provide real-time information about physical activity and such indices as calories burned. The dots connected were (1) peoples' interest in physical health and conditioning and (2) an obsession for portable electronic devices.

### Cognitive Abilities

Cognitive abilities comprise such abilities as general intelligence and abstract reasoning. Creative problem solvers characteristically have well above-average cognitive intelligence. Creative people are facile at generating creative solutions to problems in a short period of time. Creative people also maintain a youthful curiosity throughout their lives, and the curiosity is not centered just on their own field of expertise. Instead, their range of interests encompasses many areas of knowledge, and they are enthusiastic about puzzling problems. These mental workouts help sharpen a person's intelligence.

Creative people show an identifiable intellectual style: being able to think divergently. They are able to expand the number of alternatives to a problem, thus moving away from a single solution. Yet, the creative thinker also knows when it is time to narrow the number of useful solutions. For example, the divergent thinker might think of twenty-seven ways to reduce costs, but at some point he or she will have to move toward choosing the best of several cost-cutting approaches.

A hallmark of a creative businessperson's intellect is to spot opportunities that others might overlook. A case in point is Hamdi Ulukaya, a Turkish immigrant who launched Chobani brand yogurt in 2007. At the time, the Greek market share of yogurt in the United States was less than 1 percent. Today the share is over 60 percent. Ulukaya says that the growth of his enterprise began when he spotted an abandoned and dilapidated yogurt plant Kraft Foods was looking to sell. With only $3,000 left in his pocket, Ulukaya needed an opportunity to make a living.[8]

The popular belief that creative people are right-brain dominant, whereas left-brain dominant people are more logical, detail-oriented, and analytical has been challenged by brain specialists. Recent neuroscience research suggests that developing original ideas is a process, and not something that stems from one side of the brain. Based on 20 years of research, creativity specialist Ned Herrmann concluded that creativity is a mental process utilizing all the brain's special capability. A creative person is therefore "whole-brained," than left-brained or right-brained.[9] Antonio Damasio, director of the Brain and Creativity Institute at the University of Southern California, explains that there is a high level of cooperation between different parts and systems within the brain. As a result, creative problem solving is orchestrated by different parts of the brain working together. The imagination that is an integral part of creativity stems from memory because memory is necessary to recognize when something is original—a key component of creativity.[10]

A major cognitive contributor to creative thinking is **intuition**. The term refers to an experienced-based way of knowing or reasoning in which weighing and balancing evidence are done unconsciously and automatically. The *Aha!* experience is an example of intuition. The yogurt entrepreneur mentioned above showed strong intuition when he saw the possibilities in an abandoned and dilapidated yogurt plant. Take Leadership Self-Assessment Quiz 11-2 to think through your own intuition tendencies.

# LEADERSHIP SELF-ASSESSMENT QUIZ 11-2

**The Intuitive Problem-Solving Style Quiz**

Indicate your strength of agreement with each of the following statements: SD—strongly disagree; D—disagree; N—neutral; A—agree; SA—strongly agree.

| | | SD | D | N | A | SA |
|---|---|---|---|---|---|---|
| 1. | Most of my hunches prove to be correct. | 1 | 2 | 3 | 4 | 5 |
| 2. | Details tend to take care of themselves providing you are on the right track with your plans. | 1 | 2 | 3 | 4 | 5 |
| 3. | Before attempting to solve a problem, I gather a large number of relevant facts. | 5 | 4 | 3 | 2 | 1 |
| 4. | Relying on gut feel is a terrible way for a business executive to make a decision. | 5 | 4 | 3 | 2 | 1 |
| 5. | When I meet a person for the first time, I take my time in deciding whether he or she and I will get along. | 5 | 4 | 3 | 2 | 1 |
| 6. | It takes me about ten seconds to know if I am physically attracted to another person. (Skip this question if you are in a committed relationship.)☺ | 1 | 2 | 3 | 4 | 5 |
| 7. | It takes me a long time to decide whether I like the color on a vehicle I am thinking about purchasing. | 5 | 4 | 3 | 2 | 1 |
| 8. | I need, or would need, to gather a lot of facts before I would purchase stock in a specific company. | 5 | 4 | 3 | 2 | 1 |
| 9. | When making an important decision, it is much better to gather new facts rather than rely on past experience. | 5 | 4 | 3 | 2 | 1 |
| 10. | When making an important decision, it is much better to gather new facts rather than rely on past experience. | 5 | 4 | 3 | 2 | 1 |
| 11. | Common sense is an effective source of information for making decisions. | 1 | 2 | 3 | 4 | 5 |
| 12. | I usually "jump to a conclusion" when making a decision. | 1 | 2 | 3 | 4 | 5 |
| 13. | My best ideas have come from flashes of insight. | 1 | 2 | 3 | 4 | 5 |
| 14. | Unless a person is rational and systematic, he or she is unlikely to make effective decisions. | 5 | 4 | 3 | 2 | 1 |
| 15. | I am more impulsive than reflective. | 1 | 2 | 3 | 4 | 5 |
| 16. | When the "light bulb goes on" I know that I have a useful idea. | 1 | 2 | 3 | 4 | 5 |

***Scoring and Interpretation:*** Find your total score by summing the point values for each question.

- **65–80:** You probably have a strong intuitive decision-making style that facilitates being a creative thinker.

- **36–64:** You probably have a balanced approach between an intuitive decision-making style and one that relies more on facts and research.

- **15–35:** Your decision-making style probably emphasizes basing your decisions on facts and careful observation rather than on intuition which could be a deterrent to your creativity.

## Personality

Personality factors or the noncognitive aspects of an individual heavily influence creative problem solving. Creative people tend to have a positive self-image without being blindly self-confident. But because they are reasonably self-confident, they are able to cope with criticism of their ideas, and they can tolerate the isolation necessary for developing ideas. Part of the self-confidence of a creative worker focuses on the belief that he or she can solve problems creatively. Talking to others is a good way to get ideas, yet at some point the creative problem solver has to work alone and concentrate.

Self-confidence is an influential factor for enhancing the creativity necessary for successful entrepreneurship. A report on entrepreneurial success notes that "You have to be crazy-sure your product or service is something the world needs and that you can deliver it to overcome the naysayers, who will always deride what the majority has yet to validate."[11]

Creative people are frequently nonconformists and do not need strong approval from the group. They prefer to search for alternatives than worry about attaining consensus.

Many creative problem solvers are thrill seekers and risk takers who find that developing imaginative solutions to problems is a source of thrills. Larry Page, a big risk taker himself, has said that the biggest payoffs at Google have stemmed from risky ideas and investments.[12] (The self-driving car might be the next commercial success.) Creative people are also persistent, which is especially important for the verification and application stage of creative thinking. Selling a creative idea to the right people requires considerable follow-up. Finally, creative people enjoy dealing with ambiguity and chaos. Less creative people become quickly frustrated when task descriptions are unclear and disorder exists.

### Passion for the Task and the Experience of Flow

A dominant characteristic of creative people that is closely related to personality is a passion for the work. More than twenty years of research in industry conducted by Teresa M. Amabile and her associates led to the *intrinsic motivation principle of creativity*: People will be at their creative best when they feel motivated primarily by the interest, satisfaction, and challenge of the work itself—and not by external pressures.[13]

Passion for the task and high intrinsic motivation contribute in turn to a total absorption in the work and intense concentration, or the **experience of flow**. It is an experience so engrossing and enjoyable that the task becomes worth doing for its own sake regardless of the external consequences.[14] Perhaps you have had this experience when completely absorbed in a hobby or some analytical work, or when you were at your best in a sport or dance. (Flow also means *being in the zone*.) The highly creative leader, such as a business owner developing a plan for worldwide distribution of a product, will often achieve the experience of flow.

To fully understand the contribution of personal characteristics to creativity, we note the basic formula of human behavior: $B = f(P \times E)$ (behavior is a function of a person interacting with the environment). In this context, certain personal characteristics may facilitate a leader's being creative, but the right environment is necessary to trigger creative behavior. As will be described later, the right environment includes the leader encouraging creative thinking.

## Overcoming Traditional Thinking as a Creativity Strategy

A unifying theme runs through all forms of creativity training and suggestions for creativity improvement: Creative problem solving requires an ability to overcome traditional thinking. The concept of *traditional thinking* is relative, but it generally refers to a standard and frequent way of finding a solution to a problem. A traditional solution to a problem is thus a modal or most frequent solution. For example, traditional thinking suggests that to increase revenue, a retail store should conduct a sale. Creative thinking would point toward other solutions. As an example, a retail store might increase sales by shipping goods for a small fee, or by having store associates offer free fashion advice.

The creative person looks at problems in a new light and transcends conventional thinking about them. A historically significant example is Henry Ford, who was known for his creative problem-solving ability. A meatpacking executive invited Ford to visit his Chicago plant and observe how employees processed beef. The automotive executive noticed that at one end of the plant whole carcasses of steers were placed on a giant conveyor belt. As the meat traveled through the plant, workers carved it into various cuts until the carcass was consumed. A flash of whimsical insight hit Ford: What if the process were reversed, and all the pieces would become a whole steer again? Ford asked himself, "Why can't an automobile be built that way?" He took his creative idea back to the Ford Motor Company in Detroit and constructed the world's first manufacturing assembly line.[15]

The central task in becoming creative is to break down rigid thinking that blocks new ideas. At the same time, the problem solver must unlearn the conventional approach. Henry Ford unlearned the custom approach to building autos, so he could use an assembly line. (In the current era, people who have unlearned the assembly-line approach and switched to customization are considered to be creative!)

Overcoming traditional thinking is so important to creative thinking that the process has been characterized in several different ways. The most familiar is that *a creative person thinks outside the box*. A box, in this sense, is a category that confines and restricts thinking. Because you are confined to a box, you do not see opportunities outside the box. For example, if an insurance executive thinks that health insurance is only for humans, he or she might miss out on the growing market for domestic animal health insurance.

A caution about thinking outside the box: Workers still need some constraints as to how far outside the box they are permitted to think. Creativity writer Shawn Coyne contends that when people are told to think outside the box with no constraints they quickly become overwhelmed by the unlimited scope of the task. Effective project leaders establish parameters and prepare their teams for idea generation by pointing them in a specific direction. Coyne also explains that the best ideas come from "thinking inside a very carefully designed box that's not too big or too small."[16] An example might be telling team members that they need to find ways of saving the company energy costs but that no suggestions will be used that are too expensive or result in widespread employee complaints.

Management consultant Donald Sull observes that sophisticated innovators have long recognized that constraints prompt and guide innovations. To attain more disciplined innovation, organizational leaders need to add a few simple rules for innovation. An example of such a rule would be that a new product will not be launched unless there is $100 million in potential revenue.[17]

We might conclude from these concerns about thinking outside the box that imagination is still required to think outside the box within the constraints of a required framework. An example of thinking outside the box that included constraints is the Nike Flyknit shoe designed to attain high athletic performance and sustainability goals. The overall goal was to make a breakthrough product that is beautiful and sustainable, with the constraints of having one half the environmental impact. The NikeFlynit delivers on athletic performance while producing 60 percent was less waste than the traditional cut-and-sew methods used to make an athletic shoe. The outside-the-box features of the Flynit shoe are its lightness, form fitting, and new approach to making footwear including sustainability.[18]

## Organizational Methods to Enhance Creativity

To enhance creative problem solving, most organizations regularly engage in systematic approaches to develop creative and innovative ideas. We focus here on new developments in brainstorming and other creativity-enhancing methods. Programs of this nature are applied to actual problems, while at the same time they provide an opportunity to improve creative thinking.

The leader has a dual role in implementing creative problem-solving techniques: He or she facilitates group interaction and also provides a fair share of creative output. The three creativity-enhancing, problem-solving techniques described here are (1) systematically collecting fresh ideas, including the use of whiteboards and granting time to explore ideas; (2) brainstorming; and (3) the pet-peeve technique. As will be described later, creative problem-solving techniques are more likely to be effective in an organization culture that favors creativity and innovation.

A notable point about creativity-enhancing methods is that no one method is likely to be consistently better than any other method. The underlying mechanism is that each creativity-enhancing method helps bring new ideas to the surface.

## Systematically Collecting Fresh Ideas

Creativity is often referred to as a numbers game, because the more ideas you try, the greater the probability of finding one that works. Several approaches to systematically collecting fresh ideas are listed next.

1. *Straightforward collection of ideas.* A basic way of collecting fresh ideas is for employees to furnish them to a company database so that when somebody needs a fresh idea it can be accessed through a company search engine. Posting ideas on an intranet is similar to the database. Another straightforward approach to collecting ideas is for company leadership to engage more of its own staff in the search for innovation. For example, the CEO of Nike might ask the entire company, "Can you think of any piece of athletic clothing or equipment the word needs or wants that we are not already providing?"

2. *Establishing idea quotas.* To facilitate having fresh ideas, the leader or manager can establish idea quotas, such as by asking staff members to bring one new idea to each physical or virtual meeting. Although the vast majority of these ideas may not lead to innovation, a few good ones will emerge. One reason idea quotas work is that they are a goal. Another is that an environmental need (in this case, the idea quota) is an excellent creativity stimulant.

3. *Making whiteboards regularly available for sketching ideas.* The combination of a whiteboard and felt-tip pen has proven to be an effective method of sparking creative ideas. A wide range of companies encourage employees to doodle their ideas and draw diagrams to explain complicated concepts to colleagues in fields such as information technology, retailing, and real estate. Other doodling mechanisms include chalkboards and writable glass on a variety of surfaces.

   Advocates of doodling say it can facilitate idea generation, boost collaboration, and simplify communication. Everett Katigbak, a communication designer formerly at Facebook, emphasizes that even with electronic gadgets such as smartphones and tablet computers the hand is the most effective way of recording an idea. A representative example is that at Turner Broadcasting System, the strategy development team sketched tree branches and placed sticky notes on the end of the branches to think of ways to extend the Turner Classic Movie Brand. The exercise yielded more than 200 ideas, some of which proceeded to the development stage.[19]

4. *Granting tinkering time.* A formal policy approach for collecting fresh ideas is to allocate an amount or percentage of time for employees to think and experiment. Several innovative companies, including 3M, W. L. Gore & Associates, and Google, attribute some of their most successful new products to employees who were granted thinking time. The Google policy permitted its employees to spend one-fifth of their time on whatever innovative products they wished. Company leadership claimed that many of its significant advances can be traced to granting tinkering time to employees.[20] CEO Brad Smith of Intuit says that to spur innovation, his company has created 10 percent unstructured time. All 7,700 employees are granted time to work on a problem that they see as hampering customer service. Also, they can devote time to improving their own process so they can be more productive than their peers.[21]

   In recent years, Google and 3M have both restricted employee use of time off from regular responsibilities to explore innovative ideas, perhaps because the policy was regarded as an expensive employee perk. Nevertheless, "time to tinker" worked in the past and still remains another method of systematically collecting creative and innovative ideas.[22]

## Brainstorming

The best-known method for creativity improvement is brainstorming, which you have probably already done. Although brainstorming is often condemned as being superficial, it remains a key idea-generation method for even the most advanced technology companies. Furthermore, brainstorming is as much entrenched into business life as are job interviews and problem-solving meetings. A notable example of brainstorming is the firm Intellectual Ventures, whose primary mission is to develop inventions, cofounded by Nathan P. Myhrvold, the former chief technology officer at Microsoft. Myhrvold assembles groups of doctors, engineers, and scientists known for their brilliance, along with in-house inventors and lawyers, for day-long brainstorming sessions. The Intellectual Ventures staff takes ideas from the brainstorming sessions and turns them into patents. Inventors get a share of any eventual royalties. Through a combination of its own brainstorming and $5 billion in investment funds, the company has collected nearly 70,000 "intellectual assets."[23]

The Intellectual Ventures application of brainstorming emphasizes goals as an essential part of the process. The Ventures team focuses on the goal of attaining ideas worthy of a patent. Another key aspect of brainstorming is that all ideas can be stepping stones and triggers for new and more useful ideas. Any idea might lead to other associations and connections. Thus, during the idea-generating part of brainstorming, potential solutions are not criticized or evaluated in any way so that spontaneity is encouraged.

It is important to make sure that participants are prepared by studying the problem beforehand. Although it is useful to bring in employees from different departments to the brainstorming sessions, in-depth expertise on the subject may be as important as diversity in generating innovative ideas. Follow through in terms of implementing the best ideas is essential. If the good ideas are not implemented, brainstorming participants might become disillusioned and less inclined to share their creative thinking in the future.[24]

Brainstorming, much like other creative problem-solving techniques, works best in an organizational culture that fosters innovation. It is an integral part of the famous design firm IDEO, Inc., whose employees believe passionately in innovation. As a result, they are able to argue about alternative solutions to problems yet still unite to produce an effective design.[25]

As a refresher, do Leadership Skill-Building Exercise 11-1. Because the vast majority of employers use brainstorming, it is helpful to have some advanced knowledge of the topic other than that it is simply shouting out ideas.

## Using the Pet-Peeve Technique

An important part of leadership is for organizational units to find ways to continuously improve their service to external and internal customers. The **pet-peeve technique** is a method of brainstorming in which a group identifies all the possible complaints others might have about the group's organizational unit.[26] Through brainstorming, group members develop a list of complaints from any people who interact with their group. Sources of complaints include inside customers, outside customers, competitors, and suppliers. Although the pet-peeve technique is rarely mentioned, it is potentially valuable.

Group members can prepare for the meeting by soliciting feedback on themselves from the various target groups. In keeping with the informal, breezy style of the pet-peeve group, feedback should be gathered informally. Rather than approach target groups with a survey, members might tell others about the upcoming pet-peeve session and then ask in person or electronically, "What complaints can you contribute?"

During the no-holds-barred brainstorming session, group members throw in some imaginary and some humorous complaints. Humorous complaints are especially

# LEADERSHIP SKILL-BUILDING EXERCISE 11-1

## Two Brainstorming Scenarios

Presented below are two different scenarios for brainstorming. Choose one or both to work on practical business problems.

### A. Choose an Effective Brand Name

Organize into groups of about six people to play *Choose an Effective Brand Name*. An effective brand name is typically one that is easy to remember and that often appears to fit the product or service. ("Clorox," "IBM," and "Ritz-Carlton" are examples of brand names that helped build a prosperous business.) After your team has brainstormed a few possible brand names, conduct an Internet search to see if the name has not already been taken, and holds a trademark. Here are a few possible products or services to assign a brand name:

- A chain of tattoo and body piercing studios
- A micro-camera hidden in a ring or necklace
- A fat-free chocolate bar
- A chain of assisted-living residence homes for seniors
- A leadership training institute for young professionals

### B. The Next Billion Dollar Brand

Students organize into small new venture groups for your employer, Coca-Cola, PepsiCo, or Dr. Pepper Snapple Group. Although the company is a major player in its field, the CEO tasks you with the responsibility of identifying the next billion dollar brand, meaning that the brand will bring in gross revenues of about $1 billion annually. Although the CEO is giving you considerable latitude to think creatively and innovatively, the major constraint is that you are a food and beverage company. The CEO tells you that carbonated beverages have lost some of their fizz in recent years, so he or she thinks that your mission is high priority. You have twenty minutes to conduct your problem-solving/brainstorming session to think of what might be the next billion dollar brand. At the end of that short time period, present your best suggestion to the CEO.

---

important, for humor requires creative thinking. After all complaints have been aired, the group can process the information during a later session, when they can draw up action plans to remedy the most serious problems.

A pet-peeve session in the human resources department of a manufacturer of small electronic appliances generated many complaints, including the following:

"A lot of people wonder what we are doing. They think we just fill out forms and create work for ourselves."

"Some line managers think our job is to find good reasons why they shouldn't hire their best job candidates."

"Job candidates from the outside think our job is to delete résumés. They think we delete 90 percent of the résumés that arrive at the company job site."

As a result of these penetrating, albeit exaggerated, self-criticisms, the human resources department developed an effective action plan. The department leader arranged brief meetings with units throughout the organization to discuss the department's role and to answer questions.

The pet-peeve technique is potentially valuable for a leader because it can help the group improve its work processes. Because it has a good-spirited touch, it is not likely to be perceived as threatening.

## The Morality of Enhancing Creativity

Methods that help generate creative ideas, as well as the leadership and managerial actions to enhance creativity described at various places in this chapter, have ethical and moral consequences. Creativity writer Gerald Sindell emphasizes the need for creative thinkers to place their work within a moral context. He notes that creative work and output never exist in a vacuum. In contrast, every idea and product has potential harmful consequences in minor and major ways.[27]

A relevant example is the smartphone that enables millions of people to communicate readily for business and personal purposes. Yet, the unintended dysfunctional consequences have been enormous. Driving under the influence of smartphones, including texting and Internet surfing, is as dangerous as driving under the influence of alcohol. Also, productivity suffers enormously as workers become distracted by the ready availability of their smartphone for nonwork purposes. A serious ethical issue is that some scientists are concerned that excessive use of smartphones can create brain cancer.

Hundreds of other products and services also have ethical implications. For example, brilliantly developed financial products, such as derivatives, have also created harm for many consumers. Sindell recommends that creative workers should imagine all the possible misuses of an innovative product or service, and then take steps to limit the damage from the misuses.[28] Warning labels and informative advertising are at least a step in the right direction.

# Self-Help Techniques to Enhance Creative Problem Solving

Leaders and others who want to solve problems more creatively can find hundreds of methods at their disposal' Six strategies and specific techniques for enhancing creative problem solving are presented next and are outlined in Table 11-1. These strategies and techniques support and supplement the organizational programs described previously. An underlying contribution of these techniques is that they facilitate flexible thinking, or viewing the world with open and curious eyes.[29] With such a mental stance, almost anything can spark a new idea. As a warehouse manager, you might observe young people rollerblading in the park. With a creative attitude, you might conclude that your logistic specialists would be more efficient if they used Rollerblades rather than walked.

## Practicing Creativity-Enhancing Activities

An established way to sharpen creative thinking is to regularly engage in activities that encourage flexible thinking. If you enjoy photography, put yourself on assignment to take a photograph illustrating a theme. You might, for example, take photographs illustrating the proper use of your company's product. Puzzles of all types are useful in stretching your imagination; many creative people regularly do crossword puzzles. Another mind stretcher is to force yourself to write jokes around a given theme. Can you create a joke about the creativity of a leader?

Another standard technique for become a more flexible thinker is to ask yourself "what-if" questions. Such questions stretch your imagination to think of possibilities not previously given much or any thought. Two examples: "What would be the consequences if next year vehicle manufacturers switched the location of the break and accelerator pedals?" "What would happen if all consumers in the world refused to buy anything for three days?"

Learning a second (or third) language, including sign language, can facilitate creativity because you are forced to shift mental sets. For example, your second language may require you to remember the gender of every noun and to match the spelling of each adjective to the gender and number (singular versus plural) of the noun.

Leadership Skill-Building Exercise 11-2 gives you an opportunity to practice creative thinking. Doing exercises of this nature enhances creative problem solving.

TABLE 11-1 Self-Help Techniques for Creativity Improvement

| | |
|---|---|
| **1.** | Practicing creativity-enhancing activities |
| **2.** | Staying alert to opportunities |
| **3.** | Maintaining an enthusiastic attitude, including being happy |
| **4.** | Maintaining and using a systematic place for recording your ideas |
| **5.** | Playing the roles of explorer, artist, judge, and lawyer |
| **6.** | Engaging in appropriate physical exercise |
| **7.** | Solicit feedback on your performance |

## LEADERSHIP SKILL-BUILDING EXERCISE 11-2

### The Multiple Uses Technique

A standard technique for developing creativity is to find multiple uses for ordinary objects. In other words, the person doing the exercise is requested to go beyond conventional thinking in visualizing potential uses for a standard object. The point of the exercise is to develop skill in thinking flexibly. A basic example is that a soup bowl might also be used as a flower pot or paper weight. Working alone or using group brainstorming, identify about six potential uses for the following objects:

1. A paperclip[30]
2. A plastic tennis ball container
3. A shopping cart
4. An e-mail address
5. A pickup truck that no longer runs
6. A five-pound reference book

It will be instructive to share solutions with other classmates; for one thing, it helps to determine if your alternative use was not mentioned, or rarely mentioned, by others. Infrequent mention suggests a higher degree of imagination, although not necessarily practicality.

## Staying Alert to Opportunities

A key characteristic of creative leaders is that they can spot opportunities that other people overlook (as already mentioned twice in this chapter). Staying alert to opportunities can be framed as an application of the leader being mindful. Opportunity seeking is associated with entrepreneurial leadership because the entrepreneur might build an organization around an unmet consumer need. Tom Kelly, CEO of IDEO, provides a humorous example of opportunity spotting in the extreme. He was waiting for a subway train in a jammed Japanese station. Thousands of people streamed by, yet Kelly and a colleague were intrigued by one person—a young woman wearing mismatched shoes. The observers debated the reason for the mismatch, such as dressing in the dark, wearing borrowed clothes, or maybe an intentional decision. The last insight led to a company that prospers by selling mismatched socks.[31] Apparently, the unmet consumer need is to wear socks in a playful way. Does this example of opportunity spotting blow your socks off?

## Maintaining an Enthusiastic Attitude, Including Being Happy

The managerial leader faces a major hurdle in becoming a creative problem solver. He or she must resolve the conflict between being judicial and being imaginative. In many work situations, being judicial (or judgmental) is necessary. Situations calling for judicial thinking include reviewing proposed expenditures and inspecting products for quality or safety defects. Being judicial is much like a self-imposed restraint on creativity. Imaginative thinking is involved when searching for creative alternatives. Alex F. Osburn, a former advertising executive and the originator of brainstorming, notes how judgment and imagination are often in conflict:

> The fact that moods won't mix largely explains why the judicial and the creative tend to clash. The right mood for judicial thinking is largely negative. "What's wrong with this? ... No, this won't work." Such reflexes are right and proper when trying to judge.

In contrast, our creative thinking calls for a positive attitude. We have to be hopeful. We need enthusiasm. We have to encourage ourselves to the point of self-confidence. We have to beware of perfectionism lest it be abortive.[32] The action step is therefore to project oneself into a positive frame of mind when attempting to be creative. The same principle applies when attempting to be creative about a judicial task. For instance, a leader might be faced with the task of looking for creative ways to cut costs. The manager would then have to think positively about thinking negatively!

Closely related to enthusiasm as a contributor to creativity is the fact that being in a good mood facilitates creativity. The finding comes from an analysis of diaries or journals. The journal entries showed that people are happiest when they come up with a creative idea. However, they are more likely to have a breakthrough idea if they were happy the day before. One day's happiness is often a predictor of the next day's creative idea.[33]

## Maintaining and Using a Systematic Place for Recording Your Ideas

It is difficult to capitalize on creative ideas unless you keep a careful record of them. A creative idea trusted to memory may be forgotten in the press of everyday business. An important suggestion kept on your daily planner may become obscured. Creative ideas can lead to breakthroughs for your group and your career, so they deserve the dignity of a separate notebook, or computer file, or any other storage device that works for you. Many people today store their creative ideas on a mobile device. A cautious or forgetful person is advised to keep two copies of the ideas in separate places or storage devices.

## Playing the Roles of Explorer, Artist, Judge, and Lawyer

Another creativity-improvement method incorporates many of the preceding methods. Say you want to enhance your creativity on the job. This method calls for you to adopt four roles in your thinking.[34] First, be an *explorer*. Speak to people in different fields and get ideas that can bring about innovations for your group. For example, if you manage a telecommunications group, speak to salespeople and manufacturing specialists.

Second, be an artist by stretching your imagination. Strive to spend about 3 percent of your day imagining new solutions to the challenges you face. For example, the leader of a manufacturing department might ask, "Where else can we look to find people who want to become manufacturing technicians?" Also remember to challenge the commonly perceived rules in your field. A night club manager asked "Why continue to have a cover charge?" The questioning led to increased revenue because more people visited the club, resulting in higher beverage and food sales.

Third, know when to be a *judge*. After developing some imaginative ideas, at some point you have to evaluate them. Do not be so critical that you discourage your own imaginative thinking. Be critical enough, however, so that you do not try to implement weak ideas. A managing partner in an established law firm formulated a plan for opening two storefront branches that would offer legal services to the public at low prices. The branches would advertise on radio, on television, online, and in newspapers. After thinking through her plan for several weeks, however, she dropped the idea. She decided that the storefront branches would most likely divert clients away from the parent firm, rather than create a new market.

Fourth, achieve results with your creative thinking by playing the role of lawyer. Negotiate and find ways to implement your ideas within your field or place of work. The explorer, artist, and judge stages of creative thought might take only a short time to develop a creative idea. Yet, you may spend months or even years getting your breakthrough idea implemented. For example, many tax preparation firms now loan clients instant refunds in the amount of their anticipated tax refunds. It took a manager in a large tax preparation firm a long time to convince top management of the merits of the idea.

## Engaging in Appropriate Physical Exercise

A well-accepted method of stimulating creativity is to engage in physical exercise. Stephen Ramocki, a marketing professor at Rhode Island College, found that a single aerobic work-out is sufficient to trigger the brains of students into high gear—and that the benefit lasted for a minimum of two hours. Gary Kasparov, the chess champion, is a gym fanatic and has an extraordinary intellect. He has credited his physical fitness with boosting his skill in chess.

The fact that creative insights often arise during physical exercise fits the steps on the creative process referred to as immersion and incubation. Another explanation of why exercise facilitates creativity is that exercising pumps more blood and oxygen into the brain. Exercise also enhances activity in the frontal lobe, the region of the brain involved in abstract reasoning and attention.[35]

Lars Bastholm, the global chief creative officer at Google the Zoo, offers another perspective on the role physical activity plays in the creative process. He claims that while engaging in such activity a person can ruminate on a subject without having pressure on the thought process. Among these low-intensity activities are raking leaves, walking, bicycling, or cleaning a closet or garage.[36] These small accomplishments are simultaneous stress reducers, further clearing the brain to be creative.

The fact that physical exercise can boost creative thinking should not be interpreted in isolation. Without other factors going for a leader, such as a storehouse of knowledge and passion for the task, physical exercise will not lead to creative breakthroughs. Physical exercise also facilitates sleeping well, and a rested brain is helpful for creative problem solving.

## Soliciting Feedback on Your Performance

Another effective way of enhancing creativity on the job is to seek feedback on your performance from both your manager and your coworkers. Even if you are not asking for feedback on creative suggestions exclusively, the feedback process is likely to sharpen your imagination. An example of a feedback-seeking question would be "What did you think of my suggestion for reducing energy costs by encouraging employees to bring sweaters to the office?" The feedback refines your thinking, helping you develop ideas that others perceive to be imaginative.

A study demonstrating the link between feedback seeking and job creativity was conducted with 456 supervisor–employee pairs in four management consulting firms. Employees who asked for feedback directly and looked around for indirect feedback tended to be rated more highly on displaying creativity.[37] Examples of indirect feedback would be seeing positive mention of your performance in an e-mail or hearing a spontaneous comment about your work during a meeting.

## Establishing a Climate and Culture for Creative Thinking

Leaders need to develop creative ideas of their own to improve productivity and satisfaction. Establishing a climate, or culture, conducive to creative problem solving is another requirement of effective leadership. The point is that top management purposely sets about to take steps to make the organization more innovative.

A foundation step in fostering organizational creativity is to establish a vision and mission that includes creativity, such as that of DuPont: "Our vision is to be the world's most dynamic science company, creating sustainable solutions essential to a better, safer and healthier life for people everywhere." Vision statements and mission statements set the pace, but they must be supported by the right climate, or organizational culture, and extensive use of the techniques described throughout this chapter.

Information about establishing a climate for creativity can be divided into (1) fostering a culture of originality, (2) leadership and managerial practices for enhancing creativity, and (3) methods for managing creative workers. To become sensitized to this vast amount of information, do Leadership Diagnostic Activity 11-1. The instrument gives you an opportunity to ponder many of the management and leadership practices that encourage or discourage creative problem solving.

## Fostering a Culture of Originality

A macro approach to establishing a climate and culture for creative thinking is to foster a culture that favors original thinking. The larger the number of workers who think originally, the more likely that innovation will take place. Almost all the ideas expressed in the

## LEADERSHIP DIAGNOSTIC ACTIVITY 11-1

### Assessing the Climate for Creativity and Innovation

**Instructions:** Respond "mostly yes" or "mostly no" as to how well each of the following characteristics fits an organization familiar to you. If you are currently not familiar with an outside organization, respond to these statements in regard to your school.

| | MOSTLY YES | MOSTLY NO |
|---|---|---|
| 1. Company leadership wants workers to be creative. | ☐ | ☐ |
| 2. People who contribute new and useful ideas often receive financial rewards. | ☐ | ☐ |
| 3. Creative thinking is mostly the responsibility of people in creative jobs such as research and development and marketing. | ☐ | ☐ |
| 4. Workers are encouraged to spend part of their time coming up with new ideas for products or services. | ☐ | ☐ |
| 5. Creative types rarely get promoted. | ☐ | ☐ |
| 6. The company invests considerable resources in innovation. | ☐ | ☐ |
| 7. Few of our leaders appear to be innovative thinkers. | ☐ | ☐ |
| 8. Innovative thinkers are publicly recognized in our organization. | ☐ | ☐ |
| 9. People are often poked fun at for suggesting a unique idea. | ☐ | ☐ |
| 10. Constructive change is welcome in this organization. | ☐ | ☐ |
| 11. Many of our work groups are diverse both in terms of professional background and cultural factors. | ☐ | ☐ |

**Scoring and Interpretation:** The score in the direction of a climate for creativity and innovation is "mostly yes" for statements 1, 2, 4, 6, 8, 10, and 11, and "mostly no" for statements 3, 5, 7, and 9. A score of 7 or higher suggests a climate well suited for creativity and innovation. A score of 4–6 is about average, and 3 or below suggests a climate that inhibits creativity and innovation.

rest of the chapter as well in the previous sections could in some way foster original thinking. Yet here we mention several specific ideas on the topic.

Wharton School professor Adam Grant offers several ideas for generating great ideas, and therefore stimulating a culture of originality. Several of these ideas are as follows: First, it is important for workers to generate a large number of ideas because one or two might be breakthroughs. Second, look to other innovators to judge the original merits of an idea because they will tend to be more objective than the idea generator, and more positive than managers who judge original ideas. As a result, the fellow innovators are more likely to predict which ideas will be successful. Third, solicit ideas from individuals rather than groups. People can take their best ideas to the group for evaluation and refinement, but the best unit of originality is still people thinking independently.

Fourth, strike the right balance between cohesion and dissent in your organization because both are needed. Too much harmony and cohesion in the organization might lead to homogeneous thinking, producing very few new ideas. A little dissent in the form of critical thinking may spur originality.[38] For example, a middle manager at Kellogg might ask, "How long are so many people around the world going to keep on spending so much money on packaged cereal?"

A study of transformational leadership in energy companies in China offers another path for leaders to create a culture of originality. Transformational leadership facilitates followers internalizing (accepting as their own) the leader's values and standards and exhibit similar qualities. Yet to foster creative output from followers, the transformational leader must set and communicate bold expectations for original thinking.[39] An example of such activity by a leader is the behavior of Jeff Immelt, the former long-time CEO of GE. He continued to insist on transforming the company, and emphasized original thinking in many of his statements to his leadership team and to workers in general.

## Leadership Practices for Enhancing Creativity

Nine leadership and managerial practices are particularly helpful in fostering creative thinking, as revealed by the work of many researchers and observers.[40] The organizational methods already described for enhancing creativity might also be interpreted as leadership practices.

1. *Hire creative people from the outside, and identify creative people from within.* The most robust leadership and management practice for enhancing creativity is to hire people with the aptitude for, or track record in, being creative. Creativity training is helpful, yet starting with creative people enhances the potential of training. Part of the same argument is that hiring innovative people helps foster an innovative environment. Arthur D. Levinson, chairman and chief executive of Genentech, the heralded biotechnology firm, says, "If you want an innovative environment, hire innovative people, listen to them tell you want they want, and do it."[41]

2. *Intellectual challenge.* Matching people with the right assignments enhances creativity because it supports expertise and intrinsic motivation. The amount of stretch is consistent with goal theory; too little challenge leads to boredom, but too much challenge leads to feelings of being overwhelmed and loss of control. The leader or manager must understand his or her group members well to offer them the right amount of challenge. Moderate time pressures can sometimes bring about the right amount of challenge.

3. *Empowerment including freedom to choose the method.* Research with information technology workers in the People's Republic of China supported the idea that an empowering style of leadership facilitates worker creativity. Specifically, when workers are empowered they are more likely to work through the steps for creative problem solving. Part of the creativity was attributed to empowered workers having a sense of self-determination, which sparked their creative thinking.[42]

   Workers also tend to be more creative when they are granted the freedom to choose which method is best for attaining a work goal (as described in our study of empowerment in Chapter 7). Stable goals are important because it is difficult to work creatively toward a moving target.

4. *Ample supply of the right resources.* Time and money are the most important resources for enhancing creativity. Deciding how much time and money to give to a team or project is a tough judgment call that can either support or stifle creativity. Under some circumstances, setting a time deadline will trigger creative thinking because it represents a favorable challenge. An example would be hurrying to be first to market with a new product. False deadlines or impossibly tight ones can create distrust and burnout. To be creative, groups also need to be adequately funded.

5. *Effective design of work groups.* Work groups are the most likely to be creative when they are mutually supportive and when they have a diversity of backgrounds and perspectives. Blends of gender, race, and ethnicity are recognized today as contributing to creative thought, similar to cross-functional teams with their mix of perspectives from different disciplines. The various points of view often combine to achieve creative solutions to problems. Homogeneous teams argue less, but they are often less creative. Putting together a team with the right chemistry—just the right level of diversity and supportiveness—requires experience and intuition on the leader's part.

   A leadership and management practice related to work group design is encouraging face-to-face contact to facilitate innovative thinking. It is more difficult for geographically dispersed workers to think creatively. The use of whiteboards around the company, as described earlier, is one work arrangement that facilitates face-to-face contacts, as do open work spaces. Yet again, allowances must be made for people who are at their creative best when working alone.

6.  **Supervisory encouragement and linking innovation to performance.** The most influential step a leader can take to bring about creative problem solving is to develop a permissive atmosphere that encourages people to think freely. Praising creative work is important because, for most people to sustain their passion, they must feel that their work matters to the organization. Creative ideas should be evaluated quickly rather than put through a painfully slow review process.

    In addition to encouraging innovation, supervisory leaders should promote the idea that innovative thinking improves job performance. A study conducted with 238 pairs of workers and supervisors in four U.S. companies in several different industries supported the importance of employee expectations. When employees believed that innovative thinking would lead to better job performance, they were more likely to solve problems creatively. The supervisor could help in the process by explaining how innovation improves job performance.[43]

7.  **Organizational support.** The entire organization as well as the immediate manager should support creative effort if creativity is to be enhanced on a large scale. The company-wide reward system should support creativity, including recognition and financial incentives. Organizational leaders should encourage information sharing and collaboration, which lead to the development of the expertise so necessary for creativity and to more opportunities for intrinsic motivation. Executives who combat excessive politics can help creative people focus on work instead of fighting political battles. In a highly political environment, a worker would be hesitant to suggest a creative idea that was a political blunder, such as replacing a product particularly liked by the CEO.

8.  **Have favorable exchanges with creative workers.** Another insight into encouraging a creative climate is for leaders to have favorable exchanges with group members, as defined by LMX theory (see Chapter 9). A study with 191 research and development specialists found a positive relationship between LMX ratings and creativity of workers as measured by supervisory ratings.[44] When group members have positive relationships with their manager, they may have a more relaxed mental attitude that allows the imagination to flow. A useful strategy for enhancing creativity throughout the organization is to emphasize the importance of working with a sense of heightened awareness, of being alert to new possibilities.

9.  **Give financial rewards for innovation.** Creativity is self-rewarding to some extent because it is so exciting. Nevertheless, financial rewards for contributions to innovation help sustain a climate of innovation. Jeffrey Wadsworth is the chief executive of the Battelle Memorial Institute, a think tank of 23,000 employees specializing in inventions for profit. He points out that financial rewards for creativity are widespread in industry and universities. "If you publish a patent you get $1,000, or you get $1 in a frame. Or you get a piece of the action moving forward."[45] Another factor is that financial rewards have spurred useful inventions for hundreds of years. More recent research with high-tech teams suggests that financial inducements are also important for enhancing the creativity of groups. Two of the financial inducements were "provide competitive bonuses," and "offer good health care and medical insurance beyond legal requirements."[46]

Figure 11-3 presents capsule descriptions of five illustrative companies that are successful in establishing a climate and culture for creative thinking.

## Methods of Managing Creative Workers

Closely related to establishing organizational conditions favoring creativity is choosing effective methods for managing creative workers. The suggestions that follow supplement effective leadership and management practices in general.[47]

| COMPANY | JUSTIFICATION FOR BEING PERCEIVED AS INNOVATIVE |
|---------|--------------------------------------------------|
| Apple Inc. | Apple has consistently invented products that have created enormous demand for consumer-oriented digital technology, including the iPad that has been the pacesetter for tablet computers, and the iPhone. Business leaders throughout the world admire the creativity of Apple, as led by an innovative design team, and Apple products are increasingly used in the workplace. The legal staff at Apple continually fights off imitators of the company's innovations. |
| CVS Health | Although its thousands of stores (or pharmacies) sell a wide variety of everyday products, CVS Health has made considerable progress in redefining retail health care. CVS has introduced in-store clinics because about one half of their patients come in on nights and weekends, and one half do not have a primary-care physician. CVS has partnered with the Watson supercomputer to monitor the health of its patients with respect to following their prescriptions or if their health is deteriorating. |
| Nike | The best-known sports clothing and equipment company in the world, Nike continues to introduce products into the market that have a science fiction feel. One example is the FuelBand, an electronic bracelet that measures a person's movements throughout the day whether the person plays golf, jogs, or walks. Color cues help readers track activity, such as red for inactive, and green for having achieved a daily goal. |
| Trader Joe's | Beloved by its customers, this grocery chain jumped past Whole Foods to become the favorite specialty grocer in the United States. Part of the innovation is in the selection of products that are both low priced and have a gourmet appeal. |
| Fitbit | Fitbit is categorized as highly innovative for making health tracking mainstream. The company has one of the high-rank apps at the Apple App Store. Fitbit continually improves the software on its wrist bands, prompting wearers to follow and challenge their friends. |

**FIGURE 11-3** Five Consumer-Oriented Business Organizations Judged to Be Highly Innovative.

*Source: Based partially on information in Fast Company Staff "The World's 50 Most Innovative Companies,"
Fast Company, March 2016, pp. 28–110; "Most innovative Companies," October 20–22, 2016, pp. 66–118;
Alan Murray, "50 Most Innovative Companies," Fortune (www.fortune.com), December 2, 2015, pp. 1–4.*

1. ***Give creative people tools and resources that allow their work to stand out.*** Creative workers have a high degree of self-motivation and therefore want to achieve high-quality output. To achieve such high quality, they usually need adequate resources, such as state-of-the-art equipment and an ample travel budget for such purposes as conducting research.

2. ***Give creative people flexibility and a minimum amount of structure.*** Many creative workers regard heavy structure as the death knell of creativity. *Structure* for these workers means rules and regulations, many layers of approval, strict dress codes, fixed office hours, rigid assignments, and fill-in-the-blank Internet forms. (Typically, the leader/manager will have to achieve a workable compromise in this area that stays within the framework of organizational policy. Regular office hours, for example, are a must for team assignments. Also, creative people may need help with meeting deadlines because many creative people do not manage time well.)

3. ***Give gentle feedback when turning down an idea.*** Creative employees are emotionally involved with their work. As a result, they are likely to interpret criticism as a personal attack on their self-worth. (Students often feel the same way about their term papers and projects.)

4. ***Employ creative people to manage and evaluate creative workers.*** Managers of creative workers should have some creative ability of their own so that they can understand creativity and be credible as leaders. Understanding the creative process is important for evaluating the creative contribution of others. What constitutes creative output is somewhat subjective, but the output can be tied to objective criteria. At Hallmark Cards, Inc., for example, creativity is measured by such factors as how well the creative work sold and how well it performed in a consumer preference test. In general, a manager's intuition about the potential contribution of a creative idea or product still weighs heavily in the evaluation.

The accompanying Leader in Action insert describes a technology leader who is highly creative and also aware of the importance of building a creative and innovative organization.

## LEADER IN ACTION

### Gerry McGovern, Chief Creative Officer of Land Rover Leads with Passion and Inspiration

Gerry McGovern is recognized as one of the world's leading automobile designers, and also provides leadership to a team of talented and creative designers. His current job title is design director and chief creative officer for Land Rover. He is now responsible for guiding and creating visions for Land Rover, and working to ensure a consistent look among the Land Rover brands.

McGovern launched his career at Chrysler Corporation in Detroit, before returning to the United Kingdom as senior designer for Peugeot, and then joined the Rover Group. He became the lead designer for the acclaimed MGF sports care, the Land Rover Freelander, which became the bestselling compact SUV in Europe for seven years. He also led the team that designed the third-generation Range Rover. McGovern then worked for the Ford Motor Company to help rejuvenate the Lincoln–Mercury brands. After that he returned to the United Kingdom to run a design consultancy owned by Land Rover. In 2004, McGovern rejoined Land Rover, where he has remained since.

McGovern's approach to combining his own creativity with that of team members in reflected in his work at Lincoln. He states, "The challenge was to re-create Lincoln back to its glamorous heyday and I hired designers from all over the world."

Land Rover had faced difficult times, including narrow profit margins, when McGovern took over design responsibility. He said that the turnaround could not have been achieved without smarter leadership (from the top of the organization), streamlined decision making, and uncompromising design. McGovern was convinced that Land Rover's status could be improved by focusing on aesthetics—making the vehicles as well known for their striking appearance as well as for conquering rugged terrain.

McGovern headed the team that created the highly successful Range Rover Evoque. He said that the stylish new vehicle could never had gone into production as he had envisaged without the strong support for its design by the company's new owners, Tata Motors of India. (Tata bought both Land Rover and Jaguar from Ford in 2008.) Ratan Tata, Chairman of the Tata Group at the time, insisted that design must be equal with other disciplines in the business. McGovern says, "So we started to develop a vision for the brand in terms of what we wanted Land Rover to be, as opposed to what it was." In terms of his approach to leadership, McGovern says, "Our decisions are more based around how we work together and respect each other's disciplines. I don't tell the engineering director how to design his suspension system, and he doesn't tell me how to design the overall car. It's about having a vision and sticking to it."

McGovern advises other leaders, "Demonstrate your expertise in everything you do and be passionate about what you believe in. Bring people with you and learn the battles you need to fight."

After graduating with a degree in industrial design at Coventry University, McGovern earned a master's degree at the Royal College of Art in London, with a major in automotive design. His passion for design extends beyond vehicles. He is an authority on modern architecture and furniture, and is an avid collector of contemporary art.

### QUESTIONS

1. What qualifications does Gerry McGovern possess that most likely contribute to his effectiveness as a leader of automotive design groups?

2. Visualize Land Rovers you have seen recently (including photos on the Internet or one that you or someone in your network owns). What is your reaction to the appearance of these vehicles?

*Source:* Original story created from facts and observations in the following sources: Chris Maxwell, "Land Rover's Gerry McGovern," *Director Magazine* (www.director.co.uk), May 11, 2015, pp. 1–21; "How Did I Get Here? Gerry McGovern," *Bloombergbusinessweek*, October 26–November 1, 2015, p. 84; "Automotive Design Director Gerry McGovern—Land Rover," (www.landrover .com), 2016, pp. 1–4; "Innovative Leaders: Gerry McGovern, Design Director, Land Rover," *www.Landroverusa.com*, 2016, pp. 1–4.

## Leadership Practices Focused Specifically on Enhancing Innovation

Creativity in organizations leads to innovations in products, services, and processes (such as a billing system or safety improvement). All leadership and management practices that enhance creative problem solving therefore also enhance innovation. Here, we describe seven additional leadership initiatives specifically geared toward enhancing innovation.

1. *Emphasize transformational leadership if possible.* A macro-perspective on a leader's role in fostering innovation is to exercise transformational leadership. The transformational leader creates an environment of change and growth. Based on case histories, management professors Adegoke Oke, Natasha Munshi, and Fred O. Walumbwa concluded that transformational leaders are particularly well suited to jump start the innovation process.[48] This is probably because the transformational leader is good at providing intellectual stimulation.

2. *Continually pursue innovation.* A major characteristic of the Most Admired Companies, as compiled by the Hay Group consultancy for *Fortune*, is constant innovation. Translated into practice, this means that company leaders stay alert to innovative possibilities. Innovation is important because a new technology can make an industry obsolete or place it in grave danger. What will happen to petroleum refineries when (and if) electric cars and trucks dominate the market? Another practical way of pursuing innovation is to assign innovation teams freed of daily time-to-market pressures. At tool maker Stanley Works, one team based in Maryland concentrates on developing new technology to current products. A second team in the United Kingdom develops disruptive technologies. The teams are given time, money, and regular access to senior leaders. One of the first hits from the innovation teams was a motion-activated screwdriver inspired by the concept behind a Nintendo Wii controller.[49]

3. *Take risks and encourage risk taking.* "No risk, no reward" is a rule of life that applies equally well to the leadership of innovation. Even in a slow-growth economy, companies cannot win big in the marketplace by doing things just a teeny bit better than the competition. It is necessary to gamble intelligently, shrewdly, and selectively, even during a period of insecurity and instability.[50] Because most new ideas fail, part of taking risks is being willing to go down blind alleys.

4. *Emphasize collaboration among employees.* Most innovations stem from networks, that is, groups of people working in concert. The workers needed for the innovation are often dispersed throughout the organization. Choosing the right leader for a project can be the key to collaboration. The workers chosen to develop new ideas are often top performers in individual areas. However, they may be lacking the connections within the company that are vital for accomplishing the innovation task. For instance, an outstanding engineer might be selected to lead a major project. But a lower ranking engineer who has worked in more divisions of the company might be a wiser choice because he or she could tap broader knowledge and connections inside the company.

   Leaders in multiunit organizations are at an advantage for innovation because workers from the various units can share ideas that would be useful for many different products. For example, if one unit of a medical company developed a patch for delivering medicine to the body, other units might be able to profit from the same technology. The topic of encouraging idea sharing will be reintroduced in Chapter 13.

   A more direct way of attaining collaboration is to organize workers into teams for purposes of innovation. Wadsworth from Battelle notes that most of the successful innovations he has seen have come from remarkably complex teams. People from different disciplines, such as accountants, lawyers, and customer service representatives must work together smoothly for innovation to surface.[51]

5. ***Avoid innovation for its own sake.*** Leaders also have to exercise good judgment: Innovation just for the sake of innovation is not always valuable. Many gadgets are scientific marvels, yet they have limited market appeal. An example is the robot lawnmower, which arouses the curiosity of many people but does not appeal much to consumers. Most companies have loads of interesting ideas floating to the surface, but very few will even translate into a profitable product or service.

6. ***Use loose–tight leadership.*** *Looseness* refers to granting space for new ideas and exploration, whereas a tight approach means finally making a choice among the alternatives. Innovation is also enhanced when workers throughout the organization are able to pursue absurd ideas without penalty for being wrong or for having wasted some resources. An axiom of creativity is that many ideas typically have to be tried before a commercially successful one emerges.

## READER'S ROADMAP

So far, we have studied considerable information about the nature of leadership; the attributes, behaviors, and styles of leaders; the ethics and social responsibility of leaders; and how leaders exert power and use politics and influence. We then studied techniques for developing teamwork as well as motivation and coaching skills. After having studied creativity and innovation as part of leadership, we focus next on communication skills as they relate to leadership.

## SUMMARY

A creative idea becomes an innovation when it is implemented or commercialized. Creativity is an essential characteristic of leaders. A creative leader brings forth ideas or things that did not exist previously or that existed in a different form. The creative process has been divided into five steps: opportunity or problem recognition; immersion (the individual becomes immersed in the idea); incubation (the idea simmers); insight (a solution surfaces); and verification and application (the person supports and implements the idea).

Distinguishing characteristics of creative people fall into four areas: knowledge, cognitive abilities, personality, passion for the task, and the experience of flow. Creative people possess extensive knowledge, good intellectual skills, intellectual curiosity, and a wide range of interests. Personality attributes of creative people include a positive self-image, tolerance for isolation, nonconformity, and the ability to tolerate ambiguity and chaos. Passion for the work and flow are related to intense intrinsic motivation. Creative people also enjoy interacting with others. The right personal characteristics must interact with the right environment to produce creative problem solving.

A major strategy for becoming creative is to overcome traditional thinking, or a traditional mental set. Also, it is necessary to break down rigid thinking that

blocks new ideas. Yet, workers still need some constraints in terms of creative solutions to problems. Imagination is still required to think outside the box within the limits of a required framework.

Creative thinking can be enhanced by systematically collecting fresh ideas, including collecting ideas, establishing idea quotas, using whiteboards throughout the company, and granting time to tinker. Brainstorming is a key idea-generation method even for the most advanced technology companies. Goals are an important part of brainstorming. A spin off of brainstorming is the pet-peeve technique, in which a group thinks of all the possible complaints others might have about their unit. The generation of creative ideas has moral implications. Every idea and product has potential harmful consequences in minor and major ways.

Self-help techniques to enhance creative problem solving include (1) practicing creativity-enhancing exercises; (2) staying alert to opportunities; (3) maintaining enthusiasm and being happy; (4) maintaining and using a systematic place for recording ideas; (5) playing the roles of explorer, artist, judge, and lawyer; (6) engaging in appropriate physical exercise; and (7) soliciting feedback on your performance.

Establishing a climate conducive to creative problem solving is another requirement of effective leadership. Fostering a culture of originality is a major step forward. Such a culture includes expecting employees to generate a large number of ideas, and striking the right balance between cohesion and dissent in the organization.

Leadership practice for enhancing creating include (1) hire creative people from the outside and identify creative people from within; (2) provide intellectual challenge; (3) empower workers and allow them freedom to choose their own method; (4) supply the right resources; (5) design work groups effectively; (6) have supervisors encouraging and linking innovation to performance; (7) give organizational support for creativity and explain how innovation improves

performance; (8) have favorable exchanges with creative workers; and (9) give financial rewards for innovation.

Special attention should be paid to managing creative workers. One should provide excellent tools and resources, give creative people flexibility, turn down ideas gently, and employ creative people to manage and evaluate creative workers.

Leadership practices that focus specifically on enhancing innovation include the following: emphasize transformational leadership; continually pursue innovation; take risks and encourage risk taking; emphasize collaboration; avoid innovation for its own sake; and use loose–tight leadership.

## KEY TERMS

innovation 282
creativity 282

intuition 286
experience of flow 288

pet-peeve technique 291

## GUIDELINES FOR ACTION AND SKILL DEVELOPMENT

Although creativity is important for leaders, research suggests that being perceived as highly creative has a downside. Creative people are sometimes perceived as quirky, and such a perception can block a person's attempt to climb the leadership and management ladder. In studies conducted with business groups in India, and then repeated with U.S. college students, individuals who expressed more creative ideas were viewed as having less—not more—leadership talent.[52]

The way to get around this potential negative perception is for the imaginative person who wants to climb the leadership ladder to frequently remind others in a subtle way that he or she is business-oriented. If you are the creative person aspiring to climb the ladder, casually mention such concepts as the return on investment of your ideas, and how your idea might contribute to the bottom line.

In an attempt to be consumer oriented, many business leaders believe that all innovation should stem from customer desires and suggestions, as often revealed in a focus group. True product leadership, however, can sometimes stem from offering a new product or service consumers never thought they wanted or needed. During the first McIntosh team retreat, one member asked whether market research would be helpful to find out what customers wanted. Steve Jobs, replied, "No, because customers don't know what they want until we've shown them." He then quoted the famous line from Henry Ford, "If I'd asked

customers what they wanted, they would have told me, 'A faster horse!'" The point here is that the product leader's own intuition can sometimes be the source of profitable innovation.[53]

### Discussion Questions and Activities

1. Give an example of creativity in business that does not relate to the development or marketing of a product or service.
2. How might a leader being highly creative inspire subordinates?
3. Assume that you are the leader of the paperclip manufacturing division of a company. Do you think it would be worth your time and that of your group to attempt to improve the design and intended use of the paperclip? Explain your reasoning.
4. In what way does your current program of study contribute to your ability to solve problems creatively?
5. The opinion has often been expressed that too much emphasis on teamwork inhibits creativity. What do you think of this argument?
6. Describe a leadership situation in which you think a leader being a creative thinker would be more important than him or her being charismatic.
7. Several people have written that Twitter is one of the most creative developments in the history of

business and the world in general. What is your opinion about Twitter as a powerfully creative development?

8. What do you think the next great creative breakthrough in business will be that will rival e-commerce and mobile phones in importance? (Loads of product planners and business leaders are waiting for your answer.)

9. Assuming that you are convinced that creativity is a legitimate part of a leader's role, what percent of your working time do you think you should invest in creative thinking? Explain your answer.

10. Speak to the most creative person you know in any field, and find out if he or she uses any specific creativity-enhancing technique. Be prepared to bring your findings back to class.

## LEADERSHIP CASE PROBLEM A

### The T-Shirt Production Innovators

In 2011, two Brown University seniors, Walker Williams and Evan Stites-Clayton, were sad that their favorite bar in Providence, Rhode Island was closing. To commemorate the closing, the two friends decided to print T-shirts, but they were struck by the upfront costs, and the need to estimate how many of each size they would need to order. Williams built a website to take orders and measure demand, and also posted a link to the site on Facebook. By morning, hundreds of orders were received, along with a few e-mails requesting that he create similar websites for the T-shirt ideas of other people. The Aha Moment arrived for Williams, and he immediately knew that he had hit upon a commercially viable idea. The company Teespring soon followed.

Today Teespring is one of the top T-shirt vendors in the United States, and prints approximately 7 million shirts annually, with annual revenues estimated at $100 million. T-shirts have been shipped to more than eighty countries worldwide. The company has grown to over 300 employees. The business model is that individuals create Internet campaigns to sell custom T-shirts and related clothing on the Teespring website. Campaign creators are required to design and market the product themselves, but they are not required to invest money upfront, paying only when they have secured orders for their T-shirts.

Teespring's role is to fulfill order for campaigns that have attained their sale goals, and then ships the T-shirts to the buyers. T-shirts are printed on demand, thereby avoiding the problem of inventory accumulation. Teespring does all the T-shirt manufacturing and shipping for the designer, whereas the designer creates the idea and helps market the T-shirt through social media and word-of-mouth. However, the company also contributes to advertising on Facebook.

Tools on the Teespring website enable the T-shirt designer to upload their ideas and slogans. The designers can select which quality and type of shirt (traditional hoodie, or tank top) they choose to print on, and many different fonts and icons are possible. The designer then chooses how many T-shirts he or she aspires to sell, and sets a sales goal. If a minimum of five T-shirts are preordered, Teespring produces the items and ships them directly to customers, charging the designed about $9 per T-shirt. The T-shirt designer sets the retail price per item.

The Teespring model has been so successful that the founders built a printing facility in Kentucky, where all the shirts can be produced and shipped efficiently. An example of a Teespring success story is restaurant manager Benny Hsu, who earned more than $120,000 in one year with a Tee-shirt bearing the slogan, "Keep calm and let the radiation therapist take care of it."

### Questions

1. In what way have the founders of Teespring demonstrated creative and innovative leadership?
2. In what way does Teespring provide its customers an opportunity to develop their creativity skills?
3. What is your evaluation of the prospects of Teespring being sustainable in the sense of lasting a long time as a business?
4. If you were required to come up with a T-shirt to sell through Teespring, what message would you place on the T-shirt?

*Source:* Case based on facts and observations in the following sources: Alyson Shontell, "A Startup Called Teespring Has Turned 10 People Into Millionaires, and It Just Raised $35 Million To Kill Excess Inventory," *Business Insider* (www.businessinsider.com), November 18, 2014, pp. 1–7; "How to Make Money from Teespring without Spending a Penny!" *Tee Income* (www.teeincome.com), 2016; Bridget Sauer, *HackToStart-Episode 30* (http://hacktostart.com), February 3, 2015, pp. 1–6; Adam Satarino, "How Your T-Shirt Can Make You Rich," *Bloomberg Businessweek*, April 20–26, 2015.

## ASSOCIATED ROLE PLAY

One study plays the role of the operations manager at Teespring. The operations manager explains to co-founders Evan-Stites Clayton and Walker Williams that he or she doubts the company has a sustainable business model because so many enterprises can make custom T-shirts. Two other students play the roles of Clayton and Williams who are upset with the operations manager, yet they see some truth in what he or she is saying. Other students might provide feedback on the productivity of the meeting.

## LEADERSHIP CASE PROBLEM B

### "How Can We Encourage a Few Disrupters?"

Adrianna is the CEO of Luxury Designs, an office furniture company that has been in business for forty years. The company both manufactures its own furniture and assembles furniture from a few manufacturers overseas. Although Luxury Designs is profitable, revenue has declined slowly for five years. In today's meeting with her top management team, Adrianna is going to discuss the need for innovation.

"We are meeting today on a topic we have talked about in the past. I also sent you an e-mail on this topic just two days ago to give you an opportunity to think about today's meeting. My concern is that we are not doing anything radical enough to deal with today's market for office furniture. A big hurdle we face is that the market for fashionable office furniture is shrinking as more and more private offices and even cubicles are being eliminated. Almost any old work table and chairs will do in an open-space office."

Seth, the director of new product development, signaled that he wanted to comment. "We are right with you, Adrianna. We are in the design phase of some interesting concepts in open-office design. We are thinking of some really cool tables, chairs, and whiteboards that will excite our consumers."

Adrianna replied, "Seth, I am confident that you and your group will tweak our product line to have something new to offer. But the challenge I have for us as company leadership is to find a way to be disrupters. Our long-term prosperity depends on disrupting the industry, rather than just adapting to trends.

"You have heard about disruption. The PCs disrupted the mainframe computer industry a long time ago. Cell phones and smartphones disrupted the traditional telephone makers. The ZIP Cars disrupted the car rental business. Uber and Lyft disrupted the taxi business. I want somebody, somewhere in Luxury designs to come up with an idea to disrupt the office furniture industry. If we have to cannibalize some of our traditional business, that's okay."

Diane, the CFO said, "Maybe we should run a one-time disrupter campaign, and pay a big bonus for the best idea. We have to figure out how to encourage a few disrupters."

Adrianna said, "Diane, your idea has some merit. But we have to go beyond a one-time gimmick to get us on the right path. Let's all meet one week from today to reintroduce the topic of disrupting the office furniture industry."

### Questions

1. What do you recommend that leadership at Luxury Designs do to facilitate having a disrupter within the company?
2. What thought should Adrianna and the other members of the leadership team at Luxury Design give to going beyond the confines of the office furniture industry in order to be a disrupter?
3. In what way is this case about creativity and innovation?

## ASSOCIATED ROLE PLAY

One student plays the role of Seth, the head of new product development, who decides to meet with his own group of product developers for a brainstorming session. He tells them that maybe the company will be able to set up an atmosphere that encourages disruption, but in the meantime why not develop a breakthrough office furniture idea of our own. A few other students play the role of members of the product development group, perhaps including the department administrative assistant, to brainstorm ideas for a breakthrough idea in office furniture. Seth believes that the product development group can be successful at disruption. Run the role play for about fifteen minutes to see what plausible ideas you develop.

## LEADERSHIP SKILL-BUILDING EXERCISE 11-3

### My Leadership Portfolio

For this chapter's entry into your leadership portfolio, record any creative or innovative idea you have had lately in relation to organizational activity, including school. After recording the idea, ask yourself what prompted you to develop it. If you have not contributed a creative idea recently, your assignment is to develop a creative idea within the next ten days. If possible, make plans to implement the idea; otherwise, it will not lead to innovation. Here is an example of a creative community initiative taken by Alexis, a marketing major:

> In my neighborhood, there is a ten-story high-rise building. Practically all of the tenants are senior citizens who live on limited pensions. Some of the folks in the building are in their eighties or even their nineties. The building is old and not particularly warm, especially for people with poor blood circulation. I've often heard friends and family members say that we should do something to help the seniors in the high rise, but nobody seems to go beyond expressing a little sympathy.
>
> Then I got a brainstorm. I thought, "Why not organize a 'Socks for Seniors' program?" My friends and I would buy dozens of pairs of socks that usually sell for about $4.00 a pair from deep discounters like Dollar General. We could raise some of the money by returning bottles and cans with deposits. A few friends of mine made a bunch of phone calls, and we raised $200 in no time for our project. Then, one cold night, we visited the high rise, rang a few doorbells, and told the residents what we were up to. We were allowed in to start distributing the socks. The smiles and words of appreciation we received were enormous. My idea is so good, I plan to do it every year. My friends are with me, and we think that if we post this idea on a website, it might spread around the country.

## LEADERSHIP SKILL-BUILDING EXERCISE 11-4

### The Multimedia Presentation

Here is an opportunity to be creative about the topic of business creativity. Work individually or in groups to develop a multimedia presentation about the importance of creativity in business. By *multimedia*, we refer to using more than one media to develop your presentation. For example, you might make a presentation using bulleted lists, narratives, still photos, video clips, and Internet links. It might also be possible to upload your presentation to a social networking site. The presentation might also include music, art, poetry, or quotations from literary figures. Spoken words might also be considered a medium for delivering your message. If the multimedia presentations are limited to about five minutes, class time might allow for several students, or student groups, to present.

## NOTES

1. Original story based on facts and observations in the following sources: Robert McMillan and Alistair Barr, "Google Taps Director for Cloud Push," *The Wall Street Journal*, December 24, 2015, p. B5; Barb Darrow, "Google Names Diane Green to Lead Its Cloud Business," *http://foortune.com*, November 19, 2015, pp. 1–6; Ron Miller, "Diane Greene Wants to Put the Enterprise Front and Center of Google Cloud Strategy," *https://techcrunch*, May 30, 2016, pp. 1–9; Robert Hof, "Google Cloud Chief Diane Greene: Here's How We'll Catch Amazon and Microsoft," *Forbes* (www.forbes.com), May 8, 2016, pp. 1–5.

2. Emma Seppala, "How Senior Executives Find Time to Be Creative," *Harvard Business Review* (https://hbr.org), September 14, 2016. p. 1.

3. Andrew Razeghi, "Innovation: Vehicle to Greatness," *Executive Leadership*, December 2011, p. 3.

4. Warren Bennis, "The Challenges of Leadership in the Modern World," *American Psychologist*, January 2007, p. 2.

5. Graham Wallas, *The Art of Thought* (New York: Harcourt Brace, 1926).

6. Josh Quittner, "How Jeff Bezos Rules the Retail Space," *Fortune*, May 5, 2008, pp. 126–132; "Jeff Bezos: Founder and CEO, Amazon.com," *Academy of Achievement* (www.achievement.org), August 9, 2010, pp. 1–4.

7. Teresa M. Amabile, "How to Kill Creativity," *Harvard Business Review*, September–October 1998, pp. 78–79; Darrell K. Rigby, Kara Gruver, and James Allen, "Innovation in Turbulent Times," *Harvard Business Review*, June 2009, pp. 79–86.

8. Maria Bartiromo, "Entrepreneur Lives the Dream: Chobani's Ulukaya Created Greek Yogurt Craze," *USA Today*, June 18, 2013.

9. Ned Herrmann, "Is It True that Creativity Resides in the Right Hemisphere of the Brains?" *www.scientificamerican.com*, September 2, 2014, pp. 1–16.

10. Research of Damasio reported in Karen Weintraub, "Inner Workings of a Creative Brain," *USA Today*, November 9, 2013; Amy Novotney, "No Such Thing as 'Right-Brained' or 'Left-Brained,' New Research Finds," *Monitor on Psychology*, November 2013, p. 10.

11. Research reported in Joe Robinson, "Do You Have What It Takes?" *Entrepreneur*, January 2014, p. 49.

12. Cited in "Larry Page on How to Change the World," *Fortune*, May 12, 2008, p. 84.

13. Amabile, "How To Kill Creativity," p. 79.

14. Mihaly Csikszentmihalyi, "If We Are So Rich, Why Aren't We Happy?" *American Psychologist*, October 1999, p. 824.

15. "Putting Creativity into Action," *Success Workshop*, supplement to The Pryor Report, April 1996, p. 1.

16. Cited in Dawn Klingensmith, "Give Your Team Direction," *CTW Features*, March 8, 2011. Based on information in Shawn Coyne, *Brainsteering: A Better Approach to Breakthrough Ideas* (New York: HarperCollins, 2011).

17. Donald Sull, "The Simple Rules of Disciplined Innovation," *McKinsey & Company* (www.mckinsey.com), May 2015, p. 1.

18. Seppata, "How Senior Executives Find Time to Be Creative," p. 5; Rema, "Features and Benefits of Nike Flyknit Technology," *Aktors* (www.aktors.org), June 18, 2015, pp. 1–4.

19. Rachel Emma Silverman, "Doodling for Dollars," *The Wall Street Journal*, April 25, 2012, pp. B1, B8.

20. Brian M. Carney and Issac Getz, "How an Endangered Google Policy Got Results," *The Wall Street Journal*, August 29, 2013, p. A15.

21. Geoff Colvin, "Brad Smith: Getting Rid of Friction," *Fortune*, July 21, 2014, p. 24.

22. Alec Foege, "The Trouble with Tinkering Time: Company-Mandated 'Play' Is the Latest Craze—But There Are Far Better Ways to Spark Innovation," *The Wall Street Journal*, January 19–20, 2013, p. C3.

23. Michael Orey, "Inside Nathan Myhrvold's Mysterious New Idea Machine," *BusinessWeek*, July 3, 2006, pp. 54, 57; Jim Kerstetter and Josh Lowensohn, "Inside Intellectual Ventures, the Most Hated Company in Tech," *http://news.cnet.com*, August 21, 2012, pp. 1–2.

24. Dori Meinert, "Brainstorming Gone Bad," *HR Magazine*, April 2018, p. 14.

25. Michael Schrage, "Playing Around with Brainstorming," *Harvard Business Review*, March 2001, pp. 149–154; "Stock a Room to Improve Brainstorming," *Business Management Daily* (www.businessmanagementdaily.com), March 18, 2011, p. 1.

26. Anne Sagen, "Creativity Tools: Versatile Problem Solvers That Can Double as Fun and Games," *Supervisory Management*, October 1991, pp. 1–2.

27. Gerald Sindell, *The Genius Machine: The 11 Steps That Turn Raw Material into Brilliance* (Novato, CA: New World Library, 2009).

28. Sindell, *The Genius Machine*, p. 40.

29. Juanita Weaver, "The Mental Picture: Bringing Your Definition of Creativity into Focus," *Entrepreneur*, February 2003, p. 69.

30. Finding multiple uses for a paperclip might have been the first creativity development exercise in history.

31. Tom Tobin, "Inspired to Be Innovators," *Democrat and Chronicle*, May 24, 2012, p. 5B.

32. Quoted in Alex F. Osburn, "Breakthrough Ideas," *Success*, October 1990, p. 38.

33. Research cited in Bill Breen, "The Six Myths of Creativity," *Fast Company*, December 2004, p. 78.

34. "Be a Creative Problem Solver," *Executive Strategies*, June 6, 1989, pp. 1–2.

35. Richard A. Lovett, "Jog Your Brain: Looking for a Creative Spark? Hop to the Gym," *Psychology Today*, May/June 2006, p. 55.

36. Quoted in Seppala, "How Senior Executives Find Time to Be Creative," p. 4.

37. Kathleen D. De Stobbeleir, Susan J. Ashford, and Dirk Buyens, "Self-Regulation of Creativity at Work: The Role of Feedback Seeking In Creative Performance," *Academy of Management Journal*, August 2011, pp. 811–831.

38. Adam Grant, "How to Build a Culture of Originality," *Harvard Business Review*, March 2016, pp. 86–94; Interview with Adam Grant, "Six Secrets to True Originality," *McKinsey & Company* (www.mckinsey.com), August 2016, pp. 1–8.

39. Rujie Qu, Onne Janssen, and Kan Shi, "Transformational Leadership and Follower Creativity: The Mediating Role of Follower Relational Identification and the Moderating Role of Leader Creativity Expectations," *The Leadership Quarterly*, April 2015, pp. 286–299.

40. Amabile and Khaire, "Creativity and the Role of the Leader," pp. 100–109; "How to Kill Creativity," pp. 80–81; Teresa M. Amabile, Constance N. Hadley, and Steven J. Kramer, "Creativity Under the Gun," *Harvard Business Review*, August 2002, pp. 52–61; Giles Hirst, Daan van Kippenberg, and Jing Zhou, "A Cross-Level Perspective on Employee Creativity: Goal Orientation, Team Learning Behavior, and Individual Creativity," *Academy of Management Journal*, April 2009, pp. 280–293.

41. Quoted in Jena McGregor "25 Most Innovative Companies," *BusinessWeek*, May 14, 2007, p. 52.

42. Xiaomeng Zhang and Kathryn M. Bartol, "Linking Empowering Leadership and Employee Creativity: The Influence of Psychological Empowerment, Intrinsic Motivation, and Creative Process Engagement," *Academy of Management Journal*, February 2010, pp. 107–128.

43. Feron Yuan and Richard W. Woodman, "Innovative Behavior in the Workplace: The Role of Performance and Image Outcome Expectations," *Academy of Management Journal*, April 2010, pp. 323–342.

44. Pamela Tierney, Steven M. Farmer, and George B. Graen, "An Examination of Leadership and Employee Creativity: The Relevance of Traits and Relationships," *Personnel Psychology*, Autumn 1999, pp. 591–620.

45. Quoted in "The Profit Motive," *The Wall Street Journal*, September 27, 2010, p. R11.

46. Liangding Jia, Jason D. Shaw, Anne S. Tsui, and Tae-Youn Pasrk, "A Social Structural Perspective on Employee-Organization Relationships and Employee Creativity," *Academy of Management Journal*, June 2014, pp. 869–891.

47. Shari Caudron, "Strategies for Managing Creative Workers," *Personnel Journal*, December 1994, pp. 104–113; Chris Pentila, "An Art in Itself," *Entrepreneur*, December 2003, pp. 96–97.

48. Adegoke Oke, Natasha Munshi, and Fred O. Walumbwa, "The Influence of Leadership Process on Innovational Processes and Activities," *Organizational Dynamics*, January–March 2009, pp. 64–72.

49. Todd Henneman, "Brighter Ideas," *Workforce Management*, January 2013, p. 18.

50. Rob Cross, Andrew Hargadon, Salvatore Parise, and Robert J. Thomas, "Together We Innovate," *The Wall Street Journal*, September 15–16, 2007, p. R6.

51. "The Profit Motive," p. R11.

52. Jennifer Mueller, Jack A. Goncalo, and Dishan Klamdar, "Recognizing Creative Leadership: Can Creative Idea Expression Negatively Relate to Perceptions of Leadership Potential?" *Journal of Experimental Social Psychology*, March 2011, pp. 494–498; "A Bias against 'Quirky'? Why Creative People Can Lose Out on Leadership Positions," *Knowledge@Wharton* (http://knowledge.wharton.upenn.edu/), February 16, 2011, pp. 1–3.

53. Walter Isaacson, "The Real Leadership Lessons of Steve Jobs," *Harvard Business Review*, April 2012, p. 96.

## CHAPTER 12

# Communication and Conflict Resolution Skills

S outhwest Airlines has developed a reputation spanning over 45 years for a low-cost airline with exceptional service offered by happy, friendly employees who exert extra effort to satisfy their passengers. The airline serves over 100 million passengers annually. What Southwest passengers do not see, but profit from indirectly, is the communication principles and practices of the airline's leadership that facilitate such a high level of customer service.

In January 2013, Gary C. Kelly, chairman of the board, president, and chief executive officer (CEO) of Southwest presented a new corporate vision and purpose intended to motivate employees to elevate their customer service to new heights. The vision is "to become the world's most loved, most flown, and most profitable airline." The Southwest vision is supported by its purpose: "We exist to connect people to what's important in their lives through friendly, reliable, and low-cost air travel."

Company leadership and management decided to use storytelling as a key approach to assure that all the 49,000 employees pursue the vision each work day. An example of the storytelling is stories about reliability. These stories often focus on business travel. In one video a businesswoman says, "They board the fastest, they get my bags off the fastest, which is efficient. I know exactly when I will land every week, and I can easily schedule my meetings because I know they'll be on time."

Another approach to communicating with employees is Kelly's weekly Monday morning audio message that can be heard via a toll-free number and is podcast on the employee blog. The message might be about company plans, such as expansion to another city. Employee recognition is frequently contained in these messages, such as attributing much of the company's success to the people of Southwest Airline. Kelly, as do other managers, frequently remind employees that a key part of the corporate culture is to follow the Golden Rule—treat each other the way we want to be treated.

Kelly believes that a strong relationship with people is based on communication. He says, "I think communication is most effective if it includes top management. Southwest's top-down communication is carried out through a collaborative effort between Kelly and the company's communication team. The communication might be face-to-face, but digital transmission is also of major importance.[1]

The executive leader just described acts on an obvious truth that many leaders ignore—open communication between company leaders and group members helps an organization overcome problems and attain success. Effective managers and leaders listen to employees, and open communications contribute to leadership effectiveness. John Hamm notes that effective communication is a leader's most essential tool for executing the essential job of leadership: inspiring organizational members to take responsibility for creating a better future.[2]

Effective communication skills contribute to all aspects of leadership. Chapter 3 describes how charismatic leaders are masterful oral communicators. This chapter expands on this theme and also covers the contribution of written, persuasive, and nonverbal communication. In addition, this chapter describes the leadership use of communication networks, how the ability to overcome cross-cultural communication barriers enhances leadership effectiveness. Finally, because leaders spend a substantial amount of communication time resolving conflicts, the chapter also discusses conflict resolution and negotiating skills.

To focus your thinking on your communication effectiveness, complete Leadership Self-Assessment Quiz 12-1.

## Communication Networks for Leaders

A major feature of communication by leaders is to rely on networks of contacts both in-person and electronically. Without being connected to other people, leaders would find it almost impossible to carry out their various roles. Communication researchers Bruce Hoppe and Claire Reinelt note that leadership networks are a response to a rapidly changing world in which interconnectedness is important because it facilitates learning and solving complex problems. Networks provide resources and support for leaders. With networks, leaders have more impact because they influence more people.[3] Many of these contacts are within the organization, but many are also external, such as communicating with a customer, supplier, government official, or union official.

# LEADERSHIP SELF-ASSESSMENT QUIZ 12-1

## A Self-Portrait of My Communication Effectiveness

**Instructions:** The following statements relate to various aspects of communication effectiveness. Indicate whether each of the statements is mostly true or mostly false, even if the most accurate answer would depend somewhat on the situation. Asking another person who is familiar with your communication behavior to help you answer the questions may improve the accuracy of your answers.

| | | MOSTLY TRUE | MOSTLY FALSE |
|---|---|---|---|
| 1. | When I begin to speak in a group, most people stop talking, turn toward me, and listen. | ☐ | ☐ |
| 2. | I receive compliments on the quality of my writing, including my e-mail messages and social media posts. | ☐ | ☐ |
| 3. | The reaction to the outgoing message on my voice mail has been favorable. | ☐ | ☐ |
| 4. | I welcome the opportunity to speak in front of a group. | ☐ | ☐ |
| 5. | I have published something, including a letter to the editor, an article for the school newspaper, or a comment in a company newsletter. | ☐ | ☐ |
| 6. | I have my own website, and have received at least two compliments about its effectiveness. | ☐ | ☐ |
| 7. | The vast majority of my written projects in school have received a grade of B or A. | ☐ | ☐ |
| 8. | People generally laugh when I tell a joke or make what I think is a witty comment. | ☐ | ☐ |
| 9. | I stay informed by reading newspapers, watching news on television, or reading news websites. | ☐ | ☐ |
| 10. | I have heard such terms as enthusiastic, animated, colorful, or dynamic applied to me. | ☐ | ☐ |
| 11. | The text messages I send look a little better in terms of spelling and grammar than most of the text messages I receive. | ☐ | ☐ |

Total score: _____

**Scoring and Interpretation:** If eight or more of these statements are true in relation to you, it is most likely that you are an effective communicator. If three or fewer statements are true, you may need substantial improvement in your communication skills. Your scores are probably highly correlated with charisma.

**Skill Development:** The behaviors indicated by the ten statements in the self-assessment exercise are significant for leaders because much of a leader's impact is determined by his or her communication style. Although effective leaders vary considerably in their communication style, they usually create a positive impact if they can communicate well. Observe some current business leaders on CNBC News or a similar channel to develop a feel for the communication style of successful business leaders.

A focus on the communication networks of leaders is also important because much of leadership activity and effectiveness depends on working within a network.[4] The point made in chapter about leadership being a relationship between and among people is part of the network perspective on leadership. Expressed simply, the leader works within the context of a network.

Here we describe briefly how organizational leaders use face-to-face (or in-person) as well as social media networks to communicate. Recognize, however, that the categories often overlap. A leader might be speaking with a colleague from another department in the company cafeteria, and then continue the communication that evening by tweeting the network member.

## Face-to-Face Communication Networks

Developing networks of live interpersonal contacts remains an essential method for a leader building relationships, motivating others, and attaining collaboration. Even the most smartphone-obsessed executives who carry several mobile devices with them at the same time supplement their electronic messages with some personal contacts. A major reason that face-to-face communication networks are vital is that leaders achieve more engagement and credibility when they participate in genuine conversation with the subordinates and coworkers. A *conversation* in this sense is a frank exchange of ideas and information with an agenda specified or unspecified.[5] An example would be a product designer at an automotive manufacturer talking with the CEO about how the company emphasizing fuel-efficient vehicles might make sense for the environment but could be losing sales. The designer might allude to the fact that the latest growth in vehicles sales is for pickup trucks and SUVs, not small-size vehicles. The two people would talk about the issue rather than the CEO delivering as stern message about obeying his or her orders.

The ongoing value of face-to-face communication was reinforced in a survey conducted by Future Workplace and Randstad. A key finding was that although the digital natives in the workplace have different values than previous generations, 39 percent prefer in-person communication over digital forms, such as e-mail, social networking, and video-conferencing.[6] (These findings might also be interpreted that 61 percent of digital natives prefer electronic communication over the face-to-face type.)

Various types of leadership networks have been identified, with four of these types being particularly relevant. First is the *peer leadership network* that is a system of social ties among leaders who are connected through shared interests and commitments, as well as shared work. Network members share information, provide advice and support, engage in mutual learning, and sometimes collaborate together. Members of the leader's network are perceived as providing resources that can be trusted.[7]

The *operational network* is aimed at doing one's assigned task more effectively. It involves cultivating stronger relationships with coworkers whose membership in the network is clear. Some of these relationships may be part of the formal structure, such as getting cost data from a member of the finance department. *Personal networks* engage cooperative people from outside the organization in a person's effort to develop personally and advance. This type of networking might involve being mentored on how to deal with a challenge, such as dealing with the problem of sexual harassment by a senior manager. (The personal network has much in common with the peer network, except that it might include people who are not peers.)

*Strategic networks* focus networking on attaining business goals directly. At this level, the manager creates a network that will help identify and capitalize on new opportunities for the company, such as breaking into the African market.[8] Even when the manager's own company has good resources for identifying business opportunities, speaking to external people can provide a fresh and useful perspective.

## Social Media Networks

An important use of the social media is for the leader to build and maintain a professional network, much like being a member of LinkedIn. The productive leader is more likely to focus on contacts of relevance or *density* rather than focus on accumulating hundreds of superficial network members. The websites used for networking can be external (or public) as well as internal. Most consulting and management services firms, such as Accenture, have widely internal social media websites.

The *strength-of-ties* perspective explains the difference between strong and weak ties.[9] The quality of a contact in the network is particularly important for social media networks because so many contacts can be of dubious value. A key part of the theory is that there are different densities in different parts of the network. A high-density network consists of close friends or associates linked together, such as CEOs in the same industry exchanging information. In contrast, a low-density network consists of acquaintances linked together.

The relationships among the different actors in a network can be broadly classified into two major types: strong versus weak ties and direct versus indirect ties. An acquaintance would be a weak tie, whereas a close friend would be a strong tie. Strength of ties would ordinarily be measured by frequency of contact, yet some contact could be relatively superficial and others might be more emotional and intimate. Melissa might ask Trevor for status reports on his prediction about currency fluctuation, whereas she talks to Sylvie about her career and her relationship with her boss. (The conversation about the relationship with the boss would probably only take place on a social media website if it could not be observed by others.)

Direct versus indirect ties relate to whether you are directly connected to a person because of a contact you developed, or indirectly, such as a friend of a friend. Your direct contact might be Mike, but Mike is connected to Sally, so Sally is an indirect contact.

The accompanying Leader in Action box illustrates a CEO of a well-known company who makes extensive, or even excessive, use of social media in his work.

# LEADER IN ACTION

## T-Mobile CEO John Legere, Uses Twitter for Serious Business Communication

John Legere, the CEO of T-Mobile, one of the three largest mobile phone companies in the United States, contends that he spends practically every spare moment on social media, particularly Twitter. "It's something I'm doing every minute of the day. It's all I do. When I sit alone at a bar, I do Twitter. Maybe that's a little sad. But my peer CEOs would never do it, because it's way too hard and very unglamorous." Legere is such a prolific Twitter user the company gave him his own emoji, a complimentary cartoon figure of a young man with long hair (see #tweetjohn).

Legere tweets about a variety of topics but his major thrust is interacting directly with T-Mobile customers. Although the CEO, he's one of the company's go-to customer service agents. Legere credits his obsessive use of social media as one of the catalysts for T-Mobile's substantial turnaround in recent years. Several of the company's service enhancements, such as the Data Stash monthly rollover program stemmed from customer tweets.

According to Legere, he learns almost everything he needs to know to lead T-Mobile from Twitter exchanges. Information found in customer tweets is often used for executive action. Legere explains: "I take every Tweet that comes in and I read it. I forward it to my people. My executive team gets them, we reply, and at my staff meeting every Tuesday, we track social media impressions, what they are and how we responded to them. It takes a lot of time. It's a lot of fun."

Legere said that listening to customers on Twitter an monitoring customer support calls provides the leadership team information about what pain points they can resolve to give T-Mobile a competitive edge and stimulate customer growth. He sees his tweeting as a way of touching customers. He claims that some customers visit T-Mobile stores and say, "I can't believe you're on Twitter and liked my tweet. I'm switching."

Before becoming CEO of T-Mobile in 2012, Legere held executive positions at AT&T, Dell, and Global Crossing. He holds a BBA from the University of Massachusetts, Amherst, an MS from the MIT Sloan School of Management, and an MBA from Fairleigh Dickinson University.

### QUESTIONS

1. In what way does Legere make use of Twitter to improve the organizational effectiveness of T-Mobile?

2. If Legere spends practically all his time on Twitter, what other aspects of his CEO role might he be neglecting?

*Source:* Original story based on facts and observations in the following sources: David Goldman, "John Legere Credits His 'Sad' Life for T-Mobile's Turnaround," *http://money.cnn.com*, March 28, 2016, pp. 1–4; Blair Hanley Frank, "How T-Mobile Boss Uses Twitter to Stay Ahead of Rivals," *www.geekwire.com*, October 5, 2014, pp. 1–4; Matthew Hussey, "Why On Earth Did Twitter Give T-Mobile's John Legere His Own Emoji?" *http://thenextweb.com*, March 29, 2016, pp. 1–4; Kaja Whitehouse, "The F-Bomb Dropping, Maverick CEO of T-Mobile," *USA Today*, August 9, 2013, pp. 1–3.

## Group Chat as a Leadership Communication Network

Recent observations suggest that chat is becoming the backbone of many business organizations, bringing together both people and multiple software programs. Chat has been widely used as a form of customer support for many years, with many customers preferring to exchange written messages rather than engaging in conversation with a customer service or tech support representative. Chat can be both immediate and synchronous identical to a phone call or physical meeting, or asynchronous like e-mail.

The leadership communication angle to chat is that the leader can quickly connect with several group members at the same time, and receive feedback and input in the amount of time it takes to compose a sentence. Chat is also used as a tame huddle to prepare for the workday. One crowdfunding company uses a "Standup bot" whereby team members summarize what they did yesterday, what they plan to do today, and any impediments to their work.[10] The leader can play a key role by making suggestions about overcoming the impediments.

## Inspirational and Powerful Communication

Information about communicating persuasively and effectively is extensive. Here we focus on suggestions for creating the high-impact communication that contributes to effective leadership. Effective communication is frequently a criterion for being promoted to a leadership position. In this section, suggestions for becoming an inspirational and emotion-provoking communicator are divided into the following two categories: (1) speaking and writing and (2) nonverbal communication. We also discuss seven basic principles of persuasion.

## Speaking and Writing

You are already familiar with the basics of effective spoken and written communication. Yet, the basics—such as writing and speaking clearly, maintaining eye contact, and not mumbling—are only starting points. The majority of effective leaders have an extra snap or panache in their communication style, both in day-by-day conversations and when addressing a group. The same energy and excitement is reflected in both speaking and writing. Suggestions for dynamic and persuasive oral and written communication are presented next and outlined in Table 12-1.

*Be Credible*    Attempts at persuasion, including inspirational speaking and writing, begin with the credibility of the message sender. If the speaker is perceived as highly credible, the attempt at persuasive communication is more likely to be successful. The perception of credibility is influenced by many factors, including those covered in this entire section.

**TABLE 12-1** Suggestions for Inspirational Speaking and Writing

---

**A. A Variety of Inspirational Tactics**

**1.** Be credible.

**2.** Gear your message to the listener.

**3.** Sell group members on the benefits of your suggestions.

**4.** Use heavy-impact and emotion-provoking words.

**5.** Use anecdotes to communicate meaning.

**6.** Back up conclusions with data (to a point).

**7.** Minimize language errors, junk words, and vocalized pauses.

**8.** Write crisp, clear memos, letters, and reports, including a front-loaded message.

**9.** Use business jargon in appropriate doses.

**B.  The Power-Oriented Linguistic Style**

Included here are a variety of factors such as downplaying uncertainty, emphasizing direct rather than indirect talk, and choosing an effective communication frame.

Being trustworthy heavily influences being perceived as credible. A leader with a reputation for lying will have a difficult time convincing people about the merits of a new initiative such as outsourcing. Being perceived as intelligent and knowledgeable is another major factor contributing to credibility.

*Gear Your Message to the Listener, Including His or Her Needs*   An axiom of persuasive communication is that a speaker must adapt the message to the listener's interests and motivations. The company CEO visiting a manufacturing plant will receive careful attention—and build support—when he says that jobs will not be outsourced to another country. The same CEO will receive the support of stockholders when he emphasizes how cost reductions will boost earnings per share and enlarge dividends.

In order to gear your message to the listener, it is usually necessary to figure out what he or she wants, or deal with the other person's perceived self-interest.[11] Visualize the head of a customer support center who believes strongly that more funding is necessary to meet the demands placed on the department. To be convincing, the woman needs to figure out what the CEO really expects from a customer support center. Careful listening might indicate that the CEO is mainly interested in customers not asking for refunds and/or bad-mouthing the company face-to-face as well as online. The customer support head can then direct her pitch for more funding in terms of how an expanded department can reduce merchandise returns and customer complaints.

The average intelligence level of the group is a key contingency factor in designing a persuasive message. People with high intelligence tend to be more influenced by messages based on strong, logical arguments. Bright people are also more likely to reject messages based on flawed logic.[12]

*Sell Group Members on the Benefits of Your Suggestions*   A leader is constrained by the willingness of group members to take action on his or her suggestions and initiatives. As a consequence, the leader must explain to group members how they can benefit from what he or she proposes. For example, a plant manager attempting to sell employees on the benefits of recycling supplies as much as possible might say, "If we can cut down enough on the cost of supplies, we might be able to save one or two jobs."

A variation on the same theme of selling benefits is to promise, or assure, results from your suggestion. For example, if the division president wants every group in the division to reduce costs by 10 percent, the president might say, "If the entire division can reduce costs by 10 percent for the fiscal year, I promise you that the bonus pool will be increased by at least 1 percent."

*Use Heavy-Impact and Emotion-Provoking Words*   Certain words used in the proper context give power and force to your speech. Used comfortably, naturally, and sincerely, these words will project the image of a self-confident person with leadership ability or potential. Two examples of heavy-impact phrases are "We will be outsourcing those portions of our knowledge work that are not mission critical" and "We will be leading edge in both product development and business processes." However, too much of this type of language will make the leader appear that he or she is imitating a Dilbert cartoon (a long-running cartoon satire about managers and businesspeople).

Closely related to heavy-impact language is the use of emotion-provoking words. An expert persuasive tactic is to sprinkle your speech with emotion-provoking—and therefore inspiring—words. Emotion-provoking words bring forth images of exciting events. Examples of emotion-provoking and powerful words include "*outclassing* the competition," "*partnering* with customers," "*surpassing* previous profits," "*capturing* customer loyalty," and "*rebounding* from a downturn." It also helps to use words and phrases that connote being modern. Those now in vogue include *virtual organization, transparent organization,* and *seamless organization.*

A large vocabulary assists using both heavy-impact and emotion-provoking words. When you need to persuade somebody on the spot, it is difficult to search for the right words in a dictionary or thesaurus—even if you access the Internet with your smartphone. Also, you need to practice a word a few times to use it comfortably for an important occasion.

**Use Anecdotes to Communicate Meaning**    Anecdotes are a powerful part of a leader's kit of persuasive and influence tactics, as already mentioned in this chapter and in Chapter 3 about charismatic leadership. Although storytelling is an ancient art, it is more in vogue than ever as a method for leaders to influence and inspire others. A carefully chosen anecdote is also useful in persuading group members about the importance of organizational values. So long as the anecdote is not repeated too frequently, it can communicate an important message.

Zippo is a consumer products company that has hundreds of anecdotes to share about how those sturdy steel cigarette lighters saved somebody's life by deflecting a bullet. It seems that the stories originated in World War II but have continued into modern times, such as how a Zippo in the pocket of a police worker prevented a criminal's bullet from killing the officer. Zippo leaders can inspire workers with such heroic tales starring the Zippo lighter. In recent years, Zippo has shifted into many nonsmoking-related products, but the anecdotes are still inspiring for the nonsmoker.

**Back Up Conclusions with Data**    You will be more persuasive if you support your spoken and written presentations with solid data. One approach to obtaining data is to collect them yourself—for example, by conducting an online survey of your customers or group members. Published sources also provide convincing data for arguments. Supporting data for hundreds of arguments can be found on appropriate websites, in the business pages of newspapers, and in business magazines and newspapers. The Statistical Abstract of the United States, published annually, is an inexpensive yet trusted reference for thousands of arguments.

Relying too much on research has a potential disadvantage, however. Being too dependent on data could suggest that you have little faith in your own intuition. For example, you might convey an impression of weakness if, when asked your opinion, you respond, "I can't answer until I collect some data." Leaders are generally decisive. An important issue, then, is for the leader to find the right balance between relying on data and using intuition alone when communicating an important point.

**Minimize Language Errors, Junk Words, and Vocalized Pauses**    Using colorful, powerful words enhances the perception that you are self-confident and have leadership qualities. Also, minimize the use of words and phrases that dilute the impact of your speech, such as "like," "you know," "you know what I mean," "he goes" (to mean "he says"), and "uh." Such junk words and vocalized pauses convey the impression of low self-confidence, especially in a professional setting, and detract from a sharp communication image.

An effective way to decrease the use of these extraneous words is to video-record your side of a phone conversation and then play it back. Many people are not aware that they use extraneous words until they hear recordings of their speech.

An effective leader should be sure always to write and speak with grammatical precision to give the impression of being articulate and well informed, thereby enhancing his or her leadership stature. Here are two examples of common language errors: "Just between you and I" is wrong; "just between you and me" is correct. "Him and I," or "her and I," are incorrect phrases despite how frequently they creep into social and business language. "He and I" and "she and I" are correct when used as the subjects of a sentence. "Him and me" or "Her and me" are correct when used as the objects of a sentence. For example, "She and I greeted the client" and "The client greeted her and me" are both correct.

Another very common error is using the plural pronoun *they* to refer to a singular antecedent. For example, "The systems analyst said that *they* cannot help us" is incorrect. "The systems analyst said *she* cannot help us" is correct. Perhaps the worst error of all in this regard is to say something like, "I would like to speak to *them*" in reference to one person.

Using *they* to refer to a singular antecedent has become so common in the English language that many people no longer make the distinction between singular and plural. For example, nowadays most people say, "Everyone placed their order," when actually

"Everyone placed his (or her) order" is the grammatically correct statement. Staff at Facebook systematically confuse singular and plural with such statements as "What does Jessica do in *their* spare time?" Some of these errors are subtle and are made so frequently that many people do not realize they are wrong; but again, avoiding grammatical errors may enhance a person's leadership stature.

Perhaps the most common language error business leaders make is to convert hundreds of nouns into verbs. Many nouns do become legitimate verbs, such as using the noun *phone* for a verb, such as "I will phone you later." The leader has to set a limit, and perhaps not use such verb-to-noun conversions such as, "Facebook me tonight," "Focus-group this problem," and "Skype me a message." Yet, the hip leader will correctly use nouns that have been recently been converted into dual use as a verb and noun, such as "Google some potential customers for this product." Judgment is called for with respect to which nouns should be used as verbs to avoid sounding silly, and therefore weak.

When in doubt about a potential language error, consult a respected dictionary or guide to business communications. With printed information, you at least know that the suggestions have usually been edited by a knowledgeable person.

### Use Business Jargon in Appropriate Doses

Business and government executives and professionals make frequent use of jargon. (Only athletic coaches exceed businesspeople in the heavy use of jargon and clichés.) Often the jargon is used automatically without deliberate thought, and at other times jargon words and phrases are chosen to help establish rapport with the receiver. A vastly overused phrase these days is "at the end of the day," with "buckets" fighting for second place. "The end of the day" has come to replace "in the final analysis," "space" has replaced industry sector, and "buckets" replace "categories." Many businesspeople say "at the end of the day" twice in the same few sentences.

Six major executives and management professors were asked which buzzwords they would ban from conversation in the boardroom, office, and beyond: The six disliked buzzwords, or jargon words, were "push the envelope," "de-layering" (in place of downsizing), "dynamic resilience," "out-of-the-box thinking," "passionate," and "viral."[13]

Sprinkling business talk with jargon does indeed help establish rapport and adds to a person's popularity. But too much jargon makes a person seem stereotyped in thinking, and perhaps even unwilling to express an original thought—and therefore lacking power.

### Write Crisp and Clear Memos, Letters, and Reports that Include a Front-Loaded Message

Business leaders characteristically write easy-to-read, well-organized messages, both in e-mail and in more formal reports. Writing, in addition to speaking, is more persuasive when key ideas are placed at the beginning of a conversation, e-mail message, paragraph, or sentence.[14] Front-loaded messages (those placed at the beginning of a sentence) are particularly important for leaders because people expect leaders to be forceful communicators. A front-loaded and powerful message might be "Cost reduction must be our immediate priority," which emphasizes that cost reduction is the major subject. It is clearly much more to the point than, for example, "All of us must reduce costs immediately."

One way to make sure messages are front-loaded is to use the active voice, making sure the subject of the sentence is doing the acting, not being acted upon. Compare the active (and front-loaded) message "Loyal workers should not take vacations during a company crisis" to the passive (not front-loaded) message "Vacations should not be taken by loyal workers during a company crisis." Recognize, however, that less emphasis is placed on the active voice today than several years ago. Also, the passive voice may be necessary for front-loading, as in "Cloud backups are recommended by cybersecurity experts."

Suggestions for effective business writing continue to evolve, and many of these tips are worthy of a leader's or potential leader's attention. For example, using "Dear" in a salutation is practiced rarely, particularly in the United States. Yet, "Hello" beats "Hey" for appearing dignified.

***Use a Power-Oriented Linguistic Style***    A major part of being persuasive involves choosing the correct **linguistic style**, a person's characteristic speaking pattern. According to Deborah Tannen, linguistic style involves such aspects as the amount of directness, pacing and pausing, word choice, and the use of such communication devices as jokes, figures of speech, anecdotes, questions, and apologies.[15]

Linguistic style is complex because it includes the culturally learned signals by which people communicate what they mean, along with how they interpret what others say and how they evaluate others. Many of the elements of a power-oriented linguistic style are included in other suggestions made in this section of the chapter, including using heavy-impact words. Here are several components of a linguistic style that would give power and authority to the message sender in many situations, as observed by Tannen and other language specialists:[16]

- Speak loudly enough to be heard by the majority of people with at least average hearing ability. Speaking too softly projects an image of low self-confidence.
- Make frequent use of a big picture perspective rather than focusing on details. Proving an overall direction makes the person presenting the idea seem more in control. After the big picture has been presented, a few supporting details can add to the persuasiveness of the pitch. The CEO of a startup might begin a presentation to potential investors by emphasizing that her company is one the most innovative in its niche of home and small-business security systems. She would then give a couple examples of these innovative devices.
- Minimize self-deprecation with phrases such as "This will probably sound stupid, but ..." Apologize infrequently, and particularly minimize saying, "I'm sorry."
- Make your point quickly. You know you are taking too long to reach a conclusion when others look bored or finish your sentences for you.
- Emphasize direct rather than indirect talk: Say, "I need your report by noon tomorrow," rather than, "I'm wondering if your report will be available by noon tomorrow."
- Weed out wimpy words. Speak up without qualifying or giving other indices of uncertainty. It is better to give dates for the completion of a project rather than say "I'll get it to you soon" or "It shouldn't be a problem." Instead, make a statement like "I will have my portion of the strategic plan shortly before Thanksgiving. I need to collect input from my team and sift through the information."
- Know exactly what you want. Your chances of selling an idea increase to the extent that you have clarified the idea in your own mind. The clearer and more committed you are at the outset of a session, the stronger you are as a persuader and the more powerful your language becomes.
- Speak at length, set the agenda for a conversation, make jokes, and laugh. Be ready to offer solutions to problems, as well as to suggest a program or plan. All of these points are more likely to create a sense of confidence in listeners.
- Strive to be bold in your statements. As a rule of thumb, be bold about ideas, but tentative about people. If you say something like "I have a plan that I think will solve these problems," you are presenting an idea, not attacking a person.
- Frame your comments in a way that increases your listener's receptivity. The *frame* is built around the best context for responding to the needs of others. An example would be to use the frame, "Let's dig a little deeper," when the other people present know something is wrong but cannot pinpoint the problem. Your purpose is to enlist the help of others in finding the underlying nature of the problem.

Despite these suggestions for having a power-oriented linguistic style, Tannen cautions that there is no one best way to communicate. How you project your power and authority is often dependent on the people involved, the organizational culture, the relative rank of the speakers, and other situational factors. The power-oriented linguistic style should be interpreted as a general guideline.

## Basic Principles of Persuasion

Persuasion is a major form of influence, so it has gained in importance in the modern organization because of the reason described in Chapter 8: Managers must often influence people for whom they have no formal responsibility. The trend stems from leaner corporate hierarchies and the breaking down of division walls. Managers must persuade peers in situations where lines of authority are unclear or do not exist. One way to be persuasive is to capitalize on scientific evidence about how to persuade people. Robert B. Cialdini has synthesized knowledge from experimental and social psychology about methods for getting people to concede, comply, or change. These principles can also be framed as influence principles, but with a focus on persuasion.[17] The seven principles described next have accompanying tactics that can be used to supplement the other approaches to persuasion described in this chapter. (The seventh principle is a recent addition to the basic six.)

1. *Liking: People like those who like them.* As a leader, you have a better chance of persuading and influencing group members who like you. Emphasizing similarities between you and the other person and offering praise are the two most reliable techniques for getting another person to like you. The leader should therefore emphasize similarities, such as common interests with group members. Praising others is a powerful influence technique and can be used effectively even when the leader finds something relatively small to compliment. Genuine praise is the most effective.

2. *Reciprocity: People repay in kind.* Managers can often influence group members to behave in a particular way by displaying the behavior first. The leader might therefore serve as a model of trust, good ethics, or strong commitment to company goals. In short, give what you want to receive.

3. *Social proof: People follow the lead of similar others.* Persuasion can have high impact when it comes from peers. If you as the leader want to influence a group to convert to a new procedure, such as virtually eliminating paper records in the office, ask a believer to speak up in a meeting or send his or her statement of support of digital record-keeping only.

4. *Consistency: People align with their clear commitments.* People need to feel committed to what you want them to do. After people take a stand or go on record in favor of a position, they prefer to stay with that commitment. Suppose you are the team leader and you want team members to become more active in the community as a way of creating a favorable image for the firm. If the team members talk about their plans to get involved and also put their plans in writing, they are more likely to follow through. If the people involved read their action plans to each other, the commitment will be even stronger.

5. *Authority: People defer to experts.* The action plan here is to make constituents aware of your expertise to enhance the probability that your plan will persuade them. A leader might mention certification in the technical area that is the subject of influence. For example, a leader attempting to persuade team members to use statistical data to improve quality might mention that he or she is certified in the quality process Six Sigma.

6. *Scarcity: People want more of what they can have less of.* An application of this principle is that the leader can persuade group members to act in a particular direction if the members believe that the resource at issue is shrinking rapidly. They might be influenced to enroll in a course in outsourcing knowledge work, for example, if they are told that the course may not be offered again for a long time. Another way to apply this principle is to persuade group members by using information not readily available to others. The leader might say, "I have some preliminary sales data. If we can increase our sales by just 10 percent in the last month of this quarter, we could be the highest performing unit in the company."

7. ***Pre-suasion: put people in a receptive mood before asking them for something.***
Persuasion is likely to be the most effective when you get others to agree with a message before it is even sent. You attempt to get the other person in a receptive mood before asking him or her for something. A practical approach to pre-suasion is to solicit other people's advice before proposing a key initiative. For example, you might ask for advice on your idea of consolidating three office locations into one. Asking the advice makes the other people more favorable toward your idea.[18]

The developer of these principles explains that they should be applied in combination to multiply their impact. For example, while establishing your expertise you might simultaneously praise people for their accomplishments. It is also important to be ethical, such as by not fabricating data to influence others.[19]

Another principle of persuasion of potential use to leaders is **altercasting**, in which you characterize another person as a certain type of person to encourage him or her to behave in a desired manner. You cast the other person, or alter, in a role before you make a request. The approach can work as a persuasion, or influence, tactic because many people want to rise to the occasion.[20] Suppose team leader Tammy has to deal for the third time with an angry client who wants to cancel the team's contract because of a cost overrun. Tammy recognizes that she is responsible for this task, but is performing poorly. She altercasts by saying to team member Ivy, "You're so effective in resolving conflict, how about you dealing with this irate client the next time she calls?"

## Nonverbal Communication Including Videoconferencing and Telepresence

Effective leaders are masterful nonverbal as well as verbal communicators. Nonverbal communication is important because leadership involves emotion, which words alone cannot communicate convincingly. A major component of the emotional impact of a message is communicated nonverbally.

A self-confident leader not only speaks and writes with assurance but also projects confidence through body position, gestures, and manner of speech. Not everybody interprets the same body language and other nonverbal signals in the same way, but some aspects of nonverbal behavior project a self-confident leadership image in many situations.[21]

- Using an erect posture when walking, standing, or sitting. Slouching and slumping are almost universally interpreted as an indicator of low self-confidence.
- Standing up straight during a confrontation. Cowering is interpreted as a sign of low self-confidence and poor leadership qualities.
- Patting other people on the back while nodding slightly.
- Standing with toes pointing outward rather than inward. Outward-pointing toes are usually perceived as indicators of superior status, whereas inward-pointing toes are perceived to indicate inferiority. Also, opening limbs at eighteen inches or more expresses power and dominance.
- Speaking at a moderate pace, with a loud, confident tone. People lacking in self-confidence tend to speak too rapidly or very slowly.
- Smiling frequently in a relaxed, natural-appearing manner.
- Maintaining eye contact with those around you, with the ideal gaze lasting about seven to ten seconds. The ability to make eye contact has multiplied in importance as a sign of leadership because so many people are accustomed to looking at their mobile devices at every possible moment, and therefore lack skill in looking directly at people.
- Gesturing in a relaxed, nonmechanical way, including pointing toward others in a way that welcomes rather than accuses, such as using a gesture to indicate, "You're right," or "It's your turn to comment."
- Taking up a lot of space, which might include extending the arms, conveys power and confidence.

A general approach to using nonverbal behavior that projects confidence is to have a goal of appearing self-confident and powerful. This type of autosuggestion makes many of the behaviors seem automatic. For example, if you say, "I am going to display leadership qualities in this meeting," you will have taken an important step toward appearing confident.

Your external image also plays an important role in communicating messages to others. People pay more respect and grant more privileges to those they perceive as being well dressed and neatly groomed. Even on casual dress days, most effective leaders will choose clothing that gives them an edge over others. Appearance includes more than the choice of clothing. Self-confidence is projected by such small items as the following:

- Neatly pressed and sparkling clean clothing
- Freshly polished shoes, or freshly cleaned athletic shoes
- Impeccable fingernails
- Clean jewelry in mint condition
- Well-maintained hair
- Good-looking teeth with a white or antique-white (or off-white) color

What constitutes a powerful and self-confident external image is often influenced by the organizational culture. At a software development company, for example, powerful people might dress more casually than at an investment banking firm. Leadership at many law firms is moving back toward formal business attire for the professional staff. Your verbal behavior and the forms of nonverbal behavior previously discussed contribute more to your leadership image than your clothing, providing you dress acceptably.

Videoconferencing places extra demands on the nonverbal communication skills of leaders, managers, and other participants. An advance in videoconferencing, referred to as *telepresence*, places even more demands on nonverbal communication skills because it appears closer to human presence. For example, the illumination highlights the facial features of the people sitting in the telepresence studio. Some telepresence systems are custom-built meeting rooms equipped with a bank of high-definition screens and cameras. Other systems take the form of humanoid robots that are used outside of meeting rooms. Etiquette tips for making a strong nonverbal presence during a videoconference or telepresence conference include the following (and are similar to nonverbal communication suggestions in general):

- Choose what you wear carefully, remembering that busy (confusing and complex) patterns look poor on video. Also do not wear formal attire mixed with running shoes because you might move into full camera view.
- Speak in crisp conversational tones and pay attention. (The tone and paying attention are the nonverbal aspects of communication.)
- Never forget the video camera's powerful reach, such as catching you rolling your eyes when you disagree with a subordinate, or sending and receiving text messages during the conference.
- Avoid culturally insensitive gestures including large hand and body gestures that make many Asians feel uncomfortable. Asians believe that you should have long-term relationships before being demonstrative.[22]

An effective way of sharpening your videoconferencing and telepresence nonverbal skills, as well as other nonverbal skills, is to be videotaped several times. Make adjustments for anything you don't like, and repeat what you do like. Feedback on your behavior from another observer can be quite helpful.

Now that you have refreshed your thoughts on effective verbal and nonverbal communication, do Leadership Skill-Building Exercise 12-1.

# LEADERSHIP SKILL-BUILDING EXERCISE 12-1

## Feedback on Verbal and Nonverbal Behavior

Ten volunteers have one week to prepare a three-minute presentation on a course-related subject of their choice. The topics of these presentations could be as far-reaching as "The Importance of Investing in Gold" or "My Goals and Dreams." The class members who observe the presentations prepare feedback slips on 3 × 5 cards, describing how well the speakers communicated powerfully and inspirationally. One card per speaker is usually sufficient. Notations should be made for both verbal and nonverbal feedback.

Emphasis should be placed on positive feedback and constructive suggestions. Students pass the feedback cards along to the speakers. The cards can be anonymous to encourage frankness, but they should not be mean-spirited.

Persuading and inspiring others is one of the main vehicles for practicing leadership. Knowing how others perceive you helps you polish and refine your impact.

# Listening as a Leadership Skill

Listening is a fundamental management and leadership skill. Listening also provides the opportunity for dialogue and conversation, in which people understand each other better by taking turns having their point of view understood. For a leader to support and encourage a subordinate, active listening (as described in the discussion of coaching) is required. Also, effective leader–member exchanges require that each party listen to one another. The relationship between two parties cannot be enhanced unless each one listens to the other. Furthermore, leaders cannot identify problems unless they listen carefully to group members.

The relevance of careful listening to leadership effectiveness is underscored by the listening tours taken by newly appointed executives. Before making changes, such as deciding on new policies or developing strategy, the executive spends time listening to stakeholders such as employees, customers, and suppliers. When Adena Friedman returned as copresident of Nasdaq Inc, the first thing she did was embark on an international tour. (She left Nasdaq to serve as chief financial officer of an investment banker for two years.) "I met with clients and employees in every single one of our divisions across the world," said Friedman. She traveled to twenty-two cities in her first eighteen months.[23]

An effective approach to developing good listening habits is to remember to ask questions—and then listen to the answers. Bill Kanarick, the senior vice president and chief marketing officer of Sapient Corp., a global services company, believes that the organizational culture contributes to effective listening. He says that it is incumbent upon the company to create an environment that welcomes exploration and questioning.[24]

Three major impediments face the leader who wants to be an effective listener. First, the leader is so often overloaded with responsibilities, including analytical work, that it is difficult to take the time to carefully listen to subordinates. Second is the speed difference between speaking and listening. The average rate of speaking is between 110 and 200 words per minute, yet people can listen in the range of 400–3,000 words per minute. So the leader, as well as anybody else, will often let his or her mind wander. Third, multitasking is a major deterrent to listening carefully to subordinates because the leader who is involved in another task at the moment, such as glancing at a tablet computer, is not paying full attention to the speaker.

Here, we look at three leadership aspects of listening to supplement your general knowledge of listening, acquired most likely in other courses: showing respect, selective listening to problems, and making the rounds.

## Show Respect

A foundation tactic for a leader to become an effective listener is to show respect for others. Consultant Bernard T. Ferran provides the case in point of the COO of a large medical institution. He told Ferran that he could not run an operation as complex as a hospital without gathering input from staff members at all levels—from the chief of surgery to the custodial crew. The chief operating officer let everyone know that he believed each one of them had something unique to contribute. As the executive drew out the critical information, he attentively processed what he heard. Part of the COO's being liked and admired stemmed from his listening approach.[25]

A finding from a study based on 3,500 participants in a training program for managerial coaching supports the idea of showing respect. It was found that good listening included interactions that build a person's self-esteem. Good listeners made the other person feel emotionally supported and conveyed confidence in that individual.[26] An example of an esteem-building suggestion would be, "Your idea about reaching the Native American market is well thought through. Let's explore it further."

## Selective Listening to Problems

Organizational leaders are so often bombarded with demands and information that it is difficult to be attentive to a full range of problems. So the leader makes an intentional or unintentional decision to listen to just certain problems. Erika H. James notes that despite how our brains ordinarily work, success is dependent on staying open to all incoming information.[27] The busy leader must avoid listening to limited categories of information such as good news, bad news, or financial news. A CEO with a propensity to listen only to financial results might ignore any word of problems so long as the company is earning a profit.

## Making the Rounds

A robust communication channel for the leader/manager is to engage in face-to-face communication with direct reports and others, with an emphasis on listening. **Making the rounds** refers to the leader casually dropping by constituents to listen to their accomplishments, concerns, and problems and to share information. *Rounding* is a well-established concept from health care in which the physician talks to patients and other health care workers to observe problems and progress firsthand.[28] Through rounding, vital information is gathered if the physician or manager listens carefully. Making the rounds is also referred to as *management by walking around*, yet rounding seems more focused and systematic.

From the perspective of listening, the leader stays alert to potential problems. Assume that a subordinate is asked, "How are things going?" and he or she replies, "Not too terrible." This response begs a little digging, such as, "What is happening that is a little terrible?"

Leadership Skill-Building Exercise 12-2 gives you an opportunity to try out the fundamental leadership skill of listening.

# LEADERSHIP SKILL-BUILDING EXERCISE 12-2

### Leadership Listening

Six or seven students gather for a team meeting to discuss an important operational problem, such as finding new ways to reduce the cycle time required to complete their tasks, or deciding how to convince top management to expand the team budget. One person plays the role of the team leader. All of the group members take turns at making both useful

## EXERCISE 12-2 (continued)

and apparently not useful suggestions. The team leader, along with team members, displays careful listening whenever ideas surface. Students not directly involved in the group role play will take note of the listening skills they observe so that they can provide feedback later. Be particularly observant of selective listening. If class time allows, another team of six or seven students can repeat the group role play.

## Overcoming Cross-Cultural Communication Barriers

Another communication challenge facing leaders and managers is overcoming communication barriers created by dealing with people from different cultures and subcultures. Leaders typically communicate with people from other countries and with a more diverse group of people in their own country. Because of this workplace diversity, leaders who can manage a multicultural and cross-cultural work force are in strong demand. Here we give some guidelines for overcoming a variety of cross-cultural communication barriers. Implementing these guidelines will help overcome and prevent many communication problems. A useful starting point here is to take Leadership Self-Assessment Quiz 12-2 to help you think through your cross-cultural skills and attitudes.

## LEADERSHIP SELF-ASSESSMENT QUIZ 12-2

### Cross-Cultural Skills and Attitudes

*Instructions:* Listed here are various skills and attitudes that various employers and cross-cultural experts think are important for relating effectively to coworkers in a culturally diverse environment. Indicate whether or not each statement applies to you.

| | | APPLIES TO ME NOW | NOT THERE YET |
|---|---|---|---|
| 1. | I have spent some time in another country. | ☐ | ☐ |
| 2. | At least one of my friends is deaf, blind, or uses a wheelchair. | ☐ | ☐ |
| 3. | I have an approximate idea of how much the U.S. dollar is worth in comparison to the euro. | ☐ | ☐ |
| 4. | I have tried eating food from a culture much different than my own—aside from eating in a Chinese or Italian restaurant. | ☐ | ☐ |
| 5. | I can speak in a language other than my own. | ☐ | ☐ |
| 6. | I can read and write in a language other than my own. | ☐ | ☐ |
| 7. | I can understand people speaking in a language other than my own. | ☐ | ☐ |
| 8. | I can identify a religious holiday from at least three religions. | ☐ | ☐ |
| 9. | My friends include people of races different from my own. | ☐ | ☐ |
| 10. | My friends include people of different ages. | ☐ | ☐ |
| 11. | I feel (or would feel) comfortable having a friend with a sexual orientation different from mine. | ☐ | ☐ |
| 12. | My attitude is that although another culture may be very different from mine, that culture is equally good. | ☐ | ☐ |
| 13. | I would be willing to (or already do) hang art from different countries in my home. | ☐ | ☐ |

## QUIZ 12-2 (continued)

|  | | APPLIES TO ME NOW | NOT THERE YET |
|---|---|:---:|:---:|
| **14.** | I would accept (or have already accepted) a work assignment of more than several months in another country. | ☐ | ☐ |
| **15.** | I have a passport. | ☐ | ☐ |

**Scoring and Interpretation:** If you answered "Applies to Me Now" to ten or more questions, you most likely function well in a multicultural work environment. If you answered "Not There Yet" to ten or more questions, you need to develop more cross-cultural awareness and skills to work effectively in a multicultural work environment. You will notice that being bilingual gives you at least 4 points on this quiz.

1. ***Be sensitive to the fact that cross-cultural communication barriers exist.*** Awareness of these potential barriers is the first step in dealing with them. When dealing with a person of a different cultural background, solicit feedback to minimize cross-cultural barriers to communication. For example, investigate which types of praise or other rewards might be ineffective for a particular cultural group. In many instances, Asians newly arrived in the United States feel uncomfortable being praised in front of others because in Asian cultures group performance is valued more than individual performance.

   Being alert to cultural differences in values, attitudes, and etiquette will help you communicate more effectively with people from different cultures. Observe carefully the cultural mistakes listed in Table 12-2. At the same time, recognize that these *mistakes* are based on cultural stereotypes and reflect typical or average behavior of members of a particular cultural group.

2. ***Challenge your cultural assumptions.*** The assumptions we make about cultural groups can create communication barriers. The assumption you make about another group may not necessarily be incorrect, but stopping to challenge the assumptions may facilitate communication. A U.S. leader, for example, might assume that the norms of independence and autonomy are valued by all groups in the workplace. In reality, the idea of individual accomplishment does not have positive connotations for all groups. Among many Latino cultural groups, interpersonal harmony is valued over individual accomplishment.

3. ***Show respect for all workers.*** The same behavior that promotes good cross-cultural relations in general helps overcome communication barriers. A widely used comment that implies disrespect is to say to a person from another culture, "You have a funny accent." Should you be transposed to that person's culture, you too might have a "funny accent." The attitude of highest respect is to communicate your belief that although another person's culture is different from yours, it is not inferior to your culture. Showing respect for another culture can be more important than being bilingual in overcoming communication barriers.[29]

4. ***Use straightforward language, and speak slowly and clearly.*** When working with people who do not speak your language fluently, speak in an easy-to-understand manner. Minimize the use of idioms and analogies specific to your language. A systems analyst from New Delhi, India, left confused after a performance review with her manager. The manager said, "I will be giving you more important assignments because I notice some good chemistry between us." The woman did not understand that *good chemistry* means *rapport*, and she did not ask for clarification because she did not want to appear uninformed.

**TABLE 12-2** Cultural Mistakes to Avoid with Selected Cultural Groups

**Europe**

| | |
|---|---|
| Great Britain | • Asking personal questions. The British protect their privacy.<br>• Thinking that a businessperson from England is unenthusiastic when he or she says, "Not bad at all." English people understate positive emotion.<br>• Gossiping about royalty. |
| France | • Expecting to complete work during the French two-hour lunch.<br>• Attempting to conduct significant business during August—*la vacance* (vacation time). |
| Italy | • Eating too much pasta, as it is not the main course.<br>• Handing out business cards freely. Italians use them infrequently. |
| Spain | • Expecting punctuality. Your appointments will usually arrive twenty to thirty minutes late.<br>• Making the United States sign for "OK" with your thumb and forefinger. In Spain (and many other countries), this is vulgar. |
| Scandinavia (Denmark, Sweden, Norway) | • Being overly rank-conscious in these countries. Scandinavians pay relatively little attention to a person's place in the hierarchy. |

**Asia**

| | |
|---|---|
| All Asian Countries | • Pressuring an Asian job applicant or employee to brag about his or her accomplishments. Asians feel self-conscious when boasting about individual accomplishments and prefer to let the record speak for itself. In addition, they prefer to talk about group rather than individual accomplishment. |
| Japan | • Shaking hands or hugging Japanese (as well as other Asians) in public. Japanese consider the practices offensive.<br>• Not interpreting "We'll consider it" as a "no" when spoken by a Japanese businessperson. Japanese negotiators mean "no" when they say, "We'll consider it."<br>• Not giving small gifts to Japanese when conducting business. Japanese are offended by not receiving these gifts. |
| China | • Not taking a business card presented to you seriously, such as quickly putting it in your pocket.<br>• Using a strong handshake instead of a limp one. Insisting on a handshake rather than a polite bow.<br>• Making cold calls on Chinese business executives. An appropriate introduction is required for a first-time meeting with a Chinese official.<br>• Giving expensive gifts because this may obligate the person to reciprocate with something of equal value to you. Giving a clock can sometimes backfire because the Mandarin word for "to give clocks" resembles "to attend a dying relative." |
| Korea | • Saying "no." Koreans feel it is important to have visitors leave with good feelings. |
| India | • Telling Indians you prefer not to eat with your hands. If the Indians are not using cutlery when eating, they expect you to do likewise. |

**Mexico and Latin America**

| | |
|---|---|
| Mexico | • Flying into a Mexican city in the morning and expecting to close a deal by lunch. Mexicans build business relationships slowly. |
| Brazil | • Attempting to impress Brazilians by speaking a few words of Spanish. Portuguese is the official language of Brazil. |
| Most Latin American Countries | • Wearing elegant and expensive jewelry during a business meeting. Most Latin Americans think Americans should appear more conservative during a business meeting. |

A cultural mistake for Americans to avoid when conducting business in most countries outside the United States and Canada is to insist on getting down to business too quickly. North Americans in small towns also like to build a relationship before getting down to business. Also, the entire world is becoming more informal, as evidenced by people from different cultures addressing others by their first name upon first meeting.

*Source:* The first and third items about China are adapted from Eric Spitsnagel, "Impress Your Chinese Boss," *Bloomberg Businessweek*, January 16, 2012, pp. 80–81.

Speaking slowly is also important because even people who read and write a second language at an expert level may have difficulty catching some nuances of conversation. Facing the person from another culture directly also improves communication because your facial expressions and lips contribute to comprehension. And remember, there is no need to speak much louder.

5. *Look for signs of misunderstanding when your language is not the listener's native language.* Signs of misunderstanding may include nods and smiles not directly connected to what you are saying, a lack of questions, inappropriate laughter, and a blank expression. If these signs are present, work harder to apply the suggestions in point 4.[30] Also, ask questions to clarify misunderstanding, such as "Who would like clarification about what 'top-line revenue' means?"

6. *When the situation is appropriate, speak in the language of the people from another culture.* Americans who can speak another language are at a competitive advantage when dealing with businesspeople who speak that language. The language skill, however, must be more advanced than speaking a few basic words and phrases. Speaking the local language will often bring a person more insight and prevent misunderstandings. Equally important, being bilingual helps bring a person the respect that a leader needs to be fully credible.[31]

   A frustration the native English speaker who is using another language faces is that so many people around the world capitalize on an opportunity to speak English. So the leader who speaks another language to establish rapport might be rebuffed. Despite this problem, speaking another language in the workplace is likely to have a positive net effect.

   As more deaf people have been integrated into the work force, knowing American Sign Language can be a real advantage to a leader when some of his or her constituents are deaf.

7. *Observe cross-cultural differences in etiquette.* Violating rules of etiquette without explanation can erect immediate communication barriers. A major rule of business etiquette in most countries is that the participants conducting serious business together should first share a meal. So if you are invited to a banquet that takes place the night before discussions about a major business deal, regard the banquet as a major opportunity to build a relationship. To avoid the banquet is a serious faux pas.

8. *Do not be diverted by style, accent, grammar, or personal appearance.* Although these superficial factors are all related to business success, they are difficult to interpret when judging a person from another culture. It is therefore better to judge the merits of the statement or behavior. A highly intelligent worker from another culture may still be learning English and thus make basic mistakes. He or she might also not yet have developed a sensitivity to dress style in your culture, for example.

9. *Be sensitive to differences in nonverbal communication.* A person from another culture may misinterpret nonverbal signals. To use positive reinforcement, some managers will give a sideways hug to an employee or will touch the employee's arm. People from some cultures resent touching from workmates and will be offended. Koreans in particular dislike being touched or touching others in a work setting.

10. *Be attentive to individual differences in appearance.* A major cross-cultural insult is to confuse the identity of people because they are members of the same race or ethnic group. A study suggests that people have difficulty seeing individual differences among people of another race because they see so-called racial differences first; they might think, "He has the eyes of a Japanese person." However, people can learn to search for more distinguishing features, such as a dimple or eye color, and expression (serious or not so serious).[32]

## The Leader's Role in Resolving Conflict and Negotiating

Leaders and managers spend considerable time resolving conflicts and negotiating. A frequent estimate is that they devote about 20 percent of their time to dealing with conflict including negotiation. Conflict arises frequently among top executives, and it can have enormous consequences for the organization. An example of such competition would be two business units competing for resources.

Departmental competition has been regarded as the ugly underbelly of all sizes of companies, often resulting in product delays, increased costs, and dwindling market shares as departments fight each other for domination behind the scenes. Until conflict between or among the groups is resolved, collaboration is unlikely.[33] For example, if the operations group is in conflict with the human resources group, it will be difficult for the two groups to collaborate on a diversity training program.

Another type of intergroup conflict leaders might face is dealing with heavy demands from a large employee group, such as employees uniting to complain about working conditions. A frequent conflict of this type is a group of workers demanding a higher minimum wage, particularly at large discount retailers and fast-food chains. Leaders are sometimes involved in conflict with groups outside their organization, and such conflict may need to be resolved. An example is that state governments have begun demanding sales taxes from online merchants who claimed that they were exempt from such taxation.

An extensive description of conflict resolution is more appropriate for the study of managerial skills than for the study of leadership skills. The reason is because conflict resolution has more to do with establishing equilibrium than with helping the firm or organizational unit reach new heights. Here we focus on a basic framework for understanding conflict resolution styles, resolving conflict between two group members, and a few suggestions for negotiating and bargaining.

## Conflict Management Styles

As shown in Figure 12-1, a widely accepted finding is that there are five major styles of conflict management: competitive, accommodative, sharing, collaborative, and avoidant. Each style is based on a combination of satisfying one's own concerns (assertiveness) and satisfying the concerns of others (cooperativeness).[34] Leadership Self-Assessment Quiz 12-3 gives you an opportunity to think about your conflict management style.

**Competitive**

(High concern for self; low concern for other side.)

**Collaborative**

(High concern for self; high concern for other side.)

**Sharing**

(Looks for compromise; willing to go half-way.)

**Avoidant**

(Low concern for self; low concern for other side.)

**Accommodative**

(Low concern for self; high concern for other side.)

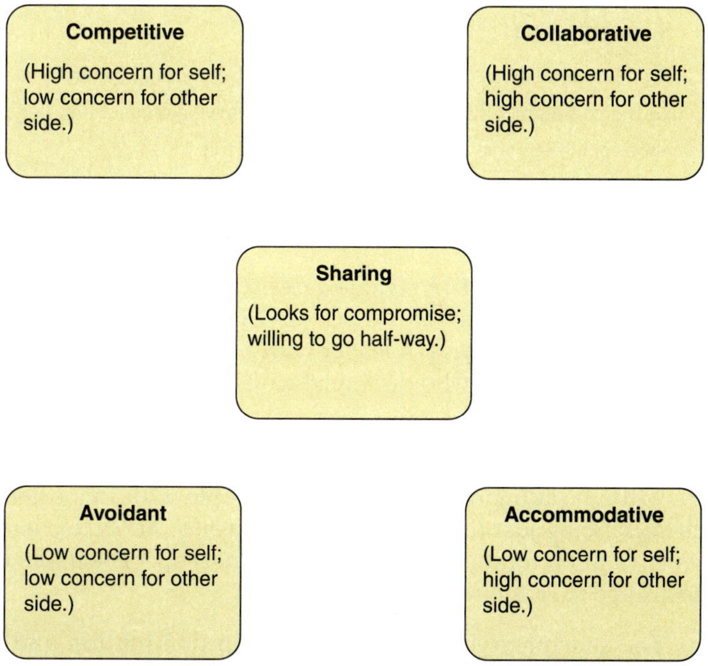

**FIGURE 12-1**    Conflict-Handling Styles According to the Degree of Cooperation and Assertiveness.

# LEADERSHIP SELF-ASSESSMENT QUIZ 12-3

### My Conflict Resolution Style

*Instructions:* Answer each of the following statements "mostly true" or "mostly false" with respect to how you have dealt with the situation, would deal with the situation, or how much you agree with the attitude expressed.

| | | MOSTLY TRUE | MOSTLY FALSE |
|---|---|---|---|
| **1.** | I see myself as a hard-hitting, smash-mouth negotiator. | ☐ | ☐ |
| **2.** | The best way to resolve conflict is to overwhelm the other side. | ☐ | ☐ |
| **3.** | When negotiating a price, I like to make sure that the other side walks away with at least some profit. | ☐ | ☐ |
| **4.** | When negotiating a price, I like to start with an outrageous demand or offer so I can eventually get the price I really wanted. | ☐ | ☐ |
| **5.** | After a successful negotiation, one side wins and one side loses. | ☐ | ☐ |
| **6.** | After a successful negotiation, both sides walk away with something of value. | ☐ | ☐ |
| **7.** | When I am in conflict with somebody else, I try to listen carefully to understand his or her point of view. | ☐ | ☐ |
| **8.** | Face it: Business is war, so why grant concessions when in a dispute? | ☐ | ☐ |
| **9.** | When working out a disagreement with a workmate, I keep in mind the fact that we will have to work together in the future. | ☐ | ☐ |
| **10.** | Nice people finish last when it comes to resolving disputes. | ☐ | ☐ |
| | **Total score:** | _____ | |

*Scoring and Interpretation:* Give yourself a score of 1 for each answer that matches the scoring key:

| | | | | | |
|---|---|---|---|---|---|
| 1. | Mostly false | 5. | Mostly false | 9. | Mostly true |
| 2. | Mostly false | 6. | Mostly true | 10. | Mostly false |
| 3. | Mostly false | 7. | Mostly true | | |
| 4. | Mostly true | 8. | Mostly false | | |

If your score is 8, 9, or 10, you most likely use the collaborative (win–win) approach to resolving conflict and negotiating. If your score is 7 or less, you most likely use the competitive (win–lose) approach to resolving conflict and negotiating. The collaborative approach is more likely to enhance your leadership effectiveness in the long run.

***Competitive Style*** The competitive style is a desire to achieve one's own goals at the expense of the other party, or to dominate. A person with a competitive orientation is likely to engage in win–lose power struggles. A leader with a competitive style might attempt to get another company leader fired who disagreed with him rather than looking to resolve differences between the two.

***Accommodative Style*** The accommodative style favors appeasement, or satisfying the other's concerns without taking care of one's own. People with this orientation may be generous or self-sacrificing just to maintain a relationship. An irate customer might be accommodated with a full refund, "just to shut him (or her) up." The intent of such accommodation might also be to retain the customer's loyalty.

***Sharing Style*** The sharing style is halfway between domination and appeasement. Sharers prefer moderate but incomplete satisfaction for both parties, which results in a compromise. The term *splitting the difference* reflects this orientation, which is commonly used in such activities as settling a patent infringement lawsuit.

**Collaborative Style**    In contrast to the other styles, the collaborative style reflects a desire to fully satisfy the desires of both parties. It is based on the underlying philosophy of the **win–win approach to conflict resolution**, the belief that after conflict has been resolved, both sides should gain something of value. The user of win–win approaches is genuinely concerned about arriving at a settlement that meets the needs of both parties, or at least does not badly damage the welfare of the other side. When collaborative approaches to resolving conflict are used, the relationships among the parties are built on and improved.

The collaborative style of conflict management has many variations, one of which is to agree with the person criticizing you. When you agree with a critic, you show that you seek a solution, not a way to demonstrate that you are right. If you agree with the substance of the criticism, you show that you are aware of the situation and ready to do what is best to solve the problem.

To illustrate, if a group member criticizes you for having been too harsh in your evaluation of him or her, you might say: "I agree that my evaluation was harsh, but I was harsh for a purpose. I want to be candid with you so you will be motivated to make what I think are necessary improvements." Your agreement is likely to spark further discussion about how the group member can improve. The collaborative style is the approach an effective leader is most likely to use because the outcome leads to increased productivity and satisfaction.

Another form of agreeing with criticism is for leaders to apologize when they have truly made a mistake. An apology often reduces conflict because the other side becomes less hostile, and the scene is set for cooperation. Visualize a scenario in which members of the executive team vote themselves large financial bonuses during a period of financial losses to the company and layoffs of employees. Saying, "We're sorry, and we goofed" to the union and/or employees can help soften the sting. Giving back some of the bonuses would be even more helpful. In general, a good apology must be perceived as genuine, with an honest appeal for forgiveness.[35]

**Avoidant Style**    Avoiders combine lack of cooperation and unassertiveness. They are indifferent to the concerns of either party. The person may actually be withdrawing from the conflict or be relying upon fate. An example of an avoider is a manager who stays out of a conflict between two team members, leaving them to resolve their own differences.

People engaged in conflict resolution typically combine several of the five resolution styles to accomplish their purpose. For example, a generally effective approach to resolving conflict is to be competitive with regard to a cost that is important to oneself but unimportant to the opponent, and at the same time use accommodation for a cost that is unimportant to oneself but important to the opponent.[36]

Deciding which mode or modes of conflict handling to use depends upon a number of variables. The major contingency factors are the importance of the conflict issue and the relative power of the opposing parties. An issue may be so important to a leader, such as preventing his or her organizational unit from being outsourced, that domination may be the most effective mode. At other times, a leader may use the accommodating mode of conflict management when the opposing side has much more power, and he or she may want to save domination for a more important issue in the future.

A variable influencing how much conflict a leader has to resolve is his or her personality. An accepting, warm, and understanding leader will have less conflict to resolve than a rejecting, cold, and noncompassionate leader. Ken Frazier, the Merck CEO, was formerly the company's general counsel and then the head of marketing. He minimizes conflict by scrupulously never making anyone look bad, including allowing scientists at the giant pharmaceutical firm do their job. Frazier says, "I am a person who does not subscribe to the hero-CEO school of thought."[37]

## Resolving Conflict Between Two Group Members

A high-level managerial skill is to help two or more group members resolve conflict between or among them. Much of the time a manager or leader invests in conflict resolution is geared toward assisting others to resolve their conflict. Often, the conflict is between the heads of two different departments or divisions. A team leader will sometimes be placed in the position of having to resolve conflict between or among team members.

A recent analysis suggests that destructive conflict stems from perceived incompatibility in the way the team members operate. Among the contributing factors are differences in personality, industry background, gender, and age.[38] An incompatibility problem that surfaces frequently is that a couple of team members might be big-picture thinkers, while a few others focus carefully on details. Big-picture-thinking Amy might say, "I see our team having a major impact on the total organization," Detail-thinking Tyler might say angrily, "Amy will you please tells us exactly what you have in mind? Be specific about we could accomplish."

The most useful approach is to get the parties in conflict to engage in confrontation and problem solving. (*Confrontation* refers to discussing the true problem, and *problem solving* refers to finding a way to resolve the conflict.) The manager sits down with the two sides and encourages them to talk to each other about the problem (rather than to the manager). This approach is preferable to inviting each side to speak with the manager or leader alone, because then each side might attempt to convince the manager that he or she is right.

During the confrontation and problem-solving session, the leader/manager is placed in a mediator role of being impartial and wanting the both sides to come to an agreement. As shown in the illustration below, the heart of the approach is *storytelling* in which each employee tells how and why the conflict started and persists. Each side must allow the other side to talk, and the leader maintains his or her impartiality.[39] An abbreviated example follows:

*Leader:* I've brought you two together to see if you can overcome the problems you have about sharing the workload during a period in which one of you is overloaded.

*Stephanie:* I'm glad you did. Josh never wants to help me, even when I'm drowning in customer requests.

*Josh:* I would be glad to help Stephanie if she ever agreed to help me. If she has any downtime, she runs to the break room so she can chat on her cellphone.

*Stephanie:* Look who's talking. I have seen you napping in your SUV when you have a little downtime.

*Leader:* I'm beginning to see what's going on here. Both of you are antagonistic toward each other, and you look for little faults to pick. With a little more respect on both sides, I think you would be more willing to help each other out.

*Josh:* Actually, Stephanie's not too bad. And I know she can perform well when she wants to. Next time I see her needing help, I'll pitch in.

*Stephanie:* I know that the name "Josh" is related to joking around, but our Josh really has a warm heart. I'm open to starting with a fresh slate. Maybe Josh can ask me politely the next time he needs help.

An effective component to this type of conflict resolution is for the leader to ask each side to restate what the other person has said.[40] In the scenario just presented, Josh might say, "I heard Stephanie say that I never want to help her." Stephanie might say, "I heard Josh say that I run to the break room to talk on my cellphone when I have a little downtime."

Conflict specialist Patrick S. Nugent believes that being able to intervene in the conflicts of group members is a management skill that grows in importance. Such competencies are useful in an emerging form of management based less on traditional hierarchy and more on developing self-managing subordinates and teams. When the conflict is between two different groups, such as online versus off-line marketing, a major goal of conflict resolution is to get the two sides to see the company's big picture.[41]

# Negotiating and Bargaining

As described in Chapter 1, negotiating and bargain is a basic leadership role. Few leaders have enough formal power to get everything they want without negotiation. Situations call for negotiation include arriving at a price for purchasing another company, receiving a tax break from a local government, or satisfying worker (or labor union) demands for adequate working conditions.

The link between negotiating and bargaining is that conflicts can be considered situations that call for negotiating and bargaining, or conferring with another person to resolve a problem. When you are trying to negotiate a fair price for relocating an office, you are simultaneously trying to resolve a conflict. At first, the demands of the two parties may seem incompatible, but through negotiation a salary may emerge that satisfies both parties. Here, we review a handful of practical negotiating tactics a leader will find helpful. The approaches to negotiation presented here emphasize a strategy of integration or collaboration, with a philosophy of win–win.

*Minimize Feeling or Looking Anxious During the Negotiation*   Negotiation specialist and assistant professor Alison Wood Brooks, at the Harvard Business School, advises us not to feel or look anxious during the negotiation session. Experiments suggest that negotiators who feel anxious tend to make weaker first offers, and are more likely to exit negotiation early. Brooks recommends that to minimizing being and looking anxious during negotiation, train, practice, and rehearse.[42] Visualize how you will conduct yourself during the negotiation and practice making some of your key statements. For example, look into the mirror or talk into a video cam, "We want you as a supplier, but your prices are 20 percent more than we are willing to pay." Role playing before the negotiation is also an effective way of reducing anxiety.

*Listen First to Investigate What the Other Side Wants*   An advanced negotiating technique is to begin by soliciting the other person's or group's point of view. You can use this information to shape the objectives of the negotiation, and figure out how you will be able to attain them.[43] For example, a business unit leader might be negotiating with executives from headquarters about outsourcing the manufacture of a product. The unit head might attempt to analyze why the headquarters group really wants to outsource. Are they attempting to reduce operating costs? Are they concerned mostly about increasing quality? Are they concerned mostly about enhancing profits?

Listening skills are essential for seeing the big picture. Bobby Covie says, "There's a saying among negotiators that whoever talks the most during a negotiation loses." Being the first to listen helps establish trust. Listening also involves paying attention to what the other side is saying.[44] A person might begin a negotiating session claiming to want a bigger share of the division budget. Yet careful listening might indicate that he or she really is looking for his or her department to receive more respect and attention. So the issue is not financial.

As shown in the example just presented, listening helps the negotiator dig for information as to why the other side wants what it does.[45] If the other side wants a bigger budget just to have more respect, there are less expensive ways to grant respect than grant a bigger share of the budget. Perhaps the leader can give the person a classier job title, rename the department, or appoint the person to head a task force. For example, the head of marketing is renamed "chief of brands," and her department, "brand development."

Negotiation specialist Gary Miller suggests that making the first offer yourself can exert a strong pull throughout the negation, referred to as an anchoring effect.[46] The first-offer approach can be compatible with listening first because after making the first offer, the negotiator can listen carefully to the reactions. So doing can lead to valuable tips for making a final offer.

*Begin with a Plausible Demand or Offer*   Most people believe that compromise and allowing room for negotiation include beginning with an extreme demand or offer. The theory is that the final compromise will be closer to the true demand or offer than if the negotiation were opened more realistically. But a plausible demand is better because it reflects good faith bargaining. An extreme demand or offer will often be perceived as insulting to the other side, leading to a possible exit from the negotiation. Assume that the owner of a startup technology company aspires to sell the company to a technology giant for $15 million. If the big company representative makes an initial offer of $1 million, the owner of the small firm might simply exit the negotiation in anger.

Also, if a third party has to resolve the conflict, a plausible demand or offer will receive more sympathy than an implausible one. For example, a judge might be unsympathetic toward a consumer and his or her lawyer who demanded $3 million because her finger was broken when a store associate bumped into her with a shopping cart.

**Focus on Interests, Not Positions**   Rather than clinging to specific negotiating points, one should keep overall interests in mind and try to satisfy them. The true object of negotiation is to satisfy the underlying interests of both sides. As professional mediator John Heister explains, when you focus on interests, all of the disputants get on the same side of the table and say, "We have a problem to solve. Based on our common interests, we need to find a solution that meets the needs of each of the stakeholders."[47]

Here is how the strategy works: Your manager asks you to submit a proposal for increasing sales volume. You see it as an important opportunity to link up with another distributor. When you submit your ideas, you learn that management wants to venture further into e-commerce, not to expand the dealer network. Instead of insisting on linking with another dealer, be flexible. Ask to be included in the decision making for additional involvement in e-commerce. You will increase your sales volume (your true interest), and you may enjoy such secondary benefits as having helped the company develop a stronger e-commerce presence.

**Be Sensitive to International Differences in Negotiating Style**   A challenge facing the multicultural leader is how to negotiate successfully with people from other cultures. Frank L. Acuff notes that Americans often have a no-nonsense approach to negotiation. A key attitude underlying the U.S. approach to negotiation is "Tell it like it is." A problem with this type of frankness and seeming impatience is that people from other cultures may interpret such remarks as rudeness. The adverse interpretation, in turn, may lead to a failed negotiation. Acuff gives a case example: "It is unlikely in Mexico or Japan that the other side is going to answer 'yes' or 'no' to any question. You will have to discern answers to questions through the context of what is being said rather than from the more obvious direct cues that U.S. negotiators use."[48] By sizing up what constitutes an effective negotiating style, the negotiator stands a reasonable chance of achieving a collaborative solution.

There are also many other differences in negotiating styles and techniques across culture. Considerable study and practice is therefore required to negotiate effectively in another culture. One of the rules of thumb offered by cross-cultural specialist Erin Meyer is to be careful about putting the final deal in writing. In the United States and Northern Europe, summarizing the agreement in writing is standard practice. Yet this seemingly efficient practice can backfire in Africa or in Asia. A spoken agreement is preferable in African and Asian countries, where relationships are more important than written contracts. A Nigerian manager explained, "If the moment we come to an agreement, you pull out a contract …I start to worry. Do you think I won't follow through? Are you trying to trap me?"[49]

**Allow for Face Saving**   While negotiating, it is important to recognize that you might want to make another deal, another day, with the same party. As a result, you want to conduct yourself in a dignified way and not attempt to maximize gain for yourself and minimize gain for the other side. Allowing for face saving is one of the principles of leadership espoused by Dale Carnegie that has considerable empirical and theoretical support. One such research finding is that when a person's face is threatened, the individual attempts to use face-saving techniques. Furthermore, if employees are allowed to save face after dealing with a problem, they are more likely to perform well and report errors.[50]

Negotiating and bargaining, as with any other leadership and management skill, require conceptual knowledge and practice. Leadership Skill-Building Exercise 12-3 gives you an opportunity to practice collaboration, the most integrative form of negotiating and bargaining, as well as conflict resolution. Practice in finding options for mutual gains is helpful for the leader because negotiating is a high-impact part of his or her job.

## LEADERSHIP SKILL-BUILDING EXERCISE 12-3

### The Minimum Wage Negotiation

One student plays the role of the Chairman and CEO of a fast-food restaurant chain who is holding a negotiation session today with an employee group. About five students play the role of the representatives of the employees. The group is asking for a $15 per hour minimum wage for all restaurant workers. Among their reasons for the demand are that (1) a full-time worker cannot support a family on the current minimum wage of $10.25 per hour, (2) many restaurant workers need food stamps to supplement their income, (3) if the restaurant

workers were paid more their increased income would stimulate the economy, and (4) the restaurant executives are highly paid. The CEO believes strongly in treating workers fairly but that a minimum wage of $15 per hour would force a loss of jobs because of automation, and that many locations would have to close because of financial losses.

Regard this negotiation as an exercise in skill development, not an opportunity to take a political stance. Both sides should attempt to put into action sensible negotiating tactics.

## READER'S ROADMAP

So far we have studied considerable information about the nature of leadership; the attributes, behaviors, and styles of leaders; the ethics and social responsibility of leaders; and how leaders exert power and use politics and influence. We then studied techniques for developing teamwork, as well as motivation and coaching skills. After studying creativity and innovation as part of leadership, we focused on communication skills as they relate to leadership. Next, we shift our study to direction setting at the organizational level: strategic leadership.

## SUMMARY

Open communication between company leaders and employees helps an organization overcome problems and attain success. Effective communication skills contribute to inspirational leadership. Nonverbal skills are also important for leadership effectiveness. A major feature of communication by leaders is to rely on networks of contacts both in-person and electronically. Without being connected to other people, it would be almost impossible for leaders to carry out their various roles.

Developing networks of live interpersonal contacts remains an essential method for a leader building relationships, motivating others, and attaining collaboration. Face-to-face communication networks allow for helpful conversations. Leadership networks include the peer, operational, personal, and strategic.

An important use of the social media is for the leader to build and maintain a professional network. The productive leader is more likely to focus on contacts of relevance or density rather than superficial contacts. The strength-of-ties perspective explains the difference between strong and weak ties. The relationships among the different actors in a network can be broadly classified into two major types: strong versus weak ties and direct versus indirect ties. Group chat is an important leadership communication network, allowing for connecting with several group members simultaneously.

Inspirational and powerful communication helps leaders carry out their roles. Suggestions for inspirational and powerful speaking and writing include the following: (1) be credible; (2) gear your message to your listener including his or her needs; (3) sell group members on the benefits of your suggestions; (4) use heavy-impact and emotion-provoking words; (5) use anecdotes to communicate meaning; (6) back up conclusions with data; (7) minimize language errors, junk words, and vocalized pauses; (8) use business jargon in appropriate doses; and (9) write crisp, clear memos, letters, and reports, including a front-loaded message.

Using a power-oriented linguistic style is another way to communicate with inspiration and power. The style includes a variety of techniques, such as downplaying uncertainty, emphasizing direct rather than indirect talks, and choosing an effective communication frame. Leaders can also improve their communication skills by following the seven principles of persuasion: liking, reciprocity, social proof, consistency, authority, scarcity, and pre-suasion. (The latter refers to putting people in a receptive mood.) Altercasting is a persuasion technique in which you characterize a person as a certain type of perhaps to encourage him or her to behave in a desired manner.

Skill can also be developed in using nonverbal communication that connotes power, being in control, forcefulness, and self-confidence. Among the suggestions for nonverbal communication are to stand erect; speak at a moderate pace with a loud, clear tone; and smile frequently in a relaxed manner. A person's external image also plays an important part in communicating messages to others.

Videoconferencing, including telepresence, places heavy demands on nonverbal communication. Videoconferences represent a powerful tool for far-flung managers to make a name for themselves at corporate headquarters. The camera magnifies small nonverbal communication errors, such as scratching your head.

Listening is a fundamental management and leadership skill. A foundation tactic for a leader to become an effective listener is to show respect for others. Three impediments for the leaders who want to listen well are (1) leaders are already overloaded, (2) people can listen to more words per minute than others can speak, and (3) the leader multitasking while listening. Leaders have to be careful about listening selectively. A robust communication channel for the leader/manager is to engage in face-to-face communication with direct reports by making the rounds. Such rounds are effective for dealing with morale problems.

Overcoming communication barriers created by dealing with people from different cultures is another leadership and management challenge. Guidelines for overcoming cross-cultural barriers include the following: (1) be sensitive to the existence of cross-cultural communication barriers; (2) challenge your cultural assumptions; (3) show respect for all workers; (4) use straightforward language, and speak slowly and clearly; (5) look for signs of misunderstanding when your language is not the listener's native language; (6) when appropriate, speak in the language of the people from another culture; (7) observe cross-cultural differences in etiquette; (8) do not be diverted by style, accent, grammar, or personal appearance; (9) avoid racial or ethnic identification except when it is essential to communication; (10) be sensitive to differences in nonverbal communication; and (11) be attentive to individual differences in appearance.

Leaders and managers spend considerable time managing conflict, including conflict with outsiders. Resolving conflict facilitates collaboration. Five major styles of conflict management are as follows: competitive, accommodative, sharing, collaborative (win–win), and avoidant. Each style is based on a combination of satisfying one's own concerns (assertiveness) and satisfying the concerns of others (cooperativeness). The collaborative style of conflict management includes agreeing with the criticizer and apologizing. When resolving conflict, people typically combine several of the five resolution styles to accomplish their purpose, such as dominating and accommodating. Which modes of conflict handling to use depends upon a number of variables such as the importance of the issue and the relative power between the parties.

A high-level managerial skill is to help two or more group members resolve conflict between or among them. The most useful approach is to get the parties in conflict to engage in confrontation and problem solving. An effective technique is for the leader to ask each side to restate what the other person said.

Conflicts can be considered situations calling for negotiating and bargaining. Specific negotiating techniques include the following: (1) minimize feeling or looking anxious during the negotiation; (2) listen first to investigate what the other side wants; (3) begin with a plausible demand or offer; (4) focus on interests, not positions; (5) be sensitive to international differences in negotiating style; and (6) allow for face saving.

## KEY TERMS

linguistic style  319
altercasting  321
making the rounds  324

win–win approach to conflict
resolution  331

## GUIDELINES FOR ACTION AND SKILL DEVELOPMENT

A subtle part of being an effective communicator—including be a good listener—is to avoid language that discourages another person from expressing his or her opinion, or worse, shuts the person up. At times you may feel like putting the lid on a subordinate. However, in the long run, silencing your team will backfire because you will lose valuable input. Here are three examples of statements leaders and managers frequently use that clamp down on communication: "I already know that," "Why would you want to change that? It's not broken," and, "Well, it's my decision and I say no."[51]

Another technique for curtailing communication is to react to a comment with a blank stare and no comment of your own. Such behavior implies that you either don't care or are denying the reality of what the person is saying.

A basic principle of negotiation, "Be hard on the problem, and soft on the on the person" applies equally well to other types of conflict resolution because it diminishes anger and a desire for revenge. "Being hard on the problem" refers to working diligently on dealing with the problem. "Being soft on the person" refers to not attacking the other side because he or she disagrees with you.

### Discussion Questions and Activities

1. Now that you have studied this chapter, what are you going to do differently to improve your communication effectiveness as a leader?

2. How could a person find out early in his or career if his or her communication skills were good enough to become a successful leader?

3. In the United States, a person who has an English (UK) accent is often at advantage to obtain a leadership position. What is your opinion of the ethics of a person developing such an accent in order to get promoted?

4. What do you see as a potential downside to using a power-oriented linguistic style?

5. In what ways does being good at public speaking enhance a leader's effectiveness?

6. Jack Dorsey, the executive chairman of Twitter and the CEO of Square, is quite soft spoken yet still very persuasive. How can that be?

7. Given that people really do defer to experts, how might the leader establish his or her expertise?

8. What concrete steps can a leader take to demonstrate that he or she respects a group member from another culture?

9. Assume that during a meeting, a middle manager is told by a subordinate that he or she is not fit for the position and should resign. What approach do you recommend that the leader take to resolve this conflict?

10. Think of any business leader you admire, and then go to YouTube to find a video of him or her talking. (You may need to try a few business leaders to find one featured on YouTube.) What do you think of that executive's communication effectiveness?

## LEADERSHIP CASE PROBLEM A

### Dani the Front-Stabbing CEO

Dani is the CEO of Bellerose Exhibits and Events—an events planning firm that coordinates all aspects of events and professional meetings. Among the many tasks Bellerose handles for clients are arranging meeting locations, providing for transportation, erecting and taking down exhibitor booths, and supervising the installation of technology for the events. At times Bellerose also organizes a theme for the event, such as pretending that participants are superheroes or superheroines, or an emphasis on charitable giving.

Dani has decided that a deterrent to Bellerose is that she as well as other staff members are too gentle in their feedback to each other. Instead of being totally honest with other about mistakes or errors in judgment, staff members tend to be too polite and indirect in their feedback to each other. Dani has read that some firms have moved toward *front-stabbing*, or complete candor in discussing problems directly with people. She decides to initiate a process of her as well as other staff members being more open in bringing problems to each other's attention. Her approach was to send an e-mail to all Bellerose workers to launch the front-stabbing initiative.

The day after announcing the initiative, Brock, an exhibits designer, asked Dani what she thought of the neon sign he used to decorate a client's booth. Dani replied, "The neon sign might work as a design to help build a retro image. But you sign was just a distraction for a company that wanted to publicize its food supplements." Brock replied, "Was my neon sign really that bad?"

The next morning Katrina, Dani's administrative assistant, dropped by her cubicle to review a few items on the budget. Dani said, "Before we get started on these budget items, I have an observation to share with you. Your appearance has deteriorated recently. Your hair is often messy, you have bags under your eyes, and your clothing combination often looks like it was chosen at random from your closet. What's wrong with you?' Katrina replied, "Dani you are being a little harsh. I have been experiencing some personal problems during the last few months."

The following Monday morning, Dani held a strategy meeting with her top management team. As she had alerted the team prior to the meeting, she would be presenting a revised vision statement. Before getting to the theme of the meeting, Dani asked if there were any other key issues that should be addressed. Lyndon, an events-planning associate, said, "Dani, I am concerned about the parking lot we all use. The snow-plowing is poor, and there is a lot of debris scattered about."

Cheryl, the chief finance officer, responded to Lyndon in these terms: "Lyndon, you are being small minded when you should be thinking big about the company vision."

Dani later presented her new vision for Bellerose, as follows: "Within five years we will become the world standard of excellence for designing and executing events to a wide variety of organizations. The events we plan will take our clients to new heights of organizational performance."

Karl, the chief technology officer, responded to Dani's vision in this manner: "Dani, have you been smoking medical marijuana? Are you creating a sensible vision for us, or are you hallucinating?"

As the meeting disbanded one hour later, Dani thought, "Has my front-stabbing initiative gone too far. Am I being nasty with my staff, and are they being nasty with each other?"

**Questions**

1. How helpful does the new candid feedback at Bellerose appear to be?
2. What suggestions might you make to Dani and her staff so that candid feedback to each other does not trigger interpersonal conflict?

## ASSOCIATED ROLE PLAY

Two students play the role of Bellerose staff members. Each role player decides now is the time to engage in front-stabbing the ideas of each other. Each role player reacts to a work-related idea of the other with a highly candid statement. Students providing feedback will look to see if the front-stabbing comments have any constructive value.

## LEADERSHIP CASE PROBLEM B

### Sean Contemplates a Delicate Confrontation

Sean is the head of the logistics group at a medium-size company that makes plastic parts for other companies, including manufacturers of printers, television sets, computers, and washing machines. His department provides a few valuable services for the company such as receiving and storing raw materials, shipping products, and disposal of waste materials. The logistics department consists of ten people including an administrative support specialist. Sean's department is meeting its goals, and Sean regularly receives average or above-average performance evaluations.

In contrast to the generally positive job situation facing Sean, he sees one irritating problem that needs resolution. Sean has received feedback from several employees inside and outside the department that Phil, one of the logistic technicians, frequently mocks him but not to his face. Karen, the administrative support person, casually mentioned to Sean recently, "Have you seen Phil do one of his impressions of you? He did one the other day during coffee break. It was kind of negative, and very unprofessional."

Sean noticed that Phil made the following post on his Facebook page: "Life isn't always so easy when you know much more than your boss." Although the post may not have been directed specifically at Sean, it was still hurtful.

Sean was thinking while driving to work, "I don't have any direct evidence that Phil is mocking me, but it sure seems to be true. I have to figure what to do about this problem."

## Questions

1. What kind of a leadership issue is Sean dealing with?
2. What do you recommend that Sean do about his conflict with Phil?

## ASSOCIATED ROLE PLAY

One student plays the role of Sean who decides to confront Phil about what could very well be a form of insubordination. Another student plays the role of Phil who is not very impressed with Sean as a leader, but he does not think he has done anything out of line in terms of reacting negatively toward him. Observers will look to see how the potential conflict in this situation might be resolved.

 ## LEADERSHIP SKILL-BUILDING EXERCISE 12-4

### My Leadership Portfolio

For this chapter's entry into your leadership portfolio, think through how you have dealt with your opportunities to communicate as a leader in your experiences. Did you have an opportunity to attempt to persuade an individual or group? Did you have an opportunity to be supportive toward another person? Did you have an opportunity to make a presentation on the job or in class? During these communication opportunities, how well did you come across as a leader? Did you impress anybody with persuasive skill or warmth? Carlos, an assistant restaurant manager, made this entry in his portfolio:

> I help manage an upscale restaurant. The wait staff has to be on top of its game when in the dining room. Without superior service, nobody is going to pay our prices, even if the food and wine are good. Late one afternoon, Rick dragged in, looking in no shape to give good service to our guests. He looked worried and distracted. Instead of telling Rick to go home, I took him aside in the office. I asked him to give me a full explanation of whatever problem he was facing. We both sat down, and I poured Rick a cup of coffee. After a minute or so, Rick opened up to tell me about how he rammed the back of his car into a two-foot-high guardrail in a parking lot. His fiberglass bumper split, and he figures it will cost him $750 to replace it. I listened to his whole story without being judgmental. I said I would check with the manager to see if we could give him extra hours this month to earn more money to apply toward his repair. Rick said, "Thanks for listening," and he left our one-on-one session feeling better and looking well enough to face the guests.

I give myself a gold star for having been a supportive leader. Ha! Ha!

**LEADERSHIP** SKILL-BUILDING **EXERCISE 12-5**

### Evaluating the Communication Skills of an Organizational Leader

So much has been said about the importance of good communication skills for an effective leader. Your assignment is to observe a specific organizational leader of your choice, such as a business executive. Methods of observing an organizational leader include (1) a live or video replay interview of an executive on a television news channel, (2) finding a brief executive presentation on YouTube or Hulu, and (3) attending a function in which an executive is either giving a talk or interacting with visitors.

In preparing your evaluation, look for such factors as persuasiveness, adequate grammar and sentence structure, and ability to establish rapport with the receiver of the message.

A side aspect of this assignment is to observe the executive's communication skills with the intent of picking up an idea or two to improve your own communication effectiveness.

## NOTES

1. Original story based on facts and observations in the following sources: Alice Grey Harrison, "Building Connections between Employees and Strategy," *Public Relations Tactics* (www.prsa.org), April 30, 2013. pp. 1–3; Carmine Gallo, "Southwest Airlines Motivates Its Employees with a Purpose Bigger than a Paycheck," *Forbes* (www.forbes.com), January 21, 2014, pp. 1–3; Kevin J. Allen, "Focus on Communication Fuels Southwest Airlines," *Health Care Communication News* (www.healthcarecommunication.com), November 11, 2007, pp. 1–2; "Southwest Citizenship," *Southwest* (www.southwest.com), © 2016 Southwest Airlines. Co.

2. John Hamm, "The Five Messages Leaders Must Manage," *Harvard Business Review*, May 2006, p. 116.

3. Bruce Hoppe and Claire Reinelt, "Social Network Analysis and the Evaluation of Leadership Networks," *The Leadership Quarterly*, August 2010, p. 600.

4. Dorothy R. Carter, Leslie A. DeChurch, Michael T. Braun, and Noshir S. Contractor, "Social Network Approaches to Leadership: An Integrative Conceptual Review," *Journal of Applied Psychology*, May 2015, pp. 597–622.

5. Boris Groysberg and Michael Slind, "Leadership Is a Conversation," *Harvard Business Review*, June 2012, p. 79.

6. Study cited in Jared Lindzon, "Communicating In-Person at Work Isn't Dead Yet, Says Gen Z," *Fast Company* (www.fastcompany.com), September 7, 2016, pp. 1–6.

7. Bruce Hoppe and Claire Reinelt, "Social Network Analysis," p. 601.

8. Networks three, four, and five are from Herminia Ibarra and Mark Hunter, "How Leaders Create and Use Networks," *Harvard Business Review*, January 2007, pp. 40–47.

9. Mark Granovetter, "The Strength of Weak Ties: A Network Theory Revisited," *Sociological Theory*, vol. 1, 1983, pp. 201–233.

10. Christopher Mims, "Chat Emerges as the Hottest Thing in IT," *The Wall Street Journal*, November 7, 2016, pp. B1, B5.

11. Carlin Flora, "The Art of Influence," *Psychology Today*, September/October 2011, p. 67.

12. Stephen P. Robbins and Phillip L. Hunsaker, *Training in Interpersonal Skills: Tips for Managing People at Work* (Upper Saddle River, NJ: Prentice Hall, 1996), p. 115. (These findings are still valid today.)

13. "Which Buzzwords Would You Ban?" *The Wall Street Journal*, January 2, 2014, p. B4.

14. Sherry Sweetham, "How to Organize Your Thoughts for Better Communication," *Personnel*, March 1986, p. 39.

15. Deborah Tannen, "The Power of Talk: Who Gets Heard and Why?" *Harvard Business Review*, September–October 1995, pp. 138–148.

16. Deborah Tannen, "The Power of Talk: Who Gets Heard and Why?" pp. 138–148; "How You Speak Shows Where You Rank," *Fortune*, February 2, 1998, p. 156; "Speak Like You Mean Business," *Working Smart* (www.nibm.net), March 2004; "Weed Out Wimpy Words: Speak Up Without Backpedaling, Qualifying," *Working Smart*, March 2000, p. 2; Joel Stein, "Could You Explain It Less Clearly?" *Bloomberg Businessweek*, July 21–27, 2014, p. 63.

17. Robert B. Cialdini, "Harnessing the Science of Persuasion," *Harvard Business Review*, October 2001, pp. 72–79.

18. Robert H. Cialdini, *Pre-suasion: A Revolutionary Way to Influence and Persuade* (New York: Simon & Schuster, 2016).

19. Robert B. Cialdini, "Harnessing the Science of Persuasion," p. 79.

20. Elizabeth Bernstein, "If You Want to Persuade People, Try 'Altercasting'," *The Wall Street Journal*, September 6, 2016, p. D1; "Altercasting" *Changing Minds* (www.changiningminds.org), p. 1. Retrieved November 19, 2016.

21. Several of the suggestions here are from Sue Shellenbarger, "Strike a Powerful Pose: Posture Can Determine Who's a Hero, Who's a Wimp; Bad News for Phone Users," *The Wall Street Journal*, August 21, 2013, pp. D1, D2; Shellenbarger, "Just Look Me in the Eye Already," *The Wall Street Journal*, May 29, 2013, p. D1; *Body Language for Business Success* (New York: National Institute for Business Management, 1989), pp. 2–29; Andy Yap et al., "The Ergonomics of Dishonesty: The Effects of Incidental Posture on Stealing, Cheating, and Traffic Violations," *Psychological Science*, November 2013, pp. 2281–2289.

22. Cited in Joann S. Lublin, "Some Dos and Don'ts to Help You Hone Videoconference Skills," *The Wall Street Journal*, February 7, 2006, p. B.

23. Bradley Hope, "Friedman to Be Nasdaq Operating Chief," *The Wall Street Journal*, December 16, 2015, p. C4.

24. "A Conversation with Bill Kanarick: The Art of Asking Questions," *Executive Leadership*, January 2014, p. 3.

25. Bernard T. Ferran, "The Executive's Guide to Better Listening," *McKinsey Quarterly* (www.mckinseyquarterly.com), February 2012, p. 2.

26. Jack Zenger and Joseph Folkman, "What Great Listeners Actually Do," *Harvard Business Review* (https://hbr.org), July 14, 2016, p. 3.

27. Erika H. James, "Selective Hearing Can Lead to a Blind Eye," *The Darden Perspective in First Person*, published in *The Wall Street Journal*, December 4, 2007, p. A16.

28. Linda Dulye, "Get Out of Your Office," *HR Magazine*, July 2006, pp. 99–100; "Making Rounds' Like a Physician," *Manager's Edge*, February 2006, p. 8.

29. Gunnar Beeth, "Multicultural Managers Wanted," *Management Review*, May 1997, p. 17.

30. "When English Is Not Their Native Tongue," *Manager's Edge*, April 2003, p. 5.

31. Kathryn Kranhold, "Lost in Translation," *The Wall Street Journal*, May 18, 2004, p. B1.

32. Siri Carpenter, "Why Do 'They All Look Alike'?" *Monitor on Psychology*, December 2000, p. 44.

33. Jeff Weiss and Jonathan Hughes, "Want Collaboration? Accept—and Actively Manage—Conflict," *Harvard Business Review*, March 2005, pp. 92–101.

34. Kenneth Thomas, "Conflict and Conflict Management," in Marvin D. Dunnette, ed., *Handbook of Industrial and Organizational Psychology* (Chicago: Rand McNally, 1976), pp. 900–922.

35. Barbara Kellerman, "When Should a Leader Apologize and When Not?" *Harvard Business Review*, April 2006, pp. 72–81.

36. Elizabeth A. Mannix, Leigh L. Thompson, and Max H. Bazerman, "Negotiation in Small Groups," *Journal of Applied Psychology*, June 1989, pp. 508–517.

37. Matthew Herper, "Merck on the Spot," *Forbes*, May 6, 2013, p. 106.

38. Ginka Toegel and Jean-Louis Barsoux, "How to Preempt Team Conflict," *Harvard Business Review*, June 2016, pp. 78–83.

39. Deb Levine, "Solutions: Advice from HR Knowledge Advisors," *HR Magazine*, October 2013, p. 18.

40. Tamara Lytle, "Confronting Conflict," *HR Magazine*, July/August 2015, p. 29.

41. Patrick S. Nugent, "Managing Conflict: Third-Party Interventions for Managers," *Academy of Management Executive*, February 2002, p. 152.

42. Alison Wood Brooks, "Emotion and the Art of Negotiation," *Harvard Business Review*, December 2015, pp. 59–60.

43. Jeff Weiss, Aram Donigian, and Jonathan Hughes, "Extreme Negotiations," *Harvard Business Review*, November 2010, pp. 68–69.

44. Cited in Brenda Goodman, "The Art of Negotiation," *Psychology Today*, January/February 2007, p. 65.

45. Deepak Malhotra and Max H. Bazerman, "Investigative Negotiation," *Harvard Business Review*, September 2007, pp. 72–78.

46. Gary Miller, "When to Make the First offer in Negotiations," *www.denverpost.com*, July 17, 2016, pp. 1–4.

47. John Heister, "Collaborate to Solve Societal Ills," *Rochester, New York, Democrat and Chronicle*, May 14, 2004, p. 18A.

48. Frank Acuff, *The World-Class Negotiator: An Indispensable Guide for Anyone Doing Business with Those from a Foreign Culture* (New York: AMACOM, 1992).

49. Erin Meyer, "Getting to *Sí, Ja, Oui, Hai,* and *Da,*" *Harvard Business Review*, December 2015, pp. 74–75.

50. Analysis presented in Tessa E. Basford and Andrea Molberg, "Dale Carnegie's Leadership Principles: Examining the Theoretical and Empirical Support," *Journal of Leadership Studies*, vol. 6, no. 4, 2013, pp. 32–34.

51. Avoid Language That Shuts People Up," *Executive Leadership*, January 2008, p. 8.

# Strategic Leadership and Knowledge Management

## LEARNING OBJECTIVES

After studying this chapter and doing the exercises, you should be able to

- Describe the development of business strategy.
- Explain how to use the SWOT model to assist in strategic planning.

- Identify a number of current business strategies.
- Describe how leaders contribute to the management of knowledge and the learning organization.

## CHAPTER OUTLINE

**The Development of Business Strategy**

The Importance of Strategic Thinking

Maintaining a Human and Emotional Aspect

Gathering Multiple Inputs to Formulate Strategy

Leadership Effectiveness and Strategy Implementation

Conducting a SWOT Analysis

**A Sampling of Business Strategies Formulated by Leaders**

**Knowledge Management and the Learning Organization**

Knowledge Management

Servant Leadership and the Creation of Knowledge

The Learning Organization

**Summary**

**Key Terms**

**Guidelines for Action and Skill Development**

**Leadership Case Problem A**

**Leadership Case Problem B**

**Notes**

A few years ago David Eun, executive vice president of the Global Innovation Center at Samsung Electronics Company, developed a winning strategy to enhance the company's success. Eun wanted to grow the electronics division by concentrating on software and services that would prompt even more extensive use the company's array of electronic devices such as television receivers and smartphones. Diversifying more into software gained in importance in 2016 when Samsung had to recall three million Galaxy Note 7 devices, after reports of overheating and exploding batteries.

The electronics wing of South Korea-based Samsung had already attained a dominant position in technology by developing exceptional hardware products and producing a full slate of smartphones and television sets that outsell those of other companies. Eun thought that the next step was to find a successful niche to ward off competitors from around the world. He and his team thought that a winning strategy would be to develop the company's own software and team up with third-party developers of software.

When asked why Samsung would have an edge over Silicon Valley companies in developing software for its products, Eun replied: "What we have is an amazing network of partners and consumers globally, so there's a lot of intelligence and a lot of scale at work here." Eun plays the leadership role of a connector, who bridges the gap between Silicon Valley startups and Samsung, one of the world's largest multinational corporations.

The Global Innovation Center, housed in headed by Eun, is the core of implementing the Samsung software strategy. The Center has offices in New York, San Francisco, Seoul, and Silicon Valley. The group works exclusively with startups because innovation in consumer software and services has usually stemmed from smaller companies and smaller groups of workers. A specific team is SmartThings that build technology that enables any home to be a smart home, meaning that home appliances and accessories connect to the Internet and to one another. SmartThings is one of many companies contributing to Samsung's push into software and services.

The mission of the Global Innovation Center is to shift Samsung from a hardware-driven company to one that is also a world leader in software and services. Eun says, "The future is about thoughtful integration of hardware and software. And that means startups." The GIC builds relationships with startup technology companies through four vehicles: investments, partnerships, acquisitions, and its Accelerator program in San Francisco and New York City. The Samsung Accelerator provides strategic capital, office space, and product support to experienced entrepreneurs so that they can build market-driven software and services.

Before Samsung, Eun held executive positions at AOL, Google, and NBC. He is highly knowledgeable about information technology but his formal education is in law and the liberal arts. He holds as JD from Harvard law School and an AB from Harvard College.[1]

The story about the Samsung executive illustrates how leaders must continually think through the direction in which the firm is headed. A key leadership role is to form a **strategy**, the organization's plan for achieving its vision, mission, and goals. For our purposes, **strategic leadership** is the process of providing the direction and inspiration necessary to create or sustain an organization.

In this chapter, we approach strategic leadership by emphasizing the leader's role rather than presenting extensive information about business strategy and the analytics that support strategy and strategic planning. First, we describe the development of business strategy including a frequently used tool for development strategy, SWOT analysis. We then examine the strategies that leaders most frequently use to bring about success. Following that is a description of a leader's contribution to an important thrust in strategy, knowledge management, and developing a learning organization.

## The Development of Business Strategy

Elaborate methods of planning are often used to help develop business strategy. The SWOT analysis presented later is a basic planning tool. In the opinion of some management specialists, the best strategy emerges from an organization having a grand purpose.[2] The effective leader, and often the founder, sets the purpose of the firm. Coca Cola began this way, as did Apple Inc., and the Sloan Kettering Cancer Institute. After the firm's purpose is established, the leader also becomes the steward of the strategy. Mintzberg argues that if you want good strategy, skip all the elaborate planning and just focus on having a great vision.[3]

Planning alone does not create strategy because strategy can also stem from inspired thinking. Corporate values also influence strategy because well-managed organizations tend to develop strategy to fit what the people in power think is important. If the company highly values innovation, it will not adopt a strategy of being successful by imitating other successful products. Piaget, for example, has remained successful for more than 200 years by staying with its own high-quality watches, and not imitating other trends in the watch industry.

While strategy often stems from planning, many business leaders choose a strategy prior to strategic planning. Once the firm has the strategy, a plan is developed to implement it. A chief executive might say, "Let's compete by becoming the most recognizable company in our field." The executive team would then develop specific plans to implement that strategy, rather than strategic planning leading to the conclusion that brand recognition would be an effective strategy. For many medium-sized and small organizations, it is strategy first, followed by plan.

Our approach to understanding the development of business strategy focuses on the importance of strategic thinking, the human and emotional aspect of strategy, gathering multiple inputs to formulate strategy, the implementation of strategy, and the SWOT analysis.

## The Importance of Strategic Thinking

Strategic planning, as well as setting the vision without the planning, shares an important purpose. It is to get managerial workers throughout the organization thinking strategically and wondering about how the firm adapts to its environment and how it will cope with its future. One of the central challenges of modern organizations is for leaders at all levels of the firm to think strategically—including seeing the overall picture as they go about their work.[4]

A strategically minded worker at any level would think, "How does what I am doing right now support corporate strategy?" The customer care center worker at Hewlett Packard Enterprises might say to himself, "Each time I help a customer solve a problem I am contributing to the strategy of having the highest quality products in all the markets we serve."

An example of high-level strategic thinking is the company leadership at Google saying it will continue "pursuing moon shots." The phrases refer to the idea that as part of its strategy, the company will continue to pursue improbable projects that will require enormous amounts of cash and great leaps of faith. Among these moon shots are self-driving cars, anti-aging drugs, and computerized glucose-sensing contact lenses for diabetics.[5]

A study of 231 upper level leaders in a large global company found that global work experience was associated with a stronger tendency to think strategically. The effect was more pronounced when the experience was in a culture distant from one's own, such as an American being on assignment in Japan.[6]

Because effective strategy begins with strategic thinking, you are invited to think through your tendencies toward being a strategic thinker by taking the Leadership Self-assessment Quiz 13-1 to explore your orientation toward thinking strategically.

## Maintaining a Human and Emotional Aspect

As implied by the creative component to strategy, strategic leaders rely heavily on intuition as to what direction the organization should take. Cynthia Montgomery, a strategy professor and former head of the Strategy Unit at Harvard Business School, says that many executives have lost the leadership and the human dimension of strategy. She believes that strategy has become too analytical, a must-do instead of a want-to-do. To make strategy more personal, leaders should answer the questions: "Does your company matter? What is your company adding to what already exists in the market?"

To illustrate the human touch in strategy, Montgomery gives the example of Gucci. The brand had become trashed and of low value because the name appeared on 22,000 products, including cigarette lighters and tennis balls. A new chief executive officer (CEO) revamped the Gucci strategy. He decided the brand should be sexy, at the leading edge of fashion, and a good value. The original Gucci market niche was high-fashion appealing to an older audience. The new CEO turned the company around to meet the new strategy, leading to survival and good profits.[7]

Most great companies start with great purposes formulated by the founder. A sterling example is IKEA's intent to offer customers "a wide range of well-designed, functional home furnishing products at prices so low that as many people as possible can afford

## LEADERSHIP SELF-ASSESSMENT QUIZ 13-1

### Are You a Strategic Thinker?

**Instructions:** Indicate your strength of agreement with each of the following statements: SD = strongly disagree; D = disagree; N = neutral; A = agree; SA = strongly agree.

| | | SD | D | N | A | SA |
|---|---|---|---|---|---|---|
| **1.** | Every action I take on my job should add value for our customers, our clients, or the public. | 1 | 2 | 3 | 4 | 5 |
| **2.** | Let company leadership ponder the future; I have my own job to get done. | 5 | 4 | 3 | 2 | 1 |
| **3.** | Strategic thinking is fluff. Somebody down the organization has to get the job done. | 5 | 4 | 3 | 2 | 1 |
| **4.** | A company cannot become great without an exciting vision. | 1 | 2 | 3 | 4 | 5 |
| **5.** | What I do on the job each day can affect the performance of the company many years into the future. | 1 | 2 | 3 | 4 | 5 |
| **6.** | It is rather pointless to develop skills or acquire knowledge that cannot help you on the job within the next month. | 5 | 4 | 3 | 2 | 1 |
| **7.** | Strategic planning should be carried out in a separate department rather than involve people throughout the organization. | 5 | 4 | 3 | 2 | 1 |
| **8.** | It makes good sense for top management to frequently ask itself the question, "What business are we really in?" | 1 | 2 | 3 | 4 | 5 |
| **9.** | If a company does an outstanding job of satisfying its customers, there is little need to worry about changing its mix of goods or services. | 5 | 4 | 3 | 2 | 1 |
| **10.** | Organizational visions remind me of pipe dreams and hallucinations. | 5 | 4 | 3 | 2 | 1 |
| **11.** | I like the idea of an organization sending a group of managers and professionals to an off-site strategy development session every couple of years or so. | 1 | 2 | 3 | 4 | 5 |
| **12.** | Strategy formulation is a bureaucratic exercise that usually gets the organization nowhere. | 5 | 4 | 3 | 2 | 1 |

**Scoring and Interpretation:** Find your total score by summing the point values for each question. A score of 52–60 suggests that you already think strategically, which should help you provide strategic leadership to others. Scores of 30–51 suggest a somewhat neutral, detached attitude toward thinking strategically. Scores of 12–29 suggest thinking that emphasizes the here and now and the short term. People scoring in this category are not yet ready to provide strategic leadership to group members.

**Skill Development:** Reflecting on your ability to think strategically is useful because leaders at all levels are expected to see the big picture and point people in a useful direction.

them."[8] Typically, the purpose comes from intuition rather than extensive analysis. Mintzberg believes that synthesizing information and thinking ahead is more important than strategic planning in developing useful business strategy.[9]

## Gathering Multiple Inputs to Formulate Strategy

Many strategic leaders arrive at their ideas for the organization's future by consulting with a wide range of interested parties, in a process similar to conducting research to create a vision. Customers are a natural source of inputs for formulating strategy, often by simply asking them what new products, services, or features they would want.

In most business enterprises, authority for the most important strategic decisions is left to the highest paid person's opinion (HiPPO). (How is that for another sample of giant-size business jargon?) The problem is that HiPPOs are often wrong due to personal biases, misinformation and other factors that can cloud one executive's opinion.[10] The solution to this problem is gathering strategy inputs through **crowdsourcing**, the use of collective intelligence gathered from the public for accomplishing tasks, often by the use of social media. One reason for gathering data for strategy formulation through crowdsourcing is to pull in diverse and end-user perspectives that are typically overlooked but potentially useful. A second reason is to build enthusiasm and alignment behind a company's strategic direction. The people whose opinions are solicited might become more committed to the new strategic direction of the company. Crowdsourcing can involve employees as well as other stakeholders, including customers and the general public.

Lego is an example of a company that makes extensive use of crowdsourcing. The company allows users to design new products, and simultaneously test demand. Any user can submit a design that is voted on by other users. The idea receiving the highest number of votes is placed in production, with the creator receiving one percent royalty on net revenue.[11] You could argue here that choosing another variation of an existing product is not true strategy. Or, you could argue that obtaining consumer input supports the strategy of diversification of goods and service.

Inputs to strategy are helpful, particularly in encouraging debate and coming up with original ideas. Strategy consultant, Melissa Raffoni, advises, however, that if staff members are asked what direction the organization should take, the executive weakens his or her leadership.[12]

## Leadership Effectiveness and Strategy Implementation

Carefully crafting a strategy and vision is not sufficient for its effectiveness. The strategy and vision must also be implemented or executed by the leader/manager. Part of being an effective leader is to implement a strategic initiative. A basic example is that Domino's managers throughout the organization successfully implemented the strategic initiative of upgrading pizza quality after the CEO decided that a high quality was necessary. The Domino example reinforces the suggestions of a three strategy specialists who emphasize that to execute their strategies, leaders must foster coordination across units.[13] For example, the pizza developers must match their pizza flavors with the claims of the marketing staff.

The cofounders of Honest Tea, Yale professor Seth Goldman and one of his students, Barry Nalebuff, have spoken to many business executives about strategy implementation. The Honest Tea partners point out that no strategy, however brilliant, can be implemented successfully unless the people with key jobs know what they need to do differently, and understand how and why they should be executing.[14] The key people must also have the necessary resources, such as every Domino manager having the correct ingredients to upgrade the Domino Pizzas after the CEO at the time initiated a strategy of high quality.

Quite often, implementation requires a series of goals that will be steps along the way to implementing the strategy. An example is the rise to prominence of VIZIO, the manufacturer of television receivers and other electronic products. The company moved gradually from being a store brand to a brand name that consumers wanted to purchase. The goals along the way included selling to more prominent retailers and creating brand recognition through advertising on television and purchasing the rights to college football games.

Field sales representatives have a major role in implementing strategy because in a business enterprise a major purpose of strategy is to sell more products or services. A major problem, however, is that company leadership embarks on a strategy without considering the realities the sales representatives face with customers. To deal with this problem, it is recommended that the sales organization should be part of every conversation about strategy.[15] A recurring example is that many office equipment manufacturers have developed a diversification strategy of obtaining a large proportion of their revenue from services rather than hardware. Such services would include taking over payroll processing for customers, or offering cloud computing. Executing the service strategy would require considerable training for existing sales representatives and/or the hiring of new reps with the right technical skills.

Formulating and implementing organizational strategy is a process that must quite often be repeated in order for the firm to be competitive and survive. Strategy researcher and University Business School professor, Rita Gunther McGrath, points out that leaders need to embrace the idea that advantage is transient. Companies must therefore launch new strategic initiatives from time to time. The result is a portfolio of advantages that can be built quickly and dropped as rapidly.[16] PepsiCo is an example of a company that has shifted its marketing strategy several times, moving away from dependence on carbonated beverages to a firm that sells a wide variety of snack foods and noncarbonated beverages.

The accompanying Leader in Action insert describes an executive who applies strategic thinking to stimulate sales at one of the world's best-known companies.

## LEADER IN ACTION

### Atif Rafiq, Chief Digital Officer at McDonald's, Works to Enhance Customer Connections

When most people hear the job title "Chief Digital Officer," they think of a person working for a large company whose products or services are directly linked to high technology. But Atif Rafiq has a different role. In 2014, he became the first chief digital officer for McDonald's. He leads the company's global digital strategy, focusing on growth in e-commerce, giving the restaurant experience a stronger technology feel, and enabling customers to use technology extensively.

Upon hiring Rafiq, his boss, chief brand officer Steve Easterbrook said, "Atif will lead a more coordinated and comprehensive digital strategy for our global organization as we deepen our connection with our customers. His cutting edge thinking, background, and expertise will help us drive even greater innovation in this arena." Before joining McDonald's, Rafiq was the chief of Kindle Direct Publishing at Amazon.

Rafiq has built a digital unit at the giant fast-food chain, partially by recruiting hundreds of digital natives from firms such as Google and Amazon. He continues to expand his team of people enhancing the digital experience for customers, with offices now located in several major cities, including Chicago and San Francisco. Among the digital initiatives of Rafiq and his team at McDonald's are home delivery of meals, hands-free payments, and automated in-store kiosks where customers can order and pay for their food. Another innovation spearheaded by Rafiq is a virtual-reality device that enables people to step into a Happy Meal.

Rafiq says that he provides strong vision for the consumer experience, continuous customer focus, along with strong execution of his vision. He says that his leadership style is hands-on from the user experience and design thinking to the launch of an initiative. He proclaims, "I'm a talent magnet, and excel at creating high-performance teams aimed at missionary work. My network of relationships is extensive."

Rafiq believes that he has built a comprehensive vision for the digital efforts at McDonald's. He remarks that he has also created a large pipeline of digital experiences and customer engagement initiatives, including business plans and strategies. He has built a massive multiple channel e-commerce solution for the company that includes retail kiosks, mobile applications, and websites for ordering food. A specific example of an innovation is restaurant music controlled by customers using their mobile devices.

Rafiq holds an MBA in finance and marketing from the University of Chicago Booth School of Business and a BA in mathematics and economics from Wesleyan University.

### QUESTIONS

1. In what ways does Rafiq appear to be a business-oriented technology leader?

2. If you happen to be at a McDonalds that offers a food kiosk, what is your opinion of (a) the usefulness of the device, and (b) whether it draws much interest from customers.

*Source:* Original story created from facts and observations in the following sources: "Tech Person of Interest: Atif Rafiq, Chief Digital Officer, McDonald's," *Fortune,* April 1, 2016, p. 41; Maureen Morrison, "McDonald's Names Atif Rafiq as Its First Digital officer," *http://adage.com,* October 3, 2013, pp. 1–3; "Atif Rafiq," *wwww.linkedin.com,* July 26, 2013, pp. 1–4; Brian McManus, "This Band's Response To McDonald's Offer to Pay Them In Hamburgers Is Hilarious," *BuzzFeed* (www.buzzfeed.com), March 5, 2015, pp. 1–7.

## LEADERSHIP SKILL-BUILDING EXERCISE 13-1

### Mapping Out a Future for an Organization

The purpose of this exercise is to give you practice on a key aspect of strategic leadership, articulating where you want your organization to be, and how to arrive at that in future. To formulate a basic organizational strategy, first choose an organization. The organization could be a present employer (including self-employment), a past employer, or any organization familiar to you.

*Step One* is to write down at the bottom of a page a brief description of where the organization (business or nonprofit) is today. This might include product or service offerings, annual revenues, and number of employees.

*Step Two* is to write down where you want the firm to be at a future date.

*Step Three* is to write down what must be done to get from Step One to Step Two. You have therefore created future goals for your organization and the strategy required to achieve those goals (or vision).

*Source:* The idea for this exercise stems from "Business Strategies for Thinking Managers," *www.thinkingmanagers.com*, June 7, 2006, p. 1.

Leadership Skill-Building Exercise 13-1 gives you an opportunity to practice a straightforward approach to developing business strategy.

## Conducting a SWOT Analysis

Strategic planning helps a manager lead strategically. **Strategic planning** encompasses those activities that lead to the statement of goals and objectives and the choice of strategy. Quite often, a firm arrives at its strategy after completing strategic planning. In practice, many executive leaders choose a strategy prior to strategic planning. As mentioned earlier, at times intuition and judgment is more important than planning in the creation of a strategy. Once the firm has the strategy, such as forming strategic alliances, a plan is developed to implement it.

Quite often, strategic planning takes the form of a **SWOT analysis**, a long-standing method of considering internal strengths and weaknesses as well as external opportunities and threats in a particular situation. A SWOT analysis represents an effort to examine the interaction between the particular characteristics of your organization or organizational unit and the external environment, or marketplace, in which you compete.[17] The framework, or technique, is useful in identifying a niche the company has not already exploited. The components of a basic version of SWOT are described next, and are also outline in Figure 13-1.

*Preparing for the Analysis*  Four steps are recommended to bring about a successful SWOT analysis. First, it is important to be clear about what you are doing and why. The purpose might be to fine-tune a present strategy or to point the business in a new direction. Second, it is important to select appropriate contributors. Select people with appropriate experience, talent, and enthusiasm. Imaginative people are particularly useful for a SWOT analysis. Usually six to ten people are enough, but involving more people can be helpful to get more people involved in the changes that SWOT might trigger. Third, allocate research and information-gathering tasks. Several members of the team might concentrate on analyzing the firm, whereas others might concentrate on analyzing the outside environment. Step four is to create a workshop environment by encouraging open communication among participants.

All present should feel free to criticize the status quo, even questioning what most people think is a company strength. A SWOT team member of a group at Starbucks might say, "Is having so many stores such a great strength? Could we be losing out to the coffee lovers who want a more unique, intimate experience?"

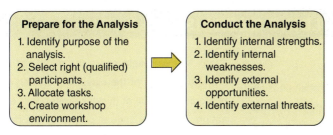

**FIGURE 13-1** The Basics of a SWOT Analysis.

***Conducting the Analysis*** The components of the basic version of SWOT are described next, as outline in Figure 13-1.

1. ***Identify Internal Strengths.*** The emphasis in this step is assessing factors within the organization that will have a positive impact on implementing the plan. (In some versions of SWOT analysis, an analysis of the external environment is included in this step.) What are the good points about a particular alternative? What are your advantages? What do you do well? Use your own judgment and intuition, and also ask knowledgeable people. As a business owner, you may have a favorable geographic location that makes you more accessible to customers than your competitor is. Another strength is that you may have invested in state-of-the-art equipment that became available only recently.

   A successful example of capitalizing on internal strengths took place when leaders at Amazon.com capitalized on its world-class capabilities for payment processing and order management for physical retailing. Soon the company offered these services to other companies, therefore becoming an outsourcing firm in addition to its many other capabilities. The specific service provided is that Amazon customers can make purchases on a company's website using the payment and shipping information stored in their Amazon accounts.[18]

2. ***Identify Internal Weaknesses.*** Here the strategy developer takes a candid look at factors within the firm that could have a negative impact on the proposed plan. Consider the risks of pursuing a particular course of action, such as subcontracting work to a low-wage country (outsourcing). What could be improved? What is done badly? What should be avoided? Examine weaknesses from internal and external perspectives. Do outsiders perceive weaknesses that you do not see? (You may have to ask several outsiders to help you identify these weaknesses.) Are there products, services, or work processes your competitors perform better than you do? You are advised to be realistic now and face any unpleasant truths as soon as possible. Again, use your judgment and ask knowledgeable people. As a manager or business owner, you may have problems managing your inventory, or you may have employees who are not up to the task of implementing a new plan or venture.

3. ***Identify External Opportunities.*** The purpose of this step is to assess socioeconomic, political, environmental, and demographic factors among others to estimate what benefits they may bring to the organization. Think of the opportunities that await you if you choose a promising strategic alternative, such as creating a culturally diverse customer base. Use your imagination, and visualize the possibilities. Look for interesting trends. Useful opportunities can derive from such events as the following:

   - Changes in technology and markets on both a broad and narrow scale
   - Changes in government policy related to your field
   - Changes in social patterns, population profiles, lifestyles, and so forth

4. ***Identify External Threats.*** The purpose of this step is to assess what possible negative impact socioeconomic, political, environmental, and demographic factors may have on the organization. There is a downside to every alternative, so think ahead,

## LEADERSHIP SKILL-BUILDING EXERCISE 13-2

### Conducting a SWOT Analysis

In small groups, develop a scenario for a SWOT analysis, such as the group starting a chain of Panini restaurants, pet-care service centers, or recycling centers for electronic devices. Because you will probably have mostly hypothetical data to work with, you will have to rely heavily on your imagination.

Group leaders might share the results of the SWOT analysis with the rest of the class. Conducting a SWOT analysis reinforces the skill of thinking strategically about a course of action. A key challenge in preparing this hypothetical SWOT analysis is to make a distinction between internal and external forces.

and do contingency planning. Ask people who may have tried in the past what you are attempting now. Answer questions such as

- What obstacles do you face?
- What is your competition doing?
- Are the required specifications for your job, products, or services changing?
- Is changing technology changing your ability to compete successfully?

Despite a careful analysis of threats, do not be dissuaded by the naysayers, heel draggers, and pessimists. To quote Nike, "Just do it."

Carrying out a SWOT analysis is often illuminating in terms of both pointing out what needs to be done and putting problems into perspective. Although much more complex schemes have been developed for strategic planning, they all include some analysis of strengths, weaknesses, and opportunities. Leadership Skill-Building Exercise 13-2 gives you an opportunity to conduct a SWOT analysis.

## A Sampling of Business Strategies Formulated by Leaders

We have been focusing on the process by which leaders and managers make strategic decisions. Also of interest to leaders and potential leaders is the content of such decisions. Business strategies are often classified according to their focus of impact: corporate level, business level, or functional level. Corporate-level strategy asks, "What business are we in?" Business-level strategy asks, "How do we compete?" And functional-level strategy asks, "How do we support the business-level strategy?" Some of the business strategies listed next might cut across more than one of these three levels. The first three of these strategies are the generic strategies espoused by Michael Porter.[19]

1. **Differentiation.** A differentiation strategy seeks to offer a product or service that the customer perceives as being different from available alternatives. The organization may use advertising, distinctive features, exceptional service, or new technology to gain this perception of uniqueness. What differentiates one of your favorite products? A challenge with the differentiation strategy is that if the product or service is successful, competitors move in quickly. An example is pioneering travel reservation websites, such as Expedia and Priceline. Dozens of competitors quickly moved into the sector, taking away market share from the original travel websites.

2. **Cost leadership.** A basic strategy is to produce a product or service at a low cost in order to lower the selling price and gain market share. ALDI, a chain of deep-discount food stores, is the eighth-largest retailer in the world. The company capitalizes on the bargain hunter who accepts private labels, limited choices, and paying 25 cents to use a grocery cart. ALDI relentlessly pursues its own brands with packaging strikingly similar to American brands. The choice of fewer brands helps cut costs. No shelving is necessary because products are wheeled in on pallets, saving the cost of hiring human

stockers. ALDI does not accept credit cards or checks and encourages customers to bring their own bags.[20]

A variety of general merchandise stores, such as Dollar General and Family Dollar, implement the cost leadership strategy. A major problem with a cost leadership strategy is that competitors can easily enter the field, creating a downward spiral in pricing.

3. **Focus or niche.** In a focus strategy, the organization concentrates on a specific regional market or buyer group. To gain market share, the company will use either a differentiation or a cost leadership approach in a targeted market. The focus strategy is a natural, commonsense approach to business because it is difficult to serve every customer well. A focus strategy is about the same thing as finding a niche, or your place in the market. Almost every successful business venture was found by locating a niche. Pawn shops that cater to the affluent exemplify how varied a niche strategy can be. One such firm is Suttons & Robertsons. CEO, Jeffrey A. Weiss, explains, "We focus on the blue-chip, wealthy crowd." The company has been in business for over 250 years and capitalizes on the fact that many people today are asset rich but have a temporary liquidity problem.[21]

4. **High quality.** A basic business strategy is to offer goods or services of higher quality than the competition does. Leaders continue to emphasize quality, even if there is less explicit emphasis today on formal quality programs than in the past. Important exceptions are the Six Sigma programs that emphasize statistical approaches to attaining quality. Leaders at GE and 3M, for example, emphasize Six Sigma. One reason that quality is classified as a strategy is that it contributes to competitive advantage in cost and differentiation. Because many customers now expect high quality, a quality strategy must be supplemented with other points of differentiation, such as supplying customized features and services that customers desire. How about Apple Inc. or the Swiss Army knife for a quality strategy? Also, all the merchandise offered at the pawn shop just mentioned is of high quality, such as diamond necklaces.

5. **Imitation.** If you cannot be imaginative, why not imitate the best? Manufacturers of popular digital devices such as digital cameras and smartphones use an imitation strategy. The company waits for the right time to introduce a lower-priced competitor. Benchmarking is a form of learning by watching. One company emulates the best practices of another company, usually without outright stealing the product or service ideas of another company. The automotive industry is rampant with one company imitating another. Next time you are in a busy parking lot or driving on the highway, see how many hoods and auto grilles you can find that resemble a Mercedes.

6. **Strategic alliances.** A modern business strategy is to form alliances, or joint ventures, with other companies to exploit a market opportunity. Strategic alliances have become more common as leaders in the high-tech industry attempt to capitalize on the strengths of other companies. Typically, the parent companies have complementary skills and assets. Strategic alliances involving food giants partnering with innovative startups have become frequent in recent years. General Mills is an industry leader in such alliances. Rather than risk being surprised by young food industry disrupters, the company is partnering with small food companies through it business development venture capital arm, 301 INC. General Mills takes an ownership stake and helps the smaller food company grow. One such partnership is between the food giant and Austin Allian, a company that makes drinkable, chilled soup.[22]

7. **Growth through acquisition.** A standard strategy for growth is for one company to purchase others. Growth in size is important, but companies may also purchase other companies to acquire a new technology or complete a product line. Buying a new technology is often less expensive than investing huge sums in R&D that might not yield a marketable product. Much of General Electric's growth over the years can be attributed to acquiring other companies. Google has already acquired over

200 companies with the largest being Motorola Mobility. The large number of acquisitions by Google fit the parent company, Alphabet's, vision of changing the world in many ways through information technology.

8. ***High-speed and first-mover strategy.*** High-speed managers focus on speed in all of their business activities, including product development, sales response, and customer service. Believing that time is money, they choose time as a competitive resource. It is important to get products to market quickly because the competition might get there first or might deliver a product or service more rapidly. Getting to market first is also referred to as the first-mover strategy. Starbucks was the first national chain of coffee bars. The many storefronts served as marketing devices to acquire more customers. A first-mover strategy sometime gives only a temporary advantage, such as the BlackBerry once being almost synonymous with smartphone. Many competitors swept in, including Samsung, Apple, and Nokia, making it difficult for BlackBerry to survive. Today, BlackBerry has turned over the production of its iconic handsets to overseas partners who license the name BlackBerry.[23]

9. ***Product and global diversification.*** A natural business strategy is to offer a variety of products and services and to sell across borders to enhance market opportunities. As described in the chapter opener, Samsung is heavily involved in a diversification strategy. Coca-Cola Co. exemplifies a company that thrives on both global and product diversification. Coke now generates 75 percent of its revenue and operating profit from countries outside the United States. Despite the company's reputation for relying too heavily on Coke, it has acquired many smaller brands of beverages in recent years, including the purchase of the organic beverage company Honest Tea of Bethesda. A key point of the acquisition is that Honest Tea is a growth company, and many consumers have made a move toward health and wellness in their beverage consumption.[24] Global diversification is such a widely accepted strategy that the burden of proof would be on a business leader who shunned globalization

10. ***Sticking to core competencies.*** Many firms of all sizes believe they will prosper if they confine their efforts to the activities they perform best—their core competencies. Corporate strategist Jim Collins calls this the Hedgehog concept: becoming very good at one thing in a world of companies that spread themselves into many areas where they lack depth.[25] Many firms that expanded through diversification later trimmed back operations to activities on which they had built their reputation.

    GE, mentioned above as a major example of growth through acquisition, is also a case history in refocusing on core competencies. A few years ago, former CEO Jeff Immelt decided that GE was drifting too far from its industrial roots, including at one time earning more than half its profits from its financial wing, GE Capital. The new strategy of simplification resulted in reducing the scope of GE Capital, the sale of NBC Universal, and a portfolio with a refocus on industrial product such as power generators and jet engines. Over a period of a few years, GE Capital sold approximately $200 billion of its assets, reducing its size by about one-half.[26] (Reducing the scope of GE Capital would include no longer making certain types of loans, such as subprime loans to restaurants.)

11. ***Brand leadership.*** As obvious as it may appear, succeeding through developing the reputation of a brand name can be considered a business strategy. The opposite strategy is to build components for others, build products that others market under their names, or be a commodity, such as cinder blocks. According to research company Interbrand, the world's ten leading brands in order of brand strength are (1) Apple, (2) Google, (3) Coca-Cola, (4) Microsoft, (5) Toyota, (6) IBM, (7) Samsung, (8) Amazon, (9) Mercedes-Benz, and (10) General Electric. An Interbrand executive says that these companies "Look inward and outward, expand into new markets, and create better experiences to grow their brands and businesses."[27] By building the reputation of their brands, senior management (assisted by countless thousands of workers) has helped these companies succeed financially.

## LEADERSHIP SKILL-BUILDING EXERCISE 13-3

### The Business Strategies of a Favorite Company

The term business strategy is used frequently in reference to business enterprises, yet which strategy or strategies a given company uses can be difficult to identify. Think of one of your favorite companies, then identify at least one specific strategy that company uses, as expressed by company management or the press. A good starting point, of course, is to enter a term into a search engine such as, "Business strategy of Kellogg." If you are unable to find the strategy for the first company you researched, try another business enterprise. After you have identified at least one specific strategy, comment on whether it fits one or more of the sampling of business strategies identified in the leadership textbook.

12. **Competitive advantage through hiring talented people.** A powerful strategy for gaining competitive advantage is to build the organization with talented, well-motivated people at every level. The most urgent need in building great companies is to find and keep great people. Microsoft and Amazon.com, along with elite business consulting firms, are examples of firms that explicitly use the hiring-talented-people strategy. Talented people may need some leadership direction, but they will think of new products and services and develop effective work processes.

   All of these impressive strategies have limited impact unless they are implemented properly, meaning that effective management must support strategic leadership. To repeat, visions must be followed up with execution. Strategies are sometimes not implemented correctly because top management is not aware of problems that threaten the business.[28] An example would be that faced with pressures to reduce costs, some manager in operating units do not report that quality is being sacrificed to hold down manufacturing costs. Another problem, as mentioned earlier, is that the sales force may not be involved sufficiently in implementing the strategy.

   Leadership Skill-Building Exercise 13-3 provides you an opportunity to dig further into business strategy.

## Knowledge Management and the Learning Organization

Another strategic thrust of leaders is to help their organizations better adapt to the environment by assisting workers and the organization to become better learners. To accomplish this, the leader manages knowledge and cultivates a learning organization. **Knowledge management (KM)** is a concerted effort to improve how knowledge is created, delivered, and applied.[29] When knowledge is managed effectively, information is shared as needed, whether it be printed, stored electronically, or rests in the brains of workers. Managing knowledge helps create a **learning organization**—one that is skilled at creating, acquiring, and transferring knowledge and at modifying behavior to reflect new knowledge and insights.[30] In the two following sections, we look first and knowledge sharing, then knowledge management in general.

### Knowledge Sharing

Knowledge management in the form of knowledge sharing has surged in importance in recent years because so many baby boomers are retiring, resulting in *tribal knowledge* leaving the firm. (Tribal knowledge refers to inside knowledge about how the organization operates.) Several firms including selected divisions of GE and the Educational Testing Service), have developed knowledge transfer programs to deal with the problem of so much useful knowledge exiting the organization.

A key part of the knowledge transfer program is for older workers to share useful knowledge with younger workers before the former depart. Technical knowledge is often included in knowledge sharing. NASA developed a program when the U.S. space agency began to lose expertise about lunar landings as senior engineers retired. Recognizing it would need the expertise for missions to Mars, NASA asked engineers who worked on the Apollo mission to share their knowledge in meetings with new engineers.[31]

The relevance of knowledge sharing to the organization is reinforced by the negative impact of knowledge hiding. When knowledge is hidden, colleagues are less likely to generate creative ideas, and the knowledge hider might also experience less creativity. The reason is that creativity often depends on information and knowledge sharing, as described in Chapter 11. A study of 240 employees in 24 groups engaged in metal manufacturing in Slovenia revealed a negative relationship between knowledge hiding and the hider's creativity. Knowledge hiding was measured by a self-quiz, whereas worker creativity was measured by supervisory ratings.[32]

Leadership Self-assessment Quiz 13-2 gives you an opportunity to think through your tendencies toward sharing or hiding knowledge.

# LEADERSHIP SELF-ASSESSMENT QUIZ 13-2

**My Attitudes Toward Sharing Knowledge**

*Instructions:* Indicate how much you agree with the following statements: disagree strongly (DS); disagree (D); neutral (N); agree (A); and agree strongly (AS).

|  | | DS | D | N | A | AS |
|---|---|---|---|---|---|---|
| **1.** | I have often helped other students with their homework. | 1 | 2 | 3 | 4 | 5 |
| **2.** | In brainstorming sessions, I usually hold back from giving my best ideas because I do not want them stolen. | 5 | 4 | 3 | 2 | 1 |
| **3.** | I enjoy helping another person with a work or school problem. | 1 | 2 | 3 | 4 | 5 |
| **4.** | I would be willing to submit some of my best ideas to a company database, such as an intranet. | 1 | 2 | 3 | 4 | 5 |
| **5.** | I am concerned about submitting my most creative ideas on a term paper because these ideas could be stolen. | 5 | 4 | 3 | 2 | 1 |
| **6.** | I enjoy working as part of a team and sharing ideas. | 5 | 4 | 3 | 2 | 1 |
| **7.** | I get a little suspicious when a coworker or fellow student attempts to pick my brain. | 1 | 2 | 3 | 4 | 5 |
| **8.** | It upsets me if I do not receive full credit for my ideas. | 5 | 4 | 3 | 2 | 1 |
| **9.** | If I had a great idea for a screenplay or novel, I would not tell anyone about it before I was finished with the idea. | 5 | 4 | 3 | 2 | 1 |
| **10.** | I have often let other people know about a good method I developed to improve work efficiency. | 1 | 2 | 3 | 4 | 5 |
| | **Total score:** _____ | | | | | |

*Scoring and Interpretation:* Tally your score by adding the numbers you circled or checked.

- **40 or higher:** You are generous with respect to knowledge sharing and would probably fit well in an organization that practices knowledge management.
- **20–39:** You have average attitudes toward sharing knowledge, with a mixture of enthusiasm and skepticism about knowledge sharing.
- **1–19:** You are quite cautious and guarded about sharing ideas. Unless you become more willing to share your ideas, you would not fit well in an organization that emphasized knowledge management.

*Note: You are authorized to share this quiz with as many people as you would like.*

# Knowledge Management

Knowledge management (KM) deals with a cultural focus on knowledge sharing. Managing knowledge is an important leadership role because very few organizations make systematic use of the collective wisdom of employees. Loads of information is often collected in databases, and even through text messaging, but little systematic use is made of the information. Here, we look at the general format of KM programs.

KM has three components, as revealed by the research and observations of Thomas H. Davenport, Laurence Prusak, and Bruce Strong.[33] *Knowledge creation* is used to spur innovation. Programs for creating knowledge solicit ideas, insights, and innovations from many sources, including rank and file workers, customers, and business partners, instead of relying exclusively on the research and development staff. For example, more than 40 percent of Procter & Gamble products have a component from external sources that is up from 10 percent ten years ago.

*Knowledge dissemination* through information technology is the most frequent activity within knowledge management. Methods of sharing knowledge include company intranets that consolidate information in one place so that it is more accessible to potential users. Also of importance are internal online collaboration networks in which workers from the same as well as geographically dispersed units share work-related information. An example is to make an intranet a one-stop information shop designed to support critical jobs and work processes. For example, Intel places on one website all of the information workers need to make a capital purchase. *Knowledge application* is the process of getting workers better at what they do. Many organizations have discovered that the most effective way of encouraging workers to apply knowledge is through basic practices such as mentoring, on-the-job training, and workshops.

*General Format of KM Programs*    KM systems often take the form of a digital system for collecting and organizing potentially useful information. However, knowledge is still disseminated through traditional approaches such as people exchanging stories about incidents that have taken place in the past. A noteworthy example is the British Royal Navy and its highly efficient informal internal network. Leadership information and stories referred to as "dits" are exchanged across the network—among layers of management, generations, branches, and social groups. Aided by these dits, the Royal Navy's collective consciousness processes new knowledge and insights while reinforcing established ones. Crews are encouraged to share their dits.[34] A dit might take this form: "A few years ago Admiral _____ visited one of the biggest vessels in the fleet. He said that he could tell our morale was high and we were battle ready because so many sailors were smiling."

A very practical form of KM is to deliver information just in time, or at the point at which it is most needed. A widely practiced method of delivering information just in time is through tablet computers, such as an insurance accessing the right information to help a customer with a complicated coverage problem. Whatever advanced technology is used to implement KM, it works best in an organizational culture that values knowledge and encourages its dissemination. A study conducted in 121 new-product development teams and 41 subsidiaries of a high-technology company quantified another factor that influences knowledge sharing. Professional workers are less likely to hoard knowledge when there is less competition across the organizational units.[35] (In other words, why share knowledge with a strong competitor?)

The organizational subculture shapes our assumptions about what constitutes knowledge and which knowledge is worth managing.[36] Professional workers in the finance division of Gap, Inc. might think that watching music channels on company time or surfing the Internet is a waste of company time. In the merchandising division, however, watching music channels and Internet surfing might be perceived as a valuable way of understanding clothing trends.

## Servant Leadership and the Creation of Knowledge

A recent theory of how knowledge is created in organizations focuses on the role of the servant leader. A key point of the theory is that servant leaders are effective in sharing leadership responsibility, and shared leadership enhances the creation of knowledge. One reason is that shared leadership leads to a free flow of information exchange among group members. Shared leadership de-emphasizes hierarchical boundaries, which facilitates servant leaders and followers communicating freely. With less power distance between group member and leader, the group members believe in the importance of their opinions and suggestions, which leads to more information exchange. The exchange of information often triggers new learning.

Caring for people is another aspect of servant leadership that facilitates knowledge creation. The reason is that caring relationships facilitate the expression of diverse ideas and foster constructive reasoning and evaluation of ideas. When people feel that they are cared for, they are more willing to disclose information and put effort into processing information.[37]

An example of this abstract theory about servant leadership and the creation of knowledge is as follows: A marketing assistant at a financial services was concerned about the portion of the company's website that dealt with customers investing in funds. The manager in his caring and sharing style could be classified as a servant leader. The assistant said that she had three relatives (who were customers of the company) who attempt to navigate the appropriate portion of the website, and all three agreed that the experience was frustrating. Furthermore, two of the relatives said the website was so goofy that they would telephone customer service rather than invest online. The manager accepted the information in a relaxed and inquisitive manner. The discussion ultimately led to getting the cooperation of the website developer in creating a more user-friendly experience for customers.

To round out your understanding of knowledge management, do Leadership Skill-Building Exercise 13-4.

## The Learning Organization

A learning organization can be viewed as a group of people working together to enhance their capacities to create the results they value.[38] Organizational leadership, however, must usually take the initiative to create the conditions whereby such enhancement of capacities, or learning, takes place. The research noted earlier in the chapter based on 20,000 executives found that strategic leaders are the focal point for organizational learning. Such leaders promoted a culture of inquiry, and they search for the lessons to be learned in both successful and unsuccessful outcomes. Strategic leaders also study their own failures and those of the team to find hidden lessons.[39] For example, a retailing executive

## LEADERSHIP SKILL-BUILDING EXERCISE 13-4

### The Knowledge-Sharing Investigation Teams

A challenge with the idea of knowledge sharing is to know what knowledge should be shared among company members. The class is organized into knowledge-sharing investigation teams. Members of each team contact two people working in a support, technical, sales, professional, or managerial position in a profit or nonprofit organization. Ask the contact persons what knowledge would be valuable to share in their place of work. Communicate using the easiest method, whether it be a phone call, a text message, or a tweet.

Discuss your findings in a group, and perhaps add opinions of your own as to what knowledge would be worthwhile sharing in an organization. Arrive at a conclusion about five specific types of knowledge within an organization worth sharing. Share your findings with members of the other groups in the class.

might conclude that going too far to attract young, more fashionable customers wound up alienating too many older, more traditional customers.

To facilitate organizational learning, several firms have created a position labeled chief knowledge officer (CKO), or its equivalent. The major justification for creating such a position is that in many companies, human skills, intuition, and wisdom are replacing capital as the most precious resource. Chief knowledge officers seek to disperse those assets throughout the firm and convert them into innovations. They are in charge of systematically collecting information and connecting people with others who might have valuable information.

WD-40, the company that makes the famous lubricant for such purposes as unscrewing a rusty bolt, exemplifies an extreme learning organization. When Gary Ridge was appointed CEO in 2009, WD-40 was used in four out of five households in the United States, and in virtually every mine, factory, and construction site in the country. CEO Gary Ridge has made learning central to the corporate culture. Ridge insists that every employee takes the "WD-40 Maniac Pledge," a commitment to become a "learning maniac." The pledge includes the phrase, "If I'm doing something others should know about, I'm responsible for telling them." Ridge has placed a premium on learning, experimenting, and improvising. Based somewhat on helping employees become more interested in what was possible for the company, WD-40 now sells its products in 176 countries.

As part of the learning organization culture, Ridge says, "My job is to create a company of learners. I like to ask my people and myself, 'When's the last time you did something for the first time?'"[40]

Here we look at a variety of leadership practices and attitudes that facilitate organizational learning.

### Transformational Versus Transactional Leadership and Organizational Learning

Research in a large European financial services firm has brought into sharper focus the leader's role in organizational learning. One major finding was that transformational leadership behaviors contribute significantly to encouraging workers to pursue exploratory innovation. An exploratory innovation deals with finding new products, services, processes, or technology. An example would be a bank finding an entirely new service to offer to the public, such as a relocation service for geographically transferred employees. Another major finding was that transactional leadership behaviors facilitate improving and extending existing knowledge and are associated with exploitative innovation.[41] Exploitation relates to learning ways to make incremental improvements in existing products, services, or processes. An example would be a bank developing a line of credit specifically geared toward the one-person enterprise.

### Leadership Initiatives for Enhancing the Learning Organization

A wide variety of leadership initiatives can create and enhance a learning organization. Understanding them will help you grasp the concept of what a leader might do to enhance organizational learning.[42]

A major building block of a learning organization is a *supportive learning environment*. Several factors comprise a supportive learning environment. Employees should not fear being belittled or marginalized when they disagree with their manager or coworkers or ask naive questions. Instead, they should feel comfortable about expressing disagreement or puzzlement. Differences in opposing views should be both accepted and appreciated. Supportive learning also includes being open to new ideas and having the time to think and reflect. In many organizations, a person seen looking out the window would be assumed to be daydreaming rather than thinking about work-related problems.

A second building block of a learning organization is *concrete learning processes and practices*. One example would be for a company to hold debriefing sessions discussing what went right or wrong with a recent program of placing product advertisements as temporary tattoos on the foreheads of paid participants.

A third building block is *leadership that reinforces learning*. For example, when leaders actively question and listen to employees, dialogue and debate as well as learning are encouraged. Most of the behaviors in the rest of this section would fit the building block of leadership that reinforces learning. Providing rewards for learning is a direct approach to reinforcing learning by individuals and teams. For example, when workers have increased their knowledge and value to the company they might be provided with new and challenging opportunities.[43]

A top-level leader should *create a strategic intent to learn*. Organizational learning then becomes a vehicle for gaining competitive advantage. *Creating a shared vision* enhances learning, as organization members develop a common purpose and commitment to having the organization keep learning. If workers at all levels believe that the company is headed toward greatness, they will be motivated to learn to help deliver greatness.

In a learning organization, *employees are empowered to make decisions and seek continuous improvement*. The idea is to develop a community of learning in which every worker believes that he or she can contribute to a smarter, more effective organization.

*Systems thinking* is almost synonymous with organizational learning. The leader helps organization members regard the organization as a system in which everybody's work affects the activities of everybody else. Systems thinking also means keeping the big picture foremost in everybody's mind and being keenly aware of the external environment. In addition to the big picture of systems thinking, the leader must encourage the little picture of *personal mastery of the job*. As team members gain personal mastery of their jobs, they contribute to *team learning*, an essential part of a learning organization. Team learning centers on collective problem solving in which members freely share information and opinions to facilitate problem solving.

*Action learning*, or learning while working on real problems, is a fundamental part of a learning organization. Participants in action learning are asked to work in teams to attack a significant organizational problem, such as decreasing the cycle time on a project. In the process of resolving an actual work problem, the participants acquire and use new skills, tools, or concepts. As the project progresses, new skills are applied while working with the problem. For example, if the team learned how to eliminate duplication of effort in one aspect of the work process, it would look to eliminate duplication at other points in the cycle.

Action learning provides another benefit that can facilitate knowledge sharing. The benefit uncovered by research is an increase of psychological safety within the group. The term refers to a shared belief by team members that the team is safe for interpersonal risk taking, such as taking one's turn in speaking up, either digitally or in person.[44] When team members feel safe in speaking up, they are more likely to share knowledge.

*Learning from failure* contributes immensely to a learning organization. A company that diversified into an area unsuccessfully might analyze why it failed, and then not repeat the same mistake. *Encouraging continuous experimentation* is another important practice for crafting a learning strategy. The leader encourages workers to learn from competitors, customers, suppliers, and other units within the organization.

For organizational learning to proceed smoothly, workers throughout the organization must have the *political skills to make connections with and influence others*. For example, if a production technician discovers an effective method of reducing water consumption, he or she must have the skill to sell an influential person on the merits of this idea.

A final perspective on creating the learning organization is that the leader must *encourage organizational members to think creatively*—to imagine possibilities that do not already exist. Research synthesized by Yukl suggests that a comprehensive way for leaders to enhance organizational learning is to "Develop, implement, and support programs and systems that will encourage and reward the discovery of new knowledge and its diffusion and application in the organization."[45] Instead of merely adapting to the environment, the organization engages in the type of breakthrough thinking described in our previous discussions of creativity and strategic leadership.

## READER'S ROADMAP

So far we have studied the nature of leadership; the attributes, behaviors, and styles of leaders; the ethics and social responsibility of leaders; and how leaders exert power and use politics and influence. We then studied techniques for developing teamwork as well as motivation and coaching skills. After having studied creativity and innovation as part of leadership, we focused on communication skills as they relate to leadership. We then shifted to strategic leadership. Next, we examine another broad challenge facing leaders: dealing with cultural diversity within the organization and across borders.

## SUMMARY

Strategic leadership deals with the major purposes of an organization or organizational unit and provides the direction and inspiration necessary to create, provide direction to, or sustain an organization. The development of business strategy is a major component of strategic leadership. Our approach to understanding such development focuses on the importance of strategic thinking, the human and emotional aspect of strategy, gathering multiple inputs to formulate strategy, the implementation of strategy, and the SWOT analysis.

Strategic leaders rely heavily on intuition as to what direction the organization should take. Many strategic leaders arrive at their ideas for the organization's future by consulting a wide range of interested parties, in a process similar to conducting research to create a vision.

Carefully crafting a strategy and vision is not sufficient for effectiveness. The strategy and vision must also be implemented or executed by the leader/manager. Strategy cannot be implemented successfully unless key people know what they need to do differently and understand how they should be executing. Quite often, implementation requires a series of goals that will be steps along the way to implementing the strategy. A SWOT analysis takes into account internal strengths and weaknesses and external opportunities and threats in a given situation. A SWOT analysis also examines the interaction between the organization and the environment.

Strategic leaders use many different types of business strategies, including the following: (1) differentiation, (2) cost leadership, (3) focus or niche, (4) high quality, (5) imitation, (6) strategic alliances, (7) growth through acquisition, (8) high-speed and first-mover strategy, (9) product and global diversification, (10) sticking to core competencies, (11) brand leadership, and (12) competitive advantage through hiring talented people.

Another strategic thrust of leaders is to help their organizations adapt to the environment by assisting workers and the organization to become better learners. To accomplish this feat, the leader manages knowledge and cultivates a learning organization. Knowledge management focuses on the systematic sharing of information, including being able to deliver information just in time. Knowledge management consists of knowledge creation, dissemination, and application.

Servant leaders are effective in sharing leadership responsibility, and shared leadership enhances the creation of knowledge. De-emphasizing hierarchical boundaries facilitates servant leaders communicating freely. People who feel cared for are more willing to disclose and process information.

The leader has many roles in a learning organization. Transformational leaders tend toward encouraging exploratory innovation, whereas transactional leaders tend toward encouraging exploitative (increments in what already exists) innovation.

Major leadership initiatives for creating a learning organization include creating a supportive learning environment and establishing concrete learning processes and practices. Leadership should reinforce learning including rewards for learning, create a strategic intent to learn, and create a shared vision. Employees should be empowered to make decision and seek continuous improvement. Also important is encouraging systems thinking, encouraging personal mastery of the job, and team learning. Action learning, or learning while working on real problems, learning from failures, and encouraging continuous experimentation are also part of the learning organization. Learning from failure is useful, and workers must have the political skills to make connections and influence others. Encouraging creative thinking is also part of the learning organization.

## KEY TERMS

strategy 343
strategic leadership 343
crowdsourcing 346

strategic planning 348
SWOT analysis 348

knowledge management
(KM) 353
learning organization 353

## GUIDELINES FOR ACTION AND SKILL DEVELOPMENT

Business strategy may be a complex subject, but the end result should be something almost everybody in the organization can understand. Three recommended rules toward making strategy understandable are as follows:[46]

1. *Make it simple.* Strategy can usually be reduced to one page that addresses in which space the organization will compete, and how it will win.
2. *Perfection is not necessary.* Strategy is not about finding perfect answers, but more about placing bets with a reasonable chance of winning.
3. *Explain the logic behind the strategy clearly.* Be clear about the changes necessary to achieve the strategic goal and mission.

To make sure that all workers understand the company's vision of where it wants to go, the vision statement should have certain key characteristics:[47]

1. *Brief.* The statement should be short enough, so employees can recall it with ease. It has been suggested that a vision should fit on an adult-size T-shirt.
2. *Verifiable.* A verifiable vision is one that ten people could agree that an organization has achieved.
3. *Focused.* Vision statements often contain too many ideas. It is better to focus on a major goal such as the vision of Ford Motor Company: "People working together as a lean global enterprise for automotive leadership." (Notice that his vision statement includes mention of both human resources and a major company product.)
4. *Understandable.* A major purpose of the vision statement is that employees will know where the organization wants to go and how to help it get there. Being understandable is therefore a key quality of the vision statement. Terms such as *world class* and *leading edge* might be subject to wide interpretation. The vision statement of Caterpillar Inc. would be understood by almost every employee: "Our vision is a world in which all people's basic needs—such as shelter, clean water, sanitation, food, and reliable power—are fulfilled in an environmentally sustainable way and a company that improves the quality of the environment and the communities where we live and work."

5. *Inspirational.* To inspire, a vision statement should make employees feel good about working for the organization and should focus them on measurable business goals.

### Discussion Questions and Activities

1. Why might being very practical minded interfere with being an outstanding strategic leader?
2. How might being very strong with business analytics (such as analyzing reams of data and preparing spreadsheets) help a person develop business strategy?
3. In what way can a business strategy motivate and inspire employees?
4. How could you adapt a business strategy to guide you in your own career as a leader?
5. Many top-level managers say that they want lower-ranking managers to think strategically. How can a middle manager or a first-level manager think strategically?
6. The Dollar Shave Club began as an online startup getting mostly free publicity on the social media. Today, this male grooming business is a serious competitor to major brands such as Gillette, and was recently sold to Unilever for $1 billion. Use your imagination or do a little research to identify the business strategy that propelled the Dollar Shave Club to success.
7. Working alone or with several team members, provide a recent example of a company that is in big trouble or went out of business because it lacked an effective strategy.
8. During the Great Recession, many consumers who had previously shopped at traditional supermarkets shifted to doing basic shopping at dollar stores and discount department stores. Furthermore, many of these shoppers remained loyal to the low-priced stores long after the recession. What are the strategy lessons here?
9. In what way might doing a good job of knowledge management give a company a competitive advantage?
10. Why do you think it has been so difficult for researchers to prove that knowledge management pays dividends to an organization?

## LEADERSHIP CASE PROBLEM A

### The Saratoga Supply Company Needs a Strategy

The Saratoga Supply Company is a distributor of a wide variety of industrial supplies to small- and medium-size companies, as well as schools, hospitals, and government agencies. The range of supplies number in the thousands including paper clips, copying paper, office furniture, desktop computers, pencil sharpeners, paper towels, and cleaning solvents. Saratoga Supply uses state-of-the-art information technology for purchasing, selling, and delivering products.

Although the company has been in business for sixty years, CEO Wes is worried about the future of Saratoga Supply. In consultation with CFO, Darleen, and head of sales, Gary, Wes notices a disturbing and steady decline in sales for almost all the products the company supplies. Wes agrees with Darleen that the downward trend in sales is accelerating (sales are decelerating) at an unhealthy rate. He also agrees with Gary's analysis that too many customers are now ordering directly from manufacturers through online sales. In the past, most manufacturers did not want to bother with small

sales to individual companies. But with e-commerce, sales can be implemented more readily without going through intermediaries such as Saratoga Supply Company.

With a concerned look on his face, Wes says to Darleen and Gary, "We need to develop a business strategy to prevent going out of business. Maybe we should meet for an all-day strategy session real soon."

### Questions

1. How should Wes and his team go about developing a survival strategy for Saratoga Supply?
2. Does Saratoga Supply really need a survival strategy? Or should the company just begin to downsize to fit the demand for its products and services?
3. From the limited evidence presented, how effectively do you think Wes is carrying out the role of a strategic leader?

## ASSOCIATED ROLE PLAY

Organize into teams of about six students because Wes has selected you to come up with a strategy for Saratoga that will enable the company to survive. Wes instructs you via e-mail: "Be as courageous as you want in giving me a strategy suggestion. We have been in business for sixty years, but we have to do something different

to survive and prosper. The handwriting is on the wall. Saratoga Supply is headed toward extinction." You have about thirty minutes to arrive at a survival strategy for Saratoga Supply. An alternative is to spend some supplementary time outside of class working on the problem. Brainstorm by e-mail or social media if you prefer.

## LEADERSHIP CASE PROBLEM B

### The Product Differentiation Strategy Team

A group of middle managers sat in a well-lit conference room overlooking the Chicago skyline. All six were impressed by the technology in the room, the furniture, and the refreshments. At 9 A.M., the meeting began, and team leader Jessica spoke first:

"We all know why we are here. Kevin, our CEO, has become convinced of the necessity of a product differentiation strategy. He thinks our conglomerate is too conventional. We go after markets in which we can compete successfully, and earn a decent profit in practically our divisions." Team member Rob asked "So

what's wrong with being successful? What's wrong with turning in good profits quarter after quarter, and seeing our stock price rise year by year?"

With a determined expression, Jessica said, "What's wrong is that we are competing in traditional spaces where the competition is too intense. Kevin wants us to compete in market space that does not already exist. We should be creating a new demand, and then filling that demand. Kevin wants us to come up with some product or service differentiation, or unique, ideas that he will then consider."

"I get it," said Kim, "We should stay in the profitable markets our various divisions already serve. But at the same time, we should get into new markets that nobody is serving. How about making smartphones that will work during outer space travel? In a few years, we might have loads of private citizens taking trips into outer space."

"Great sense of humor Kim," responded Marvin, "but the demand might be too small."

Jessica then clicked open a PowerPoint slide listing the sixty-two products and services the company already provides. She told the group, "Kevin says we should forget about these markets already being served. We have to invade new markets, maybe even create a market.

"Whoever thought 15 years ago that people would go shopping on a hand-held device while sitting in their den? Whoever thought people would pay for a package delivery service that competed with a government-backed postal service? Whoever thought people would want to read make and receive phone calls while driving in their cars, riding a bike, or sitting in a ski lift?"

Cecilia commented, "You are saying that as the product differentiation strategy team, we have to identify a multimillion dollar market space that no other company is serving right now. The world already has millions of products and services being offered. How is our humble team going to identify a market of value that does not already exist?"

Jessica said, "I don't know how we are going to find our unique strategy. But I do know that Kevin wants our report in 30 days. We're going to meet for four consecutive full-day sessions on Thursdays to get the job done. We probably will be communicating with each other between the meetings also.

"Let's get to work right now."

## Questions

1. What approaches would you recommend that the product differentiation strategy team use to identify new market space for the conglomerate?

2. How realistic is it for Kevin to delegate the task of finding a product differentiation strategy to a group of middle managers? Explain your reasoning.

3. What do you think would be the effectiveness of using the Internet to develop a product-differentiation strategy for the team? For example, why not go to Ask.com and enter the question, "What would be a new market space with no competition?"

# ASSOCIATED ROLE PLAY

One student plays the role of Jessica who has gathered the group on another Thursday strategy-development day. She is concerned that the group has not yet identified an open market space to explore. She tells the group not leave until we have at least one good idea to present to Kevin. Several other students play the role of the middle managers who will have to do some rapid brainstorming (Jessica included) to identify at least one product-differentiation strategy. Other student can provide feedback on how well the group has attained its goal this Thursday.

## LEADERSHIP SKILL-BUILDING **EXERCISE 13-4**

### My Leadership Portfolio

A major part of being a strategic leader is to think strategically. Entrapped by the necessities of the small tasks facing us daily, it is easy to "think little" instead of "think big" as required to be a strategic thinker. A "little thinker" might attend a leadership seminar and spend five minutes demanding a $5.00 rebate because he or she was served ill-prepared food at lunch. A "big thinker" might reflect on the same poorly prepared meal as a lesson in the importance of employees' taking care of small details to ensure customer satisfaction. In this installment in your leadership portfolio, enter into your journal how you capitalized—or did not capitalize—on the opportunity to think strategically during the last week, or so. An example follows:

> My friend and I visited a large shopping mall on Saturday morning. We noticed a large number of vehicles, both autos and small trucks, circling around within a block of the mall entrance. The drivers were obviously looking for a parking spot

close enough so they could avoid walking the block, or so, necessary if they parked farther from the entrance.

> My friend is a fitness nut, so he said the parking space chasers could do themselves a favor by parking a long distance from the mall entrance. In this way they could get a little physical exercise. A strategic flash went through my mind. If I, or perhaps the First Lady, could launch a national campaign for parking a distance away from mall entrances, we could make some headway on two of the major problems facing our society. First, physical inactivity is becoming almost as big a killer as smoking. Second, think of all the gas people are wasting. On a national scale, think of all the gas we would save if people would stop circling around looking for spaces. Besides, those little extra blocks of gas consumption add up. My strategic brainstorm could lead to more fitness and less energy consumption in our country.

## LEADERSHIP SKILL-BUILDING **EXERCISE 13-5**

### Developing a Business Strategy for a Small Appliance Repair Chain

Imagine that you and a few classmates are the management team of a business that is almost dead—a chain of household small appliance repair stores. Over the years, your business has been declining steadily. A major contributing factor is that most people just replace rather than repair appliances such as television sets, DVD players, irons, heaters, hair dryers, and

electric razors. Today, you are holding a business strategy session focused on the survival of your business. Be as bold as possible in your thinking, but keep in mind that your probably do not have much cash on hand and that your borrowing power is limited. Within thirty minutes, see if you can construct at least a tentative path for the survival of your appliance-repair business.

## NOTES

1. Original story created from facts and observations in the following sources: Jonathan Cheng, "Can You Build a Startup Inside of Samsung?" *The Wall Street Journal*, February 10, 2014, p. B7; Jane Onyanga-Omara and Brett Molina, "Samsung Kills Off Galaxy Note 7 Over Safety Fears," *USA Today Money*, October 12, 2016, p. 4B; "Startups: The Secret Ingredient of Samsung's Open Innovation," *Samsung Newsroom* (https://news.samsung.com), September 21, 2015, pp. 1–5; Chris Gayomali, "David Eun: For Seeding Samsung's Future," *Fast Company* (www.fastcompany.com), May 11, 2015, pp. 1–11; Kate Bulkley, "IBC Profile: David Eun, Executive Vice President, Global Media, Samsung," *The Guardian* (www.theguardian.com), September 21, 2012, pp. 1–3.

2. Cynthia A. Montgomery, "Putting Leadership Back Into Strategy," *Harvard Business Review*, January 2008, pp. 54–80.

3. Henry Mintzberg, *Managing* (San Francisco: Berrett-Koehler, 2009), pp. 162–163.

4. James R. Bailey, "The Mind of the Strategist," *Academy of Management Learning and Education*, December 2003, p. 385.

5. Jessica Guynn, "Google to Keep Shooting for the Moon," *USA Today Money*, June 4, 2014, p. 4B.

6. Lisa Dragnoni et al., "Developing Leader's Strategic Thinking through Global Work Experience: The Moderating Role of Cultural Distance," *Journal of Applied Psychology*, September 2014, pp. 867–882.

7. "A Conversation with Cynthia Montgomery: How We Think about Strategy," *Executive Leadership*, June 2012, p. 3.

8. Cynthia Montgomery, "Putting Leadership Back in Strategy," *Harvard Business Review*, January 2008, pp. 54–80.

9. Mintzberg, *Managing*, p. 162.

10. "Get the Crowd to Weigh in on Strategic Decisions," *The Management Tip of the Day from Harvard Business Review*, July 4, 2016, p. 1.

11. Kathryn Kearns, "9 Great Example of Crowdsourcing in the Age of Empowered Consumers," *TweakYourBiz* (http://tweakyyourbiz.com), p. 3.

12. Cited in "4 Subtle Leadership Traps to Avoid," *Executive Leadership*, October 2015, p. 8.

13. Donald Sull, Rebecca Homkes, and Charles Sull, "Why Strategy Execution Unravels—And What to Do About It," *Harvard Business Review*, March 2015, pp. 58–66.

14. Seth Goldman and Barry Nalkebuff, "Mission in a Bottle: Making Honest Tea," *Knowledge at Wharton* (http://knowledge.wharton.upenn.edu), October 28, 2013, pp. 5–6.

15. Frank Cespedes, "Putting Sales at the Center of Strategy," *Harvard Business Review*, December 2014, pp. 23–25.

16. Rita Gunther McGrath, "Transient Advantage," *Harvard Business Review*, June 2013, pp. 62–70.

17. Several ideas for this version of SWOT are from "SWOT Analysis," *Business Owner's Tool Kit* (http://csi.toolkit.tst.cch.com/text/P02_4341.asp), November 8, 1999; "Performing a SWOT Analysis," in *Business: The Ultimate Resources* (Cambridge, MA: Perseus Publishing, 2002), pp. 226–227.

18. "Checkout by Amazon," *Amazon Payments* (https://payments.amazon.com). Accessed January 13, 2014.

19. Michael Porter, *Competitive Strategy* (New York: The Free Press, 1980), pp. 36–46.

20. Stephanie Clifford, "Where Wal-Mart Failed, Aldi Succeeds," *The New York Times* (www.nytimes.com), March 20, 2011, pp. 1–4; The Hartman Group, "ALDI Is A Growing Menace to America's Grocery Retailers," *Forbes* (www.forbes.com), April 4, 2015, pp. 1–7.

21. Paul Sullivan, "Need Cash? Own a Bentley? Take a Pawn Ticket," *The New York Times* (www.nytimes.com), January 13, 2014, pp. 1–4.

22. Hadley Malcolm, "Food Giants Partnering with Innovative Start-Ups," *USA Today*, April 4, 2016, p. 4B.

23. Ewan Spence, "BlackBerry Admits Defeat and Exits Smartphone Manufacturing Business," *Forbes* (www.forbes.com), September 28, 2016, pp. 1–3.

24. Seth Goldman and Barry Nalkebuff, "Mission in a Bottle," pp. 1–13.

25. George Anders, "Homespun Strategist," *The Wall Street Journal*, January 6, 2004, p. B1.

26. Nathan Bomey, "GE Capital: We're Not Too Big to Fail Anymore," *USA Today*, March 31, 2016, pp. 1–2. Erika Fry, "GE Gets Back to Basics," *Fortune*, May 20, 2013, p. 31.

27. "Interbrand Releases 2016 Best Global Brands Report," *http://interbrand.com*, October 5, 2016, pp. 1–5.

28. Michael Beer and Russell A. Eisenstat, "How to Have an Honest Conversation about Your Business Strategy," *Harvard Business Review*, February 2004, pp. 82–89.

29. Thomas H. Davenport, Laurence Prusak, and Bruce Strong, "Putting Ideas to Work: Knowledge Management Can Make a Difference, but It Needs To Be More Pragmatic," *The Wall Street Journal*, March 10, 2008, p. R11.

30. David A. Garvin, "Building a Learning Organization," *Harvard Business Review*, July–August 1993, p. 80.

31. "Chowing Down On Boomers' Brains," *Bloomberg Businessweek*, January 25-January 31, 2016. pp. 19–20.

32. Matej Cerne et al., "What goes Around Comes Around: Knowledge Hiding, Perceived Motivational Climate, and Creativity," *Academy of Management Journal*, February 2014, pp. 172–192.

33. Davenport, Prusak, and Strong, "Putting Ideas to Work," p. R11.

34. Andrew St. George, "Leadership Lessons from the Royal Navy," *McKinsey Quarterly* (www.mckinseyquarterly.com), January 2013, pp. 1–5.

35. Morten T. Hansen, Marie Louise Mors, and Bjorn Lovas, "Knowledge Sharing in Organizations: Multiple Networks, Multiple Phases," *Academy of Management Journal*, October 2005, p. 790.

36. David W. De Long and Liam Fahey, "Diagnosing Cultural Barriers to Knowledge Management," *Academy of Management Executive*, November 2000, pp. 115–117.

37. Rishabh Rai and Anand Prakash, "A Relational Perspective to Knowledge Creation: Role of Servant Leadership," *Journal of Leadership Studies*, no. 2, 2012, pp. 61–85.

38. Robert M. Fulmer and J. Bernard Keys, "A Conversation with Peter Senge: New Developments in

Organizational Learning," *Organizational Dynamics*, Autumn 1998, p. 35.

**39.** Schoemaker, Krupp, and Howland, "Strategic Leadership," pp. 133–134.

**40.** Reported in Bill Taylor, "How WD-40 Created a Learning-Obsessed Company Culture," *Harvard Business Review* (https://hbr.org), September 16, 2016, pp. 1–6.

**41.** Justin J. P. Jansen, Dusya Vera, and Mary Crossan, "Strategic Leadership for Exploration and Exploitation: The Moderating Role of Environmental Dynamism," *Leadership Quarterly*, February 2009, pp. 5–18.

**42.** The three building blocks are from David A. Garvin, Amy C. Edmondson, and Francesca Gino, "Is Yours a Learning Organization?" *Harvard Business Review*, March 2008, pp. 110–114. The rest of the list is from the following sources: Robert M. Fulmer and Philip Gibbs, "The Second Generation Learning Organizations: New Tools for Sustainable Competitive Advantage," *Organizational Dynamics*, Autumn 1998, pp. 7–20; Thomas P. Lawrence,

Michael M. Mauws, Bruno Dyck, and Robert F. Kleysen, "The Politics of Organizational Learning: Integrating Power into the 4I Framework," *Academy of Management Review*, January 2005, pp. 180–191; Joe Raelin, "Does Action Learning Promote Collaborative Leadership?" *Academy of Management Learning & Education*, June 2006, pp. 152–168.

**43.** "Reward Your Team for Learning," *The Management Tip of the Day from Harvard Business Review*, October 26, 2015, p.1.

**44.** Peter Cauwelier, "Action Learning Can Accelerate Team Psychological Safety," *www.cloimedia.com*, June 9, 2016, pp. 1–4.

**45.** Gary Yukl, "Leading Organizational Learning: Reflections on Theory and Research," *Leadership Quarterly*, February 2009, p. 50.

**46.** Roger L. Martin, "The Big Lie of Strategic Planning," *Harvard Business Review*, January–February 2014, p. 81.

**47.** "Making Vision Statements 'Visionary,'" *Manager's Edge*, December 1998, p. 1.

## CHAPTER 14

# International and Culturally Diverse Aspects of Leadership

## LEARNING OBJECTIVES

After studying this chapter and doing the exercises, you should be able to

- Explain the potential, ethical, and competitive advantage from leading and managing diversity.
- Describe how cultural factors, including values, influence leadership practice.

- Explain the contribution of cultural sensitivity and cultural intelligence to leadership effectiveness.
- Explain how global leadership skills contribute to leadership effectiveness.
- Pinpoint leadership initiatives to enhance the acceptance of cultural diversity.

## CHAPTER OUTLINE

KEA (or Ikea), the well-known furniture retail chain based in Sweden, is also known for the cultural values that permeate the firm. One core value that guides the IKEA workplace is the Scandinavian tradition of the Law of Jante, a series of rules that require self-effacement and humility. In much of Scandinavian society, including its work organizations, being a loudmouth or self-promoter is strongly frowned upon. The emphasis at Ikea on modesty provides a work environment where quiet professionals and teamwork can prosper.

One report stated that global companies based in Sweden tend to be painted in 50 shades of Jante. For example, both IKEA and H&M, the clothing retailer, offer respectively simple furniture and clothing for less than affluent people at low prices yet within the framework of "attractive ordinariness."

Another core value is closely related—an emphasis on equality rather than hierarchy, status, and rank. The company's U.S. president Lars Petersson explains that "hierarchy is not a big Swedish thing." He holds the title of "country manager." Only a handful of executive even have business cards. Everyone is on a first name basis, and sit side by side at IKEA desks in an open floor plan. Egalitarianism also translates into wages for all workers that well above industry averages. A few years ago, IKEA began basing it pay on the MIT Living Wage Calculator.

The IKEA emphasis on workplace equality has also fostered gender quality. The company is equally led by men and women, and has HR policies that enable women to spend time away from work for childbirth that go far beyond legal mandates. One of the reasons IKEA emphasizes a balance of men and women holding leadership positions is to mirror society at large, and to be an outstanding place to work.

Another consequence of the egalitarian culture at IKEA is equal treatment of diverse members of the workforce. Jacqueline DeChamps, the head of HR, said that at IKEA diversity and inclusion are part of everyday business. She wrote, "Every coworker is valued and respected; and we meet our customers, develop our coworkers, and cooperate with our business partners with these values." In 2015, IKEA received a high score from the Human Right Campaign Foundation for its corporate policies and practices relating to lesbian, gay, bisexual and transgender (LGBT) workplace equality.

Petersson recognizes that not every country in which it operates has matching cultural values. Yet, he emphasizes that "We don't make different considerations in different countries. It's not that we aren't appreciative and interested in local culture. We are very much. But there are some fundamental things that we are not negotiating."[1]

The story about IKEA illustrates how cultural values can influence the leadership practices within an organization, and how welcoming diversity can benefit the organization and its employees. Because the focus on diversity includes giving many types of people an opportunity to participate fully in the organization, the word *inclusion* is often used to replace *diversity*. Not only is the work force becoming more diverse, but business has also become increasingly global. Small- and medium-size firms, as well as corporate giants, are increasingly dependent on trade with other countries. Furthermore, most manufactured goods contain components from more than one country, and global outsourcing has become a dominant trend.

A point of confusion about the emphasis on cultural diversity in organizations is that there are two different ways in which diversity is framed.[2] One frame is to emphasize differences among people, and the importance of these differences. This *value in difference* approach promotes increasing awareness of differences and biases, and suggests that these differences improve employee experiences and enhance profitability. For example, an executive at the clothing retailer Talbot might say, "Yes, we have young people running our marketing and information technology groups. And we also have women in their seventies who interact directly with our customers. That's why we are so successful."

The other diversity approach is an appeal to equality and fairness no matter what the differences among people. This *value in equality* approach emphasize that differences will not be a barrier to advancement, and that all employees are judge fairly based on merit. Almost all company leaders say, "We are an equal opportunity employer."

Our approach to cultural diversity both within and across countries emphasizes the leadership perspective. Key topics include the ethical and competitive advantage of managing for diversity, how cultural factors influence leadership practices, and how cultural sensitivity and global leadership skills contribute to leadership effectiveness. This chapter also describes initiatives that enhance the acceptance of cultural diversity. The underlying theme is that effective leadership of diverse people requires a sensitivity to and enjoyment of cultural differences.

# The Advantages of Managing for Diversity

The ethical and socially responsible goals of leaders and their organizations include providing adequately for members of the diverse work force. Ethical leaders should therefore feel compelled to use merit instead of favoritism or bias as a basis for making human resource decisions. A firm that embraces diversity is also behaving in a socially responsible manner. A leader, for example, who chose to hire five developmentally disabled, unemployed individuals, would be acting in a socially responsible manner. Hiring these people would transfer responsibility for their economic welfare from the state or private charity to the employer. (Some would argue that unless hiring these people is cost effective, the company is neglecting its responsibility to shareholders.)

According to research and opinion, managing for diversity also brings the firm a competitive advantage. Almost a decade ago, Patricia Harris, the Global Chief Diversity Officer of McDonald's Corporation, expressed the matter quite directly: "We began to diversify our operations when it became clear to us it was the best way to sell more hamburgers in minority communities."[3] The advantages of cultural and demographic (different group membership) diversity are most likely to accrue when diversity is built into the firm's strategy. In addition, the chief executive of an organization should be the champion for valuing inclusion and must establish this perspective and associated actions for others throughout the organization.[4]

Here we review evidence and opinion about the competitive advantage of demographic and cultural diversity.

1. ***Managing diversity well offers a marketing advantage.*** A representational work force facilitates the sale of products and services, and the need for such a workforce appears to be increasing. A major component of the marketing advantage of diversity is that a work force that matches the diversity of a company's customer base has an edge in appealing to those customers.

   Another marketing advantage is that many people from culturally diverse groups prefer to buy from a company with a good reputation for managing diversity. Allstate Insurance Company, Inc. is well known for its diversity initiatives, and the company has become the nation's leading insurer of African-Americans and Latinos. Allstate leadership states that inclusive diversity is one of its core values.[5] The large number of agents and customer service representatives from these two groups facilitates attracting and retaining a high percentage of African-Americans and Latinos as customers. State Farm is another example of a financial services company that promotes diversity as part of its business strategy.

   The general picture is that cultural diversity can drive business development. By reflecting the demographics of the community companies become more desirable in the global marketplace. The networks of talented employees from culturally and demographically diverse groups enable the company to connect with various audiences and expand into new markets.[6] For example, the many Latino employees at the Buick division of General Motors have helped increase the popularity of Buick cars among Latinos in the United States.

2. ***Companies with a favorable record in managing diversity are at a distinct advantage in recruiting and retaining talented people.*** Those companies with a favorable reputation for welcoming diversity attract the strongest job candidates among women and racial and ethnic minorities. Also, a company that does not welcome a diverse work force shrinks its supply of potential candidates. An organization that strives for diversity in recruiting simply has a larger talent pool in which to search for candidates. A telling example is that in recent years companies have chosen more executive leaders who are women or who are foreigners. When companies hire culturally diverse workers and provide them with all the tools, resources, and opportunities they need to succeed, those companies are more likely to display the full talents of their work force.

3. ***Heterogeneity in the work force may offer the company a creativity advantage, as well as improve its problem-solving and decision-making capability.*** Creative solutions to problems are more likely to be reached when a diverse group attacks a problem. Diversity specialist Joe Gerstandt presents a chemical analogy: By themselves, atoms of oxygen, carbon, and hydrogen are tasteless. When combined, however, they create sugar. Gerstandt believes that innovation takes place at the intersection of differences, even if getting there may bring some tensions at first.[7] Research evidence suggests that working with people who are different from you may challenge your brain to overcome its traditional thinking and sharpen its performance. Another possibility is that diverse teams are more likely to reexamine facts frequently and remain objectively.[8]

4. ***Diversity and inclusion programs help local economies thereby boosting social responsibility.*** Many large companies take the diversity initiative of purchasing from local, minority, and female suppliers. The substantial purchases aid the local economy in terms of the flow of money as well as employment. The Macy's Supplier Diversity Program is a corporate initiative aimed at fostering the promotion, growth, and development of minority- and women-owned businesses. Company leadership at the 148-year-old retailer perceives the program as a solid business investment. By supporting local and regional business enterprises, Macy's believes it can strengthen itself and expand while at the same time contribute to the financial growth of the community it serves.[9]

5. ***Enhancement of team performance.*** Similar to the creativity advantage, cultural diversity can enhance team performance, often because diverse backgrounds are associated with diverse information, knowledge, and perspectives that can be used to solve problems. Two studies conducted with students at a Dutch business school working on business simulations tasks provide some insight into when the conditions under which diversity enhances team performance. The general finding was that cultural diversity is more likely to enhance team performance when team members have a high learning approach orientation to attaining goals. (Refer back to Chapter 10.) In contrast, when team members are oriented toward the avoidance of poor performance, cultural diversity has no particular impact on team performance.[10] An interpretation here is that when the culturally diverse teammates are more concerned about developing new skills, they will perform better as a group than when they attempt to prevent looking bad.

   The potential of diversity to enhance team performance has another moderating factor. The leader of the diverse group must help members collaborate; otherwise, the advantages of diverse perspectives will be lost.[11]

The accompanying Leader in Action insert describes an executive in the tourism field who believes strongly in the business case for diversity.

## LEADER IN ACTION

### Carnival Corporation Capitalizes on Managers from Diverse Backgrounds to Reignite Growth

Arnold W. Donald, president & chief executive officer (CEO), Carnival Corporation & plc, says that diversity is a business imperative. "The key to innovation is diversity of thinking." He believes that having people from different backgrounds and different cultural experiences who are focused on a common objectives are much more likely to achieve innovation that a homogenous group. Furthermore, the same diversity of thinking is a powerful advantage.

Donald was the former chairman of the chemical company Merisant, and top executive at the weed killer division of Monsanto. He became president and CEO at Carnival Corporation in 2013, after having served on the board for thirteen years. When Donald became CEO, Carnival Corporation was reeling from several crises, including a deadly ship crash and a ship idled in the ocean in an unsanitary condition. One of his major goals was to increase the percentage of North Americans who cruise each year, which has stood at four percent for many years.

Among the better known Carnival Corporation brands are Carnival, Cunard, Holland American Line, and Princess Cruises. Each operating brands has its own unique culture based on its headquarters location, guests served, and the diversity of employees and the leaders. Arnold emphasizes that maintaining a diverse workforce promotes an open, tolerant, and positive work environment the talents and strengths of everyone can be put into play. The company works to attract, motivate, develop, and retain the best talent from the diversity within the world. Carnival leadership believes that the company's ability to be competitive and to thrive globally depends on a diverse workforce.

Donald says that "A highly talented team, with a process to work together, that is diverse will out-innovate a homogeneous team 99.9 percent of the time." In addition to being the right thing to do, diversity leads to better shareholder returns, and helps sustain business success." Jan Schwarz, president of Princess, says "Arnold is a champion of diversity and holds firm in the belief that diversity adds depth and breadth to thinking about challenges and opportunities."

The most dramatic way in which Carnival Corporation capitalizes on thought diversity is by choosing different types of people to be in charge of each of its nine brands (cruise lines). Arnold himself triggered diversity in the company leadership by being the first African-American CEO in an industry that had generally been dominated by white corporate leaders.

During his first two years at the helm Donald replaced seven of the nine cruise line heads. Four are now women, one is African-American, and one gay, and major change from a business that was once an offshoot of the European made-dominated shipping industry. Donald says that his strategy is to create an environment where differing opinions are heard and taken seriously, leading to diversity in thinking. Several of the cruise line presidents have been chosen from outside the cruise industry. For example, Orlando Ashford, the president of the Holland American line had previously been running a compensation consulting business and had never taken a cruise.

Mark Conroy, the president of a former competitor, Regent Seven Seas Cruises, commented about Donald's diverse recruiting: "You had people who grew up in the business, and they're always doing the same thing. People from the outside look at things differently." Another aspect Donald's approach to diversity is to offer special promotions to attract more young guests, rather than focusing so heavily on older people. One approach is to offer lectures on board on such topics as wine, and provide information about the locations where the ships stop.

Arnold obtained his BA from Carleton College, a BS in mechanical engineering from Washington University, and an MBA from the University of Chicago.

### QUESTIONS

1. In what way is Arnold Donald emphasizing diversity in thought as well as cultural diversity among his division leaders?

2. How is it possible that outsiders to the cruise industry would be qualified to run a cruise ship line?

*Source:* Original story created from facts and observations in the following sources: Melanie Trottman, "Cruise Lines Woo the Never-Cruisers," *The Wall Street Journal*, February 21, 2017, p. R4; Christopher Palmeri, "Carnival Rocks the Boat," *Bloomberg Businessweek*, November 16–22, 2015, pp. 22–23; Charisse Jones, "Carnival CEO Steers Cruise Giant in New Directions," *USA Today* (www.usatoday.com), January 22, 2015, pp. 1–4; "Sustainable Workforce," *Carnival Corporation & PFC* (www.carnivalcorp .com), July 29, 2016, pp. 1–5; "Diversity & Inclusion," *Carnival Corporation & PLC* (www.carnivalcorp.com), July 29, 2016, pp. 1–8.

# LEADERSHIP SKILL-BUILDING EXERCISE 14-1

### Pinpointing a Diversity Advantage

Much has been written and talked about of the advantage that a culturally diverse workforce can bring to a company, school, or government agency. Organize into teams of about five, or conduct this exercise on your own. Each person outside of class attempts to find one advantage that stemmed to an organization from having a culturally diverse workforce. Instead of relying on written information, contact one or two people in your network. Speak to your contact person or persons by phone,

text, or conduct a video interview. Ask the person to identify any workplace advantage to diversity that he or she has observed. Record the evidence you have collected, and share with group members if you formed a group. The skill builder in this exercise is that you might raise your awareness level of the advantages of a culturally diverse workforce. You might also become aware of a potential problem to diversity that you would have to manage as a leader.

To raise your level of awareness about how to capitalize on the potential advantages of diversity, do Leadership Skill-Building Exercise 14-1, which illustrates that diversity skills are another important subset of interpersonal skills associated with leadership.

# Cultural Factors Influencing Leadership Practice

A **multicultural leader** is a leader with the skills and attitudes to relate effectively to and motivate people across race, gender, age, social attitudes, and lifestyles. To influence, motivate, and inspire culturally diverse people, the leader must be aware of overt and subtle cultural differences. Although such culturally based differences are generalizations, they function as starting points in the leader's attempt to lead a person from another culture. For example, many Asians are self-conscious about being praised in front of the group because they feel that individual attention clashes with their desire to maintain group harmony. Therefore, a manager might refrain from praising an Asian group member before the group until he or she understands that group member's preferences. The manager is likely to find that many Asians welcome praise in front of peers, especially when working outside their homeland.

Here we examine two topics that help a leader learn how to manage in a culturally diverse workplace: (1) understanding key dimensions of differences in cultural values and (2) the influence of cultural values on leadership style.

## Key Dimensions of Differences in Cultural Values

One way to understand how national cultures differ is to examine their values or cultural dimensions. The cultural dimensions presented here and outlined in Figure 14-1 are based mostly on those included in Global Leadership and Organizational Behavior Effectiveness (GLOBE), a research program in sixty-two societal cultures, and builds on previous analyses of cultural dimensions.[12] We also include two other dimensions useful in working with people from other cultures—attitudes toward time and work orientation. Keep in mind that these cultural dimensions are stereotypes that apply to a representative person from a particular culture and are not meant to insult anybody. Individual differences are substantial. For example, many Americans are not assertive, and many French people are willing to work seventy hours per week (particularly during the continuing recession in France).

1. **Performance orientation** is the degree to which a society encourages (or should encourage) and rewards group members for performance improvement and excellence. Countries high on this dimension are the United States and Singapore, whereas those low on this dimension are Russia and Greece.
2. **Assertiveness** is the degree to which individuals are (and should be) assertive, confrontational, and aggressive in their relationships with one another. Countries scoring high

**FIGURE 14-1** Dimensions of Cultural Values.

on this dimension are the United States and Austria, whereas those low on this dimension are Sweden and New Zealand. Assertive people enjoy competition in business, in contrast to less assertive cultural groups who prefer harmony, loyalty, and solidarity.

3. **Future orientation** is the extent to which individuals engage (and should engage) in future-oriented behaviors such as delaying gratification, planning, and making investments for the future. Singapore and Switzerland are the examples of societies with longer time horizons, whereas Russia and Argentina are less future oriented.

4. **Time orientation** is the importance nations and individuals attach to time. People with an urgent time orientation perceive time to be a scarce resource and tend to be impatient. People with a casual time orientation view time as an unlimited and unending resource and tend to be patient. Americans are noted for their urgent time orientation. They frequently impose deadlines and are eager to get started doing business. Asians, Mexicans, and Middle Easterners, in contrast, are patient negotiators.

5. **Humane orientation** is the degree to which a society encourages and rewards, and should encourage and reward, individuals for being fair, altruistic, and caring to others. Egypt and Malaysia rank high on this cultural dimension, and France and Germany rank low.

6. **In-group collectivism** is the degree to which individuals express, and should express, pride, loyalty, and cohesiveness in their organizations and families. Asian societies emphasize collectivism, as do Egypt and Russia. One consequence of collectivism is taking pride in family members and the organizations that employ them.

7. **Gender egalitarianism** is the degree to which a culture minimizes, and should minimize, gender inequality. European countries emphasize gender egalitarianism, and so do the United States and Canada. South Korea is an example of a country that is low on gender egalitarianism and is male dominated.

8. **Power distance** is the degree to which members of a society expect, and should expect, power to be distributed unequally. Individuals who accept power and authority expect the boss to make the major decisions. These same individuals are more formal; however, being formal toward people in positions of authority has decreased substantially throughout the world in recent years. Examples of societies that score high on acceptance of power and authority are Thailand, Brazil, France, and Japan.

9. **Uncertainty avoidance** is the extent to which members of a society rely (and should rely) on social norms, rules, and procedures to lessen the unpredictability of future events. The stronger the desire to avoid uncertainty, the more likely people are to seek orderliness, consistency, and laws to cover situations in daily life. Examples of societies with high uncertainty avoidance are Singapore and Switzerland. Societies with low uncertainty avoidance include Russia and Greece.

10. **Work orientation** is the number of hours per week and weeks per year people expect to invest in work versus leisure, or other nonwork activities. American corporate professionals typically work about fifty-five hours per week, take forty-five-minute lunch breaks, and go on two weeks of vacation. Across all types of U.S. workers, the average workweek is 34.6 hours, the sixteenth longest among other countries. Mexico has the longest average workweek of 42.85 hours, with Sweden ranking last (30.94 hours) among the countries studied.[13]

How might a manager use information about differences in values to become a more effective leader? A starting point would be to recognize that a person's national values might influence his or her behavior. Assume that a leader wants to influence a person with a low power distance orientation to strive for superior performance. The low-power person will not spring into action just because the boss makes the suggestion. Instead, the leader needs to patiently explain the personal payoffs of achieving superior performance. Another example is a leader who wants to improve quality and therefore hires people who value collectivism. A backup tactic would be to counsel people who value individualism on the merits of collective action.

Leadership Self-Assessment Quiz 14-1 will help you think about how values can moderate (or influence) work performance.

## Cultural Values and Leadership Style

The values embedded in a culture influence the behavior of leaders and managers as well as the behavior of other workers. As Geert Hofstede explains, relationships between people in a society are affected by the values programmed in the minds of these people. Because management deals heavily with interpersonal relationships, management and leadership are affected by cultural values. Management and leadership processes may vary from culture to culture, but, being value based, these processes show strong continuity in each society.[14]

A few stereotypes about transcultural differences in leadership style are presented next, with an important disclaimer. As knowledge about leadership has become more widespread, managers in most cultures have placed more emphasis on collaboration and shared leadership.

*French Managers*   One example of the influence of values on management and leadership style is the behavior of French managers. France has always put a strong emphasis on class. French managers who have attended the major business schools (*Grand Écoles*) have the highest status of all. The implication for leadership style is that French managers, particularly in major corporations, are part of an elite class, and they behave in a superior, authoritarian manner. (Not every French manager follows the cultural tradition of being authoritarian, with the more modern managers being less class conscious.) The traditional style of manager would expect obedience and high respect from group members, and would tend to emphasize bureaucracy.[15] In recent years, most cultures have undergone a decrease in power distance values. As a result, a greater number of French managers are more egalitarian.

*German Managers*   Another example of a distinctive leadership style related to culture is the stereotype of the German manager. German managers were studied as part of the GLOBE project. Data were collected on culture and leadership from 457 middle managers in the telecommunications, food processing, and finance industries. A strong performance orientation was found to be the most pronounced German cultural value. German

# LEADERSHIP SELF-ASSESSMENT QUIZ 14-1

## Charting Your Cultural Value Profile

***Instructions:*** For each of the ten value dimensions, circle the number that most accurately fits your standing on the dimension. For example, if you perceive yourself to have a "high humane orientation," circle the 7 on the fifth dimension.

| | | | | | | | |
|---|---|---|---|---|---|---|---|
| **1.** | Low performance orientation | | | | | High performance orientation | |
| | 1 | 2 | 3 | 4 | 5 | 6 | 7 |
| **2.** | Low assertiveness | | | | | High assertiveness | |
| | 1 | 2 | 3 | 4 | 5 | 6 | 7 |
| **3.** | Casual time orientation | | | | | Urgent time orientation | |
| | 1 | 2 | 3 | 4 | 5 | 6 | 7 |
| **4.** | Low future orientation | | | | | High future orientation | |
| | 1 | 2 | 3 | 4 | 5 | 6 | 7 |
| **5.** | Low humane orientation | | | | | High humane orientation | |
| | 1 | 2 | 3 | 4 | 5 | 6 | 7 |
| **6.** | In-group individualism | | | | | In-group collectivism | |
| | 1 | 2 | 3 | 4 | 5 | 6 | 7 |
| **7.** | Low gender egalitarianism | | | | | High gender egalitarianism | |
| | 1 | 2 | 3 | 4 | 5 | 6 | 7 |
| **8.** | Low power distance | | | | | High power distance | |
| | 1 | 2 | 3 | 4 | 5 | 6 | 7 |
| **9.** | Low uncertainty avoidance | | | | | High uncertainty avoidance | |
| | 1 | 2 | 3 | 4 | 5 | 6 | 7 |
| **10.** | Low work orientation | | | | | High work orientation | |
| | 1 | 2 | 3 | 4 | 5 | 6 | 7 |

***Scoring and Interpretation:*** After circling one number for each dimension, use a marker, pen, or pencil to connect the circles; this gives you a *profile of cultural values.* Do not be concerned if your line cuts through the names of the dimensions. Compare your profile to others in class. Should time allow, develop a class profile by computing the class average for each of the ten dimensions and then connecting the points. If the sample size is large enough, compare the cultural value profiles of Westerners and Easterners.

One possible link to leadership development is to hypothesize which type of profile would be the most responsive and which would be the least responsive to your leadership.

middle managers thus tend to avoid uncertainty, are assertive, and are not terribly considerate of others.

German managers typically do not emphasize compassion, and their interpersonal relations are straightforward and stern.[16] (Another interpretation of these findings is that the performance orientation of German managers is so strong that they seem less interested in interpersonal relations in comparison. This does not mean that German managers and leaders are inconsiderate.) And the strong performance they expect must be packed into a short workweek!

*Malaysian Managers* The characteristic leadership style of Malaysian managers is instructive because other Asian managers use a similar style. Malaysia has become important as a trading partner of both the United States and Europe, particularly because of the outsourcing movement. The following conclusions about the Malaysian leadership style were also based on the GLOBE project.[17] Malaysians emphasize collective well-being (collectivism) and display a strong humane orientation within a society that respects hierarchical differences (high power difference). The culture discourages aggressive, confrontational behavior, preferring harmonious relationships. The preferred organizational leadership style is therefore for managers to show compassion, while at the same time be more autocratic than participative. The Malaysian work group member defers to the boss and in turn is treated with respect and compassion. A Malaysian supervisor might say typically to a worker, "Here is exactly how I want this job done, but I want you to enjoy yourself and learn something valuable while doing the job."

*Northern U.S. Versus Southern U.S. Managers*   Differences in cultural values between regions of a large country can also have an impact. An example of a cross-regional stereotype is that managers in the Southern United States are lower key and more interested in relationship building than are their brusque counterparts in the north, particularly in larger metropolitan areas. (A stereotype here is that people in smaller towns tend to more laid back and polite.) Leaders from the north have a reputation for efficiency and getting tasks accomplished quickly. Leaders from the south perceive such behavior as rude, pushy, and short on relationship building. The point here is that southern chivalry has worked its way into leadership style.

However, the stereotype of southern business leaders being more laid back and slow moving has been challenged. Business in the south may have moved more slowly in the days before air conditioning was widespread. Heat tends to slow people down. John W. Thompson, former CEO of Symantec Corporation and now chairman of Microsoft Corporation, is a Florida A&M graduate. He says there is nothing regional about attaining business results. "I was raised in the south and spent 27 years working for IBM all over the world. I don't think management style can be localized."[18]

Despite culturally based differences in leadership style, certain leadership practices are likely to work in every culture, including giving people clear directions and administering appropriate rewards for attaining goals. A comprehensive analysis of leader–member relations, conducted with studies from twenty-three countries found that high-quality relationships with subordinates facilitated task performance in countries with different values. The anchor values in clusters of values studied were individualistic versus collectivist.[19] More will be presented later about leadership practices across cultures.

## Cultural Sensitivity and Cultural Intelligence

Some managers are more effective at leading diverse groups than others. The traits and behaviors described in Chapters 2, 3, and 4 should equip a person to lead diverse groups. In addition, cultural sensitivity, cultural intelligence, and certain specific global leadership skills are essential for inspiring people from cultures other than one's own. Although they reinforce each other, here we describe cultural sensitivity and cultural intelligence separately. Global leadership skills encompass so many behaviors that they receive a section of their own.

## Cultural Sensitivity

Leaders, as well as others, who are attempting to influence a person from a foreign country must be alert to possible cultural differences. Thus, the leader must be willing to acquire knowledge about local customs and learn to speak the native language at least passably (unless the company has an English-only policy on the job). A cross-cultural leader must be patient, adaptable, flexible, and willing to listen and learn. All of these characteristics are part of **cultural sensitivity**, an awareness of and a willingness to investigate the reasons why people of another culture act as they do. Transcultural specialist and Brandeis professor, Andy Molinsky, captures the essence of cultural sensitivity in these words: "You don't need to have lived in five countries and learned five languages to be successful across borders. You do need to be thoughtful and self-aware, and you need to be willing to take that leap into the unknown."[20]

Five aspects of cultural sensitivity are described next.

1. *Recognition of nuances in customs.* A person with cultural sensitivity will recognize certain nuances in customs that will help build better relationships with work associates from another culture. Refer to Table 12-2 in Chapter 12 for a sampling of appropriate and less appropriate behaviors in a variety of countries for the purpose of overcoming communication barriers. (These are suggestions, not absolute rules.) Additional information about appropriate leadership behavior, or good etiquette, in different culture is presented in Figure 14-2.

   Another aspect of cultural sensitivity is being tolerant of the subtle differences between and among cultures. Leadership Self-Assessment Quiz 14-2 gives you an opportunity to reflect on your own tolerance for cross-cultural issues.

2. *Being a multicultural worker.* Cultural sensitivity is also important because it helps a person become a **multicultural worker**. Such an individual is convinced that all cultures are equally good and enjoys learning about other cultures. Multicultural workers and leaders are usually people who have been exposed to more than one culture in childhood. (Refer to Leadership Self-Assessment Quiz 12-2, about cross-cultural relations.) Being multicultural helps one be accepted by a person from another culture. The concept of a multicultural worker also refers to an employee who identifies with two more cultures, such as a graphics designer born in Japan, who speaks Japanese at home and works in the United States. Because multicultural workers can readily relate to people from other cultures, they are well-suited to the global workplace.[21]

   Sensitivity is the most important characteristic for leading people from other cultures because cultural stereotypes rarely provide entirely reliable guides for dealing with others. An American manager, for example, might expect Asian group members to accept his or her directives immediately because Asians are known to defer

---

**Positive Behaviors**

- Demonstrate empathy by listening carefully to employees with different experiences and perspectives. Careful eye contact will help show empathy.
- Show that you care about the other culture by learning what is important to them, such as asking about the national and local soccer teams in most countries and cities.
- Know where the country you are visiting is located; know name of the city in which the business interaction is taking place, and pronounce it correctly.
- Define acronyms, slang and jargon, such as explaining that "EBITDA" means earnings before interest, taxes, depreciation, and amortization.
- Emphasize how everybody's job is important to the team.

**Negative Behaviors**

- Touching and hugging employees without first knowing that such behavior is acceptable.
- Suggesting that the business practices from your country are superior to those of the country you are visiting.
- Display an individualist approach rather than showing humility and being group-oriented in most countries.
- Emphasizing the importance of financial incentives in motivating people.

---

**FIGURE 14-2** Suggestions for Engaging in Successful Cross-Cultural Leadership Interactions.
*Source:* Several of the ideas are adapted from Gayle Cotton, "Do This, Not That When Doing Business Overseas," (www.cnbc.com), April 8, 2013, pp. 1–5; Tina Smagala, "Empathy a Critical Skill for Leaders to Have," Democrat and Chronicle, January 21, 2014, p. 5B.

## LEADERSHIP SELF-ASSESSMENT QUIZ 14-2

### My Tolerance for Cultural Differences

**Instructions:** Indicate how comfortable you would feel in the following circumstances: very uncomfortable (VU); uncomfortable (U); neutral (N); comfortable (C); and very comfortable (VC).

| | VU | U | N | C | VC |
|---|---|---|---|---|---|
| 1. Working on a team with both men and women | 1 | 2 | 3 | 4 | 5 |
| 2. Coaching a team or club when all the members are of a different sex than myself | 1 | 2 | 3 | 4 | 5 |
| 3. Having a transgender person for a boss | 1 | 2 | 3 | 4 | 5 |
| 4. Having a person of a different race for a boss | 1 | 2 | 3 | 4 | 5 |
| 5. Having an opposite-sex person for a boss | 1 | 2 | 3 | 4 | 5 |
| 6. Having a boss older than either of my parents. | 1 | 2 | 3 | 4 | 5 |
| 7. Having dinner with someone who eats what I consider to be a pet | 1 | 2 | 3 | 4 | 5 |
| 8. Having dinner with someone who eats what I consider to be a repulsive animal or insect | 1 | 2 | 3 | 4 | 5 |
| 9. Working alongside a teammate who I know is HIV positive | 1 | 2 | 3 | 4 | 5 |
| 10. Working alongside a teammate who has served prison time for vehicular homicide | 1 | 2 | 3 | 4 | 5 |
| Total score: | | | | | |

### Scoring and Interpretation:

- **40–50:** You are highly tolerant and flexible in terms of working with a broad spectrum of people. These attitudes should help you be an effective multicultural leader.

- **21–39:** Your tolerance for working with people different from yourself is within the average range. If you learn to become more tolerant of differences, you are more likely to become an effective multicultural leader.

- **10–20:** You may be experiencing difficulties in working with people quite different from yourself. As a consequence, your effectiveness as a multicultural leader might be hampered. If you seek out more diverse cross-cultural experiences, you are likely to become more tolerant of differences.

to authority. Nevertheless, an individual Asian might need considerable convincing before accepting authority.

3. **Recognizing potential problems of cultural misunderstanding.** Problems of cultural misunderstanding leaders should be aware of cluster in five areas.[22] *Language* differences create problems because U.S. workers (most of whom are monolingual) can become frustrated by coworkers' accents and limited English skills. Non-English speakers may feel that they do not fit well into the team. Differences in *religion* are the source of many misunderstandings. In many cultures, religion dominates life in ways that Americans find difficult to comprehend. *Work habits* vary enough across cultures to create friction and frustration. Employees in some cultures are unwilling to spend personal time on work. Problems can also stem from office rituals, such as having coffee or tea together during work breaks, or singing songs together at the start of the workday.

*Women's roles* may differ considerably from those in the United States. Women in many countries may not have the same independence or access to education and higher-level jobs as American women. Workers from various countries may therefore have difficulty accepting the authority of an American manager who is female.

What constitutes *acceptable personal appearance and behavior* varies considerably across cultures. Grooming, office attire, eating habits, and nonverbal communication may deviate significantly from the U.S. standards. Many workers around the world may perceive American workers as overfriendly, aggressive, or rude.

A key item in personal appearance is choosing appropriate attire when working in another culture. Cultural sensitivity helps you detect what type of clothing is appropriate. In some countries wearing flip-flops to the office would be considered unacceptable. Many faux pas are possible, including that many Hindus in India may be offended by a finely tooled leather belt and briefcase because steers have religious significance. In some parts of Asia, white is the color of mourning. A cross-cultural guideline for professionals is that a dark, well-made business suit and conservative accessories such as ties and simple jewelry are acceptable for business around the world.[23]

A frequently occurring area of cultural misunderstanding is the importance of punctuality in terms of arriving to work and to meetings at a specified time, and submitting work at an agreed upon dates. "On time" has different meanings in different cultures, so it is important for the leader to be very specific about starting times and due dates. In a culture with lax attitudes toward completing projects on time, it is helpful to ask for needed work early than really needed. It is also important to explain why Western-style punctuality is important.[24]

*Generational differences* are another manifestation of cultural differences, quite often within a leader's national culture. For example, young people typically want more frequent recognition and rewards as well as flexible scheduling. Older people might want more deference to their knowledge and experience.

4. ***Transgender employees.*** The reality of greater number of *transgender* employees in the workplace requires considerable cultural sensitivity on the part of the leader or manager. (A transgender person goes beyond cross-dressing, and converts to the opposite sex through a combination of surgery and hormone treatments.) A recent development is that some companies are offering sex reassignment benefits as a method of attracting LGBT employees.[25]

Managers may have to deal with their own tolerance toward the transgender (or transsexual) workers, as well as the tolerance and flexibility of employees and customers. A particular need for cultural sensitivity is to begin referring to an employee as "him" or "her," when the person was formerly "her" or "him." A general guide is that transgender employees are rare, but are still part of a culturally diverse workforce, and they have some legal protections with respect to job discrimination.

5. ***Flexibility in dealing with others.*** Cultural sensitivity is enhanced by cultural training, and also by simply listening carefully and observing. A key principle is to be flexible when dealing with people from other cultures. Cultural sensitivity is also enhanced by asking questions, such as whether it is reasonable to expect people to work on Saturday and Sunday. When cross-cultural issues about performance arise, the leader/manager is advised to ask: "My job requires that I manage your performance. Your job is to meet or exceed our performance standards. How can I help you do that?"[26]

6. ***Eliciting ideas and giving critical feedback.*** Two more areas in which cross-cultural communication can break down are in eliciting ideas from subordinates and providing them feedback. Cultural norms about expressing ideas vary across cultures. Team members from relatively egalitarian cultures, such as the United States, may be accustomed to voicing their candid opinions and ideas. In contrast, team members from more hierarchical cultures such as Japan and China, tend to speak up only after more senior colleagues have provided their input. Furthermore, in some cultures, such as Scandinavian countries, workers tend to wait until they have carefully developed an idea for fear of seeming foolish. In a culture that that accepts half-processed

(or Tweet-like) ideas, such as the United States, many workers will express ideas that they have carefully reasoned.

Giving critical feedback presents transcultural challenges because feedback is perceived differently depending somewhat on the culture. Executives from more individualistic and task-oriented cultures such as the United States and Canada, usually perceive critical feedback as an opportunity for personal development, and therefore as advantageous. People from more collectivistic and relationship-oriented cultures might feel uncomfortable in receiving critical feedback, particularly in a group setting.[27] (Despite cultural differences, the leader is advised to apply in any culture, one of the most basic human relations principles: Praise in public, and criticize in private.)

## The English-Only Policy and Cultural Sensitivity

To facilitate communication in global enterprise, a growing number of companies have declared English as the official language for conducting business. For example, Honda Motor Co. has switched it official corporate language for international communications within the company to English by 2020. English has been a key part of its operations for several years. The decision to make English the corporate lingua franca recognizes the global presence of the company.[28]

A key argument for an English-only policy in companies involved in cross-cultural activity is that multilingualism without restriction interferes with accomplishing business goals.[29] Without clearly understood communication, sales are lost, physical accidents occur, and post-merger cultures are difficult to integrate. (The accidents might occur with respect to misunderstanding safety directions or not taking precautions.) Many businesspeople from all over the world are proud of their ability to speak English that tends to minimize negative attitudes toward an English-only policy.

Despite the general acceptance of English as the language of business, problems of cultural sensitivity remain. Some people may regard the policy as an affront to their cultural identity and may resent the implication that English is the superior language. Furthermore, some businesspeople may not feel comfortable speaking about complicated topics in English if their English-speaking ability is not strong. One approach the leader can take to demonstrate cultural sensitivity in this area is to emphasize that English-only policy applies mostly to formal meetings, and he or she wants to listen to the sound of another language at other times. Insisting that workers speak English during informal interactions is an Equal Employment Opportunity Commission (EEOC) violation.[30] Also, if the leader speaks another language well, he or she might exchange a few words in that language before the formal meeting gets started.

Should a company adopt an English-only policy, it is strongly recommended that the leadership team spearhead assessments in English skills and training for all nonnative speakers. A rule of thumb is that approximately 3,500 words of English are sufficient for conducting business in the language. (A naïve aspect of this rule of thumb is that knowing 3,500 nouns and adjectives is not sufficient. You also need to know how to conjugate verbs.) Language training, which might include apps, the Internet, and CDs, should be held during work hours. An accessible on-site location should be available.[31]

## Cultural Intelligence

A refinement and expansion of cultural sensitivity is **cultural intelligence (CQ)** : an outsider's ability to interpret someone's unfamiliar and ambiguous gestures the way that person's compatriots would.[32] For example, an American might be attending a business meeting in Europe. He or she might pick up the clue that the Europeans present prefer to discuss U.S. politics and trade agreements (or current events) for twenty minutes before discussing the business purpose of the meeting. So the cross-border visitor engages in a

Another area where tolerance for ambiguity is a success factor lies within providing leadership to cross-cultural teams. One of the more pronounced cross-cultural differences is that various members of the team nay have differing attitudes toward hierarchy and authority (or power distance). Team members from some cultures may have difficulty with the flat structure of most teams. If team members defer to a higher-status team member, their behavior will be regarded as appropriate when most of the team derives from a hierarchical culture. In contrast, team members who defer to authority may damage their stature and credibility if most of the team comes from a culture of low power distance (egalitarian). One manager of Mexican heritage who belonged to a cross-cultural team lamented:

> In Mexican culture, you're always supposed to be humble. So whether you understand something or not, you're supposed to put it in the form of a question. You have to keep it open-ended, out of respect. I think that actually worked against me, because the Americans thought I really didn't know what I was talking about. So it made me feel like they thought I was wavering on my answer.[39]

A potential leadership intervention to the problem of status and hierarchy is to talk about the problem in advance, and to encourage behavior that will fit most team members. The team leader might mention several times that the structure is flat, and that all team members have an equal voice. Because cultural values control behavior so strongly, the message will have to be repeated frequently.

A confusing skill issue for many international workers is the importance of having a good command of a second language. Part of the confusion comes from the fact that English has become the standard language of business, as well as technology, engineering, and science. However, when you are trying to influence a person from another culture, you are more influential if you can speak, read, and write very well in his or her language. (We assume that even with an English-only policy, some conversations take place outside of group meetings. Also, not every company has an English-only policy.) Another point of confusion is that most businesspeople from around the world speak English, and look for the opportunity to converse in English. Nevertheless, a command of a second language also enhances the person's charisma.

## Motivating and Inspiring Workers in Other Cultures

The discussion of expectancy theory in Chapter 10 provided the best general clue to motivating people in other cultures—figure out which rewards have high valence for them. Workers who lack basic necessities in life would rather be rewarded with a scooter or bicycle than a $500 luxury fountain pen or watch. Workers will be motivated and inspired to the extent that need satisfaction will be forthcoming.

Here are a few examples of transcultural differences in the effectiveness of rewards: Team members from Asian cultures are more motivated by rewards that emphasize group harmony, such as a group reward. American workers appreciate rewards for individual accomplishment, but also take pride in receiving team rewards. Mexican-American workers often respond well to financial rewards because they are family oriented, and like to send money to family members in Mexico. (Again we are presented with cultural stereotypes that work much of the time but not all the time.)

## Understanding Which Leadership and Management Practices Function Well in a Specific Culture

A general challenge confronting the global leader is that techniques that work well in one culture may not necessarily work well in another culture. For example, in a culture that highly respects the authority of the boss, granting decision-making authority to the group may not be so effective. In cultures such as those of India and Japan, the manager is supposed to make most decisions. Most workers in India and Japan would therefore consider it a sign of weakness if the manager called on them to make most decisions.

An example of how a specific management practice might not work well in another culture comes from a large high-technology company that had established an innovation center in one of their U.S. offices. Most of the employees at the center were entrepreneurial, engaged, and excited to come to work. As a result many new-product ideas were forthcoming. One element of the innovation center was open office space, in a location removed from the main campus. Managers believed that on balance, the open, flexible workplaces fostered collaboration and innovation.

An attempt at using open office space at a new innovation center in China was poorly received. Open offices were unusual in China, and the product developers were puzzled by the expectation of being more collaborative. Instead, they continued their cultural practice of working alone at their desks, with limited interaction except for lunch and physical meetings. Furthermore, they saw the separation from the main campus as isolating. The innovation center was eventually closed, enabling the workers to return to the main campus.[40]

So who is an example of a leader with global leadership skills—one person who has most of the attributes described in this section? A highly visible example is Carlos Ghosn, the chief executive of both Nissan and Renault, known as the "hottest car guy on earth." In 2017, Ghosn left his CEO post at Nissan but remained as chairman. He is also the chairman of the board of Mitsubishi Motors that Nissan acquired in 2016. Three key aspects of his leadership style that facilitate his ability to lead two companies in different cultures are his embrace of diversity, his penchant for listening, and his collaborative approach.

Ghosn travels around the world in a corporate jet that can fly between Paris and Tokyo nonstop, and also spends considerable time visiting the U.S. operations of Nissan. He carries two briefcases, one for Renault and another for Nissan. He crosses time zones and cultures with great facility. After many years being the CEO of two companies, Ghosn recommended that two CEOs be hired to eventually replace him, stating, "Being in charge of two companies and having to run between two countries is extremely taxing on people." Born in Brazil to Lebanese parents and college-educated in Paris, Ghosn speaks several languages and enjoys cuisine from many countries.[41]

Do Leadership Skill-Building Exercise 14-3 to sensitize you even more to cross-cultural experiences.

## LEADERSHIP SKILL-BUILDING EXERCISE 14-3

### Gaining International and Cross-Cultural Experience Inexpensively

Gaining international and cross-cultural experience is valuable for occupying a leadership role. Learning to relate comfortably with people from different cultures alone is useful. Acquiring international and cross-cultural experience can be time consuming and quite expensive, such as spending three months in another country. Organize into brainstorming groups of about five people to identify ways in which class members can acquire international and cross-cultural experience inexpensively, or at no cost. (One student doing this exercise said she would have breakfast at IHOP [International House of Pancakes] at least once a month!) After the groups have identified about six specific suggestions for gaining international and cross-cultural experience, share the results across groups.

## Leadership Initiatives for Achieving Cultural Diversity

For organizations to value diversity and inclusion, top management must be committed to it. The commitment is clearest when it is embedded in organizational strategy, as well as in the life and culture of the organization. Company leadership should dedicate time to work personally on diversity and inclusion initiatives.[42] Diversity initiatives should be deep rather than superficial.[43] A true diversity strategy should encourage all employees to contribute their unique talents, skills, and expertise to the organization's operations, independent of race, gender, ethnic background, and any other definable difference. In addition, leaders should take the initiative to ensure that many activities are implemented to support the diversity strategy. Table 14-1 lists the six leadership initiatives for encouraging diversity that are discussed in the following text.

### Hold Managers Accountable for Achieving Diversity

A high-impact diversity initiative is for top-level organizational leaders to hold managers accountable for diversity results at all levels. If managers are held accountable for behavior and business changes in the diversity arena, an organizational culture supportive of diversity will begin to develop. A group of CEOs whose organizations are well known for their diversity practices agreed that metrics are essential because, "What gets measured gets done." Bank of America, for example, includes questions about diversity and inclusiveness in its biannual employee engagement survey, and results are compared against a normative group of companies. CEO Brian Moynihan says, "We've also built a diversity-and-inclusion index that tells us if people here feel they are treated fairly and to help us ensure that people of diverse backgrounds can succeed at Bank of America."[44]

Accountability for diversity results when achieving diversity objectives is included in performance evaluations and when compensation is linked in part to achieving diversity results. Another way of making managers accountable for diversity is to consider the attainment of diversity and inclusion a factor in being promoted to a higher-level position.

### Establish Minority Recruitment, Retention, and Mentoring Programs

An essential initiative for building a diverse work force is to recruit and retain members of the targeted minority group. Because recruiting talented members of minority groups and women is competitive, careful human resources planning is required.

Efforts at recruiting a culturally diverse work force must be supported by a leadership and management approach that leads to high retention. To increase retention rates, diversity consultants advise employers to strengthen cultural training programs, recognize employees' hidden skills and talents, and give diversity committees clout with top management.[45] Retaining employees is also a function of good leadership and management in general, such as offering workers challenging work, clear-cut goals, feedback, and valuable rewards for goal attainment. Mentoring is a key initiative for retaining minority group members, as well as for facilitating their advancement.

**TABLE 14-1** Leadership Initiatives for Achieving Cultural Diversity

1. Hold managers accountable for achieving diversity.
2. Establish minority recruitment, retention, and mentoring programs.
3. Conduct diversity training.
4. Conduct anti-bias training.
5. Avoid group characteristics when hiring for person–organization fit.
6. Attain diversity among organizational leaders.

A study of 829 midsize and large U.S. firms found that college recruitment targeting minorities is an effective diversity initiative. Recruiting at historically black schools typically yields a group of qualified minority group members. The same study found mentoring to have an especially positive impact. Leaders who sponsored women and minorities come to believe that through increased contact that the people they mentored deserve the training and opportunities they receive.[46]

## Conduct Diversity Training

**Diversity training** has become a widely used method for enhancing diversity within organizations. The purpose of diversity training is to bring about workplace harmony by teaching people how to get along better with diverse work associates. Quite often the program is aimed at minimizing open expressions of racism and sexism. All forms of diversity training center on increasing people's awareness of and empathy for people who are different from themselves in some important way. Diversity training often emphasizes leveraging diversity to enhance business performance.[47] The enhancements to performance were described at the outset of the chapter.

Training sessions in valuing differences focus on the ways in which men and women, or people of different races, reflect different values, attitudes, and cultural backgrounds. These sessions can vary from several hours to several days or longer. Sometimes the program is confrontational, sometimes not.

An essential part of relating more effectively to diverse groups is to empathize with their point of view. To help training participants develop empathy, representatives of various groups explain their feelings related to workplace issues. Leadership Skill-Building Exercise 14-4 gives you the opportunity to engage in an effective diversity training exercise. Relating effectively to coworkers who are different from you in some meaningful way adds to your interpersonal effectiveness.

A frequently mentioned concern about diversity training is that it reinforces stereotypes about groups. Participants are informed about group differences, such as cultural values, and tactics might be suggested for coping with these differences—such as using more body language when relating to Latinos.

Leaders of diversity training exercises are cautioned to guard against encouraging participants to be too confrontational and expressing too much hostility. Companies have

# LEADERSHIP SKILL-BUILDING EXERCISE 14-4

### The Diversity Circle

Some diversity trainers use the *diversity circle* exercise to help workers appreciate diversity and overcome misperceptions. The exercise adapts well for classroom use. Form a group of about ten students. Arrange your chairs into a circle, and put one additional chair in the center of the circle. A group member who feels diverse in any way volunteers to sit in the center chair and become the first awareness subject. Because most people are diverse in some way, most people are eligible to occupy the center chair.

The person in the center tells the others how he or she has felt about being diverse or different, and how people have reacted to his or her diversity. For example, an Inuit described

how fellow workers were hesitant to ask him out for a beer, worrying whether he could handle alcohol. Another name for this exercise is "How I Felt Different" because each person describes how he or she felt different from others at one point in his or her life.

An equally effective alternative to this procedure is for each class member to come up in front of the class to describe a significant way in which he or she is different. After each class member has presented, a discussion might be held of observations and interpretations.

What lessons did you learn about interpersonal relations from this exercise that will help you be a more effective leader?

found that when employees are too blunt during these sessions, it may be difficult to patch up interpersonal relations in the work group later on. Sometimes the diversity trainer encourages group members to engage in outrageous behavior, such as by having women sexually harass men so the men know what it feels like. Key themes of negative reactions to diversity training are charges of political correctness and white male bashing.

A review of 178 articles found that when diversity training was integrated into a system of other diversity-related activities, the outcomes were more likely to be positive, such as participants believing that they learned to interact more effectively with other cultural groups. Another key finding was that programs that focus on a more general, positive, and inclusive approach—rather than singling out one demographic group—may be better received by all participants.[48]

Voluntary adversity training tends to be more effective that making such training mandatory. Research suggests that when training is voluntary about 11 percent more black men, Hispanic men, and Asian-American men and women are promoted to management positions five years later. At the same time no decreases in white or black women in management were found.[49]

## Conduct Anti-Bias Training

Closely related to diversity training are programs to help employees discover their unconscious biases that may adversely affect certain demographic and cultural groups. Examples include being more likely to call back a white than black applicant than for a second interview, and automatically not inviting a worker in his or her sixties to join a team on a high-tech venture. An unconscious bias is a hidden, reflex-like preference that can shape a person's view of the world. Such biases also can shape diversity by rejecting people for certain assignments and not valuing their ideas. For example, a project manager at a mine in northern Alaska might not give a key assignment to an Inuit because the manager has an unconscious bias suggesting that an Inuit has a weak work ethic. Facebook and Google make extensive use of unconscious bias training.[50] The Facebook class concentrates on identifying and neutralizing racial, age, gender, and other forms of bias that might be present in the workplace. More recently Facebook has also focused on political bias when the company was accused of giving too little space on its website to conservatively toned news.[51]

Unconscious bias training usually includes administration of the Implicit Association Test that is based on the logic of describing what comes to mind when a specific demographic group is mentioned. For example, "What associations do you make to *Mexican*?"

Research conducted at Google indicates almost everyone is a little bit sexist or racist. Training can help us become aware of our unconscious biases and make appropriate adjustments. For example, a leader might have the bias that Chinese workers want to occupy strictly technical roles, and are therefore not well suited for supervisory roles. After training, the leader would recognize that many Chinese-American workers are interested in and skilled at supervisory positions. (The CEO of Blackberry, turnaround specialist John Chen, is Chinese in origin.)

After anti-bias training people may not change their attitudes completely, but they may be willing to explore if their perceptions are correct. Favorable experiences can then lead to a change in attitude. In the example of Chinese people, after observing Chinese people as managers, the leader would not think, "I guess I was wrong. A lot of Chinese workers are good at management."

## Conduct Cross-Cultural Training

For many years, companies and government agencies have prepared their managers and other workers for overseas assignments. The method frequently chosen is **cross-cultural training**, a set of learning experiences designed to help employees understand the customs, traditions, and beliefs of another culture. Foreign language training is often included in cultural training.

A major thrust to cross-cultural training is improving internal and external communications, including overcoming cross-cultural communication barriers. Improved communication would include knowing how to build trust in different cultures, and how to give criticism. In many cultures trust is built by slowing developing a relationship though such means as frequent exchange of polite messages. Feedback differences include the tendency for French managers to provide direct, blunt feedback. American and British managers tend to accentuate the positive aspects of performance, and softly introduce negative feedback.[52]

The multicultural leader needs to know that English is spoken differently in the United States, Great Britain, Australia, and South Africa, among other countries. Four examples follow:

- Britons say "keen" whereas Americans say "enthusiastic."
- Britons say "to table (an idea)," whereas Americans say "to put (an idea) out for discussion."
- Britons say "to put (an idea) aside," whereas Americans say "to table (an idea)."
- Britons say "lift," whereas Americans say "elevator."
- Britons say "sorry" when they accidentally get in your way, whereas Americans say "excuse me."[53]

Cross-cultural training usually includes the type of information about cross-cultural bloopers included in Chapter 12. In addition, the art of facial cheek-kissing is an amusing, yet important, aspect of cross-cultural training. Americans favor handshakes for greetings, yet in most countries outside of Asia, light kisses on the cheek of the other person are more acceptable. The kisses are given to people of the same and opposite sex for greeting purposes; however, kissing a business acquaintance of the opposite sex is even more expected and appropriate.

Another development in intercultural training is to train global leaders in cultural intelligence. Following the model of cultural intelligence described earlier in this chapter, global managers receive training in the cognitive, physical, and emotional or motivational domains. The training is highly complex, with the leader being expected to learn dozens of different concepts and behaviors, as well as insights.[54] A recurring example is learning how to interpret a smile from a person in another culture. The smile could have such different meanings as (1) thinking what you said was amusing, (2) mocking what you said, (3) agreement, and (4) indifference.

Again, cultural intelligence is a refinement of cultural sensitivity. The international leader who remains alert to cues in the environment can go a long way toward building relationships with people from different cultures.

## Avoid Group Characteristics When Hiring for Person–Organization Fit

An important consideration in employee recruitment and hiring is to find a good *person–organization fit*, the compatibility of the individual with the organization. The compatibility often centers on the extent to which a person's major work-related values and personality traits fit major elements of the organization culture. Following this idea, a person who is adventuresome and prone to risk taking would achieve highest performance and satisfaction where adventuresome behavior and risk taking are valued. Conversely, a methodical and conservative individual should join a slow-moving bureaucracy.

Many business firms today are investing time and effort into recruiting and hiring employees who show a good person–organization fit. A selection strategy of this type can lead to a cohesive and strong organizational culture. The danger, however, is that when employers focus too sharply on cultural fit in the hiring process, they might inadvertently discriminate against protected classes of workers. Specifically, the hiring manager might focus on superficial aspects of conformity to culture, such as physical appearance and which schools the candidates attended.

The selection of candidates who look alike and act alike conflicts with a diversity strategy. Leaders can take the initiative to guard against this problem. The way to circumvent it is to avoid using group characteristics (such as race, sex, ethnicity, or physical status) in assessing person–organization fit. The alternative is to focus on traits and behaviors, such as intelligence or ability to be a team player. Leaders at Microsoft and Amazon emphasize hiring intelligent people only because bright people fit their culture best. Being intelligent is an individual difference rather than a group characteristic.

## Attain Diversity Among Organizational Leaders

To achieve a multicultural organization, firms must also practice **leadership diversity** — that is, have a culturally heterogeneous group of leaders. Many global firms have already achieved leadership diversity with respect to ethnicity. Sex is another key area for leadership diversity, with many organizations today having women in top executive positions. An organization with true leadership diversity also has a heterogeneous group of leaders in such positions as supervisors, middle managers, and team leaders. McDonald's Corporation and General Motors Corporation are two examples of well-known companies whose C-level executives include minority group members and women. One of the executive positions at McDonald's is chief diversity officer, a practice also followed by several other large business firms including PepsiCo.

Top-team diversity appears to be associated with the financial success of the enterprise. A study of 180 firms conducted by the consulting firm, McKinsey & Company, measured diversity in terms of women and foreign nationals on senior teams. Firms in the top quartile of executive diversity, in comparison to the bottom quartile, had a 53 percent higher return on equity. The same firms had scored 14 percent higher on earnings before interest and taxes.[55] (Another interpretation of these results is that more prosperous firms are more willing to recruit diverse leaders.)

### READER'S ROADMAP

So far we have studied the nature of leadership; the attributes, behaviors, and styles of leaders; the ethics and social responsibility of leaders; and how leaders exert power and use politics and influence. We then studied techniques for developing teamwork as well as motivation and coaching skills. After studying creativity and innovation as part of leadership, we focused on communication skills as they relate to leadership. We then shifted our attention to strategic leadership, after which we discussed another broad challenge facing leaders: dealing with cultural diversity within the organization and across borders. Next, we deal with the capstone topic of developing leaders and choosing successors for executives.

## SUMMARY

The modern leader must be multicultural because corporate success, profit, and growth depend increasingly on the management of a diverse work force. The ethical and social responsibility goals of leaders and their organizations include providing adequately for the members of the diverse work force.

Managing for diversity brings a competitive advantage to the firm in several ways. Marketing can be improved because a representational work force facilitates selling products and services, and a good reputation for diversity management may attract customers. Companies with a favorable record in managing diversity are at an advantage in recruiting and retaining talented minority group members. Managing diversity also helps unlock the potential for excellence among employees who might otherwise be overlooked. A heterogeneous work force may also offer an advantage in creativity and problem solving. Diversity and inclusion programs also help local economies partly because of the reliance on minority suppliers, and team performance is often enhanced. Diversity can enhance team performance because diverse backgrounds provide diverse information, knowledge, and perspectives useful in solving problems.

To influence, motivate, and inspire culturally diverse people, the leader must be aware of overt and subtle cultural differences. Differences in cultural values help explain differences among people. Ten of these values are as follows: (1) performance orientation, (2) assertiveness, (3) future orientation, (4) time orientation, (5) humane orientation, (6) in-group collectivism, (7) gender egalitarianism, (8) power distance (acceptance of formal authority), (9) uncertainty avoidance, and (10) work orientation.

Cultural values influence leadership style as well as the behavior of other workers. For example, French managers believe in a class system. Another way to understand how culture influences leadership is to compare leadership styles across cultural groups. For Malaysian managers, the preferred organizational leadership style is to show compassion while at the same time being more autocratic than participative. Cultural differences in leadership style within the same country exist also, such as the stereotype of U.S. Southern managers being more interested in building relationships than their Northern counterparts.

Cultural sensitivity is essential for inspiring people from different cultures. Part of this sensitivity is the leader's willingness to acquire knowledge about local customs and to learn to speak the native language. A person with cultural sensitivity will recognize certain nuances in customs that help him or her build better relationships with people from different cultures. Cultural misunderstandings tend to cluster in five key areas: (1) language differences, (2) religious differences, (3) work habits, (4) women's roles, and (5) personal appearance and behavior.

Choosing appropriate attire for conducting business in another culture requires careful observation. The reality of a greater number of transgender employees requires considerable sensitivity by the leader or manager. A key principle is to be flexible in dealing with people from other cultures. Transcultural differences are often found in the best way to elicit ideas from work associates and give feedback.

To facilitate communication in international enterprise, many companies have declared English as the official language for conducting business. Despite the general acceptance of English as the official language of business, problems of cultural sensitivity remain, and speaking a second language well still gives the leader an edge.

Cultural intelligence helps an outsider interpret someone's unfamiliar and ambiguous gestures the way that person's compatriots would. Such intelligence has three facets: (1) cognitive (head), (2) physical (body), and (3) emotional/motivational (heart).

Global leadership skills help improve a company's reputation and contribute to a sustainable competitive advantage. Excellent global leaders have a leadership style that generates superior corporate performance. Among the success factors for international management positions are cultural sensitivity; cultural adventurousness (or being a global explorer); emotional intelligence; and tolerance for ambiguity. Having a command of a second language is helpful for influencing a person from another culture. An effective way of motivating people from another culture is to figure out which rewards have a high valence for them. A general challenge confronting the global leader is that techniques that work well in one culture many not necessarily work in another culture.

Top management commitment to valuing diversity is clearest when valuing diversity is embedded in organizational strategy. Specific leadership initiatives for valuing diversity can be divided into eight categories: (1) hold managers accountable for diversity; (2) establish minority recruitment, retention, and mentoring programs; (3) conduct diversity training; conducting anti-bias training; (4) conduct cross-cultural training; (5) avoid group characteristics when hiring for person–organization fit; and (6) attain diversity among organizational leaders.

## KEY TERMS

## GUIDELINES FOR ACTION AND SKILL DEVELOPMENT

When working with people from another culture, it is natural to focus on differences in values and behaviors to avoid mistakes, such as assuming that money is that person's primary motivator. Focusing on differences, however, is insufficient for building connections. A recommended approach for building connections is to focus on similarities. Casual conversations will often reveal similarities. A representative example for an American visiting Europe would be to notice that the work associate is a strong fan of football (soccer). The American could then comment that soccer is the fastest growing sport among children in the United States, and how professional soccer leagues are also flourishing.[56]

A major problem to manage in developing a diverse work force is for company leadership to reduce turnover among the employees they have worked so hard to recruit. A report that surveyed 490 minority professionals in finance suggests that companies that work so hard to get diverse employees in the building don't try nearly hard enough to keep them from leaving. Among the suggestions made in the report were to include communicating a clear path for employee advancement and providing suggestions for development as part of performance evaluation. The report also stated that "Professionals of color are, or perceive themselves to be, outside of the informal mechanisms of information sharing and social networks, including lunch or coffee with peers, being invited to drinks, and socializing with managers."[57]

A related problem is that when blacks and Latinos do not perceive themselves as having good promotional opportunities, they often leave the firm. The Financial Services pipeline, a group of sixteen financial institutions in Chicago, found that the percentage of blacks and Latinos shrink considerably in the senior ranks. The problem is that they encounter a "choke point" of advancement at the manager level, and show high rates of attrition.[58]

### Discussion Questions and Activities

1. A wheelchair user is conducting a job search to land a middle management position. Given that so many companies are attempting to build a more culturally diverse group of managers, should this job hunter include a photo of himself in a wheelchair on his job resume? Explain your reasoning.

2. With so much business being conducted over the Internet, including e-mail, why is it important to understand cross-cultural differences in values?

3. Suppose an American manager is assigned to be the general manager of a division in Sweden. During the first week in her position, she is confronted by a group of workers who say that because they are Swedish they do not respect rank and status. They insist that she should share her executive salary with the production and clerical staff. If you were the American manager, how would you respond?

4. If a business leader is regarded as charismatic by many people in one culture, to what extent do you think the leader would be perceived as charismatic in many other cultures?

5. What actions might a leader take to demonstrate that his or her interest in diversity goes beyond rhetoric?

6. Assume that a manager becomes the leader of a division in which the vast majority of the workers are under twenty-five, such as a restaurant chain. Would you recommend that the leader get some body piercing and tattoos to help establish rapport with the division work force? Explain your reasoning.

7. Walmart (the well-known store that is part of Wal-Mart Inc.) has such a diverse workforce in both its management ranks and store associates that it appears the majority of workers are minority-group members. Why do you think that Walmart receives such little publicity for being culturally diverse?

8. Should a company such as McDonald's restaurants that already has a highly diverse workforce and customer base require managers and franchise owners to attend diversity training? Explain your reasoning.

9. Suppose you are a team leader and one of your team members has a strong work ethic, based on his or her cultural values. Is it fair to assign this member much more work just because he or she is willing to work longer and harder than the other team members?

10. What can you do this week to help prepare yourself to become a multicultural leader?

# LEADERSHIP CASE PROBLEM A

## Cultural Sensitivity at Pacific Pods

Ava is the operations manager of Pacific Pods, a manufacturer and distributor of the large containers. Small businesses and individuals use these containers to store items for which they have no room in their workspace or residences. A company that owns these pods typically transports them to a person's workplace or home, loads the pods, and then charges a storage fee. Customers who rent a pod usually can visit the site of the storage company and have access to their goods.

Revenues at Pacific Pods are growing steadily. With the high cost of office space and housing in northern California, many people lack enough space to house all their goods. Turnover at Pacific Pods is relatively low (about 15 percent), and the workers seem to be reasonably engaged in their work. Ava recognizes that manufacturing pods does not represent exciting work for all employees.

The workforce reporting to Ava is culturally and demographically diverse, and she values their talent and dedication. Ava herself represents cultural diversity, with a Mexican father and a Chinese mother. After talking to the HR director and reading many articles on the subject, Ava decides that if she displayed even more cultural sensitivity than she does now, employee retention and engagement might be even higher. She then embarks on an initiative to display even more cultural sensitivity.

The first target of Ava's enhanced cultural sensitivity is Deon, a middle-aged supervisor who is African-American. Toward the end of a conversation about recruiting more production technicians with a better understand of math, Ava says, "I hope that you and your family have a great Kwanza this year." Deon responded good-naturedly, "And a happy *cinqo de mayo* to you and your family."

The second person Ava approached to display more cultural sensitivity is Gloria, a parts assembler in her late sixties. Gloria is pleasantly surprised that Ava dropped by her work station. The two engage in small talks for several minutes, and then Ava says, "Do you and your neighborhood friends play a lot of shuffle board and bingo? My folks and their friends do." Shrugging her shoulders, Gloria said, "I don't care about shuffle board and bingo, Instead I text back and forth with my four grandchildren."

The next person Ava approached to display what she believed to be enhanced cultural sensitivity was Tyler, a young accountant and wheelchair user. After chatting about a couple of financial ratios related to Pacific Pods quarterly results, Ava commented, "Tyler, I have wanted to tell you for a long time how much I admire your courage. A lot of professionals who use a wheelchair would look for work at home, instead of going through the rigors of commuting. Tyler replied, "I'm no different from anybody else. I accept challenges."

Next, Ava approached Lindsay, an information technology specialist with many visible tattoos and several body piercings. After chatting about cloud computing for a few moments, Ava said, "Please don't ever think that your tattoos and body piercings will ever hold you back from promotions at Pacific Pods. We are an equal opportunity employer." With a quizzical look on her face, Lindsay said, "Why is my body even a subject for discussion?"

Ava thought, "I think I am going to wait for any informal feedback about how my cultural sensitivity is working before I continue."

### Questions

1. What is your evaluation of appropriateness and effectiveness of Ava's cultural sensitivity initiatives?
2. What suggestions can you offer Ava to be even more effective in displaying cultural sensitivity?
3. Explain if you found any one of Ava's four cultural sensitivity initiatives to be offensive.

# ASSOCIATED ROLE PLAY

One person plays the role of Ava who will attempt each one of the cultural sensitivity initiatives described in the above case. Four other students choose one of the roles of Deon, Gloria, Tyler, and Lindsay. The role players should react in the manner they would if they were actually the recipient of Ava's cultural sensitivity initiatives. Other students might provide feedback on the effectiveness of Ava's initiatives, as well as the plausibility of the responses of the four Pacific Pods workers.

## LEADERSHIP CASE PROBLEM B

### An Affinity Group for Workers 60 and Over?

Penelope is the vice president of HR at a large utility company, Power Energy. The company prides itself for its culturally diverse workforce, including a leadership team that is demographically and culturally diverse. One of the company initiatives for recognizing the rights of different groups are the company sponsorship of affinity groups. Power Energy affinity groups (also referred to as employee network groups) include the Latino Association, The Black Tech Workers Group, The Gay Workers Alliance, and the Lesbian Rainbows. The groups receive both encouragement and a modest financial budget from the company.

Penelope is the official coordinator for these groups, and has helped each group form a charter and organize meetings. Last week she received an e-mail from five workers who have decided to form another affinity group, Power Energy employees 60 years of age and older. Skeptical of the purposes of such a group, Penelope holds a meeting with the group who is attempting to form the new affinity group, "The Splendid Seniors."

During the meeting, members of the Splendid Seniors explain to Penelope that the company has a large number of workers aged 60 and over who collectively have special interests. Ron, the leader of the group, explains that many senior workers like to talk about retirement, as well as their concerns that Power Energy might soon cut their retirement and medical benefits. Ron also pointed out that if the company can sponsor affinity groups for Latinos, Blacks, Gays, and Lesbians, the company should be willing to support a group organizing itself by age.

Penelope explains to the group that an affinity group is usually reserved for EEOC-protected groups such as race, gender, and sexual orientation. She also asks why outside of talk about future retirement, workers over 60 have any particular concerns that would warrant a company-sponsored affinity group.

Ron replied, "I and the rest of the group are disappointed. We thought that Power Energy really believed in demographic diversity." Penelope replied that she would give the subject of an affinity group for people 60 and over some more thought.

### Questions

1. What do you recommend that Penelope do with the request to form a company-sponsored affinity group, The Splendid Seniors?
2. What concerns, if any, do you have about Penelope's commitment to demographic and cultural diversity at Power Energy?

## ASSOCIATED ROLE PLAY

One student plays the role of Ron, who has requested a private meeting with Penelope to reinforce the group meeting. However, Ron is much more aggressive in his demands that Power Energy form the affinity group, "The Splendid Seniors." He also hints of possible legal action because Penelope might be in violation of Equal Employment Opportunity legislation. Another student plays the role of Penelope who wants to be a firm but fair leader in this situation. Observers should look to evaluate the extent to which Penelope demonstrates effective cultural sensitivity and leadership.

## LEADERSHIP SKILL-BUILDING EXERCISE 14-5

**My Leadership Portfolio**

To be an effective cross-cultural leader, you need to work effectively with people from demographic and cultural groups different from your own. Describe what experiences you have had lately in working with and/or relating effectively to a person quite different from you. If you have not had such an experience, take the initiative during the next week to relate meaningfully to a person quite different from you in terms of culture or demographic group membership. Finance major Stephanie had this to say:

> Claire, a special education teacher, lives on my block. Claire goes to work every school day in spite

of being legally blind. She can read with visual assists, including reading what is on her computer screen. Yet paper forms are difficult for Claire to navigate. I telephoned Claire one night and asked her if she could use my assistance in preparing her income tax this year. Claire agreed, and it worked out well. I now feel more comfortable working side by side with a visually handicapped person. Also, I picked up some practical experience in preparing a complicated tax form.

## NOTES

1. Original story based on facts and observations in the following sources: Beth Kowitt, "At Ikea: No Ranks, No Rancor," March 15, 2016, pp. 202–203; Natalia Brzezinski, "Values-Based Leadership Empowering Women: Interview With CEO of IKEA Group," *Huffington Post* (www.huffingtonpost.com), February 19, 2014, pp. 1–6; David Zweig, "What Work Cultures Around the World Can Teach Us About Leadership," *Huffington Post* (www.huffingtonpost.com) September 30, 2015, pp. 1–5; "IKEA US Receives Notable Score of 90 in the 2015 Corporate Equality Index," *IKEA* (www.ikea.com), November 19, 2014, pp. 1–3.
2. Evan Apfelbaum, "Why Your Diversity Program May Be Helping Women, But Not Minorities (or Vice Versa)," *Harvard Business Review* (https://hbr.org), August 8, 2016, pp. 2–3.
3. Patricia Harris, "The McDonald's Diversity Story," *Guest Insights* (http://views.washingtonpost.com), November 25, 2009, p. 1.
4. Susan Meisinger, "Diversity: More Than Just Representation," *HR Magazine*, January 2008, p. 8.
5. "Workforce Diversity," *www.allstate.com/diversity.aspx*, © 2017 Allstate Insurance Company.
6. Juan Baron, "Workforce Diversity: Building a Stronger Future," *www.hispanicbusiness.com*, September 18, 2013, p. 1.
7. Quoted in Diana Louise Carter, "The Diversity Dilemma," *Democrat and Chronicle*, December 15, 2013, p. 5E.
8. David Rock and Heidi Grant Halvorson, "Why Diverse Teams Are Smarter," *Harvard Business Review*, November 4, 2016, pp. 1–2.
9. "About Us—Community Relations—Vendor Development Program—Macy's (www1.macys.com). © 2016 Macy's Inc.
10. Anne Nederveen Pieterse, Daan Van Knippenberg, and Dirk Van Dierendonck, "Cultural Diversity and Team Performance: The Role of Team Member Goal Orientation," *Academy of Management Journal*, June 2013, pp. 782–804.
11. Katherine J. Klein and David A. Harrison, "On the Diversity of Diversity: Tidy Logic, Messier Realities," *Academy of Management Perspectives*, November 2007, p. 31.
12. Mansour Javidan, Peter W. Dorfman, May Sully de Luque, and Robert J. House, "In the Eye of the Beholder: Cross Cultural Lessons in Leadership from Project GLOBE," *Academy of Management Perspectives*, February 2006, pp. 69–70. Similar dimensions were described in Geert Hofstede, *Culture's Consequences: International Differences in Work Related Values* (Beverly Hills, CA: Sage Publications, 1980); updated and clarified in Hofstede, "Who Is the Fairest of Them All, Galit Ailon's Mirror," *Academy of Management Review*, July 2009, pp. 570–571. Dimensions 4 and 10 are not included in the above research.
13. G. E. Miller, "The U.S. is the Most Overworked Developed Nation in the World—When Do We Draw the Line?" *20 Something Finance* (https://20somethingfinance.com), September 11, 2016, pp. 1–3; Benjamin Snyder and Stacy Jones, "Americans Work Hard, But People in these 15 Countries Work Longer Hours," *http://fortune.com*, November 11, 2015, pp. 1–5.

14. Geert Hofstede, "The Universal and the Specific in 21st-Century Global Management," *Organizational Dynamics*, Summer 1999, pp. 35–37.

15. The observation about bureaucracy is from Javidan, Dorfman, de Luque, and House, "In the Eye of the Beholder," p. 79.

16. Felix C. Brodbeck, Michael Frese, and Mansour Javidan, "Leadership Made in Germany: Low on Compassion, High on Performance," *Academy of Management Executive*, February 2002, pp. 16–30.

17. Jeffrey C. Kennedy, "Leadership in Malaysia: Traditional Values, International Outlook," *Academy of Management Executive*, August 2002, pp. 15–26.

18. Del Jones, "North vs. South: Leaders from Both Sides of the Mason-Dixon Line Have Strong Opinions About the Styles of Their Regionally Different Peers," *USA Today*, July 9, 2004, p. 5B.

19. Thomas Rockstuhl, James H. Dulebohn, Soon Ang, and Lynn M. Shore, "Leader-Member Exchange (LMX) and Culture: A Meta-Analysis of Correlates of LMX Across 23 Countries," *Journal of Applied Psychology*, November 2012, pp. 1097–1130.

20. Cited in an Interview by Sarah Cliffe, "Companies Don't Go global, People Do," *Harvard Business Review*, October 2015, p. 85.

21. Stacey R. Fitzsimmons, "Multicultural Employee: A Framework for Understanding How They Contribute to Organizations," *Academy of Management Review*, October 2013, pp. 525–549.

22. Carla Johnson, "Cultural Sensitivity Adds Up to Good Business Sense," *HR Magazine*, November 1995, pp. 83–85.

23. Christina Binkley, "Where Yellow's a Faux Pas and White Is Death," *The Wall Street Journal*, December 6, 2007, p. D8.

24. Andy Molinsky and Ernest Gundling, "How to Build Trust on Your Cross-Cultural Team," *Harvard Business Review* (hbr.org), June 28, 2016, pp. 1–2.

25. Rita Pyrillis, "A Transgender Transition," *Workforce*, July 2016, p. 14.

26. "Managing Diversity: When Cultures Collide," *Managing People at Work*, sample issue, 2008, p. 7.

27. Ginka Toegel and Jean-Louis Barsoux, "3 Situations Where Cross-Cultural Communication Breaks Down," *Harvard Business Review*, June 8, 2016, pp. 2–3, 4–5.

28. "Honda Makes English Official," *The Japan Times* (www.japantimes.co.jp), July 18, 2015, p. 1.

29. Tsedal Neeley, "Global Business Speaks English: Why You Need a Language Strategy Now," *Harvard Business Review*, May 2012, pp. 116–124.

30. Cited in Amanda Shelby, "EEOC to Update Guidance on English-Only Policies?" *HR Hero* (http://blogs.hrhero.com), January 19, 2014, p. 1.

31. Tsedal Neely and Robert Steven Kaplan, "What's Your Language Strategy?" *Harvard Business Review*, September 2014, pp. 70–76.

32. Christopher Earley and Elaine Mosakowski, "Cultural Intelligence," *Harvard Business Review*, October 2004, pp. 139–146.

33. Ming Li, William H. Mobley, and Adrian Kelly, "When Do Global Leaders Learn Best to Develop Cultural Intelligence? An Investigation of the Moderating Role of Experiential Learning Style," *Academy of Management Learning & Education*, March 2013, pp. 32–50.

34. Javidan, Dorfman, de Luque, and House, "In the Eye of the Beholder," p. 85.

35. Joseph A. Petrick, Robert E. Scherer, James D. Bodzinski, John F. Quinn, and M. Fall Ainina, "Global Leadership Skills and Reputational Capital: Intangible Resources for Sustainable Competitive Advantage," *The Academy of Management Executive*, February 1999, pp. 58–69.

36. Gretchen M. Spreitzer, Morgan W. McCall Jr., and Joan D. Mahoney, "Early Identification of International Executive Potential," *Journal of Applied Psychology*, February 1997, pp. 6–29.

37. Research cited in Douglas T. Hall, Guorong Zhu, and Amin Yan, "Developing Global Leaders: To Hold on to Them, Let Them Go," *Advances in Global Leadership*, Vol. 2, 2001, p. 331.

38. Javidan, Dorfman, de Luque, and House, "In the Eye of the Beholder," p. 85.

39. Jeanne Brett, Kristin Behfar, and Mary C. Kern, "Managing Multicultural Teams," *Harvard Business Review*, November 2006, p. 87.

40. Pamela Hinds, "Research: Why Best Practices Don't Translate Across Cultures," *Harvard Business Review* (https://hbr.org), June 27, 2016, p. 4.

41. "Carlos Ghosn Leadership Style," *Advise America* (www.adviseamerica.com), pp. 1–8, © 2016; "Renault-Nissan's Ghosn Recommends Two Successors: Report," *Reuters.com* (www.reuters.com), January 10, 2014, p. 1; Paul Ingrassia and John Stoll, "Hottest Car Guy on Earth," *The Wall Street Journal*, January 14, 2006, p. A8.

42. Boris Groysberg and Katherine Connolly, "Twenty-Four CEOs on Creating Diverse and Inclusive Organizations," *Harvard Business Review*, September 2013, p. 76.

43. Todd Campbell, "Diversity in Depth," *HR Magazine*, March 2003, p. 152.

44. Groysberg and Connolly, "Twenty-Four CEOs," p. 73; "Culture, Inclusion, People," *http://careers.bankofamerica.com*, pp. 1–3. © 2016 Bank of America Corporation.

45. Marc Adams, "Building a Rainbow One Stripe at a Time," *HR Magazine*, August 1998, pp. 73–74.

46. Frank Dobbin and Alexandra Kalev, "Why Diversity Programs Fail: And What Works Better," *Harvard Business Review*, July–August 2016, p. 59.

47. Rohini Anand and Mary-Frances Winters, "A Retrospective View of Corporate Diversity Training from 1964 to the Present," *Academy of Management Learning & Education*, September 2008, pp. 356–372.

48. Katerina Bezrukova, Karen A. Jehn, and Chester S. Spell, "Reviewing Diversity Training: Where We have been and Where We Should Go," *Academy of Management Learning & Education*, June 2012, pp. 207–227.

49. Dobbin and Kaley, "Why Diversity Programs Fail," p. 55.

50. Farhad Manjoo, "Exposing Hidden Bias at Google," *New York Times* (www.nytimes.com), September 24, 2014, pp. 1–4; Jessica Guynn, "Facebook Develops Unconscious Bias Training," *USA Today*, July 30, 2015, p. 3B.

51. Deepa Seethharaman and Natalie Andrew, "Facebook to Train Against Bias," *The Wall Street Journal*, June 24, 2016, p. B3.

52. Raju Chebium, "A Common Language: Training Across Borders," *HR Magazine*, January/February 2015, pp. 52–56.

53. DeeDee Doke, "Perfect Strangers," *HR Magazine*, December 2004, p. 64; Terry Eagleton, "Sorry, But Do You Speak English?" *The Wall Street Journal*, June 22–23, 2013, p. C3.

54. P. Christopher Earley and Randall S. Peterson, "The Elusive Cultural Chameleon: Cultural Intelligence as a New Approach to Intercultural Training for the Global Manager," *Academy of Management Learning and Education*, March 2004, p. 105.

55. Thomas Barta, Markus Kleiner, and Tilo Neumann, "Is There a Payoff from Top-Team Diversity?" *McKinsey Quarterly* (www.mckinseyquarterly.com), April 2012, pp. 1–4.

56. Andy Molinsky and Sujin Jang, "To Connect Across Cultures, Find Out What You Have in Common," *Harvard Business Review* (https://hbr.org), January 20, 2016, pp. 1–4.

57. Michael Todd, "Report: Companies Should Help Workers Get Comfortable, Stay Awhile," *Hispanic Business*, March 2007, p. 44.

58. Alexia Elejalde-Ruiz, "Some Financial Firms Tackle Diversity Gap Head-on, Say they Can't Afford Not To," *Chicago Tribune* (www.chicagotribune.com), July 15, 2016, p. 2.

# Leadership Development and Succession

The Ritz-Carlton hotel chain, a subsidiary of Marriott International, is one of the world's best-known luxury brands, including a reputation for superior customer service. To help sustain its reputation and high-quality service, top-level management has invested resources into leadership and management development for many years. A key component of Ritz-Carlton's efforts in this area is the Voyage global leadership development program, sponsored by the Marriott.

The Voyage program is aimed at recent college graduates, and is available in 40 countries worldwide. The fulltime program lasts for twelve to eighteen months at full pay, and offers several opportunities for career enrichment, including the following: (1) Hands-on training in a specific discipline geared to specific interests such as food and beverage operations, culinary, engineering, revenue management, and sales and marketing. The acquisition of knowledge in a discipline is the foundation for becoming a manager and leader. (2) Immersion in the operations of an individual hotel. (3) Comprehensive understanding of the global scale of the Marriott operations, and global brands. (4) Opportunities to interact with and learn from the senior global leadership at the Marriott. (5) Experience with the Virtual Hotel Simulator, a gaming experience that enables Voyagers to compete globally to manage a hotel and test their knowledge.

Voyagers who successfully complete the program transition into an entry-level management or supervisory position suited to the capability and interests. The entry-level position is the building block for becoming a leader within Ritz-Carlton or Marriott. The Voyage program is sometimes combined with the leadership and management development program at one large hotel. A hotel-specific example of leadership development at the Ritz-Carlton is the program at the Al Bustan Palace, located in Oman, a sultanate of the southeast Arabian Peninsula on the Gulf of Oman. In one year, the Omani Leadership Development program enrolled eleven high potential "ladies and gentlemen"

for an eleven-month leadership course. The participants were supervisors from different departments within the hotel, but all had the ambition and potential to become leaders in hospitality. Held during working hours, the curriculum included instructor-led training, and individual and team projects designed to develop strategic thinking and teamwork. Also included were written assignments and cross-exposure to another country during a familiarization to other Ritz-Carlton properties around the world.

The Ritz-Carlton chain has developed a world-wide reputation for high levels of customer service combined with luxury to the point many companies want to study its success. This fact combined with the success of the leadership and management training programs at Ritz-Carlton fostered the development of the Ritz-Carlton Leadership Center. The Center provides training and development programs that help organizations improve their cultures, enhance employee engagement, and develop high-level customer service environments that create significant competitive advantage.[1]

The huge amount of time and resources the Ritz-Carlton invests in leadership development illustrates the importance organizations attach to the development of leaders and managers. Based on Association for Talent Development data it is estimated that approximately $20 billion is spent annually on leadership development.[2] Sydney Finkelstein, the Director of the Leadership Center at the Tuck School of Business at Dartmouth College, further emphasizes the importance of leadership development. He contends that generating and regenerating talent is more important for success than strategy, technology, and even products.[3]

The previous chapters in this book have included information and activities designed to develop leaders and enhance their effectiveness. This chapter describes how self-development can enhance leadership effectiveness, as well as the processes organizations use to develop current and future leaders. Such activities and processes are typically referred to as leadership development or management development.

The primary emphasis in leadership development is on building and using interpersonal competence, even when it appears that a trait or behavior is the focus of development.[4] For example, a leader might work on enhancing his or her self-discipline, yet being more self-disciplined might help the leader to remember to provide feedback and recognition to group members.

In addition to describing various approaches to leadership development, this chapter also describes leadership succession. Leadership succession is included here because an important part of leadership development is being groomed for promotion. The text concludes with a glimpse of the challenges newly appointed leaders face.

## Development Through Self-Awareness and Self-Discipline

Leadership development is often perceived in terms of education and training, job experience, and coaching. Nevertheless, self-help also contributes heavily to developing leadership capabilities. Self-help takes many forms, including working on one's own to improve communication skills, to develop charisma, and to model the behavior of effective leaders. As the self becomes developed, the leader is able to engage in more effective interactions with people. Research suggests that individuals with a strong career growth orientation are more skilled at self-development of leadership characteristics and behaviors. *Career growth orientation* involves greater career exploration and feedback-seeking activities.[5] Two major components of leadership self-development are self-awareness and self-discipline.

## Leadership Development Through Self-Awareness

An important mechanism underlying self-development is **self-awareness**, insightfully processing feedback about oneself to improve one's effectiveness. Part of self-awareness is being able to understand how the individual is perceived by others.[6] For example, a leader might say, "I come across to others as a person of passion and commitment." If others perceive the leader in the same way, the leader has good self-awareness. In contrast, if most subordinates perceive the leader as unexcited about attaining group goals, the leader's self-awareness is low.

According to two specialists in leadership assessment, many big mistakes in careers and organizations result from gaps in self-awareness.[7] For example, a department leader might observe that three key group members left her group over a six-month time span. The leader might defensively dismiss this fact with an analysis such as, "I guess we just don't pay well enough to keep good people." Her first analysis might be correct. With a self-awareness orientation, however, the leader would dig deeper for the reasons behind the turnover. She might ask herself, "Is there something in my leadership approach that creates turnover problems?" She might ask for exit interview data to sharpen her perceptions about her leadership approach.

The late Chris Argyris has coined the terms *single-loop learning* and *double-loop learning* to differentiate between levels of self-awareness.[8] **Single-loop learning** occurs when learners seek minimum feedback that might substantially confront their basic ideas or actions. As in the example of the high-turnover leader, single-loop learners engage in defensive thinking and tend not to act on the clues they receive. Argyris offers the example of a thermostat that automatically turns on the heat whenever the room temperature drops below 68 degrees Fahrenheit (20 degrees Celsius).

**Double-loop learning** is an in-depth type of learning that occurs when people use feedback to confront the validity of the goal or the values implicit in the situation. The leader mentioned earlier was engaged in double-loop learning when she questioned the efficacy of her leadership approach. To achieve double-loop learning, one must minimize defensive thinking. Many people are blind to their areas of incompetence and do not know their vision is blocked. Figure 15-1 illustrates the difference between single-loop learning and double-loop learning.

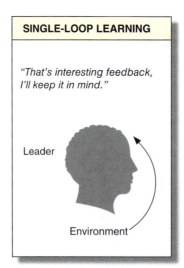
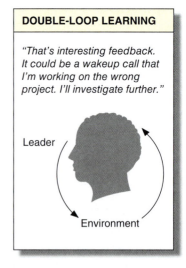

**FIGURE 15-1** Single-Loop Learning Versus Double-Loop Learning.

An important contribution of double-loop learning is that it enables the leader to learn and profit from setbacks. Interpreting the reason that a setback occurred may help the leader to do better the next time. Faced with a group in crisis, a leader might establish a vision of better days ahead for group members. The leader observes that the vision leads to no observable changes in performance and behavior. Perhaps the group was not ready for a vision. In a comparable situation in the future, the leader might hold back on formulating a vision until the group is headed out of the crisis.

A fruitful area of self-awareness is for leaders to recognize their standing on two key dimensions of leadership: forceful versus enabling leadership, and strategy versus operational. Bob Kaplan explains that the leader should not go overboard on each dimension, such as being too forceful or too enabling (empowering). A leader should also not spend so much time strategizing that operations become neglected, or so much time focusing on operations that strategy is neglected.

The process of self-awareness on these two dimensions is much like volume control—raise or lower the volume to get the best result. Figure 15-2 outlines this area of self-awareness in terms of the extremes, or being lopsided. The ideal point is to be just right in forcefulness versus enabling, and strategic versus operational. Feedback from others helps a leader become self-aware of his or her standing on these two dimensions.[9]

Self-awareness can also be helpful in understanding how close an individual is to his or her concept of an ideal leader.[10] Many people develop perceptions of who they consider to be an ideal leader, even without a conscious process of searching for such a person. A person with high self-awareness might think, "I'm getting close to behaving like ____, but I still have to develop my charisma and strategic thinking further to get there."

## Leadership Development Through Self-Discipline

As with other types of personal development, leadership development requires considerable self-discipline. In the present context, **self-discipline** is mobilizing one's effort and energy to stay focused on attaining an important goal. A key component of being a self-disciplined learner is to set goals for development such as, "I am going to think more strategically about my work."[11]

Self-discipline is required for most forms of leadership development. Assume, for example, that a leader is convinced that active listening is an important leadership behavior. The leader reads about active listening and also attends a workshop on the subject. After the reading and workshop are completed, the leader will need to concentrate diligently in order to remember to listen actively. Self-discipline is particularly necessary because the pressures of everyday activities often divert a person's attention from personal development.

Self-discipline plays an important role in the continuous monitoring of one's behavior to ensure that needed self-development occurs. After one identifies a developmental need, it is necessary to periodically review whether one is making the necessary improvements. Assume that a person recognizes the developmental need to become a more colorful communicator as a way of enhancing charisma. The person would need self-discipline to make the conscious effort to communicate more colorfully when placed in an appropriate situation.

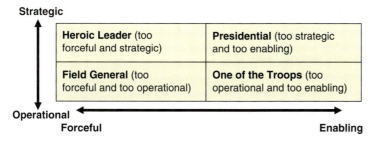

**FIGURE 15-2**    Four Kinds of Lopsided Leaders.

*Source:* Based on concepts from Bob Kaplan with Rob Kaiser, The Versatile Leader: Make the Most of Your Strengths—Without Overdoing It (San Francisco: Pfeiffer, 2006).

Leadership Self-Assessment Quiz 15-1 gives you the opportunity to examine your own tendencies toward being self-disciplined. Leadership Self-Assessment Quiz 15-2 contains an interpersonal skills checklist that will help you identify your own developmental needs related to interpersonal relationships.

# LEADERSHIP SELF-ASSESSMENT QUIZ 15-1

## My Self-Discipline Tendencies

Indicate the extent to which each of the following statements describes your behavior or attitude by circling one number. The numbers refer to disagree strongly (DS), disagree (D), neither agree nor disagree (N), agree (A), and agree strongly (AS). Consider enlisting the help of someone who knows your behavior and attitudes well to help you respond accurately to the statements.

| STATEMENT RELATED TO SELF-DISCIPLINE | DS | D | N | A | AS |
|---|---|---|---|---|---|
| **1.** I usually stay focused on whatever goal I am pursuing. | 1 | 2 | 3 | 4 | 5 |
| **2.** I have a mission or purpose in life. | 1 | 2 | 3 | 4 | 5 |
| **3.** Saving or investing for the future makes little sense when you can have fun with the money in the present. | 5 | 4 | 3 | 2 | 1 |
| **4.** If a person is highly talented he or she does not have to invest much time in practicing the skill related to that talent. | 5 | 4 | 3 | 2 | 1 |
| **5.** I am able to work on my job for an entire hour without checking to see if I have a phone message, a text message, or an e-mail message. | 1 | 2 | 3 | 4 | 5 |
| **6.** I have developed a new skill in the last twelve months without being forced to by my employer or an instructor. | 1 | 2 | 3 | 4 | 5 |
| **7.** I almost never bother retaining facts any longer because I can find whatever facts I need on the Internet. | 5 | 4 | 3 | 2 | 1 |
| **8.** My days rarely turn out the way I hope. | 5 | 4 | 3 | 2 | 1 |
| **9.** Given a choice between receiving a gift of $1,000 today versus receiving a gift on $3,000 three months from today, I would wait for the $3,000. | 1 | 2 | 3 | 4 | 5 |
| **10.** I would be willing to devote fifteen minutes per day for two years to learn another language. | 1 | 2 | 3 | 4 | 5 |
| **11.** Working sixty hours per week for even a short period of time is something that I would never do. | 5 | 4 | 3 | 2 | 1 |
| **12.** I tend to daydream a lot even on the job or during quite moments with family and friends. | 5 | 4 | 3 | 2 | 1 |
| **13.** I usually read the owner's manual before I spend much time operating a new vehicle or complicated piece of electronic equipment. | 1 | 2 | 3 | 4 | 5 |
| **14.** When I'm involved in an important work project, I can enjoy myself fully at a recreational event after hours. | 1 | 2 | 3 | 4 | 5 |
| **15.** I feel that I'm moving forward a little bit at every day toward achieving my goals. | 1 | 2 | 3 | 4 | 5 |
| **16.** I accomplish very little unless I am closely supervised. | 5 | 4 | 3 | 2 | 1 |
| **17.** Several people have described me as being conscientious. | 1 | 2 | 3 | 4 | 5 |
| **18.** My work area is neat, clean, and well organized. | 1 | 2 | 3 | 4 | 5 |
| **19.** I become bored easily. | 5 | 4 | 3 | 2 | 1 |
| **20.** I am willing to work hard and long at a task even if the payoff is uncertain. | 1 | 2 | 3 | 4 | 5 |
| **21.** It makes sense for a marathon runner to keep going even when it appears that he or she has almost no chance of being among the top group of finishers. | 1 | 2 | 3 | 4 | 5 |

## QUIZ 15-1 (continued)

| STATEMENT RELATED TO SELF-DISCIPLINE | DS | D | N | A | AS |
|---|---|---|---|---|---|
| 22. I frequently misplace or lose items such as my keys, wallet, smartphone, or glasses. | 5 | 4 | 3 | 2 | 1 |
| 23. Planning is difficult because life is so unpredictable. | 5 | 4 | 3 | 2 | 1 |
| 24. I am able to concentrate on an entire news story if the subject interests me. | 1 | 2 | 3 | 4 | 5 |
| 25. I'm terrible at remembering names of people I meet only one or twice. | 5 | 4 | 3 | 2 | 1 |

*Scoring and Interpretation:* Calculate your score by adding up the numbers circled:

- **110–125:** You are a highly self-disciplined person who should be able to capitalize on your skills and talents.
- **61–109:** You have an average degree of self-discipline.
- **25–60:** You appear to have a below-average degree of self-discipline that could be interfering with your accomplishing goals and achieving satisfaction.

# LEADERSHIP SELF-ASSESSMENT QUIZ 15-2

### The Interpersonal Skills Checklist

*Instructions:* Following are a number of specific aspects of behavior that suggest that a person needs to improve his or her interpersonal skills related to leadership and influence. Check each statement that is generally true for you. You can add to the reliability of this exercise by asking one or two other people who know you well to rate you. Then compare your self-analysis with their analysis of you.

| DEVELOPMENTAL NEEDS AND AREAS FOR IMPROVEMENT | |
|---|---|
| 1. I am too shy and reserved. | ☐ |
| 2. I bully and intimidate others frequently. | ☐ |
| 3. I tell others what they want to hear rather than emphasizing the truth. | ☐ |
| 4. I have trouble expressing my feelings. | ☐ |
| 5. I make negative comments about group members too readily. | ☐ |
| 6. Very few people pay attention to the ideas I contribute during a meeting. | ☐ |
| 7. My personality is not colorful enough. | ☐ |
| 8. People find me boring. | ☐ |
| 9. I pay too little attention to the meaning behind what team members and coworkers are saying. | ☐ |
| 10. It is very difficult for me to criticize others. | ☐ |
| 11. I am too serious most of the time. | ☐ |
| 12. I avoid controversy in dealing with others. | ☐ |
| 13. I do not get my point across well. | ☐ |
| 14. It is difficult for me to make small talk with others. | ☐ |
| 15. I boast too much about my accomplishments. | ☐ |
| 16. I strive too much for individual recognition instead of looking to credit the team. | ☐ |

## QUIZ 15-2 (continued)

**DEVELOPMENTAL NEEDS AND AREAS FOR IMPROVEMENT**

| | | |
|---|---|---|
| **17.** | Self-confidence is my weak point. | ☐ |
| **18.** | My spoken messages are too bland. | ☐ |
| **19.** | I rarely ever speak to people any longer. Instead I rely on text messages. | ☐ |
| **20.** | I relate poorly to people from cultures different from my own. | ☐ |
| **21.** | I read people poorly. | ☐ |
| **22.** | I display a lot of nervous mannerisms when I am working in a group. | ☐ |
| **23.** | I do a poor job of making a presentation in front of others. | ☐ |
| **24.** | I multitask, such as receiving a phone call, while talking to another person face-to-face. | ☐ |
| **25.** | _____ | ☐ |

(Fill in your own statement.)

Now that you (and perhaps one or two others) have identified specific behaviors that may require change, draw up an action plan. Describe briefly a plan of attack for bringing about the change you hope to achieve for each statement that is checked. Ideas might come from personal development books or from leadership development and human relations workshops. After formulating an action plan, you will need self-discipline for its successful implementation. For example, if you checked, "People find me boring," you might want to expand your fund of knowledge by extensive reading and by talking to dynamic people. You will then need the self-discipline to continue your quest for ideas and to incorporate some of these ideas into your conversation.

Another approach to this exercise is for each student to choose one developmental need, combined with an action plan, that he or she is willing to share with others. Next, students present their developmental need and action plan to the rest of the class. After all students have presented, a class discussion is held about whatever observations and generalizations students have reached.

A key part of making self-awareness and self-discipline vehicles for personal development is to have a healthy belief in personal growth. According to psychology professor Carol Dweck, some people have a healthy belief in growth, whereby they assume that they will develop their talents during their personal and work lives. In contrast, others possess a fixed mindset, whereby they believe that talents are innate and will carry them to the top without the need for modification.[12]

## Development Through Education, Experience, and Mentoring

Much of leadership development takes place through means other than self-awareness and self-discipline or leadership development programs. Leadership is such a comprehensive process that almost any life activity can help people prepare for a leadership role. Three important life and work experiences that contribute to leadership development are education, experience as a leader, and mentoring. In the next several pages, we look at the link between each of these three factors and leadership.

### Education

Education generally refers to acquiring knowledge without concern about its immediate application. If a potential leader studies mathematics, the logical reasoning acquired might someday help him or her solve a complex problem facing the organization. As a result, the leader's stature is enhanced. Reading biographies and autobiographies about successful people is a good source of ideas about leadership. Formal education is positively correlated with achieving managerial and leadership positions. Furthermore, there is a positive relationship between the amount of formal education and the level of leadership position attained.

Another key contribution of formal education to leadership development is that enhances a person's learning agility (the ability to learn). Michael Trusty, the head of capability consulting at Rolls Royce, observes, "The pace at which information now flows means that those who are the most ready for change, particularly in knowledge-drive organizations, don't just apply what the know but can quickly seek out and assimilate new information."[13] The link between learning agility and leadership is that leaders are required to learn regularly.

The correlation between education and leadership status, however, may not reflect causation. Many people get the opportunity to hold a business leadership position *only if* they have achieved a specified level of education. A more important issue than the statistical association between leadership and formal education is *how* education contributes to leadership effectiveness.

Most high-level leaders are intelligent, well-informed people who gather knowledge throughout their career. The knowledge that accrues from formal education and self-study provides them with information for innovative problem solving. Being intellectually alert also helps them exert influence through logical persuasion.

## Experience

On-the-job experience is an obvious contributor to leadership effectiveness. Without experience, knowledge cannot readily be converted into skills. For example, you will need experience to put into practice the appropriate influence tactics you studied in Chapter 8. Leadership experience also helps build skills and insights that a person may not have formally studied. Many company leadership development programs focus on giving participants varied experiences, such as Yum! Brands requiring that executive leaders obtain experience managing a store.

*Challenging Experiences*   The best experiences for leadership development are those that realistically challenge the manager, including dealing with stressful problems. A recommended approach to developing as a leader is to step outside your comfort zone and gain novel experiences.[14] Novel experiences that are complex are even more important for development. Claudio Fernández-Aráoz observes that the most successful leaders are those who continue to learn and grow, and the best way to do that is through assignments of increasing complexity. Aráoz gives the example of a leader within a multinational conglomerate who was exposed to new complexities. He was successfully rotated through financial, marketing, and production roles in his domestic Argentine market, as well as U.S. markets, and those in Europe. As a result he was ready for the leadership assignment of launching a new business that would compete with the company's clients.[15]

Creating an environment for development requires that an organization first rid itself of the belief in survival of the fittest. The goal of leadership development is to provide meaningful development opportunities, not to push managers to the point where they are most likely to fail.[16] An example of a stretch experience for many managers is being placed in charge of an organizational unit with low productivity and morale. The manager would need to apply many leadership skills to improve the situation.

Failure is a special type of challenging experience that contributes enormously to reaching one's leadership potential. One reason is that people who have never failed have avoided taking big risks. Richard Branson, the flamboyant chair of Virgin Atlantic Airways Limited, claims that "the best developer of a leader is failure." An effective way of capitalizing on failure is to reflect on what you might do differently in the future. Ask yourself questions such as "What would have to change inside me to enable me to do things differently?"[17] For example, perhaps the project failed because you did not provide enough guidance to the group and did not communicate a sense of urgency. In the future, you might lead with more control and assertion. Table 15-1 lists a number of powerful learning experiences for developing leadership and managerial skills.

An important part of capitalizing on challenging experiences is for the leader or manager to be given leeway in choosing how to resolve the problem. A team leader, for example, might be told, "Increase productivity by 10 percent and, at the same time, decrease costs by 10 percent." The team leader would have the developmental opportunity of finding a solution to this challenge.

Challenging experiences are the most likely to result in leadership development when the leader receives some coaching and guidance about the lessons to be derived from these experiences.[18] Imagine that middle manager Max is given a three-month assignment to help turn around a distribution center that has been suffering from financial losses and poor morale. Max is successful, and then goes over an intense debriefing with his boss and the HR director as to why he succeeded. Max then achieves the insight, "It looks like I expressed confidence that the workers could resolve the problems. I also pointed people in the right direction."

**TABLE 15-1** Powerful Learning Experiences for Developing Leadership Skills

Research with managers has revealed fifteen types of powerful learning experiences that contribute to one's development as a leader and manager.

1. *Unfamiliar responsibilities.* Responsibilities are new, quite different, or much broader than previous ones. As a result, the situation requires skills and abilities beyond a person's current competencies.
2. *Proving yourself.* There is pressure to show others that one can get the job done.
3. *Developing new directions.* The leader is responsible for starting something new, implementing a reorganization, or responding to rapid changes in the business environment.
4. *Inherited problems.* The manager must fix problems created by a former manager or is handed the responsibility for problem employees.
5. *Downsizing decisions.* The manager must make decisions about shutting down operations or reducing staff.
6. *Dealing with problem employees.* The group members lack adequate experience, are incompetent, or are resistant.
7. *Facing high stakes.* The manager is faced with tight deadlines, pressure from senior management, high visibility, and responsibility for success and failure.
8. *Managing business complexity.* The job is large in scope, and the manager is responsible for multiple functions, groups, products, customers, or markets.
9. *Role overload.* The size of the job requires a large investment of time and energy. An example is that suddenly you deal with a customer request far beyond the capacity of the company to handle.
10. *Handling external pressure.* The manager is forced to deal with external factors that affect the business, such as negotiating with unions or government agencies or coping with serious community problems.
11. *Having to exert influence without authority.* To accomplish the job, it is necessary to influence peers, higher management, external parties, or other key people over whom one has no formal control.
12. *Adverse business conditions.* The business unit faces a drop in revenues or a drastic budget cut. For example, it becomes necessary to raise funds from investors and you have to be humble and almost beg for money.
13. *Lack of top management support.* Senior management is reluctant to provide direction, support, or resources for the manager's major work activities or for a new project.
14. *Lack of personal support.* The manager is excluded from key networks and receives little encouragement from others about the work activities.
15. *Difficult boss.* A personality clash with the boss is evident, or he or she is incompetent.
16. *Solving difficult problems around the world.* IBM deploys a Corporate Service Corps in which emerging leaders work as volunteers to solve difficult problems in developing countries.

*Source:* Adapted from Cynthia D. McCauley and Morgan W. McCall Jr. (Eds.), *Using Experience to Develop Leadership Talent: How Organizations Leverage On-the-Job Development* (San Francisco, CA: Wiley, 2014); Cynthia D. McCauley, Marian N. Ruderman, Patricia J. Ohlott, and Jane E. Morrow, "Assessing the Developmental Components of Managerial Jobs," *Journal of Applied Psychology*, August 1994, pp. 544–560. Point 1 is also derived from Gretchen M. Spreitzer, "Leadership Development Lessons from Positive Organizational Studies," *Organizational Dynamics*, no. 4, 2006, p. 307. Points 7 and 12 are also derived from "Moments of Truth: Global Executives Talk About the Challenges That Shaped Them as Leaders," *Harvard Business Review*, January 2007, pp. 16–17.

Another contributing factor to profiting from experiences is the leader having the right mental set for learning. According to the theorizing of Peter A. Hesling and Lauren A. Keating of the UNSW Australian Business School, leaders learn more from their challenging leadership experiences when they are in a *learning mode*. The mode refers to intentionally framing and pursuing each element of learning through experience with more of a growth than a fixed mindset. A leader in a learning mode has a motive of self-improvement and self-enhancement. Assume that a leader is placed in charge of a global task force to find ways to penetrate markets in underdeveloped countries.  In a learning mode, the leader would reflect, "Here is a great opportunity to learn how to really work smoothly with workers and consumers from other cultures."

The learning mode contains many different elements, yet its nature is reflected in growth mindset-related assumptions such as the following: "Leadership ability is not limited by genetics or carved in stone." "Frustrating mistakes contribute to learning, so should not be feared." "Disappointing results often indicate where more learning is needed." [19]

**Sources of Experience**    The two major developmental factors in any work situation are work associates and the task itself.[20] Work associates can help a person develop in myriad ways. An immediate superior can be a positive or negative model of effective leadership. You might observe how your boss skillfully confronts a cost overrun problem during a staff meeting. You observe carefully, and plan to use a similar technique when it becomes necessary for you to confront a problem with a group. In contrast, assume that your boss's confrontational approach backfires and the group becomes defensive and recalcitrant. You have learned how not to confront. Members of upper management, peers, and reporting staff can also help a worker profit from experience. For example, by trial and error, the worker might learn which type of praise is best for influencing others.

Work-related tasks can also contribute to leadership development because part of a leader's role is to be an effective and innovative problem solver. The tasks that do most to foster development are those that are more complex and ambiguous than a person has faced previously (as mentioned above). Starting a new activity for a firm, such as establishing a dealer network, exemplifies a developmental experience.

An extreme approach to developing leadership skills is to be assigned responsibility for an area in which you lack the appropriate skills or knowledge of the business. An example would be appointing an operations manager as the director of marketing. According to Matt Paese of Development Dimensions International, leadership ability is the most effective way of succeeding in areas where you lack technical expertise. Among the specific leadership skills would be consulting with people who have the necessary expertise and exuding self-confidence, yet not being arrogant.[21]

**Broad Experience**    Many aspects of leadership are situational. A sound approach to improving leadership effectiveness is therefore to gain managerial experience in different settings. An aspirant to executive leadership is well advised to gain management experience in at least two different organizational functions, such as marketing and operations.

A widespread practice is to assign managers to cross-functional teams to give them experience in working with other disciplines. The more urgent the purpose of the team, the more likely meaningful leadership development will take place. Achieving broad experience fits well with the current emphasis on growth through learning new skills rather than a preoccupation with vertical mobility. For example, more professionals today than in the past are willing to take a lateral move instead of a promotion if there is an opportunity to acquire new skills. For example, the manager of market research might be content to become a sales manager (a position at about the same level) in order to enhance his or her skill portfolio.

A particularly effective type of broad experience early in a career is to perform technical work in one's specialty, and combine it with frontline supervision. A representative example is a person with a specialty in materials management who receives an assignment of managing order delivery technicians.

As implied by double-loop learning, experience is the most beneficial when the person extracts value from what is happening. People with this capability have the capacity to scan for new ideas, the intellectual skills to absorb them, and the practical intelligence to translate that new learning into productive action for customers and organizations.[22] For example, the materials management supervisor just mentioned might spot a way to stack inventory to save enough space to avoid having to construct a new wing to the distribution center.

The leadership portfolio that you have been maintaining will help you capitalize on experience as a source of leadership development. The accompanying Leader in Action insert describes a person whose broad experience helped catapult him into a major executive slot.

## LEADER IN ACTION

### Broad Experience Helped David S. Taylor Earn Top Position at P&G

About one week after graduating from Duke University with a B.S. degree in electrical engineering in 1980, David S. Taylor joined Procter & Gamble as a production manager in the Greenville, North Carolina plant. Thirty-five years later he was appointed as chairman of the board, president, and chief executive officer (CEO) of the company. His major task as CEO was to spark substantial sales growth at the company, particularly with existing products (organic growth) rather than through acquisitions.

Jim McNerney, lead director of P&G's board, and former CEO of Boeing Corporation, made the following comments about Taylor upon his promotion to the head of the consumer products giant: "David is a proven leader who has the experience and track record of delivering results. He has a broad understanding of P&G's business, having worked on several categories in multiple regions around the world. He has helped build many of the Company's most successful brands and businesses. The Board is confident that David will lead P&G to executive the company's strategies to win with consumers, and improve shareholder value."

One of first proclamations in his new position was that P&G needs to become more nimble in its decision making. (P&G has faced fierce competition from house brands and lower-price competitors in recent years. Frugal consumers also create problems in terms of selling name brands.) At an analyst conference, Taylor said, "A few years ago we got too central and global and too slow to address market opportunities. We need more direct ownership from our regional managers all the way to the store shelf."

During his career with the company, Taylor helped build many of P&G's core businesses, including baby care, family care, hair care, and home care. He has provided leadership to global businesses, and lived in worked in North America, Europe, and Asia. Prior to the top position, Taylor served as group president of global beauty, grooming and health care—a collection of products that accounted for approximately one-half of P&G revenues.

Among the well-known brands for which Taylor has held leadership roles include Pampers, Crest, Oral-B, Pantene, Head & Shoulders, Gillette, and Vicks. Among the many job titles Taylor held during his first thirty-five years with the company are as follows: operations manager, Albany, Georgia; brand manager, Pampers; general manager, Greater China Hair Care and Anti-Counterfeiting; vice president, North American Family Care; and group president Global Health & Grooming.

Taylor is committed to dealing with the problem of food insecurity in the United States. For eight years he served on the board of directors for Feeding America, including two years as board chair.

### QUESTIONS

1. To what extent do you think that Taylor's various roles within P&G give him credibility as the company's leader?

2. Taylor's joined a large company right after college graduation, and then stayed with that company for the rest of his career. Why might his career path be regarded as old-fashioned?

3. What take away might Taylor's employment history have for you in your leadership career?

Source: Original story created from facts and observations in the following sources: "David Taylor Appointed P&G President & CEO," Spray (www.spraytm.com), pp. 1–2; "Why P&G's CEO Says the Company Needs to Be More Nimble," Reuters (www.fortune.com), February 19, 2016, pp. 1–5; Ellen Byron, Serena Ng, and Joann S. Lublin, "Lafley to Hand Over Reins at P&G," The Wall Street Journal, July 28, 2015, pp. B1, B7; "David S. Taylor: Chairman of the Board, President and Chief Executive Officer," P&G (www.us.pg.com), July 16, p. 1; "David S. Taylor: Group President, Beauty, Grooming and Health Care," P&G (www.us.pg.com), July 2015, p. 1.

# Mentoring

Another experience-based way to develop leadership capability is to be coached by an experienced, knowledgeable leader. Quite often this person is a **mentor**, a more experienced person who develops a protégé's abilities through tutoring, coaching, guidance, and emotional support. Mentoring others is an important leadership responsibility. In some companies, every manager from the CEO on down is supposed to be an active mentor. The mentor, a trusted counselor and guide, is typically a person's manager. However, a mentor can also be a staff professional or coworker. An emotional tie exists between the person mentored and the mentor.

*Informal Versus Formal Mentoring*    Mentoring is traditionally thought of as an informal relationship based on compatibility or spark between two personalities. A key aspect of informal mentoring is that the mentor and the protégé identify with each other. Identification includes the thought that the protégé vies the mentor as a model of someone he or she wants to be in the future.[23] At the same time the mentor might think, "I was just like you when I was getting started in my leadership career."

All mentoring does not take place in the context of a spontaneous relationship between two people. Employers often formally assign a mentor to a new employee to help him or her adjust well to the organization and to succeed. Mentoring is so widely accepted as a valuable approach to development that most large organizations have a formal mentoring program.

Another approach to mentoring is **shadowing**, or directly observing the work activities of the mentor by following the person around for a stated period of time, such as one day per month. The protégé might be invited to strategy meetings, visits with key customers, discussions with union leaders, and the like. The protégé makes observations about how the mentor handles situations, and a debriefing session might be held to discuss how and why certain tactics were used.

*Online Mentoring*    Online, or virtual, mentoring is popular because sending e-mail messages and social media posts helps overcome barriers created by geography, limited time, and voice mail. Exchanges of tweets are popular for mentoring also because of the brevity and pointedness, such as a mentor sending this message to the person being mentored, "Good presentation but avoid getting defensive when questioned. Ask for clarification rather than getting angry." Another positive feature of online mentoring is that the protégé might pose a career or work question to the mentor and receive a helpful reply that day. A major advantage of online mentoring is that it offers a wide pool of possible mentors and better matches between the mentor and the person mentored. Going online, you might be working in Chicago, yet have a good fit with a manager in San Francisco or London.

One innovation in online mentoring is websites that link mentors and mentored employees via profiling software, modeled after dating websites. Another innovation is virtual mentoring that makes face-to-face contact rare. With one system, an employee searching for a mentor logs onto an intranet and enters up to three career interests or skills he or she wants to develop. Video transmissions, such as webcams and Skype, can also be effective for mentoring.

Despite the efficiency advantage of online mentoring, some face-to-face contact with a mentor is recommended to help keep the relationship vibrant. Can you imagine somebody recommending you for promotion after having communicated with you exclusively by an e-mail and a website?

*Effective Mentoring Behaviors*    Because many mentors are leaders, effective mentors are likely to engage in many of the behaviors of effective leaders described throughout this book. Interviews with professionals in service firms, such as consultancies and accounting firms, suggest that the following behaviors in particular are characteristic of a good mentor:

- Highly credible, and whose integrity shows through whether the message delivered is positive or negative
- If necessary, will tell you things you do not want to hear, but listens to you

- Interacts with you in a way that makes you want to improve your effectiveness
- Makes you feel secure enough to be willing to take risks
- Helps boost your self-confidence enough to put aside your inner doubts and fears
- Encourages you to set stretch goals for yourself
- Presents opportunities and points to challenges you might not have seen on your own
- Instead of giving a definitive answer to your problem, shares a way of thinking about a problem you may not have thought about[24]

The behaviors just listed are examples of contributions by a mentor that can assist the protégé develop as a leader.

**Impact on Leadership**  Mentors enhance the career of protégés in many ways, such as by recommending them for promotion and helping them establish valuable contacts. High-level leaders sometimes use mentors as a way of obtaining useful feedback. Coaching can be a component of mentoring. Mentors demonstrating a high level of involvement tend to coach apprentices on how they handle certain leadership assignments. The mentor is usually not physically present when the protégé is practicing leadership. An important role for a mentor is to coach and guide the person being mentored on leadership situations the person is facing or will be facing. Jeff Immelt, the longtime CEO of General Electric, explains how a former mentor guided him in an aspect of strategic leadership:

> I started my career selling plastic in Detroit and my first boss was a sales manager, a guy named Pat Bayes, and he was awesome. He really taught me how to see the company through the eyes of the marketplace and through customers. He told me to have a healthy skepticism of headquarters, which I still have today. I think there's value in the CEO having a healthy skepticism of what corporate people do. He taught me in a constructive way how to be agnostic about corporates and see the company through the eyes of the customer. I still carry that with me today.[25]

A challenge in having a strong mentor is to at some point graduate from mentorship. Your mentor may have given you credibility and connections for a long time, but at some point you have to emerge from the shelter of that shadow in order to be perceived as a leader with your own strengths. Detaching yourself from a strong mentor is often facilitated by a few accomplishments of your own, outside your mentor's jurisdiction.[26]

A study conducted with 260 graduate business students and information systems students provides evidence that mentoring can impact a person's leadership behaviors. Approximately 80 percent of the students held full-time positions while attending school. The results of the study indicated that participants who had a mentor had slightly more political skill than did participants without a mentor. The presence of a mentor, in general, did not have an impact on leadership self-efficacy. (Political skill and self-efficacy were measured by questionnaires rather than by observing the participants in action.) Yet having a higher-quality mentoring relationship was associated with significantly higher leadership self-efficacy but not with increased political skill.[27] An important implication of this study is that having a good mentor can help a person develop leadership self-efficacy but might not further enhance political skill.

**The Importance of Having More than One Mentor**  Having a backup mentor is important because mentoring relationships are often fragile, and problems can occur. Also, your mentor in the company might leave the organization. As expressed by financial executive Michael J. Mardy, "You don't want to hitch your horse to one post."[28] One potential problem is that the mentor might perceive the protégé to be a rival and therefore attempt to damage the latter's career through such means as badmouthing. A more common problem is that the mentor may wind up neglecting the protégé because the former becomes preoccupied with his or her own job responsibilities. Having more than one mentor at a time helps alleviate both problems.[29]

Kate Mitchell, a venture capitalist, uses the term *composite mentor* to refer to a collection of people you draw lessons from, including enhancing strategic thinking and

## LEADERSHIP SKILL-BUILDING EXERCISE 15-1

### Finding a Mentor or Mentors for Leadership Development

The vast majority of successful leaders have had or currently have one or more mentors. Yet finding an effective mentor is not always so easy. Organize into brainstorming groups to identify at least three ways of finding a mentor who could be a positive force in your leadership development. Keep in mind that for a mentoring relationship to work you have to find a person with whom you have rapport. After the brainstorming groups have accomplished their task, share your results across groups. Look to see if the same method for identifying a mentor showed up in all the brainstorming groups. Also look for creative suggestions, and remember that "useful" is embedded in the definition of creativity.

creativity. A composite mentor is important because challenges typically evolve. Relying on multiple sources enables you to zero in on the best advice for different situations.[30]

Leadership Skill-Building Exercise 15-1 is designed to make you proactive bout finding a mentor.

## Leadership Development Programs

A time-honored strategy for developing prospective, new, and practicing leaders is to enroll them in leadership development programs. Many management development programs are also aimed at leadership development. The difference, however, is that management development programs offer courses that cover hundreds of topics within the functions of planning, organizing, controlling, and leading. Table 15-2 lists a sample of leadership development programs.

An analysis conducted by *Fortune* concluded that no matter what business a company is in, the real business is building leaders. Without a cadre of effective current and future leaders, a company would lose its competitive edge. Part of the reason is that leaders are either responsible for providing innovative ideas or for creating the conditions that foster innovation (refer back to Chapter 11).

Developing and training leaders is far more complex than merely sending aspiring leaders to a one-week seminar. The leadership development program has to be appropriately sponsored, carefully designed, and professionally executed. Although online learning supplements other forms of leadership development, face-to-face interaction with other leaders and course presenters will most likely remain popular. Leadership development programs for C-level executives are unlikely to be conducted online because executives believe that face-to-face contact with professors and other executives is an important part of the learning process.

### Types of Leadership Development Programs

In practice, the various programs for developing leaders often overlap. For ease of comprehension, we divide these programs into six categories: feedback-intensive programs, those based on skills, conceptual knowledge and awareness, socialization, action learning, and coaching and psychotherapy. We also comment on the effectiveness of leadership development.

*Feedback-Intensive Programs*  As implied at many places in this text, an important vehicle for developing as a leader is to obtain feedback on various aspects of your behavior. A **feedback-intensive development program** helps leaders develop by seeing more clearly their patterns of behaviors, the reasons for such behaviors, and the impact of these behaviors and attitudes on their effectiveness. Such a program also helps leaders or potential

**TABLE 15-2** A Sampling of Leadership Development Programs Offered by Universities and Training and Development Firms

High-Performance Leadership

Strategic Business Leadership: Engagement, Performance, and Execution

Transforming Your Leadership Strategy

Reinventing Your Business Strategy

Business Ethics for the Professional Manager

The Disney Approach to Leadership Excellence

Leading Change and Innovation

Building Better Work Relationships

Think Like a Leader

Managing People for Maximum Performance

Building Leadership Capital

Developing Exemplary Leaders: Key Practices for Achieving Results

The Voice of Leadership: How Leaders Inspire, Influence, and Achieve Results

Leading Into the Future: Managing in a Changing World

Capitalizing on Social Media for Marketing and Internal Communications

The Power of Persuasion

*Note:* Organizations offering such seminars and courses are the Wharton School of the University of Pennsylvania, the University of Michigan Business School, the University of Chicago Graduate School of Business, the Cornell University School of Industrial and Labor Relations, the Northwestern Kellogg School of Management, the Massachusetts Institute of Technology, MIT Sloan School of Management, the Center for Creative Leadership, Chicago Booth (the University of Chicago), Dale Carnegie Training, the World Business Forum, Stanford Executive Briefings and DVDs and Video Streaming, Tuck Executive Program at Dartmouth, and the Disney Institute.

leaders find more constructive ways of achieving their goals. 360-degree is widely used in organizations of every type, including corporate government, non-profit, military, and education. As described in Chapter 4, 360-degree feedback is a prominent process for facilitating leadership development.[31]

An instructive point about feedback-intensive programs, as well as practically all forms of leadership development, is that the person being developed needs to follow up. If you learn that you tend to shut people off with an angry smirk on your face, unless you practice removing that smirk, you have not gained much from the feedback. In the words of well-known leadership coach Marshall Goldsmith, "If you go to a class and don't do any follow-up, it's a complete waste of time."[32]

**Skill-Based Programs**   Skill training in leadership development involves acquiring abilities and techniques that can be converted into action. Acquiring knowledge precedes acquiring skills, but in skill-based training the emphasis is on learning how to apply knowledge. A typical example would be for a manager to develop coaching skills, so he or she can be a more effective face-to-face leader. Skills training, in short, involves a considerable element of how to.

Five different methods are often used in skill-based leadership training: lecture, case study, role play, behavioral role modeling, and simulations. Because the first three methods are quite familiar, only the last two are described here. *Behavioral role modeling* is an extension of role playing and is based on social learning theory. You first observe a model of appropriate behavior, and then you role-play the behavior and gather feedback. A person might observe a video of a trainer giving positive reinforcement, then role-play giving positive reinforcement. Finally, the classroom trainer and the other participants would offer feedback on performance.

*Simulations* give participants the opportunity to work on a problem that simulates a real organization. In a typical simulation, participants receive a digital packet of information about a fictitious company. The participants are given details such as the organization chart, the company's financial status, descriptions of the various departments, and key problems facing the organization and/or organizational units. Participants then play the roles of company leaders and devise solutions to the problems. During the debriefing, participants receive feedback on the content of their solutions to problems and the methods they used. The group might be told, for example, "Your decision to form a strategic alliance was pretty good, but I would have liked to have seen more group decision making."

According to simulation developer and founder of the online training company, Enspire Learning, Bjorn Billhardt, the most effective training involves competition. He says that having teams go up against each other is a powerful motivator for people to test and hone their skills. Another advantage of simulations for leadership training is that making mistakes and learning from a simulation is better than failing in the outside world.[33]

Simulations are also used to give managers the opportunity to work on problems that approximate those faced by the company. For example at Macy's Leadership Institute in Cincinnati, Ohio teams of four or five middle managers tackle problems such as contending with an underperforming juniors department.[34]

*Conceptual Knowledge and Awareness Programs*    A standard university approach to leadership development is to equip people with a conceptual understanding of leadership. The concepts are typically supplemented by experiential activities such as role playing and cases. Conceptual knowledge is very important because it alerts the leader to information that will make a difference in leadership. For example, if a person studies how a leader brings about transformations, he or she can put these ideas into practice. Table 15-2 presents examples of the types of conceptual knowledge contained in leadership development programs. One of the reasons for the continuing acceptance of university-based conceptual knowledge programs for leadership development is that these programs often address topics of immediate concern to business. For example, programs have been developed in recent years to help managers provide leadership in using social media, particularly for users of mobile devices, to the company's advantage.

*Socialization Programs*    From the company standpoint, an essential type of leadership development program emphasizes becoming socialized—becoming acclimated to the company and accepting its vision and values. Senior executives make presentations in these programs because they serve as role models who thoroughly understand the vision and values participants are expected to perpetuate.[35] Many of the other types of programs presented so far also include a segment on socialization, particularly in the kickoff session. Quite frequently, the chief executive makes a presentation of the company's vision and values. An important purpose of a socialization program is to help leaders sustain the organizational culture, such as placing a high priority on honest dealing with each other and customers.

*Action Learning Programs*    A directly practical approach to leadership development is for leaders and potential leaders to work together in groups to solve organizational problems outside their usual sphere of influence. You will recall that action learning is part of the learning organization, as described in Chapter 13. Much of the development relates to problem solving and creativity, yet collaborating with a new set of people from your firm can also enhance interpersonal skills.

About one decade ago, executives at Goodyear Tire & Rubber Co, decided to change the business from a volume tire supplier to one that focused on market segments, such as tires for construction equipment. A deep leadership bench was required to bring about these changes. An action learning format was included in developing the necessary number of leaders. (Other aspects of the leadership development program included virtual learning overseen by a business school professor.) Program participants identified areas they wanted to learn more about, and found learning partners to assist them. The executive team developed the learning projects by identifying real business issues. High-impact projects were chosen, including a cost-reduction plan that had a major impact on the supply chain. One measure of the success of the program is that within a year after the program began, one half of the members received new assignments or increased responsibilities, and 22 percent received promotions.[36]

*Coaching and Psychotherapy*    Executive coaching as described in Chapter 10 is clearly a form of leadership development because the managers coached receive advice and encouragement in relation to their leadership skills. A coach, for example, might advise a leader that giving more recognition for good performance would make him a more dynamic leader. Coaching is perhaps the most direct approach to leadership development because the person might be able to improve in an area that is preventing him or her from becoming a leader, or blocking further progress as a leader.

Leadership coach Julie Cohen describes how she helped an SAP sales support executive move into a new leadership role by reshaping his image of being quiet and reflective. He was encouraged to present himself as an innovator and expert on public sector clients. Cohen suggested that he promote himself and his skills rather than assuming "people would see his ability and tap him on the shoulder." The client advanced so rapidly in his interpersonal skills that an SAP executive commented, "I barely recognized him."[37]

Another highly personal way of enhancing leadership effectiveness is to undergo treatment for emotional problems that could be blocking leadership effectiveness. For example, a leader who has difficulty giving recognition might not improve in response to coaching. The person might have underlying problems of being so hostile toward people that he or she really does not want to boost their morale. Psychiatrist Kerry Sulkowicz notes that change from psychotherapy does not always take place quickly. However, executives are accustomed to getting quick results, which can make them highly motivated patients.[38]

In general, leaders who score low on the personality dimension of emotional stability might become more effective in their interpersonal relationships with the benefit of psychotherapy. Some of the bizarre behavior exhibited by executives, such as swearing at and belittling subordinates, sexually harassing subordinates, and arbitrarily firing workers, are symptoms of emotional instability. The hostility is often directed at people who disagree with them, even about technical and design issues.

*Evaluation of Leadership Development Programs*    Many companies evaluate their leadership development programs to see if they are cost effective. In a large company, for example, a comparison would be made of the ratings from superiors and subordinates for those leaders who participated in the program versus those who did not. Another method of evaluating the outcome of a leadership development program would be to compare the financial results of participants versus nonparticipants.

According to a leadership development benchmarking survey of 329 organizations around the globe, about 75 percent of organizations said their leadership development programs are not very effective. Yet the satisfaction with the programs was high under certain conditions: A specific leadership development strategy was in place; the financial investment in leadership development is substantial; and the leadership development program has been in existence five years or longer.[39]

## Leadership Succession

In a well-managed organization, replacements for executives who quit, retire, or are dismissed are chosen through **leadership succession**, an orderly process of identifying and grooming people to replace managers. Succession planning is vital to the long-term health of an organization, and therefore an important responsibility of senior leadership. Instead of engaging in a flurry of activity after a key person leaves the organization, the planning is done in an orderly way over time.

Succession planning is linked to leadership development in two important ways. First, being groomed as a successor is part of leadership development. Second, the process of choosing and fostering a successor is part of a manager's own development. Our approach to understanding the leadership aspects of succession focuses on five topics: (1) how the board chooses a new chief officer; (2) the emotional aspects of leadership succession; (3) developing a pool of successors; (4) promotion from within; and (5) characteristics of an effective leadership development program. Understanding these factors should lead to more success in new appointments to leadership positions.

## How the Board Chooses a Successor

A major responsibility of the board of directors is to select a successor to the chief executive, typically a CEO. The general approach is to follow standard principles of human resource selection, such as thoroughly screening candidates, including speaking to several people who have worked with the individual. Conducting a background investigation to uncover any possible scandalous or illegal behavior is also important. When the successor is an outsider, boards consistently use executive search firms (also known as *headhunters*) to locate one or several candidates. Even when the board has an outside candidate in mind, a search firm might be hired to act as an intermediary.

A major challenge in choosing a new CEO is that many executives who want the top job lack experience as the chief executive officer. Yet few other roles in a company adequately prepare someone to become a CEO. Boards often select a person who has general manager experience, thinking that such a role is comparable to that of a CEO. Josi Trammell, a contributor to *Forbes*, thinks that being a small-company CEO is better preparation for being a CEO at a larger company than is general manager experience.[40]

George D. Kennedy, a person with experience on many boards, provides a few specifics of a representative approach to selecting an internal candidate for the top executive position. First, the information from a development program for successors must be carefully reviewed, including documentation of performance. Second, the board should have direct and regular contact with all of the promising candidates. Some of the contact should be formal; for example, the candidate should make regular presentations at board meetings. Informal connections are also important. Board members should invest the time to develop a feel for the personal chemistry of the candidates through such means as casual conversations over dinner and lunch.[41]

Whether selecting an insider or an outsider to succeed a given leader, the board is encouraged to obtain objective data about the candidate's performance in addition to opinions about his or her effectiveness.[42] Among these objective performance indicators would be profits, changes in stock price, new product introductions, employee turnover, and cost control.

## The Emotional Aspects of Leadership Succession

Leadership succession should not be regarded as a detached, objective management process. Even financially independent executives are likely to experience an emotional loss when they are replaced; they might yearn for the power and position they once possessed. Leadership succession in family-owned firms is a highly emotional process for many reasons. Family members may fight over who is best qualified to take the helm, or the owner and founder may not feel that any family member is qualified. An intensely emotional situation exists when the owner would like a family member to succeed him or her, yet no family member is willing. The business may therefore have to be sold or simply abandoned; in any case, its identity will be lost.

The emotional aspects of leadership succession are also evident when a business founder is replaced by another leader, whether or not the enterprise is a family business. After the sale of his or her company, the business founder often stays on in some capacity, perhaps as a consultant or chair. Watching the new owner manage the business can be uncomfortable for the founder. The issue transcends concerns about delegation.

Entrepreneurial leaders typically are emotionally involved in the firms they have founded and find it difficult to look on while somebody else operates the firm.

Emotional reactions to leadership succession also take place at the workgroup level, as described in a theory developed by Gary A. Ballinger and F. David Schoorman. For example, when a departing leader is well liked by the group or team, it will be more difficult for the new leader to exert his or her authority or to be accepted. Another problem is that when the previous leader was well liked, turnover in the group will be higher and productivity might be lower. Yet, on the positive side, if the previous leader was disliked, turnover might be lower and productivity might be higher.[43]

## Developing a Pool of Successors

Developing a pool of successors goes beyond succession planning, which usually involves identifying one or two candidates for a specific job. The following steps are involved in developing a pool of successors (or succession management):[44]

- Evaluate the extent of an organization's pending leadership shortage. Planning should begin several years in advance of when the new leaders will be needed.
- Identify needed executive competencies based on the firm's future business needs, values, and strategies.
- Identify high-potential individuals for possible inclusion in the pool, and assess these individuals to identify strengths and developmental needs to determine who will stay in the high-potential pool.
- Establish an individually tailored developmental program for each high-potential candidate that includes leadership development programs, job rotation, special assignments, and mentoring. Rising stars should be given the opportunity to change responsibilities every three to five years.
- Select and place people into senior jobs based on their performance, experience, and potential. While in these positions, the leaders should have access to board members including making presentations. The managers develop a sense of what matters to directors, and directors get to see firsthand the talent in the pipeline.
- Continuously monitor the program and give it top management support.

Developing a pool of candidates, therefore, combines evaluating potential with giving high-potential individuals the right type of developmental experiences. To the extent that these procedures are implemented, a leadership shortage in a given firm is less likely to take place.

To help preserve a strong pool of candidates for future assignments, financial services giant Aetna focuses on mentoring young managers with high potential. A specific program is that eight high-level Aetna managers, including the chief executive, meet one-on-one with eight target candidates for an hour each month for a year. To qualify, the protégés must have at least a decade of experience at the company and have received high-performance evaluations.[45]

## Promotion from Within

A continuing debate related to succession planning is whether a company should promote an insider or an outsider to a top position. Approximately 20–30 percent of boards replace outgoing CEOs with outside executives.[46] Yet research and analysis suggest that promoting insiders with an outside perspective may be the best solution. Joseph Bower found in his analysis of 1,800 successions that companies performed substantially better when they appointed insiders to CEO.

Other researchers have reached similar conclusions. A study conducted by the consultancy Booz & Co. found that CEOs hired from outside a company are more than twice as likely to be dismissed as those promoted from within. A major problem is that the outsider often does not understand how to bring about change within the company.[47]

Furthermore, newcomers often misread the political situation or overestimate the organization's willingness to abandon old traditions and behaviors.[48] An example of misreading the political situation would be not recognizing who are the most influential people at the company.

Recognizing the potential advantages of promotion from within, Macy's recently appointed an insider, Jeff Genette, as the new CEO replacing a longtime CEO (as described in the case opener to Chapter 2). Gennette was serving as the company president, and had been with the company for thirty-three years. The board thought that he was the right person to help Macy's compete in a quickly changing retail market.[49]

Promotion from within also offers the advantage of more hope to insiders because they believe they have more opportunity for advancement within their own company. Company insiders promoted to a top position know the company, its culture, and its people but often do not see clearly the need for radical change. Also, their many political ties may inhibit them from making some necessary personnel shifts. Outsiders may recognize the need for a new approach but may be limited because they do not understand the company culture or the industry. Bower recommends that companies nurture *insider–outsiders*—internal candidates who have developed an outside perspective.

Insider–outsiders are frequently those who have considerable experience away from the company mainstream (and away from headquarters), and experience in taking on challenging opportunities. A frequent example is an executive who spends several years running a division of the company in another country. For instance, a U.S. executive at Walmart might be assigned to the position of president of Walmart of Canada for several years.

A study indicated that board members who are appointed as CEO outperformed other types of candidates because they represent a strong blend of insider and outsider. Board members have more company knowledge than a pure outsider. Yet, at the same time, they don't have the constraints of a pure insider with respect to making politically unpopular decisions or bring about painful changes. For example, it is often difficult for an insider to lay off a well-liked but underperforming executive.[50]

## Characteristics of an Effective Leadership Development Program

Leadership development programs have been presented in a separate section in this chapter, yet leadership development also includes succession, and promotion from within. Here we highlight five characteristics of an effective leadership development program.[51]

First, the program *should involve both cognitive and experiential components.* For example, the leader might study advanced coaching techniques, and then try out these techniques in role playing or on the job. Second, *the developers should have both applicable academic credentials and experience in working with managers and leaders.* Academic credentials are particularly useful because the leadership development specialist is more likely to take a research-based view of what is likely to work rather than simply promoting a fad.

Third, *senior executives should participate in program.* The participation of C-suite members enhances the credibility of the program, and also increases the probability that the content of the program will be implemented in the organization. For example if middle managers are taught how to think strategically, executives should also implement more strategic thinking.

Fourth, *a key part of leadership development is for leaders to understand their own strengths and weaknesses.* 360-degree evaluations are useful in helping leaders develop more self-awareness, such as helping a person know what he or she has to do to become a better listener. Fifth, *heavy emphasis must be placed on sustained use of what knowledge and skills are learned in the leadership development program.* One of the most frequent criticisms of development program is that the leader is a changed person for about one week after the program, but then reverts to his or her typical behavior.

## Challenges of Being a New Leader

People participate in leadership development programs for two broad purposes: (1) preparing to become a leader for the first time, or (2) enhancing their leadership skills, knowledge, and behavior for a current position or advancement into more leadership responsibility.

Everything that has been written in this book and discussed in your leadership course fits these two broad purposes. Another way of preparing for becoming a leader for the first time is to think through some of the inevitable challenges in the role. The information about the rewards and frustrations of occupying a leadership role in Chapter 1 points to the challenges of occupying a formal leadership position for the first time. In addition, consider these five additional challenges for the first-time leader:

1. *Uncertainty about how much time to spend leading versus doing individual tasks.* From the first-level supervisor of entry-level workers to the chairperson of the board, leaders spend some time as individual contributors, including preparing budgets, thinking of ideas for new products, and making financial deals. As a new leader, you have to work with your manager and perhaps your direct reports to find the right balance between doing and leading.

2. *Overcoming the resentment of the people in the group who wanted your leadership position.* If you are selected from among the group to be the new leader, you will have to deal with the resentment and envy of several direct reports who wanted your position. It can be helpful to deal openly with the issue with such statements as, "I know that other people would be equally qualified to be the leader of the group. Yet management has chosen me for this position, at least for now. I respect your expertise, and I need your contribution. I also want your respect for me in my job as the chosen leader."

3. *Building relationships and fostering teamwork quickly enough.* As a new leader, a high priority is to build constructive relationships with subordinates as quickly as possible, using many of the techniques described in Chapter 9. Several direct reports who were your former coworkers may attempt to manipulate you and take advantage of prior friendships to receive special treatment. It is essential to build a professional, merit-based team climate as soon as possible. In the words of career coach Aya Fubara Eneli: "Friendships work best between equals. If you were already friends with some of the staff, expect those relationships to change. It's difficult to be a friend while giving orders and judging performance."[52]

4. *Having realistic expectations about how much you can accomplish right away.* The role of a leader/manager is not like that of a house painter—you typically do not see sparkling results right away. Patience is necessary. Many organizational leaders as well as elected officials proclaim, "Everything will be different from day one." Leadership involves building relationships, so the process will take more time than the implied in the two previous statements.

5. *Overcoming the need to be liked by everybody.* The most admired leaders at every level are rarely liked by everybody. By the nature of their roles, leaders make decisions that not everybody agrees with. The changes you bring about may hurt the feelings of some people and jeopardize their positions. Your role is to establish and implement goals that will result in the greatest good.

Leadership Skill-Building Exercise 15-2 may give you a few good insights into the type of leader you are becoming and how well you fit the role of a new or experienced leader.

# LEADERSHIP SKILL-BUILDING EXERCISE 15-2

### Building for the Future

Our close-to-final skill-building exercise, the use of a feedback circle, encompasses many aspects of leadership covered in this and the previous fourteen chapters. Ten members of the class arrange their chairs in a circle. One person is selected as the feedback target, and the other nine people take turns giving him or her supportive feedback. Assume it is Linda's turn. Each person in the circle gives Linda two pieces of feedback: (1) her best leadership attribute, and (2) how she needs to develop for the future.

The feedback should take about thirty seconds per feedback giver. After receiving input from all of the circle members, Linda is free to comment. It is then the next person's turn to be the feedback target. Class members who are not in the circle observe the dynamics of what is happening and report their observations after the circle finishes. With diligence, the whole process will take about ninety minutes. If time permits, a new feedback circle can form. Alternatively, the class can break into several circles that operate simultaneously, or run just one circle with ten volunteers.

## SUMMARY

Leadership and management development are widely practiced in a variety of organizations and take many forms, including self-development. Self-awareness involves the insightful processing of feedback about oneself to improve personal effectiveness. Single-loop learning occurs when learners seek minimum feedback that may substantially confront their basic ideas or actions. Double-loop learning occurs when people use feedback to confront the validity of the goal or values implicit in the situation; it enables the leader to learn and profit from failure. A promising area of self-awareness is for leaders to recognize their standing on two key dimensions of leadership: forceful versus enabling, and strategy versus operational.

Leadership development requires considerable self-discipline. For example, self-discipline is needed to monitor one's behavior to ensure that the necessary self-development takes place.

Education, leadership experience, and mentoring are all major contributors to leadership development. Most high-level leaders are intelligent, well-informed people who gather knowledge throughout their career. Learning agility is also important. The best experiences for leadership development are those that realistically challenge the manager. An important part of capitalizing on challenging experiences is for the leader/manager to be given leeway in how to resolve the problem. Two important aspects of leadership experience are work associates and the task itself (such as a complex and ambiguous assignment). An extreme approach to developing leadership skills is to be assigned responsibility for an area in which you lack the appropriate skills or knowledge of the business. Being in a learning modes also facilitates learning from experience.

Broad experience is important for leadership development, as suggested by membership on a cross-functional team. An effective type of broad experience early in a career is to perform technical work in one's specialty, combined with frontline supervision. People who profit from their experience have good potential for leadership.

Another experience-based way to develop leadership capability is to receive mentoring. Although usually an informal relationship, mentoring can also be assigned. The human resource department often coordinates a formal mentoring program. Shadowing is a form of mentoring, and online mentoring is widely used. Mentors enhance the career of protégés in many ways, such as by recommending them for promotion and helping them establish valuable contacts. Also, the mentor can serve as a model for effective (or ineffective) leadership. Having more than one mentor is helpful because a mentoring relationship can fail.

Feedback-intensive development programs help leaders develop by seeing more clearly their patterns of behavior, the reasons for such behaviors, and the impact of these behaviors and attitudes on their effectiveness. Skill training in leadership development involves acquiring abilities and techniques that can be converted into action. Such training involves a considerable element of *how to*. Five methods of skill-based training are lecture, case study, role play, behavior role modeling, and simulations. During simulations, participants play the role of company leaders and devise solutions to problems. Simulations can also involve working on hypothetical company problems. Feedback on performance is provided.

A standard university approach to leadership development is to equip people with a conceptual understanding of leadership. The concepts can be applied to leadership situations. From the company standpoint, an essential type of leadership development is becoming socialized in the company vision and values. Action learning is a directly practical approach to leadership development and may be directed at areas outside the participant's expertise. Coaching and psychotherapy are two highly personal ways of developing as a leader. Psychotherapy is called for when the leader has emotional problems that lower his or her effectiveness.

Leadership succession is linked to leadership development because being groomed as a successor is part of a leader's development. Boards of directors use standard selection methods in choosing a CEO. In addition, they look for both formal and informal contact with insiders. When recruiting an outsider, organizations often employ executive search firms. Leadership succession is highly emotional for the leader who is being replaced, especially when a founder sells a business. The succession problem in a family business often leads to conflict among family members. Large family-run businesses are more likely to identify leadership successors. One way to cope with potential shortages of leaders is to identify a pool of high-potential individuals and provide them with developmental experiences. Promotion from within to top-level leadership positions is often more effective than recruiting an outsider. Research and analysis suggest that promoting company insiders with an outside perspective may be the best solution to succession through an internal versus an external candidate.

One way of preparing for becoming a first-time leader is to think through some of the inevitable challenges in the role, including the following: uncertainty about how much time for leading versus doing individual tasks; overcoming resentment of people who wanted your job; quickly building relationships and fostering teamwork; having realistic expectations about quick accomplishments; and overcoming the need to be liked by everybody.

## KEY TERMS

**self-awareness** 398
**single-loop learning** 398
**double-loop learning** 398

**self-discipline** 399
**mentor** 407
**shadowing** 407

**feedback-intensive development program** 409
**leadership succession** 412

## GUIDELINES FOR ACTION AND SKILL DEVELOPMENT

A major determinant of whether a person will develop as a leader later in life is the *motivation to lead*. Typically, this motivation develops early in life. The motivation is manifested in such activities as volunteering for leadership roles, as well as taking the initiative to lead in sport, club, or neighborhood activities.[53] It is therefore important to assume leadership roles in both work and personal life as early in your career as possible.

An important method for enhancing both the acceptance and the effectiveness of leadership development is needs analysis, the diagnosis of the needs for development. A needs analysis is based on the idea that there are individual differences among leaders and future leaders. For example, Jasmine might have excellent conceptual knowledge about leadership but limited team experience. She might be a good candidate for outdoor training. Jordan might be an excellent team leader with limited conceptual knowledge. He might be a good candidate for a leadership development program concentrating on formal knowledge about leadership. Sources of data for assessing leadership developmental needs include the following:

1. Self-perceptions of developmental needs, including the results of many of the diagnostic instruments presented in this text
2. Perceptions by superiors, subordinates, and peers of the person's developmental needs, including 360-degree survey results
3. Psychological evaluation of developmental needs
4. A statement of organizational needs for development, such as the importance of leaders who can deal effectively with diversity (within the company, with customers, and globally)

Multiple sources of data are useful because of possible errors in perception, biases, and favoritism.

### Discussion Questions and Activities

1. The Fire Department of New York (FDNY) offers a leadership development program that includes simulating being a firefighter by going through emergency drills such as rescuing passengers from a subway accident. Assuming that you have the physical capabilities, would you be willing

to participate in such a challenge as part of your leadership and teamwork skills development? Explain your logic.

2. Many business executives believe that playing team sports helps a person develop as a leader. Based on your knowledge of leadership development, where do you stand on this issue?

3. In terms of developing as a leader, should an executive take seriously nasty comments made about him or her on Facebook, Twitter, and Instagram?

4. Suppose you aspired to become a senior manager in a large company. How would working as an office supervisor, production supervisor, or manager in a quick-service restaurant help you achieve your goal?

5. Why is being a member of a cross-functional team considered to be helpful experience for a future leader?

6. According to the Corporate Productivity Institute, companies whose leaders participated in a leadership development program experienced better customer satisfaction, more revenue growth, and reduced employee turnover. Why might have such good results come about?

7. Identify at least one developmental need with respect to leadership skills for the current president of the United States. Point to any specific behavior of the president that indicates the need for the particular development you specify. (Attempt to be objective rather than political in your answer.)

8. What can you as a parent, future parent, or close relative do to help a child under ten-years old become a leader later in life?

9. Ask an experienced leader what he or she thinks is the most effective method of developing leadership skills. Bring your findings back to class.

10. Now that you have completed a course in leadership, what do you think of this ancient adage: "Leadership shouldn't be a popularity contest."?

## LEADERSHIP CASE PROBLEM A

### Holly, the Potential Team Leader

Holly works as an environmental engineer at a pollution prevention institute in Philadelphia, Pennsylvania. The institute is funded by the state, and helps companies become more sustainable for workers, the public, the environment, and the economy. The institute has been growing based on the many useful and money-saving suggestions offered to business firms. For example, Holly and her colleagues have help companies save money by recycling water and reducing food waste. The demands on Holly's team have expanded to the point that the manager of the group, Malcolm, has decided to create the position of team leader.

Today Malcolm, the director of the institute, is interviewing Holly to recommend whether she should be promoted to team leader. If Malcolm thinks Holly is qualified to be team leader, she will be interviewed also by two other managers at the institute. A partial transcript of the interview follows:

*Malcolm:* As I explained in my e-mail, we want to talk about the possibilities of you becoming the first team leader for the environmental engineering group. Your performance has been outstanding. I am aware also that you majored in environmental engineering, and took a cross-major in business administration. Do you have any interest in becoming the team leader of your group?

*Holly:* The thoughts of becoming a team leader intrigue me. Yet, I would only want to be the team leader if I still had the opportunity to do environmental engineering. I am passionate about my chosen field.

*Malcolm:* What kind of leadership experiences have you had so far, both on and off the job?

*Holly:* I've always loved technical work and math since early childhood. As a teenager I was a little nerdy (laughs). So I didn't jump in and do leadership. Yet I did form an environmental club in high school that lasted about six months. We would go around different neighborhoods giving people tips on how to protect the environment if we saw a problem. Come to think of it though, I did head up a subgroup in our department to analyze what toxic and recyclable materials were being placed in dumpsters. It was a dirty job, but somebody had to do it (laughs).

*Malcolm:* What about your personality, Holly? What leadership traits do you have?

*Holly:* People do ask my opinion about environmental engineering topics, as well as information technology problems. I get along with people pretty well, and I also set a good example of being a hard worker. I think that's important for a leader.

*Malcolm:* What is your long-term career goal?

*Holly:* I wanted to be known as an environmental engineer who helped create a better environment without being a fanatic or a pest.

*Malcolm:* Would you accept the team leadership position if it were offered to you within two weeks.

*Holly:* My tentative answer is yes, but I would have to have more details about what the position would entail. Becoming a team leader would be a big step for me.

*Malcolm:* It's been a pleasure interviewing you, and you will be hearing back from me soon.

## Questions

1. Based on her interview responses, explain whether Malcolm should recommend that Holly be promoted to team leader.
2. What has Holly revealed that would suggest she might be an effective team leader?

## ASSOCIATED ROLE PLAY

One student plays the role of Malcolm who regards Holly as a good possibility for the team leadership position. However, he is going to dig deeper today as to whether Holly has leadership potential. Another student plays the role of Holly who has decided she really wants the position. As a result, she will attempt to present to convince Malcolm that she is the woman for the job. Feedback from other students is welcome in terms of Holly's qualification and the interviewing skills of Malcolm.

## LEADERSHIP CASE PROBLEM B

### Kaitlin the New Mentor

Kaitlin is the sales manager at a lumber supply company, so successful in its geographic region that it employs 250 full-time workers and 50 part-time workers. In addition to selling lumber to builders, the company also makes steps, doors, deck material, and molding. Kurt, the CEO, asked Kaitlin if she would mentor Misty, a newly hired marketing researcher. Kurt explained to Kaitlin that the marketing research position is vital to the future of the company. He believes that the market for the company's main product line is leveling off, and that a market researcher might be able to explore new markets and product expansion for the company.

Kaitlin said that she was eager to mentor Misty because she thinks that the new market researcher has considerable potential to help the company. Kaitlin said, "I've already begun mentoring Misty, and she seems receptive." Three days later, Kaitlin met with Misty for the first mentoring session. The session included the following comments by Kaitlin:

"Misty, as your official mentor, I want you to do the following things. First, dress more professionally. It looks like you outfit yourself at stores for low-income people. I will recommend a few better stores for you in an e-mail. Second, I have a list of websites I want you to track every day. I have sent you an e-mail listing these sites because they are excellent for picking up marketing trends. Third, I want you to spend at least one day a week out in field speaking to new potential users of our products."

Three weeks later, Kaitlin sent Misty a text message saying, "Report back to me immediately on your progress. Send me a summary of your website searches. Also, send me a few photos of any new office clothing you have bought."

Later that day, Kaitlin sent Misty a brief text message that stated, "Remember to focus on your daily work tasks. Don't be a dreamer."

During lunch with Pete, the company information systems administrator, he asked Misty how she enjoyed being mentored by Kaitlin. Misty responded, "Did you say being mentored or being smothered?"

### Questions

1. What is your evaluation of the most likely effectiveness of Kaitlin's approach to mentoring?
2. What recommendations would you make to Kaitlin to improve her mentoring effectiveness?
3. What do you recommend Misty do to profit more from the mentoring and leadership provided by Kaitlin?

## ASSOCIATED ROLE PLAY

One student plays the role of Kaitlin who meets with Misty to discuss how well she is responding to her mentoring. Kaitlin is concerned that Misty is resisting her mentoring and leadership. One student plays the role of Misty who feels that she is being micromanaged rather than mentored. Yet she does not want to offend her boss, and she believes that the marketing research position will be a great learning opportunity.

## LEADERSHIP SKILL-BUILDING EXERCISE 15-3

### My Leadership Portfolio

The final entry for your leadership portfolio deals more with the future than the present. As you build your leadership career in either a formal or informal leadership position, update your journal from time to time, perhaps once a quarter. Review what experiences you have had that contribute to your development as a leader. Entries might take forms such as the following:

- In January, my company sent me to a seminar about dealing with difficult people. I came away with a few good insights about helping to turn around a difficult person, such as explaining how his or her behavior was hurting productivity and morale. I also learned that many difficult people are crying out for attention, so I will try to pay more attention to a difficult person should I encounter one.

- We had a major flood in the area last week, and our office became inundated. We had to do something quick before we were damaged so badly that we could not serve our customers. Our supervisor was out of town. I called her on her phone and asked for her authorization to be in charge of organizing our salvage operation. I spearheaded an effort that helped salvage a lot of equipment and computer records. I think I really polished my crisis management skills.

## LEADERSHIP SKILL-BUILDING EXERCISE 15-4

### Analyzing a Local Leader

As an individual or group project, identify a leader in your community who you would like to analyze from the standpoints of strengths, weaknesses, and needs for development. Among the possibilities of a leader to analyze would be a prominent business person, the president of your learning institution, or an athletic coach. Use information from anywhere in the text, plus your own thoughts, to identify both the positive and negative personal characteristics, along with the developmental needs of this particular leader.

If this is a group project, look to see if there is any consistency across groups with respect to the traits, behaviors, and developmental needs of the leader chosen. If you think the analysis is constructive, you might send a copy to the leader in question.

## NOTES

1. Original story based on facts and observations in the following sources: Melanie Dorange, "Al Bustan Palace, A Ritz-Carlton Hotel Develops the Next Generation of Omani Hoteliers," *Al Bustan Palace* (www.ritzcarlton.com), pp. 1–4. Retrieved September 11, 2016; "Ritz-Carlton Internships," *The Ritz-Carlton*® (www.marriott.com), Retrieved September 12, 2016; "The Voyage Global Leadership Development Program," (www.marriott.com), September 12, 2016, pp. 1–2.

2. Data presented in Jeffrey Pfeffer, "Leadership BS," *HR Magazine*, July/August 2016, p. 24.

3. Sydney Finkelstein, "Why We Loathe Leadership Training," *BBC – Capital* (www.bbc.com), July 20, 2016, p. 1.

4. Ronit Kark, "Games Managers Play: Play as a Form of Leadership Development," *Academy of Management Learning & Education*, vol.10, no. 3, September 13, 2011, p. 507.

5. David V. Day et al., "Advances in Leader and Leadership Development: A Review of 25 Years of Research and Theory," *The Leadership Quarterly*, February 2014, p. 68.

6. Scott N. Taylor, Mo Wang, and Yujie Zhan, "Going Beyond Self-Other Rating Comparison to Measure Leader Self-Awareness," *Journal of Leadership Studies*, vol. 6, no. 2, 2012, p. 7.

7. Robert Hogan and Rodney Warrenfeltz, "Educating the Modern Manager," *Academy of Management Learning and Education*, March 2003, p. 74.

8. Chris Argyris, "Teaching Smart People How to Learn," *Harvard Business Review*, May–June 1991, pp. 99–109; Chris Argyris, "Double-Loop Learning, Teaching, and Research," *Academy of Management Learning and Education*, vol. 1, no. 2, December 2002, p. 206.

9. Bob Kaplan and Rob Kaiser, *The Versatile Leader: Make the Most of Your Strengths—Without Overdoing It* (San Francisco: Pfeiffer, 2006).

10. Roseanne J. Foti, Bethany C. Bray, Nicole J. Thompson, and Sarah F. Allgood, "Know Thyself, Know Thy Leader: Contributions of a Pattern-Oriented Approach to Examining Leader Perceptions," *The Leadership Quarterly*, August 5, 2012, p. 703.

11. Herminia Ibarra, "The Authenticity Paradox," *Harvard Business Review*, January–February 2015, p. 59.

12. Cited in Jared Sandberg, "Cubicle Culture: Why Learn and Grow on the Job? It's Easier to Feign Infallibility," *The Wall Street Journal*, January 22, 2008, p. B1.

13. Cited in Vadim Liberman, "Will Your People Be Ready?" *The Conference Board Review*, December 10, 2016, p. 5.

14. Dori Meinert, "Fake It 'Til You Make It'," *HR Magazine*, October 2015, p. 19.

15. Claudio Fernández-Aráoz, "To Grow as a Leader, Seek More Complex Assignments," *Harvard Business Review* (https://hbr.org), July 20, 2016, p. 2.

16. Morgan W. McCall, "Leadership Development Through Experience," *Academy of Management Executive*, August 2004, pp. 127–130; Jean Martin and Conrad Schmidt, "How to Keep Your Top Talent," *Harvard Business Review*, May 2010, p. 58.

17. "How Great Leaders Benefit from Failure," *Manager's Edge*, November 2004, p. 3; Steven Snyder, *Leadership and the Art of the Struggle: How Great Leaders Grow through Challenge and Adversity* (San Francisco: Berrett-Koehler Publishers, 2013).

18. Cynthia D. McCauley and Morgan W. McCall Jr. (Eds.), "Using Experience to Develop Leadership Talent: How Organizations Leverage On-the-Job Development" (San Francisco, CA: Wiley, 2014), p. 5.

19. Peter A. Heslin and Lauren A. Keating, "In Learning Mode? The Role of Mindsets in Derailing and Enabling Experiential Leadership Development," *The Leadership Quarterly*, June 2017, pp. 367–384.

20. Richard L. Hughes, Robert C. Ginnett, and Gordon J. Curphy, *Leadership: Enhancing the Lessons of Experience* (New York: McGraw-Hill/Irwin, 2006), pp. 58–61.

21. Cited in Joann S. Lublin, "Leadership Skills Ease Stressful Promotion to Uncharted Area," *The Wall Street Journal*, July 3, 2007, p. A7.

22. Douglas A. Ready, Jay A. Conger, and Linda A. Hill, "Are You a High Potential?" *Harvard Business Review*, June 2010, p. 82.

23. Beth K. Humberd and Elizabeth D. Rouse, "Seeing You In Me: Personal Identification in the Phases of Mentoring Relationships," *Academy of Management Review*, July 2016, p. 435.

24. Thomas J. DeLong, John J. Gabarro, and Robert J. Lees, "Why Mentoring Matters in a Hypercompetitive World," *Harvard Business Review*, January 2008, p. 117; "The Give and Take of Mentoring," *The Wall Street Journal*, May 23, 2013, p. B5.

25. "GE's Jeff Immelt on Leadership, Global Risk and Growth," *Knowledge@Wharton* (http://knowledge.wharton.upenn.edu/), April 30, 2013, p. 3.

26. Joann S. Lublin, "Protégé Finds Mentor Gave Her a Big Boost, but Shadow Lingers," *The Wall Street Journal*, September 7, 2004, p. B1.

27. Suzette M. Chopin, Steven J. Danish, Anson Steers, and Joshua N. Hook, "Effects of Mentoring on the Development of Leadership Self-Efficacy and Political Skill," *Journal of Leadership Studies*, no. 3, 2013, pp. 17–32.

28. Quoted in Joann S. Lublin, "How to Cope When Your Mentor Moves On." *The Wall Street Journal*, November 23, 2016, p. B5.

29. Dawn E. Chandler and Lillian Eby, "When Mentoring Goes Bad," *The Wall Street Journal*, May 24, 2010, p. R3.

30. Cited in "The Give and Take of Mentoring," *The Wall Street Journal*, p. B5.

31. Day et al., "Advances in Leader and Leadership Development," p. 70.

32. Quoted in Jared Sandberg, "The Sensitive Me," *The Wall Street Journal*, April 11, 2006, p. B1.

33. Lori Hawkins, "Using Role-Playing to Create Real-World Success," *Austin American Statesman*, January 14, 2014.

34. Leadership Development: The Secret to Success at Macy's" www.bts.com. Copyright © 2015 BTS, pp. 1–2.

35. Jay A. Conger and Beth Benjamin, *Building Leaders: How Successful Companies Develop the Next Generation* (San Francisco: Jossey-Bass, 1999), p. 79; Conger, *"Can We Really Train Leadership,"* www.strategy-business.com, 2006.

36. Gary Vander Lind and Amy Alexy, "All for Tomorrow's Leaders," *HR Magazine*, August 2013, pp. 27–28.

37. Sue Shellenbarger, "Career Makeover: Shaking Off a Shy Image," *The Wall Street Journal*, January 15, 2014, p. D3.

38. Cited in Carol Hymowitz, "More CEOs Seek Psychotherapy," *The Wall Street Journal*, June 22, 2004, pp. B1, B3.

39. Lorri Freifeid, "Survey: Leadership Programs Lack Effectiveness," *Training* (www.trainingmag.com), September 30, 2013, pp. 1–3.

40. Josi Trammell, "What Are the Right Criteria for Selecting a New CEO?" *Forbes* (www.forbes.com), February 9, 2015, p. 2.

41. Cited in Jay W. Lorsch and Rakesh Khurana, "Changing Leaders: The Board's Role in CEO Succession," *Harvard Business Review*, May–June 1999, p. 100.

42. Todd Henneman, "Most Companies Err on Prepping Heir Apparents," *Workforce Management*, January 2012, p. 8.

43. Gary A. Ballinger and F. David Schoorman, "Individual Reactions to Leadership Succession in Workgroups," *Academy of Management Review*, January 2007, pp. 118–136.

44. William C. Byham, "Grooming Next-Millennium Leaders," *HR Magazine*, February 1999, pp. 46–50; Joseph Weber, "The Accidental CEO," *BusinessWeek*, April 23, 2007, p. 068; Henneman, "Most Companies Err on Prepping Heir Apparents," p. 8.

45. Victoria Barret, "Talent Search," *Forbes*, March 1, 2010, p. 26; "Professional Development," *Aetna* (www.aetna.com), Copyright © 2001–2016, Aetna, Inc., pp. 1–2.

46. Even Harrell, "Succession Planning: What the Research Says," *Harvard Business Review*, December 2016, p. 73.

47. Joseph L. Bower, "Solve the Succession Problem by Growing Inside-Outside Leaders," *Harvard Business Review*, November 2007, pp. 90–96.

48. Ram Charan, "The Secrets of Great CEO Selection: An Insider's Guide," *Harvard Business Review*, December 2016, p. 63.

49. Balley Bischoff, "Will a New CEO Give Macy's a Boost?" *The Christian Science Monitor* (www.csmonitor.com), June 24, 2016, pp. 1–2.

50. James M. Citrin and Dayton Ogden, "Succeeding at Succession," *Harvard Business Review*, November 2010, pp. 29–31.

51. Deborah Rowland, "Why Leadership Development Isn't Developing Leaders," *Harvard Business Review* (https://hbr.org), October 14, 2016, pp. 1–7; Finkelstein, "Why We Loathe Leadership Training," pp. 2–3; Meinert, "5 Characteristics of Companies with Top Leaders," p. 20.

52. Quoted in Sonja D. Brown, "Congratulations, You're a Manager, Now What?" *Black Enterprise*, April 2006, p. 104.

53. Ronald E. Riggio and Michael D. Mumford, "Introduction to the Special Issue: Longitudinal Studies of Leadership Development," *The Leadership Quarterly*, June 2011, p. 454.

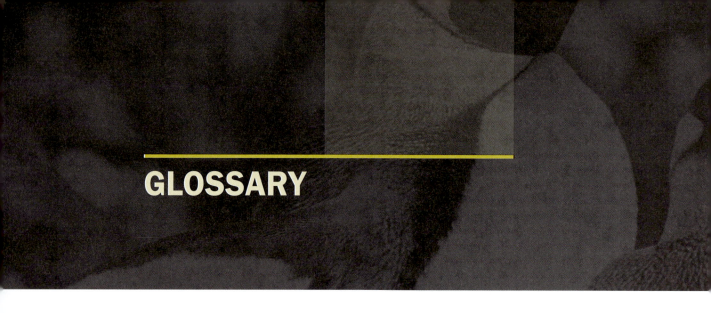

# GLOSSARY

*NOTE:* The number in brackets following each term refers to the chapter in which the term first appears.

**Abusive supervision**   A dysfunctional leadership behavior that adversely affects its targets and the organization as a whole. [6]

**Achievement motivation**   Finding joy in accomplishment for its own sake. [2]

**Altercasting**   A principle of persuasion in which you characterize another person as a certain type of person to encourage him or her to behave in a desired manner. [12]

**Apprising**   Influence tactic in which influence agent explains how carrying out a request or supporting a proposal will benefit the target personally, including advancing the target's career. [8]

**Assertiveness**   Forthrightness in expressing demands, opinions, feelings, and attitudes. [2]
   As a cultural value, the degree to which individuals are (and should be) assertive, confrontational, and aggressive in their relationships with one another. [14]

**Authenticity**   Being genuine and honest about your personality, values, and beliefs, as well as having integrity. [2]

**Autocratic leader**   A person in charge who retains most of the authority for himself or herself. [4]

**Charisma**   A special quality of leaders whose purposes, powers, and extraordinary determination differentiate them from others. [3]

**Coalition**   A specific arrangement of parties working together to combine their power. [8]

**Coercive power**   The power to punish for noncompliance; power based on fear. [7]

**Cognitive factors**   Problem solving and intellectual skills collectively. [2]

**Commitment**   The most successful outcome of a leader's influence tactic: The person makes a full effort. [8]

**Compliance**   Partial success of an influence attempt by a leader: The person makes a modest effort. [8]

**Consensus leader**   The person in charge who encourages group discussion about an issue and then makes a decision that reflects general agreement and that group members will support. [4]

**Consideration**   The degree to which the leader creates an environment of emotional support, warmth, friendliness, and trust. [4]

**Consultative leader**   A person in charge who confers with group members before making a decision, but who retains the final authority to make decisions. [4]

**Contingency approach to leadership**   The contention that leaders are most effective when they make their behavior contingent upon situational forces, including group member characteristics. [5]

**Cooperation theory**   A belief in cooperation and collaboration rather than competitiveness as a strategy for building teamwork. [9]

**Co-opt**   To win over opponents by making them part of your team or giving them a stake in the system. [8]

**Core self-evaluations**   A broad personality trait that captures bottom-line self-assessment, composed of self-esteem, locus of control, generalized self-efficacy, and emotional stability. [2]

**Corporate social responsibility**   The idea that firms have obligations to society beyond their financial obligations to owners and stockholders, and also beyond those prescribed by law or contract. [6]

**Creativity**   The production of novel and useful ideas. [11]

**Crisis leadership**   The process of leading group members through a sudden and largely unanticipated, intensely negative, and emotionally draining circumstance. [5]

**Cross-cultural training**    A set of learning experiences designed to help employees understand the customs, traditions, and beliefs of another culture. [14]

**Crowdsourcing**    The use of collective intelligence gathered from the public for accomplishing tasks, often by the use of social media. [13]

**Cultural intelligence (CQ)**    An outsider's ability to interpret someone's unfamiliar and ambiguous gestures the way that person's compatriots would. [14]

**Cultural sensitivity**    An awareness of and a willingness to investigate the reasons why people of another culture act as they do. [14]

**Debasement**    Demeaning or insulting oneself to control the behavior of another person. [8]

**Delegation**    The assignment of formal authority and responsibility for accomplishing a specific task to another person. [7]

**Democratic leader**    A person in charge who confers final authority on the group. [4]

**Dependence perspective**    The point of view that a person accrues power by other being dependent on him or her for things they value. [7]

**Diversity training**    A learning experience designed to bring about workplace harmony by teaching people how to get along better with diverse work associates. [14]

**Double-loop learning**    An in-depth style of learning that occurs when people use feedback to confront the validity of the goal or the values implicit in the situation. [15]

**Drive**    A propensity to put forth high energy into achieving goals and persistence in applying that energy. [2]

**Effective leader**    One who helps group members attain productivity, including high quality and customer satisfaction, as well as job satisfaction. [4]

**E-leadership**    A form of leadership practiced in a context where work is mediated by information technology. [9]

**Emergent leader**    A group member who significantly influences another group member even though he or she has not been assigned formal authority. [1]

**Emotional intelligence**    The ability to do such things as understand one's feelings, have empathy for others, and regulate one's emotions to enhance one's quality of life. [2]

**Empowerment**    Passing decision-making authority and responsibility from managers to group members. [7]

**Engagement**    The high levels of personal investment in the tasks performed on a job. [10]

**Entitlement**    In relation to unethical behavior by executives, the idea that some CEOs lose their sense of reality and feel entitled to whatever they can get away with or steal. [6]

**Ethical mind**    A point of view that helps the individual aspire to good work that matters to their colleagues, companies, and society in general. [6]

**Ethics**    The study of moral obligations, or separating right from wrong. [6]

**Evidence-based leadership or management**    The approach whereby managers translate principles based on best evidence into organizational practices. [5]

**Executive coaching**    A one-on-one development process formally contracted between a coach and a management-level client to help achieve goals related to professional development and/or business performance. [10]

**Expectancy**    An individual's assessment of the probability that effort will lead to correct performance of the task. [10]

**Expectancy theory**    A theory of motivation based on the premise that the amount of effort people expend depends on how much reward they can expect in return. [10]

**Experience of flow**    An experience so engrossing and enjoyable that the task becomes worth doing for its own sake, regardless of the external consequences. [11]

**Farsightedness**    The ability to understand the long-range implications of actions and policies. [2]

**Feedback-intensive development program**    A learning experience that helps leaders develop by seeing more clearly their patterns of behaviors, the reasons for such behaviors, and the impact of these behaviors and attitudes on their effectiveness. [15]

**Flexibility**    The ability to adjust to different situations. [2]

**Future orientation**    As a cultural value, the extent to which individuals engage (and should engage) in future-oriented behaviors such as delaying gratification, planning, and making investments for the future. [14]

**Gender egalitarianism**    As a cultural value, the degree to which a culture minimizes, and should minimize, gender inequality. [14]

**Gig economy**    Workers who are involved in some form of freelancing, contorting, often based on outsourcing. [9]

**Global leadership skills**    The ability to exercise effective leadership in a variety of countries. [14]

**Goal**    What a person is trying to accomplish. [10]

**Hands-on leader**    A leader who gets directly involved in the details and process of operations. [8]

**Humane orientation** As a cultural value, the degree to which a society encourages and rewards, and should encourage and reward, individuals for being fair, altruistic, and caring others. [14]

**Implicit leadership theories** Personal assumptions about the traits and abilities that characterize an ideal organizational leader. [8]

**Influence** The ability to affect the behavior of others in a particular direction. [8]

**In-group collectivism** As a cultural value, the degree to which individuals express, and should express, pride, loyalty, and cohesiveness in their organizations and families. [14]

**Initiating structure** Organizing and defining relationships in the group by activities such as assigning specific tasks, specifying procedures to be followed, scheduling work, and clarifying expectations of team members. [4]

**Innovation** The creation of new ideas and the implementation and commercialization. [11]

**Insight** A depth of understanding that requires considerable intuition and common sense. [2]

**Instrumentality** An individual's assessment of the probability that performance will lead to certain outcomes. [10]

**Integrity** Loyalty to rational principles, thereby practicing what one preaches, regardless of emotional or social pressure. [6]

**Intergroup leadership** Leading a number of teams within the organization. [9]

**Intuition** An experienced-based way of knowing or reasoning in which the weighing and balancing of evidence are done unconsciously and automatically. [11]

**Knowledge management (KM)** A concerted effort to improve how knowledge is created, delivered, and applied. [13]

**Leader–member exchange (LMX) model** An explanation of leadership proposing that leaders develop unique working relationships with group members. [9]

**Leader political support** Political acts and influence behaviors performed by leaders to provide followers with valuable resources to advance individual, group, or organizational objectives. [7]

**Leadership** The ability to inspire confidence and support among the people who are needed to achieve organizational goals. [1]

**Leading by example** Influencing others by acting as a positive role model. [8]

**Leadership by storytelling** The technique of inspiring and instructing group members by telling fascinating stories. [3]

**Leadership diversity** The presence of a culturally heterogeneous group of leaders. [14]

**Leadership effectiveness** Attaining desirable outcomes such as productivity, quality, and satisfaction in a given situation. [1]

**Leadership polarity** The idea that leaders are often either revered or vastly unpopular. [3]

**Leadership style** The relatively consistent pattern of behavior that characterizes a leader. [4]

**Leadership succession** An orderly process of identifying and grooming people to replace executives. [15]

**Learning organization** An organization that is skilled at creating, acquiring, and transferring knowledge and at modifying behavior to reflect new knowledge and insights. [13]

**Legitimate power** The lawful right to make a decision and expect compliance. [7]

**Linguistic style** A person's characteristic speaking pattern. [12]

**Machiavellians** People in the workplace who ruthlessly manipulate others. [8]

**Management openness** A set of leadership behaviors particularly relevant to subordinates' motivation to voice their opinion. [4]

**Making the rounds** The leader casually dropping by constituents to listen to their accomplishments, concern, and problems and to share information. [12]

**Meaningful work** The feeling of doing work that matters or makes a difference. [10]

**Mentor** A more experienced person who develops a protégé's abilities through tutoring, coaching, guidance, and emotional support. [15]

**Micromanagement** The close monitoring of most aspects of group member activities by the manager or leader. [9]

**Mindfulness** A state of nonjudgmental attentiveness to and awareness of moment-to-moment experiences. [2]

**Moral identity** The extent to which an individual holds morality as part of his or her self-concept. [7]

**Morals** An individual's determination of what is right or wrong influenced by his or her values. [6]

**Multicultural leader** A leader with the skills and attitudes to relate effectively to and motivate people across race, gender, age, social attitudes, and lifestyles. [14]

**Multicultural worker** A worker who is convinced that all cultures are equally good and enjoys learning about other cultures. [14]

**Narcissism** A relatively stable personality trait characterized by a sense of personal superiority, a desire for power, and a sense of self-importance. [3]

**Normative decision model** A view of leadership as a decision-making process in which the leader examines certain factors within the situation to determine which decision-making style will be the most effective. [5]

**Open-book management** An approach to management in which every employee is trained, empowered, and motivated to understand and pursue the company's business goals. [9]

**Organizational politics** Informal approaches to gaining power through means other than merit or luck. [7]

**Outcome** Anything that might stem from performance, such as a reward. [10]

**Participative leader** A person in charge who shares decision making with group members. [4]

**Path-goal theory** An explanation of leadership effectiveness that specifies what the leader must do to achieve high productivity and morale in a given situation. [5]

**Performance orientation** As a cultural value, the degree to which a society encourages (or should encourage) and rewards group member for performance improvement and excellence. [14]

**Personal brand** Your basket of strengths that makes you unique. [3]

**Personal magnetism** A captivating, inspiring personality with charm and charismatic-like qualities. [8]

**Personal power** Power derived from the person rather than from the organization. [7]

**Personalized charismatic** A charismatic leader who exercises few restraints on the use of power in order to best serve his or her own interests. [3]

**Pet-peeve technique** A method of brainstorming in which a group identifies all the possible complaints others might have about the group's organizational unit. [11]

**Political skill** An interpersonal style that manifests itself in being socially astute and engaging in behaviors that lead to feelings of confidence trust, and sincerity. [7]

**Positive psychological capital** An individual's positive psychological state of development, characterized by four psychological resources: self-efficacy, hope, optimism, and resilience. [7]

**Power** The potential or ability to influence decisions and control resources. [7]

**Power distance** As a cultural value, the degree to which members of a society expect, and should expect, power to be distributed unequally. [14]

**Practical intelligence** The ability to solve everyday problems by using experience-based knowledge to adapt to and shape the environment. [2]

**Prestige power** The power stemming from one's status and reputation. [7]

**Proactive personality** A relatively stable tendency to effect environmental change. [2]

**Pygmalion effect** The situation that occurs when a managerial leader believes that a group member will succeed and communicates this belief without realizing it. [4]

**Resistance** The state that occurs when an influence attempt by a leader is unsuccessful: The target is opposed to carrying out the request and finds ways to either not comply or do a poor job. [8]

**Reward power** The authority to give employees rewards for compliance. [7]

**Self-awareness** Insightfully processing feedback about oneself to improve personal effectiveness. [15]

**Self-discipline** The ability to mobilize one's efforts to stay focused on attaining an important goal. [15]

**Self-efficacy** The confidence in one's ability to carry out a specific task. [10]

**Self-leadership** The idea that all organizational members are capable of leading themselves, at least to some extent. [7]

**Servant leader** One who serves constituents by working on their behalf to help them achieve their goals, not the leader's own goals. [4]

**Shadowing** An approach to mentoring in which the trainee follows the mentor around for a stated period of time. [15]

**Single-loop learning** A situation in which learners seek minimum feedback that might substantially confront their basic ideas or actions. [15]

**Social entrepreneurship** The use of market-based methods to solve social problems. [6]

**Socialized charismatic** A charismatic leader who restrains the use of power in order to benefit others. [3]

**Strategic contingency theory** An explanation of sources of power suggesting that units best able to cope with the firm's critical problems and uncertainties acquire relatively large amounts of power. [7]

**Strategic leadership** The process of creating or sustaining an organization by providing the right direction and inspiration. [13]

**Strategic planning**   Those activities that lead to the statement of goals and objectives and the choice of strategy. [13]

**Strategy**   An integrated, overall concept of how the firm will achieve its objectives. [13]

**Substitutes for leadership**   Factors in the work environment that provide guidance and incentives to perform, making the leader's role almost superfluous. [1]

**SWOT analysis**   A long-standing method of considering internal strengths, weaknesses, and external opportunities and threats in a given situation. [13]

**Team**   A work group that must rely on collaboration if each member is to experience the optimum success and achievement. [9]

**Teamwork**   Work done with an understanding and commitment to group goals on the part of all team members. [9]

**Territorial games**   Also referred to as turf wars, political tactics that involve protecting and hoarding resources that give one power, such as information, relationships, and decision-making authority. [7]

**Time orientation**   As a cultural value, the importance nations and individuals attach to time. [14]

**Tough question**   One that makes a person or group stop and think about why they are doing or not doing something. [4]

**Transformational leader**   A leader who brings about positive, major changes in an organization. [3]

**Trust**   A person's confidence in another individual's intentions and motives and in the sincerity of that individual's word. [2]

**360-degree feedback**   A formal evaluation of superiors based on input from people who work for and with them, sometimes including customers and suppliers. [4]

**Uncertainty avoidance**   As a cultural value, the extent to which members of a society rely (and should rely) on social norms, rules, and procedures to lessen the unpredictability of future events. [14]

**Upward appeal**   A means of influence in which the leader enlists a person with more formal authority to do the influencing. [8]

**Valence**   The worth or attractiveness of an outcome. [10]

**Virtuous circle**   The idea that corporate social performance and corporate financial performance feed and reinforce each other. [6]

**Vision**   The ability to imagine different and better conditions and ways to achieve them. [3]

**Whistleblower**   An employee who discloses organizational wrongdoing to parties who can take action. [6]

**Win–win approach to conflict resolution**   The belief that after conflict has been resolved, both sides should gain something of value. [12]

**Work orientation**   As a cultural value, the number of hours per week and weeks per year people expect to invest in work versus leisure, or other nonwork activities. [14]

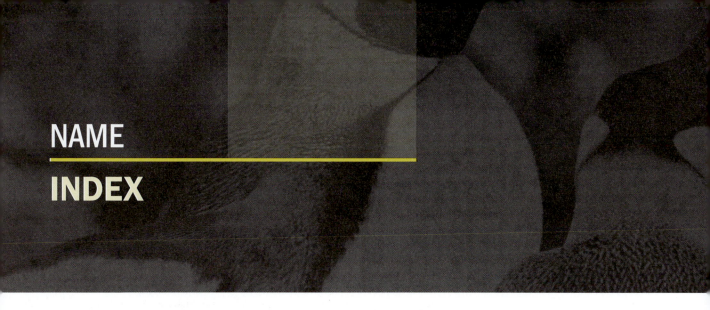

# NAME INDEX

# COMPANY INDEX

# SUBJECT

# INDEX